Understanding Decision Support Systems and Expert Systems

Understanding Decision Support Systems and Expert Systems

Efrem G. Mallach
University of Massachusetts at Lowell

Boston, Massachusetts   Burr Ridge, Illinois   Dubuque, Iowa
Madison, Wisconsin   New York, New York   San Francisco, California   St. Louis, Missouri

Irwin/McGraw-Hill

A Division of The ***McGraw-Hill*** *Companies*

This symbol indicates that the paper in this book is made of recycled paper. Its fiber content exceeds the recommended minimum of 50% waste paper fibers as specified by the EPA.

Sponsoring editor: Rick Williamson
Associate editor: Rebecca J. Johnson
Editorial coordinator: Christine Wright
Project editor: Karen M. Smith
Production manager: Jon Christopher
Designer: Larry J. Cope
Art coordinator: Heather Burbridge
Art studio: Precision Graphics
Compositor: J.M. Post Graphics, Book Division, Cardinal Communications Group, Inc.
Typeface: 10/12 Palatino
Printer: R. R. Donnelley & Sons Company

Library of Congress Cataloging-in-Publication Data

Mallach, Efrem (date)
Understanding decision support systems and expert systems/Efrem G. Mallach.
p. cm.
Includes bibliographical references and index.
ISBN 0-256-11896-5
1. Decision support systems. 2. Expert systems (Computer science) I. Title.
T58.62.W35 1994
658.4'03—dc20 93–6186

Printed in the United States of America
5 6 7 8 9 0 DO 0 9 8 7

To my students,
who have taught
me more
than I have
taught them

Preface

Understanding Decision Support and Expert Systems is intended as a textbook for a one-semester course in DSS, in which expert system technology plays a substantial role. With the addition of enrichment material in expert systems, it fits a quarter system: the DSS portion of the book fits one quarter and the expert systems portion can easily be expanded to fit another. The book is suitable for these environments:

- Management (business administration) programs, at either the advanced undergraduate or the master's level.
- Programs in computers and information systems (CIS) or in an application-oriented computer science program, typically at the advanced undergraduate level.
- Workshops for practicing professionals who need a grasp of this important area of technology.

Why This Book?

I wrote this book for the same reason that most authors write textbooks: I taught the subject for several semesters and was not satisfied with any of the available texts. This book is meant to offer several advantages over the alternatives that were available as it was being written:

- It has a realistic objective: to help the student understand decision support systems, not to create an experienced professional.
- It was written as a unified whole in which each chapter relates its content to what has gone before and is, in turn, related to what will follow.

- As a result, topics are reinforced by continued use rather than being touched upon and subsequently forgotten.
- It focuses throughout, not just on how things are, but on *why* they are that way. It does not present facts or research results without explanation and context.
- Along the same lines, it does not attempt to provide exhaustive coverage of every fact or research result that exists. It focuses on what is (in the author's humble opinion) important.
- It presents expert systems, not as somehow different from (or contrasted to) DSS, but as a technology which is often useful in DSS and has other application areas as well.
- It makes realistic assumptions about what students have already studied. It neither assumes they remember every nuance of introductory finance nor insults them by assuming they never saw the subject.
- It offers many accessible, often non-technical, examples of difficult concepts.
- It includes a running case that enables the students to apply the concepts in the chapters to a familiar situation.

How This Book is Organized

Understanding Decision Support and Expert Systems is divided into four major parts. They are described further in Section 1.6, "The Plan of This Book." Each major part opens with a brief introduction to the entire part.

Part I, Chapters 1–4, provides an overview of decision support system fundamentals: how people make decisions, how systems work, where models fit into the DSS picture, what the benefits of DSS are, and several ways to classify them. The purpose of this classification is this: if we know something about the types of decisions and the types of DSS, and if we know what DSS have been useful with certain decisions in the past, we have a head start in developing a DSS for a similar decision today.

Part II, Chapters 5–8, covers technical and non-technical DSS development issues. Chapter 5 covers the ways in which information systems can be developed, which fit DSS best, and why. Again, the intent is to be able to apply the best method to a new situation. Chapters 6 and 7 cover the hardware and software technologies that go into DSS. The non-technical side, including implementation and some ethical issues, is in Chapter 8.

Part III, Chapters 9–13, goes into particular types of DSS and important aspects of many DSS in more detail. These chapters cover, respectively, the major kinds of models that are useful for decision support, optimization, group decision support systems, and executive information systems. Chapter

13 has some DSS cases to help unify the concepts of the preceding chapters.

Part IV, Chapters 14–18, covers expert systems. It opens with an introduction to artificial intelligence and continues through various aspects of expert systems. In parallel to the DSS cases of Chapter 13, Chapter 18 contains several expert system cases.

Finally, Part V contains Chapter 19, which summarizes the book.

Each chapter (except Chapters 13 and 18, which contain only cases) includes:

- A chapter outline.
- A set of learning objectives for the chapter.
- An introduction, which explains why the chapter is important.
- A summary, which recaps the major points made in the chapter.
- A list of key terms introduced in the chapter.
- A set of simple review questions to check the reader's understanding. These require only reference to the appropriate paragraph(s) of the chapter.
- A set of more involved discussion questions to apply the material. These require additional thought and, in some cases, use of a computer.
- References, covering both citations in the chapter and sources of further depth in the chapter topics.
- A case, about a small environmental engineering firm named Envoyance, to show how the concepts and principles of that chapter are applied. Envoyance is introduced at the end of Chapter 2. There are discussion questions for each episode of this running case.

SUPPLEMENTS

Adopters of this book can obtain the following items, in addition to the book itself:

- An instructor's manual with suggestions for presenting the material, ideas for class projects, and other information that will help make a DSS course successful.
- The student edition of EXSYS, which is packaged in the instructor's manual.
- A test bank with true/false, multiple-choice, and short essay questions.
- Computest 3, the computerized version of the printed test bank.

ACKNOWLEDGMENTS

No person can sit down at a word processor and hope to arise some time later with a finished manuscript. I am indebted to many people for much that is in these pages. In particular, I wish to thank:

- The over one hundred DSS students at the University of Massachusetts, Lowell, who suffered through several versions of this book in the form of class notes and whose comments improved it substantially.
- The reviewers who pointed out many errors and opportunities for improvement. Since I ignored their advice in a few places, I retain the blame for any remaining problems. These reviewers were: Johannes Aarsen, Wichita State University; Yvonne Antonucci, Widener University; Jane Fedorowicz, Boston University; William L. Harrison, Oregon State University; W. J. Kenny Jih, University of Tennessee, Chattanooga; Christine T. Kydd, University of Delaware; Albert L. Lederer, Oakland University; Jane M. Mackay, Texas Christian University; Brother Matthew Michelini, Manhattan College; Roger Alan Pick, Louisiana Tech University; Stephen Richards, Ambassador College; Jeanne Ross, Worcester Polytechnic Institute; and Laurette Simmons, Loyola College.
- The editors and production staff at Richard D. Irwin, Inc., particularly Rebecca Johnson, who kept after me to ensure that the book was as good as I was capable of making it.
- The many educators and MIS professionals who have worked in DSS and related fields over the past several decades and who have taken the time to record what they have learned. I hope I have added some useful insight here and there but, as with any textbook, I can claim truly original authorship for only a small part of its content.

If this book helps students become practicing professionals who really understand what DSS are about and how to construct DSS that match decision makers' support needs, it will have achieved its most important objective.

Efrem G. Mallach

Brief Contents

PART IV

Introduction to Artificial Intelligence and Expert Systems

PART V

Summary

Contents

Part I

Introduction to Decision Support Systems

PART IV

Introduction to Artificial Intelligence and Expert Systems

PART V

Summary

Part I Introduction to Decision Support Systems

We understand things—items, entities, ideas—by putting them into a frame of reference. To a biologist, categorizing a newly discovered creature as an "insect" conveys a great deal of information, and that information can help understand how it functions. Once we establish (based on size, skeletal structure, and number of legs, etc.) that a creature is an insect, we know certain things about its digestive system, its reproductive mechanisms, and so on. These may, on rare occasions, not all apply fully to a particular insect, but they are a helpful jumping-off point. Without such a framework, entomologists would be forced to discover these facts anew for every species of insect. There are millions of insect species, so the waste of effort would be enormous.

So it is with computer-based information systems. You have learned there are many types of IS: transaction processing systems, office automation systems, computer-aided design systems, and more. You studied their characteristics—transaction processing systems access a shared database; office automation systems incorporate word processing capabilities; computer-aided design systems run on powerful workstations with high-resolution graphics. These generalizations, like an insect's digestive system, are usually true but have exceptions as well. The IS specialist, like the entomologist, must understand both the value of the generalizations and the exceptions to them.

This book is about one particular type of information system, called a *decision support system*. DSS exist to help people make better decisions than they could make on their own. There are many different types of people: they vary in their personalities, their decision-making preferences, and the role they play in the organizations where they work. There are also many different types of decisions. Some recur regularly; some arise once. Some are based on hard data, some on "gut feel." Some are emotionally neutral, but others involve strong feelings and a need to communicate. There are, correspondingly, many different types of decision support systems.

The first four chapters of this book will give you a framework by which to look at DSS. After a brief introduction, you'll see how people make decisions. This is basic information if we are to develop computer systems to help that process. We'll get a perspective on how systems work in general in Chapter 3, and move on to different types of DSS in Chapter 4. At that point you'll be ready to get into more specific DSS issues in Part II.

CHAPTER 1 Introduction to Decision Support Systems

Chapter Outline

Introduction

This chapter will introduce you to decision support systems, the subject of this book. Decision support systems are, in a nutshell, information systems that help people make decisions. In this chapter you'll get an idea of what decision support systems are, how they were originally used, how they are used today, what benefits they provide to organizations, and why it makes sense for you to study them over the next few months.

Chapter Objectives

After you have read and studied this chapter, you will be able to:

1. Define decision support systems.
2. Describe how decision support systems evolved.
3. Discuss where decision support systems fit into the information systems picture.
4. Identify how all types of information systems can also be used for decision support.
5. Outline the benefits of decision support systems.
6. Understand why it is important to study decision support systems.

1.1 Evolution of Information Systems

As you learned in an introductory course, the first computers were used to automate repetitive calculations. They originally processed numerical data, as in solving equations. Many advances in computing were made under the pressure of World War II needs. During that conflict, computers calculated the effective range of depth charges and optimal trajectories for artillery shells. Computing power in that era was typically measured by the roomsful of mathematicians that an "electronic brain" could replace, a popular comparison that ignored the difference between a clerk operating a calculator and a true mathematician. (Those clerks, incidentally, were often called "computers"—sometimes "computors," to distinguish them from the electromechanical kind.)

Electronic computers found commercial uses in the 1950s. Their first large-scale use to process business-like data was a Univac I at the U.S. Census Bureau in 1951. It has been stated that, without computers, the 1950 census data could not have been tabulated before it was time to carry out the next census a decade later.

By the mid-1950s, large corporations had adopted computers for their own repetitive calculations, such as processing the corporate payroll. This activity was known as *automatic data processing*—a term used earlier for electromechanical punched card processing as well—or *electronic data processing*. These terms were shortened to just *data processing* as computers came into wide use and manual data processing became a historical relic. Later, when "data processing" often meant all computer applications, the term *transaction processing* was coined to describe this type of computing.

Managers were quick to realize that transaction data was, if suitably summarized, of potential decision-making value. They asked for information that could be obtained from data that was already in computers. At the time, direct-access storage devices and on-line terminals, to say nothing of integrated databases with query software, were not in general use. There was therefore no easy way to obtain one data element on request. The only way to satisfy these needs was to produce voluminous reports that contained every data element that could possibly be wanted. *Information reporting systems* (IRS) thus arose. Managers found thick reports, typically on 17-inch wide paper with green and white horizontal bars for easy reading across the page, on their desks every Monday morning. In some cases these reports got lots of use. In others, they were discarded untouched when the following Monday's report arrived.

Outmoded as paper-based IRS might seem in the mid-1990s, they did demonstrate that computers contained a great deal of useful management data. As technology evolved in the 1960s to permit instant access to this data, albeit at a high cost in hardware and custom programming, the concept of a *management information system* (MIS) evolved with it. The idea behind an MIS was to store all the firm's data: customers, orders, inventory, production schedules, suppliers, employees, payroll, and so forth for access and correlation on demand by nontechnical managers. While this dream did not come true in that form at that time, in part because technologies such as distributed databases were not yet available, many firms are approaching a similar concept today by integrating their systems into a coordinated whole. The major vestige of those early efforts today is the continued use of "MIS" to refer to commercially oriented information systems as a whole. Your introductory information systems course, your previous textbook, or both may possibly have used this name.

Despite their lack of general success, efforts to produce a corporate MIS showed that decision-making data did not have to come from thick reports. This lack of success may have been a benefit in disguise: Managers saw that they didn't need a global MIS in order to have useful information. As a result, more modest systems to help make specific types of decisions came to the fore in the 1970s. These were, and are, called *decision support systems,* or DSS.[1] This book is about such systems: what they do, how they do it, how they are built, how they are used.

1.2 What Is a DSS?

In order to understand decision support systems or DSS, we must first agree on what they are. This is not easy: As Davis points out in his preface [DAVI88]: "Ask someone to explain the concept and application of DSS, and the answer given will most often depend on who you ask."

One way to try to understand the essence of decision support systems is to look at several definitions that have been put forth. A sampling follows. Some of these definitions were taken from popular introductory MIS textbooks, perhaps including the one you used. Others are from more specialized writings in the DSS field.

> An integrated set of computer tools that allow a decision maker to interact directly with computers to create information useful in making unanticipated semistructured and unstructured decisions. [HICKS93]

> Decision support implies the use of computers to (1) assist managers in their decision processes in semistructured tasks; (2) support, rather than replace, managerial judgment; (3) improve the effectiveness of decision making rather than its efficiency. [KEEN78]

[1]We'll use the abbreviation DSS to stand both for decision support system in the singular and decision support systems in the plural. You shouldn't have any difficulty deciphering which is meant in a particular instance.

> Information systems featuring an integrated system composed of decision models, database, and decision maker to support decision making. [SPRA79]

> A set of computer-based tools used by a manager in connection with his or her problem-solving and decision-making duties. [LEIG86]

> A computer-based system that is used on an on-going basis by managers themselves, or their immediate staffs, in direct support of managerial decision making. [KEEN79]

> . . . a computer-based information system that affects or is intended to affect how people make decisions. [SILV91]

> Decision support systems are used for less structured problems . . . where the art of management is blended with the science. [KANT92]

> . . . a set of tools, data, models, and other resources that managers and analysts use to understand, evaluate and solve problems . . . [in] unstructured problem domains. [KROE92]

Ralph Sprague, in his pioneering work on DSS [SPRA80], made a serious attempt to define DSS from a theoretical point of view and in terms of what it means in practice. His compromise, based on observations of many DSS of that era, includes these four characteristics:

- They tend to be aimed at the less well structured, underspecified problems that upper level managers typically face.
- They attempt to combine the use of models or analytic techniques with traditional data access and retrieval functions.
- They specifically focus on features that make them easy to use by noncomputer people in an interactive mode.
- They emphasize flexibility and adaptability to accommodate changes in the environment and the decision-making approach of the user.

Several themes come through as we read these definitions:

1. *Decision support systems are information systems.* This might seem obvious, but this seemingly trivial statement has great significance: It means that everything you know about information systems applies to DSS as well. There may be a slight shift in emphasis here and there, but the basic concepts still work.

2. *Decision support systems are used by managers.* This is part of many definitions of DSS, but it's a bit too restrictive. A manager is someone who achieves results through other people. DSS are used by the broad category of *knowledge workers* in general. Knowledge workers include nonmanagement staff such as stockbrokers, urban planners, production coordinators, travel agents, college admissions officers, and many more. Anyone who makes decisions, in business, in government, or in the nonprofit sector, is a potential DSS user.

3. *Decision support systems are used in making decisions.* Making decisions

is the foundation of corporate success: What products should we manufacture? What services should we provide? How should we market and sell them? How should we raise capital? Who should be assigned to each task? DSS can therefore have an enormous impact on an organization's "bottom line."

4. *Decision support systems are used to support, not to replace, people.* Decision support systems are not decision-making systems, though the dividing line can be fuzzy at times and borderline cases do exist. If there isn't, as a minimum, some human review of the system's recommendation, it isn't a DSS.

5. *Decision support systems are used when the decision is "semistructured" or "unstructured."* We'll define what decision "structure" means more completely in Chapter 4. For now, lack of structure means essentially that we can't program a computer to make the decision to our total satisfaction in all cases. A decision that is not structured is a decision that requires some human judgment.

6. *Decision support systems incorporate a database of some sort.*[2] That is because all decisions are based on information. A database is where computers store information. (More precisely, it is where computers store data that we can process into or interpret as information.)

7. *Decision support systems incorporate models.* A model is a computer representation of reality that lets us investigate the impact of a possible decision.[3] This capability is, obviously, of great value when a lot is at stake.

Two points are worth noting about these elements of DSS:

- The very name DSS reflects points 1, 3, and 4. In contrast to many other MIS terms, this one actually makes sense.
- The first four points are true of all DSS. The last three are typical of most DSS but may not apply to a particular one. DSS experts differ on their importance. (Not only do experts disagree, but "the field cannot even agree on how it disagrees!" [SILV91]) When an author puts one of the last three points in a definition that is intended to characterize all DSS as a group, it tells us something about that author's perspective and the types of DSS we can expect him or her to discuss.

The definition of DSS we'll use in this book is as follows:

A decision support system is an information system whose primary purpose is to provide knowledge workers with information on which to base informed decisions.

---

[2]The term "database" is used here in its informal sense as a collection of data. We'll get more precise about database concepts in Chapter 6.

[3]This is not a general definition of a model, but applies to the models in most DSS. We will consider models in more detail—with a more general definition—in Chapter 3.

This definition incorporates the essential elements of the above definitions, without restricting us to a specific technology, approach, or set of system elements. It is a broad definition. We can't avoid this in a definition that must cover all the types of DSS that exist. As we proceed further in our study of DSS, we will uncover many types of DSS with narrower definitions.

Note the words "primary purpose" in our definition. Many DSS provide, as a by-product, reports or other aspects of conventional data processing systems. These incidental features, which often cost little or nothing to add and can be of real value, do not make a system non-DSS-like as long as they are secondary to the main reason for developing it.

1.3 DSS IN THE INFORMATION SYSTEMS PICTURE

1.3.1 Types of Information Systems

As you know, organizations use several different types of information systems. We've just mentioned three of them:

- Transaction processing systems (TPS), which record and process information about transactions: events, often but not always financial in nature, that take place during the operation of an organization.
- Information reporting systems (IRS, also sometimes known as management information systems, MIS, in yet another usage of that term), which provide members of the organization with information based on these transactions.
- Decision support systems (DSS), which provide members of the organization with information on which to base informed decisions.

Figure 1–1 compares some characteristics of these types of information systems.

In addition, you may have encountered these types of information systems as well:

- Office information systems (OIS), which improve the efficiency and effectiveness of handling information (words, images, schedules, and so forth) in an office.
- Executive information systems (EIS), by which the top management of an organization can obtain information to guide its decisions. (This makes them a type of DSS, so there's a chapter about EIS in this book.)
- Personal information systems, developed and used by one individual (in a process often known as *end-user computing*) to improve his or her personal productivity and effectiveness. That effectiveness can

FIGURE 1–1

Table of Information System Characteristics

System Charcteristic	*Transaction Processing Systems*	*Information Reporting Systems*	*Decision Support Systems*
User community	Clerical and supervisory	Supervisory and middle management	Individual knowledge workers, all management levels
Usage volume	High	Moderate	Moderate to low
Database usage	Some reading, heavy updating	Read-only	Primarily read-only
Typical software base	Third-generation languages	3rd and 4th generation languages	Specialized languages, packages
Emphasis on ease of use	Low	Moderate	High
Emphasis on processing efficiency	High	Moderate	Low
Reason for development	Cost savings, customer service	Reporting requirements, basic information for decision making	Improved decision-making effectiveness

involve decision making. A personal information system used for this purpose is a DSS too.

- Work group information systems, used to improve communication and coordination within members of a group who collaborate on a set of joint tasks.
- Expert systems, which follow rules similar to those a human might use in order to reach a recommendation or conclusion from available data. If the rules are those a human might follow to reach a decision, an expert system can be a DSS also.
- Strategic information systems (SIS), through which an organization can obtain a competitive advantage over its rivals, or prevent its rivals from obtaining a competitive advantage over it.

These are not distinct categories. They overlap, they interact, and they supplement each other. Several of them, as we noted above, are closely related to DSS. Some of them, such as work group systems and expert systems, are technologies as much as they are types of information systems.

Take the first—and oldest—category of transaction processing systems. It is easy to put these down as "old hat," yet no modern organization could function for long without its TPS. Today's transaction processing systems often form the foundation for powerful strategic information systems. Examples include airline reservation systems and the "Tootie" automated order entry system, which uses the customer's touch-tone telephone, that enables

Home Shopping Club to adjust its prices on the air using up-to-the-second order rate data. The combination of transaction processing and an on-line link to the customer, on which both these applications are based, is a powerful one. In both of these cases it is hard to define exactly where the TPS stops and where the SIS begins. Fortunately, we don't have to.

We could find similar examples for any of the other areas. Applying information technology intelligently can transform the way an organization works. It is no exaggeration to state that information systems can reshape the nature of competition in an industry.

1.3.2 Information Systems and Decision Support

Consider the types of information systems listed above. With the possible exception of TPS, and then only if we define them in the narrowest possible way, every one can support people as they make decisions:

- IRS: An accounting clerk, looking at an aged accounts receivable report, decides which customer to call for payment.
- EIS: The vice president for strategic planning, seeing that our Model A-100 is gaining market share, decides to expand in that market segment with a smaller Model A-80 and a larger Model A-150.
- OIS: A marketing director, having been informed by an automated calendar and scheduling system that six product managers can't meet as a group for the next three weeks, decides to meet with four of them the day after tomorrow and talk to the other two individually later.
- Personal IS: A department manager tries out several different budget possibilities before deciding which one to submit upward.
- Work group IS: Regional sales managers must decide, as a group, what type of national advertising they would like their firm to use.
- Expert system: A family doctor must decide how to treat a patient with a rare blood disease that the general practitioner has never seen before.
- SIS: The two above examples support customer decisions. Airline passengers and their travel agents use information from on-line reservation systems to choose their flights. Home Shopping Club viewers make purchase decisions on the basis of the price offered at the moment. If it's too high, they won't buy. If it's too low, HSC loses potential revenue. These customer decisions tie into internal business decisions: What flights should we schedule? How should we adjust the price of the product now being sold on the air?

The point here is that computer support of decision making is all-pervasive. We can't put it in a slot called "DSS" with walls between that slot and adjacent slots. All types of information systems have some relationship to decision support. A DSS, as we defined the term above, is a system built with decision support as its primary purpose. That puts it at one end of the spectrum. We can visualize this spectrum as in Figure 1–2.

There are two ways to look at computer support for decision making: via systems that have decision support as their primary task, DSS as we have defined them, or via the decision support capabilities that most computer-based information systems possess. We will take the former approach in this book. Doing so will enable us to focus on decision support, without being overly distracted by other issues that arise in discussing any broad-based information system. Yet because decision support is not the sole province of a particular category of system, what you will learn about computer-based support for decision making in a pure DSS context will help you work on other types of systems as well.

1.3.3 *Using Computers for Decision Support*

Consider the three decision problems outlined below.

1. We have budgeted $100,000 to advertise our new line of nongreasy green, pink, and yellow sunscreen lotion next summer. We know something about the types of people who buy sunscreen lotion. (We decided to concentrate on converting existing sunscreen lotion users to our product rather than persuading nonusers to start using sunscreen lotion. Computers might have helped us make that decision as well.) Demographic survey data tell us what types of people read various magazines and watch various TV shows. We

FIGURE 1–2

ISS Spectrum with DSS at One End

Approximate decision support content of different types of information systems:

100%	
	Decision support systems
	Executive information systems
Decision	Expert systems
Support	Information reporting systems
Content	Work group information systems
	Personal information systems
	Office information systems
	Transaction processing systems
0%	

These categories are approximate and overlap considerably.

can relate these demographic data to what we know about sunscreen buyers. Research studies have provided data about the impact of size and color usage in a print ad, and the impact of commercial duration for TV and radio, on brand awareness. We want to spend our $100,000 to give our ads the greatest brand awareness impact on our target market.

2. We have budgeted $100,000 to invest in common stocks. We decided that we want to invest in firms with a good growth record over the past five years, which have had a recent drop in earnings so their stock price is down and which pay a dividend of under 3 percent so they can reinvest their earnings in more growth.[4] There are thousands of stocks on major stock exchanges that might meet these criteria.

3. We have budgeted $100,000 for new equipment to improve the productivity of our factory. There are dozens of things we could do with the money: upgrade our milling machines, install conveyor belts, buy robotic assembly systems, install a computer to schedule jobs better, hire more workers, rearrange the existing equipment, give our current work force a raise, and so forth.

People can make all these decisions, and many others like them, more effectively (not necessarily more efficiently, though this often happens, but more effectively) with computers. One possible way—not necessarily the best—in which a computer could help us make each decision is outlined below.

1. *Advertising budget.* We enter a combination of print ads and commercials into a computer, which already has the cost of specific advertising vehicles in its database, so that the computer can figure the cost of this combination. We repeat this process until we have a program that costs approximately $100,000. The computer then figures out its awareness impact on our target market by using impact formulas and readership demographic data, which are also in its database. We repeat this process several times until we are happy with the results or feel that we can't improve them much more. (You can read about an actual system of this type in [RATH92]).

2. *Investment decision.* We have a computer scan a database of all the stocks on the New York and American Stock Exchanges for stocks that meet these criteria. The third one, dividend rate, is easy to get from current price data. Several publicly available databases have five-year stock price records. We must define a "recent earnings drop" more precisely if we want the computer to scan for that as well. Even without that, the computer can give us a short list of all the stocks that meet the other two criteria and print their earnings history for us to inspect.

[4]This is not necessarily a good investment strategy. If you try it and it doesn't work, don't blame this book!

3. *Factory upgrade.* We can develop a model of our production process: what steps each product goes through, how long each one takes, what equipment is required for it, what has to happen between each step and the next. We can calibrate this model by plugging in data for our present production process and verifying that the model predicts its present output with acceptable accuracy. We can then plug in changes, such as a milling machine that carries out step 6 in half the time or a conveyor belt that reduces the time between steps 8 and 9, and see what difference each $100,000 mix of alternatives makes. To figure out the effect of giving our workers a raise, we would have to make assumptions about the impact the raise would have on job performance, employee turnover (which affects performance), or other factors that affect factory output.

All three of these possible computer systems are decision support systems. If you take another look at the seven themes that came through the definitions of a DSS in Section 1.2, you can see that all three of these example DSS meet the first five points. The first and third DSS here use models: Example 1 uses a model of responses to advertising; example 3 uses a model of factory production. The value of these DSS is largely in their ability to carry out many complex calculations quickly so we can use the results. The first and second DSS both use databases: an ad medium demographics database in the first case, one or more corporate financial history and stock performance databases in the second. The second DSS doesn't do much computing. Its value to an investor lies primarily in its ability to scan these massive databases far more quickly than a person could.

1.3.4 *The Value of Computer-Based Decision Support*

The types of information systems we've been discussing span all levels of every organization. Yet each type is not necessarily used at every level. It is unlikely that the president of Galactic Industries Inc. will personally update its accounts payable files. It is equally unlikely that an accounts payable clerk will make the final decision on the per-share price that Galactic will offer for its chief rival, Universal Manufacturing, in a merger proposal. Each type of system has its main purpose, primary user community, and business impact.

The impact of pure transaction processing systems is usually in improving the efficiency of existing processes. No customer will choose a supplier because that supplier handles its payroll especially well or produces its general ledger with unusual elegance. TPS tend to be used primarily by employees at lower levels of the organization and tend to be used in high volume. Even though organizations have grown dependent on them and couldn't continue to function without them for long, the difference between one organization's TPS and another's generally has a comparatively small bottom-line impact.

The benefits that come from providing managers with information to make better decisions are far greater. That's where DSS come in: in making the organization more effective and giving it a competitive advantage. DSS are typically used by fewer people than use TPS, although their usage is spreading as organizations empower more and more of their workers to make decisions independently. DSS users typically use DSS less frequently; some decisions are made only at intervals, and in other cases some "think time" is needed between computer runs. For both these reasons they usually consume only a fraction of the firm's computer resources. Yet DSS make a bigger bottom-line difference than the transaction processing applications that eat up so many CPU cycles. This is analogous to the management hierarchy: People near the top are few in number compared with those further down, but they have a disproportionately large impact—for good or for bad—on the future of the organization. Figure 1–3 shows the analogy graphically. It shows no dividing lines because the boundaries are, at best, fuzzy. It gives a general idea of the relationships. Don't let it force your thinking into narrow boxes where each type of system is "supposed" to fit.

Increased use of information for decision making, as opposed to control, is a clear trend. Management "guru" Peter Drucker has written extensively on his vision of the corporation of the twenty-first century. He sees it as having fewer levels of management and far fewer managers than does today's typical corporation [DRUC88]. These managers will be empowered to make decisions on their own, as the massive controlling structures of today will no longer exist. They will make these decisions on the basis of organized feedback from colleagues, customers, and corporate headquarters: in short, information. This information-based, knowledge-based organization will depend heavily on computer-based decision support systems.

Early DSS were designed to provide useful information for individual decision makers. As both management styles and computer technology evolved, a new type of DSS has come into being that focuses on supporting the way groups of people make decisions jointly. These systems are called *group DSS,*

FIGURE 1–3

Twin Pyramids of Organizational Structure and Information System Usage

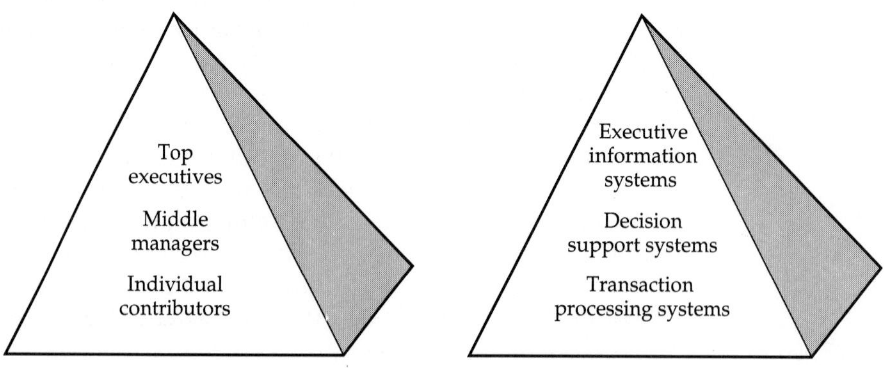

GDSS for short. In the early 1990s, GDSS are the fastest growing area in DSS. They are likely to be quite important to you in your work: developing them, implementing them in an organization that wants their benefits, and using them for your own decisions.

1.4 SPECIFIC DSS BENEFITS

Organizations, and people within organizations, adopt decision support systems in order to improve some aspect of their operation. We must make this vague desire more specific if we are to plan and develop effective DSS. This section will tell you about specific ways in which DSS can help an organization. The benefits are not mutually exclusive: It is possible, indeed desirable, for one DSS to help an organization in more than one way. For example, a DSS that facilitates communication (see Section 1.4.3) may also, if managers are part of the improved communication process, increase organizational control (see Section 1.4.5).

These categories of DSS benefits were originally described by Steven Alter [ALTE80]. Alter's research is about 15 years old as this book is being written. Nonetheless, we will cite it several times because people and their decision support needs haven't changed much. The technologies used to support DSS today would impress an observer from the late 1970s, but the benefits of those technologies in supporting decisions—with a few exceptions noted below—are much the same.

1.4.1 Improving Personal Efficiency

Many DSS don't do anything a person couldn't do himself or herself. They just do it far faster and with less chance of error. People prepared budgets for centuries before spreadsheet software came into use. Today, few spreadsheet users would willingly revert to manual techniques.

We mustn't confuse efficiency with effectiveness or productivity. A spreadsheet may allow a budget analyst to assess the consequences of a set of choices in a few seconds. People in this situation often fall victim to "computer syndrome": repeated iterations of a problem well after the incremental improvement from one iteration to the next has passed the point of diminishing returns. Without a spreadsheet program, our hypothetical budget analyst might have spent a day on the budget, tried five options, and stopped with a fully satisfactory result. With the program, the same analyst might try 200 options in two days with no measurable improvement in the outcome. Efficiency went up 20-fold, from 5 options evaluated per day to 100. Productivity was cut in half because the budgeting process took two days instead of one.

1.4.2 Expediting Problem Solving

The previous category referred to efficiency in carrying out a specific calculation or data retrieval task. This category of DSS benefits refers to solving the overall problem of which that task is a part. A DSS can make it possible for a person or a group to solve a problem faster or better than they could without it. There is a relationship between the two, of course: Increasing the efficiency of a small task hopefully contributes to solving the problem as a whole.

Solving a problem faster is self-explanatory. Some decisions must be made quickly, before the value of a correct decision erodes or more nimble competitors move in. In other cases a job consists largely of making decisions, and productivity is a direct function of the time spent on each. A loan officer who can evaluate two applications per hour is twice as productive, all else being equal, as one who evaluates just one per hour. A bank that can double the productivity of its loan officers needs only half as many of them, saving the costs associated with the other half. If those savings exceed the cost of the system that makes the savings possible, the system is financially justified. (The social costs of job elimination and dislocation are a separate issue, but managers must not ignore them. It is increasingly difficult, due to both legal and social pressures, to ignore these social costs.)

Solving a problem better may reflect objectively improved decision quality. If stockbrokers without a DSS can pick stocks that perform 20 percent better than the market average and if equally capable ones with a DSS can pick stocks that outperform the market by 30 percent, the benefits of the DSS are clear. The benefit of improved problem solving—better performance of the selected portfolio—is distinct from the increased efficiency with which the DSS retrieves stock information or compares alternative investments. DSS that are used many times for similar decisions, and that replace manual systems that performed the same task in the past, allow us to quantify their benefits in this way.

Solving a problem better may also mean increased consistency of decisions. Judicial sentencing is one example. Intelligent and well-informed individuals have debated "correct" sentencing for millennia without agreement. Most people agree, however, that sentencing should be consistent. One motorist should not get 30 days in jail for passing a stopped school bus if the next is fined $5 and sent home. A DSS can help ensure consistency in this as well as in other, less emotional, decisions.

DSS can improve consistency by providing decision makers with information about similar decisions that have been made in the past or with information that constrains a set of similar decisions to be made in the future. Salary increases are an example of data about a group of future decisions. Many large firms give their managers salary increase guidelines but allow managers latitude in interpreting these guidelines. A persuasive low-level manager can obtain a larger slice of a higher level manager's salary increase budget, or one manager can give widely varying increases that average out to the right figure while another keeps all raises within 1 percent of the prescribed average. Such inconsistencies are bad for morale. They can be reduced with a DSS. DSS can also help ensure consistency by making sure that all decision makers use the same assumptions and formulas in reaching their decisions.

The technology of expert systems can improve consistency by recommending, on a consistent and unemotional basis, decisions that make sense when given a particular set of facts. That's one of the many close connections between expert systems technology and decision support applications. We'll look at expert systems in detail in the second half of this book.

1.4.3 Facilitating Interpersonal Communication

Alter found that DSS facilitate interpersonal communication in several ways [ALTE80]. In addition, technology developments that have occurred since his research have opened up new ways for DSS to provide this benefit.

One way in which DSS facilitate communication is as a tool for persuasion: that a particular action should be taken in the future (*offensive* use) or that a particular action was taken properly in the past (*defensive* use).

> *Example of offensive use:* A carefully constructed spreadsheet can persuade a manager to approve a subordinate's budget request. That subordinate may, as a result, obtain more resources than other subordinates whose requests are not as well documented.
>
> *Example of defensive use:* A financial forecast can explain, after the fact, why a project that failed was nonetheless a good bet based on what was known when it was approved.

Both these examples involve decisions that initially appear to be individual decisions, but that turn out in effect to be group decisions when viewed in a broader organizational context. The proliferation of graphic embellishment capabilities in modern spreadsheet packages is eloquent testimony to the importance of such situations in the business world.

DSS also facilitate communication by providing a common basis for decision making, including standardization of concepts, mechanics, and vocabulary. These are important in group decisions. Two people may disagree over the implications of a decline in "last year's sales," when the real disagreement is over just what "last year's sales" consists of. Does it refer to sales in units, as production people normally measure them, or in dollars, as marketing people do? (Many electronics firms currently have increasing unit sales and decreasing revenue.) Does it mean the previous calendar year or the most recent 12 months? Does it count what was booked, what was shipped, what was accepted by customers, what was installed, or what was paid for? Does it reflect returns made this year of goods sold last year? If the word "sales" is defined in terms of specific data elements to be retrieved from a database, this source of disagreement is removed. Similarly, if it is agreed that all business forecasts should assume 5.5 percent inflation, the forecasts will be consistent on this point.

A new form of DSS that is designed specifically to provide this type of benefit is called *groupware.* Groupware is decision support software designed to accommodate the way in which a group reaches decisions and to support its activities as a group. To deal effectively with group interactions during the decision-making process, groupware must fulfill an interpersonal communication function. We'll discuss groupware again briefly in Section 4.5 and in more detail in Chapter 5.

Some forms of groupware facilitate communication by providing more convenient communication vehicles than were formerly available. Electronic mail is an elementary example of this genre, as are computerized "bulletin boards" and various forms of electronic conferencing. Others provide clerical support to decision makers, such as by automatic scheduling of meetings for times when all participants are available. These capabilities are helpful—decision makers do send messages, and they do sometimes have to meet—but they are more properly classified as office automation tools or office information systems than as DSS. (This is another example of the point we made earlier: The boundaries between types of information systems are seldom clear cut.)

True group DSS reflect the nature of the group decision-making process. This may appear in automatic routing of documents so that each participant in a group decision can contribute at the right time. Insurance claims can be routed to the right people in the right order, with each person having available what was done before and being able to add his or her contribution in the right place.

1.4.4 Promoting Learning or Training

Improved learning was seldom a goal of early DSS. However, it often occurred as a by-product of their use. Today it is often deliberately incorporated into DSS design.

Improved learning is often associated with DSS that follow a human-like process in reaching a decision, as opposed to DSS that simply provide information for humans to use. Expert systems, which we cover in detail beginning in Chapter 12, can be designed to provide this type of benefit. Most expert systems include an interface facility that allows users to ask why the system made a particular recommendation and receive an answer couched in nontechnical terms. After seeing many such explanations, expert system users begin to understand the reasoning of the experts who contributed to system development. They can make better decisions without the system than they could have made previously. Learning can properly be said to have taken place.

1.4.5 *Increasing Organizational Control*

This factor refers to using a DSS to constrain individual decisions to conform to organizational norms, guidelines, or requirements. By requiring managers to develop salary increase forecasts using a computerized system, a firm can ensure a level of consistency across organizational units.

DSS can also report information about an individual's decisions to his or her management group. This information can then be used to assess the productivity of the individuals in question. Such capabilities, even if available in a system, should be used with caution. Their use may encourage people to make "safe" decisions, which may not be in the organization's best interests. They can also damage morale. If taken to an extreme, this use of DSS raises legal and ethical privacy issues.

1.5 Why Study DSS?

One reason is that they matter to your future—or, if you're in an information systems-related job now, your current—employer. You should know something about them because you'll probably be working on them soon. We could stop there. But there are more reasons, perhaps even more important ones, that apply even if you won't be working specifically with DSS in your career.

One reason is that DSS may well be the only type of information system you will be able to pursue in depth during your course of study. Your DSS course is not, of course, your only information systems course. Yet, your other courses probably apply to several types of information systems. Systems analysis is important for defining and designing any type of system. Programming languages work with any application. Database, networking . . . all these courses are quite general.

DSS uses all these areas. If you've already studied some or all of these topics, now you'll be able to see how they come together for a specific type of application. If you haven't yet studied these areas in detail, knowing how decision support systems use them will put you in a better position to appreciate them when you get to those courses. In short, studying DSS will help you integrate what you already know, and what you are yet to learn, about MIS and about computers.

The second reason, which we hinted at in Section 1.3.2, is that virtually every information system has decision support aspects. If you understand DSS, whose primary purpose is decision support, you will be in a better position to work on the decision support side of almost any other information system as well.

A third reason, which applies even if you will not have a career as an MIS professional, is that you will be using computers in your career in any field. Much of your use will be for decision support. You will be expected to develop personal DSS via end-user computing, to be an active contributor to the development of group DSS for your work group, and to provide recommendations for enterprise-wide DSS. You will be expected to use such systems, whoever they might be developed by. The more you know about DSS, the more you will be an intelligent and informed DSS consumer—and the better your decisions, made with the help of a DSS whose capabilities and limitations you understand, will also be.

1.6 The Plan of This Book

The objective of this book is simple: to help you (together with your teacher, your classmates, and your own hard work) truly understand what DSS are all about. At the end of this course, you should be able to look at a corporate decision-making situation and see three things:

- *What* decisions are involved.
- *Where* computers could help.
- *How* computers could help.

You should then be able to make DSS recommendations that fit both the business situation and the technology. You should be able to join a team developing a DSS with a good understanding of what that DSS will do for its sponsor—your employer. In short, when it comes to DSS, you should be able to earn your keep on the job.

To help you reach this goal, this book is divided into four major parts. The first part, through Chapter 4, covers DSS in general. You'll learn about how people make decisions, how systems work, and about the characteristics of all decision support systems. You'll see how certain types of DSS fit certain types of decisions, or certain types of decision makers, best.

You'll learn how DSS are developed in Chapters 5 through 8. We'll look at the ways in which information systems can be developed, which fit DSS best, and why. You'll read about the hardware and software technologies that go into DSS. We'll also cover the nontechnical side of putting a DSS into use, including some of the ethical issues that DSS developers may face.

The next part of the book will tell you more about particular types of DSS and important aspects of many DSS. You'll learn about the major kinds of models that are useful for decision support, about systems designed to support decisions made by groups of people, and about systems designed to support decisions made by top executives. In Chapter 13, you'll see some real DSS in use and will see how the concepts of the preceding chapters all come together in practice.

Chapters 14 through 18 cover expert systems. You'll learn how these systems fit into the field of "artificial intelligence" and how they work. You'll see how they can be used to mimic the human decision-making process. This makes them uniquely suited to supporting decision makers who may not know as much about a decision as the experts do. We'll also learn about combining expert systems with other types of DSS. Just as Chapter 13 described some real DSS, Chapter 18 describes several real expert systems so you can see the types of contributions that they are making in business today.

Finally, in Chapter 19, we'll pull the picture together and put you in it as you embark on—or continue—your career.

Most of the chapters include a case that shows how the principles of that chapter work out in practice. These cases all involve a small environmental engineering firm named Envoyance. You'll meet Envoyance at the end of Chapter 2. While you don't have to be an environmental engineer to understand these cases, by the time you finish the book you may feel like one!

Summary

Decision support systems are information systems whose primary purpose is to provide knowledge workers with information on which to base informed decisions.

Decision support systems evolved when managers who used transaction processing system output recognized that it could be of value in decision making. First, they called for this data to be organized in ways that would facilitate its decision-making usage. Later, they called for the development of systems designed explicitly for this purpose. Other types of information systems also have value for decision support but are not as clearly focused on it.

Common characteristics of most or all decision support systems include their use by managers and other knowledge workers, their use of a database, and their use of models. DSS are generally used when a computer cannot be programmed to make a decision for all cases. They support, but do not replace, human decision makers.

As a general rule, decision support systems are used by people who are higher in the organization than those who use transaction processing systems. Each decision that one of these people makes has more bottom-line impact than does each transaction which a TPS processes. Their use of the system tends to be more sporadic, less steady, than does TPS use.

Decision support systems are designed to provide their sponsoring organizations with certain benefits. These benefits can be categorized as (1) improving personal efficiency, (2) expediting problem solving, (3) facilitating interpersonal communication, (4) promoting learning or training, and (5) increasing organizational control.

Key Terms

database 7
data processing (DP) 4
decision support systems (DSS) 7
defensive (DSS use) 17
electronic data processing (EDP) 4
end-user computing 8
executive information systems (EIS) 8
expediting problem solving (DSS benefit) 16
expert systems 9
facilitating interpersonal communication (DSS benefit) 17
group decision support systems (group DSS, GDSS) 14
groupware 18
improving personal efficiency (DSS benefit) 15
increasing organizational control (DSS benefit) 19
information reporting systems (IRS) 4, 8
management information system (MIS) 4
model (in a DSS) 7
offensive (DSS use) 17
office information systems (OIS) 8
personal information systems 8
promoting learning or training (DSS benefit) 18
strategic information systems (SIS) 9
transaction processing, transaction processing system (TPS) 4, 8
work group information systems 9

Review Questions

1. What is a decision support system?
2. Were DSS the first use of electronic computers? If not, what was?
3. What are seven common characteristics of most DSS?
4. In addition to DSS, list eight categories of information systems.
5. Can other types of information systems, besides DSS, have value in supporting management decisions? If so, give an example.
6. Are DSS more often used by people at the bottom of an organization or above the bottom?
7. Are the decisions made with the help of DSS of value to the organization? Why or why not?
8. Do DSS generally use most of the organization's computing resources and power?
9. State five potential areas in which DSS can benefit an organization.
10. What is the difference between improving personal efficiency and expediting problem solving?
11. In what ways can a DSS be used to facilitate communication?
12. What do we call a DSS specifically designed to help the way a group reaches joint decisions?

13. What is one type of DSS that is well suited to help its users learn how to make the decision on their own?
14. Give three reasons why it is worth your while to study DSS.
15. What three things should you be able to see in a decision-making situation after you finish this book (and this course)?

Exercises

1. Look at recent issues of information systems–oriented publications, such as *Computerworld, Information Week,* and *Datamation,* or general business publications, such as *Business Week* and *Fortune,* for examples of firms using computers to help make decisions and ads for products that claim to help people make decisions. What decisions are involved in these situations? What are the benefits of these systems or products to their users? In what ways (according to the article or the ad, which may not be objective) is using the system or product better than the alternatives?
2. Your college probably uses computers to store student records, produce class rosters, produce grade reports, print transcripts, etc. (If it doesn't, or if you're not sure, assume it does.) What decisions could the information it uses for these purposes also help with? (Hint: There is at least one decision you make every term.) Who are the decision makers in these cases? What information could the computer provide them with to help make these decisions?
3. Your firm has budgeted $100,000 to improve the performance of its central corporate computer. Options include augmenting the existing disk drives with additional ones of the same type, replacing the existing disk drives with faster ones, expanding main memory, upgrading the central processor to a faster model, rewriting some time-consuming applications for greater efficiency, adding a front-end communications processor to take some of that load off the main system, getting a stand-alone minicomputer to handle some tasks that don't require access to the central database. Which of the three example decisions in Section 1.3.2 does this decision resemble? Would the same solution work? What changes would have to be made in the approach, if any?
4. The decision examples in Section 1.3.2 were all described as individual decisions. The DSS that went along with them were, correspondingly, designed to support one person making them. Could these be group decisions? If they could, what could a group DSS do to support the group aspect of making the decision that would not help an individual decision maker?

5. Consider each of the following decisions:
   - Travel agents selecting vacation destinations for clients.
   - Individual investors deciding when to buy and sell stocks.
   - A firm's purchasing agent selecting the best supplier for parts on the basis of price quotations and the suppliers' history of part quality and on-time delivery to the firm.
   - Jet engine mechanics diagnosing engine problems as part of deciding what repairs to perform.
   - A firm's MIS steering committee deciding which new application projects it will fund.

   For each of these five decisions:

   a. Could a computerized DSS help the decision makers make these decisions? If not, why not? If so, how?

   b. State the benefit(s), in terms of the categories of Section 1.4, of each of the DSS you thought would be helpful.

References

ALTE80 Alter, Steven L, *Decision Support Systems: Current Practice and Continuing Challenges.* Addison-Wesley, Reading, Mass. (1980).

DAVI88 Davis, Michael W. *Applied Decision Support.* Prentice Hall, Englewood Cliffs, N.J. (1988).

DRUC88 Drucker, Peter F. "The Coming of the New Organization." *Harvard Business Review* 66, no. 1 (January–February 1988), pp. 45–53.

HICK93 Hicks, James. *Management Information Systems,* 3rd ed. Richard D. Irwin, Homewood, Ill. (1993).

KANT92 Kanter, Jerome. *Managing with Information,* 4th ed. Prentice Hall, Englewood Cliffs, N.J. (1992).

KEEN78 Keen, Peter G. W., and Michael S. Scott Morton. *Decision Support Systems: An Organizational Perspective.* Addison-Wesley, Reading, Mass. (1978).

KEEN79 Keen, Peter G. W., and G. R. Wagner. "DSS: An Executive Mind Support System." *Datamation* 25, no. 12 (November 1979), pp. 117–22.

KROE92 Kroenke, David M. *Management Information Systems,* 2nd ed. Mitchell McGraw-Hill, Watsonville, Calif. (1992).

LEIG86 Leigh, William E., and Michael E. Doherty. *Decision Support and Expert Systems.* South-Western Publishing, Cincinnati, Ohio (1986).

RATH92 Rathnam, Sukumar; M. R. Arun; Abhijit Chaudhury; and P. R. Shukla. "MUDRAPLAN—A DSS for Media Planning: From Design to Utilization." *Interfaces* 22, no. 2 (March–April 1992), pp. 65–75.

SILV91 Silver, Mark S. *Systems that Support Decision Makers.* John Wiley & Sons, New York (1991).

SPRA80 Sprague, Ralph H. Jr. "A Framework for the Development of Decision Support Systems." *MIS Quarterly* 4, no. 4 (December 1980), pp. 1–26.

SPRA79 Sprague, Ralph H, Jr., and Hugh J. Watson. "BIT-BY-BIT: Toward Decision Support Systems." *California Management Review* 22, no. 1 (Fall 1979), pp. 560–68. Reprinted in *Decision Support Systems: A Data-Based, Model-Oriented, User-Developed Discipline,* William C. House, ed. Petrocelli, New York (1983).

CHAPTER

2 Human Decision-Making Processes

Chapter Outline

Introduction

Decision support systems, by definition, exist to help people make decisions. They do not make decisions by themselves. This is why they are called decision *support* systems, not decision-*making* systems. Since DSS must work with human decision makers, they must fit into the style in which humans work—or, at least, into a style in which humans can be persuaded to work. A system that does not fit into human decision-making styles will not be used. If an organization forces its people to use an unsuitable system, it will create resentment, poor morale, and high turnover. DSS designers must therefore understand human decision-making processes.

Chapter Objectives

After you have read and studied this chapter, you will be able to:

1. Discuss what a decision is and how decisions are characterized.
2. Describe three phases every decision must go through.
3. Identify two important ways of categorizing decisions: on the basis of their structure and on the basis of their scope.
4. Outline the nine decision types.
5. Discuss several methods managers use to make decisions.
6. Identify four preferences which determine personality type.
7. Outline the eight stages of the Kepner-Tregoe decision-making method.

2.1 WHAT IS A DECISION?

A *decision* is a reasoned choice among alternatives. We make decisions regularly in our daily lives. Personal decisions include what to have for dinner, which courses to take, and whether to do homework or to see a movie. Business decisions include what to charge for a product, where to advertise a new service, how to finance construction equipment, and which candidate to hire for job. Business decisions may seem more significant and may get more space in the daily paper, but all are part of the same picture.

Making decisions is part of the broader subject of problem solving. Problem solving is the overall process of closing the gap between reality and a more desirable situation. To solve a problem, we must first realize that the problem—the gap—exists. We must then conclude that the problem is important enough to do something about. Having done this, we will probably discover that there are obstacles preventing us from reaching the desired state immediately and effortlessly.

In most cases there will be no one obvious way to overcome some of these obstacles. Upon reflection, possibly involving a group of people and creativity techniques such as "brainstorming," we will usually uncover several possible approaches. This leads directly to a need for one or more decisions. Once those decisions are made, they must be put into effect (implemented). The implementation must be monitored to make sure our decisions are solving the problem. If they are not, we have a new or modified problem, and the process repeats.

Each decision is characterized by a decision statement, a set of alternatives, and a set of decision-making criteria. These always exist, though we are not always aware of them.

The *decision statement* states what we are trying to decide. A clear decision statement is important to intelligent decision making. It keeps our thinking focused clearly on the main subject and away from irrelevant side issues. If a decision is to be made by a group of people, a clear decision statement ensures that all members of the group are trying to decide the same thing. Decision support tools such as electronic mail (a *group* decision support tool, which we'll focus on in Chapter 11) can help people in different locations communicate about a joint decision statement.

If you do not have a clear decision statement, you cannot develop the best system to support people making that decision. Begin every DSS development project by getting—or at least trying to get—a clear understanding of the decision(s) to be made with the help of the proposed system.

The *alternatives* are the possible decisions we can make. Sometimes there are few alternatives: a stadium vendor offers only pizza and hot dogs, or there are only two candidates for a job that must be filled now. In other situations there are thousands: to pick an investment from all the firms whose stock is traded on major stock exchanges or to choose the mix of options to be installed in a factory-ordered automobile. For these, the decision maker needs to narrow the range down to a reasonable number. Decision support tools such as selective information retrieval systems can help with this task.

Decision making criteria are what we want to optimize in a decision. In making an investment we may be concerned with income, growth, and safety of principal. In choosing a car we care about appearance, comfort, performance, economy of operation, reliability, safety, and initial cost. It may not be possible to maximize all these at the same time. Stocks with above-average growth potential often have above-average risk. Most high-performance cars are not economical to operate. Compromises are mandatory. Decision makers often cannot define their approach to compromises in a precise mathematical way. Indeed, they often cannot define their decision-making criteria precisely. However, the criteria and the approaches to compromise exist even if the decision maker cannot specify them. Where the selection process among alternatives can be put in numerical terms, computers can help carry out the evaluation. Even where this is not the case, computers can assist in presenting the alternatives in a form that facilitates making a decision.

2.2 The Decision Process

Every decision must go through three phases, which were first defined by Herbert Simon in [SIMO60]. These phases are called *intelligence*, *design*, and *choice.* The emphasis on each phase, and the relationships among the phases, often differ from one decision to another because

- Different people may emphasize one phase or another, as we'll see when we discuss preferred styles of behavior in Section 2.5.
- Different decision-making situations call for spending more time in one phase or another.
- We often bounce back and forth among the phases: We may try to select an alternative only to discover we don't know enough to do that yet, so we go back and collect more data.

Despite these facts, and despite the fact that we are not always consciously aware of what we are doing when we make a decision, all three phases exist in some form in every decision we make. It is important for the prospective developer of a DSS to understand these phases because the type of support a computer can best provide depends on the decision phase that is under way.

2.2.1 The Intelligence Phase

The intelligence phase consists of finding, identifying, and formulating the problem or situation that calls for a decision. (This has been called *deciding what to decide.*) The intelligence stage may involve, for example, comparing the current status of a project or process with its plan. The end result of the intelligence phase is a decision statement.

Example. At about 6 o'clock one evening, we suddenly realize we are hungry and haven't made any preparations for dinner. We have at this point identified a situation that calls for a decision. The decision statement is simple: What to do about dinner?

It is important not to confuse the symptoms of a problem with the underlying problem itself. Suppose a customer calls to complain about late deliveries. If we think in terms of alleviating the symptom, we may arrange for that customer to receive future shipments via an overnight air courier service. If the underlying problem is an understaffed shipping department, however, this will merely placate one of many unhappy customers without identifying, let alone dealing with, the real issue.

The name of this phase, "intelligence," can be confusing. Intelligence, as we usually use the term informally in talking about decision making, is what we use after we know a decision must be made. Simon borrowed the term from its military meaning, which involves the gathering of information without necessarily knowing what it will lead to in terms of decisions to be made. In business decision making, we must often collect a great deal of information before we realize that a decision is called for.

Military intelligence can also, of course, be more focused: We might try to determine an enemy's troop distribution in order to concentrate an attack on its weak points. That type of information gathering falls into the next phase of decision making.

2.2.2 The Design Phase

The design phase is where we develop alternatives. This phase may involve a great deal of research into the available options. During the design phase we should also state our objectives for the decision we are to make.

Example. In deciding what to do about dinner, we have two broad categories of choices, cooking or letting someone else cook. Both can be broken down further. If we cook, we can either use ingredients that are already in our kitchen, or we can go to the store. If we let someone else cook, we can try to get a free meal at a friend's house, or we can go to a restaurant in any of several categories.

The Importance of Creativity

What creative alternatives can you come up with? That's your goal for the design phase of the decision. The classic story helps illustrate what a creative alternative is.

A physics professor asked his class on a midterm exam, "How could you use a barometer to find the height of a building?" He wanted the standard answer that uses a barometer's unique capability to measure atmospheric pressure: Measure the pressure on the roof, measure it again at ground level, then calculate the height from the difference. He also got these creative (and totally correct) responses:

- Drop the barometer from the roof. With a stopwatch, time its fall until it crashes into the sidewalk. Use the formula for acceleration under gravity to find the height.
- Tie a long string to the barometer. Lower it from the roof to just above the sidewalk. Swing it from side to side and time its oscillations. Use the formula for oscillation frequency as a function of pendulum length to find the height.
- Walk up the stairs from the ground floor to the roof. Place the barometer against the wall as you go, thus measuring the building in units of barometer length. Then, measure the barometer with a ruler, and convert the result to feet and inches.
- Place the barometer in the sun near the building. Measure its shadow and that of the building. Then measure the height of the barometer. Calculate the height of the building from the length of its shadow and the ratio of the barometer's height to the length of the barometer's shadow.

My personal favorite, however, is this:

- Take the barometer to the building superintendent's office. Say to the superintendent, "I have this fine brass and wood barometer. I will give it to you, if you will look at the plans of this building and tell me how high it is."

2.2.3 *The Choice Phase*

In the choice phase, we evaluate the alternatives that we developed in the design phase and choose one of them. The end product of this phase is a decision that we can carry out.

Example. We might select a dinner option on the basis of speed, cost, and food quality. Their relative importance varies from person to person and from time to time for a given person. If we're in a hurry, on a budget, and just want to fill our stomach, we can eat a container of yogurt or make a peanut butter and jelly sandwich. Given more time and money, we might go to the new restaurant down the street.

The three decision phases are not as separate as this description implies. As Simon points out:

> The cycle of phases is, however, far more complex than the sequence suggests. Each phase in making a particular decision is itself a complex decision-making process. The decision phase, for example, may call for new intelligence activities; problems at any given level generate subproblems that in turn have their intelligence, design, and choice phases, and so on. There are wheels within wheels.

The message is that decision making is often an iterative process. We start by making a decision. We then proceed to put that decision into effect. At that point we may encounter an unanticipated difficulty: a shortage of parts for our product design or a price tag of $35,000 on that "cute little car." We return to an earlier stage and consider additional alternatives in the light of our new information. We may even revise our decision-making criteria if we realize, having looked at our first choice in more detail, that we left one or more important ones out. We may even build iterations into our decision-making process. A common example is in the development of a major information system, where management schedules periodic project reviews and, at each one, decides whether or not to continue with the next phase of the effort.

Despite this truism, knowing which decision phase we are in can help us design the right computer system to support that phase. In the intelligence phase, we may need broad-based information gathering capabilities. In design, more focused information retrieval or perhaps brainstorming aids could be useful. In the choice phase, optimization tools can help.

2.3 Types of Decisions

Decisions can be categorized in several ways. This is useful because decisions of the same type often have common characteristics. They can therefore benefit from similar computer support. If, as DSS developers, we can categorize a decision, then we will be able to see which DSS have been used to good effect with that type of decision in the past and can expect similar DSS to help with the problem at hand.

Following Keen and Scott Morton [KEEN78], we can organize decisions along two dimensions: the nature of the decision to be made and the scope of the decision itself. By dividing each dimension into three categories, we obtain nine decision types as shown in Figure 2–1. The three categories shown down the left side of Figure 2–1 (from [KEEN78]) extend Simon's earlier concept of programmed versus nonprogrammed decisions. Those categories are as follows:

- A *structured* decision is one for which a well-defined decision-making procedure exists. A structured decision could be given over to a

FIGURE 2–1

3 × 3 Decision Type Grid

Decision	*Operational*	*Tactical*	*Strategic*
Structured	1	2	3
Semistructured	4	5	6
Unstructured	7	8	9

computer program, although the economics might not justify developing such a program in every case. More precisely, a structured decision is one for which the inputs, outputs, and internal procedures of all three decision phases discussed in Section 2.2 (intelligence, design, and choice) can be specified. Each decision phase for which this is true is called a *structured decision phase.* Structured decisions can be left to a clerk or a computer.

- An *unstructured* decision is one for which all three decision phases are unstructured. We don't know how to specify at least one aspect of each phase: its inputs, its outputs, or its internal procedures. This may be because the decision is so new or so rare that we haven't studied it carefully. Computers can still help the decision maker, but only with a lower level of support.
- A *semistructured* decision has some structured aspects but cannot be completely structured. This usually means that one or two of its three phases is structured but the other one (or two) isn't. Computers can provide a great deal of specific help with semistructured decisions. Conveniently, most organizational decisions are of this type.

The proper placement of a decision within these three categories is not always clear cut. Sometimes our approach to a problem defines, for us, how we think about it. One decision maker may feel that an optimum selling price can be determined via analysis of product costs and price-demand curves. This person would consider the choice phase of this decision to be structured. Another might argue that these curves do not reflect all the factors that affect customer response to a particular price level and that several important ones cannot be quantified. That person would, equally correctly, consider the choice phase of this decision to be unstructured.

The three levels of decision scope across the top of Figure 2–1 (originally from [ANTH65]) are as follows:

- A *strategic* decision is one that will affect the entire organization, or a major part of it, for a long period of time. Strategic decisions affect organizational objectives and policies. Strategic decisions are generally, but not always, made at the upper levels of organizational management.

- A *tactical* decision, also called a management control decision, will affect how a part of the organization does business for a limited time into the future. Tactical decisions generally take place within the context of previous strategic decisions. Tactical decisions are generally made by "middle managers"—those who are below the top executives who set strategic policies but are high enough to determine how an entire category of future actions will be taken.
- An *operational* decision is one that affects activities taking place in the organization right now but either has little or no impact on the future or—if it does—is made within the confines of a controlling policy. Operational decisions relate to activities whose tasks, goals, and resources have already been defined via prior strategic and tactical decisions. Operational decisions are generally made by lower level managers or by nonmanagerial personnel.

Decisions of these three types vary in their information requirements: from detailed to aggregated, near-present to future, etc. Figure 2–2, from [KEEN78], shows the key information characteristics of each decision level. Using this table, if you know the scope of a decision being made, you will have a good idea of the type of data your DSS will require.

The two decision characteristics are not unrelated. As a general rule, operational decisions tend to be more structured. Strategic decisions tend to be less so. Here are examples of the nine decision types to help give you a feel for the categories:

1. *Structured/Operational:* deciding how to cut a log into boards in order to minimize wastage. In most sawmills this decision is not made by computers, although computers have been proven to be good at it; it is usually made by experienced saw operators. One practical difficulty is measuring each log precisely and entering its dimensions—not just its overall length and diameter, but all its twists and variations—into a computer quickly enough for the result to be useful.

We can see why this decision is considered structured by looking at the three decision phases. The intelligence phase is trivial: If a log arrives at the mill, it must be cut. The design phase is likewise fixed: The products that the mill produces, and hence the acceptable types of cuts, are not within the purview of the saw operator. The choice phase is subject to mathematical optimization: The value of each potential board can be determined from business considerations, and the number of boards that can be obtained via various combinations of cuts is a problem in solid geometry.

Inventory reordering also falls into the structured/operational category, particularly if the organization has enough experience with a specific item (or a good enough forecast of its future use) to benefit from the mathematical models that have been developed for this field.

FIGURE 2–2

Information Characteristics by Decision Scope

Information Characteristic	*Operational*	*Tactical (management)*	*Strategic*
Accuracy	High	⟷	Low
Level of detail	Detailed	⟷	Aggregate
Time horizon	Present	⟷	Future
Frequency of use	Frequent	⟷	Infrequent
Source	Internal	⟷	External
Scope of information	Narrow	⟷	Wide
Nature of information	Quantitative	⟷	Qualitative
Age of information	Current	⟷	Can be older
Flexibility of organizing information*	Can be rigid	⟷	Must be flexible

*Added to Keen's original figure.

2. *Structured/Tactical:* choosing the way in which to depreciate corporate assets. There are many options, including straight-line depreciation and various accelerated depreciation formulas, that provide earlier tax benefits than does the straight-line method. Accelerated depreciation, however, may have drawbacks as well, such as making the depreciated asset ineligible for investment tax credits. The issues are complex and vary with every revision of the tax code but—if the depreciable life of this type of asset is specified by the tax code and if the choice can be made on a net-present-value or similar numerical basis—are entirely quantitative and can be dealt with mechanically.

Resource allocation problems that can be solved by linear programming methods are also in this category. As with inventory management, the issue is whether the problem to be solved meets the requirements for this approach to apply.

3. *Structured/Strategic:* This is a rare combination. An example might be a decision that is usually tactical in nature but that, because of its size, becomes one of the "you-bet-your-company" variety. Deciding whether or not to proceed with a research and development (R&D) project on the basis of projected return on investment (ROI) might normally be a tactical decision, but if the proposed project will tie up 80 percent of the firm's R&D staff for the next two years, it becomes strategic. (If factors other than projected ROI enter into the decision, it might not be structured.)

A plant location decision could be in this category if the only factors in the decision are quantifiable, such as transportation costs of known raw materials from known locations and of known products to known markets.

4. *Semistructured/Operational:* deciding to accept or reject an applicant to a selective college. Some parts of this decision are quite structured: An applicant with a combined SAT score of 1400 is, all other things being roughly equal, more likely to succeed academically than one with a combined score

of 600. Other issues, such as a desire to balance the nonacademic characteristics of an entering class and the degree to which unusual talents, such as playing third base or double bass, can offset below-average grades, are not subject to quantitative evaluation.

5. *Semistructured/Tactical:* choosing an insurance carrier for an employee health program. Cost per employee is an important and objective factor in this decision. Intangible factors include the acceptability of a carrier to the employee population and the relative importance of different benefits: Is 100 percent hospitalization coverage with a $250 deductible amount better or worse than 80 percent coverage with no deductible?

6. *Semistructured/Strategic:* deciding whether or not to enter a new market segment. Sales projections, marketplace growth data, development cost estimates, and marketing expense forecasts can combine to provide a profit-and-loss forecast. This forecast, however, cannot take into account the myriad factors that could make it totally worthless. The judgment of experienced managers is needed for that final step.

7. *Unstructured/Operational:* dealing with a machine breakdown. If the machine in question doesn't break down often, there is probably no set procedure for what to do while awaiting the repair service.

8. *Unstructured/Tactical:* Hiring decisions typically fall into this area, especially if the job to be filled is above the level where aptitude and ability tests can be relied on as performance indicators. Civil Service procedures have attempted to structure the hiring task for years. The wide use of "escape hatches," such as allowing a police chief to choose the next captain from the three top-scoring lieutenants on a promotion exam, is eloquent testimony to their lack of complete success.

9. *Unstructured/Strategic:* deciding how to respond to an unfriendly takeover proposal made by a competitor. The range of options is so wide, they differ so much from each other, and the issues are so hard to quantify, that direct comparison is all but futile.

2.4 How Managers Make Decisions

Managers' decisions have a great impact on a corporate success, making their study of obvious interest. The subject of managerial decision making has therefore been studied at great length. The many methods by which managers make decisions can be categorized along three dimensions: rationality, politicality, and flexibility [DEAN91].

Rationality in decision making is the extent to which the decision makers collect and analyze information objectively and choose among the alternatives on the basis of these alternatives' relationship to predetermined objectives.

Politicality is the extent to which a decision involves competition among decision makers and the extent to which the decision depends on the distribution and use of organizational power.

Flexibility is the extent to which decision makers free themselves from tradition and structure, potentially making choices that "break the mold."

2.4.1 The Rational Manager

Rational management is the classical assumption about how managers make, or are supposed to make, decisions. The rational manager presumably obtains all possible facts, weighs the likelihood of the alternative outcomes, and chooses the one with the highest statistically probable value to the firm.

In terms of the three dimensions just listed, the rational manager is clearly high on the rationality scale. This does not, however, necessarily imply that he or she is low on the other two. As Dean and his colleagues point out, an acceptable decision can be the product of both rational and political factors, perhaps by using rational analysis to select among politically viable options.

Decision trees are a useful way to represent the options facing the rational manager. Decision trees presume a sequence of events of the from "if I do A, then X or Y might happen; if Y happens I can do B or C, in which case R, S, or T might happen." They reflect the rational manager's thought process in choosing among those options. Figure 2–3 is an example of a decision tree. This tree has two levels. The first represents the management decision. The second represents the possible "states of nature" that will result. A decision tree may have more than two levels but will always have an even number. It always starts with a decision, the two types of nodes always alternate, and states of nature are always at the ends of the branches.

FIGURE 2–3

Decision Tree for Truck Engine Decision

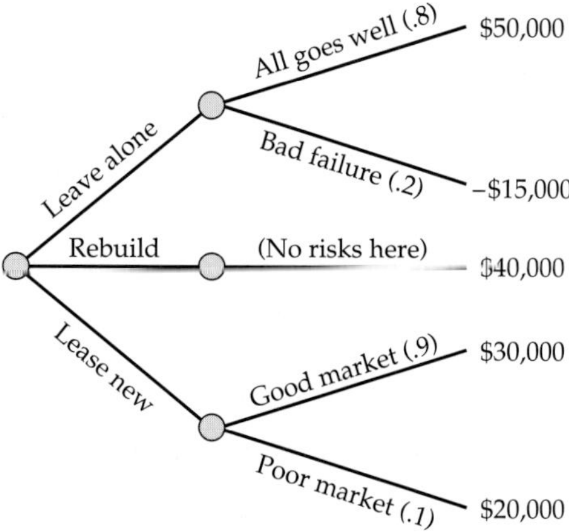

The decision to be made in Figure 2–3 is, Should we rebuild a truck's worn engine, leave it as is, or replace the truck? Leaving it alone costs nothing today, will enable us to make a profit of $50,000 over our two-year planning horizon with a likelihood of 80 percent, but also presents a 20 percent chance of incurring a $15,000 loss due to unexpected failures. Rebuilding costs $5,000 and ensures a $45,000 operating profit over the two years, for net profit of $40,000. (We would have made the other $5,000 while the truck will be off the road having its engine rebuilt.) A new truck will cost $50,000 to lease for two years, will enable us to earn an $80,000 profit during the two years since it will be both faster and more economical to operate than our present rig, but has a 10 percent probability of a $10,000 charge at the end of the lease if the market value of this type of truck is low at that time.

The decision tree allows us to evaluate the probable payoff of each option. The probable payoff of rebuilding the engine is $40,000 since we have assumed that no chance misfortunes can befall that choice. The probable payoff of letting nature take its course with the engine is 8 × $50,000 + 0.2 × (−$15,000) = $40,000 − $3,000 = $37,000. A similar calculation, working back from the end nodes and their probabilities, shows that the probable payoff of leasing a new truck is $29,000. Accordingly, the rational manager opts to rebuild the engine.

A tree is not the only possible way to evaluate the possible outcomes of a decision such as this. Other approaches include decision tables and formulas. Figure 2–4 shows a decision table for a business that must choose a small, medium, or large computer and that may encounter high or low customer acceptance of its services. Palvia and Gordon compare the three approaches in [PALV92], from which the example in Figure 2–4 is taken. They found that the table method was preferable overall for the sample task used in their study but that this varies with the specific task and with the characteristics of the decision maker. The truck engine example above is difficult to express as a decision table because the "state of nature" possibilities vary depending on the choice we make; that is, the factors that determine the resale value of a new truck at the end of the lease are not the same as those that determine whether an old engine, if not repaired, will fail on the road.

FIGURE 2–4
Decision Table Example

	Profit as Function of Computer System Choice and Customer Acceptance of Firm's Services	
Decision Alternative	*High Customer Acceptance (30% probable)*	*Low Customer Acceptance (70% probable)*
Lease large computer system	$200,000	(−$20,000) (loss)
Lease medium computer system	$150,000	$20,000
Lease small computer system	$100,000	$60,000

Tables work better in situations such as the one in Figure 2–4, where all the choices are subject to the same chance effects. In the example of Figure 2–4, a rational manager who wants to maximize the statistically expected profit would choose the small computer system.

Statistically expected profit is not the only possible decision criterion. At one extreme, a risk-averse manager might want the best possible result if the worst state of nature occurs. That is the $60,000 profit in the bottom right cell of the figure. This manager would make the same choice as the rational manager: get the small computer. A "high roller," however, might go for the maximum possible payoff even at the risk of high losses if the best state of nature does not occur. This manager would see the $200,000 possible profit in the top row and would get the large computer. Neither of these two philosophies is truly rational in the traditional sense, but they do exist.

2.4.2 *Subjective Utility*

Human beings are not, as you have probably noticed by this stage in your life, entirely rational. Suppose the rebuilding work in the decision tree (Figure 2–3) cost $10,000 rather than $5,000. The expected profit would then be highest if we let nature take its course. The rational manager would instruct the driver to fill the tank, head for the loading dock, pick up the next load, and hope for the best.

However, the average person looks at things differently. A manager who recommends a rebuilt engine will probably not be questioned. Nothing much can go wrong if that choice is made. But what if the manager recommends staying with the status quo? At first, he or she can justify a decision on the basis of the numbers and will probably get a small pat on the back for not tying up the truck for repairs. Suppose, though, that the engine fails while the truck is halfway from Miami to Seattle with a perishable, time-critical shipment for the firm's biggest customer. At that point the manager will be in serious trouble. A year-old decision tree that showed a $3,000 statistical profit expectation will not be of much help in his or her defense against charges of professional incompetence.

What happened here is that the individual manager's *utility curve* does not match the linear one that rational managers are presumed to have. A person's utility curve defines the relationship between the amount of something that the person has and its value to the person. Most utility curves flatten as the amount of a good that one possesses increases. For example, the value of owning an automobile is, to the typical single suburban professional, high. The value of having a second automobile is considerably lower, that of a third lower yet, and that of a fourth essentially zero. Economists measure utility in units called *utils*. While each of the above four automobiles may be worth the same number of dollars, their value in utils differs. Our suburbanite may decide that the first car is worth more utils than having another $20,000 in the bank is worth but that the second one isn't.

Figure 2–5A shows this person's subjective feelings about the value of owning zero or more cars and of having money in the bank, expressed in utils. The automobile curve flattens out rapidly after the first one. The money curve is straighter, reflecting the fact that additional money is potentially useful, while a person can only use one car at a time. The straighter money curve also reflects the assumption that our decision maker has more than $80,000 in the bank, so the zero point on the curve is to the left of that part in Figure 2–5. If we were looking at the utility value of one's first $20,000, it might well be higher. Few people who have a total of $20,000 to their name would spend every last penny of their net worth on a car.

Figure 2–5B flips the money curve horizontally so the points corresponding to each possible decision line up: no cars and no change to the bank balance, one car and $20,000 less in the bank, etc. We can see by eye that the total height of both curves is greatest when one car is purchased. That is, therefore, the chosen decision.

Economists call this type of utility theory, which measures utility in terms of an objective yardstick, *cardinal utility*. Some economists, pointing out that

FIGURE 2–5

Cardinal Utility Curves

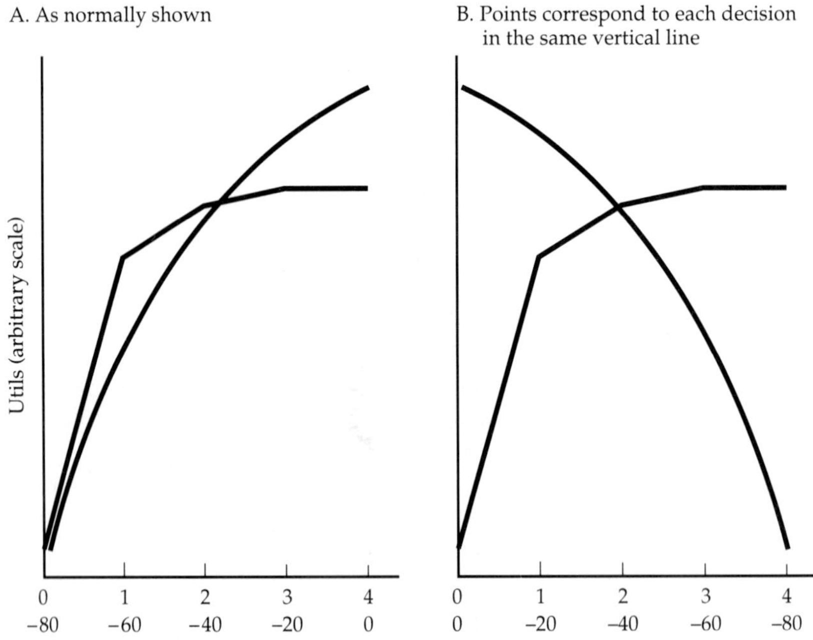

Upper scale: Automobiles purchased.
Lower scale: Change in bank balance (in units of $1,000).

none of us has had any experience with a util, prefer to deal with *ordinal utility.* Ordinal utility theory defines utility in terms of combinations of goods that the decision maker considers to be of equivalent value. In terms of ordinal utility, the automobile purchaser might rank the utility of the available options as follows:

1. One automobile, $20,000 less in the bank (highest utility).
2. Two automobiles, $40,000 less in the bank.
3. No automobiles, bank balance unchanged.
4. Three automobiles, $60,000 less in the bank.
5. Four automobiles, $80,000 less in the bank (lowest utility).

Figure 2–6 shows this decision maker's *indifference curves.* The purchaser considers each combination of automobiles and money along a given curve to be of equivalent subjective value. The curves are "higher," in some unspecified sense, as we move to the upper right of the figure. The highest value curve is the one that passes through the point (one automobile, −$20,000 in the bank). This curve also passes through the point (two automobiles, −$30,000 in the bank). This suggests that if our purchaser could get the second automobile for less than $10,000, he or she would buy it. This is, of course, an unlikely event. The third curve passes through (zero automobiles, bank balance unchanged). This curve also passes, approximately, through (one automobile, −$38,000). This suggests that if an acceptable automobile cost up to about $38,000, it would be purchased; above that amount, it would not.

FIGURE 2–6

Automobile Purchase Indifference Curves

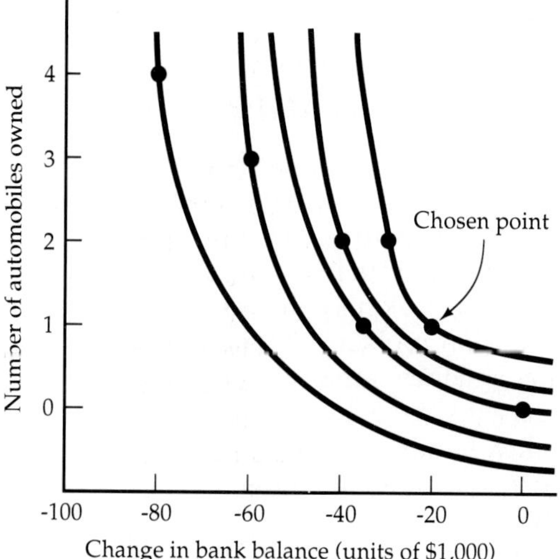

Having made this ranking, or at least the top part of it, our purchaser buys one car and is happy.

Ranking alternatives in this way can be a useful decision aid. Suppose you are asked to expedite the Bell shipment to be sure it gets out this week. You know that doing this will delay another customer's order. So you ask your boss, "How long a delay in shipping the Danforth order will you accept if I can get the Bell shipment out this week? A one-week delay? Two weeks?"

Knowing the answer to such a question can often save a great deal of detailed analysis. Suppose the answer is, "Get the Bell order out this week as long as it doesn't impact the Danforth shipping date by more than five weeks." You may be able to figure out in five minutes that the impact on the Danforth order can't possibly be more than three weeks, so you expedite the Bell order. Without this information, you might have wasted a great deal of time trying to ascertain if the impact on the Danforth order was two weeks and two days or two weeks and three days—which has absolutely no effect on the decision.

In the truck engine example, the positive utility value to an individual salaried manager of a slightly larger profit is small. The negative utility value to this same manager of a loss, where the loss is directly traceable to his or her decision, is enormous. Measured in utils, the −15,000 on the second arm of the decision tree is far too low. A figure of −1,500,000 would be closer to the manager's subjective perception of career disaster if this event should occur. This figure puts the option of leaving the engine alone in a distant third place.

In terms of the three dimensions of decision making, subjective utility is likewise high on rationality—if we define rationality appropriately, in terms of utils rather than dollars. Since utility is defined in a context of the decision maker's views about the future distribution and use of power, it has a clear political aspect as well.

2.4.3 *Systematic Decision Making*

There are several decision-making processes that, while they do not yield a decision that is optimal in a mathematical sense and, therefore, do not qualify for the "rational management" label, do let a decision maker approach an issue in a manner free from personal bias.

Systematic decision-making processes in this sense are usually applied to "multiattribute decision problems," where the alternatives are described by a several attributes and they cannot all be optimized simultaneously. Choosing a car is such a decision: The potential buyer must consider cost, performance, economy, reliability, handling, styling, carrying capacity, convenience of service locations, cost, and more. (It is often cost that forces a compromise among the other attributes.)

It is often possible to reduce the number of alternatives being considered by determining their "envelope." The envelope eliminates all the alternatives that are inferior to some other alternative on all attributes, or, at best, equal on some and inferior on the others. This process may not reduce the number of alternatives to one, so it must be followed by something else in order to reach a decision. Still, reducing the number of alternatives to consider can't hurt and is often of considerable benefit.

Suppose we must choose an instructor for a financial accounting course next term. Published evaluations by previous students rank the five available instructors in terms of the workload each one assigns (which we would like to be low) and how much students felt they learned in the course (which we would like to be high). This list is shown in the following table.

Instructor	*Workload (10 = low)*	*Learning (10 = high)*
Kahn	3	9
Keady	9	3
Kilroy	7	7
Kosinski	4	6
Kuchar	6	4

We plot these rankings in Figure 2–7. The envelope is the line starting at 9 on the workload axis, connecting Keady, Kilroy and Kahn, and ending at 9 on the learning axis. This method allows us to eliminate Kosinski and Kuchar as options. We could have probably done that more easily in this simple,

FIGURE 2–7

Chart of Instructor Choice Options

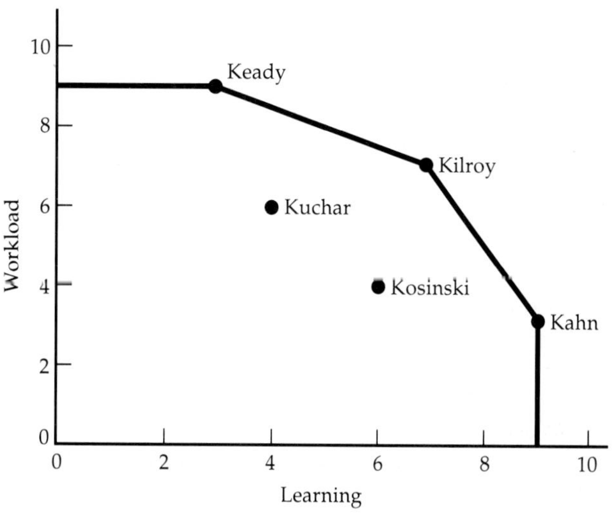

two-variable case, but most practical situations have more than two variables and more than five alternatives. (They are also harder to represent in a graph on two-dimensional paper, but computers take that type of complexity in their stride.) We still have to choose one of the remaining three instructors. That will depend on our feelings about the relative importance of the factors. The following systematic decision-making methods help deal with this part of the decision.

"Lexicographic elimination" starts with the most important attribute and keeps the alternative that ranks highest on that score. If two or more are tied, it proceeds to the next and so on until either one alternative has been selected or the remaining ones are tied on all attributes. Here, if we decide that learning is the most important attribute in selecting an instructor, the lexicographic elimination method would lead us to sign up for Professor Kahn's section.

The "elimination by aspects" method [TVER72] considers one attribute at a time and compares it against a predetermined minimal acceptable standard. Any alternatives that do not meet this standard are discarded. If we want to learn at least as much as a score of 5 on that scale would indicate, we can eliminate Professor Keady from further consideration. We would then apply the workload standard to try to choose one of the others. If we were willing to work up to an 8, elimination by aspects would leave us with a choice between Professors Kahn and Kilroy. Systematic decision-making methods such as this one often do not narrow the choice down to one alternatives.

"Conjunctive decision making" [TODD92] applies the same concept as elimination by aspects—comparing attributes against predetermined minimal acceptable levels—but in the other order. Instead of comparing the same attribute of all alternatives against its criterion and proceeding through the attributes, it compares all attributes of one alternative against all criteria and proceeds through alternatives. The end result is the same. The amount of work done to get there may differ.

Other methods attempt to integrate the values of all attributes into an overall score for each alternative based on the importance of each attribute expressed as a numerical weight. The "additive linear" model computes a score for each alternative by multiplying its score on each attribute by a predetermine weight for that attribute. The "additive difference" model [TVER69] weights the difference between scores of two alternatives on each attribute by a predetermined weight for that attribute and discards the lower ranking alternative. This continues until only one alternative remains.

Many other such strategies have been proposed as ways to formalize the often informal process of searching for the best alternative. Twelve such strategies are described in [SVEN79]. The implementation effort required for several strategies is discussed in [TODD91].

Systematic decision-making methods rank high in rationality and relatively low in terms of politicality and flexibility—although there are opportunities for both of these to arise in the values set for weights, the ordering of attributes, and the thresholds for rejecting an alternative.

2.4.4 *Satisficing*

The term "satisficing" was coined by Simon to describe the actions of a decision maker who wants a decision that's "good enough" [SIMO60]. If management has set a goal of a 20 percent cost reduction and a decision maker has reached 21.7 percent, there may be little reason to see if yet another change will raise this figure to 24 percent. As Ackoff and Sasieni put it [ACKO68], "satisficing appeals to planners who are not willing to stick their necks out."

Satisficing is not always bad. This may be a perfectly sensible thing for a decision maker to do: It is often not possible to discover, let alone investigate, all of the options. Furthermore, the resources that would be expended in looking for further improvements must perforce be taken from some other activity, which also has a payoff. Leaving well enough alone in terms of one decision may actually be optimal, in a more global sense, by letting a decision maker focus attention on things that really matter.

Satisficing contains elements of rational and political decision making. It is low on flexibility; in fact, it is often felt to characterize rigid bureaucrats who do well enough to get by but have no interest in achieving the outstanding results that could come from a more flexible approach.

2.4.5 *Organizational and Political Decision Making*

The preceding three approaches to decision making apply largely to an individual decision maker. Many decisions, however, involve more than one person. In those cases, the interpersonal aspects of decision making can take on a great deal of importance.

The organizational description of decision making recognizes that organizations consist of people and subunits [CYER63]. Each of these has its own goals, priorities, "rights" (as it perceives them), information that it feels it "owns," and standard operating procedures. Decisions, and the overall decision-making process, must reconcile all of these. Where they are in conflict, the decision-making process can be difficult and painful. Where they are not in conflict, recognizing them permits us to design systems specifically to support the information flow and decision processes of the organization. Such DSS are called *group decision support systems*, GDSS for short. We'll cover them in detail in Chapter 11.

Viewing decision making as an organizational process combines rationality with politicality. Each unit of the organization (in the limit, each individual) is using a rational process internally in terms of its perception of its own goals. Organizational decision making does not conflict with a rational approach to the overall decision either, as long as the application of this approach does not infringe on what the subunit perceives as its territory.

Where the driving factor in arriving at a decision becomes bargaining among the participants, we have what is often called *political* decision making. The work "political" has negative overtones in our society. It calls forth images of hidden, often unethical, decisions made in back rooms by people whose only motivation is their own self-interest. The use of the term in a decision-making context, however, is not necessarily negative. It is the realistic recognition that people may legitimately have different goals, that people committed to a goal can be expected to fight for it, that bargaining is required to reconcile the different goals to a single decision, and that power—interpreted broadly—is an inherent component of any bargaining process.

The nature of the bargaining process depends on the importance of the decision as it is perceived by the decision-making group [KERR92]. The ability, and hence the tendency, of the majority to prevail grows or declines with the importance of the issue. So does the tendency of the decision to polarize the group. A management team may almost come to blows over a strategic decision between a new R&D project versus overseas sales expansion but is likely to agree amicably on the color of the corporate bowling team's shirts.

However unpleasant it may be to admit that well-intentioned managers can disagree, however difficult it may be to treat disagreement through formal management science optimization methods, the fact is that managers do disagree. DSS can help isolate areas of disagreement, can help articulate common goals, and can help create a common vision by facilitating structured, nonjudgmental sharing of information. These capabilities, too, fall under the category of group DSS.

DSS can also help resolve differences through electronic voting or the Delphi approach. In a truly political environment, though, this type of DSS usage may not be acceptable to the participants. Those who lost the vote may try to overturn the result by going around or above the DSS.

Politics has been described as "the art of the possible." Political decision making is characterized by compromise. "I'll give a little here, if you give a little there." A "win-win" outcome can often be achieved by discovering what issues are truly important to each participant. The DSS developer in a political decision-making environment must be attuned to what is possible, within the organizational culture and power structure, and develop systems that conform to their constraints.

2.5 The Impact of Psychological Type on Decision Making

The pioneering Swiss psychiatrist Carl Jung realized in the 1920s that individuals have personality traits that stay in place over time [ISAC88]. Their behavior in new situations can be predicted, at least in part, from their past behavior in similar ones. Furthermore, people can be placed into categories whose members all tend, as a general rule, to respond similarly to similar situations.

Katharine Briggs and Isabel Briggs-Myers refined Jung's concepts and showed that humans have four key behavioral characteristics [BRIG57]. Each of these is characterized by a spectrum ranging from one behavioral tendency to its opposite. Each characteristic reflects an individual tendency, or preference, to use one of two alternative approaches to a given area. Every person is at some point on this spectrum in terms of each of the four characteristics. For example, one person may prefer to evaluate issues logically and objectively, while another prefers to evaluate issues subjectively and personally. Since each of the four characteristics can take on either of two preferences, this approach yields a total of $2 \times 2 \times 2 \times 2 = 16$ psychological types.

These four preferences, unless they are indulged when a different behavior is called for, are not "good" or "bad." They reflect a person's mental preferences in the same sense—and with the same lack of inherent value—as a person's physical preference to write with the left or right hand. Similarly, the 16 categories, called *types*, are not good or bad, either, and are not related to aptitude or intelligence. Psychological type affects a person's behavioral tendencies in many areas, including decision making.

Psychological type is determined by a questionnaire (not a test, as people associate the word "test" with a good or a bad score) of several dozen questions. Each question asks which of two behaviors a person would be more likely to choose in a specified situation. Taken as a whole, and interpreted by a trained professional, the Myers-Briggs Type Inventory[1] or MBTI[2] can provide a great deal of insight into one's behavioral preferences. These preferences, in turn, can yield a great deal of insight into the way a person tends to approach decision-making tasks.

According to Briggs and Briggs-Myers, the four preferences that determine personality type (summarized primarily from [PROV90]) are:

1. *Introversion (I)/extraversion (E).*[3] This preference suggests whether individuals prefer to direct their energy toward the outer world (E) or the inner world (I). Extraverts understand the world through acting and reacting to it; they need to externalize things to understand them. Introverts understand their world through careful contemplation. They prefer to act or respond after thoughtful consideration of an issue.

2. *Sensing (S)/intuition (N).*[4] This function refers to a person's preferred perception process. It indicates how people take in information and become aware of things, people, events, and ideas. Sensing means finding out about things through the senses and through careful, detailed observation. People who prefer intuition perceive patterns or relationships among ideas, people,

---

[1]Myers-Briggs Type Inventory® is a registered trademark of Consulting Psychologists Press, Inc.

[2]MBTI™ is a trademark of Consulting Psychologists Press, Inc.

[3]Personality type workers use this spelling rather than the more common "extroversion." This is not a frivolous idiosyncrasy. The reasons for this usage are spelled out in [BRIG57].

[4]The letter "N" is used to denote the intuitive type. This prevents confusion with using "I" for Introversion. (If you play chess, you may have noticed that some chess notation schemes use "N" to denote knight for the same reason, to prevent confusion with "K" for king.)

and events. Intuitives trust perception based on intuitions and reading between the lines, while sensors confine their attention to what is real and verifiable.

3. *Thinking (T)/feeling (F).* This function refers to a person's preferred judgment process. It describes how people prefer to come to conclusions or make decisions about what they have perceived. Thinking means considering pros and cons or consequences and coming to a logical choice, decision, or conclusion. Feeling involves weighing personal values and others' reactions: Will there be conflict or harmony, approval or disapproval? Those with a feeling preference often neglect logical reasoning and fail to consider consequences. Those with a thinking preference often neglect taking other people's reactions—even their own emotional responses—into account.

4. *Judgment (J)/perception (P).* This is a "lifestyle" preference. It describes whether one tends to let a perception process (S/N) or judgment process (T/F) run one's outer life. People who have a judging preference want to have things settled, decided, planned, and managed to the plan. They are often seen as decisive and organized, and they enjoy working in structured organizations. People with a perception preference are often seen as flexible, spontaneous, and uncomfortable with much structure and planning. They want to keep plans to a minimum to be able to adapt flexibly to new situations.

One of the two middle functions (S, N, T, or F) is each person's "favorite" function, the one that a person prefers to use in his or her preferred world (internal or external). This function is referred to as that person's *dominant* function. With extraverts, who prefer dealing with the outer (external) world, the dominant function is the one indicated by his or her J/P preference, as that preference indicates which type of process a person tends to use in the outside world. With introverts, who prefer dealing with the internal world, the dominant function is the one *not* indicated by the J/P preference. In other words,

If your E/I and J/P preferences are	*Then your dominant function is*
Extraverted, judging (EJ)	T or F*
Extraverted, perceiving (EP)	S or N
Introverted, judging (IJ)	S or N
Introverted, perceving (IP)	T or F

*Whichever is your preference.

As an example of using the dominant function, consider people with type INFP. They tend to let their perception preference (here, intuition) run their *outer* lives. However, as they are introverts, the outer world is not their preferred world. Their dominant function is feeling, but they use it primarily in their inner world and don't show it easily. They "have a great deal of warmth but may not show it until they know a person well . . . Although their inner loyalties and ideals govern their lives, they find these hard to talk about. Their deepest feelings are seldom expressed; their inner tenderness is masked by a quiet reserve" [MYER90].

As Provost puts it [PROV90],

> It is important to remember that the Myers-Briggs Type Indicator indicates natural preferences—the ways we prefer to be. Often, however, we may act differently from our preferences because the situation demands it or because we are not comfortable with using our preferences. We all express each of these eight preferences at different times in different circumstances, but the MBTI tells us which four we prefer to express most of the time.

The four dimensions create the 16 types shown in Figure 2–8. You can find easily understood descriptions of all sixteen types in [HIRS90, ISAC88, KEIR84, MYER90, and PROV90] and in several other books.

The impact of personality type on decision-making style is important to the DSS developer because a DSS must reflect the decision-making methods of the people who will use it. Knowing that a DSS user's type is INTJ, for example, suggests that certain types of automated decision support are likely to be useful but that others are not. If a DSS is to be developed for a large user community with members of varying types, it should have features designed to support their varied decision-making preferences. Should that be impractical, management must be alert to the fact that the DSS is not well suited to the decision-making preferences of some staff members. It can then make allowances for this via extra training or alternative approaches to decision support.

The four personality characteristics affect decision making in these ways:

1. *Introversion/extraversion.* This preference affects the way in which a decision maker might approach group decisions. An extravert will prefer to

FIGURE 2–8

Myers-Briggs Personality Type Chart

	Sensing (S)	*Sensing (S)*	*Intuitive (N)*	*Intuitive (N)*	
Introverted (I)	ISTJ*	ISFJ	INFJ	INTJ	*Judging (J)*
Introverted (I)	ISTP	ISFP	INFP	INTP	*Perceiving (P)*
Extraverted (E)	ESTP	ESFP	ENFP	ENTP	*Perceiving (P)*
Extraverted (E)	ESTJ	ESFJ	ENFJ	ENTJ	*Judging (J)*
	Thinking (T)	*Feeling (F)*	*Feeling (F)*	*Thinking (T)*	

*A boldface letter indicates the dominant functions of eaxh type.

thrash matters out in a group. An introvert will prefer to mull over an issue in private and present fully formed conclusions to the group.

2. *Sensing/intuition.* This preference shows up in the way a decision maker will gather information for a decision. The sensor will want, in the words of the old Dragnet show, "just the facts, ma'am"—and all of them. The intuitive may need fewer facts: just enough for his or her intuition to put them together and reach a conclusion.

3. *Thinking/feeling.* This preference affects the decision-making process directly. The thinker can be the very model of the classical "rational manager," basing decisions on carefully thought-out logic but often ignoring human factors. A person with a feeling preference will have less use for "management science" approaches.

4. *Judgment/perception.* This preference influences whether, in working with others, the decision maker will focus on the information-gathering parts of the decision process or on the analysis and decision-making parts. A judging person may want to rush the information gathering and get right to the heart of the matter. A perceptive will want to postpone the decision as long as possible, keeping options open while more and more information is collected.

Huitt [HUIT92] summarizes the preferred decision-making techniques of the eight personality types as shown in Figure 2–9. Note that several techniques match more than one personality type. For example, the random word association technique ["how can the word 'sardine' (selected randomly from a dictionary, or suggested by a computer program that is designed to help people generate ideas) relate to this problem?"] match both sensing and perceiving types. It follows that an individual whose type includes SP would be especially attracted to it.

Psychological type also affects how well people work together.[5] This doesn't mean that all members of a decision-making group should be of the same type or similar types. The varying approaches brought to a group decision by people of different types can improve decision quality dramatically. In this case, it is important for the team as a whole to be aware of their varying styles. Team members can then make allowances for the fact that other members, while their styles may differ, can still make a significant contribution to the group. If type information is available to suitably trained managers or human resource professionals in an organization, it can be used to help plan a good decision-making group. Automated support for deciding group composition is itself a potential DSS application area.

---

[5]In some parts of the country, such as the Minneapolis area, "personals" ads often state psychological type. Prospective partners can use this information to help gauge their likely compatibility with the advertiser.

FIGURE 2–9

Types and Decision-Making Techniques

Type	*Preferred Techniques*
Extravert (E)	Brainstorming in group Outcome psychodrama (evaluating scenario through role playing) Thinking aloud
Introvert (I)	Brainstorming privately Incubation (doing something else as subconscious works on problem)
Sensing (S)	Share personal values, ideas Overload (deliberately considering too many facts to see individually) Inductive reasoning (developing rules from specific instances) Random word technique
Intuitive (N)	Classify, categorize Deductive reasoning (applying rules to specific instances) Challenge assumptions Imaging/visualization Synthesizing
Thinking (T)	Classify, categorize Analysis Network analysis (e.g., critical path method, PERT) Task analysis
Feeling (F)	Share personal values Listen to others' values Values clarification
Judging (J)	Evaluation (comparison with a standard or preestablished norm) Plus-minus-interesting technique (for evaluating alternatives) Backward planning (identify conditions needed to reach goal) Select a single solution
Perceiving (P)	Brainstorming Random word technique Outrageous provocation (absurd statement as bridge to idea) Taking another's perspective

In Section 4.5, after we've discussed the different kinds of DSS that exist, we'll discuss which are best suited to decision makers of each psychological type.

2.6 THE KEPNER-TREGOE DECISION-MAKING METHOD

The decision-making method described next was developed by Charles Kepner and Benjamin Tregoe to improve human decision making before computers became common decision aids [KEPN65, KEPN73]. The Kepner-Tregoe (K-T) method helps focus attention on critical issues and get to the crux of the matter without wasted effort. It can also be used in group decision making.

While it is not the only systematic way to make decisions, it is a good one. Its concepts can help DSS developers in two ways: to see where computers can fit into the decision-making process and to outline a method computers can use to take over some of the decision making task. The method consists of the steps shown in Figure 2–10 [KEPN73].

In terms of the decision-making approaches discussed in Section 2.4, K-T uses the additive linear method with a few twists. (If you put this fact together with the previous section, you may conclude correctly that the K-T method is best suited to decision makers with a thinking preference.) However, appearances can be deceiving. The K-T method accepts the facts of organizational decision making as well and, in that sense, has a political aspect. Furthermore, it is designed not to inhibit flexibility overmuch. It is not well suited to a truly political environment. The "wheeler-dealers" who

FIGURE 2–10

Graphical Representation of K-T Steps

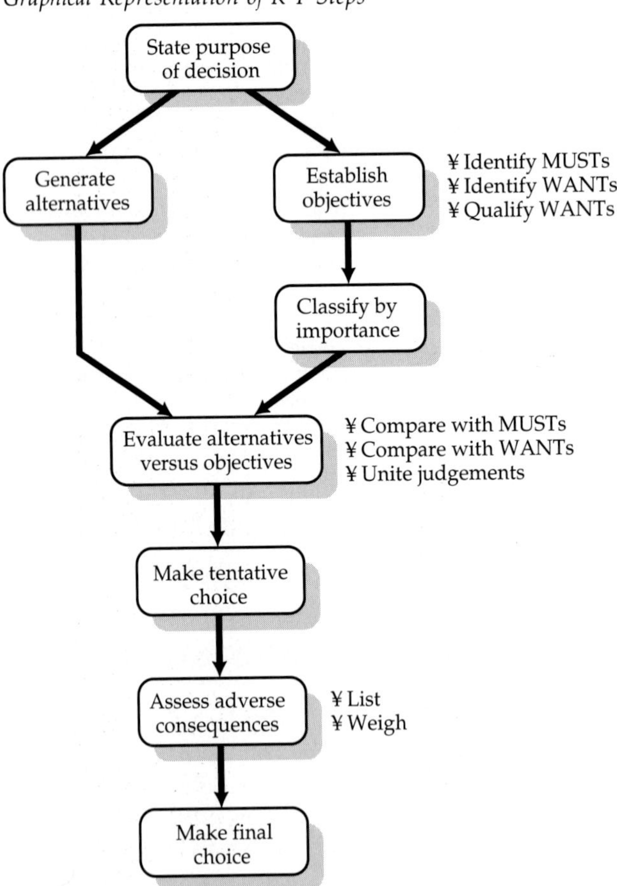

thrive on that type of decision making may chafe under its constraints and look for ways to sabotage the K-T process if they do not see its outcome tending in the direction they prefer.

2.6.1 *State the Purpose of the Decision*[6]

The Kepner-Tregoe method assumes that the intelligence phase is essentially complete and needs only to be formalized by obtaining agreement on the decision statement. In other words, we have already realized that a decision is needed and is worth spending some time on.

It takes self-control to focus on the purpose of the decision and the evaluation criteria first. Most of us like to think about alternatives, as they are concrete and easy to visualize. However, we must resist the impulse to discuss alternatives prematurely. Doing so will get the decision off on the wrong foot by overinflating the factors that favor a (perhaps subconsciously) desired alternative. That, in turn, may affect the quality of the eventual result.

The first step in the decision process is preparing a written decision statement. All participants in the decision must agree on this statement. If two managers making a joint decision have different unspoken objectives, they will never agree on a mutually satisfactory solution. By forcing a joint decision statement, we make the issues visible and force a compromise set of objectives. A compromise at this stage will be more acceptable than a compromise at the solution stage. A compromise then is likely to be a "split the difference" decision that leaves neither participant satisfied.

2.6.2 *Establish Objectives*[7]

Just as a decision has a broad purpose, it should also accomplish necessary and desired results. A certain *output* is expected. Also, certain *input* resources may be available to limit the choice of alternatives.

Decision outputs may include, among others,

- People: attitudes, skills, performance, development, health, safety.
- Organization: relationships, communications, responsibilities, coordination.
- Facilities and equipment: space, location, flexibility, adaptability, compatibility.
- Materials: sources, availability, handling, storage.
- Money: costs, expenses, return.
- Production output: quality, quantity, pace, timing.
- Personal: goals, family, strengths, weaknesses.

[6]This step corresponds to the intelligence phase of decision making.

[7]The design phase of decision making starts here and continues through Section 2.6.4.

2.6.3 *Classify According to Importance*

Not all objectives are of equal importance. Some are essential; any acceptable solution *must* achieve them. You *want* others, but they are not absolutely necessary. Some want objectives are more important than others. In this step you divide the objectives we just determined into these two categories. You then determine the relative values of the want objectives.

Identify Must Objectives

For a result objective to be a must, you must be able to answer the question, "Can you image *any acceptable solution at all* that would not meet this result?" with a firm "No!" With a resource, you must be able to answer "No!" to "Can you imagine any acceptable solution at all that uses more than the upper limit (or less than the lower limit) of this resource?" If the applicable question elicits, "Well, maybe if . . . ," the objective in question is a want.

To qualify as a must objective, the target must be measurable: "completion in two weeks," "absenteeism 10 percent lower within three months," "cost not over $10 million." There should be no possible room for disagreement over whether or not an alternative meets a must objective.

Must objectives are sometimes called *filter criteria*. They are standards by which you will filter out unsatisfactory alternatives.

Identify Want Objectives

Want objectives include those that remain after all the must objectives have been identified. Want objectives may include "contribute to employee growth" for a programming project, "have air conditioning" for a car, "maximum market share in 24 months" for a marketing plan.

Other want objectives reflect a premium for being better than the must limit. A personal computer may have an absolute cost limit of $5,000. At the same time you might want to keep the cost lower. Quantitative must objectives should be checked to see if there is any value in exceeding the filter level.

Quantify Want Objectives

Not all want objectives are equally important. Their relative importance must be weighed. While there are many ways to do this (high, medium, low, etc.) the most rigorous is a numerical value. Numerical ratings lend themselves to group consensus and to computerization. A scale from 1 to 10 is sufficiently fine to show shades of importance while not getting bogged down in meaningless differences between 67 and 68.

You now have a decision statement and two lists of objectives: musts and wants. The wants have numerical values. Other people might disagree with your lists or with those of any other decision maker. The important thing is for the lists to reflect the criteria of the people who are making the decision.

2.6.4 Generate Alternatives

Finding alternatives cannot be a hit-or-miss affair. Only a systematic search can turn up the number of quality alternatives you need to make an appropriate decision.

One approach to finding alternatives is to use the must/want objectives as your blueprint. Each objective is a tool to open up new possibilities. Thinking of ways to accomplish each objective helps you generate a broader range of alternatives.

Suppose one of your must objectives for a car is "bright orange paint." In considering this objective you will realize that George's Auto Body on Chestnut Street will paint any car this color for $500. You might then broaden your search, adding $500 the price of cars that are not already bright orange to pay for the paint job.

K-T is not an idea-generating or creativity-boosting method. While it urges the decision maker to search for all possible alternatives, it assumes that he or she can do so. It works well with any creativity-oriented technique, such as brainstorming, for generating them, but those approaches are not part of K-T itself.

As you search for alternatives, new objectives may come to mind. If they are valid, add them to your must/want lists. Be sure that the new factor is really a desired objective, not just a feature of an emotionally attractive alternative.

2.6.5 Evaluate Alternatives against Objectives[8]

To evaluate alternatives against objectives we must have the best, most accurate, and most timely information about each alternative. First, we make the evaluation for musts. Later, we repeat the process for each want alternative in the order of their importance.

Compare with Must Objectives

The only question that matters here is, "Does this alternative meet the standard?" If it does, keep it for further investigation. If it doesn't, drop it.

Borderline values require judgment. Criteria are often set as round numbers: "costs no more than $3,000." Alternatives do not always yield round numbers. A personal computer, when the prices of its component parts are added, may come to exactly $3,001.29. If you eliminate it, you risk not considering an alternative that meets all the other musts and compares favorably on the wants as well. If you accept it, you in effect concede that your must limit wasn't really a limit after all. Stretch the limit, stretch it a bit more . . . soon

[8]The choice phase of decision making begins with this step and continues through the rest of the process.

the entire decision-making process falls apart. You may want to retain such an alternative while noting it is borderline.

If the must comparison eliminates all your alternatives, you will either need more alternatives, or you will have to relax your criteria. In making this decision, ask, "Are any standards too tight? Do all reflect absolute requirements?"

If, on the other hand, no alternatives are eliminated at this stage, it might again be well to think through your must objectives again. Ask, "Are all the requirements reflected? Are the standards too loose?"

Compare with Want Objectives

Now turn to the alternatives that have satisfied all the musts. Search out the best available information on all of them relative to each want. A brief key point summary of information on each alternative may make accurate comparisons easier.

Alternatives may differ in the degree to which they satisfy a want objective. A way to compare them is needed. Here again, numbers that reflect your judgments provide a consistent, comparable yardstick. A good approach is to assign a value of 10 to the information describing the alternative that best satisfies each want objective. The information on each other alternative can then be compared with the best alternative and valued from 10 down to 0 as appropriate.

In assessing the value of the information about each want, ignore the weight assigned to the relative importance of the objective. Cover it up if necessary.

Unite Separate Judgments

To make an overall judgment, you must combine your separate judgments into one evaluation. Here again, numerical yardsticks show their worth. Multiply the weight assigned to the objective with the score assigned to the information for each alternative. If an objective has a weight of 10 (the maximum) and an alternative was rated as 10 on that objective (also the maximum), the weighted score for that alternative on that objective is $10 \times 10 = 100$.

Now sum the weighted scores for each alternative. The total weighted scores give the relative standing of each alternative and provide a reasoned, visible comparison. The closer two or more alternatives compare, the more necessary it is to double check both the information and your evaluation.

2.6.6 Tentatively, Choose the Best Alternative

You are now ready to make a tentative decision, which must still be tested. Select the alternative, or a very few alternatives, with the highest total weighted score(s) as your tentative choice(s).

2.6.7 Assess Adverse Consequences

Your tentative selection meets all your must criteria and best satisfies your want objectives. The information you used in your analysis is from the past and the present, but your decision will be implemented in the future. Many things can go wrong in the future. Before you commit to a final choice, you must test your chosen alternative by attempting to determine how well it will hold up in the future, how it will respond to changing conditions, and what the impact of overlooking key factors could be. The right decision should yield the best possible result if all goes well. It should also offer reasonable protection against things not going well.

List Possible Adverse Consequences

What could go wrong with your decision? Lots of things. List them all. A used car might fall apart after 200 miles. That fantastic English professor for whose course you signed up could stay in Tahiti as a beach bum and be replaced by an incompetent substitute. You could take a January ski vacation and encounter the warmest weather Vail has seen in decades. The objective categories in Section 2.6.2 are a good checklist for your search.

When we evaluated alternatives, we evaluated all the alternatives against the same set of criteria. The adverse consequence lists for each alternative, however, will usually not be the same. One computer system alternative may have the adverse consequence "little third-party software available," while another may suffer from "sales representative is obnoxious."

Weigh the Adverse Consequences

In evaluating the adverse consequences of any alternative, consider the following:

- The likelihood that the consequence will occur. This is its *probability.* Probability is a score here, not a mathematical probability from 0 to 1.
- The impact if the consequence happens. This is its *seriousness.*

Assign each adverse consequence a value of 10 (virtually certain) to 1 (highly unlikely) for probability. Similarly, evaluate its seriousness on a scale of 10 (catastrophic) to 1 (slightly annoying). A 10-10 rating means we are dead certain of catastrophe. Obviously, any alternative with such a consequence is unsatisfactory. A 1-10 rating means that catastrophe is remotely possible. The obnoxious computer salesperson might get a 10-1 score. We're sure it will happen, but we can live with it.

All actions carry risks. Looking at the probability and seriousness of adverse consequences is intended to put risk into perspective, not to panic everyone into inaction. Think of it as a tool for (1) identifying alternatives that are clearly unsatisfactory and (2) helping minimize what goes wrong with the alternative that is eventually chosen by alerting you to the need for contingency planning.

Using The Kepner-Tregoe Method

This is a brief example of how the Kepner-Tregoe decision making method could be applied in a practical situation. The number by each step indicates the section of the text in which that step is discussed.

Decision purpose (2.6.1): To pick a speaker for the next dinner meeting of our civic organization.

Objectives (2.6.2): To find a speaker who will speak at no charge, will inform meeting attendees about a topic of current interest, will entertain them, will motivate guests attending the meeting to join the organization by showing them how valuable its programs are, and will provide material for a good newspaper report on the meeting.

Importance (2.6.3):

- Must: Speak at no charge.
- Want: Inform 10
  Motivate 8
  Article 6
  Entertain 4

Alternatives (2.6.4):

- President of our organization.
- Town high school principal.
- U.S. representative in Congress from our district.
- Executive from local biotechnology firm.

Evaluation against objectives (2.6.5):

- Must (2.6.5.1):
  All Yes except representative in Congress, maybe.
- Wants (2.6.5.2) (see the table below):

Unite separate judgments (2.6.5.3): Multiplying each of the above scores by the weights we derived earlier, the candidates rank as follows:

1. U.S. Representative: 232.
2. Biotechnology executive: 212 (a close second).
3. High school principal: 164.
4. Our president: 140 (funny, but otherwise not very suitable).

Choose best alternative tentatively (2.6.6): We opt to invite our district's representative in Congress.

Assess adverse consequences (2.6.7):

- May turn us down (probability 6; seriousness 10).
- Having accepted, may cancel at last minute (1–10).
- May turn out to be a dud as a speaker (5–5).

Make a final choice (2.6.8): The key to accepting the tentative first choice is our ability to deal with its highest scoring adverse consequence, which is that the representative may turn down our invitation. We plan to deal with this by asking for an early answer and, if it is negative, turning to the biotechnology executive. We believe we will be able to get our biotechnology executive with six weeks' notice. Accordingly, we direct our corresponding secretary to invite the representative and to obtain an answer at least six weeks in advance of the meeting. Knowing that members of Congress typically schedule speaking engagements at least this far in advance, we do not think this is an unreasonable request.

	Our President	*High School Principal*	*United States Representative*	*Biotech Executive*
Inform	4	6	10	8
Motivate	6	6	8	10
Article	2	4	10	6
Entertain	10	8	2	4

2.6.8 Make a Final Choice

If your tentatively chosen alternative has no significant adverse consequences, or if you can see how to deal with those which it has, make the choice.

If you are not satisfied with its level of risk, consider the alternative that next best satisfied your want objectives and test its consequences.

If two or more alternatives are close, review each closely to

- Assess the degree to which each consequence is both probable and serious for each alternative.
- Judge (sum) the total impact of all consequences for each alternative.

If one alternative has a low total impact and no 10-10 (or very close: 10-9, 9-10, etc.) consequences, make this choice. If two are close on total impact but one has no 10-10 consequences, make this choice. If one has a somewhat higher total impact but no 10-10 consequences while the other has a lower total impact but does have 10-10 consequences, choose the one with the higher total impact. If all have a high total impact and one or more 10-10 consequences, think carefully about considering more alternatives. If you can't come up with some acceptable ones, your plans will have to include provisions for reducing the likelihood or the seriousness of the adverse consequences. Preventive actions and contingency plans cost money, but it is often money well spent. The process of assessing adverse consequences, by alerting you to the need for such plans and actions before disaster strikes, will help prevent disasters from happening.

Summary

A decision is a choice among alternatives. Each decision is characterized by a decision statement, a set of alternatives, and decision-making criteria.

Decision makers go through intelligence, design, and choice phases in the process of reaching a decision. In the intelligence phase, the need for a decision is determined. In the design phase, alternatives are developed and researched. In the choice phase, the alternatives are evaluated, and one of them is chosen.

Decisions can be categorized according to their degree of structure: structured, semistructured, or unstructured. They can also be categorized on the basis of their organizational impact: strategic, tactical (managerial control), and operational.

Managers make decisions with varying degrees of rationality, politicality, and flexibility. Common combinations of these attributes yield the decision approaches of rational management (seldom found in its pure form), rational management based on subjective utility, satisficing, and organizational or political decision making.

The way in which people approach decisions, and the decision-making phases on which they prefer to focus, depends on their personality type. Personality types can be characterized in terms of four preferences: introversion/extraversion, sensing/intuition, feeling/thinking, and judgment/perception. These preferences yield a total of 16 personality types. Knowing the personality type of a decision maker will help design appropriate tools to support that person.

A systematic decision-making process helps ensure that all aspects of decision making receive proper consideration and lends itself, at least in part, to computerized support. One such process, the Kepner-Tregoe process, goes through the stages of (1) stating the decision purpose, (2) establishing objectives, (3) classifying the objectives by their importance, (4) generating alternatives, (5) evaluating the alternatives against the objectives, (6) making a tentative choice, (7) assessing its potential adverse consequences, and (8) making a final choice.

Key Terms

adverse consequences 57
alternatives 28
cardinal utility 40
choice phase (of decision making) 29
criteria (singular: criterion) 29
decision 28
decision statement 28
decision tree 37
design phase (of decision making) 29
dominant function 48
extraversion (psychological type) 47
feeling (psychological type) 48
filter criteria 54
flexibility 37
indifference curve 41
intelligence phase (of decision making) 29
introversion (psychological type) 47
intuition (psychological type) 47
judgment (psychological type) 48
Kepner-Tregoe method 51
must objectives 54
operational decision 34
ordinal utility 41
organizational decision making 45
perception (psychological type) 48
political decision making 45
politicality 36
probability (of an adverse consequence) 57
psychological type 46
rationality 36
rational decision making 37
satisficing 45
semistructured decision 33
sensing (psychological type) 47
seriousness (of an adverse consequence) 57
strategic decision 33
structured decision 32
structured decision phase 33
tactical decision 34
thinking (psychological type) 48
unstructured decision 33
utility 39
want objectives 54

Review Questions

1. What is a decision? Give three examples.
2. Define the three elements of a decision.
3. Define the three phases of decision making.
4. What is a structured decision? A semistructured decision? An unstructured decision?
5. What are the three levels of decision scope? Define each.
6. Describe three dimensions along which managers differ in the ways they make decisions.
7. Why do managers seldom make purely rational decisions?
8. What is satisficing? Do you ever make decisions that way?
9. Give an example of political decision making.
10. What are the four preferences that determine one's psychological type?
11. How will an introvert and an extravert differ in their preferred decision making style? A judging person versus a perceiving person?
12. List the stages of the Kepner-Tregoe decision-making process. Describe each in a line or two.

Exercises

1. A-Plus Manufacturing is a $1.6 billion per year firm with four plants and a nationwide distribution network. The product moves through 38 branch offices and 312 distributors, all of which maintain some inventory. Distributors generate 37 percent of the orders but only 24 percent of the dollar volume. A-Plus products are classified into 176 groups representing 12,000 finished goods listed in the catalog. Of these, 3,600 are carried in inventory (in one or more of the 350+ possible locations) and 8,400 are made to order. About 1,500 new items enter the product line annually. A similar number are discontinued. A-Plus can deliver 90 percent of orders according to customer requests, if they are consistent with lead times stated in the catalog, with no delays or adjustment of dates. They hope to improve this service level to 95 percent with a new computer system, giving them a competitive advantage.
   a. What, precisely, is the decision they must make here? Write a clear, concise decision statement.
   b. Where does this decision fall in the grid of Figure 2–1?
   c. Do you expect this decision to be made rationally? Why or why not?

2. What is wrong with each of the following decision statements? Give a corrected decision statement for each case.
   a. For a college admissions office DSS, which predicts the academic success of applicants on the basis of their secondary school records and their standardized exam scores: "to predict how well applicants will do at our college."
   b. For a fast food chain DSS, which determines the likely revenue of new restaurants based on characteristics of their location: "to build our next restaurant where it will generate the most revenue."
3. Write down three decisions you made within the past week. Place each of them in the appropriate box of Figure 2–1.
4. Call or speak to a manager or executive—a businessperson you know, the dean of your school, a town official. Ask this person about a recent decision that he or she made on the job. Answer Exercise 1, parts *a*, *b*, and *c*, for that decision.
5. What do the intelligence, design, and choice phases consist of for the following decisions?
   a. Buying a car.
   b. Applying to graduate school.
   c. Deciding which of three proposed, nonoverlapping information systems projects to undertake, if your budget can only cover one of them.
6. Assume you own an automobile dealership. State one decision you or your employees would make that fits in each box of Figure 2–1. Put your answers on a grid in the form of Figure 2–1.
7. Section 2.2.2 has a box on creative alternatives for finding the height of a building by using a barometer. What is the characteristic of a barometer that makes it useful in each of the alternative methods of finding the height of the building? What other object (there are many; just name one) has each of these properties? What criteria would you use for choosing one of these methods to find the height of the building using the barometer?
8. Draw a decision tree (see Section 2.4.1) of the following situations:
   a. You are considering buying a car. One option is a new car. It costs $11,000 and will last for the four years you plan to keep it. It will be worth $6,000 at the end of that time unless it is in a major accident, which you think is 25 percent likely, in which case it will be worth $4,000. Your other choice is a used car that costs $6,000. It has a 50 percent chance of lasting the four years and of being worth $3,000 at that point. It also has a 50 percent chance of needing major repairs, becoming worthless, and requiring another expense estimated at $6000 to buy a second used car during this period. This second used car will be worth $4,000 at the end of the period. Ignoring the time value of money, which should you do?

b. (This is a multi-level decision tree.) Think a bit more about what might happen to your used car in Exercise 8*a*. If it needs major repairs, you can carry them out for $4,000. They will last the rest of the planning period, and the car will again be worth $3,000 when you go to sell it. You still have the option of buying a second used car as in Exercise 8*a*. You can also, if you're feeling rich at that time, lease a new car for the remaining (estimated) two years of your planning period at $2,000 per year. Again ignoring the time value of money, what should you do?

9. At the end of Section 2.4.1, we said "a rational manager [faced with the decision in Figure 2–4] who wants to maximize the statistically expected profit would choose the small computer system." Justify this statement.
10. Talk to a counselor trained in the MBTI. Obtain his or her opinions about the ways in which different personality types approach decision making. Compare these with the comments in the text. (Since we are talking about general tendencies and since there is a great deal of variation among individuals, you should expect some minor differences.) What does he or she suggest a decision maker should do (*a*) to recognize when his or her preferences do not match the needs of a decision-making situation and (*b*) to deal with this mismatch?
11. Apply the Kepner-Tregoe decision-making method (Section 2.6) to
    a. Buying a new (new to you, if not newly manufactured) car.
    b. Choosing an advertising program for Baa-Bits ("the only sheep food that your sheep ask for by name").
    c. Choosing a college major.
12. Apply the Kepner-Tregoe decision-making method *by yourself* to decide where to locate a warehouse for Baa-Bits (see Exercise 9*b*) and Moo-Bits (its bovine equivalent). Then use the method in a group of three or four students, and reach a group decision. Assess (*a*) the time it took to reach an individual versus a group decision, (*b*) how easy it was, and (*c*) the quality of the result.
13. Your employer, a computer vendor, is to participate in a trade show 2,000 miles from your headquarters. You have developed a project plan to build a booth, ship a new prototype computer to the show, write demonstration programs, staff the booth, and provide enough literature for the expected demand. List at least six things that could go wrong with your plan (the adverse consequences). Assess the probability and seriousness of each. State which three you would concentrate on for either preventive action or a contingency plan.
14. For each step of the Kepner-Tregoe decision-making process (i.e., each of Sections 2.6.1 through 2.6.8) state how a computer could be used to support
    a. An individual decision maker.
    b. A group decision.

15. Discuss which psychological preferences might affect a person's effectiveness in carrying out each step of the Kepner-Tregoe decision-making process. What does this suggest to you about the composition of a group formed to carry out this process for a joint decision?

References

ACKO68 Ackoff, R. L., and M. W. Sasieni. *Fundamentals of Operations Research.* John Wiley & Sons, New York (1968).

ANTH65 Anthony, Robert N. *Planning and Control Systems: A Framework for Analysis, Studies in Management Control.* Harvard University, Graduate School of Business Administration, Cambridge, Mass. (1965).

BRIG57 Briggs-Myers, Isabel, and Katharine C. Briggs. *The Myers-Brigs Type Indicator.* Educational Testing Service, Princeton, N.J. (1957).

CYER63 Cyert, R. M., and J. G. March. *A Behavioral Theory of the Firm.* Prentice Hall, Englewood Cliffs, N.J. (1963).

DEAN91 Dean, James W. Jr.; Mark P. Sharfman; and Cameron M. Ford. "Strategic Decision-Making: A Multiple-Context Framework." In *Advances in Information Processing in Organizations* 4. James R. Meindl, Robert L. Cardy, and Sheila M. Puffer, eds. JAI Press Inc., Greenwich, Conn. (1991), pp. 77–110.

HIRS90 Hirsh, Sandra Krebs, and Jean M. Kummerow. *Introduction to Type in Organizations,* 2nd ed. Consulting Psychologists Press, Palo Alto, Calif. (1990).

HUTI92 Huitt, William G. "Problem Solving and Decision Making: Consideration of Individual Differences Using the Myers-Briggs Type Indicator." *Journal of Psychological Type* 24 (1992), pp. 33–44.

ISAC88 Isachsen, Olaf, and Linda V. Berens. *Working Together: A Personality Centered Approach to Management.* Neworld Management Press, Coronado, Calif. (1988).

KEEN78 Keen, Peter G. W.; and Michael S. Scott Morton. *Decision Support Systems: An Organizational Perspective.* Addison-Wesley Publishing, Reading, Mass. (1978).

KEIR84 Keirsey, David, and Marilyn Bates. *Please Understand Me: Character and Temperament Types.* Prometheus Nemesis, Del Mar, Calif. (1984).

KEPN65 Kepner, Charles H., and Benjamin B. Tregoe. *The Rational Manager: A Systematic Approach to Problem Solving and Decision Making.* Kepner-Tregoe Inc., Princeton, N.J. (1965).

KEPN73 Kepner-Tregoe Inc. *Problem Analysis and Decision Making.* Kepner-Tregoe Inc., Princeton, N.J. (1973).

KERR92 Kerr, Norbert L. "Issue Importance and Decision Making." In *Group Process and Productivity.* Stephen Worchel, Wendy Wood, and Jeffry A. Simpson, eds. SAGE Publications Inc., Newbury Park, Calif. (1992).

MYER90 Myers, Isabel Briggs. *Introduction to Type.* Consulting Psychologists Press, Palo Alto, Calif. (1990).

PROV90 Provost, Judith A. *Work, Play, and Type.* Consulting Psychologists Press, Palo Alto, Calif. (1990).

PALV92 Palvia, Shailendra, and Steven R. Gordon. "Tables, Trees and Formulas in Decision Analysis." *Communications of the ACM* 35, no. 10 (October 1992), pp. 104–113.

SIMO60 Simon, Herbert A. *The New Science of Decision Making.* Harper & Row, New York (1960).

SVEN79 Svenson, O. "Process Descriptions of Decision Making." *Organizational Behavior and Human Decision Process* 23, no. 1 (1979). pp. 86–112.

TODD91 Todd, Peter, and Izak Benbasat. "An Experimental Investigation of the Impact of Computer Based Decision Aids on Decision Making Processes." *Information Systems Research* 2, no. 2 (June 1991), pp. 87–115.

TODD92 Todd, Peter, and Izak Benbasat. "The Use of Information in Decision Making: An Experimental Investigation of the Impact of Computer-Based Decision Aids." *MIS Quarterly* 16, no. 3 (September 1992), pp. 373–93.

TVER69 Tversky, Amos. "Intransitivity of Preferences." *Psychological Review* 76, no. 1 (January 1969), pp. 31–48.

TVER72 Tversky, Amos. "Elimination by Aspects: A Theory of Choice." *Psychological Review* 79, no. 4 (July 1972), pp. 281–99.

ENVOYANCE
THE FIRST MEETING*

Most chapters of this book will let you apply what you are learning to Envoyance, a small environmental engineering firm. Here Doug and Adrienne, seniors majoring in MIS at nearby Harwich University, meet Envoyance co-founder Dan Woods. He describes the firm to them prior to their embarking on a semester project to plan and design decision support systems for Envoyance.

"There are about 15 of us here at Envoyance," opened Dan after the three introduced each other. "We all work in the general area you could call 'environmental engineering.' We don't really have a formal organization, so I won't draw you a chart. Basically, Sandra Halpern and I are in charge, but we try not to make too big a deal over that."

"What do you include when you say 'environmental engineering?' " asked Adrienne. "I mean, I know what the environment is, and I know what engineering is, but I don't see people going out and engineering the environment!"

"You're right about that, Adrienne. Perhaps 'environmental engineering' is a bad term, but everyone in the field uses it so we're stuck. In any case, to use that term

*The author is grateful to Eric Wood, P. Hg., CGWP (certified ground water practicioner), president of EnviroSense Inc., for his careful review and thoughtful comments on this and the other Envoyance episodes.

means three things: First, it means helping our customers arrange their operations to avoid environmental damage. This means designing a process to minimize harmful by-products, arranging for the proper disposal of the by-products that can't be avoided, or both. We might also do a business analysis here; for instance, it might initially cost more to clean an assembly with a nonpolluting solvent, but there would be savings in disposing of it. We can evaluate the total costs of both approaches. We also get involved in permitting—"

"I've never heard anyone use that as a verb before," Doug interrupted. "I assume it has something to do with getting a permit?"

"Yes, it does, such as a permit to build a factory in an area that has air pollution problems," agreed Dan. "We do tend to use a lot of jargon around here, and that was probably about the simplest part of it. Environmental engineers talk about RCRA, CWA, CAA, CERCLA, SARA, and a whole lot more. We'll try to keep to English when we talk to you. If there's anything you don't understand, just ask!

"Meanwhile, Number Two on our list is evaluating situations where an area is being polluted now or was polluted in the past. This includes going back in history to find out what was done and inspecting the soil, water, or whatever to find out what's there now. We have an in-house lab that handles most of our chemical analyses, and we send a few of the rarer ones out. In fact, we've used a few faculty members at the Harwich chemistry department to help us. The evaluation typically involves defining the problem and then doing what we call "risk assessment:" deciding what would happen if everything is left alone.

"Third, we clean up messes. Some of these, like sewage, are unavoidable, although there are ways to minimize their impact. Others might have been avoided if we had been there in the first place. Of course, a lot of these date back to a time when nobody understood the long-term impacts of pollution, and firms like ours were not around. It's hard to blame someone for not being a prophet 40 years ago! Still, the messes are there, and they have to be cleaned up. We do the design work for that cleanup. We use subcontractors to do most of the physical work; for instance, we don't own a bulldozer or a truck bigger than a pickup. We provide full-time, on-the-job supervision.

"We also do a few other things, such as giving expert testimony in court, but those are a pretty small part of our business picture. We don't really plan for them, make a big effort to market them, or count on them."

"What kinds of people does it take to do all these things?" asked Doug.

"About half of us are technical specialists of one sort or another," responded Dan. "We've got a biologist, a hydrologist, two toxicologists, a hydrogeologist—that was my background, by the way—a chemist, and a soil scientist. Those folks focus on areas such as using microbes to chew up nasties in the ground or developing computer models of how pollutants are dispersed through the soil or the groundwater. Most of the rest are generalists and cover the entire field with less depth in any one area. That's Sandra's background. They prepare bids, getting help from specialists as they need it. They manage projects and carry out specific tasks that don't demand a real specialist in one area. They also try to sell new projects. Our marketing and sales efforts aren't terribly well focused or coordinated right now; we know we have to do something about this. We also have a bookkeeper, a receptionist, and a typist who handle whatever the professional staffers don't do on their own word processors."

"Speaking of word processors," continued Doug, "what sort of computers does Envoyance use?"

"Our information systems are even more fragmented than our sales efforts," laughed Dan. "We use a bunch of micros, but they don't tie into each other. Our bookkeeper does her thing; our engineers do theirs. Most of us do use Microsoft Word for word processing, but even there we have three versions: one each for plain MS-DOS, MS-DOS with Windows, and Macintosh. Our biggest compatibility problem there, oddly enough, isn't with the Mac; it reads 3-1/2 inch disks from the IBM side quite nicely, and most of our data files convert with no sweat. The biggest problem is the 5-1/4 inch disks on a few old Zenith and IBM PCs. A couple of the PCs are high-end configurations with big screens for computer-aided drafting and design work. Besides the micros, two of our technical specialists have Sun workstations to do their calculations. Today they might get a high-end PC or Macintosh instead, but those lines just didn't have the power a few years ago when we bought the Suns."

"You mentioned using the computers for word processing, for bookkeeping, and for calculations," Adrienne commented. "Do you use any of this equipment to help make decisions?"

"Not really," Dan admitted. "That's a big part of the reason you two are here. Our decision-making processes are pretty free-wheeling because we don't have much bureaucratic structure. Either Sandra or I has to approve anything major, like a bid or a new hire. Project managers have a good deal of latitude within their projects. In practice, we talk to each other a lot, so hardly anything gets decided without half a dozen people putting in their two cents' worth. We all know each other and what the others can do, so we make sure the right people get into the act. If we grow as quickly as we plan to grow, that won't work 12 to 18 months from now."

Envoyance players, in the order you'll meet them, include:

Dan Woods and Sandra Halpern, co-founders
Jim, a "generalist" working on several projects involving pollution cleanup
Chris, senior technical staff member
Jackie and Ed, staff members
Hakeem, who works with Chempact
Steve Klein, legislative expert
Peggy Letendre, newly hired sales representative
Bob, who tinkers with Mike the robot
Miguel, "expert" on dealing with asbestos problems

Exercises

Consider these two Envoyance decisions:

A. Oxbow Chemicals plans to hire an environmental engineering firm to assess groundwater pollution in an area where they have stored chemicals since 1957. If a problem is found, it will have to be cleaned up. In that case, the firm performing the assessment will have the inside track (but no guarantee) for the cleanup contract. Envoyance must quote a price for this job, knowing that its competitors will most likely bid low because of the increased likelihood of profitable follow-on work at standard rates.

B. Dan and Sandra are screening resumes for the newly created position of sales manager. The good news is that the economy is down, so they are flooded with resumes. The bad news is that environmental engineering is booming, so few applicants have any relevant experience. They feel they may have to hire someone with good sales skills who can learn enough about Envoyance's environmental engineering business to sell the firm's services effectively.

For each of the above decisions:

1. What do the intelligence, design, and choice phases consist of for this decision?
2. Where does the decision fall in the grid of Figure 2–1?
3. How do you feel this decision will be made, in terms of the approaches listed in Section 2.4?
4. Suppose you know that Sandra's psychological type is ENFJ. What does this tell you about her probable preferred approach to this decision?
5. Suppose Dan's psychological type is INTP. What does this tell you about his probable preferred approach to this decision? What conflicts might arise because of the differences between Dan's and Sandra's psychological types?
6. Would the Kepner-Tregoe decision-making method help with this decision? Why or why not?

CHAPTER

3 Systems and Models

Chapter Outline

Introduction

The third word in "decision support systems" is *systems.* It is not used by accident. A decision support system is a particular type of system. We must therefore understand systems if we hope to understand DSS. Also, as you saw in the sample definitions of DSS in Chapter 1, many DSS contain models. For that reason we must also understand something about models before we get further into the types of DSS in the next chapter. Since a model is a representation of a system, this chapter discusses these two closely related subjects together.

Chapter Objectives

After you have read and studied this chapter, you will be able to:

1. Define a system and describe its characteristics.
2. Define an information system.
3. Use data flow diagrams to represent systems.
4. Explain how information systems fit into the overall category of information systems.
5. Explain why we use models in decision support systems.
6. Identify several types of models used in decision support systems: static versus dynamic, continuous versus discrete event, deterministic versus stochastic, and more.
7. Understand the need for simplification in designing a DSS model.

3.1 ABOUT SYSTEMS

You probably have an informal, intuitive idea of a "system." Chances are that you use the word fairly often in your daily conversations: the school system, the nervous system, your old car's blasted electrical system. In order to study systems properly, we need a more precise definition that will allow us to know exactly what we mean when we refer to one:

> A system is a group of interacting components with a purpose.

The key words in this definition are

- *Group.* A system must consist of more than one item. A piece of paper, unless one cares about its molecular structure, is not a system.
- *Interacting.* The components must operate in some relationship to each other. A collection of components that are not connected to each other, such as a piece of paper in one room and a pencil in another, is not a system. These same components would comprise a writing system if they were brought into close proximity.
- *Components.* The components may be elementary items incapable of (for our purposes) further subdivision. Alternatively, they may be systems in their own right: smaller systems, to be sure, but systems nonetheless. Small systems that are components of a larger system are often referred to as *subsystems* of the larger system.
- *Purpose.* Without getting into metaphysics or religion—Does the earth, as an ecological system, have a purpose? Does the solar system have one? Do we? We note here that the systems discussed in this book all have one purpose. Knowing the purpose of a system helps us understand it or redesign it to carry out this purpose better.

Every system also has a *boundary.* The boundary of a system separates the components of that system, which are inside it, from the rest of the world, which is outside the system. Objects or information can cross the boundary of most systems: inward, outward, or in both directions. If nothing crosses the boundary of a system in either direction, that system is called a *closed system.* Otherwise, it is called an *open system.* Completely closed systems are rare in the real world. It is, however, sometimes useful to simplify the analysis of a system by treating it as closed. For example, we might study the performance of a computer system by assuming it runs a certain mix of programs indefinitely. In the real world, each job terminates after a while and is replaced by another job for the computer to process. In the real world, computer jobs also receive input from, and send output to, entities outside the system itself.

Systems can be of many types. Consider a few from everyday life:

- Your body. Its components include the circulatory system, the skeletal system, the digestive system, the respiratory system, the nervous system, the immune system, and several more you can find in anatomy books. Each of these, as its name suggests, is itself a system; for example; your circulatory system consists of your heart, your veins, your arteries, and your capillaries. Your body's systems interact in many ways: The digestive system puts nutrients into the circulatory system, the nervous system sends out electrical signals that control the other systems, and so on. The purpose of the system, again avoiding metaphysics and religion, is to sustain its existence and to perpetuate the species. Its boundary is your skin. Air, food, and drink cross the boundary of the system in the inward direction; used air, digestive waste, and occasional flakes of dry skin cross it outward. Information enters the system via your senses and leaves it via your voice and actions.

- A metropolitan area transportation system. Its components are roads, cars, trucks, buses, railroad lines, trains, signals, drivers, traffic control officers, passengers, and more. They interact by intersecting in space (as at a road crossing), by exchanging passengers, by giving information to each other (traffic officer to driver, signal to train engineer, bus driver to passenger), and in several other ways. Its boundary depends on the purpose for which we are studying the system: For some purposes we would include railroad station buildings in the system; for other purposes we might not. It also has a geographic boundary that determines which roads and railroad tracks are part of our system and which are not. Passengers, vehicles, and so on cross the system's boundary in both directions. So does information, as in a radio traffic report giving information about conditions in the area to drivers outside it. The purpose of this system is to move goods and people within the defined area.

  As with the human body system, each important component of the transportation system is itself a system. Some people might be concerned only with the rail component of the transportation system. At a lower level, people who work for a locomotive manufacturer might consider the locomotive to be their system and let others worry about the uses to which it might later be put. The locomotive's diesel engine is a complex system in its own right but is a single component to the locomotive designer. To another person the fuel system of that locomotive is the system. Moving down further, a combustion chemist might be concerned with a small aspect of the fuel system. The breakdown doesn't stop until we reach elementary particles in the domain of the nuclear physicist. Clearly, studying combustion chemistry inside a diesel engine is of little practical value to a regional transportation planner.

As these examples suggest, the ways in which the components and boundary of a particular system are defined are largely up to the person studying it. The value of a system study depends vitally on studying the right system: not too much and not too little, not in too great detail or at too high a level of generalization. The officer controlling traffic at an intersection can't worry about subway schedules or the fuel injection system of every passing car. He or she must focus on the overall motion of vehicles that are within a few hundred feet of the intersection and moving toward it. This type of focus is intuitive to all traffic control officers who survive their first day on the job. The equivalent focus in an information system is not nearly as intuitive but is just as important for the career survival of information system professionals.

Systems often incorporate *feedback*. Feedback is output from a system component that becomes, perhaps after additional processing, input to a system component. When you pass a button in an elevator, it activates a motor to change the position of the elevator. Elevator position information is *fed back* into the system via sensors along the elevator shaft. This information, in turn, is used by the elevator's control circuits to determine when to stop the motor in order to align the elevator with the requested floor. Systems that use feedback to adjust their outputs, based on how well the result of those outputs matches the desired result, are called *closed loop* systems. Those that do not use feedback to adjust their outputs are called *open loop* systems.

Feedback can be *internal* to a system, as in this elevator example, or *external* to it. In many DSS the important feedback is a function of the system's environment and is thus external to the system. The system diagrammed in Figure 3–1 is an example of this: The choice of an advertising program has an effect on customer purchases, which in turn influences our future choices of advertising programs. This effect takes place through customer reactions and sales data. Since customers are outside our advertising selection system, this system has external feedback.

The study of systems in general and the (often unexpected) ways they behave is the subject of *general systems theory*. You can read more about general systems theory in books such as [RAPO86], [VONB68], [WILS90] or any of several others that your library probably has indexed under that subject heading.

FIGURE 3–1

Diagram of Ad Selection System with Feedback

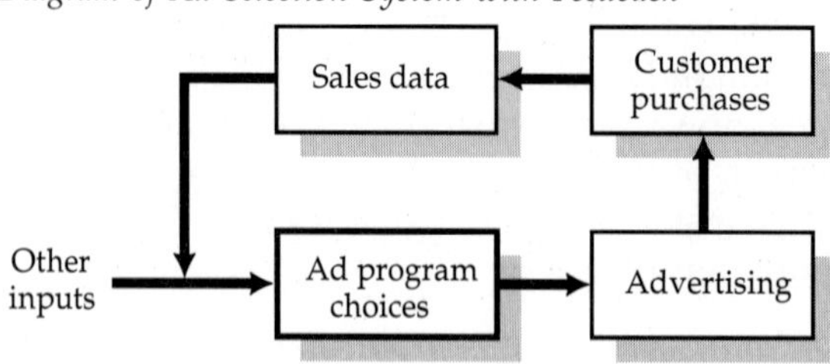

3.2 Information Systems

An *information system* is a system whose purpose is to store, process, and communicate information.

In the 1990s we associate information systems with computers. Many information systems, and virtually all large ones, use computers today. Yet an information system need not use computers. Computers first became widely available in the 1950s. They were initially too expensive for all but the largest businesses and government agencies. People stored, processed, and

Precomputer Information System Technology

Information systems technology is not a new concept. It has just changed a bit over the years.

Centuries ago, the Incas of Peru used an accounting system based on string technology [MENN69]. It was totally solid state, required no electricity, and was proof against most natural disasters except fire. To guard against that eventuality, they used what we would call a distributed database today, with important records duplicated in widely separated geographic locations.

The Inca system, called *quipu,* used a horizontal rope about 1 ft. 8 in. (50 cm) long from which hung 48 secondary cords, each about 1 ft. 4 in. (40 cm) long. These cords were colored to designate the various areas of government: tribute, land, economic productivity such as crops and herds, wars, religious rituals. Each cord had three knots: The knot closest to the main rope designated hundreds, the next one down designated tens, and the third one designated individual units. One style of knot represented the digit "1," while another type of knot with two to nine loops represented any of those digits.

Several of the cords hanging from the main rope could be grouped with a loop of string. A "head string" was then added to the loop, containing the sum of the entries on the individual strings. (In today's terminology, they entered the total as a separate database record—usually a poor idea, but reasonable for unchanging historical data when calculation times are long compared with record retrieval times.) In this way, individual villages could send their crop counts to the regional capital. A regional official would tie the village cords to the regional quipu and create a head string representing the crop count of the entire region. A duplicate head string was forwarded to the national capital in Cuzco. There, it became one of many regional quipu, which were in turn totaled to give national crop data.

Each Inca village had four official quipu keepers called *camayocs.* In addition, regional commanders and officials at Cuzco—military commanders, judges, the heads of noble families—used the system. Just as information processing and today's computers influence our thought patterns, quipu influenced those of the Inca. Early European visitors to South America reported that the Inca made efforts to translate everything they were told to quipu-based numerical terms. They had a great deal of difficulty understanding concepts that did not translate properly into those terms, such as the religious idea of the trinity.

transmitted information for centuries before then. They used a variety of devices—paper and pencil, abaci, and more—to store data, to calculate with it, and to communicate it to other people. Some of these devices are still in use and may still be the best way to deal with an information handling task. Part of an information system designer's job is to determine which parts of an information processing task are best done by computers and which, on the other hand, should be done by humans or by "low-tech" methods.

The payroll system diagrammed in Figure 3–2 is a typical information system, albeit not a DSS. Its components include people (payroll clerks), a variety of paper forms, checks, and a computer. Information enters the system via forms and exits via check stubs and reports. Information is also transmitted among the components of the system, in part via forms and in part electronically. Data are stored partly on paper forms, partly in computer files. Processing is done largely in the computer.

FIGURE 3–2

Data Flow Diagram of Payroll System

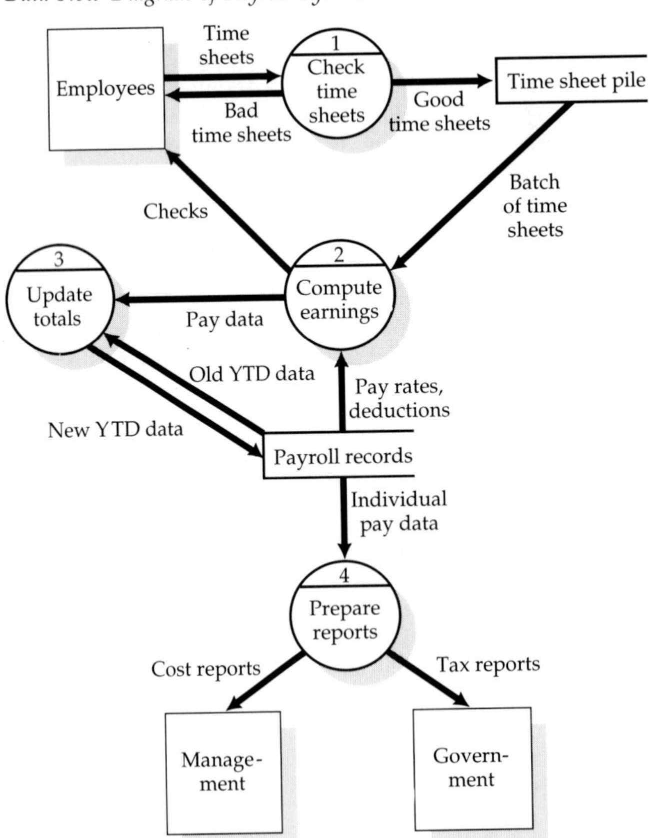

3.3 DATA FLOW DIAGRAMS

Figure 3–2 represents the payroll system as a *data flow diagram,* or DFD.[1] A DFD is a popular way to describe an information system. A DFD shows the components of the system: processes, shown as rounded rectangles in the DFD, and data stores (computer or paper files), shown as open-ended rectangles.[2] Where a component of a system is itself a system, it can be described in a lower level DFD. A DFD shows interactions among the components in the form of data flows among the processes and data stores. It shows the boundary of the system implicitly: The processes and data stores are inside the system, while the square boxes represent external entities that communicate with the system.

A data flow diagram is not a complete description of a system. It doesn't show, among other things, the purpose of the system. Fortunately, we can usually infer a system's purpose from other information sources. A DFD also does not show the timing relationships among the processes in the system. The DFD in Figure 3–2, for example, does not tell us if paychecks are produced daily, weekly, monthly, or at some other interval. As with the purpose of the system, we must find this information elsewhere.

Data flow diagrams are important because they help people communicate about what the components of a system are, how the system works, and what it does. They are more precise than normal English for this purpose. They communicate a great deal of information via a few easily understood pictures. When a system becomes too complex to show in one DFD, we can use a layered set of data flow diagrams: one like Figure 3–2 to show the overall system, and additional ones to show how its components work internally. Figure 3–3 amplifies payroll Process 2, Computer Earnings. The processes in Figure 3–3 are all numbered 2.*n* to show that they are parts of Process 2, Compute Earnings, in the top-level DFD of the payroll system.

We'll use DFDs regularly to describe systems through the rest of this book. If you haven't already studied data flow diagrams in your introductory MIS or systems analysis course, you can read more about them in Appendix A. That appendix also explains this payroll system example in more detail.

---

[1]Some authors use "dataflow" as one word. Expect to see both forms used.

[2]If you've studied systems analysis, you may have used either Gane-Sarson DFDs like this one or Yourdon-DeMarco DFDs, which use slightly different symbols. Both work the same way. Their differences are purely cosmetic.

FIGURE 3–3
DFD of Earnings Computation

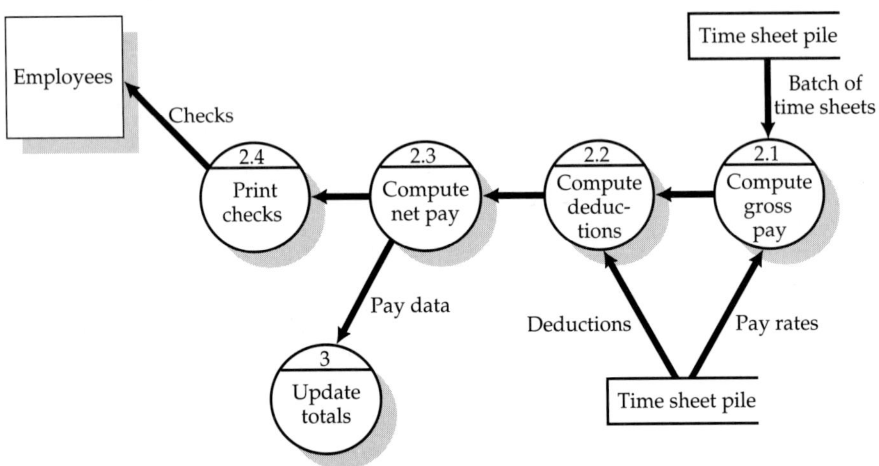

3.4 DSS AS INFORMATION SYSTEMS

A decision support system is a specific type of information system. If we know that an information system is a DSS, we can infer some conclusions about it that do not apply to all types of information systems:

- A DSS usually uses one or more data stores (databases or sets of files) that provide information to support the decision. Some of these may be maintained by the DSS itself. Some may be maintained within the organization that uses the DSS. A DSS may also use external (often public) information sources, such as stock market price data or airline flight schedules.
- The DSS generally does not update the databases that it uses as external information sources. They are updated by suitable transaction processing systems, either within the organization using the DSS or outside it.
- The DSS communicates with the decision maker. Depending on the situation, we may depict the decision maker as an external entity or as part of the system. The choice will often depend on whether we are studying an entire decision process on the one hand or a system to support the way decisions are already being made on the other.
- In all likelihood, the decision maker supplies the DSS with specific information defining the decision to be made within the general category of decisions that the DSS can help with. That information tells the DSS what data to extract from its data stores.

FIGURE 3–4

Data Flow Diagram of Generic DSS

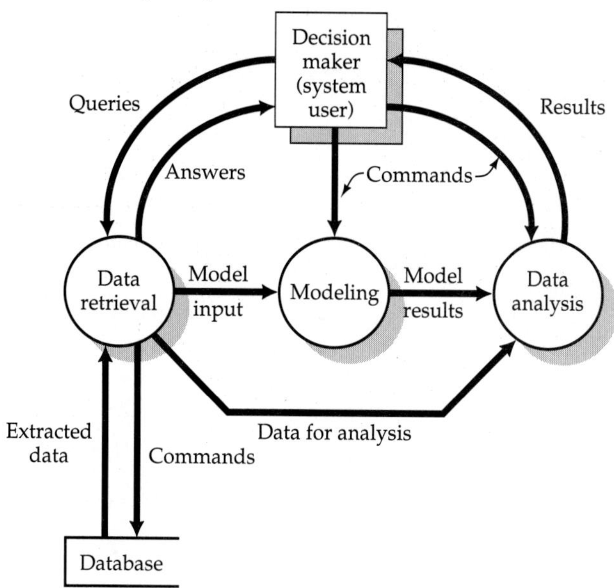

A general schematic of a DSS that conforms to this description is shown in Figure 3–4. This figure is not tied to a specific DSS application. It applies equally to a loan approval system or to a system that selects media for an advertising campaign. In the case of a specific system, we would replace the generic component names with names that reflect the specific components of that system. For example, the component shown as "database" in Figure 3–4 might be labeled "credit history database" for a loan approval system. The emphasis on each component of a DSS, and the specific lower level components into which we could break down each higher level element, also vary widely from one DSS to another.

Before embarking on the design of any DSS, whether in this course or on the job, you should start by defining it as a system. There are two ways to view the overall system you will design: as a decision support system or as a decision-making system. In the former case, illustrated in Figure 3–5, the decision maker is outside the system you are studying. In the latter case, illustrated in Figure 3–6, the decision maker is inside the overall system though still outside its DSS component. The design choices that are open to you depend in part on the point of view you choose to take.

To start designing your DSS, ask yourself these questions:

- What is the purpose of the DSS, in terms of the decision being made and the outputs it must supply? (Be as specific as you can.)

FIGURE 3–5

Context Diagram of DSS as System

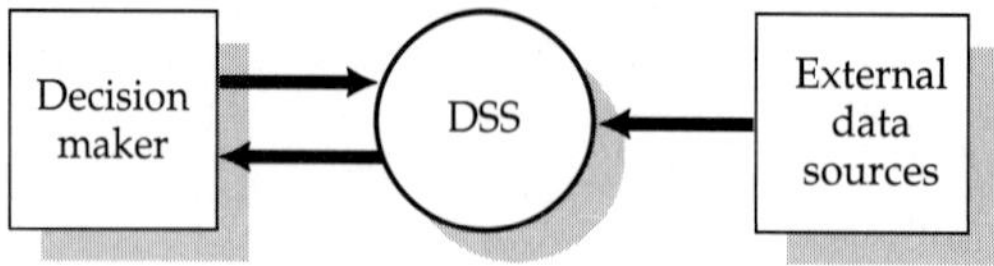

FIGURE 3–6

Decision-Making System Incorporating DSS as Component

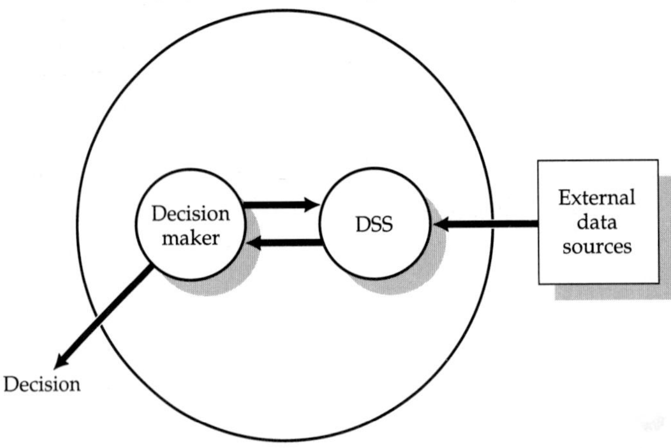

- What are the external entities (decision makers, information sources) with which the DSS communicates? What are the data flows to and from these external entities?
- What are the internal data files the DSS uses? Where do they get their information? If they get it from outside the system, what are the external entities that provide it?
- What are the major processes in the DSS? What are the data flows among them?

You may not be able to answer all these questions when you start to define a system. The exercise of trying to take a "first cut" at them will still pay off, both in terms of increasing your understanding of the system and in telling you what you don't yet know and must therefore make an effort to find out. Just remember that the first cut *is* a first cut. Don't get so attached to it that you can't see its flaws later on.

If you can answer these questions, you will understand your DSS as a system. One test of this understanding is being able to draw it as a data flow diagram. Success in diagramming your system means you are well on your way to its successful design.

3.5 Models

Now that we understand what a system is we are in a position to deal with the concept of a *model:* a replica of a real system or object. This definition applies to all types of models: model trains, clay models used by automobile stylists, and model legislation that is intended to be adopted with local variations by several states. People use models to capture important aspects of the real item while eliminating other aspects that cause difficulties in a particular situation. For instance,

- A model railroad lets hobbyists capture the appearance, much of the atmosphere, and the operating challenge of a real railroad. However, it does not require an area the size of a small state; several dozen permits from state, local, and national regulatory bodies; and a budget of several hundred million dollars.
- A styling model lets people see how an automobile design will look. It does not require investing in tooling for shaped metal parts or assembling mechanical and interior components that do not affect the external appearance of the finished product.
- Model legislation lets experts debate the merits of an issue without becoming embroiled in the political issues and bargaining that arise in any real legislature and without having to answer to constituents or special-interest groups for having cast an "unpopular" vote.

Models often have advantages over the "real thing" for their specific purposes. A model railroad lets its designer determine landscape features that the planner of a real railroad, constrained by nature, cannot alter. If a deep gorge provides dramatic scenery or an opportunity to build an intricate model of a wooden trestle, in it goes. A clay mockup can be changed more easily—to round a fender, to lower a headlamp—than a production vehicle. Their deficiencies (neither a model railroad nor an automobile styling mockup can haul passengers or cargo) are not significant for their users' purposes.

In decision support systems, we use models to predict the outcome of decision choices we might make. Models have several advantages over the real thing for this purpose. One advantage of models is ease of access and manipulation. It is often impractical to test business alternatives in practice. A firm choosing among six factory equipment layouts would find it quite impractical to set up six factories, one with each layout, to compare their operating costs. Yet that firm may be able to develop computer models of the six layouts, using methods we'll discuss in detail in Chapter 9, and choose the best.

In some cases it is literally impossible to compare all the alternatives, even without cost constraints, since running one experiment changes the conditions enough to invalidate the second one. For example, the U.S. Federal

Reserve Board cannot set the rate of interest it charges to member banks, then watch the national economy for six months to see the results, and finally pick a different rate retroactively if it didn't like the effects of its first choice. With a computer model, the Federal Reserve Board can try several possibilities. It can reset the starting conditions of its model to today's economic situation before each experiment and predict what the impact of each possible interest rate is likely to be. While the result of this process is seldom perfect, it's better than guessing.

As a second advantage, it is often easier to collect data from a computer model than from the actual system. To understand the production bottlenecks in a real factory we would have to station an observer at each work station to note and record where work in process builds up and where equipment or people are idle. A computer can collect this data easily as a by-product of running a model.

Third, given a sufficiently fast computer, a model can compress time and yield results more quickly than the real world could. The expected results of a year of production, or several years of economic policy, can be made available to decision makers in minutes. This, too, contributes to the practicality of evaluating several decision options via computer models.

There are many different types of models. We saw examples of a *graphical model* earlier in this chapter: the data flow diagram. A *narrative model* describes a system in a natural language such as English: the definition of a DSS in Section 1.1 is a highly simplified narrative model of a decision support system. A *physical model* is a smaller or idealized representation of the real system, such as a model railroad or a clay styling mockup. These three types of models, while often useful, are generally not part of decision support systems. (You might use a graphical model or a narrative model to describe a decision support system, but describing a DSS isn't the same as being part of a DSS.) Several types of models are shown in Figure 3–7.

Since decision support systems are information systems, the models used in DSS represent reality by information about reality. (Strictly speaking, they represent reality by data, which can be processed into or interpreted as information.) This is a fourth type of model, often called a *symbolic model* or a *mathematical model*. Despite its name, a mathematical model need not involve a great deal of what you have studied in your math courses. Indeed, the term *information-based model* would probably be better than either of the usual terms, although it is unfortunately not in general use. The data elements in a symbolic model can be of any of the data types that computers and computer programs can deal with:

- True/false, also called Boolean, values: that an investor should, or alternatively should not, invest in common stocks.
- Character strings: that this investor might consider a common stock represented by the letters GM, GE, or IBM.

FIGURE 3–7
"Family Tree" of Model Types

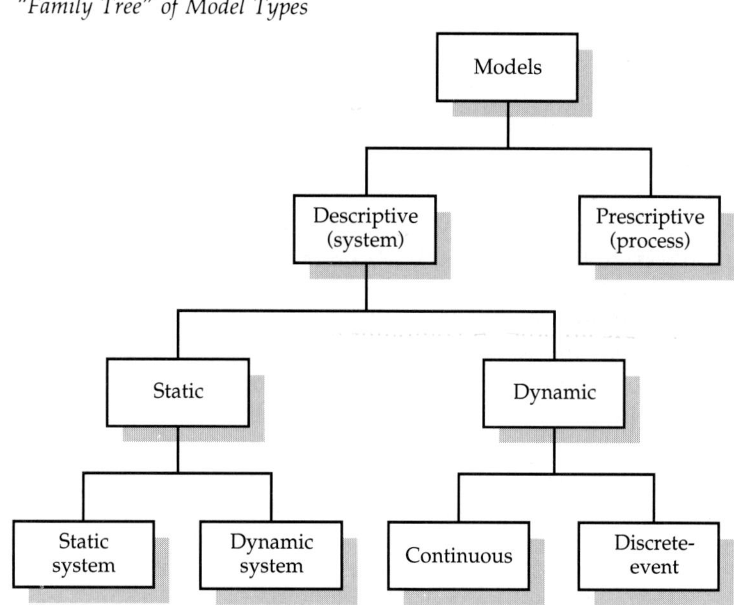

- Numerical values: that this investor should purchase 200 shares, or should buy if the price per share drops to $35. The "mathematical" aspect of the model, where the DSS has one, usually emphasizes its numerical data elements.

Models incorporate procedures and formulas to manipulate their data elements. These procedures and formulas derive the value of new data elements from values of other data elements in the model and from external values entered into the model. These external values can come from the user, from a database, or from a device such as a product inspection system or a stock exchange "ticker tape." A procedure that accessed suitable information sources could derive a per-share price of $42.125 and an annual dividend payment of $1.32 from the character string "T," the New York Stock Exchange symbol for AT&T common stock. A formula could then determine that the annual yield of this security is 3.13 percent. A useful characteristic of most models, which applies even to this mini-example, is that the model remains valid when the data change. That allows us to change one variable and see the effect. Here, we can ask, "What would the percentage yield be if the price of a share rose to $44?" and the model could tell us. In other models, the procedure may enable a model to reflect the passage of time: The closing inventory of one day may become the opening inventory of the next, or the component that enters a painting process may emerge, a half hour later, all painted and ready for the next step.

3.5.1 Types of Models

A DSS can incorporate several different types of mathematical models. The next few sections cover the major categories. We will discuss some of the most important types of DSS models in more detail in Chapter 9.

System versus Process Models: What Are We Modeling?

A mathematical model, as we mentioned earlier, is an information-based representation of an actual system. In the case of decision support systems we want to use this model to help us make decisions. Two types of models can help us toward this goal. One type of model, called a *system model,* models the system that we wish to study. The other type, called a *process model,* models the process that humans follow in making a decision about the system. The two types of models have different strengths and weaknesses and different areas of applicability in DSS.

To understand the distinction between these two types of models better, consider a DSS intended to help a corporate tax planner decide how to depreciate an asset. The options are accelerated depreciation, with several allowable variations, or straight-line depreciation plus an investment tax credit (ITC). A system model would incorporate the tax formulas for each case and a present-value algorithm based on a (user-specified or database-extracted) hurdle rate. A process model would incorporate rules of thumb used by experienced tax planners, such as "If the depreciable life of the asset is 10 years or greater, take the ITC."

When its rules apply, the process model can be more efficient. It reaches the same conclusion—take the ITC—with far fewer steps. However, a process model does not incorporate the "deep knowledge" of a system that would let it adapt easily to unforeseen circumstances. If the hurdle rate changes, the process model would be utterly lost since its rules of thumb assume a certain relationship between the present and the future values of funds. A system model could simply plug a new hurdle rate into its formulas and obtain the correct answer for the new situation.

Process models form the basis of most expert systems, which we fit into the DSS picture in Chapter 14. Group decision support systems, which bring people together electronically to help them reach a decision and which we discuss in Chapter 11, often also incorporate models of a decision process.

Some authors, by the way, differentiate between *descriptive* and *predictive* or *prescriptive* models. To them, a descriptive model describes what a system did in the past or is doing at the present, whereas a predictive (or prescriptive) model describes what the modeler expects it to do in the future. Both types are based on a model of the system itself. They differ primarily in the source of their input data. The descriptive model (according to this distinction) uses actual past or present data, while the predictive model uses assumed or statistically described future data. The difference is thus not really in the model itself. We will lump both types under the heading "process models" or "descriptive models," but don't be surprised if you see the separate terms elsewhere.

Static versus Dynamic Models: Cause and Effect Over Time

An important distinction between two types of descriptive models is the distinction between static and dynamic models. As Gordon puts it [GORD78]: "Static models show the values that system attributes take when the system is in balance. Dynamic models follow the changes over time that result from system activities."

A *static model* can model either a *static system* or a *dynamic system*. A static system is one in which the passage of time does not play a part. In a dynamic system, the passage of time, with cause-and-effect relationships connecting one time period to the next, is essential to what is being modeled.

A static model describes relationships that exist among the data values describing a system at any instant in time. In a static system, this is always the case. A static model can apply to a dynamic system as well, if it is in equilibrium. For example, it is a fact that income for a period is equal to revenue less expenses (static system), that the weight of a truck equals its empty weight plus the weight of its cargo (static system for this purpose, even if the truck is moving), or that, over a period of time, the number of customers entering a store must equal the number of customers who leave it (dynamic system in balance). In such a *static model* any given data element, once calculated, remains stable. Many financial planning models behave this way: Once we enter the data, the result will not change unless we change the input.

In a *dynamic model,* the flow of time is inherent, not only in the system, but also in our modeling process. Data values change over time. An assembly line model works this way as it tracks products through their manufacturing process. When a subassembly finishes one step of the manufacturing process, the next step can begin. A model of traffic flow at an intersection, which we might use to minimize delays by adjusting the signal timing, works this way as well. Or, a model of consumer response to advertising could relate the impact of one ad to the number of prior ads for the same product to which the consumer has already been exposed. In these and other dynamic models, what happens at one instant in time affects the modeled system at future instants in time.

The distinction between static and dynamic models can be confusing because a collection of static models can also appear to show a quantity varying over time. Consider three spreadsheet models of a corporate budget, each showing the major revenue and expense categories for 1994 through 1997.

Each of the three looks exactly like Figure 3–8. They vary only in their formulas, which we can't see.

- If all four data columns are calculated independently, this is a static model even though it shows how profits are predicted to vary over the four years. Each of the four one-year models is separate from the others. No relationship between one year and another is built into the numbers.
- If the spreadsheet used a formula to enter revenue increases of 10 percent per year, it is still a static model. We can use a formula in cells C3, D3, and E3 to simplify data entry and make it easier to model different assumptions about revenue growth, but that does not affect the model itself.[3] The 1994 revenue does not cause 1995 revenue to be 10 percent higher.
- If a spreadsheet formula relates one year's R&D and advertising revenues to the next year's sales revenues, it becomes a dynamic model. Here we are modeling *cause-and-effect relationships.* R&D spending leads to better products and hence to higher sales. Advertising leads to increased customer awareness and hence to higher sales. This cause-and-effect relationship between one time period and succeeding ones is the essence of a dynamic model.

As noted above, we may choose to use a static model of a dynamic system. Such a model can tell us where a dynamic system reaches equilibrium, also

FIGURE 3–8

Corporate Budget Spreadsheet

	A	B	C	D	E
1	KITSON CORPORATION SUMMARY FINANCIAL FORECAST ($MIL)				
2		1994	1995	1996	1997
3	Revenue	2.00	2.20	2.42	2.66
4	R&D costs	0.25	0.30	0.35	0.40
5	Advertising costs	0.10	0.12	0.14	0.16
6	Cost of goods sold	0.80	0.87	0.95	1.04
7	General and administrative	0.45	0.50	0.55	0.60
8	Total costs	1.60	1.79	1.99	2.20
9	Profit before tax	0.40	0.41	0.43	0.46

[3]A well-designed spreadsheet that took this approach would put the 10 percent figure in a visible and clearly labeled cell rather than hiding it in a formula that was replicated across a row.

called its "steady state." Its output might say, for example, that a box office window with specified customer arrival and service time statistics has an average of 3.5 customers waiting in line after it has been open long enough for arrivals and departures to balance statistically. The system is dynamic—customers arrive, buy tickets, and depart—but a static model can determine where it settles down. Since the model is static, it won't tell us anything about how individual customers move through the system or how line length varies over time, but for some decisions that doesn't matter. We'll cover this type of model, which we can solve mathematically via the equations that define its equilibrium, in Section 9.2.

Continuous versus Discrete-Event Models: How Do Quantities Vary in the System?

Dynamic system models mimic the behavior of a real system over time, allowing us to examine this behavior and thus learn about or optimize the system. The system in question can be a physical system: We might want to study blood pressure in an artery, temperature in an engine combustion chamber, or the trajectory of a space vehicle as it passes through the gravitational fields of various bodies in the solar system. It can be a socioeconomic system, where we are interested in income, population, and resource consumption trends. In business, it might be a manufacturing system where we must choose among factory arrangements or equipment.

Dynamic system models can be divided into two categories: *continuous-system* models and *discrete-event* models.

Continuous-system simulation models describe physical or economic processes in which the numbers that describe the system vary continuously. For example, blood pressure varies continuously over time. It does not jump instantaneously from one value to another. Rather, there are processes that cause it to rise or to fall at given rates. (There may be events, such as stress, that cause its rate of change to jump instantaneously from one value to another, but the value of the pressure itself is still continuous.) For every time interval, no matter how small, there may be a change in pressure. When the blood pressure increases from one value to a higher one, it passes through every intermediate value on the way. The same is true of the location of a train along a track, the position of a piston in an engine, and most other physical phenomena.

Simple continuous systems can be studied via calculus and differential equations. The differential equations that describe complex systems are usually too complex to solve in closed form: that is, too complex to get the answer as a formula which we can evaluate. They can, however, be solved numerically.

Discrete-event models deal with systems in which discrete, identifiable *events* occur at identifiable points in time and change the state of the system instantaneously from one value to another one. For example, the arrival of an order at a firm may change the state of the system from "2 Type 4 desks on order" to "3 Type 4 desks on order." The system does not go through intermediate states of "2.5 Type 4 desks on order" or "2-7/8 Type 4 desks on order," whereas a continuous system would progress smoothly through all the values between 2 and 3 before settling down at its new level. We treat the arrival of the third order as an instantaneous event. No matter how finely we divide time, there is a precise instant at which we say this order arrives. There are exactly two orders on hand before this event occurs, exactly three on or after that instant.

Business systems are usually characterized by identifiable events that cause instantaneous change in the system: an order arrives; a product is shipped. Business situations therefore usually don't lend themselves to continuous models. Socioeconomic planners use continuous models, but their work—while undeniably important—is not in the mainstream of corporate DSS. Since discrete-event models suit most business planning needs, they are the only type of dynamic system model we will discuss further in this book.

Deterministic versus Stochastic Models: Statistical Uncertainty

Another categorization of descriptive (system) models involves our confidence that the relationships in the models hold true in the real world. Some models reflect certainty. Others involve uncertainty or risk. There is no uncertainty only when all the relationships in a model are true by definition or by decree.

Most models have elements of both certainty and of uncertainty. A corporate financial planning model may reflect certainty in the accounting relationships among its variables, but there may still be some uncertainty in its developer's mind as to future sales. A manufacturing model may reflect uncertainty in the time to assemble a product, but the relationships among production quantities and parts inventory withdrawals is still certain. A traffic control model may use a formula with no uncertainty to represent the timing intervals between signal changes but incorporate some uncertainty in its description of cars' arrival rate at an intersection.

We call a model *deterministic* if its outputs are fixed for a given set of inputs, *stochastic* if they reflect an element of statistically defined uncertainty. A deterministic model of a three-step assembly process might have each step takes exactly one hour, so the entire process takes three hours. A stochastic model's output, for a given set of inputs, varies randomly over a range of possible outcomes. A stochastic model of the same assembly process might have the duration of each step vary around its one-hour average. If we run this model many times we will obtain many different answers, clustered around three hours. Their variance from this mean, or any other measure of their disperson, will depend on the way the duration of each step varies around its one-hour mean.

We can deal with uncertainty by describing the statistics of a data element: its mean and its variance if it follows a normal distribution, its cumulative distribution function for continuous distributions in general, or the discrete probabilities that the data element will take on each value in a set of possible individual values.

However we describe the statistics of a random variable, there are two ways a model can use its statistical description:

- One is to carry the statistical description through the model and produce the answer in the form of a statistical description at the end. We might be able to say, for example, that if next year's estimated revenues are normally distributed with a mean of $1.5 million and a standard deviation of $0.2 million, then next year's net profits before tax will be normally distributed with a mean of $150,000 and a standard deviation of $100,000.
- Another approach is to choose a value for each statistically described variable, each time it is needed, and use this value in the model. To do this we would pick a random value from the given distribution of next year's revenue: say, $1,546,873. We would carry this figure through the model and obtain a profit figure of $173,436. We would then repeat the process: our second try might pick $1,412,890 for revenue and obtain $106,445 as the corresponding profit. After a large number of samples, we could analyze or plot the expected profit distribution.

With the second approach, the outcome of each run varies according to the choices made from the given statistical distributions for that run. We must exercise such a model many times to get an accurate statistical picture of its predictions. This increases the computer time required to get a useful result, often substantially. However, this approach always works. In modeling complex systems, it is often mathematically impossible to carry the statistics of all the distributions through to the final result.

It is important to distinguish between uncertainty in the model itself and uncertainty in its inputs. Consider the financial model of a few paragraphs back in which next year's revenue was estimated statistically. The model which translates revenue into profits is deterministic. All its relationships are true by accounting definitions. This model, though, is a component of a larger model of the overall business. The larger model should incorporate some uncertainty in estimated sales. Our decision to characterize a model as deterministic or stochastic depends on what we put inside the model and what we put outside it.

This little example, by the way, points out the need to agree on the boundary of a system. If one person considers the uncertainty in revenue forecast to be inside the system and another considers this uncertainty to be outside the system, they might argue endlessly over the nature of the model (and its validity as a prediction of the future of the business) without realizing that their differences revolve merely about where each one draws the system boundary.

The familiar spreadsheet is a useful tool in dealing with deterministic models. Indeed, the first use of microcomputer spreadsheets in the late 1970s was to carry out accounting calculations, although they have found many more applications since then. Financial planning software can also be used for this purpose. Sophisticated financial planning packages, and some state-of-the-art spreadsheet packages, can deal with uncertainty in the inputs to the accounting model as well. We'll discuss financial planning software in Chapter 6.

In the next chapter we'll encounter the terms *accounting model* and *representational models.* These correspond closely to deterministic and stochastic models. We mention the terms here because many writers on DSS, including Steven Alter whose work we cite there, used them.

3.5.2 Simplification in Models

All models simplify the real world. Even accounting models, which at first glance seem totally precise, use simplifications. For example, no firm calculates the depreciation of individual pencils. This simplification is sanctioned by tax codes and by generally accepted accounting practices, so it's not much of a "simplification." If the purpose of our model is to predict how a tax return will look, it isn't one. Yet, conceptually, ignoring depreciation on a 29¢ pencil does simplify reality. The modeler must determine which simplifications are acceptable and which are not. Some simplification is essential to make models practical. Too much simplification, such as ignoring depreciation on a $2 million corporate jet, can make a model useless. Guidelines for builders of most business models are usually not as clear cut as the tax code definition of a depreciable asset.[4]

As another example, consider a model of a traffic intersection. Transportation planners use such models to determine how to optimize traffic flow: how long to make each part of the light cycle, whether or not to use dedicated left turn lanes and/or left turn light cycles, whether allowing right turns on red lights will improve vehicle flow, etc. A complete model of a four-way intersection will be quite complex, and even so, it is likely to be incomplete. The signals at other nearby intersections are likely to affect the arrival rates of cars at the intersection we are studying—thus making a model that treats one intersection in splendid isolation doomed to inaccuracy, if not total irrelevance, before we start.

Yet traffic planners do use single-intersection models successfully. They really can improve traffic flow by following the recommendations of simple models. Even a model of the simplest possible intersection, two one-way streets, can be useful because:

[4]As any of your accounting instructors will confirm, the U.S. tax code is not considered an example of clarity.

- Building a simple model teaches us a great deal about the process of modeling the type of system we wish to study. A simple model is therefore a good starting point even if we plan to move on to more complex models of our system.
- Many complex models can use simple models as components. If we can build a good model of how a disk drive behaves in a large computer system, we can later incorporate this model into a more complex model of the computer system as a whole.
- Examining a simple model may show general principles of how the system in question behaves. This might be hidden behind the mass of detail we would get from a more complex (or more complete) model. For instance, a model of the simplest two-one-way-streets intersection will show us that total motorist waiting time is minimized if the light turns yellow in each direction as soon as all the waiting cars (including those that join the line after it begins to move) have passed through. Once this rule is known, it can be used to optimize complex intersections as well.

The assumption of individual, discrete events taking place in a business, while central to many models, may also be a simplification of reality. For instance, to model a supermarket, we would assume that customers arrive at discrete instants in time. At one instant there are 16 customers inside, then another arrives, and an instant later there are 17. In fact, the customer enters the market as part of a continuous process: first the toe of one foot or the hand pushing the door open, then the rest of the body in stages, finally the heel of the trailing foot. This level of detail is unnecessary for business modeling of what goes on in a supermarket. All models involve simplifications. The assumption of discrete, instantaneous events is among the most widely accepted, and acceptable, ones.

Summary

A decision support system is a system. More specifically, it is an information system.

A system is a group of interacting components with a purpose. In addition to its components and its purpose, every system has a boundary that separates the components of the system from the world outside the system. A system may incorporate feedback. Feedback can occur within the system or outside it.

An information system is a system whose purpose is storing, communicating, and processing information. Most large information systems in business today incorporate computers, but many important information systems do not. It is important to consider noncomputerized information processing methods as solutions to business problems.

Data flow diagrams are a convenient and widely accepted way to record and communicate (1) the processes and data stores that comprise a system and (2) the information flows among them and between them and the outside world. Data flow diagrams do not, however, show the timing relationships among system activities, the conditions under which certain activities occur, or the reasons why they occur. For this reason they must be augmented by other system description methods.

Decision support systems, as information systems, usually use data stores that are created and updated by other systems. They communicate their results, not to other information systems, but to human decision makers.

A model is a simplified representation of a real system or object. Models are used in decision support systems because (1) they are easier to manipulate than the real systems whose behavior we want to study, (2) it is easier to extract data from them, and (3) they generate results more quickly. For a model to be useful we must be sure not to simplify the description of the real system so far that the usefulness of the model is lost.

One important distinction among the many types of symbolic models we could use in a computer-based decision support system is that between descriptive models, which show how a system behaves, and process models, which prescribe what humans should do in the situation being modeled. A further division of descriptive (system) models is between static models, which describe the system at a moment in time, and dynamic models, which show how it evolves through time. Within dynamic models, system activity can be modeled as a process of continuous change or by numerical data that jump instantaneously from one value to another as events take place in the system.

Another aspect of all descriptive models is the statistical uncertainty that may apply to one or more aspects of system behavior. There are several ways to handle uncertaintly in a model.

Key Terms

accounting model 90
boundary (of a system) 72
closed loop system 74
closed system 72
continuous model 87
data flow diagram (DFD) 77
data store (in a DFD) 77
descriptive model 84
deterministic model 88
discrete-event model 87
dynamic model 85
dynamic system 85
environment (of a system) 72
event 87
external entity (in a DFD, of a system) 77
external feedback 74
feedback 74
graphical model 82
information-based model 82
information system 74
internal feedback 74
mathematical model 82
model 81

narrative model 82
open loop system 74
open system 72
physical model 82
predictive model 84
prescriptive model 84
process (in a DFD or system) 77
process model 84
representational model 90
simplification (in a model) 90
static model 85
static system 85
stochastic model 88
subsystem 73
symbolic model 82
system 72
system model 84

Review Questions

1. What is a system? What are the key characteristics of a system?
2. Give one example of a system with internal feedback and one example of a system with external feedback, other than the ones in this chapter.
3. How does an information system differ from a system in general?
4. What does a data flow diagram show? What doesn't it show?
5. How does a decision support system differ from an information system in general?
6. What is a model? Give two examples of noncomputer models, other than the ones in this chapter. For each, state one feature it shares with the real system that it models and one feature it does not share with the real system.
7. What are three reasons to use computer models to support decision making?
8. State the differences between descriptive (system) and prescriptive (process) models.
9. How do static and dynamic models differ?
10. What is the difference between a continuous and a discrete-event model? Which type can use differential equations in its solution?
11. What characteristic distinguishes a stochastic model from a deterministic model?
12. Describe two ways of dealing with statistically defined phenomena in models.
13. Why do models simplify the real world?

Exercises

1. Make a photocopy or sketch of Figure 3–2, then draw the boundary of the payroll system.

2. Consider your DSS course as a system. What are its inputs? Its outputs? Its major processes?
3. Describe your college or university registration system as a system. Specify its purpose, its components, and their interactions.
4. Draw a data flow diagram for the above system.
5. Consider a corporate photocopying center. Employees who need copies of documents come to the center with the original document. They fill out a form stating the number of copies required; requirements such as stapling, binding, or colored paper; the requestor's name; and the department number to be charged for the job. The job is ready for pickup some time later: within an hour for short jobs (under 20 original pages, under 25 copies, no binding, unstapled or standard top left corner stapling, white paper without prepunched holes); during the next half-day for medium-sized jobs (a less restrictive definition); and within 24 hours, not counting weekends and holidays, for large jobs or those with unusual requirements. These are upper time limits that the center promises to meet under any and all circumstances. Most jobs are ready much sooner.
   a. Describe the photocopying center as a system. What parts of the above description didn't you need for this purpose?
   b. Draw a data flow diagram of this system.
   c. A manager asks a secretary for copies of a report. The manager's secretary takes the originals to the photocopying center and, at a later time, returns to pick up the finished copies. Is the secretary part of the system? Why or why not?
6. Insurance companies hire people to evaluate claims and determine how much, if anything, the company should pay. The decision process includes evaluating the amount of damage or some other measure of how much money the claimant might be due, determining if the type of claim is allowable under the policy, and examining the terms of the policy to determine how much of the claim should be paid. Each of these parts can be quite complex. Simple situations that involve small amounts of money, such as reimbursement for prescription drugs under a medical insurance policy, can be dealt with in minutes by relatively low-skilled personnel. Complex situations involving larger amounts of money, such as a long-term disability claim for a 35-year-old person injured at work, may require months of investigation by skilled medical and rehabilitation professionals.
   a. Pick a specific insurance situation of your choice. Draw a data flow diagram for its claim processing.
   b. In part *a*, you put a claimant either inside or outside the system. Justify your choice.
   c. Expand one of the processes in your DFD into a lower level DFD.
7. You have prepared a spreadsheet outlining how you plan to spend your advertising budget for each of the 12 months of next year: so much on each of several TV programs, so much on direct mail, so much on mag-

azines of various types, etc. Your spreadsheet shows totals by category and the grand total for each month.

a. Is this a static or a dynamic model? Why?

b. You enhance your spreadsheet to show the number of people who will be exposed to your message each month and, for each month, the number of people who will have been exposed to your message a given number of times from January 1 to the end of that month. Is your spreadsheet now a static or a dynamic model? Why?

8. You have been hired by an airline to model the effects of last-minute gate changes for aircraft at an airport. "Last-minute" means that people are already at the gate at which the aircraft was originally supposed to park, either to greet arriving passengers or to board the aircraft for its next flight. If the gate assignment is changed, these people will have to go to the new gate. Your model is to predict the time it takes them to reach the new gate so that the airline can determine if the switch will impact its flight schedule. Define three dynamic, descriptive models, having different degrees of simplification, that you could apply to this problem. State which is the simplest model that you think would give useful results for airline planners to use.

References

GORD78 Gordon, Geoffrey. *System Simulation,* 2nd ed. Prentice Hall, Englewood Cliffs, N.J. (1978).

MENN69 Menninger, Karl. *Number Words and Number Symbols: A Cultural History of Numbers.* English translation: MIT Press, Cambridge, Mass. (1969); German original: Vandenhoek & Ruprecht, Göttingen (1958).

RAPO86 Rapoport, Anatol. *General Systems Theory: Essential Concepts and Applications.* Abacus Press, Cambridge, Mass. (1986).

VONB68 von Bertalanffy, Ludwig. *General Systems Theory: Foundations, Development, Applications.* Braziller, New York (1968).

WILS90 Wilson, Brian. *Systems: Concepts, Methodologies, and Applications.* John Wiley & Sons, New York (1990).

ENVOYANCE
THE STAR-BRITE CRISIS

As Doug and Adrienne entered the Envoyance reception area at 8:55 A.M. on the following Tuesday, they could not help noticing the tension in the air. The receptionist looked up at them and said, "Sandra just called everyone into the conference room for 9 o'clock. I'm sure you're included."

Jim and the rest of the Envoyance staff were already seated around the conference table as Doug and Adrienne took places near the back of the room. Sandra opened the meeting with these words: "Some of you may remember the Star-Brite Paint cleanup. For the more recent arrivals, Star-Brite went out of business in the early sixties after making paint for the better part of the century. Like a lot of companies back then, they had been spilling anything and everything all over the place without giving it a second thought. The site was vacant until three years ago. That's when Perry Construction decided to put in a mixed-income housing development. We cleaned the place up, keeping in mind that there would be a lot of little kids playing in the dirt, digging in it, and once in a while eating a mud pie or two. Perry built the Fox Glen complex, and they're managing it today."

Sandra paused and looked around before continuing. "We got a phone call from Perry's lawyers at 8:15 this morning. Two children from the same family at Fox Glen are having neurological symptoms such as dizzy spells. They're assuming that the cause is earth they put in their mouths and are suing Perry. Perry, in turn, is coming to us."

"Are they suing us, or what?" asked Chris, one of the senior Envoyance technical staff members.

"Not at this point, though it could come to that," responded Sandra. "Right now we have to show that the site was clean when we finished, at least as regards anything that could possibly cause those kids' symptoms. If we can do that, then Envoyance is off the legal hook, though we might have to appear in court if this goes to trial.

"Assuming we can do that—and it may not be easy—then either something was brought in since we left, which is possible, or the kids picked up their symptoms outside Fox Glen, or the cause is totally unrelated to pollution. In the first case Perry could still be held liable. They may want our help in defending themselves against the possibility."

"There seem to be an awful lot of possibilities," commented Jim. "What happens next?"

"You're right about the possibilities, Jim. Dan and I talked this over and we have to move in a lot of directions at once. First, we'll have to find out what chemicals could be associated with the children's symptoms, as well as what other medical causes—perhaps hereditary ones, since both kids have the same two parents—there might be.

"Once we have that, we'll have to see if Star-Brite ever used any of them. This will involve checking their records, historical data on paint formulations from the late 19th century through 1963 and our pre-cleanup assessment work. Unfortunately, Eric, who headed the Star-Brite project, left last year to start his own company. We could still call him if we had to, but I'd rather not.

"If there were, or could have been, any potentially guilty substances on the site, we'll have to go through our cleanup records to make sure they were eliminated. This involves making sure we did the right things and did them correctly. It will also involve reviewing our post-cleanup data.

"We will also have to find out if any such substances could have been introduced during or after construction.

"Finally, if it comes to that, we may have to look at the other places the two children went together. They're in the same family, and they both attend the West Mitchell Avenue school, but they're in different grades and participate in totally different kinds of activities. Since the other West Mitchell children aren't, as far as I know, showing similar symptoms, the most likely candidate outside Fox Glen would be somewhere they went on a family outing. It's also possible that other West Mitchell kids *are* showing symptoms. We may not have heard about them simply because they don't live at Fox Glen, so nobody would have a reason to tell us. That would be good to know too, as it would probably get Perry out of trouble instantly."

"Is that all?" asked Chris.

"Isn't that enough? We're not even getting paid for this, though we might be later on if we have to defend Perry against any post-cleanup charges. And, of course, we need it all in a hurry. So—

"Jackie, I'd like you to find out the most likely substances that could cause the symptoms these kids have reported, along with other known medical causes that can have the same kind of effect.

"Ed, you make sure we can get at Star-Brite's and the industry's chemical history. It ought to be in our files already, but please make sure you know where it is and that it's complete. No sense searching it until we know what to search for, but we have to be ready when Jackie comes back with that.

"Sandy, see if you can find out if anyone else at West Mitchell has had these dizzy spells. Try not to get into the papers at this point.

"Jim, while we're waiting for Oxbow to make up their minds on your proposal, you dig out Eric's records, familiarize yourself with what's in there, and make sure you'll be able to find what we need in them.

"Any questions?"

"Yes, Sandra. How about digging up Fox Glen now?"

"We may have to do that, Sue. Drilling cores and analyzing them could get very expensive, as we know, so I'd rather save it as a last resort. Besides, if we did find something, it may not be easy to prove when or how it got there. So we'll need the data in any case."

As the group filed soberly out of the conference room, Sandra stopped by Adrienne and Doug. "What do you think of this mess?"

"Well, it's not quite like business school!" Adrienne answered quickly. "We always talk about strategic plans with no time pressure and no surprises."

"In that case, welcome to the *real* world! Could your computers help us now?"

Exercises

1. State briefly and clearly the specific decisions Envoyance faces here. Are they:
   - Operational, tactical, or strategic?
   - Structured, semistructured, or unstructured?
2. Where do the tasks that Sandra has assigned fit into the design-intelligence-choice decision framework?
3. You know that Sandra's psychological type is ENFJ (see the case in Chapter 2). What does this suggest to you about her probable next step? What might Dan, whose psychological type is INTP, do differently? Do you have any ideas as to which of the two was more likely to suggest, when Dan and Sandra met privately, the steps she outlined in the meeting?
4. Diagram the earth in the Fox Glen children's play area as a system. Show its inputs (going back several decades) and outputs.
5. Draw a data flow diagram of what Sandra knows about the Fox Glen site as a result

of the activities she set in process at the meeting. Treat her knowledge as a data store.

6. Consider a model of the process through which the earth around Fox Glen might have become polluted by Star-Brite Paint.
   a. Is this a continuous or a discrete-event model? Why?
   b. Is this a deterministic or a stochastic model? Why?
7. Describe possible narrative, graphical, and physical models of the Fox Glen site. When or how might each one be useful?
8. Answer Sandra's last question. If you say "No," explain why. If you say "Yes," explain how.

Chapter 4

Types of Decision Support Systems

Chapter Outline

Introduction

The variety of decision support systems is overwhelming. As we've seen, a DSS can range from a spreadsheet on a PC to a custom-written system for hundreds of users, accessing a multi-gigabyte database, running on mainframe computers costing tens of millions of dollars. DSS differ in their scope, the decisions they support, the people who use them, and what they do for those people.

Fortunately, we can place decision support systems into categories. This is helpful because we can learn what tools, techniques, and approaches have worked in each category. Then, when we face a new situation, we can begin by deciding what categories that situation fits. Approaches and techniques that have worked in those categories before have a good chance of working in the new situation as well.

Chapter Objectives

After you have read and studied this chapter, you will be able to:

1. Describe the seven basic types of DSS, and explain how each can be applied to a real decision-making situation.
2. Identify how the seven types of DSS can be grouped into broader categories.
3. Explain why each type of DSS is best suited to different types of decisions.
4. Define individual, multi-individual, and group DSS, and explain how each type tends to provide different benefits.
5. Discuss how different types of DSS match the needs of decision makers of different psychological types.
6. Describe the usage methods of DSS, the types of people they involve, and how they have changed with technology changes.
7. Explain how and why an institutional DSS and an ad hoc DSS differ.

4.1 THE DSS HIERARCHY

Steven Alter, whose DSS work was mentioned in Chapter 1, divided decision support systems into the seven levels shown in Figure 4–1 [ALTE80]. This hierarchy is based on the capabilities of a DSS. While these categories don't fit every system that exists today, and while there are grey areas between some adjacent categories, they are still an excellent place to start. From the bottom to the top, the seven DSS types and Alter's original definitions are:

File drawer systems allow immediate access to data items.

Data analysis systems allow the manipulation of data by means of operators tailored to the task and settings or operators of a general nature.

Analysis information systems provide access to a series of databases and small models.

Accounting models calculate the consequences of planned actions on the basis of accounting definitions.

Representational models estimate the consequences of actions on the basis of models that are partially nondefinitional.

Optimization systems provide guidelines for action by generating the optimal solution consistent with a set of constraints.

Suggestion systems perform mechanical work leading to a specific suggested decision for a fairly structured task.

4.1.1 *The Seven DSS Types*

In this section we'll look at the seven DSS types in a bit more detail. We'll cover them in the order given above. Don't, however, think of the latter types as being "better" in some philosophical sense than the earlier ones. They are actually more of a continuum. The first ones are better suited to dealing with less structured problems. The later ones are better for more structured situations.

FIGURE 4–1

*DSS Hierarchy**

Top	Suggestion systems
	Optimization systems
	Representational models
	Accounting models
	Analysis information systems
	Data analysis systems
Bottom	File drawer systems

*Source: [ALTE80].

File Drawer Systems

These are the simplest DSS, yet they can often be of value. Retrieving a desired piece of information can help reach decisions. When a bank teller gives you your savings account balance, when a travel agent informs you that there are no seats left on a flight you asked about, when an order-entry operator tells you that your credit limit will not cover the full amount of an order, they are using file drawer systems. In every case the decision maker is then in a position to make an act: to move funds from one account to another, to choose between an earlier and a later flight, to forego a purchase or to use a different method of payment.

Data Analysis Systems

It is a rare data management system today that cannot also carry out operations such as conditional retrieval of records and elementary arithmetic summaries of selected data. In the 1990s pure file drawer systems are found only in dedicated end-user applications such as checking your bank balance at an ATM. Almost all software packages and systems used as file drawer systems also have some *data analysis* capability. Any SQL-based relational database management system can find the sum and average of the data it retrieves: these operations are built into the lowest level of the SQL standard.[1] The airline reservation system that tells your travel agent "no more seats on that flight" can also display a list of alternate flights to the same destination at about the same time. With few exceptions, the distinction between the first two DSS categories is now usually more a function of how a system is used than of its underlying capability.

Integrated software packages that combine a spreadsheet with data management capability are useful data analysis systems for desktop microcomputers, though modern spreadsheet programs have modeling and analysis capabilities beyond what this category requires.[2] Where their data management capabilities do not suffice, most spreadsheet packages can import files from other data or database management software. Setting up the transfer may require some technical skills, especially if the files in question reside on a system other than the micro. Once a person with the requisite skills sets up the connection and the importing procedures, the process of actually importing the latest data for local analysis does not tax the typical end user.

---

[1]SQL is an acronym for the Structured Query Language, a standard way of accessing data in relational databases. You'll learn more about SQL in Section 6.3.1.

[2]While many microcomputer users refer to this capability as *database* management, MIS professionals and users of larger systems reserve the term "database" for software that can associate data from several files. We will retain the historically precise usage and insist that a database manager must have multifile capability. (Database managers are discussed in Section 6.3.1). You should not, however, expect all end users to make this distinction.

Analysis Information Systems

Alter's name for this category sometimes causes confusion. If the second category is called "data analysis systems," shouldn't this one be "information analysis systems?" The emphasis in this category name, however, is on the "analysis." The last two words mean that an information system carries out the analysis.

The key distinguishing feature between the preceding category of DSS and this one is that we are now combining information from several files. In other words, we have a true database. An analysis information system could let a user compare the sales growth trend of one firm's products, calculated from its internal sales data, with industry-wide data from an external source.

Accounting Models

The term *accounting model* refers to a model with no uncertainty and where the calculations in each time period depend only on other data from that time period. Such models arise frequently in accounting. Balance sheets and income statements are accounting models, where certain calculations must be performed in order to yield the correct results. The most common business tool used to represent accounting models is the spreadsheet program, invented by two Harvard Business School students to automate the accounting calculations they had to do for a case analysis. (Their program was later commercialized as Visicalc for the Apple II product line.) Other tools can also be used, especially if the accounting model is a small part of a larger DSS.

Material requirements planning (MRP) systems, widely used by manufacturing firms, incorporate accounting models. The bill of materials (BOM) for a product states which components, and how many of each, go into that product. If the BOM of a desk calls for four legs, precisely four legs are needed: not 3, not 3.5, not an average of 4 with a standard deviation of 0.3.

While an accounting model itself cannot incorporate any uncertainty, its inputs—as we mentioned in Chapter 3—may not be known precisely. For example, Alter discusses a model used by a shipping firm to calculate its costs and, hence, its charter prices. Two factors in this calculation are fuel consumption and the unit cost of fuel at the time of the voyage. Both are subject to uncertainty, although historical data for the vessel in question allow us to estimate its fuel consumption with a high degree of accuracy and forecasts of fuel prices are available from several sources. Once we have made our estimate, though, the model itself behaves as if the figures were known precisely and does not take their possible variation into account. The model in this DSS is therefore an accounting model. Similarly, we will call a budget forecast that uses an estimated future inflation rate, or any such model, an accounting model in the context of these seven categories.

Representational Models

Representational models reflect uncertainty, often in individual or collective human behavior, or represent the dynamic behavior of systems over time.

Representational models are widely used to forecast the future effect of a decision: the productivity of one factory setup versus another, the stockout frequency of one ordering policy versus another, the response time of one computer system configuration versus another. By representing how we expect a real-world system to respond to certain inputs, we can consider different decisions (system inputs) and choose among them on the basis of their predicted results (system output). We'll cover several types of representational models in Chapter 9.

Optimization Systems

Given a suitable model, we can estimate the effect of various decision alternatives. If the alternatives can be enumerated or laid out along mathematical axes, a program can choose the one that yields the best results. While the best mathematical forecast is not always the only basis for decision making—using it alone corresponds to the "rational manager" of Chapter 2—it is often helpful to give a decision maker this information. A system that selects the best of several alternatives on a numerical basis is called an optimization system. We'll discuss optimization methods in Chapter 10.

Suggestion Systems

It is often a short step from determining a mathematically optimal decision via a descriptive (system) model to suggesting that the decision maker should make that decision. When decisions are highly structured it may be practical for a DSS to make such a suggestion. Such DSS are called, appropriately, suggestion systems.

Another type of suggestion system uses a prescriptive (process) model to mimic the reasoning process a human expert would use in reaching a decision. It then suggests that the user make the same decision that this reasoning process would yield. This approach works well where human expertise can be codified into a reasonable number of rules. The technology of expert systems is often used to construct this type of suggestion system. Chapters 14 through 18 are about expert systems.

4.1.2 Applying the DSS Types to Airline Yield Management[3]

A concrete example will help clarify the distinctions among these seven types of DSS. Yield management is a business problem that is simple enough to understand (not really simple: real-world problems seldom are) yet complex enough to need computer support. The first industry to practice deliberate yield management as a profit-maximizing strategy was the airline industry, although it has since spread to other areas. Industries that can use yield

[3]The author is grateful to Professor Peter Belobaba, of the MIT Department of Aeronautics and Astronautics, for his constructive comments on a draft of this section.

management are generally characterized by high fixed costs, low variable costs, a product or service that loses value rapidly if not used, and several types of customers with different characteristics who use what is essentially the same product or service. (You may have run into the term "price discrimination" when you discussed these concepts in your economics course.)

The Yield Management Problem

Most airlines offer a variety of fares on a given flight segment. It is often said that an airline can fill a flight with no two passengers paying the same fare with precisely the same terms and conditions. Airlines expend a great deal of effort on *yield management:* deciding what conditions will apply to each discount fare and how many seats the airline will make available at each discount level.

Suppose a flight has two coach class fares. The higher fare is called *full coach fare.* It is available until the plane takes off and is refundable in full at any time—even after the flight, if the ticket was not used for any reason. A full-price coach ticket can be rewritten for any other flight to the same destination. The lower "SuperSaver" fare has several restrictions. One possible set of restrictions is that SuperSaver tickets must be purchased at least 30 days before the flight, is available only for round trips that include a Saturday night stay at the destination, can be rewritten for a different flight only at a substantial additional charge, and is not refundable if it is not used on the ticketed flight.

Many vacationers plan their trips more than a month ahead, stay at their destination at least one Saturday night, and are willing to plan around specific flights in return for substantial savings. Most business travelers plan trips on shorter notice, want to return home as soon as their meetings are over, and need flexibility to deal with unforeseen events. Therefore, many vacationers can qualify for SuperSaver fares, but most business travelers cannot.

The airline's dilemma is this: It doesn't have enough business travelers to fill a plane. It has, however, enough potential vacationers to fill a plane—or can generate them by setting the discount fare low enough. If it sets a low SuperSaver price and allows vacationers to fill the plane, the flight will fill up a month before it takes off. The airline will then have no seats left for business travelers who need them at the last minute. Since business travelers pay a higher fare, the airline's profits will be less than they might be. In addition, business travelers—who are any airline's most profitable customers—will be unhappy and may transfer their allegiance to another carrier.

To avoid these problems airlines limit the number of seats they sell at discount fares. For example, an airline may decide that only 40 of 100 coach seats can be sold at the SuperSaver price. If a 41st traveler requests this fare, it will not be offered—even if the traveler meets the conditions of 30 days' advance notice, a Saturday night stay, etc. If it sets the limit too high, business travelers will be turned away because the plane is full of low-fare vacationers. If it sets the limit too low, the plane will take off with empty seats that could have held vacationers who bought SuperSaver tickets. SuperSaver tickets may be less profitable than full-fare tickets, but they are more profitable than empty seats.

Suppose full-fare sales form a normal distribution with a mean of 40.5 full-fare ticket sales in a 100-seat airplane. Half the time, we sell 41 or more full-fare seats. The other half of the time, we sell 40 or fewer. Suppose we could fill the plane with SuperSaver travelers if we allowed that to happen. How many SuperSaver seats should we sell?

The answer depends on the relationship between the two price levels.[4] If the SuperSaver fare is exactly half the full coach fare, we should sell 59 or 60 SuperSaver seats; it doesn't matter which. When we change the limit from 60 to 59, we give up a sure SuperSaver sale in return for a 50 percent chance of a full-fare sale. Given the 2:1 price relationship between the two fares, the two revenue streams are statistically equivalent and will even out in the long run.

Suppose we make more than 60 SuperSaver seats available. Since we have a better than even chance of selling 40 full fare seats, we are giving up (statistically) more than 50 percent of a full-fare sale for a half-fare sale. That's a bad deal. If we offered fewer than 59 SuperSaver seats, we would give up (again statistically) half-fare seats for a less than 50 percent chance of full-fare sale. That's a bad deal, too.

If a SuperSaver ticket cost two-thirds of the full-fare price, we would raise the limit. We would now want a two-thirds chance of filling all the full-fare seats. For a normal distribution, the two-thirds point is about 0.43 standard deviations above the mean. We would reserve 0.43 standard deviations fewer tickets for full-fare passengers. If full-fare sales, which we already know have a mean of 40.5, have a standard deviation of 14, we would offer 65 or 66 SuperSaver seats. We have increased the likelihood that some potential full-fare passengers won't find room. We accept this because selling a SuperSaver ticket is now, at two-thirds of the full-fare price, relatively more desirable to the airline than it was at only half of full coach fare.

Conversely, if the SuperSaver price were one-third of the full coach fare, we would lower the limit to give us a one-third chance of filling the plane. For the above distribution, we would make only 53 or 54 SuperSaver seats available. We accept a higher likelihood of the plane taking off with empty seats because SuperSaver seat sales are now less desirable than before. All these situations can be visualized in terms of the decision tree of Figure 4–2. It is clear from the decision tree that the correct decision is to keep the seat empty if the price of a full-fare ticket times the probability that a full-fare

[4]More precisely, it depends on *profit* levels: price less variable costs such as meals and extra fuel, plus average profit on drinks and headsets. Since these variable costs are small compared with either price or the flight's share of fixed costs, using price here is close enough for practical purposes.

FIGURE 4–2

Airline Discount Ticket Seat Quota Decision Tree

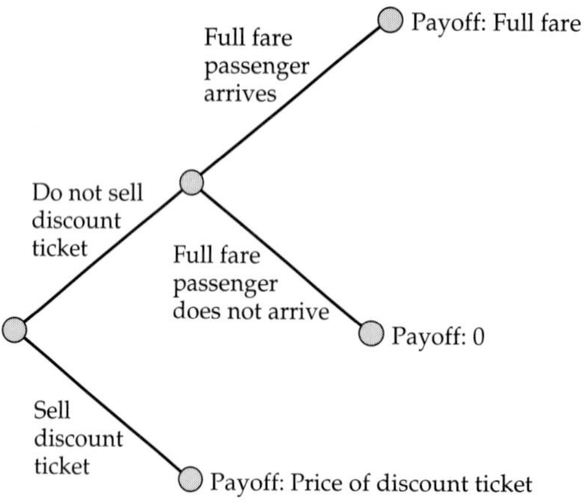

passenger will arrive (or that the disappointed traveler who can't get a discount ticket will agree to pay the full fare) exceeds the price of a SuperSaver ticket.

The yield management process is complicated in practice by the presence of far more than two coach fares.[5] There are full fares and SuperSaver fares, more or less as described. There may be 14-day, 7-day, and 3-day advance purchase fares with fewer or no restrictions. There are discounts for passengers above and below certain ages, for those traveling with a full-fare passenger, for those willing to leave after a certain hour at night. There are discounts for people attending conventions that have agreed to feature the airline in their publicity materials. There are free tickets for frequent travelers who have flown a certain number of miles on the airline and have earned them as a reward. Other tickets are given to travelers who held confirmed reservations but were "bumped" from an oversold flight or to travel agents to let them sample the airline's service first-hand. Each has its own limits and special considerations. The decision tree for this situation is considerably more complex, as it must reflect all the higher priced fares and their probabilities.

Yield managers can manipulate three variables for each fare:

- *The number of seats the airline will sell at a given fare level.* This can be adjusted at any time. Many airlines adjust the number of discount seats available daily or even more frequently. If high-priced seats are

---

[5]Historically, the variety of fares has fluctuated widely. The industry undergoes a simplification process every few years: the fare structure is streamlined, and many deeply discounted fares are eliminated. The most recent such process took place in the spring of 1992. Fares are then slowly added back until a new simplification is needed.

selling more quickly than expected, the number of discount seats is reduced, and vice versa.

Airlines generally *nest* their seat quotas: The number of seats available at any given fare is never greater than the number available at any higher fare. If a fare is sold out, so are all less expensive fares. If a fare is available, so are all more expensive fares.

- *Price.* All airline fares are subject to change without notice. Full fares and most discount fares can and do change daily. A few discount fares are harder to "fine-tune" via minor adjustments because of competitive pressures and widespread advertising.
- *The restrictions that apply to discount tickets.* These are somewhat flexible, but the travel industry is used to certain types of restrictions (e.g., a Saturday night stay as a requirement for the lowest fares), and too much originality might encounter travel agent resistance.

Matters become more complicated when we consider the entire route structure of an airline. Consider, for example, Delta Air Lines' 3:50 P.M. Flight 1455 from Wilkes-Barre/Scranton, Pennsylvania, to Atlanta.[6] This flight, whose route is highlighted in Figure 4–3, is part of Delta's "hub" system. Westbound flights from several eastern U.S. cities converge on Atlanta within a half-hour period. They stay on the ground for an hour or so, allowing passengers to move from one plane to another. They then take off at about the same time to various West Coast destinations. Soon after, the process repeats in the eastbound direction. The hub approach is quite popular. Delta has additional hubs at Cincinnati, Dallas-Fort Worth, and Salt Lake City. Different airlines use different cities: TWA's major east-west hub is in St. Louis; American's and United's are in Chicago. The same principles apply to all.

Some of Flight 1455's passengers want to go to Atlanta. Some will stay on the plane as it continues its travels. The majority will transfer to other flights: Delta's westbound flights to Dallas, Salt Lake City, Los Angeles, or Seattle; commuter flights to smaller cities throughout the southeastern United States; flights on other airlines. Delta can, if it wishes, collect passenger preference statistics in this regard.

Suppose a traveler wants a SuperSaver ticket from Wilkes-Barre/Scranton to Los Angeles and back. The Wilkes-Barre/Scranton–Atlanta leg has no more SuperSaver seats available, but the Atlanta–Los Angeles leg (whose flight, no. 187, originated in West Palm Beach) does, as do the desired return flights. Should Delta sell this SuperSaver ticket or not? If it sells the ticket, it loses the statistically expected additional profit on a full-fare seat sale for the Wilkes-Barre/Scranton–Atlanta leg. If it does not sell the ticket, thus keeping the Wilkes-Barre/Scranton–Atlanta seat open for the statistically expected full-fare passenger, it runs the risk of letting the Atlanta–Los Angeles flight and the

[6]The flights in this example existed in March 1993. Delta's schedules may have changed since then, but the concepts have not.

FIGURE 4–3

Delta Route Map Centered on Atlanta

Delta Gives Wilkes-Barre/Scranton National Coverage.

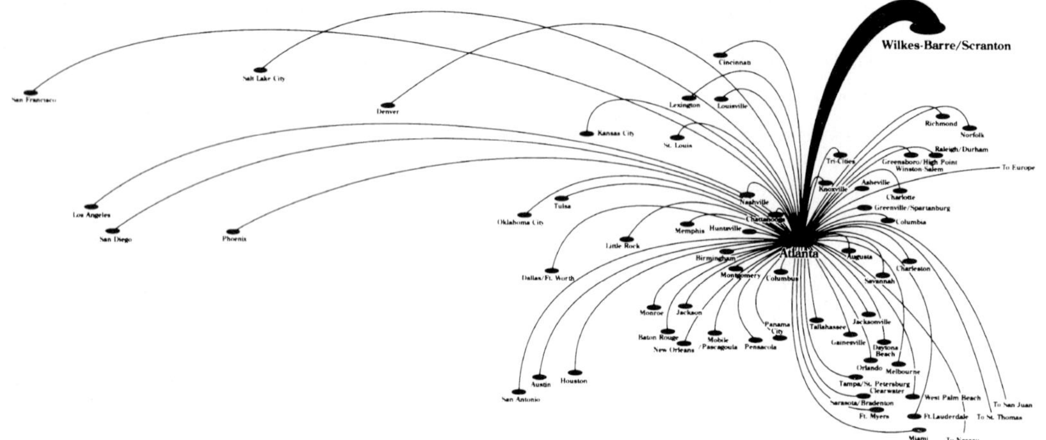

Announcing New Nonstop Service To Atlanta And Beyond.

No matter where you want to go from Wilkes-Barre/Scranton, Delta Air Lines is here to give you the coverage you deserve.

Delta now offers two nonstop flights a day to Atlanta, departing at 9:00 in the morning and 3:50 in the afternoon. With either flight, we'll give you easy access to cities throughout the South, West and West Coast.

And wherever you fly with us, you'll always get the best service in the sky. Delta has the best overall record for passenger satisfaction of any major U.S. airline.†

Earn Free Trips With Delta's Bonus Plus Program.

If you're a Delta Frequent Flyer, take advantage of our Bonus Plus Program. With it, you'll earn free trips to just about anywhere in the world we fly, both faster and easier than ever before.

For more information on Delta's Bonus Plus Program or to become a Delta Frequent Flyer, see your Travel Agent. Or call Delta at 1-800-323-2323.

You deserve national coverage, and that's what you get from Delta.

return flights take off emptier than they have to be. There's no simple answer to this question. It is complicated, in this case, by the fact that the Wilkes-Barre/Scranton–Atlanta leg is short and, hence, inexpensive, while the total of the Atlanta–Los Angeles leg and the two return flights is longer and, hence, more expensive. As of 1993 general industry practice is not to sell a discount ticket if the fare is sold out on any of the flight segments involved. That decision rule is simple to state and to administer but is probably not optimal. Some major airlines are developing *origin-destination yield management systems* to make this decision on the basis of a traveler's entire itinerary.

Travelers' flight time flexibility adds yet another dimension of complexity. A Boston-based business traveler with a morning appointment in Dallas may not be willing to leave until mid-afternoon of the previous day. A vacationing couple who finds all the deeply discounted fares sold out on their first choice of flights, a month or more in the future, can adjust their plans with little or no inconvenience. Yield management thus has the desirable (to the airline) effect of pushing low-fare travelers toward flights that are less popular with the more profitable business travelers. This evens out the airline's passenger load and smooths demand over the time of day and day of the week—leading, in turn, to better utilization of equipment, facilities, flight crews, and ground staff.

Applying DSS to Yield Management

Yield management analysts can use decision support systems to help set the capacity limits of the various fares. Corresponding to the seven levels of the DSS hierarchy, some DSS they could use are:

File drawer system. Yield management analysts could find out how many seats were sold on a given flight at a given fare with a given set of restrictions. Using this information, they could (manually or with another system) choose prices, conditions, and capacity limits for future flights.

Data analysis system. Such a system would simplify extracting the historical data from the database. It could calculate averages, trends, and similar aggregates from the raw data.

Analysis information system. This type of system might present historical average booking data for a given type of ticket at a given fare in the form of a graph; see Figure 4–4. This tells us that, historically, the SuperSaver fare did not sell out by its purchase deadline (which, for purposes of this example and this chart, is four weeks before the flight). If planes on this route generally take off with empty seats, we should consider lowering our SuperSaver price further or creating other incentives. Suppose, however, the curve looked like Figure 4–5. In this case, SuperSaver tickets sold out before the cutoff date. Presumably some customers for this type of ticket, who arrived four or five weeks before the deadline but after the capacity limit was reached, were turned away. This suggests that we could make the tickets less attractive and still sell out by the deadline.

FIGURE 4–4

Graph 1 of Ticket Bookings over Time—SuperSaver Tickets Still Available after Cutoff Date

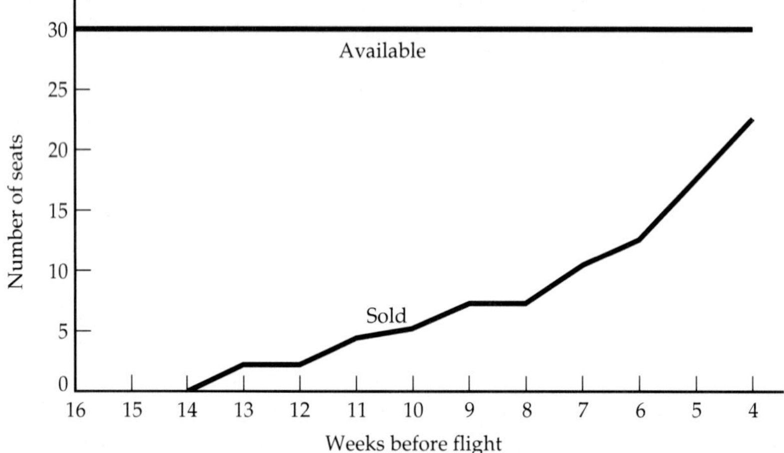

FIGURE 4–5

Graph 2 of Ticket Bookings over Time—SuperSaver Tickets Sell Out before Cutoff Date

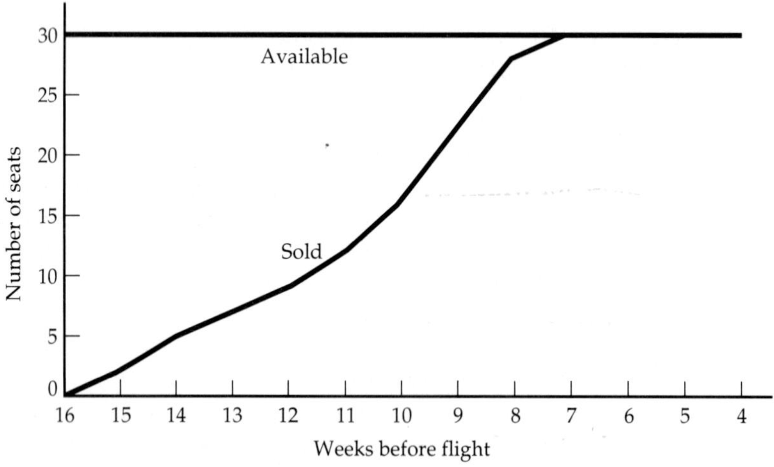

One way to do this is to raise the fare for such tickets. Or, we could tighten the conditions: perhaps keep the current fare for 45-day advance purchase, which history tells us would usually sell out, and institute a slightly higher fare with more available seats for 30-day advance purchase. *Accounting model.* An accounting model could calculate the expected revenue for a given seat allocation. An analyst might expect to sell seats as follows:

Fare Type	*Price*	*Quantity*	*Revenue*
Unrestricted coach	$800	30	$24,000
3-day advance purchase, refundable	$750	20	$15,000
7-day advance purchase, refundable	$650	20	$13,000
14-day advance purchase, $100 cancellation penalty, $50 charge to change flights	$500	20	$10,000
30-day advance purchase, nonrefundable, no changes, Saturday night stay required	$350	20	$7,000
		Total:	$69,000

An accounting model could calculate the expected revenue, as shown in the right-most column, and the corresponding profit. A spreadsheet program is well suited to such calculations.

Representational model. Here we start to consider human behavior. The usual method of considering human behavior in a situation such as this is via the price-demand elasticity curve of classical economics. If we reduce a particular fare by $50, what will happen to demand? Airline managers can't answer this question directly, but they have accumulated vast amounts of historical data that describe the general shape of elasticity curves quite accurately. Given one or two points on the actual curve for a particular fare and flight segment, they can estimate the complete curve well enough for practical purposes.

By combining representational and accounting models, we could estimate the revenue that will accrue from any mix of restrictions (among those for which we have historical data), prices, and capacity limits. Such a model would allow analysts to choose a set and evaluate its effect. Based on its effect, they could make another, hopefully better, set of choices. They could repeat this process until they feel that more changes will not improve the result.

Optimization system. The variables under our control are few in number, at least on any given flight segment, and known precisely. It is relatively easy to program a computer to evaluate them over the range of interest and return the "best" answer. This process, however, would be limited to a single flight segment. When several flight segments interact with each other, a solution requires the application of complex network optimization algorithms. It also requires origin/destination passenger data that most airlines, as a practical matter, do not have.

Suggestion system. This type of system could cope with the issues that arise when several flight segments interact. An expert system, with rules that describe what managers do in the situations that normally arise, might be able to help with the system-wide optimization problem. It couldn't do anything that managers couldn't also do in principle, given enough time, but its ability to process large amounts of data quickly might allow it to produce recommendations while they are still useful.

The expert system would have a large number of rules and an even larger number of data points with which to deal. It would utilize a historical database covering hundreds of tickets sold on each of hundreds of flights per day over a period of many months. It would be expected to recommend capacity limits for every fare type for a given flight on the different days of the week. Such a system would be a major undertaking but could confer a significant strategic advantage on the airline that developed it.

Yield management has been called the most significant strategic airline information system application after reservation systems. In 1993, seats on every airline of significance are available through every major reservation system, so the use of such a system no longer confers a strategic advantage on the airline that sponsors it. Yield management is therefore perhaps the most important strategic information system an airline can have today. It ties in directly to the mainstream operations of the firm. It directly affects the bottom line. It is not surprising that major airlines use DSS to help them make yield management decisions. (You can read about American Airlines' DINAMO yield management DSS in [SMIT92].)

4.2 Generalizing the DSS Categories

We can collapse the seven DSS categories into two broader categories. As [ALTE80] points out, this simplification loses some information, but it is still helpful in taking a first look at a new system.

The bottom three levels of the hierarchy focus almost entirely on their database. Above the file drawer level they have some analysis capabilities, but these capabilities do not involve a detailed model of a system or a business situation. We refer to these and similar DSS as *data oriented*.

The upper levels concentrate more on the model of a business system, less on the database. The database component may still be present, and may even be as large as it is in one of the first three types, but is relatively less important as the modeling components dominate this type of DSS. Such a DSS is called *model oriented*.

These distinctions are useful in a general sense but do not always apply precisely. Analysis information systems, in particular, may fall into a gray area between data-oriented and model-oriented DSS.

Decision support systems that incorporate a model generally rely less on massive databases than do the lower types of DSS in the hierarchy. That is why we categorized the first three levels as "data oriented" and the top four levels as "model oriented." There are exceptions, but databases in model-oriented DSS are often small, self-contained, and constructed solely for use by the model.

The models in the higher levels can be either system models or process models in terms of the distinction we drew in Section 3.5.2. Those at the fourth and fifth levels, accounting and representational models, are system models. Those at the top two levels, optimization and suggestion models, are often process models: either purely process models or incorporating aspects of both system and process models. It is sometimes convenient to refer to a DSS based only on a process model as a *process-oriented* DSS. This focuses our attention on the way such a DSS mimics the human decision-making process.

4.3 Matching DSS to the Decision Type

DSS can be categorized according to the type of decision they help with: structured, semistructured, or unstructured.

Fully structured decisions may be below the level at which DSS is useful. They can be programmed into a computer and made without human assistance. A data-oriented DSS can be useful if the data on which to base the decision are not known in advance and must be determined by humans before the decision can be made. Where a fully structured decision must be reviewed by humans, a suggestion model can suggest the right course of action with its recommendation either confirmed (normally) or overridden (occasionally) by a person.

Semistructured decisions lend themselves to model-oriented DSS, most often using system models. The model can predict the effect of choosing alternatives, but the human must still assess the unstructured factors, or deal with the unstructured decision phases, and make the final decision.

Unstructured decisions are the realm of data-oriented DSS. Where there is no structure, we cannot build a model. All a DSS can do is to present the available information to decision makers in the format they want and with as much predigestion as the circumstances permit. A process-oriented DSS may also be helpful here, as a way of making sure that the necessary factors are considered and the necessary decision-making steps are taken.

4.4 Individual and Group DSS

Decision support systems can also be categorized on the basis of the type of group, if any, that they support. Certain DSS are used by individuals making individual decisions. A marketing manager deciding on next year's ad budget is in that situation. This person wants to pick the ideal advertising budget for his or her firm. The final decision is made by the marketing manager alone, although many people would discuss the options with colleagues and seek their advice.

At the lowest level, a data-oriented DSS that provides information on the cost, reach, and likely impact of different media choices can help this person make an informed decision. An analysis information system could automate some simple calculations on these data. Moving up from there, an accounting model could consolidate the data and calculate the total exposure of an overall advertising program: seven half-page black-and-white ads in *Time,* a one-minute commercial every week for a month on the major league baseball Game of the Week, ... This model could provide a chart that tells the marketing manager how many people will see one of the ads, how many will see two, etc. A representational model could predict the impact of these impressions on purchase decisions over time, providing guidance not only in selecting the right advertising program but also in making sure enough stock is in the stores to satisfy the anticipated demand.

Other DSS are used by individuals, but these are by individuals who make the same types of decisions that are made by many other people within an organization, and consistency is required. A bank may want to make sure that all its loan officers apply certain criteria to the applications they review, even though the loan officers make each decision individually. We call such DSS *multi-individual* DSS.

Finally, some DSS support decisions that are inherently made by a group as a whole. Such *group DSS* must take into account not only the models and data of the decision but also the dynamics of the group decision-making process. Software designed to support the work of a group is often called *groupware.* This term includes both group DSS and other packages, such as electronic mail or meeting scheduling, that are inherently group oriented but that are not usually considered decision support systems as such. We'll discuss group DSS in Chapter 11.

An individual or multi-individual DSS takes on some group DSS characteristics if the individuals' managers review and comment on the decisions in question. A department manager may use a spreadsheet program to develop a budget for the department. For that purpose the spreadsheet—or the model built with its help—is an individual DSS. If the budget is subject to review and approval by the division manager, however, the decision is a group decision: a mere two-person group but a group nonetheless. Any tool used to help make that decision therefore has aspects of a group DSS.

The expectation of using an essentially individual DSS in this fashion may affect its design. The department manager in the previous paragraph may format and label the budget spreadsheet beyond his or her own informational needs. This is done with a view to showing the spreadsheet to the division manager, justifying its contents, and possibly vying with other department managers for a share of the divisional resources.

4.5 Matching Benefits to DSS User Community

There is a strong relationship between the type of people who use a DSS and the benefits, as discussed in Section 1.4, that the DSS provides. As a general rule—which, like all other rules, is subject to many exceptions—the overall tendencies are shown in Figure 4–6. An "H" in this table, for high applicability, means that the benefit listed at the left is a common primary benefit for DSS intended for this type of usage, often the main intent of the system as a whole. An "M" (moderate) means that it is usually an incidental benefit but is not uncommon and may be reflected in system design. An "L" (low) means that this benefit does not usually apply to the type of usage indicated at the head of the column.

The first row indicates that improving personal efficiency generally applies to individual and multi-individual DSS. The focus of most group DSS is on the decision-making process of the group as a whole, not on the personal productivity of any one of its members.

Improved problem solving can apply to individual, multi-individual, or group DSS. Speed and objective quality improvements apply to all three. Consistency improvements relate primarily to multi-individual DSS.

Interpersonal communication is primarily a factor in group situations, so improved interpersonal communication applies most strongly to group DSS. It may also be a factor in multi-individual DSS. Where it applies to individual DSS, it is usually because the output of the DSS is used as a "convincer."

Improved learning applies primarily to individual and multi-individual DSS.

Improved organizational control is often a major motivating factor in the development of multi-individual DSS. It can also apply to group DSS, as management can define the decision-making process that the DSS supports. The group will then be forced to use that process. For example, a group DSS can make sure that insurance applications above a certain amount of coverage are approved by an underwriter before being returned to the agency that submitted them.

Figure 4–6

Relationship Between DSS Users and DSS Benefits

	Individual	*Multi-Individual*	*Group*
Improving personal efficiency	H*	H	L
Expediting problem solving	L	M	H
Facilitating interpersonal communication	L	L	H
Promoting learning or training	M	H	H
Increasing organizational control	L	H	M

*H = High applicability; M = Moderate applicability; L = Low applicability.

4.6 Matching DSS to the Decision Maker's Psychological Type

In Section 2.3 we discussed psychological type and its impact on decision-making style. Since decision-making styles differ and since DSS are intended to support human decision-making styles, DSS must reflect these differences. It should not come as a surprise, then, to learn that people of different psychological types are best served by different types of DSS.

Sometimes a decision maker must use a DSS best suited to a person of different psychological type. This may be for reasons of corporate standardization or because a better suited DSS is not available. In this case, he or she should be aware that using this DSS calls for using nonpreferred behavioral styles. Since, as we noted in Section 2.3 in a quotation from [PROV90], the styles are preferences—not behavioral dictators—using a nonpreferred style is always possible. It may call for a conscious effort, though, particularly if an individual preference is strong.

In organizations that use psychological type as a team-building tool, a manager will often be aware of his or her subordinates' types. This knowledge, properly applied, can help managers match DSS characteristics to employees' preferred working styles.

The impact of the four psychological preferences on DSS usage is given below. This breakdown discusses each type in isolation. A more complete discussion would cover each of the 16 four-letter types shown in Figure 2–3 individually. Such a discussion can be found in several sources such as [HIRS90] and [PROV90].

4.6.1 Introversion/Extraversion

As we noted in Section 2.3, introversion (I)/extraversion (E) does not affect a person's decision making directly. It does, however, affect the type of interaction a person tends to prefer during the decision-making process.

The extraverted type enjoys discussing ideas and options with other people and is productive in this free-wheeling mode of interaction. If he or she uses electronic meeting aids, for example, those aids would ideally provide for concurrent use by several people interacting at one time.

The introverted type tends to be less comfortable with immediate interaction. This person prefers to mull over a decision and reach a position before discussing it with others. Delayed electronic interaction, such as via electronic mail, may be more comfortable to such a person.

When a group decision is to be made, it is not possible to customize the DSS to the needs of an individual. In that case, it may be desirable to develop a DSS that can be used in different ways. Here we might provide an "electronic town meeting" capability for interactive discussion and allow other group members to review the dialogue and add their comments at a later time.

4.6.2 *Sensing/Intuition*

A person with a preference for sensing (S) may want a large number of facts and may therefore tend to be well served by a data-oriented DSS or by complete, detailed models. One with an intuitive (N) preference will tend to reach a conclusion on the basis of "hunches" that require less in the way of data. The type of model needed to support this person's intuitive approach may not have to be as detailed or exhaustive as the one that the person who prefers sensing may like to use. However, the intuitive who reaches a conclusion on the basis of highly simplified models may have trouble justifying this conclusion to others of a more sensing preference.

4.6.3 *Thinking/Feeling*

As we noted in Section 2.4, the Thinker (T) bases decisions on carefully thought out logic but sometimes ignores human factors and values. They approach the concept of the "rational manager" in this regard. Thinkers may opt to make a decision solely on the basis of an optimization or suggestion model DSS.

People with a feeling (F) preference may focus on people in their decision making. Left on their own, they would gravitate less toward this type of DSS. They will find decision support tools that support interaction among people, including many of the "groupware" tools discussed in the next chapter, to be useful. This is true even for individual decisions since these people are concerned with how other people will react to the decision in question.

People with both preferences can benefit from an optimization or suggestion model DSS, but the way in which they use that system may differ. The thinking decision maker may tend to give the DSS output too much weight; the feeling decision maker may give it too little. By being aware of these tendencies, decision makers and managers can use the combined strengths of both types to reach decisions that satisfy both numerical and human criteria.

4.6.4 *Judgment/Perception*

The person with a judging (J) style prefers to reach closure on a subject quickly, gathering only as much data as he or she feels necessary for this purpose. Model-oriented DSS suit this personality type well. The danger here is that this type of person may tend to make a decision even when the decision is not urgent, when deferring the decision could allow gathering additional useful information.

The perceptive (P) has the opposite tendency: to gather as much information as possible while keeping the decision options open. They like data-oriented DSS. However, their information-gathering tendency may mean putting off the decision itself as long as possible. Perceptives are often seen as procrastinators by their judgment-oriented colleagues.

A process-oriented DSS that automates a decision-making process such as that of Kepner-Tregoe, which we discussed in Section 2.5, can help both types by forcing both to spend enough time—but not too much time—on both the information-gathering and decision-making parts of the process.

4.6.5 Combinations of Preferences

Huitt [HUIT92] has studied the types of assistance that are required by people having different combinations of types, or "temperaments" [KEIR78]. It turns out that, when it comes to problem solving, the S-N dimension is the key variable, but the second variable is different for S's and N's. For sensing types, the J-P preference is the second to be considered: Should the existing data be organized and structured (the J tendency), or should additional data be gathered (the P tendency)? For intuitives, the second dimension to consider is T-F: Is the tendency to make the decision on the basis of logic or impact on people? Figure 4–7 shows the relationships he put forth.

We can use this information to select the most appropriate types of decision support systems for a group if we know something about the personality types of its members. For example, if the group consists primarily of SJ's, it will most likely need help in generating creative alternatives. Support for brainstorming techniques, as is provided by electronic meeting systems (see discussion of TeamFocus in Section 5.6.1), can be useful here. If it consists largely of the more visionary and idealistic NF's, however, there will be plenty of creative alternatives; the issue will be which ones can realistically be implemented. Brainstorming support will be of little use in answering this question. Software that helps evaluate potential difficulties and adverse consequences will be more to the point.

FIGURE 4–7

*Relationship between Temperament and Decision Support Needs**

Temperament	*Need Help in . . .*
SP	Coherence of plan Following selected solution
SJ	Categorizing and classifying Generating creative alternatives
NT	Attending to facts and details Looking at impact on people
NF	Attending to facts and details Developing realisic alternatives Monitoring implementation carefully

*Source: [HUIT92].

4.7 Usage Modes

Different DSS are used in different ways by the people they support. This is important to understand since the ideal user interface for a DSS depends on how it is going to be used.

Alter identified four major usage modes for DSS. These modes are quite general. Today's DSS still fall into these modes, although their shares of DSS usage have shifted since Alter's work. He called these four modes *subscription mode, terminal mode, clerk mode,* and *intermediary mode.*

Subscription mode refers to situations where a decision maker receives DSS output on a regular basis. This term traditionally referred to piles of paper arriving on decision makers' desks at predictable intervals. That usage mode has not disappeared but has become rarer, as more managers have desktop microcomputers linked directly to their firms' databases.

Another form of subscription mode, which Alter did not foresee, arose in the 1980s. This form consists of preprocessing data into reports and charts that remain in a system's mass storage files. The reports and charts can then be retrieved without delay when they are needed for decision making. This preprocessing can take place at night when computer workload is low, with digested data available to managers in the form of summaries and graphs the following morning. Many executive information systems, which we'll discuss in Chapter 12, work this way.

Terminal mode refers to direct use of the computer by the decision maker. The word "terminal" implies a decision maker interacting by terminal with a multi-user computer at a distance from his or her office. Today's interaction is as likely to be with a microcomputer located on the decision maker's desk. The direct interaction is the same in either case, as one cannot determine solely from the interaction whether a desktop microcomputer or a remote multi-user computer is supporting the screen and the keyboard. Terminal mode is increasing in popularity, at the expense of both the preceding and the following modes of operation.

Clerk mode means that a decision maker fills out a form to specify the information to be retrieved, or the operations to be performed, by the DSS. A clerk then enters the data into the computer, directly or via an off-line device such as the once-ubiquitous keypunch machine. After the DSS performs its operations its output is delivered to the decision maker.

Clerk mode is seldom encountered now that personal computers permeate the workplace from the shop floor or the checkout counter to the executive suite. Decision makers may still need professional assistance with a DSS, but that is not the same as needing clerical help. Professional help falls under the next heading.

Intermediary mode refers to situations where a decision maker uses the DSS via a professional assistant, who contributes actively to posing the problem to the DSS. This contribution involves the assistant's professional skills, not just keying in the content of a filled-out paper form. Decision makers use intermediaries in three roles. These may at times be combined in one individual:

- *Staff assistants* are general helpers to top executives. They perform tasks that the executive is also able to perform but that do not demand his or her unique talents. A staff assistant's job is to save the executive's valuable time.
- *Technical support staff* have specific skills in the computer aspects of using a decision support system. For instance, retrieving information from a database may require mastering a query language. If a busy manager does not need to use this query language often, it may be more cost effective for the manager to explain the need to a specialist who already knows the language and to let that person interact with the DSS.
- *Business analysts* are people with specific skills in management science, operations research, production planning, financial analysis, or other fields. They can assist decision makers by figuring out exactly what question should be posed to the DSS, by designing simulation models, by carrying out linear programming optimizations, and more. Many managers know what these tools are and, in a general way, how they can be of value, but they do not have the professional skills to use them themselves.

The skills of several individuals may be needed to solve a problem or reach a decision. This is especially true of strategic decisions that are made rarely but have far-ranging impact, such as choosing the location of a new factory.

A given type of system can work in a combination of usage modes. A university registration system may have aspects of all four:

Subscription mode. Students receive schedule sheets before every term and grade reports after it ends. Faculty members receive class rosters for their courses when the course starts, after the period for course changes ends, and just before final grades are due. These documents appear automatically, without the need for specific requests on the part of the students or faculty members in question.

Terminal mode. Administrators can access the system directly from their offices when they need information. In some universities, students can also use it directly to verify their enrollment status or to register for an upcoming term by using conveniently located terminals on the campus.

Clerk mode. Where students do not have direct access to terminals, they can check their registration status by asking a clerk in the registrar's office. This clerk does not perform any operations that are beyond the capabilities of a student—in fact, the clerk is often a student in a work-study job—but adds a measure of security when a registration system lacks safeguards against one person's accessing information about another.

Intermediary mode. In choosing courses, students often consult faculty advisors who have printouts of the students' records and interpret them to suggest courses the students might take next. Faculty advisors correspond to the "business analyst" intermediary role above: They are chosen for their expertise is in the subject matter of the decision—advising students—and not for their expertise in using a computer.

Obtaining registration status information from a staff member of the registrar's office may have aspects of intermediary mode if using the system requires a great deal of technical training or practice. The staff member in this case performs a technical support intermediary role.

The staff assistant role generally does not apply to student registration systems. The purpose of a staff assistant is to save the decision maker's time. Colleges and universities seldom provide students with this type of staff support.

4.8 Institutional versus Ad Hoc DSS

An important characterization difference of decision support systems, which will affect how you go about developing and implementing them, is between *institutional* and *ad hoc* DSS.

An *institutional* DSS is one that is part of the fabric of an organization. It is used regularly, usually by more than one person. Using an institutional DSS becomes part of the way a particular decision is made. Its users cannot usually imagine doing business without it. A system that advertising agency staff members use to compare the cost per exposure of several potential ad media, within a target group defined by age, sex, and income level, would usually be an institutional DSS.

An *ad hoc* DSS is developed for one-time use, often by a single individual, with the expectation that it will be discarded after the need for it has gone away. Many managers develop such "mini-DSS" using spreadsheet or data management packages.

A system initially developed as an ad hoc DSS may turn out to have a life far beyond its developer's initial expectations. As a personal example, the author of this book developed an ad hoc DSS using a spreadsheet that calculated course grades on the basis of homework, exam, and term project grades. (This was a decision support system, not a decision making system, as I adjusted the spreadsheet output to reflect class participation and other nonquantifiable factors before submitting the grades to the registrar.) I found myself re-creating an essentially identical spreadsheet the following term and eventually developed a template that could be customized to the number of homework assignments, exam weights, etc., of a given course. I now use this template as a starting point for grading each course. If my colleagues make copies of the template and begin to use it, it will have evolved fully from ad hoc to institutional DSS. At that point all the perils of widespread distribution of any "quick and dirty" software—DSS or other—will begin: lack of documentation, minimal input validation, poor or nonexistent error messages, and the potential vulnerability of other template users to my departure.

Summary

Knowing the different types of decision support systems is useful because it enables us to zero in quickly on types of tools and techniques that are likely to be useful with a new problem. DSS can be divided into categories in several ways.

One basic set of categories divides DSS into seven major categories: file drawer systems, data analysis systems, analysis information systems, accounting models, representational models, optimization systems, and suggestion systems.

We can group these seven DSS categories into three major categories: data oriented, model oriented, and process oriented. Data-oriented DSS include file drawer systems, data analysis systems, and analysis information systems. Model-oriented DSS include accounting models, representational models, optimization systems, and suggestion systems. Optimization and suggestion systems whose recommendations are based on a human decision-making process rather than on analysis of an underlying system are process-oriented DSS.

Different DSS categories help make different types of decisions. Suggestion systems are often well matched to structured decisions. Other types of model-oriented DSS usually fit semistructured decisions well. Data-oriented DSS are most useful with unstructured decisions.

DSS can also be categorized according to whether they support decisions made by one individual, by several individuals whose decisions must show some consistency (multi-individual decisions), or by groups operating as a whole. The benefits to be derived from a DSS depend in large part on its usage mode modes in this sense.

Different types of DSS suit the needs of people having different personality types. An introverted person may prefer a group DSS that allows for thinking before responding, while an extravert would lean toward interactive discussion. A sensing person will want larger amounts of data than an intuitive. Both thinking and feeling people can use model-oriented DSS, but the thinker will tend to rely more on its output. Judgment-oriented people will tend to use a data-oriented DSS for a long time, while perception-oriented people will generally close off its use and make their decision sooner. A further breakdown by combinations of types or temperaments can also be valuable in choosing appropriate decision support tools.

Decision support systems can be used in four modes: subscription, terminal, clerk, and intermediary. Intermediary mode may involve staff assistants, technical support staff, and business analysts. Clerk mode is little seen today. The other three are all appropriate to some decision makers and decision-making situations.

Finally, decision support systems can be designed for one-time (ad hoc) use or for regular, repeated (institutional) use. The expected usage affects the documentation, error handling, user interface, training, and technical support that the DSS must have.

Key Terms

accounting model 102
ad hoc DSS 123
analysis information system 102
business analyst 122
clerk mode (usage) 121
data analysis system 102
data-oriented DSS 114
file drawer system 102
group DSS 116
individual DSS 116
institutional DSS 123
intermediary mode (usage) 121
model-oriented DSS 114
multi-individual DSS 116
optimization system 102
process-oriented DSS 115
representational model 102
staff assistant 122
subscription mode (usage) 121
suggestion system 102
technical support staff 122
temperament 120
terminal mode (usage) 121
yield management 106

Review Questions

1. What are the seven basic DSS categories?
2. Which categories of DSS are considered data oriented? Which are considered model oriented?
3. What is a process-oriented DSS? To which DSS categories do they correspond?
4. Which types of DSS are most helpful with structured decisions? With semistructured decisions? With unstructured decisions?
5. Define individual, multi-individual, and group decisions.

6. What DSS benefits are most often associated with individual DSS? With multi-individual DSS? With group DSS?
7. How would the difference between introverted and extroverted personality types affect DSS usage?
8. How would the difference between sensing and intuitive personality types affect DSS usage?
9. How would the difference between thinking and feeling personality types affect DSS usage?
10. How would the difference between judging and perceiving personality types affect DSS usage?
11. What are the four basic DSS usage modes? Give examples (other than the university registration example in Section 4.7).
12. What are the three types of DSS usage intermediaries? What is the benefit of using each?
13. What is the difference between an institutional and an ad hoc DSS? Why does it matter?

Exercises

1. Consider the examples of DSS Section 1.3.3 (pages 11–12). Place each of those examples in the appropriate category per each of Sections 4.1, 4.2, 4.4, 4.7, and 4.8.
2. You work in the admissions office of a selective university. Each year, you and your colleagues have three months (from the mid-January application deadline to mid-April, when applicants are notified) to review about 12,000 application folders and make about 3,000 offers of admission. Each folder contains test scores, secondary school transcript(s), letters of recommendation, applicant essays, lists of activities and honors, and perhaps additional information. Each folder is first read by two admissions officers. If they agree, their decision is forwarded to the director. If they disagree, a third reader breaks the tie. The director personally reviews, and may reverse, all rejections of alumni children, recruited athletes, and ethnic minority applicants. The director also reviews a random sample of other decisions to check the consistency of decision making by staff members. Suggest how (*a*) a data-oriented DSS, (*b*) a system-model-oriented DSS, and (*c*) a process-oriented DSS could be used to help your office in its work. In your answers to parts *a*, *b*, and *c*, also state whether your suggested system would be an individual, multi-individual, or group DSS.

3. Describe a specific DSS that the admissions office of Exercise 2 could use. State which psychological types (Section 4.5) might tend to work well with that system and which might not. Keep in mind that people of all preferences *can* learn to use the system.
4. Quantify the benefits of each DSS type discussed in the airline yield management example (section 4.1.3) as much as possible. Express your answer in terms of quantities that an airline would be expected to know, such as the number of flights per day, the total salary of its yield management analysts, total revenue on the flights in question, etc.
5. In Section 4.1.3, we stated that a policy of refusing to sell a low-fare ticket on a multisegment route, if the limit of such tickets has been reached on any of the segments involved, is "probably not optimal." Do you agree? Can you think of a better decision rule? How could your rule be administered with the aid of computers?
6. In terms of the DSS benefits listed in Section 1.4, what is the benefit of each additional step up the DSS hierarchy with the airline yield management DSS of Section 4.1.3? Does each step contribute to reduced cost, more effective decisions, or improve communications, or does it provide some other benefit?
7. Carry out a literature search, preferably using an automated document retrieval system, for articles about yield management DSS. How do the systems you found fit into the frameworks discussed in this chapter?
8. Describe how you could apply yield management concepts to promotional rates in the car rental industry or another type of business.
9. Colleges and universities use yield management in several ways, although they may not call it by that name. For example, they can (and do) offer above-normal financial aid to students who plan to major in unpopular fields, who can contribute to athletic success, or who have other desirable attributes. Define a DSS that a college financial aid office could use to optimize its allocation of scholarship funds in this sense.
10. Describe how each of the four usage modes (Section 4.7) could apply to a DSS used by the admissions office of Exercise 2. For intermediary mode, answer for each of the three types of intermediaries. (All told, you will have six answers.)
11. Reread your answer to Exercise 5 of Chapter 1. State if each of the systems in your answer to 5*a* is an individual, multi-individual, or group DSS. Draw a copy of Figure 4–6 without the letters in the cells. For each benefit you identified in part 5*b* of that exercise, put a check mark in the cell in the benefit row and the DSS type column. See how closely your pattern of check marks matches the high-moderate-low relationships shown in the figure.

References

ALTE80 Alter, Steven L. *Decision Support Systems: Current Practice and Continuing Challenges.* Addison-Wesley, Reading, Mass. (1980).

CORR91 Correa, Arlene. "On-Line Conference." *Digital Review* 8, no. 19 (May 13, 1991), p. 16.

HIRS90 Hirsh, Sandra Krebs, and Jean M. Kummerow. *Introduction to Type in Organizations.* Consulting Psychologists Press, Palo Alto, Calif. (1990).

HUIT92 Huitt, William G. "Problem Solving and Decision Making: Consideration of Individual Differences Using the Myers-Briggs Type Indicator." *Journal of Psychological Type* 24 (1992), pp. 33–44.

KEIR84 Keirsey, David, and Marilyn Bates. *Please Understand Me: Character and Temperament Types.* Prometheus Nemesis, Del Mar, Calif. (1984).

PROV90 Provost, Judith A. *Work, Play, and Type.* Consulting Psychologists Press, Palo Alto, Calif. (1990).

SMIT92 Smith, Barry C.; John F. Leimkuhler; and Ross M. Darrow. "Yield Management at American Airlines." *Interfaces* 22, no. 1 (January–February 1992), pp. 8–31.

ENVOYANCE: THE STAR-BRITE CRISIS (*continued*)

After the Tuesday 9 AM meeting (see the Envoyance case at the end of Chapter 3) Doug and Adrienne stayed in the rapidly emptying conference room to discuss what they had heard. Sandra's parting words echoed in their heads: "Could your computers help us *now*?"

As they began to think of possibilities, Jackie Boyle, whom Sandra had asked to look at possible causes of the children's symptoms, passed the conference room door on the way back to her office from the coffee maker. On seeing Doug and Adrienne still in the room, she stopped to chat.

"You know, I'm not even sure where to begin with this job," she confessed to open the conversation. "It seems to be so open ended!"

"How do you mean?" asked Adrienne.

"Well, for one thing, it seems as though someone, somewhere, ought to have looked at this question before! I'm not much of a computer type, though. I can write a memo with my word processor, and that's about it. I've heard about using computers to help with this sort of problem, but I'm not sure how to go about it."

"How do you think computers might be able to help you?"

"That's what I was hoping you two could help me with. Frankly, I suspect that some of the other folks on this task were hoping the same!"

Exercises

1. What is Jackie's immediate, personal decision statement?
2. What criteria should she consider in making this decision?
3. Define, briefly, five DSS that could help Jackie determine which substances could have caused the children's symptoms. Put each into one of the seven DSS categories. If you don't have one in at least every other category, keep defining more DSS until you do.
4. Which of the DSS in your answer to Exercise 3 do you think would be the most useful to Jackie in practice? Why? For this DSS,
   - Would this be an individual, multi-individual, or group DSS (Section 4.4)?
   - What would be its usage mode (Section 4.6)?
   - What would be its major benefits (Section 1.4)?
5. At the end of the last episode Sandra stated that the "real world" is more crisis driven (and hence, she implied, less plannable) than your business school courses suggest.
   - Do you agree?
   - Of the seven DSS you suggested in your answer to Question 3, which DSS could Envoyance reasonably have put in place ahead of time—perhaps not knowing that this specific problem would arise, but expecting them to become useful someday?
6. How could Jackie benefit from a commercial database, assuming the right sort of database existed? If you were designing the ideal database for her purpose, what information would it contain? (Be creative; think of anything that could possibly be relevant.) With what keys might she assess this database?[7]
7. Using printed directories and electronic information retrieval capabilities of your school library, identify one or more commercial databases that could provide the type of information Jackie would need. How close do they come to the ideal you defined in your answer to Question 5? Would using more than one of them provide more information than using just one database alone?

[7]A *key* in a database is a data element that can be used to select desired records. Keys in a student database usually include the student's name and ID number.

Part II Building and Implementing Decision Support Systems

Now you know what a decision support system is, how it's used, and what it's good for. You've also seen several examples of DSS. Though most of these were written to make a specific point, they were realistic and should have given you a feel for how DSS work in practice. Now you're ready to see how DSS are actually put together.

This part of the book will cover the important areas of developing a real decision support system. In its first chapter, Chapter 5, you'll read about the process of developing a decision support system. This process has a lot in common with the process of developing any other information system—DSS are, after all information systems—but has significant shifts in emphasis because of the specialized nature of DSS. You'll also read about the user interface to decision support systems: a crucial part of their design because of their demanding user community and their often sporadic usage pattern.

In Chapters 6 and 7 we'll focus on the two complementary components of any information system: application level software (Chapter 6) and the hardware/operating system platform (Chapter 7). As regards software, some DSS use specialized components, some of which you may not be familiar with from your earlier coursework. In hardware, DSS must run on the same types of equipment as do other information systems, but here again there are some differences in emphasis and suitability. As we discuss hardware, we'll also cover some of the most recent trends in information systems platforms, such as client/server computing, massively parallel computers, and the movement toward open systems.

Once you have a DSS that works (or seems to!) it is necessary to "roll it out" to the user community and obtain their willingness to use it. That is more of an issue with DSS than with some other types of systems, as there is usually an alternate way to make most decisions that DSS might support. Chapter 8 covers these implementation issues. It will give you some procedures you'll be able to use on the job to make your system implementation go smoothly.

CHAPTER 5

Building a Decision Support System

Chapter Outline

Introduction

As noted at the start of the previous chapter, a decision support system is an information system. Just as it uses the same fundamental software building blocks as any other information system, it is built through the same conceptual steps as any other information system: determining user requirements, choosing hardware, obtaining whatever software packages may be of use, programming the rest, testing the whole, and putting it into operation. Within this general framework, however, there are major differences between DSS and most other information systems. The person about to embark on a DSS project should be aware of them, as these differences can mean project success or project failure.

Chapter Objectives

After you have read and studied this chapter, you will be able to:

1. Explain the importance of information system architecture.
2. Describe the DSS architecture and identify the factors you should account for in planning a DSS architecture.
3. Describe the traditional system development life cycle and discuss its advantages and disadvantages in decision support system development.
4. Describe two approaches to prototyping and how well each matches decision support system development needs.
5. Identify how and when end-user development matches decision support system development requirements.
6. Discuss several types of operating system and decision support system user interfaces.
7. Identify factors to consider and steps to take when defining the user interface of a decision support system.
8. Understand the guidelines for using color in your user interface.
9. Summarize several emerging technologies that will help you design decision support system user interfaces during your career.

5.1 DEFINING THE DSS ARCHITECTURE

The *architecture* of an information system refers to the way its pieces are laid out, what types of tasks are allocated to each piece, how the pieces interact with each other, and how they interact with the outside world. Information system architecture is a high-level concept: The architecture does not specify that an IBM PS/2 Model XYZ will be installed in each purchasing agent's office, that the manufacturing LAN (local area network) will support precisely 17 users, or that a market planning model will become operational in June 1995. The following definition of an information systems architecture, from [MART91], applies well to DSS:

> A written expression of the desired future for information use and management in an organization, that creates the context within which people can make consistent decisions.

The most appropriate analogy to an information system architecture outside the information system field is not with the architecture of a building, despite the use of the same word. An information system architecture corresponds more closely to a city master plan. The plan estimates future needs and builds on those estimates. It lays out areas for homes, shopping, and industry; indicates what type of roadways will be needed and approximately where; and suggests when infrastructure elements such as sewage treatment facilities will need expansion. But it does not state that a two-family house will be built in September 1996, at 120 Elm Street or that parking along Chestnut Street will be limited to one hour on weekdays from 9 A.M. to 6 P.M.

Having a well-defined and well-communicated decision support system architecture provides an organization with significant benefits. Nontechnical benefits include the ability to create a common vision that keeps all project participants working in tandem, the ability to communicate system concepts to management (leading to a greater likelihood that their expectations will be met), the ability to communicate needs to potential vendors, and the ability of other groups to implement systems that must work with this DSS. Technical benefits of a DSS architecture include the ability to plan systems in an effective and coordinated fashion and to evaluate technology options within a context of how they will work rather than abstractly. Achieving all these benefits requires that both information system professionals and prospective system users—who, after all, are the ones who understand the problems that the system is to help solve—must cooperate closely in developing the architecture.

The overall architecture of a DSS should be laid out and understood before specific decisions are made. The nature of this architecture depends on the DSS. Mini-DSS developed by individuals for their own use do not justify an architectural planning effort, although the overall information system architecture of the organization may make a statement about how and where they fit into the picture. Enterprise-wide DSS do require careful advance planning if they are to succeed.

To lay out a DSS architecture you must consider the spectrum of DSS that your organization will be using. To do this systematically, you should consider:

- Strategic, tactical (management control), and operational decisions.
- Unstructured, semistructured, and structured decisions.
- All levels of management in the organization.
- All major functional, product or line of business, and geographic divisions of the organization.

If your DSS architecture allows for needs in all these categories, it will be sufficiently comprehensive and robust to stand the test of time. Your DSS architecture must reflect these elements:

- Its database or databases, including any existing databases, internal or external to the organization and any databases that are created specifically for DSS use. The architecture should state who is responsible for different types of databases—at the personal, departmental, and enterprise levels—and for ensuring their accuracy, currency, and security.
- Its model or models, including information about their sources of data, the organizational responsibility for maintaining them, limits on access to them, etc.
- Its users, including any assumptions about their locations, jobs, levels of education, and any other factor that may affect their use of the DSS. "Location" in this context means both geographic location, type of working environment (e.g., office, factory, construction site, home, truck cab) and any other factors that will affect the delivery of decision support system services to the user.
- Software tools through which the users access the database and the models, over and above those provided by the hardware and software platforms that support them.
- Software tools through which system administrators manage the database and the models, again over and above those provided by the hardware and software platforms that support them.
- Hardware and operating system platforms, at a generic level, on which the databases and models reside, on which the programs run, and through which users access the DSS. Any constraints, such as a policy to standardize on products of a particular vendor or products that use a particular operating system, should be stated here. This applies both to overall corporate standards and to standards that apply only to the DSS.
- Networking and communication capabilities through which these platforms are interconnected. These must reflect individual needs to connect to one or more servers and databases, work group needs to

communicate within the group, and enterprise needs to link work groups to each other or to shared data.

In many DSS situations the interconnection mechanism will simply be the corporate network, either an existing one or one that is planned within an overall corporate information systems architecture. Should this be the case it must be examined to make sure it meets present and future DSS needs, which may not have been foreseen when the network concepts were first defined.

- The culture of the organization that will use the DSS. If its culture is centralized, it may be acceptable (or even desirable) to have a central database, a central library for models with central control over its contents, and system-wide standardization on one or a few software packages of each major type. If its culture is decentralized, it may be more appropriate to give each part of the organization control over its own information resources, with provision for sharing or merging where this is called for. Similar considerations apply to the question of user versus MIS control over these resources and the uses to which they are put.

Figure 5–1 shows a generic view of a DSS architecture. Figure 5–2 shows a specific DSS architecture. Both diagrams must, of course, be supplemented by a great deal of explanatory text. The general elements of Figure 5–1 have become more specific in Figure 5–2, although not to the point of constraining the designers of specific DSS unduly or limiting the use of as-yet-unknown technologies and products. If this architecture meets the needs of its sponsoring organization, we can conclude certain things about that organization: It has a centralized culture; it exercises a great deal of management control. It is, however, open to new technologies since it has standardized on some fairly recent ones. This is typical: No one DSS will have all the elements of a "standard" DSS in precisely the average proportions.

Once you have an overall DSS architecture—not the work of a few minutes, or even a few hours—the development of your specific DSS can now begin. The rest of this chapter discusses the kinds of user interfaces you can give it and the development approaches you can use. The next chapter goes into specific types of DSS-related software packages in more detail, including your choice among packages, customized packages, and custom programming. Chapter 8 does likewise for hardware platforms.

5.2 DSS Development Project Participants

Any DSS development project requires the use of several complementary skills. In all but the most trivial cases, you will not be able to find these skills in one person. It will be necessary to assemble the right mix of contributors

FIGURE 5–1

Conceptual DSS Architecture

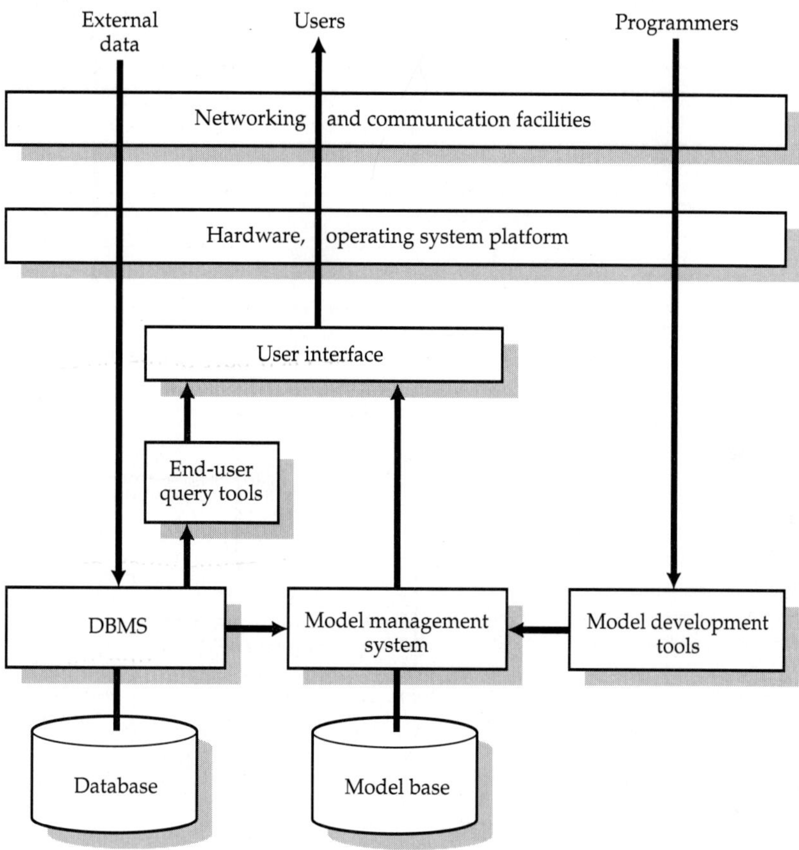

in the DSS project team. The key DSS development roles, as originally put forth in [SPRA80], are listed below in order of increasing technical expertise (and decreasing business expertise).

When Sprague originally described these roles, he assumed an approach to DSS development that made sense for the technology of that era. As you'll see early in the next chapter, that approach is not always appropriate today. The descriptions of each role that follow adjust Sprague's original concepts, which remain valid, to today's technology.

The user (or users). This is the person or group responsible for solving the problem that the DSS is to help with. Users are generally nontechnical people in functional areas of the business: marketing, finance, etc.

The intermediary. This is the individual who will help the user or users use the DSS. Using an intermediary implies the intermediary usage mode

(support people)

FIGURE 5–2
Specific DSS architecture

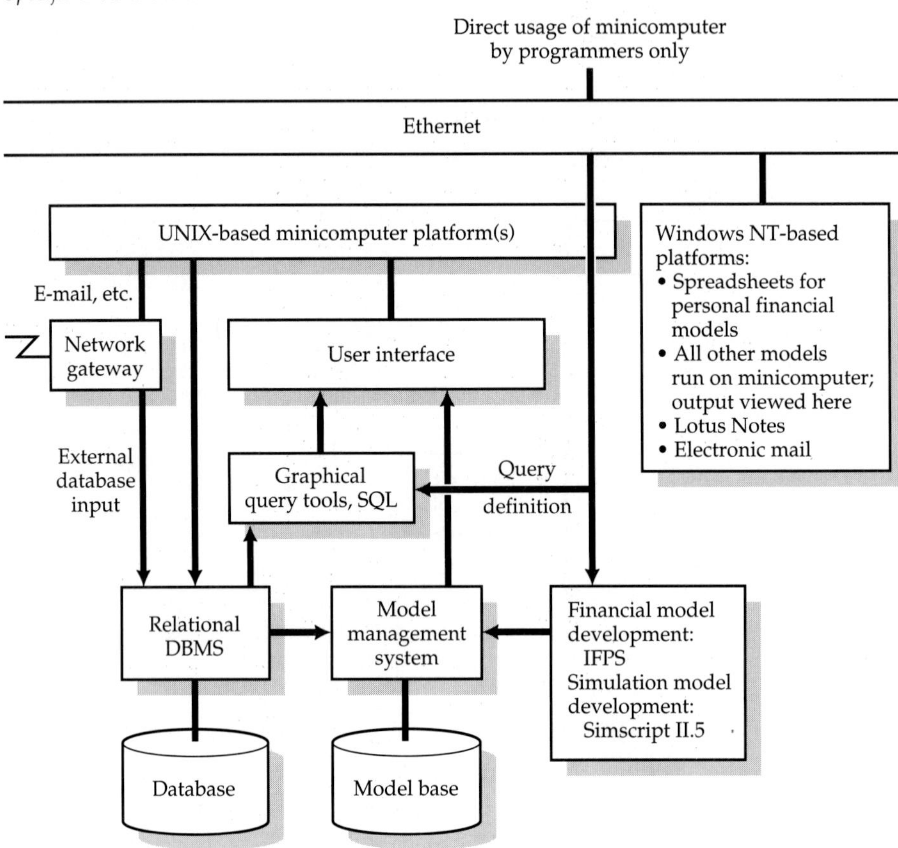

discussed in Section 4.7, where we listed three common types of intermediaries. If the DSS is to be used in a different mode, the intermediary role does not apply. Creating a spreadsheet model would be done by this type of person.

The DSS builder or facilitator. This is the technical expert who will make the technical decisions about the software tool(s) to use (see Chapter 6), the hardware platform(s) to use (see Chapter 7), the models and/or databases to incorporate into the DSS, and how they will be integrated with each other. This is generally a person with a great deal of experience who understands both the business problem and the available technologies.

The technical support person. This is the programmer who integrates existing packages into one overall system and carries out custom programming that contributes directly to DSS functionality. His or her responsibility begins with the packages that will comprise part of the DSS and ends with a functional DSS for the user.

The toolsmith. This person focuses on the tools that will be used in constructing the DSS and the packages that will be combined into it. He or she is an expert on these tools and packages and their effective use. This is the person who creates underlying capabilities, often not visible to the user, but required for the technical support personnel to carry out their more user-oriented jobs effectively.

A large DSS project may involve several people in some of these roles. A small one may have one person covering several roles. In one common example, users with sufficient computer literacy often create their own spreadsheet models. When they do this, they are filling the role of an intermediary with respect to the DSS in question.

Before embarking on a DSS development project, review the list of roles in this section and make sure that they are all adequately covered—or that you have good reason to believe that the roles that are not covered do not apply to that project.

5.3 THE DSS DEVELOPMENT PROCESS

Three approaches to information system development are commonly used:

1. The traditional SDLC, or system development life cycle, approach.[1]
2. The prototyping approach, with two major variations.
3. End-user development, often with professional support.

5.3.1 *The SDLC Approach*

The SDLC approach is based on a series of formal steps. Figure 5–3 shows a typical series of steps. While different versions of SDLC vary in the precise number of steps and in the detailed definitions of those steps, all follow this general pattern.

Each SDLC step culminates in a written document that must be reviewed and approved before the next step can begin. Reviewers include both prospective users of the system, who verify that the documented functionality and external interfaces meet their needs, and its developers, who verify that the system's internal interfaces are consistently defined and meet all technical requirements.

[1]Not to be confused with the other common meaning of these initials: synchronous data link control, a data communication protocol first used with IBM's system network architecture (SNA).

FIGURE 5–3
Chart of Typical SDLC Stages

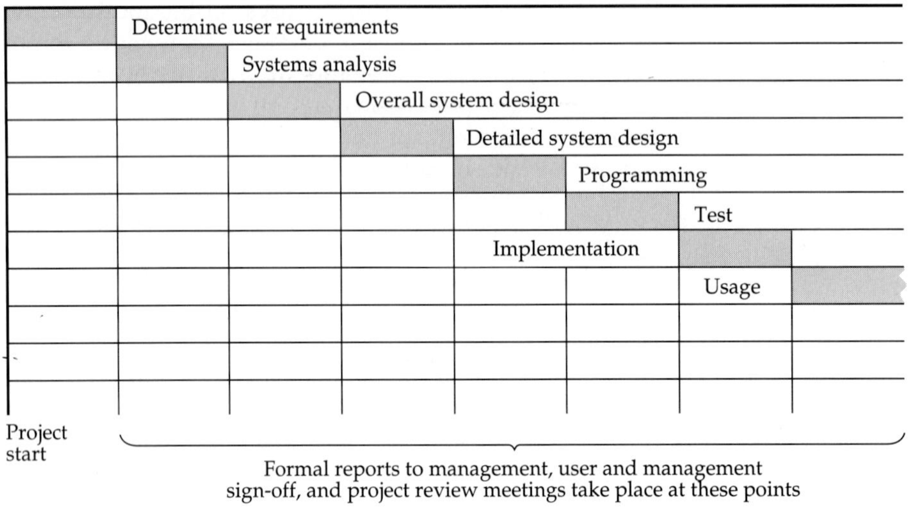

Determine user requirements
Systems analysis
Overall system design
Detailed system design
Programming
Test
Implementation
Usage

Project start

Formal reports to management, user and management sign-off, and project review meetings take place at these points

Advantages of SDLC

When the SDLC approach was first formalized in the mid-1970s, it was a big improvement over the then-common state of anarchy. System development was commonly practiced as a "black art" with little or no management control. The idea of a standardized series of steps, with formal documents and formal procedures for proceeding from each step to the next, was traditional in engineering disciplines but revolutionary in programming. The SDLC approach did indeed provide important discipline to system developers. It was soon adopted for transaction processing systems, which were the norm in that era. It is still widely used for this purpose. It is especially common today when a formal contractual relationship exists between the developers of an application system and its eventual users, as it provides written evidence that can be used to arbitrate any disputes.

Drawbacks of SDLC

The SDLC approach is too rigid for systems whose requirements change rapidly. User requirements, agreed upon at the first stage of the process, are frozen forevermore. Any change forces nearly a complete restart of the entire development cycle, as subsequent documents are based on the originally agreed user needs. Changes are therefore not often attempted: in fact, SDLC can be described as a means of preventing change rather than a way of dealing with it and accommodating it. When a system emerges at the end of the SDLC development cycle, months or years later, it may meet user needs as originally described—but those needs might no longer exist or might have changed beyond recognition.

Another drawback of the SDLC approach is that specification documents are poor user-developer communication vehicles. Users have a hard time articulating what they need in a system. Responses to "What would you like to have?" tend to be of two varieties: either incremental improvements over the present system, to correct its deficiencies without extending it significantly, or "blue sky" wish lists that cannot be satisfied outside a science fiction novel. The useful middle ground, which is the systems analyst's goal, is hard to elicit. If a systems analyst perseveres and defines a meaningful new system, its 200-page technical description is not likely to be read and reviewed in any case, even if it avoids technical terminology and uses easier-to-comprehend descriptions such as data flow diagrams.

These disadvantages are more telling in a DSS context than they are in a transaction processing context. As a result, the SDLC approach is usually less appropriate than one of the following approaches for DSS development. The SDLC approach may still make sense for large DSS projects that will be used by many people. Such DSS are generally used for operational, and occasionally for tactical, decisions.

5.3.2 *Prototyping*

Prototyping, which follows either the steps shown in Figure 5–4 or those shown in Figure 5–5, evolved in response to the deficiencies of the SDLC. In the prototyping approach, systems analysts sit down with potential users and develop a system that appears to work—on the surface—approximately the way the eventual system will work. They use tools such as fourth-generation languages (4GLs) that support rapid development, at the expense of efficient computer utilization if necessary. They omit (only for now!) error checking, access to a real database, "help" screens, little-used options, and all the other minutiae that account for the overwhelming majority of development time. The result is something that users can try out, react to, comment on, and eventually approve with a high confidence level that it really meets their needs. Missing features will be added later, once users are satisfied with the way the prototype works.

Once approved, the prototype can be used in either of two ways. In one scenario, a prototype is used as a surrogate specification. This specification is turned into an operational system using the same tools that would be used had the specification been written on paper. In the other approach to prototyping, the prototype evolves directly into the finished product. It is attached to a live database and features are added to it, but it remains written in the 4GL or other high-level tools originally used.

The first approach, often called *throwaway prototyping,* picks up the SDLC stages midway through the development process. It is well suited to transaction processing system (TPS) applications. Such systems are used heavily by many people to process large volumes of data. Efficiency of application

FIGURE 5–4

Chart of Typical "Throwaway" Prototyping Stages

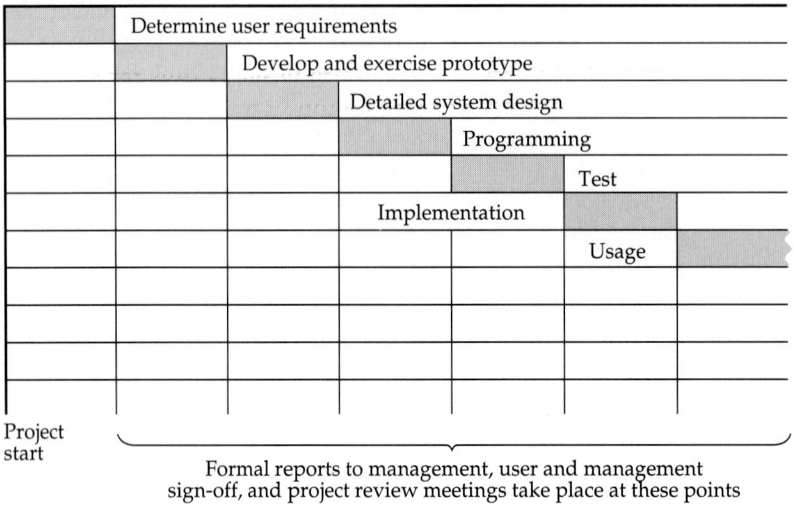

Determine user requirements
Develop and exercise prototype
Detailed system design
Programming
Test
Implementation
Usage

Project start

Formal reports to management, user and management sign-off, and project review meetings take place at these points

FIGURE 5–5

Chart of Typical "Evolutionary" Prototyping Stages

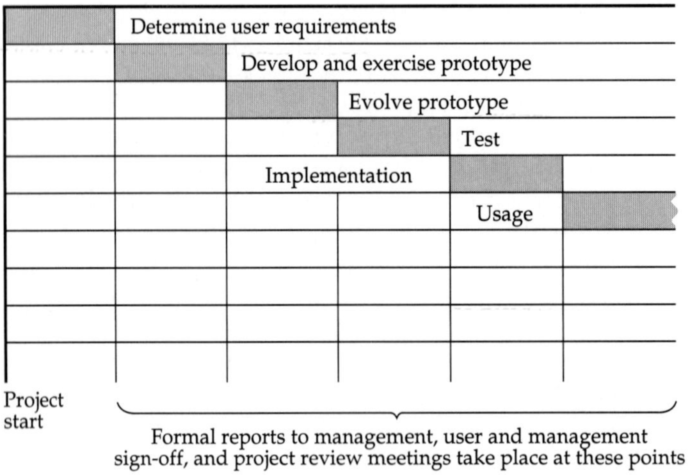

Determine user requirements
Develop and exercise prototype
Evolve prototype
Test
Implementation
Usage

Project start

Formal reports to management, user and management sign-off, and project review meetings take place at these points

execution is therefore paramount. The run-time inefficiencies and hardware resource requirements of 4GLs and other high-level development tools, while far smaller than they once were, cannot be tolerated.

Throwaway prototyping is less well suited to DSS because DSS typically have different usage patterns. Most DSS are used by fewer people than are most TPS and are used less regularly. If run on an individual decision maker's desktop computer, inefficiency is irrelevant unless it calls for an expensive upgrade or creates unacceptably long run times. If run on the corporate mainframe, DSS usually account for only a small fraction of its load. The impact of inefficient hardware usage is thus far smaller than it would be for a TPS. The value of DSS to the organization, and hence the value of having them available quickly, exceeds the cost of a little hardware. These factors usually make the second approach, called *evolutionary prototyping* or *rapid application development,* better suited to DSS since keeping the prototype as the foundation of the application, and continuing to use its high-level development tools, speeds the programming process.

Evolutionary prototyping is especially appropriate for what is often called a *quick-hit* DSS [SPRA82]: a DSS developed for a one-time situation where there is a recognized need and a high potential payoff. The drawbacks of limited DSS applicability and inefficient hardware usage are nearly irrelevant in this situation. The importance of having the DSS as soon as possible is paramount.

Advantages of Prototyping

Compared with the SDLC approach, prototyping improves user-developer communication. It introduces deliberate flexibility and responsiveness into the development process. Change is no longer something to be avoided; it is built into the process and encouraged. The system that is developed is more likely to meet user needs than is a system developed through SDLC.

Disadvantages of Prototyping

Prototyping can extend the development schedule if it is improperly used. The inclination to "tinker" with systems, to make minute changes that do not really improve the usability of the finished product, is always tempting. Both users and developers must control their all-too-human tendencies in this regard in order to obtain a useful system within their lifetimes.

Prototyping raises the possibility of using the wrong tools or of using the right tools in the wrong way. Developers, especially, must understand the limitations of screen forms packages, 4GLs, and other rapid prototyping tools.

Finally, the nearly finished appearance and interface of a prototype may mislead users into thinking the system itself is nearly done. They may have unreasonable expectations about the time required to turn a prototype into a functional product. A prototype resembles the visible tip of an iceberg: 80 percent of the system is below the surface and not visible to its users, but that 80 percent must still be developed if the system is to work. Education is the best solution to this problem. Developers must take the time to describe the missing features, point out that they are usually more technically complex than the visible ones and that they take more time to work out, and explain what would happen if they were skipped.

5.3.3 End-User Development

In prototyping there is a cooperative relationship between users and developers, but the developers are ultimately responsible for creating a working system. End-user development puts the responsibility for creating a DSS on the shoulders of the decision makers themselves.[2]

End-user computing is often associated with desktop microcomputers. Affordable personal computers were, without a doubt, the key factor in its rapid spread during the 1980s. They remain the most popular end-user computing platform today. However, there is no inherent connection between the two. Today's minicomputer and mainframe software, much of it developed in the mold of popular microcomputer tools, provides a suitable environment for end-user computing as well. More and more end-user–oriented packages, among them Lotus 1-2-3, Focus, Oracle, IFPS, and many more, are available in microcomputer, minicomputer, and sometimes mainframe versions. Some of these, such as Lotus 1-2-3, originated in the microcomputer world and were "ported" to larger systems. Others, such as Focus, originated at the large system level and were brought down to micros as the latter became powerful enough to support them. In either case, the end-user computing tool, and hence the ability to do end-user computing, is available on both small single-user and large multi-user computers.

The lowly spreadsheet is a common end-user development tool. Using a spreadsheet program, a manager can analyze the impact of different budget options and select one that best meets a department's needs. Market analysts can study different breakdowns of a market into segments, while making sure that all segments sum to the right overall totals and show the correct trends. With today's permeation of personal computers into medium-sized and large organizations, with "spreadsheet literacy" a requirement of every college business curriculum, managers and professionals are increasingly expected to be able to carry out such analyses on their own. More advanced packages, such as Crystal Ball, which you'll read about in Section 9.1.7, are also often written so as to be usable by end users.

More complex end-user projects can be carried out with the aid of professional support. Many firms have a department in the MIS group whose task it is to provide such support. (This group is often called an *information center,* a term that originated in IBM Canada in the 1970s.) With the help of this support staff, managers can explore the use of database accessing tools such as 4GLs to satisfy their own information needs. Most information centers provide training classes, telephone help, and walk-in or by-appointment consultation for users with information-processing needs. Many also set organ-

[2]The term end user refers to the individual who personally has the business problem that the DSS is meant to help solve. It is used to distinguish such people from MIS professionals, whose job is to develop systems to help solve other people's problems.

izational standards for essential hardware and software components of personal information systems. Such standards help ensure compatibility among personal systems developed throughout the firm, make it possible for a central group to provide support without having to know about many different packages that satisfy similar user needs, and may enable the firm to negotiate substantial volume purchase discounts with software suppliers.

An end user developing any DSS beyond the most trivial could benefit by considering the formal stages of the SDLC. Each is there for a reason. Each has been found, over time, to provide a benefit, even if that benefit is not immediately apparent. While it isn't necessary for the end user/developer to go through the full detail of every SDLC step, every major topic deserves some thought. The developer should think about objectives before starting, think about costs and benefits, plan how the system will eventually be tested, etc.

Today's managers and professionals are, in historical terms, in the most difficult situation that ever existed or will ever exist regarding end-user system development. Knowledge workers of the past were not expected to be able to develop their own systems. Those of the future will have tools we can only dream of to make system development easier. The managers and professionals of today—you, on the job in the next few years—are often expected to develop their own systems, but they must know a good deal about computers to do it well.[3]

Advantages of End-User Computing for DSS Development

The greatest advantage of end-user development is that the person with the problem feels, *and is,* in control of its solution. This control manifests itself in several ways: physical control over the hardware (if a desktop microcomputer is being used), lack of conflict with other projects for developer time, and the understanding that comes with having put the DSS together from the ground up.

There can also be significant time and cost savings associated with end-user development. Instead of explaining a problem to a programmer—or, worse, explaining it to a systems analyst, who in turn attempts to explain it to a programmer, who is then expected to program it—the user programs it directly. The time that would be taken up by communication is eliminated and can be used for more productive purposes. The errors introduced in the communication process, that must be removed at the cost of more user and developer time, are likewise eliminated.

[3]The situation resembles that of automobile drivers around 1920. A generation earlier, automobiles were not a factor in most people's lives. A generation later, electric starters and automatic transmissions had made the driver's job far easier. The driver of 1920 was caught in the middle. The pace of change in computing is, of course, far faster.

Disadvantages of End-User Computing for DSS Development

Users may get carried away with the computer aspects of a problem, at the expense of their primary jobs. A $75,000-per-year marketing director should not do work that a $35,000-per-year programmer could do—and could often do better. Small end-user development projects save money because the need to communicate with a system developer is eliminated. Large ones may waste money because people are working outside their professional field and are therefore not working cost effectively.

A second danger is that most professionals and managers are not trained in, or even aware of, system development discipline. As with the spreadsheets we'll discuss in Section 6.3.3, they usually do not test their systems thoroughly or document them carefully. They tend to be casual about backing up files and ensuring adequate data security. Again as with spreadsheets, some of these attitudes may be acceptable in a system developed for one-time use over a short period by one individual. Unfortunately, and the analogy to spreadsheets still applies, many systems that were planned for one-time, one-person use turn out to be far more widely used, for far longer, than their developers could possibly have anticipated. Problems that result from lax development attitudes and incomplete or sloppy testing can cost more in the long run than proper development discipline, with the involvement of information systems professionals, would have cost in the first place.

A third danger is that end-users may get carried away "playing graphic designer." They spend time trying out fancy fonts, putting borders around spreadsheet cells and shading behind paragraphs, and generally tinkering with the appearance of a document instead of concentrating on its content. Sadly, they all too often overestimate their own graphic design abilities and create distracting "visual clutter" when a straightforward printout would do a better job.

5.4 DSS User Interfaces

Since decision support systems are intended to work closely with human decision makers in carrying out their tasks, a DSS can only be as effective as its interface with those humans permits. Compared with the clerical and administrative workers who are the primary users of data processing systems, the knowledge workers and managers who use DSS tend to have the following characteristics:

- They use the DSS for only a fraction of their working day, spending the rest of their time performing tasks that do not call for its use. In many cases, these other tasks do not call for using a computer at all.
- They are chosen for their positions based on other factors than facility with (or willingness to use) a computer.

- Their tasks are less standardized.
- Each execution of one of their tasks has a higher impact on organizational performance.
- They have more latitude to exercise individual judgment as to the best way to perform their tasks.
- Their high pay makes it cost effective to accommodate their personal wants at the expense of additional system development effort or computer resources.
- Their relatively high organizational status (compared with, e.g., order entry operators or payroll clerks) conditions them to expect more organizational accommodation of their individual needs.

5.4.1 Factors to Consider in User-Interface Design

All the user characteristics listed above influence the design of a DSS user interface. James Larson [LARS82] points out the following DSS factors that are determined, or at least affected, by its user interface:

- *Time.* How long does it take the end user to perform his or her task?
  Some fraction of task time is determined by actual DSS execution time. DSS execution time, while developers have some control over it by choosing software tools and hardware that are fast enough to provide the desired responsiveness, is not a user interface issue. Proper user-interface design can, however, minimize *wasted* time on the user's part.
- *Learning.* How long does it take a novice to learn the system?
  No one over one week old is a true "novice" at everything. Proper design for learning must take into account what the user knows and how the user's mind fits that knowledge together.
- *Recall.* How easy is it for an end user to recall how to use the system after he or she has not used it for some time?
  This is a more important factor for DSS than for data processing systems because managers often return to a DSS after a long interval of nonuse. Some systems, for example, are intended to help with decisions that recur predictably on an annual basis. Eleven months might elapse from a manager's last use of the system on one annual cycle until his or her first encounter with it on the next. A user interface that facilitates recall will reduce the time it takes to "get back up to speed" each year.
- *Versatility.* Can the system be used to perform a variety of end-user tasks?
  The DSS must be versatile enough to accommodate the full range of tasks for which decision makers will want to use it. Once a system becomes widely used, tasks related to its original purpose—but

distinct from that purpose—will often arise. While it is reasonable for these new tasks to require new development work, it should be possible to incorporate them into the existing user-interface framework.

- *Errors.* How many errors does the end user make, and how serious are those errors?

  The most serious errors lead to wrong decisions as a result of system misuse. Following closely behind are errors that corrupt a corporate database. Then come errors that bring down ("crash") the computer, followed finally by errors that waste the user's time but have no other bad effects. Fortunately, most user errors will be in the last category. Within this group there are variations, depending on the amount of wasted time. Don't make a user start entering a series of 70 numbers from the beginning just because he or she mistyped the 67th!

  Understanding the users' usual decision-making process can help minimize errors. If a user is used to entering dates in the sequence month-day-year, don't require them in the sequence year-month-day—even if that's how the computer will ultimately organize them internally.

  It is possible to instrument a system to keep track of its users' errors so that the most common ones can be identified and dealt with through interface improvements. If a DSS project doesn't justify this level of effort, it may still be feasible to watch users exercise an early version of the system. If they tend to make mistakes in a particular area, don't argue with them or show them the documentation section they should have read more carefully. Change the system to make the error less likely, or at least to make recovering from it as easy, quick, and painless as possible.

- *Help.* Does the system provide help when the end user has trouble?

  On-line help facilities are becoming the norm for "industrial-strength" DSS. More and more development tools make it easy to incorporate on-line help into a system. Wherever possible, help should be *context sensitive:* The Help facility should recognize what the user is trying to do, or at least what screen the user is looking at, and provide help that is tailored as closely as possible to the current need.

  On-line help should be meaningful. The on-line help for a field clearly labeled "Telephone Number" should say more than "Enter the telephone number." It could usefully read, "Customer's daytime telephone number, area code first."

  Expert systems have unique requirements in this area since they are often expected to explain to their users why they are asking for a particular data item or how they reached a particular conclusion.

We'll cover the specialized user-interface requirements of expert systems in Chapter 15.

- *Adaptability.* Does the system adjust to the end user's level of competence as he or she becomes more experienced? Does it tailor itself to the habits and styles of different users?
  It may be difficult or impractical for the system to be truly self-tailoring in this sense. It is easier, and may be sufficient, to let the experienced user select an "expert user" mode in which prompts are minimized. In a graphical user-interface environment, it is helpful to provide keyboard equivalents for commonly used mouse-and-menu commands, as some users prefer mice and others prefer keystrokes.
- *Concentration.* How many things must an end user keep in mind while using the system?
  Most people have difficulty keeping more than six or seven active facts in mind at any one time. One way to reduce the memory load is to label screens and output with the parameters of the current scenario: "Profit Projection: 6% inflation, 10% sales growth, Model 47 shipments start 4/94. . . ."
- *Fatigue.* How quickly does the user tire while using the system?
  Physical fatigue—or, more seriously, repetitive strain injuries such as carpal tunnel syndrome—is seldom a factor with DSS because usage frequency is not high enough to lead to such problems. Mental fatigue can arise, however. Minimize it by keeping the necessary concentration within reason (see the previous point) and by asking for information in the sequence in which users normally use it.
- *Uniformity.* Are the commands of this system identical to equivalent commands of other systems?
  Studies performed during the late 1980s, comparing usage of Macintosh and MS-DOS systems, indicate that the greater user acceptance of the Macintosh results primarily from interface consistency among all applications that follow Apple's Macintosh interface guidelines. The inherent merits of a graphical user interface over the character-oriented variety are a far smaller factor. People can learn any esoteric interface if they want to. What is difficult is learning (and remembering) two, three, or more interfaces, be they esoteric or simple, and switching frequently among them.
  A DSS developer must be aware of other systems that the intended DSS users are familiar with. If their standard word processor invokes on-line help via function key F1, don't use Alt-F2 or control-? for that purpose. If any standards control some of their user interfaces, such as IBM's Common User Access (CUA) standard under its System Application Architecture, developers should conform to these if possible.
  Terminology is a factor in making commands look uniform. Many

VAX users call the Alt(ernate function) key on their keyboards the "Gold Key" because VAX terminals have colored it gold since the late 1970s. The documentation of many application packages that were first developed for the VAX uses the same term, even retaining it when the software is ported to other platforms (often without anyone realizing that people who are used to systems from other suppliers, whose keys do not use Digital's color scheme, might not have the vaguest notion what a "gold key" is). If that's what your users call it, that's what you should call it. Paint all your users' PCs' Alt keys gold if it makes them happy—or if it reduces support calls.

- *Fun.* Does the end user enjoy the system?

  This does not mean "funny" error messages or jokes on the screen. Those grow stale quickly. It means you should keep users informed about what the system is doing, warn them of time-consuming operations, provide progress displays or reports as a long operation is being carried out, and generally try to minimize frustrations that come from using an uncooperative system.

Another user-interface issue, unique to DSS and often not adequately considered, is the type and amount of guidance that a DSS provides its users in the decision-making process [SILV91a]. This guidance can be inadvertent: Users tend, all other things being equal, to select the first or last items from menus, which can influence their choice of a statistical analysis method or graph type. If, as is common practice, a system provides a default menu selection—often the item selected the previous time the same menu appeared—it has the same effect and can perpetuate a practice that is no longer appropriate.

Decisional guidance can also be deliberate: intentionally built into a system by its designer, presumably after determining that a particular decision approach or process is better than what many users, unaided, would chance upon by themselves. This type of guidance is distinct from the typical on-line help facility, which focuses on guidance in the mechanical aspects of operating the system. On-line help assumes that the user has already decided what to do but doesn't know how to do it.

Some DSS give the developer more of an opportunity to provide decisional guidance than others. A DSS that does not provide for many discretionary user judgments in its use cannot benefit greatly from such a facility. A DSS that lets users choose among several decision methods, several alternative models, several ways to cross tabulate a set of data, several forecasting techniques, or even alternative sequences of activities does provide an opportunity to provide decisional guidance. Most DSS today—or, more accurately, their developers—do not take full advantage of this opportunity. You should consider it in DSS development. Silver [SILV91a] suggests areas to look at, with several concrete examples.

The following sequence of steps for developing a DSS user interface has been suggested. There is room for decisional guidance (at least) in steps 3, 4, 5, 8, and 9.

1. Determine who your user is.
2. Determine what the user will use the system for.
3. Determine what sequence of steps the user must follow to accomplish a task.
4. Diagram the steps in item 3 and the decision tree involved. Review them with the user.
5. Determine which of these steps require interaction with the system.
6. Determine information and decision requirements for each interaction (both system and user).
7. Select the categories of dialogue (menus, prompts, forms, etc.).
8. Diagram the flow of dialogue, showing all decisions and their information requirements. Review these with the user.
9. Design screens.
10. Try it, analyze it, simplify it, change it, try it. . . .
11. Update the decision diagrams.
12. Bulletproof the dialogue (i.e., what if the user does something unexpected?)

While this list focuses primarily on the SDLC development approach, every step in the process has to be performed in some way for any other development approach as well. Even if you will develop your DSS via prototyping, you must still understand who your user is, what the user will use the system for, what sequence of steps he or she will follow, etc. You may be able to skip over some of the formal diagramming steps, such as steps 4, 8, and 11, in favor of exercising a prototype, but the same understanding has to be there in either case.

A Cautionary Note

Color is often recommended as a means of enhancing user-interface design. Appropriate use of color can undoubtedly enhance the aesthetics of an interface for most people. Color can call attention to exceptional data, help users differentiate among items on a chart, and convey information at a glance. Blue creates a sense of trust; green means "go" or "all clear;" red indicates danger.

However, system developers must remember that about 4 percent of the North American and European populations have significant color vision deficiency. This deficiency may be limited to certain pairs of (usually complementary) colors. The most common form of color vision deficiency is inability to distinguish between red and green. In total color blindness, all colors appear as shades of gray. Color vision deficiencies are sex linked: about 1 man in 12 suffers from the problem but only about 1 in 200 women.

As a result, always follow these two guidelines for your use of color:

1. Never allow color to be the only way your system conveys any information. Augment use of color with other cues that can be used by people who cannot see the color difference. Include numerical values in addition to color codes, provide cross hatching on top of color, use blinking characters, or make sure that the colors you choose are perceived as substantially lighter or darker than each other. (Canary yellow and navy blue will be perceived as different even by a person who cannot tell "yellowness" from "blueness.")

2. Where your underlying hardware and software permit, allow the user to customize an application's use of color. Some color vision deficiencies can be compensated for (as they affect ability to use an application) by changing, for example, red to blue, so that a user who cannot distinguish red from green can tell the two colors apart. In some systems, colors that cover an area, such as a region on a map, can be replaced by monochrome patterns such as dots, stripes, and cross hatching.

A third guideline for the use of color, which is not related to color vision capability, is that light pastel colors create fewer annoying reflections than do dark ones. This is especially true in an office environment with fluorescent lights. As a result, try to use light colors to cover large areas of the screen. Reserve darker ones for smaller "spot" usage.

5.4.2 *User-Interface Styles*

There are four general ways to control computers today: command-line interfaces, graphical interfaces, menu interfaces, and question-and-answer dialogues. Each has its place in the DSS user interface picture. They can often be combined usefully in a single application or set of related applications.

Command-line interfaces are the oldest form of computer control, dating back to the days in which each command was entered on a punched card. They still dominate user interaction with operating systems, all the way from the MS-DOS "C:\> prompt" at the desktop level to the complex job control languages of mainframe systems. They require a user to enter a command telling the system what to do next. It is the user's responsibility to know what commands are available and how to phrase those commands with their parameters. Such interfaces can be quite powerful, giving their users detailed control over system operation, but there is a cost. They are hard to learn. Most people who are not primarily computer professionals never learn more than a fraction of any command language and make frequent mistakes in command entry. While such mistakes can usually be corrected, they exact a cost in time and make users feel frustrated in trying to deal with an unforgiving, detail-ridden system.

Graphical user interfaces (GUIs) are an increasingly popular alternative at the desktop level and on minicomputers using the UNIX operating system.

Figure 5–6 shows a GUI screen display. Each small picture, called an *icon*, represents a program or a data file. A pointing device (typically a *mouse* but possibly a trackball, joystick, or any of several other possibilities) allows the user to select one or several of them. The *menu bar* or *action bar* at the top of the screen lists menus of operations that can be performed on programs and files. To run a program, the user points at the program's icon, clicks a button on the mouse to select that program, points at a menu, moves the mouse to point at an entry on the menu that drops down from the menu bar, and releases the button. (This process takes far less time to perform than it took

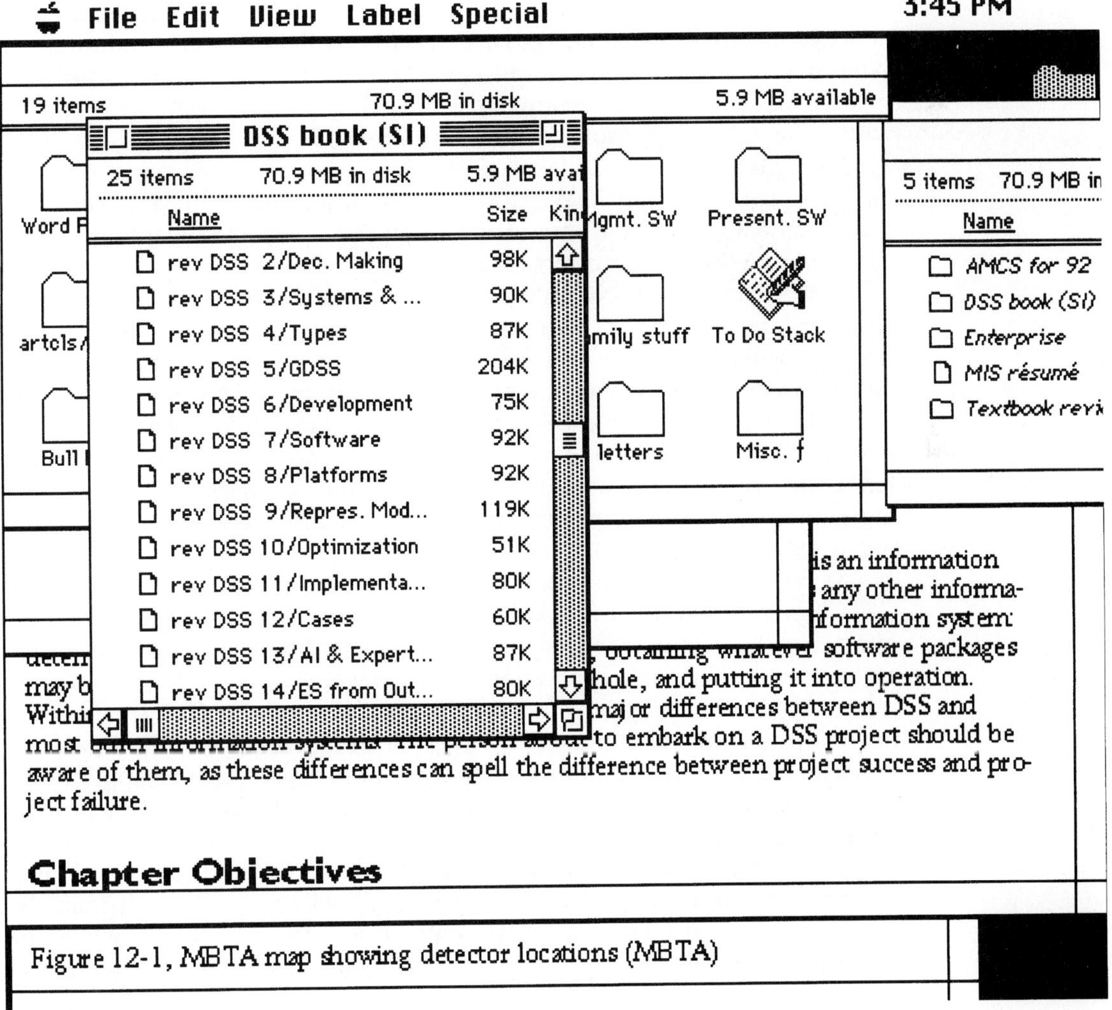

FIGURE 5–6
GUI Screen Shot

you to read about it. In addition, most popular GUIs provide *keyboard shortcuts* that allow the user to perform common operations from the keyboard, and either multiple mouse buttons or multiple button-clicking patterns to reduce menu access needs.) The specifics of button clicking vary from one GUI to the next, but the principles are common to all.

The fundamental psychological principle underlying the spread of GUIs is that *recognizing a command is easier than recalling it.* If a user forgets that the Print command is in the File menu (which some consider an odd place for it, although it is standard GUI practice) he or she simply pulls down a few menus until it appears. There is no way to make a mistake in the command format, to type the wrong letter, to forget a parameter, or to enter options in the wrong order.

The most popular GUIs at the desktop level are Microsoft Windows, which runs under MS-DOS, and the operating system of the Apple Macintosh. Two new GUI-oriented operating systems for IBM-compatible microcomputers are Windows NT from Microsoft and OS/2 from IBM. Both of these operating systems offer, with some restrictions, the ability to run programs originally written for either Microsoft Windows or MS-DOS.

Most minicomputer GUIs use a standard computer-to-terminal communication protocol called X Windows. X Windows allows an application to describe the windows that should appear on the screen and what they should contain in a powerful, succinct, and device-independent language that minimizes the data traffic between the application and the software that manages the user interface. It also allows the user-interface software to send data to the application: what key has been pressed on the keyboard, which mouse button was pressed, where the mouse was pointing when that button was pressed. Many GUIs have been built with the basic X Windows "toolkit," among them Motif and Open Look. Several vendors offer "X terminals:" terminals that have the user-interface side of the X Windows protocol built in. In addition, X Windows emulation programs are available for all popular microcomputers.

At first glance it might seem that the question of command lines versus GUIs affects the use of the operating system, not the way application programs interact with their users. This is only true to a degree. The use of a GUI environment affects the application in two ways:

1. Application programs that are meant to run under a GUI are expected to conform to the standards set by the GUI designers. This conformance is important if the GUI is to fulfill one of its major promises: that all applications in its environment work in the same way, reducing learning time and facilitating training. A GUI-conformant application should use windows, menus, and a pointing device as decreed by the standards of that GUI. Developing an application for this environment is considerably more difficult than developing one whose commands are entered as character strings when the application decides to ask for them. This realization came as a rude awakening

to many suppliers of MS-DOS application programs in the mid-1980s, when they decided to convert their programs to the then-new Apple Macintosh with its GUI. However, application developers who moved their software among the Macintosh, Windows, and OS/2 in the 1990s found the conversion far easier. The first GUI-based development had taken care of the conceptual issues.

2. Developers of applications with a graphical user interface benefit from the facilities provided by a GUI-oriented operating system. It is possible to develop graphical applications that run under a character-oriented operating system. Early computer-aided design (CAD) packages worked this way because they had no choice. They supported windows and a mouse even though the operating system didn't use them. However, GUIs give the application developer system interfaces to create, move, and resize windows; create menus; create standard dialogue boxes; detect and respond to mouse clicks; and handle all the other minutiae of the GUI environment. Creating the same interface functionality from scratch is far more difficult.

If your DSS is to run under a GUI you must decide whether full conformance with its standards is worth the added development effort. If you are developing a DSS package for commercial sale you have no practical choice but to conform. If your system will be used only within one firm, you need not do so. In this case, your decision will often be guided by the availability of programmers who have experience in developing applications for that GUI. If such programmers are not available, it is not advisable to delay deploying a valuable DSS while its developers learn the niceties of a new interface style. Get the basic system working with a simpler interface, let the company derive its benefits, and then enhance its user interface for full GUI conformance.

DSS that do not run under a GUI-oriented operating system can still incorporate GUI-like features. PC/Focus screens resemble Figures 6–18 and 6–19 (in the next chapter) even when PC/Focus runs under nongraphical, nonwindowed MS-DOS. Providing a GUI-like appearance at the application level is of value because even the most technically illiterate end user can learn enough operating system commands to get into an application. Most of the user's interaction then takes place within the application itself. Thus, the ease-of-use advantages of a graphical user interface are applied where they do the most good. It is, as noted above, not easy to add a full GUI-like appearance when the underlying platform is not oriented toward that mode of operation. It may be worth the effort when a DSS is intended for a large community of nontechnical users who will use it sporadically and therefore will never become fully familiar with all its commands and options.

DSS developers who do not develop their DSS entirely from scratch often use a tool that provides some user-interface functionality. This constrains the type of interface that the developer can create. If this is important, the user interface may be a consideration in selecting a DSS development tool. To jump ahead a bit, any dialogue box created with Microsoft Excel will have the basic appearance of Figure 5–7, although its elements and their locations can be customized to each application's needs. If that appearance is unacceptable for any reason, Excel may not be the right development tool.

Menus, which the application displays on the screen, can be used to enter user commands into a DSS. A menu in this context differs from the menus in a GUI because GUI menus are always present at the top of the screen. The GUI user can always invoke a menu command, and the system must always be ready to respond appropriately. Option menus displayed on the screen, however, are shown only when the application program decides that the user should make a choice among the options. The real difference is not the cosmetic one of whether menus drop down from a menu bar or are displayed in the center of the screen. It is the deeper, philosophical difference of whether the system or the user decides what to do next.

Question-and-answer dialogues are appropriate when the user must specify data values or other parameters before the system can carry out a desired operation. A DSS used to plan a retirement financial plan might ask for the age of the individual for which the plan is to be developed, his or her marital status, ages of children being supported, annual income, etc. The user responds to each question by typing the appropriate answer.

Here, too, there is a difference between the character-oriented dialogue approach and the way in which most GUIs would handle the same issue. Under a GUI, the user would be presented with a dialogue box such as the

FIGURE 5–7

GUI Dialogue Box

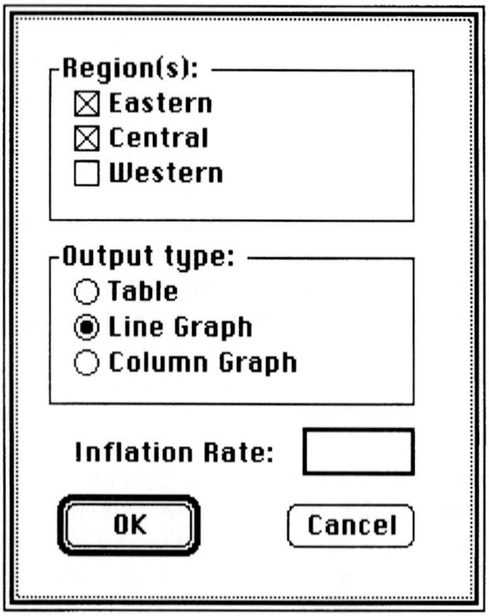

one in Figure 5–7. (This dialogue box was created with Microsoft Excel, a spreadsheet package that runs on IBM-compatible and Macintosh computers and has extensive application customization features.) There is room for all the same entries, but the user is not forced to go through them in the order that the system prefers. He or she can enter any answer by clicking on the appropriate box and typing: selecting regions before output type, vice versa, or even mixed—first selecting the Eastern region, then choosing a line graph, then deciding that the Central region ought to be on the graph too. The user can even click on "OK" before entering all the values. The system must incorporate enough error checking to deal with this situation—in the case of Figure 5–7, the user has specified the desired regions and output type, but not the inflation rate—as well as with all the errors that users can make in typing the individual entries.

Each user interface style suits certain situations. Several modes can be combined in one DSS: for example, a menu that lists available calculation options, followed by a question-and-answer dialogue to enter the parameters that apply to the chosen one. A DSS that operates under a GUI can still display "dialogue boxes" in which a user may make choices or answer a question. Your DSS is unlikely to use a command-line interface style unless it incorporates an existing program that uses this style.

User data entry will usually be via the keyboard. Some GUI-based applications use graphical "sliders" to enter numerical data as in Figure 5–8. These sliders resemble the front panel of a graphic equalizer in a stereo system. To use them, the user points at the control bar on the slider with the mouse (or other pointing device), holds down the mouse button, moves the mouse, watches the slider move on the screen, and releases the mouse when it is in the right place. A numeric display, as shown above each slider in Figure 5–8, can confirm the current slider position and give the user the alternative of entering a numeric value via the keyboard. A series of such sliders might represent a decision maker's estimate of the growth rates of several markets, of the relative importance of several product design factors, or, as in the figure, of expected inflation rates over the next few years.

When accepting keyboard data, any application should provide as much prompting and error checking as possible. This is especially important for DSS, whose users are not generally professional typists and who are therefore likely to make keying errors. Menus of choices are better than blanks to be filled in. If there is no alternative to free typing, the program should perform as many reasonableness and validation checks on the input data as possible. The core temperature of a living human, for example, can be required to be between 85°F and 110°F or 30°C and 45°C. If your DSS must allow an occasional unusual data item, it should at least ask the user, "Do you *really* mean that?"

Data entry methods, limited to keyboards since the computer's infancy nearly half a century ago, are evolving. Pen-based computers (which use a special stylus, not a real pen with ink) are coming into general use today. They are well suited for applications that require an easily carried computer

FIGURE 5–8

Application Interface with "Slider"

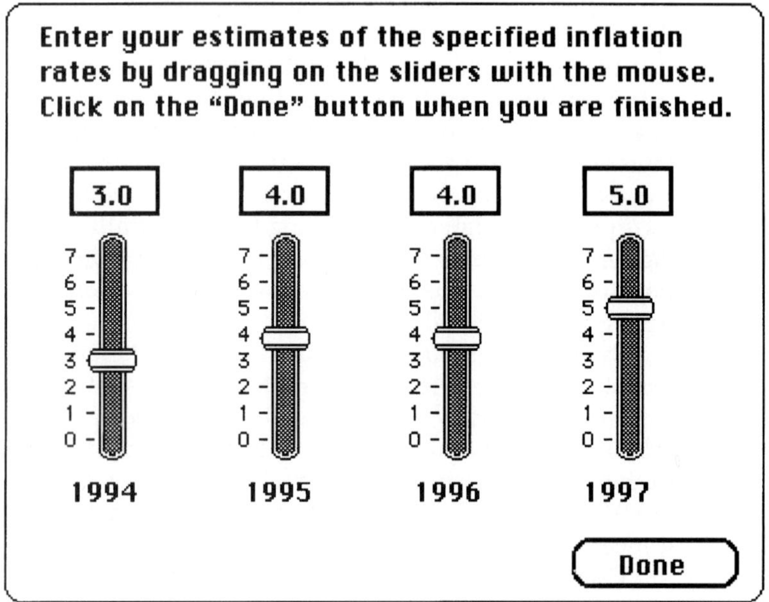

and do not call for entering large amounts of data. For example, United Parcel Service (UPS) personnel use pen-based computers to enter package delivery information. Despite recent advances in handwritten character recognition, however, the keyboard remains the most practical way to enter character strings with speed and reliability.

Voice recognition is likely to be the next step after pen-based computing. Coming not too long after pen-based computing, this new technology may limit the future of pen computers to environments in which the sound of speech is unacceptable—such as taking notes in a lecture or retrieving information from a database while speaking on the telephone.

DragonDictate exemplifies the 1992 state of the art in microcomputer-based speech recognition systems.[4] With a vocabulary of 30,000 words this program is usable for general dictation. It supports only *disconnected speech,* in which users must pause between words. This is awkward at first but typical users can reach speeds of 30 to 40 words per minute. DragonDictate learns its user's voice via an interactive training process, so people with severe speech impediments can use it as long as they pronounce each word consistently from one time to the next. Other potential users include workers in

[4]DragonDictate is available from Dragon Systems, Inc., Newton, Mass., for about $9,000; it requires a MS-DOS microcomputer with 80386 processor and 8MB RAM.)

"hands-busy" environments and businesspeople who can't, or won't, type. This last characteristic applies to many DSS users.

5.4.3 Hypertext/Hypermedia

Hypertext refers to an electronic document whose parts are electronically linked in such a way as to avoid the limitations of traditional linear media such as clay tablets, papyrus scrolls, or bound books. *Hypermedia* extends hypertext by combining text, graphics, animation, and sound in the same electronic "document." Together, hypertext and hypermedia offer the promise of navigating through computer-based information in a fashion dictated by the needs of the user rather than by the structure of a database or the limitations of a computer program. A user faced with the hypertext screen shown in Figure 5–9 can click on any of the highlighted words to get another screen with more information about that topic. Alternatively, he or she could click on any part of the map to get more information about that state—perhaps including photographs of its cities and scenery, the sound of its name spoken correctly, or a summary of any articles about it that appeared in yesterday's *New York Times.* The screen that appears could have hypertext links to other screens, which could be linked to others, which are linked to others. . . . The process is limited only by the content of the available databases and the imagination of the developer.

Information retrieval applications are a natural match to hypertext. An

FIGURE 5–9

Hypertext Screen with Map and Text

New England
The six New England states are located in the northeast corner of the United States. They were among the first parts of North America to be settled by Europeans in the seventeenth century.
New England states include Connecticut, Maine, Massachusetts, New Hampshire, Rhode Island, and Vermont.
Click on any part of the map or on any underlined word for more information.

FIGURE 5–10
Screen Shot of Hypertext Sales Graph

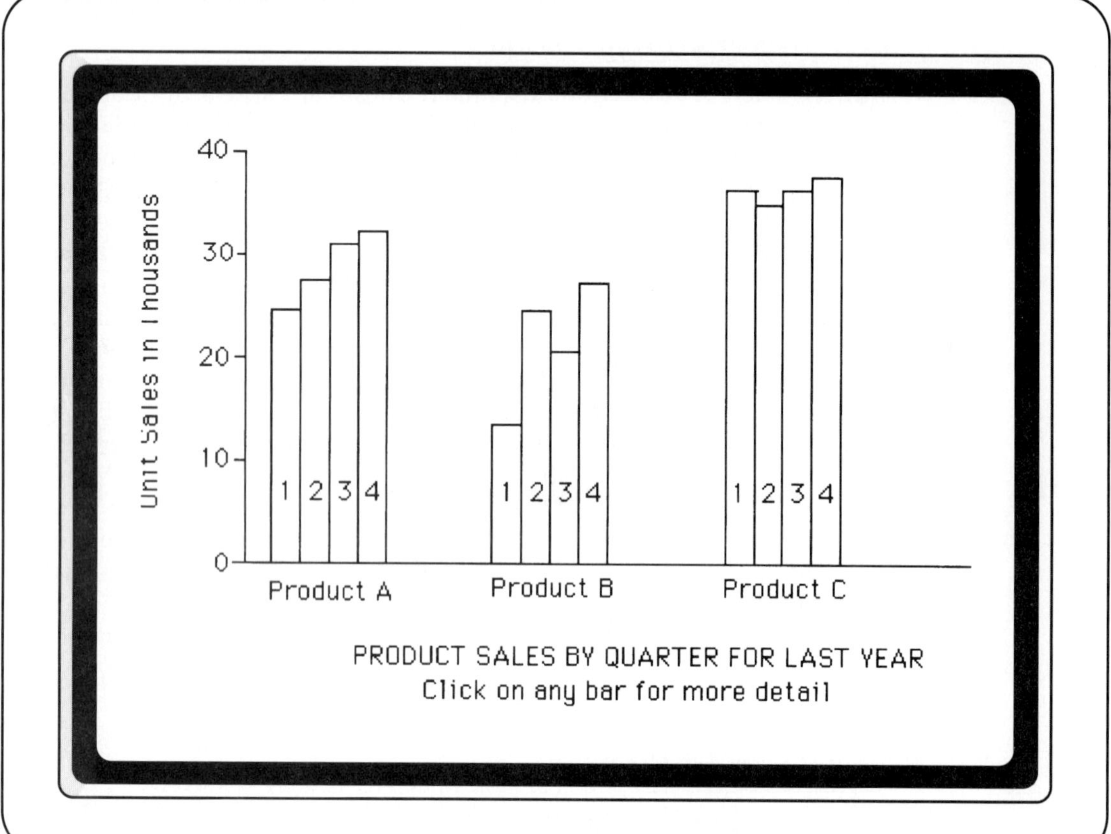

executive information system (which we'll discuss in more detail in Chapter 12) might show a column graph of sales by product as shown in Figure 5–10. If its user clicks on one of the columns in the graph—in this case one that shows a drop in sales—the system could display the dialogue box shown in Figure 5–11. Clicking on one of the three "buttons" in that dialogue box would lead the system to display the requested sales breakdown or to cancel the request. (It is especially important to give the user an opportunity to cancel a request if it will take a long time to execute or lead the user to a part of the system from which it is difficult to return to the current location.) Note that the chosen column is highlighted on the underlying graph so the user can verify visually that he or she clicked in the right place. If the wrong column is highlighted, usually due to a user error but perhaps reflecting a bug in the routine that calculates columns from mouse click coordinate data, the user can cancel the request and click again.

Hypertext is supported by a wide range of products at the mainframe,

FIGURE 5–11
Same Screen as Figure 5–10 with Superimposed Dialogue Box

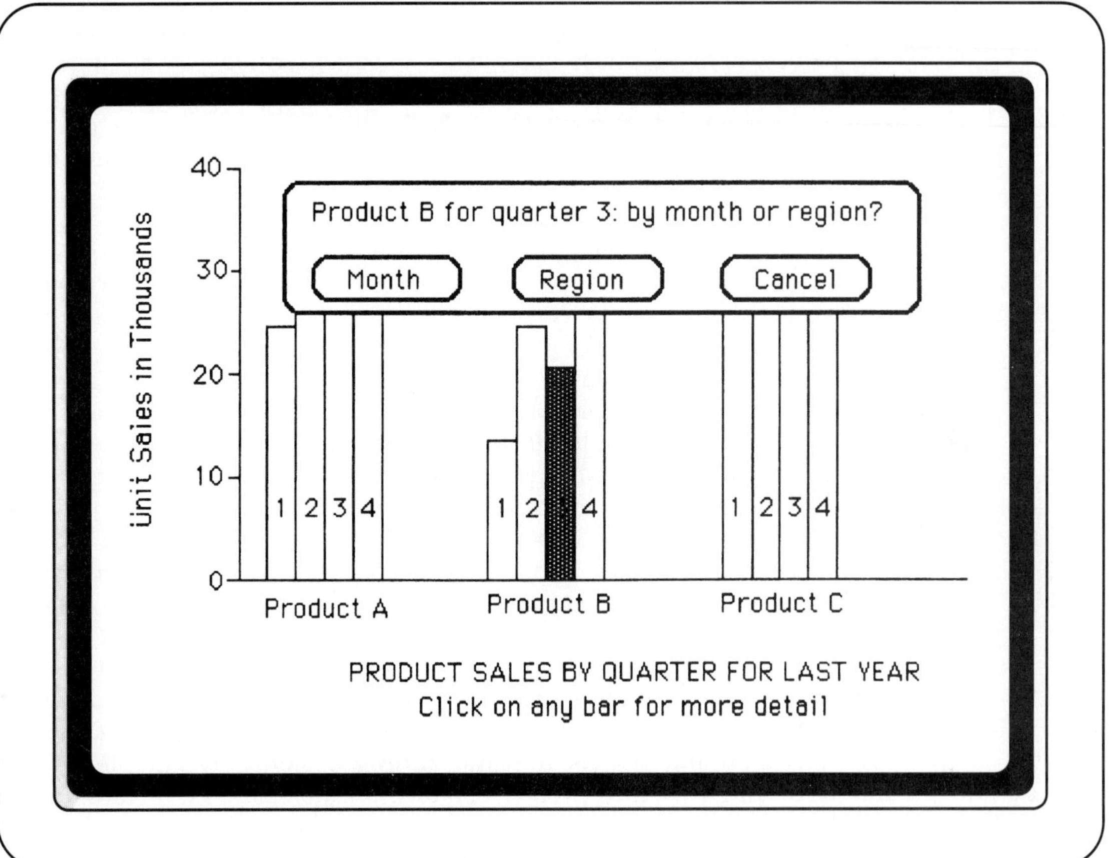

minicomputer, and microcomputer levels. It is most popular, however, at the desktop. Easy-to-use products such as HyperCard from Apple and ToolBook from Asymetrix have contributed to its popularity. So have their distribution strategies: these two products are bundled with, respectively, every Macintosh and every copy of Microsoft Windows.[5] These products, and others such

[5]Strictly speaking, only the "reader" portion of ToolBook is bundled with Windows. A prospective hypertext developer must purchase the authoring tools, but any Windows user will be able to use the resulting document. Apple originally shipped a full-featured version of Hypercard with every Macintosh. In 1987 they began to ship a version that looked like a "reader" and was accompanied only by reader-level documentation, but whose full capabilities could be unlocked by typing a simple code. In early 1993 they changed their policy again and began shipping only a true "reader" (called, in this case, "player") version. As with Windows, a prospective Hypercard developer must now purchase the authoring version, but any Macintosh user can use the resulting "stack."

as SuperCard and Plus, offer capabilities beyond hypertext: They support limited animation, limited database management, and *scripting* languages that allow users to write computational procedures with less training than they would need to use a traditional third-generation language (3GL). This mix of capabilities, none of which match what a specialized tool can do in its own area (e.g., animation), makes it difficult to categorize these products and others like them and often creates confusion as to what hypertext is all about. Despite this confusion over their essential nature, such products have made it possible to develop prototypes of fully graphical applications, and in some cases fully operational applications, with a minimum of effort.

Another emerging way of interacting with computers is *virtual reality*. Virtual reality incorporates technologies such as graphical displays in the form of eyeglasses to give the sense of inhabiting a computer-created "space," and input devices in the form of gloves to allow the user to manipulate "objects" in this space. Using virtual reality, a store manager could evaluate alternate store floor layouts by "walking" through them to get a feel for how they would look if actually built. He or she could push a display shelf a few feet to one side, lengthen or shorten a checkout counter, or move the customer information booth. The result of these manipulations could be stored in a database. This database could later be input to a CAD program to produce architectural drawings. A somewhat more limited application, for custom kitchen design, is described in [BYLI91].

Virtual reality is still a laboratory technology being developed for specialized uses. Its "goggles and gloves" incarnation is not a reality in DSS today, nor will it be for some time. One reason is that, today, anything more than flat, cartoon-like images requires an investment of several hundred thousand dollars in basic hardware alone. Yet graphical user interfaces and hypertext were laboratory technologies, or dreams in the minds of a few visionaries, when today's mid-career managers were in school. Virtual reality is almost certain to have mainstream business applications during your career.

Summary

Before embarking on the development of any major decision support system, you should have a clear idea of both its architecture and the overall DSS architecture of your organization. Knowing these will help you communicate your DSS vision to management and will help you plan systems that will continue to meet user needs in the future.

You should also have a clear idea of who will fill each development role on the project or that the role does not apply. The roles to consider are user, intermediary, DSS builder (or facilitator), technical support person, and toolsmith.

Systems can be built by the MIS department on the basis of a fixed user specification, by the MIS department on the basis of a user-approved prototype, or by the end users themselves with professional help and support.

If a prototype is used, it can either be used as a machine-executable specification or evolved into the finished application. The first approach usually yields higher performance and may be more appropriate to transaction processing applications. The second often produces the application more quickly and therefore may suit DSS better.

Planning the user interface is an important part of planning any DSS: perhaps more so than with most other types of information systems. DSS users have more sporadic and more varied needs than do most other information system users, and their activities tend to have higher organizational impact. Factors to be considered in planning the DSS user interface include minimizing task performance time, minimizing learning and recall time, maximizing system versatility, minimizing errors (and making it as easy as possible to recover from those that do occur), and adapting to different user needs, including the availability of help for those who need it. Additional factors to take into account are the user's ability to keep several things in mind, user fatigue, and command consistency with other systems the users are familiar with.

Color can often enhance a user interface but must be used with due consideration for those users who cannot see a difference among the developer's color choices.

The four most common user-interface styles are commands typed by the user, menus of choices for the user, blanks for the user to fill in, and graphical user interfaces (GUIs). Each of these applies both to the DSS itself and to the operating system under which the DSS runs. While there is no forced connection between the two, the user interface of the operating system has an indirect impact on that of the DSS: It creates expectations as to how the DSS will operate, and it provides capabilities within which the DSS must exist or that the DSS can use. Developing an application that conforms fully to the standards of a GUI is, despite the availability of operating system facilities, more difficult than developing a comparable application that operates via menus and typed-in commands.

User-interface technology is evolving. Pen input is practical today, especially if the user is willing to print uppercase characters with reasonable care. Voice recognition is unable for disconnected speech (with pauses between words) for constrained subject areas. Hypertext and hypermedia, as ways of combining different types of information and letting the user navigate flexibly through the resulting "information universe," are also proving useful. Virtual reality, in which the computer creates the illusion that the user is actually manipulating the system under study, is still in the laboratory but shows great promise.

Key Terms

action bar 153
architecture 134
builder (see DSS builder) 138
command-line interface 152
DSS builder (development role) 138
end-user development 144
evolutionary prototyping 143
facilitator (development role) 138
graphical (user) interface 152
hypermedia 159
hypertext 159
icon 153
information center 144
intermediary (development role) 137
keyboard shortcut 154
menu (interface) 156
menu bar 153
mouse 153
prototyping 141
question-and-answer dialogue 156
quick-hit DSS 143
rapid application development 143
system development life cycle (SDLC) 139
technical support person (development role) 138
throwaway prototyping 141
toolsmith (development role) 139
user (development role) 137
user interface 146
virtual reality 162
X Windows 154

Review Questions

1. What is an information systems architecture?
2. Why is it good to have an information systems architecture?
3. How does a DSS architecture differ from an overall corporate information systems architecture?
4. Give eight factors that a DSS architecture must take into account or reflect.
5. Explain the five major DSS development roles.
6. What are the three basic methods of developing an information system?
7. For what types of DSS is the SDLC approach best suited?
8. What is a prototype?
9. What are the two basic approaches to prototyping? Which is usually better suited to DSS development?
10. Who is responsible for creating the DSS when end-user development is used?
11. What is an information center? What does it do?
12. What are three dangers in end-user computing?
13. What factors make the user-interface design issues of a decision support system different from the user-interface design issues that arise with transaction processing systems?

14. Give at least 10 factors to consider in DSS user-interface design.
15. Why should you not rely exclusively on color to convey information to a DSS user?
16. What are the four basic user-interface styles?
17. How does the use of a graphical user interface by the operating system influence the use of a GUI by a DSS application?
18. Name two alternatives to keyboard data entry.
19. What is hypertext?

Exercises

1. Develop a DSS architecture for a retail clothing chain's marketing department. It must include at least three databases: *(a)* sales information from all stores, *(b)* product availability and pricing information from warehouses and suppliers, and *(c)* industry market share and trend information from an external public information supplier. Its models will include at least *(a)* an advertising response model, *(b)* a financial model for ordering clothing that considers the need to dispose of unsold merchandise via end-of-season sales or by selling it to discounters, and *(c)* a model that compares the income to be gained by selling the firm's mailing list with the lost profits if the customers buy from competitors who bought the list. The chain's stores are located throughout the United States and Canada. Its suppliers are located all over the world. Its marketing staff is located primarily in Terre Haute, Indiana. Its advertising agency is located in New York, as is a small marketing staff to deal with the many clothing suppliers based there. Include all the elements discussed in the text, not just those that show up in Figures 6–1 and 6–2.
2. You have been asked to develop a DSS to help the staff of a large credit card company decide how to deal with overdue accounts. They become involved in the process only when an account is 90 days overdue since for the first two months the computer automatically appends a note (friendly the first time, firmer the second) and a finance charge to the monthly bill. The staff has access to information about the cardholder, his or her credit history, and any other information they could reasonably expect to have under the circumstances. Their options include simply letting finance charges build and accumulate, calling the cardholder, writing a letter to the cardholder, cutting off credit temporarily, canceling the account, garnishing the cardholder's wages, turning the account over to a collection agency,

instituting legal action, and various combinations of these. What development approach would you choose for this DSS? Why?

3. It has been suggested that end-user development might be good for *ad hoc* DSS but not for institutional DSS. Suggest one argument in favor of this position and one against it.
4. Create a written description of the screen display in Figure 5–10 and its behavior, without using any pictures. Comment on how well you feel this description conveys what the screen will look like compared with *(a)* Figure 5–10 plus a written description of its behavior, (b) Figures 5–10 and 5–11, and (b) seeing it on a computer screen.
5. Must a personal computing application use a personal computer? Why or why not?
6. Why is it important to determine who your user is before designing a user interface? As an example, consider a student course selection advising system to be used by *(a)* students, *(b)* faculty advisors, and *(c)* professional counselors who spend about a third of their time counseling students on course selection and the rest counseling them on other issues. How would the ideal user interfaces differ for these three types of users?
7. Find and read one or more articles on virtual reality. Suggest some potential applications for this technology in managerial decision making. Don't use trivial variations on the architectural design examples in Section 5.4.3.

References

BYLI91 Bylinsky, Gene. "The Marvels of 'Virtual Reality.' " *Fortune* 123, no. 11 (June 3, 1991), pp. 138–50.

GRAY89 Gray, Paul, and Lorne Olfman. "The User Interface in Group Decision Support Systems." *Decision Support Systems* 5, no. 2 (June 1989), pp. 119–37.

LARS82 Larson, James A. *End User Facilities in the Nineteen Eighties*. IEEE Computer Society, Los Alamitos, Calif. (1982).

MART91 Martin, E. Wainwright; Daniel W. DeHayes; Jeffrey A. Hoffer; and William C. Perkins. *Managing Information Technology: What Managers Need to Know*. Macmillan, New York (1991).

SILV91a Silver, Mark S. "Decisional Guidance for Computer-Based Decision Support." *MIS Quarterly* 15, no. 1 (March 1991), pp. 105–22.

SPRA80 Sprague, Ralph H., Jr. "A Framework for the Development of Decision Support Systems." *MIS Quarterly* 4, no. 4 (December 1980), pp. 1–26.

SPRA82 Sprague, Ralph H., Jr., and Eric D. Carlson. *Building Effective Decision Support Systems*. Prentice Hall, Englewood Cliffs, N.J. (1982).

ENVOYANCE: JIM'S DECISION

"Jim, you've already met Doug and Adrienne," Dan opened. "They're in the Harwich University MIS program and are trying to figure out how we could use computers in our decision-making processes. I thought you might discuss some of your current decision-making needs with them for a while. I'll be back in about half an hour to go over that air quality situation down south."

"Sounds good to me—we can use all the free help we can get!" laughed Jim. "Seriously, I'm happy to see you here. How can I help you?"

"Well, Jim, we understand you're one of the 'generalists' that Dan told us about. He also said you're in charge of the Mitona Creek cleanup and the Oxbow Chemicals bid."

"He got that part right. He may not have mentioned that assignments like the Oxbow bid change, if not from day to day, at least from month to month. When we submit the bid I go on to something else. If we win the job I might be the project manager, or I might not. That would depend on how busy I am with other things and who else is available."

"Does this create a problem?" asked Doug.

"In some ways it does," Jim agreed. "The new project manager has to meet the key players at Oxbow and come up to speed on the details. However, there are only four or five reasonable candidates, and they're all aware of the bid from our Tuesday morning staff meetings. The biggest problem for a new project manager is reading through a lot of paper. I'd personally like to get rid of it—I could use the filing space!"

"Sandra told us a bit about the Oxbow bid," Doug continued,[6] "Pricing it sounded almost like random guesswork, trying to estimate how much everyone else will cut their bids now to improve their chances later."

"That's true to a point," conceded Jim, "but not totally. We went about it this way:

"First, we estimated the current job, the assessment, on the basis of our standard costs and margins.

"Second," Jim continued as he ticked off the points on his fingers, "we estimated the cleanup job based on what we know now, which is enough for a rough first cut.

"Third, we estimated the likelihood that a cleanup will be needed at all.

"Fourth, we estimated our chances of winning the cleanup job given that we do the assessment and given that we don't. The difference is the increased probability of getting the cleanup job as a function of winning the assessment contract.

"Fifth and finally—which is a good thing because I don't have any more fingers—we applied the last two probability factors to the estimated cleanup profit. That told us how much the future prospect of that job is worth. This, in turn, is how much we can afford to cut our assessment bid and still, on a probability basis, come out ahead in the long run."

[6] See Decision 1 under Exercises for "Envoyance: The First Meeting" in Chapter 2, p. 65.

"That's a great process—it sounds like something Professor Khan does in our business strategy course! I do have two questions, though," continued Sandra. "Did you use a computer to help you, and did you finally bid what this approach suggested?

"We did use computers, but only in a limited sense," Jim responded. "We used some simple spreadsheets to estimate the costs of the assessment and cleanup jobs, given estimates of the resources they would take and how much each resource costs. This is our standard estimating procedure, and we've gotten pretty good at it. We've got templates on disk that include our standard labor categories, the most common subcontracting categories, and the hourly rates for all of these. We factored in the probabilities with a calculator.

"As for your second question: No, we didn't take the answer as our bid. It turned out that the cleanup job, with any reasonable assumptions we could make, is huge compared with the assessment work. Even a fraction of its profit swamped the assessment costs. We could have justified giving the assessment away. In fact, the numbers would have justified paying Oxbow to let us do it."

"You obviously couldn't do *that*," Doug stated as the others nodded agreement, "so what *did* you do?"

"Basically, we went in at our direct cost with no markup, no profit margin, and no contribution to overhead. We feel that it's important to be able to justify our bids, line by line and number by number, to our prospects. We bid the lowest figure we could justify to them if they asked us to."

"How did they react?"

"We don't really know yet. Bids were due on the 10th and we haven't heard since then. We would have heard by now if we had been thrown out in their initial screening, but that was never too likely. The initial screening is where their contract administrator makes sure we filled out all the forms and that we have all the right sections in our proposal. We didn't really expect to be rejected for anything like that."

"Assuming you get picked, what next?"

"As I said earlier, we'll need to pick a project manager. Actually, we'll need to pick a whole team, perhaps including some subcontractor help. In this case we picked some of the specialized subcontractors in advance and included them with our bid. We try to do that all the time, but it doesn't always work out smoothly. Staff planning is always a challenge. We're trying to hire, but there aren't a whole lot of qualified environmental engineers out there looking for jobs."

"To change the subject," interposed Doug, "can we talk about the Mitona Creek cleanup? For instance, what sort of decisions does a project like that involve?

"Once we get started on a project, the staffing decisions are hopefully nailed down. We're left with the technical decisions: what processes and materials to use, how far to dig, and so on. Some of these get settled at the assessment stage, but we still have to be able to modify the plan as we get into the cleanup and uncover new information.

"Making these decisions accurately often involves formulas and equations that describe, for instance, how quickly a given pollutant seeps through a given type of soil. I have—actually, all of us here have—some PC programs that deal with the simple cases. Once you get into unusual ones, like odd-shaped rock domes beneath the surface, it takes a lot of computing power. It also helps to understand PDEs—"

"PD what?"

"PDEs, partial differential equations. Mathematicians use them to describe things that change along more than one dimension at a time. Don't worry; you won't have to know anything about them."

"That's a relief!"

"Anyhow, we have two gurus here who solve PDEs for fun. Even if I could work through a set myself, they know six ways to solve them where I muddle through with the one I learned in college. Chances are they can pick one that will be an order of magnitude faster once they know the specific problem they're dealing with. It's worth going to them for the time savings—my time and the computer time."

"That covers quite a range of decisions: pricing, staffing, and highly technical calculations," said Doug. "Can we generalize from you to the other engineers at Envoyance?"

"As far as the generalists go, 90 percent of the basic issues are similar," answered Jim. "The technical specialists each have their own particular problems. The issues a biologist faces don't have much in common with what a hydrogeologist would worry about."

"They'll be meeting one or two of our technical experts down the road," Dan put in as he returned for his meeting with Jim. "From the number of pages they've just covered with notes, it sounds like you've given them a lot to chew on for now!"

Exercises

1. List the databases that would be used in all the DSS described in this episode, the models that would be used, the person or people who would be responsible for maintaining them, and the type of networking that would be required.
2. What development approach would you use to developing a DSS for proposal bid pricing? A DSS for deciding how to clean up situations such as Mitona Creek?
3. Envoyance has developed a DSS that compares alternative cleanup approaches for situations such as Mitona Creek. It incorporates, among other features, three alternative numerical methods for solving partial differential equations. How should its user interface differ, depending on whether Jim or one of the two "gurus who solve PDEs for fun" is to be its user? How would you design the user interface for the system to be used by either?
4. Suggest a way in which the creek cleanup DSS could use virtual reality.

Chapter 6 DSS Software Tools

Chapter Outline

Introduction

A decision support system is an information system. It uses the same building blocks as any other information system. However, it uses them in specialized ways that the DSS builder must be aware of. This chapter covers what you have to know about software for DSS, with emphasis on the types of software that are especially useful for decision support purposes, without trying to repeat what you already know from your introductory MIS course.

Chapter Objectives

After you have read and studied this chapter, you will be able to:

1. Outline four methods of obtaining a DSS, and explain how the choice among them depends on organization size and problem uniqueness.
2. Identify the types of database management systems and their usefulness in decision support applications.
3. Discuss how Structured Query Language (SQL) can retrieve information for decision support.
4. Describe the types of specialized languages used to build decision support models, to perform statistical analyses, to forecast future values of important business variables, and more.
5. Identify what programming languages are used for DSS and why fourth-generation languages are popular for this purpose.
6. Briefly explain how programs written in one leading 4GL look and work.

6.1 DSS Software Categories

There are four fundamental ways to obtain any software capability: to purchase a turnkey package, to customize a package, to use specialized tools or "generators" designed for the task at hand, or to write the necessary programs from scratch in a suitable language. Since a decision support system is software, these approaches apply to DSS as well. The choice between packages (customized or not) and custom software usually depends on two factors:

- The degree to which your needs resemble those of many other organizations. This determines the likelihood that software developers will have found the market for the capability you need attractive enough to develop packages.
- The financial impact of the application, which determines the value of even a small difference between the capability you want and those available in standard packages. The size of your organization is a factor here. A system that costs $300,000 and that could increase the profits of General Motors by 1 percent of gross sales would be a wise investment. The same $300,000 investment would not be advisable if the result was to be the same (proportionate) 1 percent of sales increase in the profits of Sid's and Suzie's Sandwich and Soda Shoppe.

  The reason size is a factor is that the development cost of a computer program is only loosely related to the size of the organization that will use it. If S&SS&SS has gross sales of $100,000 a year, General Motors is approximately 100,000 times its size by that measure. GM's payroll, inventory, etc., are more complex than Sid's and Suzie's, but not 100,000 times more complex. The ratio of application benefit to cost therefore goes up with the size of the organization.

  As another example of this phenomenon, consider the system that American Express uses to help its staff members decide whether or not to authorize a credit purchase. It cost many hundreds of thousands of dollars to develop this system, not including the cost of deploying it across the firm. This development expense was justified because of the enormous annual credit volume, and the correspondingly large potential losses, of the American Express credit card business. Allen's Hardware annual credit losses on its charge accounts, even if they could be eliminated in full by a computer system, wouldn't justify the same expenditure.

These factors, and the areas where each approach is usually applicable, are shown graphically in Figure 6–1. This suggests that you should look toward standard packages and tools where your application is common to many firms or where your firm is small. If your application is unique and

FIGURE 6–1

Graph of Application Uniqueness versus Company Size

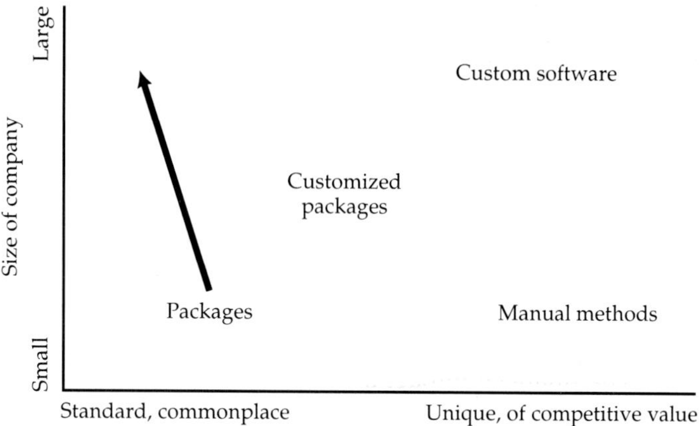

your organization is large, consider custom development. Below that part of the graph, in medium-sized organizations and for applications with some standard features, customized packages play a part.

If your application is unique and your firm is small, you may have to forego a computer-based DSS unless you can find a creative way to reduce its cost. A few such possibilities are:

- Develop a system for future resale to other firms with similar needs. In a well-known example, the Mrs. Field's Cookies chain developed outstanding software to forecast cookie demand as a function of time of day, day of week, weather, holidays, store location (business street, shopping mall), etc., and then recouped much of its cost by going into the software business.

  There is a business decision to be made here: If we resell the package, will we not aid our competitors? If your firm can keep the package secret and thus sustain the competitive edge that it provides, it would be unwise to sell the package. In most cases, however, if the concept of a DSS is valuable, others will develop similar software as soon as word of it gets out, and your competitors will be able to obtain the capability whether or not your firm decides to sell its software. You cannot prevent them from doing so. You can only give them the option of paying you for the software instead of paying another supplier.
- Sharing the cost with similar firms that do not compete directly with yours, either because their lines of business are not quite the same as yours or because another factor, such as geographic sales territories, limits competition.

- Finding information system students who will develop your system as a term project. A small family-owned ice-cream shop on Cape Cod uses a sophisticated demand forecasting and supply ordering program of which any large firm would be proud—because one of its owners' children needed a senior project in operations management.
- Working with software suppliers who believe that your experience will help them penetrate a new market.
- Finding a software developer—perhaps a startup firm—who needs user assistance in developing a new program and who will in turn work with you to apply that program to your needs.
- Persuading one of your larger suppliers to develop the program for later licensing to you and to their other customers.

This list barely scratches the surface. The moral: Don't let lack of resources deter you from obtaining computer-based decision support capabilities without trying to "brainstorm" a creative way out of your difficulties.

6.2 Standard Packages

Standard packages to help make specific decisions have been developed for a few common decisions.

Scan the back pages of any microcomputer magazine. You're sure to find several ads for investment software. This software can generally dial up an on-line financial information service on a schedule you specify (usually daily), put the current prices of stocks you're interested in into its database, create a variety of performance charts, and recommend what you should buy or sell. Such programs follow the "technical" approach to stock price prediction: They predict future price behavior from past trading patterns. The "fundamentals" approach requires analysis of products, management, and future earnings potential, making it less amenable to automation.

The characteristics of this decision that make it attractive to package suppliers are

- Many people make these decisions; that is, the potential market is large.
- The decision has financial importance to many of these people.
- The underlying factors are the same for all of them. (Individual investors vary in the importance they attach to different performance measures and in the set of stocks of potential interest, but a price-volume chart is a price-volume chart to them all.)
- The support infrastructure—public databases designed to provide the necessary data to anyone for a small fee—already exists.

Decisions having these characteristics are, unfortunately, rare, and especially so in the business world. Where they exist, and where companies have developed DSS to help with them, these companies often do not want to give away their secrets to their competitors. The likelihood of your finding a ready-to-use package that will give you meaningful help with a business decision is next to zero. What you *can* find is a large number of tools that you can combine to create the decision support capability you need. We therefore turn to those next.

6.3 Specialized Tools and Generators

While few decision support applications are sufficiently general to justify the development of packages that do nothing else, many DSS applications do have common features. *DSS tools* and *DSS generators* allow DSS developers to utilize standardized "building blocks," which support these common features, to develop their own custom applications. As a potential DSS developer, you should be aware of the tools that are available so you can choose the best one for your needs on each project.

The terms "DSS tool" and "DSS generator," both quite common in the DSS literature, create a great deal of confusion. As Sprague originally conceived them [SPRA80, SPRA82; discussed in SILV91, p. 201ff], DSS tools would generally be used to create DSS generators, which in turn would generate the specific DSS used by decision makers. He associates the use of DSS tools in this sense with the toolsmith role discussed in Section 5.2. The use of DSS generators is associated with the higher level, more business-oriented, roles.

The proliferation of customizable packages such as spreadsheet programs has made this approach less the order of the day than it once was. (It wasn't universal in 1980 either. Part of Sprague's message was that it ought to be.) Adapting Sprague's concepts to the 1990s, we can say that a DSS generator will usually have the capability to become or to create an entire DSS. The software that supports a financial modeling programming language, such as the IFPS language that we discuss in Section 6.3.3, would be a generator. A blank spreadsheet package, before we insert formulas and macros, would usually be considered a generator as well. A DSS tool deals with part of the DSS but not all of it. A graphing package that graphs data from some other source, and is useless without such a source, would be a DSS tool. So would database management systems, if we consider them as tools for organizing and accessing data without the higher level capabilities, such as end-user query packages, that are often sold along with them.

The major categories of specialized software used to assist DSS development are

1. Database management packages.
2. Information retrieval (query and reporting) packages.
3. Specialized modeling packages (including spreadsheets) and languages.
4. Statistical data analysis packages.
5. Forecasting packages.
6. Graphics packages.

These are described in the following sections.

6.3.1 Database Management Systems

A *database management system* allows users to store data in an organized form and retrieve it on the basis of specified selection criteria [BRAD87, COUR88]. Products within this broad category range from under $100 to over $100,000, with a correspondingly wide range of features and capabilities. However, "more expensive" does not always mean "better for the specific purpose at hand."

The simplest so-called "database managers" do not, according to computer scientists, deserve this name. (We noted this briefly in a footnote in Chapter 4.) To a database expert, one critical defining characteristic of a true database is its ability to integrate data from several files: for example, pulling out lists of students with unpaid bills from one file, their schedules from another, their instructors' office addresses from a third in order to send notices to the students' instructors alerting them to the situation. Many microcomputer-based packages, such as pfs:File for character-mode MS-DOS and FileMaker for Macintosh and Microsoft Windows, can only deal with one file at a time. In the interests of technical accuracy we will call such one-file-at-a-time programs *file managers* or *data managers* here. You should expect to hear many end users refer to these programs as database managers, especially those whose computing experience has been primarily with desktop machines.

Data managers can be quite useful as personal filing systems, allowing a decision maker to recall data quickly when it is needed to make a decision. In the DSS spectrum of Section 4.1, data managers are file drawer systems. The more capable ones can calculate totals, averages, trends, and more on selected data elements from a file. These capabilities bring them up to the category of data analysis systems.

Data managers can also be used as a "back end" to a system in a higher category. For example, a data manager could supply input to a model that calculates the results to be expected from a particular marketing program aimed at selecting customers from a list. When the data manipulation requirements of such a high-level DSS are modest, data managers provide an easy way to meet them. If one is willing to get involved in custom programming, it is perfectly practical to process data from multiple files even if one's data accessing package can only work with one at a time. In most cases, however, if the application calls for integrating data from more than one file, it's a good idea to start with a tool that can handle the job.

Moving up from data managers, we come to full-fledged database managers that can associate records from several files with each other. Using such a system, a decision maker could (for example) see what percentages of the motors in vacuum cleaners returned for warranty work last year came from each supplier, versus the percentage of motors that each supplier provided overall. If one vendor supplied only 5 percent of all vacuum cleaner motors but its motors were responsible for 30 percent of the warranty claims, a purchasing manager might decide not to get more motors from that firm or to insist on documented quality improvements before any more purchases.

Any database reflects a conceptual *data model.* The data model specifies the entities about which the database contains data and the ways in which these entities are related. The data model is often illustrated as an *entity-relationship diagram (ERD).* Figure 6–2 shows such a diagram for part of a college bookstore database. According to this diagram, the database contains data on courses, textbooks, and authors. The crows'-feet and circles at the ends of the line describe the nature of the relationships among the entities:

- Each department offers zero or more courses. (Some "departments" may be administrative conveniences that do not offer courses.)
- Each course is offered by one department. (Our database design does not allow for joint course offerings. One reason for developing an entity-relationship diagram is that it makes this type of assumption explicit and visible.)
- Each course has zero or more textbooks. (This covers all the possibilities.)
- Each textbook is used for zero or more courses. (We store data on all texts used in the recent past because they might be used again.)
- Each textbook has one or more authors. (This is an assumption. It may not always be appropriate.)
- Each author wrote one or more textbooks. (We do not store data on potential authors or on authors of books in which we have no interest.)

The entity-relationship diagram also shows the attributes of each entity. The example in Figure 6–2 shows a few of these attributes. Attributes that identify the entity, also called *key attributes,* are underlined.

The ERD of the entire database would be far more complex—courses are divided into sections, each section has an instructor, courses are taught during terms (important because FIN 301 may have different instructors and textbooks in different terms), etc. However, the same concepts apply as the diagram expands to include these.

FIGURE 6–2

College Bookstore Entity-Relationship Diagram

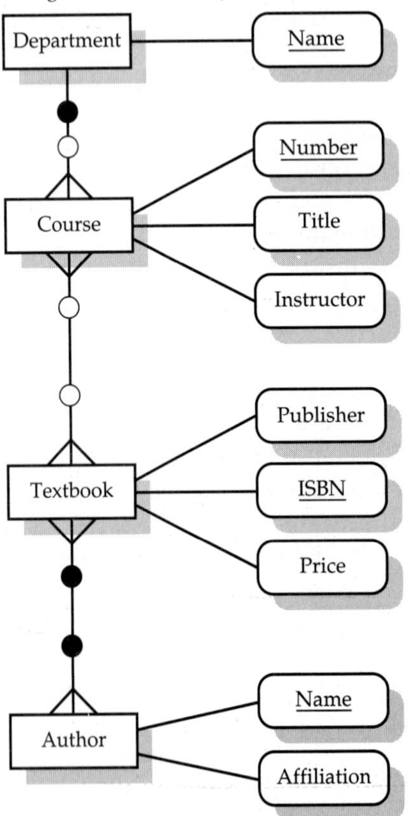

You will encounter data models in (at least) these ways as a DSS developer. They are listed in increasing order of the technical demands they place on you:

1. Data models, ideally, describe the relationships among business data independently of how it might be stored in a computer [FINK89, SCHE92]. Using them will help you understand the business data that your DSS will use. For this purpose you need not be precise about the formal, technical aspects of entity-relationship diagramming. However, as we saw in the above example, it is important to be quite precise about the business relationships that it conveys.

2. Your DSS uses an existing database. Examining its data model, presuming it exists (it should!) is a good way to understand what it contains and how its elements are interrelated.

3. Your DSS must present its users with different views of an existing database. Drawing their ERDs is a good way to understand what data must

be extracted from the database and to communicate this understanding to your system's users.

4. You must design a database for your DSS. Database design should always begin with a conceptual data model, usually expressed as an ERD. Database management courses and books can teach you what you have to know for this purpose.

Database managers are categorized according to the way in which they organize their data. There are three basic database structures: hierarchical, network (or CODASYL), and relational.

A *hierarchical* database manager links records of different types in a strict hierarchy from top to bottom, as shown in Figure 6–3. Each record, except those at the top level, is associated with a specific parent record. Each parent record can have several child records of different types. The linkages are made via pointer fields in the records in question. The pointer fields are defined as part of each record when the database is defined. (While they occupy storage and hence must be taken into consideration in calculating database space requirements, they do not appear as part of the user-visible record format.) Records can only be linked where predefined pointers exist. In the example of Figure 6–3, it would be difficult to find a doctor with a given specialty who lives in the same town as a particular patient.

The earliest mainframe database management system (DBMS) followed the hierarchical model. Most popular low-end microcomputer database managers, such as the dBase family, are of this type as well. A hierarchical structure is well suited to representing simple data structures, such as customer/invoice/line item. It is weaker in handling more complex relationships, such as many-to-many relationships. In the example of Figure 6–3, a hierarchical database could not deal easily with a situation in which each

FIGURE 6–3

Hierarchical Database Example

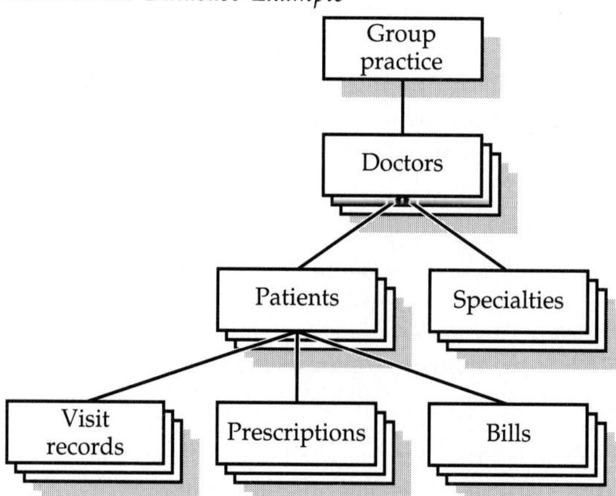

doctor can have several patients (as in the figure) and each patient can also have several doctors (not as in the figure).

A *network* database structure provides more flexibility in the way different files are linked. (The use of the term "network" to describe a database structure does not refer to data communication networks. A database whose parts are spread over a communication network is called a distributed database, not a network database.)

Figure 6–4 shows an example of a network database structure. Here, a "product" is associated with several higher level entities: the invoice on which it was sold, the warehouse in which it is stored, and the supplier from which it was obtained. Several of these relationships can be many-to-many: a warehouse contains multiple products, and a widely used product can be stored in several warehouses. An invoice can be for several products, and a product may appear on more than one invoice. A supplier may supply several products, and a product may come from more than one supplier. The diagram uses the common convention of an arrowhead to indicate the "many" end of a relationship. The only single-valued relationship here is the one between invoices and customers: a given invoice is associated with one—and only one—customer.

Compared with hierarchical DBMS, network DBMS software is more complicated because its pointers must be able to represent more complex data structures. A large-scale network DBMS usually requires a full-time database administrator. Most mainframe DBMS in use today are of this type.[1] Many network DBMS follow the *CODASYL* (COnference on DAta SYstems Languages) standard. Such databases are often referred to as CODASYL databases.

A *relational* DBMS stores its data in the form of two-dimensional tables as shown in Figure 6–5.[2] There are no pointers in the records of a relational database. (They may exist behind the scenes, often in an index created by a database administrator to improve performance on common actions, but they are not user visible, and users can proceed as if they did not exist.) Rather, the database management software links records from several tables by matching corresponding fields. This is the greatest strength and the greatest weakness of the relational model: a strength because information retrieval is not constrained to predefined links, a weakness because the links must be created (at least in theory) each time they are used. In this example, if a night tele-

---

[1]You may hear that IBM's widely used IMS mainframe DBMS is hierarchical. Its early versions were, but IMS has supported the network database structure for years.

[2]Many people, especially those whose computing experience is only with microcomputers, think the word "relational" comes from the ability of a database to relate files, so any database that can deal with multiple files is relational. This is incorrect. This term comes from the mathematical concept of a *relation*. In essence, it means that all data elements in a record relate to the same entity. This error is even found in DBMS ads and sales literature (perhaps because "relational" sounds good), and some otherwise knowledgeable authors have fallen into this trap.

FIGURE 6–4

Network DBMS Example

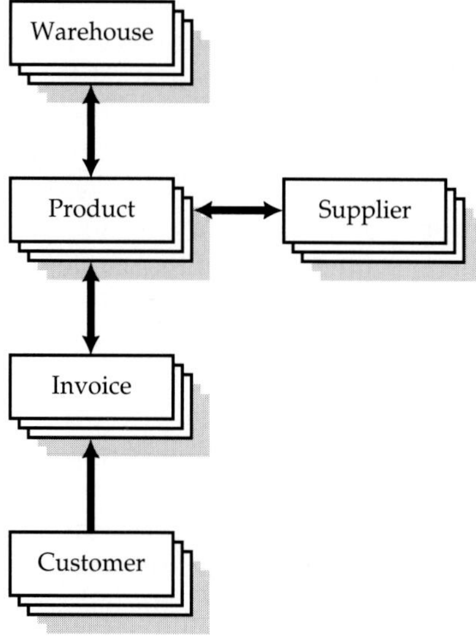

FIGURE 6–5

Relational DBMS Example

Doctor Table

Name	*Specialty*	*Home Town*	*Phone Number*
Jones	Hematology	San Jose	408-555-9876
Kelly	Cardiology	Fremont	510-555-1234

Patient Table

Name	*Insurance*	*Home Town*	*Complaint*
Smith	Blue Goose	Mountain View	Sniffles
Wilson	Improvident	Fremont	Heartburn
Davis	None	Santa Clara	Tonsilitis

phone operator responding to a call from Wilson wants a cardiologist who lives in Wilson's home town, Dr. Kelly's name can be found easily—without having to find out where Wilson lives and then searching the database for cardiologists living in Fremont.

Relational DBMS were developed after the other two types, coming into commercial use in the 1980s. Minicomputers were also coming into commercial use at about this time. Most minicomputer DBMS therefore follow the relational model today. Relational DBMS were slow to catch on with microcomputers because early microcomputers lacked the processing power to handle them with acceptable response times. As microprocessors became more powerful, relational DBMS came into use at the desktop. At the mainframe level, users' decades of investment in network DBMS prevent rapid conversion to the relational approach, but surveys of mainframe users' future purchase plans point to a move in this direction.

Relational DBMS are better suited to DSS applications than are the other types. This is because their records do not contain predefined links to associated records in other files. This provides them with greater flexibility in retrieving data based on previously unplanned criteria. If a market planner wants a list of all customers located in cities that have a warehouse in them, a relational database can satisfy the query easily. Answering the same query with a hierarchical or network database would require either predefined links from warehouse records to customer records or a special program. Neither of these is within the capability of the typical end user.

A second advantage of relational DBMS is that their retrieval operations inherently return the set of all records satisfying a given set of conditions. Other DBMS return one record and require programming to get more than one, although some DBMS packages include query capabilities to handle this programming for common cases. Since many decisions involve looking at or summarizing many records, the set orientation of a relational DBMS is helpful.

A final advantage of relational DBMS is interface standardization. SQL (Structured Query Language, often pronounced "sequel") is used by all major relational DBMS vendors [AGEL88]. While SQL is not fully standardized and while existing SQL standards do not address all aspects of database manipulation, partial standardization is better than none. Translators exist to allow applications written for one relational DBMS to access others. Apple Computer's Data Access Language (DAL), for example, allows users of Apple Macintosh microcomputers to access many popular relational DBMS. The Macintosh user or application program creates a data access request in the DAL language. The DAL processor translates it into the particular dialect of SQL used by the target database. This is possible only because all SQL variants share the same fundamental underlying concepts. Since DSS must often obtain and correlate data from several preexisting transaction processing systems, this ability to access a variety of different DBMS is important. Similar products exist for many other platforms, such as DataLens for importing data from many sources into Lotus 1-2-3 under MS-DOS.

A fourth type of database management system, which is entering commercial use in the 1990s, is the *object-oriented* DBMS. Object-oriented DBMS store information about objects: entities that an application treats as units. We'll discuss object-oriented technology concepts in Chapter 16.

6.3.2 *Information Retrieval Packages*

Information retrieval packages can either be included as part of a DBMS-based system or sold separately. DBMS suppliers, mindful of the difficulties inherent

Data Retrieval for Decision Support Using SQL

Suppose we have two tables in our employee database. One gives employee names, numbers, and home towns. The second gives employee numbers and the languages that the employee speaks:

EMPDATA Table

EMPNO	NAME	TOWN
101	Able	Arlington
102	Baker	Bedford
103	Chan	Concord
104	Dinsmore	Dracut
105	Exley	Everett

EMPLANG Table

EMPNO	LANGUAGE
101	French
101	Spanish
102	German
103	Chinese
103	Russian
104	Italian
104	French

Getting an employee list with addresses is simple:

```
SELECT NAME, TOWN FROM EMPDATA
```

To get the same list, aphabetically by employee name:

```
SELECT NAME, TOWN FROM EMPDATA ORDER BY NAME
```

Finding out how many different towns our employees live in is a bit more complex:

```
SELECT COUNT (DISTINCT TOWN) FROM EMPDATA
```

We can combine, or *join* in relational terminology, two tables to learn which of our employees speak, say, French. This might be helpful in picking someone for an overseas assignment or, perhaps less interestingly to the employee, to escort a group of French visitors through our factory:

```
SELECT NAME FROM EMPDATA, EMPLANG
WHERE EMPLANG.LANGUAGE = 'FRENCH'
AND EMPDATA.EMPNO = EMPLANG.EMPNO
```

The second line specifies that we want only the numbers of those employees who speak French. The third line joins the two tables, using their common employee number field, to give us the names corresponding to those employee numbers: Abel and Dinsmore.

As a final example, suppose we want to find out which of our employees speaks more than one language: [Note that indented lines would in reality be a continuation of the line(s) above.]

```
SELECT NAME FROM EMPDATA, EMPLANG
WHERE EMPDATA.EMPNO = EMPLANG.EMPNO
AND EMPNO = (SELECT DISTINCT EMPNO)
      FROM EMPLANG FIRST
      WHERE EXISTS SELECT *
      FROM EMPLANG SECOND
      WHERE FIRST.EMPNO = SECOND.EMPNO
      AND FIRST.LANG NOT = SECOND.LANG)
```

continued

concluded

This query goes through the EMPLANG table twice for each entry in the table. In the outer loop, it goes through the table once and finds the employee number and language. It then executes the inner loop for each row of the table. In the inner loop, it scans the entire table for instances of the same employee number (next-to-last line) with a different language (last line). It records all it finds, eliminating (because of the keyword DISTINCT on the third line) duplicate employee numbers. Once it has the desired list of employee numbers, it uses the EMPDATA table to translate them to names: Abel, Chan, and Dinsmore.

You can see how SQL, deceptively simple in easy examples, gets difficult quickly for complex queries. Queries that are not carefully planned can also run for a very long time. The execution time of this last example grows with the square of the EMPLANG table. If this table has 1,000 rows, the DBMS will make a million comparisons. That's not too bad, but "industrial-strength" DBMS may have many million rows. Queries that perform trillions of comparisons are best avoided. A "back of the envelope" execution time estimate, done by a trained analyst in a few seconds or minutes, should be undertaken whenever an end-user query runs for what seems to be a long time without results. Quite often, it will show that the results would not appear for another month, or before the user retires. If the query is important, proper database organization—again a task for a trained professional—can usually make its execution time acceptable.

in end-user attempts to access a database via SQL, vie with each other for the best offering in this area. Many information retrieval packages combine both capabilities: They incorporate their own database management capability but can access data stored by other DBMS as well.

The strength of a good information retrieval package lies in its combination of power and ease of use. Power, in this context, refers to the ability to specify complex queries. Ease of use means that end users can master the package, or enough of the package to obtain the results they need, without getting a graduate degree in computer science. As we just saw, SQL provides power in the hands of a trained professional but not ease of use. Simple microcomputer-based packages provide ease of use but not power. The challenge to the developer of an information retrieval package lies in combining the two. Since specialized information retrieval packages compete with the query capabilities built into most DBMS packages, they must offer more than database management systems offer in at least one of those two areas if they are to find a market.

Information retrieval packages, whether built into a DBMS or obtained separately, provide three data accessing capabilities:

- Select: the ability to choose the records that will be displayed (or graphed, or totaled, etc.). We used selection to obtain the names of employees who speak French but not those who speak other languages in the previous example.

- Join: the ability to combine information from two record types. We used this capability when we obtained the name of an employee from one table and the languages that he or she speaks from another.
- Project: the ability to specify which data fields are to be retrieved. We used projection when we printed out only the names of employees who speak French, not their home towns.

These capabilities are independent of database organization: They apply to hierarchical and network databases as well as relational. However, their visualization and their implementation are often more natural in a relational database environment.

Information retrieval packages provide interfaces by which end users can invoke these capabilities without knowing SQL or a similar retrieval language. This interface first displays the files or tables that it is able to access. The user specifies which ones are of interest. The software then uses the data dictionary of the DBMS to obtain a list of the fields in each record. The user indicates which fields are to be retrieved (projection) and what conditions are to be applied to them (selection).

In a hierarchical or network database environment, joins are implied by the pointers that were defined for the database and will be used automatically if the user specifies fields that span more than one record. In relational DBMS, the user must also specify the fields that are to be matched in creating a join. A good information retrieval package will suggest suitable fields—perhaps because their names match or because their data types match—and warn a user who requests a seemingly improper join. Graphically oriented information retrieval packages may let a user specify a join by dragging the on-screen pointer from a field in one table to a matching field in another.

6.3.3 *Specialized Modeling Languages*

As we noted earlier, many DSS incorporate models of various types. Models of a given type tend to have many characteristics in common. For that reason, standard packages have been developed to deal with many popular types of models. These packages do not incorporate any models themselves. They simply make it easier for the user to define the characteristics of his or her model to the computer. This section deals with languages used for financial, or accounting, models. We'll discuss dynamic discrete-event models, including an example of the specialized language GPSS, in Chapter 9.

The term "accounting model," which we introduced in Chapter 4, refers to a static model with no uncertainty. As we mentioned there, the familiar spreadsheet is the standard tool with which most knowledge workers and managers manipulate accounting models.

A spreadsheet, in its basic form, looks like a two-dimensional grid of cells. Each cell can contain a number, a formula that uses the contents of other cells to yield a number, or text for annotation. Figure 6–6 shows a simple example. Cells A1, A2, A3, and A4 in this spreadsheet contain labels. (In most spreadsheet packages, a label too long to fit into one cell spills over into adjacent ones if they are blank. That is why the label in cell A1 seems to be in cell B1 as well.) Cells B2 and B3 contain constants (numbers). Cell B4 contains the formula "B2 − B3." The spreadsheet program carries out the specified computation and displays the result in the cell. The formula itself can be inspected by switching the spreadsheet to "display formulas" mode or by selecting cell B4, which causes the spreadsheet program to display that cell's formula at the top of the screen.

Most modern spreadsheets can do more than this. They include dozens, often hundreds, of built-in functions for mathematical and business computations: loan amortization, net present value calculations, statistics, and more. They have conditional computation capabilities where different calculations can be carried out depending on the result of a formula. They can create several kinds of graphs automatically from the data they calculate. They may extend the two-dimensional grid to three or more dimensions. They can treat the contents of each row as a simple database, with form-based data entry, sorting, and retrieval. They provide "macros" to automate repetitive procedures. They may have enough formatting capability—font choices, sizes, borders, character attributes, and color—to create finished presentation materials. But the basic concept—an array of cells that contain numbers, text, or formulas—remains as it was pioneered by Visicalc on the Apple II in the late 1970s.

As the spreadsheet is essentially an electronic reproduction of an accountant's and financial analyst's paper-and-pencil tool, it fits the financial analyst's needs well. However, spreadsheets have several disadvantages for this purpose. Consider, for example, the spreadsheet in Figure 6–7. This spreadsheet has one change from that of Figure 6–6: Profits are given as

FIGURE 6–6

Spreadsheet Example

	A	B	C	D
1	INCOME STATEMENT FORECAST			
2	INCOME	$10,000		
3	EXPENSES	$9,000		
4	PROFIT	$1,000		
5				

$2,000, not as $1,000. The error could have been introduced in either of two ways: via an error in the formula used to calculate cell B4 or by simply entering the figure $2,000 into that cell next to the label "Profit." The first cause could result from honest error. A malicious user might use the latter method, knowing that most spreadsheet readers would assume that a number next to such a label was actually calculated from a suitable formula. (While a person is unlikely to introduce a deliberate error into a spreadsheet meant only for his or her use, many spreadsheets are used to recommend or justify decisions to other people.) There is no way to tell by looking at the spreadsheet how the error was introduced.

In the spreadsheet of Figure 6–7, which has three data cells and round numbers, most people would spot this error in a few seconds. In a spreadsheet with 186 rows and 55 columns, full of arcane formulas and complex calculations leading to a nonobvious answer at the bottom right, an equally serious error would not be nearly as noticeable. Spreadsheet packages, however, provide little protection against human error or malice.

Specifically, spreadsheets have (at least!) the following drawbacks:

- Because each cell is independent of every other cell, formulas that are supposed to be identical in several cells are independent of each other. While all spreadsheets provide a "copy" or "replicate" capability to eliminate repetitive typing, the potential for error still exists. This capability does nothing to ensure that the right formula was replicated into the right cells or that the replicated formulas remain identical thereafter. A formula may be correct in one cell but incorrect in an adjacent one that supposedly carries out the same calculation. Modifications made to a spreadsheet after it has been in use for a while are especially likely to cause such errors. People selecting a range of cells to modify, whether with cursor keys or

FIGURE 6–7

Spreadsheet Example of Figure 6–6 with Error

	A	B	C	D
1	INCOME STATEMENT FORECAST			
2	INCOME	$10,000		
3	EXPENSES	$9,000		
4	PROFIT	$2,000		
5				

with a mouse, are prone to going one cell too far or stopping one cell short of the correct position.

- Because formulas are normally hidden from the user and are scattered all over a spreadsheet, it is difficult to ascertain just what is "inside" a spreadsheet by inspecting it. Moreover, data references in a spreadsheet are often in cryptic row-column format, where the referenced cells themselves contain the results of calculations involving yet other cells. Most spreadsheet packages let their users name ranges and use the range name rather than a row-column reference, but spreadsheet developers often find it easier to select a desired range directly on the screen than to go through the range-naming process. (This is, in a way, a negative side effect of GUIs: Users who might have named a range to avoid repetitive entry of its coordinates or the need to select it with cursor keys may find it so easy to select the range with a mouse that they don't go to the trouble of naming it.)
- For both of these reasons, spreadsheets are susceptible to malicious change by anyone with an ax to grind and few ethical scruples about how he or she grinds it.
- The limitations of the basic spreadsheet paradigm, cells containing formulas that direct calculations on data in other cells, are too confining for some applications.

The rest of this section discusses approaches that have been developed to bypass these constraints. To alleviate the first and second of the preceding problems, many firms have turned to software that was developed specifically for financial modeling. The most widely used package of this type is IFPS from Execucom. IFPS runs on most major computing platforms from mainframe to desktop.[3]

The IFPS model in Figure 6–8 shows a corporate income forecast for four years. Figure 6–9 shows the output of this model. It resembles a spreadsheet on the surface. The difference is that the model exists as a separate, easily visible, and easily auditable entity. For example, the last line of the model ensures that every element in the output line labeled "Net Profit" will be calculated from the same formula and shows us what that formula is. It is not possible, by accidental slip of a finger on cursor key or mouse, to copy a revised formula up to but not including the last cell of its intended range. It is also not possible to alter deliberately a formula in one out-of-the-way cell: When the model is listed, there are no out-of-the-way cells.

[3]While most IFPS variants use the name IFPS, perhaps with a suffix indicating its hardware environment, the Macintosh version is called Mindsight. Perhaps Execucom felt that Macintosh users are more "folksy."

FIGURE 6–8

IFPS Model

```
Columns 1993 . . . 1996
Revenues = Price * Units Sold
Price = 150, previous * 1.05
Units Sold = 1000, previous * 1.15
Cost of Goods Sold = Units Sold * Unit Cost
Unit Cost = 100, previous * 1.05
Gross Margin = Revenues - Cost of Goods Sold
Utilities = 4950, previous * 1.05
Overhead = 8250, previous * 1.1
Depreciation = 3025
Selling Expenses = .10 * Revenues
Gen and Admin = .115 * Revenues
EBIT = Gross Margin - sum (Utilities thru Gen and Admin)
Interest Expense = Annual Rate * Debt
Annual Rate = .11
Profit Before Tax = EBIT - Interest Expense
Tax = .46 * Profit Before Tax
Net Profit = Profit Before Tax - Tax
```

FIGURE 6–9

IFPS Financial Model Output Example

	1993	1994	1995	1996
Revenues	150000.00	181125.00	218708.44	264090.44
Price	150.00	157.50	165.38	173.64
Units Sold	1000	1150	1323	1521
Cost of Goods Sold	100000.00	120750.00	145805.63	176060.29
Unit Cost	100.00	105.00	110.25	115.76
Gross Margin	50000.00	60375.00	72902.81	88030.15
Utilities	4950.00	5197.50	5457.38	5730.24
Overhead	8250.00	9075.00	9982.50	10980.75
Depreciation	3025.00	3025.00	3025.00	3025.00
Selling Expenses	15000.00	18112.50	21870.84	26409.04
Gen and Admin	17250.00	20829.38	25151.47	30370.40
EBIT	1525.00	4135.63	7415.62	11514.71
Tax	701.50	1902.39	3411.19	5296.77
Net Profit	823.50	2233.24	4004.44	6217.94

This IFPS model shows some of the basic features of IFPS:

- Output cells are referred to by row and column names. Cryptic letter-and-number cell references do not exist.
- Formulas apply to an entire row unless stated otherwise. Formulas can be applied to part of a row, but this must be stated explicitly in

the model. For example, the Total column is computed differently from the others.

- A backward reference uses the word "previous" instead of an obscure cell reference. If the element taken from the previous column is not on the same row, this must be stated explicitly.

Consider line 4 of Figure 6–7. In English, it instructs IFPS to set the first year's sales to 1,000 units and each subsequent year's sales to 1.15 times the prior year's value. Had a spreadsheet user entered 1.25 rather than 1.15 here, by mistake or by malice, the error would have been hidden in the formulas underlying the output and would have been hard to see in the output alone. (If first quarter sales were 1,458 units rather than a nice, round 1,000, nobody would notice.) In the IFPS model, the 1.15 is clearly shown. Any attempt to override it for one column—say, to nudge predicted 1996 gross margin over $90,000 or to move an R&D project up in a competitive corporate ranking process—would jump out at a glance.

IFPS capabilities include goal-seeking, "what if?" testing of alternatives, and a full set of financial and mathematical functions. Modern spreadsheet programs include these as well. The major difference between financial modeling programs and spreadsheet programs is the way in which the model is set up.

Auditing packages, which are available for the major spreadsheets, help find both accidental and malicious errors in standard spreadsheets. Several studies have shown that spreadsheets in regular business use often contain inadvertent errors. Davies and Ikin examined 19 Lotus 1-2-3 spreadsheets and found that 4 of them had major errors [DAVI87]. Simkin cites a consultant for an accounting firm who found 128 errors in the spreadsheets of only 4 clients [SIMK87]. Some of these spreadsheets were used to make multi-billion-dollar decisions. He also cites the case of a manager in a Florida construction firm who forgot to adjust formula references when he inserted a new row into a spreadsheet, so his firm's bid on a project was over $250,000 lower than it should have been. The firm won the bid but wished it hadn't.[4]

Spreadsheet auditing packages such as The Cambridge Spreadsheet Analyst display all the formulas of a spreadsheet, highlighting items that appear to violate the rules of logic that most correct spreadsheet models follow.[5] They provide a global view of patterns, showing exactly how far a particular formula

[4]The construction firm then sued Lotus Development Corporation, claiming that a Lotus 1-2-3 bug caused its low bid. Upon investigation it proved otherwise. The suit was withdrawn but only after a great deal of time, technical and legal professional work, expense, and publicity on both sides.

[5]For more information on the Cambridge Spreadsheet Analyst, contact Intex Solutions, Needham Heights, Massachusetts.

was replicated: If all the formulas for 1993 were replicated through 1998 except for the one in the Units Sold row, this will be immediately evident. They check for circular references: situations where the formula in one cell uses data in a second cell, whose formula in turn uses the data in the first cell (perhaps with more steps along the way). This is occasionally a useful modeling technique but is usually a mistake. They can provide cross references between cells and formulas in other cells that refer to them: a *trace,* which lists the sources of input to a given cell, and a *probe,* which lists the users of a given cell's output. Spreadsheet auditing package users report that they uncover many previously unsuspected errors, almost universally due to human error and often potentially costly.

Figure 6–10A shows a simple spreadsheet. Unit sales were supposed to grow 5 percent per year from 1993 through 1996. In order to predict higher profits in 1996, someone removed the formula from the 1996 column of the Unit Sales row, where it would have forecasted sales of 1,159 units, and replaced it with the constant 1,200. An auditing package, in this case the Worksheet Auditor macro bundled with Excel, produced the worksheet map shown in Figure 6–10B. It is instantly obvious that cell E5 differs from its predecessors in row E: It contains a numeric constant, not a formula. (A clever person bent on deception, knowing that only this check was to be done, could enter a formula that was precalculated to yield 1200, rather than a constant. Other spreadsheet auditing packages, however, will flag formulas that differ from those in the cells to their left.)

The fourth spreadsheet problem noted above, that its fundamental paradigm does not suit all requirements, is the reason other types of software exist.

FIGURE 6–10A

Spreadsheet with Deliberate Error

	1993	1994	1995	1996
Unit Sales	1000	1050	1103	1200
Unit Price	$1.00	$1.00	$1.10	$1.10
Net Sales	$1,000.00	$1,050.00	$1,212.75	$1,320.00
Expenses	$900.00	$1,000.00	$1,100.00	$1,200.00
Profit	$100.00	$50.00	$112.75	$120.00

FIGURE 6–10B
Audit Map

Map of Worksheet1

	A	B	C	D	E
1					
2					
3		9	9	9	9
4					
5	T	9	F	F	9
6	T	9	9	9	9
7	T	F	F	F	F
8	T	9	9	9	9
9	T	F	F	F	F

LEGEND	
T	Text
F	Formula
9	Number
L	Logical
#	Error

6.3.4 Statistical Data Analysis Packages

Virtually every decision involves an attempt to predict what will happen in the future if a given course of action is chosen. Will I like this restaurant's mustard sauce, or will their Hollandaise taste better? How much will sales increase if we cut our prices by 10 percent?

A fundamental premise of decision making is that the future is in some way tied to factors we can change. By determining how a system—be it our taste buds or a business system—has reacted to these factors in the past, we hope to estimate how it will react in the future and thus gauge the likely outcome of our decisions. These relationships are often statistical. Specialized software helps us deal with the statistics.

The simplest type of prediction is based on regression calculations such as you studied in your statistics classes. Consider Figure 6–11A. It plots average gasoline mileage as determined by Consumers Union versus weight for 48 1992-model-year cars and small vans [CONS92]. There is clearly a relationship: Heavier cars tend to get worse mileage. At the same time, the data points do not all fall on a perfectly straight line, so other factors must be at work as well. Most adults of the late 20th century are sufficiently familiar with automobiles to guess what a few of these might be: engine size, body shape. (Many factors that affect mileage, such as engine condition and tire pressure, are controlled in CU's tests.) By calculating the "best-fit" line through the given points we can accomplish two things:

FIGURE 6–11A

SYSTAT Plot of Vehicle Mileage versus Weight

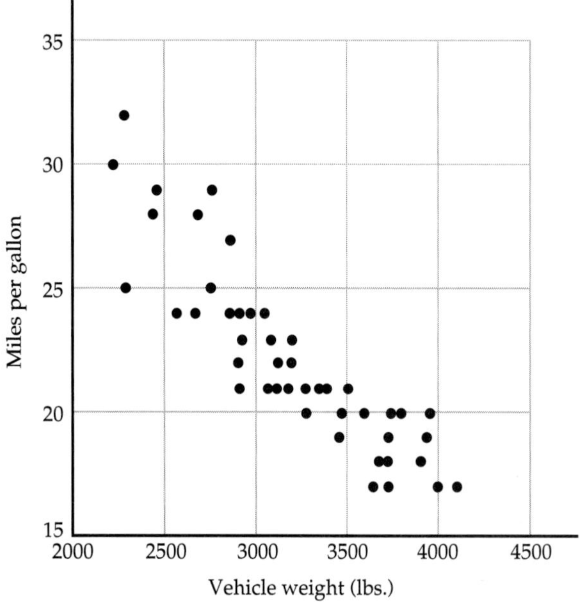

1. We can develop a formula (in this case the equation of a straight line, but a more complex shape if the data or our knowledge of the underlying system suggest one) to predict, approximately, what highway mileage an unknown car of a given weight will obtain. Figure 6–11B shows the same data as Figure 6–11A, with the best linear fit and 95 percent confidence bands added. We can conclude from this chart that an unknown car weighing in at 3,500 pounds is likely to get between 19 and 21 miles per gallon, while a 2,500-pound vehicle is likely to achieve about 27 mpg.

2. We can determine the *correlation* between this estimating formula and the actual mileage figures. That, in turn, tells us statistically how much of the mileage variation from one vehicle to the next is explained by vehicle weight and how much of it must be due to other factors. The correlation between vehicle weight and gasoline mileage, as determined by the Pearson correlation formula, is −0.891. In other words, vehicle weight appears to account for about 89 percent of the variation in fuel consumption, while other factors explain the other 11 percent.

This calculation, by the way, points out an important consideration in using statistical software. SYSTAT provides a number of correlation tools—Pearson, Spearman, Kendall Tau-B, and more—that can produce different results. (Pearson correlation calculations, e.g., can be more susceptible to

FIGURE 6–11B

SYSTAT Plot of Vehicle Mileage versus Weight with Best Linear Fit and 95 Percent Confidence Intervals

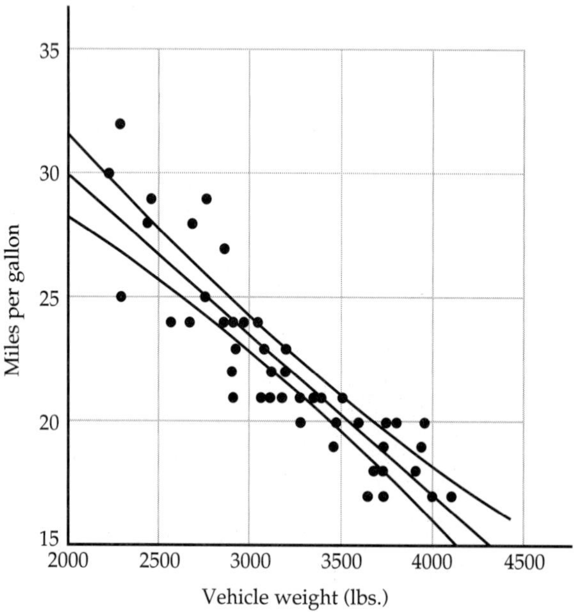

influence by a few outlying points than are Spearman.) And correlation calculations are one of the simpler statistical analyses. The moral: Be sure you know what you're doing with statistics before you use one of these packages. They enable the novice to create a great deal of impressive-looking, laser-printed statistical garbage in short order. If you're incorporating this type of software into a larger decision support system for users who may not be trained in statistics, be sure to provide adequate guidance in the appropriate calculations to perform and how far to trust their results.

As an example of the potential of drawing unwarranted conclusions from the data, consider the statement in the paragraph before the last: ". . . weight appears to account for about 89 percent of the variation in fuel consumption. . . ." The words "appears to" were deliberate. Vehicle weight is itself highly correlated with, at least, engine size (heavier cars need larger engines in order to achieve acceptable performance) and aerodynamic drag (heavier cars tend to be larger). The danger lies in assuming that statistical correlation implies a cause-and-effect relationship. We do not know from the given data how much of the difference in fuel consumption is due to weight and how much to these other factors that tend to go along with weight. If we took a 3,500-pound car which got the typical 20+ mpg, and by use of exotic lightweight materials reduced its weight to 2,500 pounds while making no changes to its engine or its physical bulk, would we get 27 mpg? We don't know. An automobile firm executive who ordered a weight reduction program based on these data, in the expectation of that improvement, would be on shaky ground indeed.[6]

SYSTAT and many competing packages are available in versions to run on most popular microcomputer and larger systems. Most statistical packages allow a decision maker to deal with more than one dependent variable at a time, although it is difficult to show more than one—and impossible to show more than two—via typical graphical output methods.

Statistics packages have other capabilities as well. They can create cross tabulations to analyze data from market research questionnaires as a basis for marketing decisions: How, for example, does pizza consumption vary by age group? Other forms of statistical analysis allow decision makers to identify clusters in data: what types of people buy purple refrigerators, what eating patterns are associated with a particular medical problem. Both of these are well supported by most statistics packages. They also allow users to delve more deeply into aspects of the data that appeal to them. For example, a SYSTAT user can point at the highest mileage point at the top left of Figure 6–11A or 6–11B with the mouse. Upon his or her doing so, the data list will scroll to show the Hyundai Scoupe—rated at 32 miles per gallon—at the top. The same process works on any desired group of data points by selecting a "rope" tool and drawing a line around the points in question. All will be highlighted in the data list.

Computer industry periodicals review and compare statistics software regularly. The four-product review in [FRID90] is typical. He compared four statistics packages for IBM-compatible microcomputers running MS-DOS: Minitab 7.1 (Minitab, State College, Pa.), SPSS/PC+ 3.1 (SPSS, Chicago, Ill.), Statgraphics 4.0 (STSC, Rockville, Md.), and SYSTAT/Sygraph 4.1 (SYSTAT Inc., Evanston, Ill.). He evaluated them in terms of 10 characteristics, which he selected on the basis of extensive experience using this type of software. After using all four to carry out a predetermined set of tasks, he gave them the rankings in Figure 6–12.

We're not showing them here to persuade you that Fridlund's first choice (SYSTAT/Sygraph) is best for you a few years later. For one thing, he didn't review all the packages that exist; for another, the current releases are better; for a third, the ranking depends on what factors matter to you and your users. (Another reviewer, Barry Keating, found that ease of use and ability to handle complex economic statistics were inversely related [KEAT89].) The purpose

---

[6]We also don't know, for that matter, that a correlation isn't due to chance. Out of every 20 statistical correlations that each have less than a 5 percent chance of being due to chance, 1, on the average, *will* be due to chance alone. We can improve the odds by insisting on a higher certainty factor, but we can never totally eliminate chance as a possible cause of a statistical correlation.

FIGURE 6–12
*Statistics Package Comparison Chart**

	Minitab 7.1	*SPSS/PC+ 3.1*	*Statgraphics 4.0*	*SYSTAT/ Sygraph 4.1*
Data management	Satisfactory	Excellent	Satisfactory	Excellent
Analytical capability	Satisfactory	Excellent	Very good	Excellent
Graphics	Satisfactory	Good	Very good	Excellent
Speed	Very good	Very good	Good	Very good
Documentation	Very good	Excellent	Very good	Very good
Ease of learning	Good	Good	Good	Very good
Ease of use	Very good	Very good	Very good	Excellent
Error handling	Poor	Good	Satisfactory	Satisfactory
Support policies	Good	Very good	Good	Very good
Technical support	Excellent	Excellent	Satisfactory	Good

*Data taken from [FRID90].

is to show you the type of information you can expect to find when you have to make this sort of decision. After reading a few reviews, you'll be able to narrow your choice to a small number of packages. You can then purchase these and evaluate them in detail.

As with so many other types of software, many packages that were originally meant for statistical analysis have evolved well beyond that. The SAS system, whose roots go back for decades and which runs on a variety of platforms from several vendors, is an example. Its name originally meant "statistical analysis system," but (like NCR Corporation, whose initials once stood for "National Cash Register") it kept the initials while removing their original, literal meaning. The SAS system still incorporates advanced statistical tools, forecasting methods, time-series analysis, regression and variance analyses, multivariate analysis, spectral analysis, tools for econometric modeling, and optimization methods for operations management. It includes the variety of graphical output methods that one would expect from a dedicated statistics package. However, it has been extended to include data access capability for many popular DBMS, the ability to create easy menu-driven access, and an end-user report generation tool. The result is a package that can be of use to people whose DSS needs include statistical analysis but are not necessarily limited to it.

6.3.5 Forecasting Packages

Forecasting can be defined as predicting the future based on facts known at the present. The word is used to mean two different things in business:

- One type of forecast is a pure prediction of a phenomenon that will take place in the future. This includes a variety of activities, including customer order forecasting and lottery number forecasting (which, according to most experts, doesn't work). This type of forecast is usually based on some type of historical data and statistical trend analysis.

- Another type of forecast is derived from a model of how known (or, perhaps statistically, predictable) factors influence other factors that cannot be predicted as easily.

You can find good descriptions of all types of forecasting commonly used by business managers in any of several books such as [BARR85], [ELLI90], [WEBS86], [WILL87], or [WILS90]. A good source of up-to-date information on forecasting, including real-world case studies, is the quarterly *Journal of Business Forecasting Methods and Systems.*

A common forecasting problem is time-series forecasting. Many phenomena reflect two (or more) underlying trends over time: a long-term, or secular, trend and one or more periodic cycles. Demand for skis, for instance, is seasonal and also responds to the long-term rise and fall in the popularity of skiing over several years or decades. Demand for restaurant tables is affected by the time of day, day of week, and, in locales such as ski resorts, by the season as well. Such trends may also be influenced by external factors, such as the state of the economy.

Developing a time-series forecast involves three steps:

1. Determine the secular trend of the phenomenon in question. The secular trend can often be found, or at least visualized, by a moving average long enough to cover one periodic cycle of the phenomenon. If external factors influence the variable being forecasted, they can be used to adjust the secular trend.

Figure 6–13 shows table reservations at a restaurant, day by day, for a period of five weeks with a seven-day moving average. While individual days vary greatly, showing a strong weekend peak, smoothing out the daily variations by averaging over a week shows longer term trends more clearly.

2. Determine the periodic cycles of the phenomenon. Some phenomena react to more than one cycle: perhaps a weekly cycle, a seasonal cycle, plus some sensitivity to overall business cycles. In this case, it is necessary to identify all the major cycles to which the phenomenon is sensitive.

3. Determine how much of the historical variation in the phenomenon can be explained by these two factors and, hence, how much remains to be explained by other factors. This corresponds to the correlation step in static statistical analysis.

It can be dangerous to trust a forecast too much. All forecasts assume that nothing of importance is going to change from the base period to the period being forecasted. Economic factors caused a drop in airline traffic during the last part of 1980 and the beginning of 1981. No time-series forecast that did not take economic conditions into account could possibly have predicted this drop. A forecast that did attempt to take economic conditions into

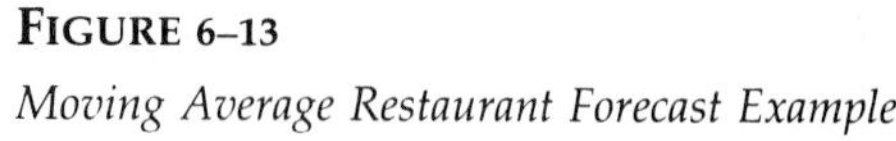

FIGURE 6–13

Moving Average Restaurant Forecast Example

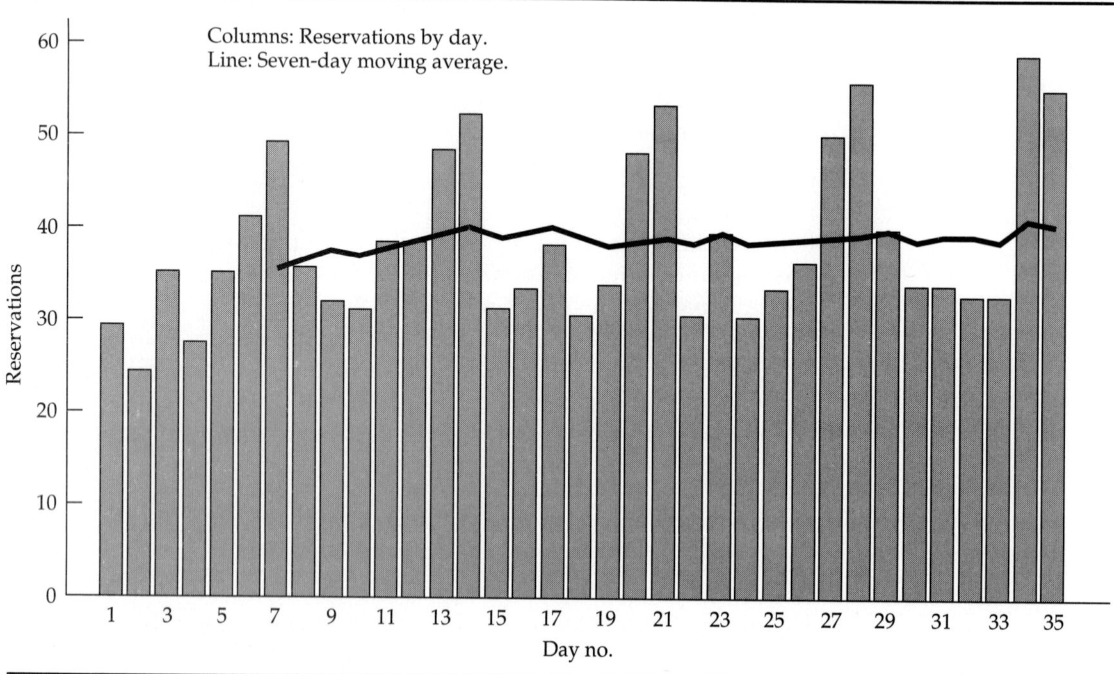

NOTE: This graph might correspond to a newly opened restaurant. A restaurant that had been in business for more than a few months would probably not show much change over a five-week period unless seasonal factors were at work.

account would have been at the mercy of economic forecasters. While economic forecasters' predictions are hardly perfect, to the dismay of managers, politicians, and investors everywhere, they are usually better than nothing.

6.3.6 *Graphing Packages*

Most people assimilate data most readily in the form of a picture. While graphs cannot convey differences among numbers smaller than about 1 percent of their full scale, higher precision is usually wasted in decision support applications. (DSS differ in this respect from transaction processing applications. An accounts payable program that generated supplier checks whose amounts were accurate to within 1 percent or so would not be acceptable.) Most decisions are based on trends or differences that are clearly apparent on a graph.

Today's spreadsheet and statistical data analysis packages include built-in graphing capabilities that suffice for most users' everyday needs. Stand-alone graphing packages offer more options for visual data analysis to those whose needs are more complex. Using such a package is not much harder than using a spreadsheet with its own graphing capability since these packages are all designed to import data in common spreadsheet formats. Getting data from the spreadsheet to the graph requires switching from one program to another and using a system-supplied "clipboard" or an intermediate data file. This is not so complex as to tax the typical PC user because specialized graphic packages are of necessity designed to make it as simple as possible. Data transfer is becoming even simpler as system capabilities, such as Dynamic Data Exchange and Object Linking and Embedding in Microsoft Windows and Publish and Subscribe on the Apple Macintosh, become standard data interchange methods in their respective environments. (These names refer to system-supported capabilities for moving data directly from one application to another.)

Competition has led to rapid improvement in microcomputer spreadsheet package graphing capabilities. The more graphically oriented Microsoft Excel forced Lotus to upgrade the capabilities of Lotus 1-2-3 in this area. Then, Lotus's better integration of graphs with the spreadsheet on which they are based forced a Microsoft response. Meanwhile, other competitors such as Wingz—realizing that there is a limit to users' appetite for still more mathematical functions—tout their graphics features as advantages over the market leaders. While the need for specialized graphing packages is not likely to disappear when the utmost in flexibility and graphical appeal is called for, their applicability will continue to narrow as spreadsheet and statistics packages become better able to satisfy nearly all needs with their built-in capabilities.

Graphing packages, by the way, should not be confused with "graphics packages." (Some people use the term "charting packages" for what we have called graphing packages here to reduce the potential confusion.) There are many software packages on the market whose purpose is to create attractive or useful drawings: for advertising, for publications (such as many of the illustrations in this book), for architecture, for engineering, for training, etc. While graphics packages are important to business, they do not usually have a major role in DSS.

6.4 Programming Languages for DSS

The final approach to DSS development is to write the necessary software from scratch. "From scratch" is a bit of a misnomer here since true "from scratch" software development is a rarity today. Few if any DSS would not take advantage of at least some capabilities listed in the previous section. However, important components of many DSS cannot be satisfied by standard tools and are still written in a programming language of some type.

6.4.1 *Third-Generation Programming Languages*

While so-called experts have been predicting their demise for decades, third-generation languages (3GLs) such as COBOL and Pascal remain the mainstay of system developers in the early 1990s. Despite substantial progress in more advanced languages and standard software packages, most programmers still work at the procedural (3GL) level.

Third-generation languages have the advantage of standardization. Chances are you have been, or will be, exposed to at least one popular 3GL during your academic career. You will then be able to use that language, with a bare minimum of additional system-specific training, on any hardware platform and under any operating system you encounter. In addition, the concepts underlying most 3GLs are close to one another. An experienced Pascal programmer, for example, has a big head start in learning C.

Compilers for popular 3GLs have been refined over the years and produce code that utilizes hardware efficiently. If one is writing a program that will be used regularly by many people over an extended period of time, so that the hardware resources needed to support the application are significant to the organization, hardware resource utilization considerations usually make a 3GL the approach of choice. High-volume transaction processing programs fall into this category.

Efficiency is less of a consideration with most DSS, as we noted in Section 5.2.2 while discussing the two approaches to prototyping. DSS are usually used less intensely: A manager will examine a forecast, think about it, discuss it with a colleague, change a parameter, and then request the computer to generate another forecast. This is quite different from the work of an order-entry clerk who does nothing but enter orders all day long. Furthermore, an organization is likely to have fewer managers who use a DSS than it has employees in computer-intensive jobs. While this doesn't mean a DSS developer should take a "hardware cost be damned" attitude, it is less likely, as a rule, for hardware usage efficiency to be a major factor in the overall cost of a DSS.

The bottom-line impact of DSS usage on the firm is also more substantial than is the impact of most transaction processing applications. No customer will choose a particular supplier because it processes its accounts payable or its payroll especially well. The value of having a new accounts payable or payroll program running a month earlier is therefore relatively small. The value of having a new decision-making tool running a month earlier, by contrast, can be enormous.

The net effect of these considerations is to justify an attitude of "let it be inefficient, just get it to me right away!" on the part of managers who need a DSS. There are exceptions, of course, but they tend to be exceptions. In most cases, the added value of having the DSS available quickly more than makes up for any inefficiencies in how it uses the hardware. For these reasons fourth-generation languages, or 4GLs, are often the approach of choice for DSS development.

6.4.2 Fourth-Generation Programming Languages

The defining characteristic of a fourth-generation language is that its user specifies *what* the computer is to do, not *how* the computer is to do it. Do you need a sales report by region for the past three years? List the items to be reported on, how you want them organized and totaled, and let the 4GL do the work. A COBOL programmer, by contrast, must specify in detail how the program should cycle through the regions and the years and must write the necessary statements to accumulate the desired totals. This process is labor intensive, time consuming, and error prone. Logic mistakes, such as omitting the first or the last item on a list from a total, are often detected only after a program has been in use for months or years. By this time many decisions will have been based on its output.

This small example serves to point out the key differences between 3GLs and 4GLs. The 4GL user is trading off flexibility and run-time efficiency for speed of development. Where the built-in capabilities of the 4GL suffice and where the utmost in machine utilization efficiency is not required, a 4GL can cut application development time by an order of magnitude.

If we evaluate these characteristics in the context of DSS, we find that

- The flexibility of a modern 4GL is usually sufficient to get the job done. Most current 4GLs offer nearly all the flexibility of their COBOL counterparts. Programmers can use complex commands where necessary and still take advantage of 4GL conciseness throughout the vast majority of their code.
- The greater hardware resource utilization of most 4GLs is usually not a major issue with DSS, as they tend to be used by a small user community making decisions having a big financial impact on the organization.
- Quicker application development time is often an important 4GL advantage with DSS. Time spent waiting for the DSS to become available is time during which the best decisions are not being made. It is also often necessary to modify DSS quickly to react to changing conditions. Modifications to transaction processing systems, to respond to changes such as a modification to the tax code or new accounting standards, generally allow more lead time.

For these reasons 4GLs are usually a better DSS development tool than 3GLs. The most widely used 4GL today is Focus.[7] Focus runs on the most popular computing platforms: MS-DOS and Macintosh at the desktop level, VAX VMS and UNIX in the mid-range level, and IBM MVS at the mainframe level. Many other 4GLs exist: some offered by computer system vendors (MAPPER and LINC from Unisys); some from database management system suppliers such as Oracle, Informix, and Progress to work with their DBMS; some, like Mark

[7]Focus is available from Information Builders, Inc., of New York City.

IV from Informatics, originally developed as data extraction and reporting tools and substantially enhanced over the years. The APL language, despite its odd (to the uninitiated) character set and inscrutable statements, has its adherents as well, especially in the financial and investment community.

Figure 6–14 is an example of a program in the 4GL Focus. Figure 6–15 shows its output. This program reads a file SALES and organizes it by store code (called STORE_CODE). For each store it first prints out an informative heading. It then prints a list by product giving the product code, units sold, units rejected (damaged units plus returned units), and percentage of units

FIGURE 6–14

FOCUS Program Example

```
TABLE FILE SALES
HEADING
""PRODUCT SALES REPORT"
"" ''
SUM UNIT_SOLD
COMPUTE
TOT_REJ = RETURNS + DAMAGED;
PCT_REJ/D5.2 = TOT_REJ/UNIT_SOLD * 100;
BY STORE_CODE
BY DATE
BY PROD_CODE
ON STORE_CODE RECOMPUTE PAGE-BREAK
END
```

FIGURE 6–15

One Page of Output Produced by FOCUS Program Example

PRODUCT SALES REPORT

STORE_CODE	DATE	PROD_CODE	UNIT_SOLD	TOT_REJ	PCT_REJ
14Z	10/3	B10	30	5.00	16.67
		B17	20	3.00	15.00
		B20	15	1.00	6.67
		C17	12	.00	.00
		D12	20	5.00	25.00
		E1	30	11.00	36.67
		E3	35	6.00	17.14
*TOTAL STORE_CODE		14Z	162	31.00	19.14

sold that rejects represent. The rejection percentage is printed in a five-character field with two places to the right of the decimal point, as specified after the first slash on line 8 of the program. The other fields, whose formats are not explicitly specified in the program, will be printed in their (wider) standard formats. The program finally prints the total of UNITS_SOLD because it is so directed in the SUM command and carries out the reject computations of the total line as well. It repeats the process for each store until there are no stores left.

Many introductory MIS texts show such a 4GL program with its COBOL equivalent, one or two pages long. The intent is to convince the reader that 4GL programs are shorter than equivalent 3GL programs. Most people find this side-by-side comparison quite convincing.

A program such as the one in Figure 6–14 is still a program. It must follow precise rules of statement order and statement formation. Consider the first line, TABLE FILE SALES. It means that the program is to create a **table** (as opposed to a graph, for example) using data from a **file** called **SALES.** While this line is easy to understand when it is explained, a nontechnical end user can hardly intuit that a Focus program ought to start this way. Businesspeople can learn a 4GL in a one-week workshop, but they will forget all they have learned in a month or two unless they use it regularly on the job. This explains why you may encounter people with similar technical backgrounds (or nontechnical backgrounds) who hold widely differing opinions as to the value of a 4GL to end users.

Because of this natural tendency to forget the details of programming language syntax, most modern 4GLs offer a graphical development interface that handles these nit-picking details via menus and graphical screen painting. Via these developmental tools, Focus under MS-DOS (known as PC Focus) lets you:

- Define a new database, including field names and characteristics. Figure 6–16 shows a database being defined. The user is now choosing a specific format for the field named DATE, which has the alias (alternative name) DTE and has already (in the box you can see part of peeking out under the "Select a date format" box) been specified to contain a date. This box appears automatically as soon as the Date option is chosen for the content of this field. You can see how the various options for date formats are all displayed for the user to choose from. The database definition step is not necessary if an existing database will be used, as Focus can read the data dictionaries of most popular DBMS packages.
- Design attractive data-entry screens, including data validation (numerical values within a range, values on a list, values included in another named file) and context-sensitive help for the operator.
- Create complex database queries via the TableTalk facility. As a query is formulated, Focus displays the actual Focus code (as in Figure

FIGURE 6–16

Database Field Characteristic Definition Screen Shot

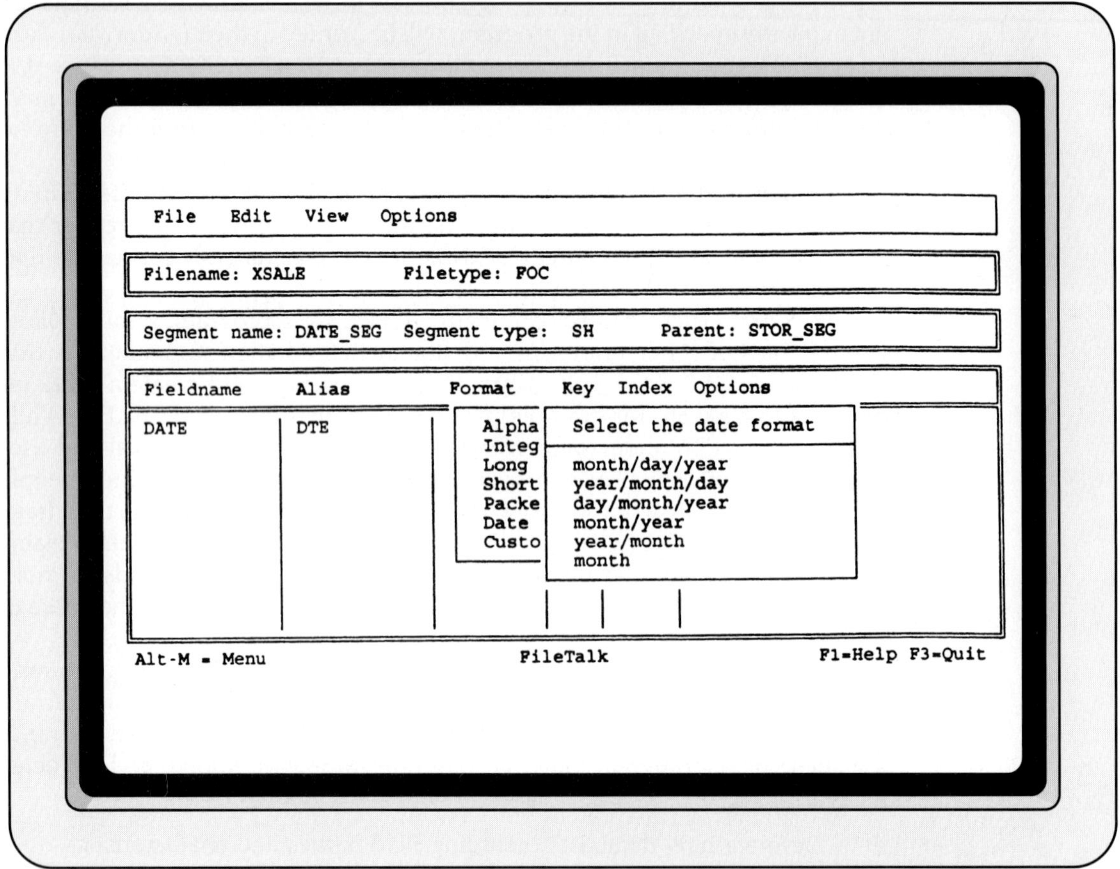

SOURCE: *PC/FOCUS Getting Started* (manual), p. 5-20. Copyright 1993 Information Builders Inc. Used with permission.

6–14) being created in a window at the bottom of the screen. A manager can use this code as a learning aid, modify it if the query is beyond TableTalk's limits, or ignore it. Figure 6–17 shows a user composing a query. At this point the user has identified the file to be used—the same file, SALES, as in the previous example—and is about to specify what is to be printed (actually a generic term for output, as "printing" can go to the user's screen) in the first column of the requested report. The list of options in the left window is longer than what is shown, as indicated by the downward pointing arrow in its top right corner. Options change as the report definition progresses. TableTalk can define reports that join data from several files, sort data, calculate aggregates (sum, count, average, etc.), put in control breaks when a sort variable changes, incorporate page headers and footers, and have any desired format.

FIGURE 6–17

Screen Shot of Query Composition

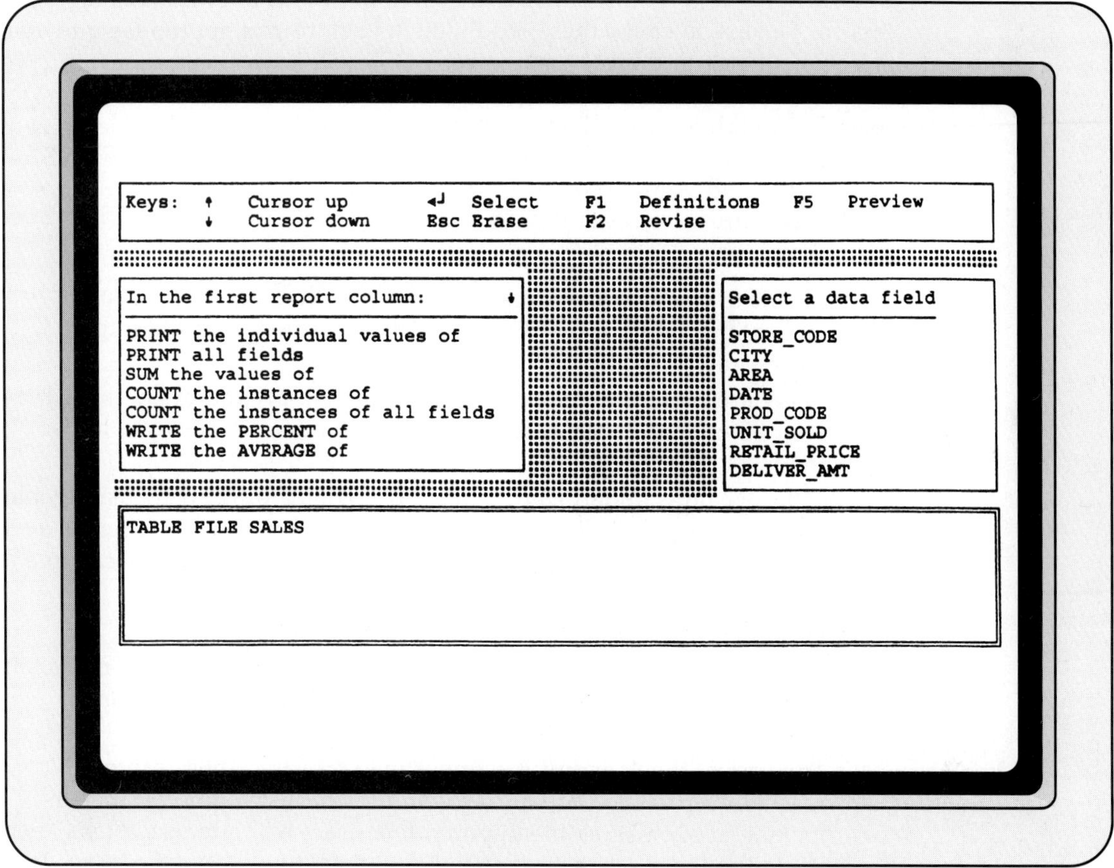

SOURCE: *PC/FOCUS Getting Started* (manual), p. 10–25. Copyright 1993 Information Builders Inc. Used with permission.

- Plot data as a line chart, vertical or horizontal bar chart, scatter diagram, or pie chart.
- Enter data into the FOCALC spreadsheet component of the Focus system, which provides the capabilities of popular spreadsheet packages.
- Define menus that let another user enter any of several different modules. This capability is useful to MIS professionals developing a multimodule application for end users.

The need to interface to one or more existing databases and to modules written in a 3GL are often important factors in 4GL choice (or, indeed, the decision to use one in the first place.) Most 4GL packages, even those that incorporate their own database management capability, can access the most widely used third-party databases: dBase III and its relatives under MS-DOS,

Oracle and Sybase under UNIX, etc. Below the top few database formats, however, the need for database access may narrow your choices. So it is with 3GLs: interfaces to C and COBOL are common, those to other languages are less so. Be sure to check these requirements before you get too far into 4GL selection. When in doubt, assume your DSS will have to access every conceivably relevant database in sight. It is better to eliminate a 4GL with potentially useful features than to discover, six months into a development project, that accessing the manufacturing database has become a DSS requirement—and your chosen 4GL can't read it.

If 4GLs are so wonderful, why aren't they more widely used? There are several reasons:

- Most existing systems are written in COBOL. It is easier to modify and extend these in COBOL rather than restructuring them to incorporate 4GL and COBOL modules.
- There are more trained and experienced 3GL programmers than there are trained and experienced 4GL programmers. People tend to use the tools that they know.
- 4GLs are not standardized, while most 3GLs are. A Focus user would have to learn Progress or MAPPER almost from scratch, whereas a VAX or MS-DOS Pascal programmer can adapt easily to Pascal on a Sun workstation.
- Force of habit. It may not be defensible, but it is a fact.
- The continued concern of many veteran information system managers with run-time efficiency. This may influence their decisions even when objective analysis suggests it shouldn't.
- The cost of the 4GL and its supporting software. These can easily reach six figures for a mainframe-and-micro installation. Managers looking at such sums to support a few users will often say "let's keep using the languages we've already got," as it would take a great deal of saved programmer time to make up this cost.

Despite these factors, 4GL use is increasing. The business advantages, especially in a DSS context, are too great to ignore.

Summary

Decision support systems can be obtained as a complete package, as a customized package, or as custom software. Totally turnkey packages are not usually available. Custom software is appropriate for large firms solving important problems, although smaller firms can often find creative ways of reducing its cost. Customized packages or systems that use a great deal of "canned" software are common.

Types of software that you can use in DSS development include database management packages, information retrieval (query and reporting) packages, specialized modeling packages (including spreadsheets) and languages, statistical data analysis packages, forecasting packages, and graphics packages.

Database management packages support one of three database structures: hierarchical, network, or relational. The hierarchical structure is most common on desktop microcomputers, the network structure on mainframes, and the relational structure on microcomputers and workstations. The relational structure offers more flexibility in responding to unforeseen information retrieval requests than do the others. This makes it more suitable for most decision support system uses. Fortunately, relational DBMS are moving down to the microcomputer level.

Most relational databases are accessed via queries in Structured Query Language, or SQL. While SQL is not fully standardized, its variants are sufficiently similar for a person who knows one of them to learn another quickly. Unfortunately, complex queries are difficult to express in SQL and can take a long time to run. Most relational DBMS vendors therefore also offer end-user query packages that make it easier to access their databases.

In addition to the information retrieval capabilities built into many DBMS, one can buy a separate information retrieval package. These tend to be either more powerful than those offered with the DBMS, easier to use, more general (in the sense of accessing more than one type of database), or, in a few cases, less expensive.

There are several types of financial modeling tools. The simplest is the spreadsheet. It consists of an array of cells. Each cell can contain text, a number, or a formula. Formulas operate on the contents of other cells and produce, in most cases, numbers. These numbers can be used as input to other formulas. The results can be displayed in numerical form or graphed.

Spreadsheets are error prone in several ways. For that reason, two other types of software exist: spreadsheet auditing packages, which help detect (accidental or intentional) spreadsheet errors, and financial modeling languages such as IFPS, which formalize the "loose" spreadsheet approach to defining a financial model.

Statistical data analysis packages automate standard statistical operations: finding means, spreads, patterns, and correlations; determining statistical confidence levels; creating cross tabulations; and more. While a package cannot tell you to use statistical methods, it can help you use them once you determine the need.

Forecasting is the application of statistical techniques to predict the future value of some variable based on its past behavior. The need for sophisticated forecasting methods, combined with the fact that the same methods are used by managers in every industry, has led to wide availability of packages that perform this task.

Most spreadsheet, statistical, and forecasting packages can produce graphic output. Yet their basic purpose is not graphics, so their capabilities are often limited in this regard. Specialized graphing packages can take their output, in a number of standardized data interchange formats, and create a wider variety of charts and graphs with it than the original package could. The need for graphing packages is dropping as the graphing capabilities of other types of software improve.

Where programming is necessary to develop a decision support system, one can use either a third generation language or a fourth generation language.

Third generation languages are widely known to programmers and reasonably well standardized. However, they involve a long and error-prone programming process. Fourth generation languages, while not quite as flexible and somewhat less efficient in their use of computer time, permit faster application development. Their capabilities are normally sufficient for DSS needs, and their computer usage inefficiency is not normally a barrier in a DSS application. They are therefore usually better suited to DSS development than are 3GLs. Many 4GLs include end-user facilities through which a nontechnical person can retrieve information from a database, sort it, tabulate it, and generate simple reports to support his or her decision-making needs.

Key Terms

cell (in spreadsheet) 185
charting software package 199
correlation 193
data management, data manager 176
data model 177
database 176
database management, database management system 176
DSS generator 175
DSS tool 175
entity-relationship diagram 177
file manager 176
financial modeling software 188
forecasting, forecasting software 196
formula (in spreadsheet) 186
fourth-generation (programming) language 201
graphing software package 198
hierarchical database 179
join (in a relational database) 185
key attributes 177
modeling software package 188
network database 180
probe (in spreadsheet auditing context) 191
regression 192
relational database 180
spreadsheet 185
SQL 182
statistical software 192
third-generation programming language (3GL) 200
trace (in spreadsheet auditing context) 191

Review Questions

1. What are the four ways you can obtain any software capability?
2. Why are most custom DSS developed by large companies?

3. If you are not in a large company, should you assume you can't develop a custom DSS? Why or why not?
4. Why are standard packages to support many business decisions not widely available?
5. Contrast a DSS tool with a DSS generator.
6. What is an entity-relationship diagram? Why are they useful?
7. What are the three basic database structures?
8. What is the essential difference between the hierarchical and network database structures on the one hand and the relational database structure on the other?
9. Why are relational databases better suited to decision support than the other types?
10. What is SQL? What types of databases is it meant to work with?
11. What are the three basic database access capabilities of an information retrieval package?
12. What noncomputerized object does a spreadsheet screen resemble?
13. What are some disadvantages of using spreadsheets for business planning?
14. What are two approaches to overcoming some of these disadvantages?
15. What do statistics packages do?
16. What are the basic steps in developing a time-series forecast?
17. Why are graphing packages losing importance?
18. What are some popular third-generation programming languages?
19. What is the essential difference between a 3GL and a 4GL?
20. Give two factors that make 4GLs undesirable for high-volume transaction processing applications but that are not serious drawbacks in most decision support applications.

Exercises

1. You work for a car rental firm that wants to develop a decision support database with information on its rental offices, fleet, customers, and rentals. Draw entity-relationship diagrams for the following three cases:
   a. All cars "belong" to one rental office, are always rented there, and are always returned there.
   b. All cars "belong" to one rental office but may be returned elsewhere. They may remain away from their "home" for a considerable time.
   c. Cars do not belong to a particular office.
2. Sketch four relational tables for Exercise 1*a*.

3. Using a spreadsheet package, decide if your firm should take an investment credit on its corporate income tax return, given the following information:
   - Your firm's internal rate of return (IRR) requirement is 15 percent per year. (Your tax rate is 50 percent.)
   - The asset for which this decision is to be made has a depreciable life of five years and has no salvage value at the end of that period.
   - If you take straight-line depreciation, you are eligible for a 10 percent investment credit in the first year. (That is, your taxes are reduced by 10 percent of its purchase price.)
   - If you forego the investment credit, you can take sum-of-digits accelerated depreciation: 5/15 of purchase price in the first year, 4/15 in the second, 3/15 in the third, 2/15 in the fourth and 1/15 in the fifth year.
4. Obtain population data for your state at 10-year (U.S. Census) intervals going back 50 years. (If you don't live in the United States, use comparable data for your country or region.) Fit a straight line to them—using a forecasting package if you have one, otherwise a spreadsheet package if yours has the necessary functions, or by hand—to predict what the population will be 10 years from your last data point. Do you think this forecast will be accurate? Give two reasons why it might not be.
5. In Section 6.3.5 we took the moving average over precisely one cycle, which was seven days for the restaurant example of Figure 6–13. What would have happened if we had taken a different period, say five days or eight days? Would any period other than seven days give meaningful results?
6. Find a review of a 4GL, or a comparative review of several 4GLs, in a newspaper, magazine, or reference service volume. What charactersitics did the writer consider important? What features of the package did the writer like or dislike? Did the system reviewed provide graphical end-user development tools like those of PC Focus? For what applications did the writer recommend using the 4GL or 4GLs?
7. Interview a programmer who has used at least one 3GL and at least one 4GL in his or her work. Find out how easy it is, in his or her opinion, to develop systems, to debug them, and to modify them when requirements change. What advantages and disadvantages does this person see to the two types of languages? Which does he or she prefer? Why?

References

AGEL88 Ageloff, Roy. *A Primer on SQL*. Times Mirror/Mosby, St. Louis, Mo. (1988).

BARR85 Barron, Michael, and David Targett. *The Manager's Guide to Business Forecasting*. Basil Blackwell, New York (1985).

BRAD87 Bradley, James. *Introduction to Database Management in Business* (2nd ed.). Holt, Rinehart and Winston, New York (1987).

CONS92 *Consumer Reports* 57, no. 4 (Annual Auto Issue, April 1992), pp. 226–37 (mileage); pp. 272–75 (weight).

COUR88 Courtney, James F., Jr., and David B. Paradice. *Database Systems for Management.* Times Mirror/Mosby, St. Louis, Mo. (1988).

DAVI87 Davies, N., and C. Ikin. "Auditing Spreadsheets." *Australian Accountant* (Dec. 1987), pp. 54–56.

ELLI90 Ellis, Dennis, and Jay Nathan. *A Managerial Guide to Business Forecasting.* Graceway Publishing, Flushing, N.Y. (1990).

FINK89 Finkelstein, Clive. *An Introduction to Information Engineering.* Addison-Wesley, Reading, Mass. (1989).

FRID90 Fridlund, Alan J. "Number-Crunching Statistics Software," *Infoworld* 12, no. 9 (February 26, 1990), pp. 59–69.

KEAT89 Keating, Barry. "Statistics Software for Economists: Macintosh." *Business Economics* 24, no. 3 (August 1989), pp. 54–57.

SCHE92 Scheer, August-Wilhelm, and Alexander Hars. "Extending Data Modeling to Cover the Whole Enterprise." *Communications of the ACM* 35, no. 9 (September 1992), pp. 166–72.

SILV91 Silver, Mark S. *Systems That Support Decision Makers.* John Wiley & Sons, New York (1991).

SIMK87 Simkin, M. G. "How to Validate Spreadsheets." *Journal of Accountancy* (Nov. 1987), pp. 130–38.

SPRA80 Sprague, Ralph H., Jr. "A Framework for the Development of Decision Support Systems." *MIS Quarterly* 4, no. 4 (December 1980), pp. 1–26.

SPRA82 Sprague, Ralph H., Jr., and Eric D. Carlson. *Building Effective Decision Support Systems.* Prentice Hall, Englewood Cliffs, N.J. (1982).

WEBS86 Webster, Charles E. *The Executive's Guide to Business and Economic Forecasting.* Probus, Chicago (1986).

WILL87 Willis, Raymond E. *A Guide to Forecasting for Planners and Managers.* Prentice Hall, Englewood Cliffs, N.J. (1987).

WILS90 Wilson, J. Holton, and Barry Keating. *Business Forecasting.* Richard D. Irwin, Homewood, Ill. (1990).

ENVOYANCE: A BUSINESS PLAN FOR PLASTIC RECYCLING

Doug was shouting, "I Eat Plastic! I Eat Plastic!" at the top of his lungs as he and Adrienne approached the Envoyance building on Tuesday afternoon.

"Shut up, Doug!" Adrienne whispered in exasperation. "Honestly, I don't know why I ever agreed to do this project with you!"

Just then they reached the reception area for a presentation by PlasticEater Inc. of Terre Haute, Indiana. A few Envoyance staff members were already in the conference room. Others made their way in as the students approached. The overhead projector was set up and the screen was pulled down. Two men Doug and Adrienne had never met, dressed a bit more formally than the average Envoyance staffer, sat near the projector.

Sandra opened the meeting precisely at 2 o'clock. "For those of you who haven't been involved in this project until now," she began, "we're here to start looking at one of the options for The Bag Man. They make, not surprisingly, bags—specifically plastic bags, about $50 million worth every year. They make the shopping bags you get in stores and supermarkets, garbage bags, wastepaper basket liners, hotel laundry bags . . . you name it. If it's a plastic bag, they make it. They're all made from a type of plastic called high-density polyethylene, or HDPE for short.

"Recently The Bag Man has become interested in making their products from recycled plastic. Part of the reason, of course, is that everyone is becoming more conscious of environmental issues. A bigger part of this reason, in their case, is that their customers are demanding it. Green is in, as it were. Shoppers ask supermarkets what the bags are made of, so the supermarkets move up the chain and pressure their suppliers. The Bag Man doesn't know anything about plastic recycling, but they know us from the air quality project we did for them a couple of years ago. So they asked us what they should do about converting their production.

"A big question mark in their minds is the cost of recycled plastic. Right now you can get brand-new HDPE resin for about 29¢ a pound, delivered to your loading dock. Recycled pellets cost about 34¢ or 35¢ a pound, which is about a 20% premium in the cost of their raw materials. Since you can use about 50% recycled material in thin bags like supermarket bags, that means you pay a net premium of about 10% of your materials cost if you want to use recycled resin. The Bag Man is wondering about two things:

"First, are the bottom-line benefits of 'green marketing' worth 10%? A lot of people feel that the benefits to the planet are worth more than 10%, but that's not the question. They might buy that argument if the numbers come out close enough to make the decision a coin toss, but they still want to see a hard-nosed business analysis.

"Second, is there any way to reduce this premium? That's why we're meeting here this afternoon. One of their options is to recycle their own plastic: to take in post-consumer waste and generate their own pellets. This would essentially mean going into the recycling business in addition to their current 'bag-blowing' business. They're willing to consider this, again if the numbers to the bottom line work out right, but it's not a step they would take lightly.

"With that in mind, I'd like to introduce Jim Davidson and Frank Mayo from PlasticEater Inc.," as she pointed to the two men seated near the overhead projector. "Their firm builds a system that The Bag Man could use to recycle bottles and other HDPE products. In a nutshell, used bottles go in one end and clean HDPE pellets come out the other. There's more to it than that, of course. I'll let Jim and Frank fill in the details."

"Thank you, Sandra," said Frank as he turned on the overhead projector. "Your nutshell summary was 100% accurate. From what you told us on the phone when we set up this meeting, we feel that we have a good solution for your client, and we appreciate this opportunity to discuss it with you.

"Our system looks like this when it's installed," pointing to a photograph on the screen as his colleague Jim put an overhead slide on the projector glass. "If you stretched it all out in a row, it would be over 100 feet long. Most of our customers don't install it that way because most of them don't have facilities that look like a bowling alley.

"Starting with a bale of bottles, this system processes the plastic in six stages:

"First, the bale-breaker unit breaks up bales of bottles as they arrive on a truck from a recycling center.

"Next, a vibrating conveyor belt and a magnet here," he continued as he pointed to part of the diagram that had replaced the photograph on the screen, "separate out debris and magnetic metals. The aluminum caps and rings are still in place, as well as the paper or light plastic labels.

"Third, the separator system here"—he pointed again—"gets rid of nearly all the paper and the light plastic labels.

"Fourth, we wash the rest of them and the glue off here. This system can run open loop, but we usually install it with a water recycling subsystem. That way it can reuse about 1,000 gallons of water continuously after cleaning it. Since one of the major points of recycling is to minimize the environmental impact of industrial processes, we don't want to add more pollution ourselves!

"Then we separate out the aluminum and PET—that's polyethylene terephthalate—from the HDPE. This unit takes advantage of the specific gravity differences between HDPE and anything else to separate them. Naturally, it's closed loop too.

"Now that we have nothing but clean HDPE left, we pelletize it here. This is what the end product looks like," he said as Jim passed around a few clear sandwich bags with small, translucent white plastic pellets.

"To get right to the point," said Sandra when she realized that Frank had paused, "how much does all this cost?"

"That is, as your client would say, the 'bottom line,'" Frank laughed. "I'm just the technical type. Jim can take over now and cover the dollars-and-cents side."

"A lot depends on the volume that The Bag Man will use," began Jim as he replaced Frank at the podium. "You said they do about $50 million in business per year. As a rough guess, they could probably use about six million pounds of recycled HDPE per year. If you work through the numbers, that comes out to processing about a thousand pounds per hour on a three-shift basis.

"A system that can handle this volume would sell for somewhere under a million dollars. We'd have to look at The Bag Man's specifics to get more precise. Again in rough numbers, add about as much again for the building and all the other costs to get it up and running. Total investment: between $1.5 and $2 million.

"You also have your operating costs. Scrap milk bottles will cost you about a nickel a pound, give or take a penny, delivered in bales to your loading dock. It will cost you about 15¢ a pound to process them. The exact figure depends on your exact costs for labor, electricity, and so on, which we can look at. You also have to amortize your initial investment, which at a 10-year life and the volumes we've talked about will add about 3¢ a pound. Put all these together, and your net cost per pound is somewhere in the range of 20¢ to 26¢. Not only is this cheaper than buying recycled pellets on the open market, it's even cheaper than new resin."

"Putting it that way makes it look very attractive," agreed Sandra. "But what are its downside risks?"

Exercises

1. Use the Kepner-Tregoe method (Section 2.6) to answer Sandra's closing question by assessing the adverse consequences of The Bag Man's purchasing a PlasticEater Inc. recycling system.

2. Using a financial planning program such as IFPS if one is available to you, or a spreadsheet program otherwise, determine the expected 10-year rate of return on this investment. Choose average figures where Jim Davidson presented ranges. Ignore all tax consequences. (In the "real world," taxes can be a significant factor in this type of decision, especially if an investment tax credit is available.)
3. Determine the sensitivity of your results in Exercise 2 to the cost figures reaching *(a)* the lower, and *(b)* the upper, ends of their stated ranges.
4. How could Envoyance use the following types of software packages to help them reach the right decision for The Bag Man?
   a. Statistical data analysis.
   b. Forecasting.
   c. Graphing.
5. Suppose Envoyance expected to make plastic recycling recommendations to its clients repeatedly over the next year or two. Could that justify developing a standard DSS for this purpose rather than applying general-purpose tools such as financial planning packages? Why or why not?
6. Regardless of your answer to Exercise 5 above, Envoyance has decided to develop a DSS for this purpose. (If you didn't think it was a good idea, assume that an MIS student will develop this DSS for them at no cost as a term project.) Answer these questions as part of their system development effort:
   a. How, if at all, could it use a database? What would be in that database? What organization would you recommend for it?
   b. Recommend a programming language for this DSS. Explain your choice.
   c. Design a suitable user interface for this DSS. Explain your design choices.

CHAPTER 7 DSS Hardware and Operating System Platforms

Chapter Outline

Introduction

Computer applications run on hardware, under an operating system. Decision support systems are no exception. If you will be involved in planning a DSS, you will have to decide what environment it will run in. You will have to choose among mainframes, minicomputers, and microcomputers. Your choices will differ in their hardware and in the operating systems they use. You will also have to consider different approaches to linking several computers and sharing the workload among them. Each of these options has its pros and cons. Picking the right one combination can help make your DSS more responsive and successful. Picking the wrong one can help it fail.

Even if you will be using a DSS planned and developed by others, it helps to know what you can expect from its hardware/software/networking environment. This section will tell you about the major environments in which DSS run.

Chapter Objectives

After you have read and studied this chapter, you will be able to:

1. Describe the types of hardware environments used for decision support systems.
2. Outline the advantages and disadvantages of each type of hardware environment.
3. Explain how an information base is useful in DSS.
4. Explain why client/server computing is becoming more popular.
5. Describe why the use of open systems is increasing.
6. Explain why DSS are often the reason an organization moves toward open systems.
7. Discuss how downsizing figures in the choice of hardware/software platforms.
8. Outline several factors to consider in selecting a hardware/software environment for a DSS.

7.1 The Major Options

The term "platform" refers to the combined hardware/software environment that supports the applications, in this case decision support systems. DSS can work on several types of platforms:

1. The central corporate system.
2. A separate system that obtains data from the central system.
3. A combination of linked systems, each doing the part it does best.
4. A stand-alone system.
5. A combination of the above.

Each approach has several variations. Each also has its advantages and disadvantages. The following sections discuss the four major approaches. In reading them, keep in mind that there are grey areas between the approaches that are described here. Systems that follow any of the four cleanly, purely, and totally are the exception.

7.2 DSS on the Central Corporate System

Virtually every organization of any size, and every major division of large organizations, has a central computer system. These systems run transaction-oriented applications such as accounting, order entry, and time billing. They also often run strategic applications such as electronic data interchange with customers or facilities for rapid inquiry into the status of critical orders. These central systems usually use an integrated database management system for most, if not all, of the organization's important information. The hardware platform is usually a mainframe or a large minicomputer. Users usually access the system through terminals or through microcomputers equipped with a terminal emulation package. (In some hardware environments, the microcomputer requires a special adapter card to "emulate" the terminals that the central system supports.)

Given that the central mainframe already exists, it is tempting to put new applications on it. In fact, this is where most new corporate applications are expected to run. *Capacity planners* within the MIS organization monitor the central system's load as new applications are developed and as the number of users grows. They watch response time statistics, the remaining amount of space on disk storage units, and communication line usage. Using mathematical tools (based on concepts we will discuss in Chapter 9) they predict how the system will perform under its expected load increases. When they see that response time or capacity will soon become inadequate, they decide how best to improve the system. The required changes may be as simple as adding another disk drive or more main memory. At the other extreme, it may be time for complete system replacement. Where total replacement is called for, the new system is usually a larger model of the same family as the old. Exceptions to this rule arise when the system to be replaced is the largest model of its product line, when its product line has become obsolete since it was originally selected, or when changes in the nature of the workload make it no longer suitable. As soon as the system expansion, upgrade, or replacement is complete, the load monitoring process resumes until the next expansion or upgrade is required.

If corporate applications are generally put on the central system and if this mode of regular load increases and upgrades is considered normal, a new DSS can be put on the central system as well. This has the following advantages and disadvantages:

Advantages of Using the Central System

1. MIS staffers are already familiar with the system and its software.

2. Many users already know how the system works. (All users are not created equal. Even when a system is widely used within an organization, you must make sure that the specific individuals who are to use the proposed DSS are familiar with it.)

3. The necessary hardware (terminals, communication links) to use the system is in place in the organization. (As with the previous point, it may be in the organization in general but not on the desks of the specific managers and professionals who will use the proposed DSS.)

4. DSS applications can access the central database directly for up-to-date information, as they reside on the same system and run in the same programming environment.

5. The processing power of a large system can run complex DSS, such as large simulation models, thousand-rule expert systems, or massive information retrieval tasks, in acceptable elapsed times.

6. Most mainframes have a variety of available DSS tools such as 4GLs, database managers, simulation packages, expert system shells, and EIS (executive information system; see Chapter 12) software.

Disadvantages of Using the Central System

1. The central system was probably not originally selected for DSS applications and may not be well suited to them. This applies to the hardware and to the systems software: operating system, database manager, etc. Mainframe operating systems are often designed for efficiency and throughput where DSS need interactivity and responsiveness.

2. The cost of additional mainframe resources to run a DSS may exceed the cost of smaller computers to handle the same task. Much of the cost of a mainframe reflects its ability to move massive amounts of data quickly and to be shared effectively by many users. These capabilities are vital to many applications but are often of marginal value to DSS.

3. There may be a tendency to force unsuitable software tools into DSS use because they are already there, rather than getting suitable ones. This is especially true of database management systems. Most mainframes in 1993 use either hierarchical or network database structures. As we saw in the last chapter, these are less flexible, hence less suitable for DSS, than the relational structure.

4. DSS responsiveness may be affected by other loads on the system. It may be organizationally unacceptable to give the DSS users a high enough priority for system resources to avoid this problem, as doing so would mean degraded response times for the users whose needs justified the mainframe in the first place.

5. DSS users may have to wait in line behind other application development efforts. As with the previous point, this is in principle under management control, but the reality of the situation may put others first.

6. The user interface of most mainframes is not as easy for nontechnical people to use (as "user friendly," in the vernacular of the 1990s) as that of most smaller systems. The operating system tends to be command oriented and designed for close control of the system by a professional programmer. Graphical user interfaces, such as many desktop systems offer, are generally nonexistent.

7. Support for graphics may be poor. Even if a mainframe application can handle graphics, existing terminals may be alphanumeric, and existing communication links may not be up to the increased load of graphs and pictures.

Popular Mainframe Systems

IBM's MVS and VM operating systems, running on hardware from IBM and a few smaller firms with "plug-compatible" products, account for about 80 percent of all mainframes sold in the United States. It is not surprising that most third-party DSS software runs under them. Unisys has about 10 percent of the market, but, for historical reasons, three incompatible product lines. These have 4GLs and modern database management software but few third-party packages. The remaining market is divided among several U.S., European, and Japanese firms.

7.3 DSS with an Information Base on a Separate System

Many organizations have chosen to cope with the disadvantages of using the central corporate system, while not completely losing access to the central database, by obtaining a new computer for DSS use and copying all or part of their central database to it.

The new system can range from a personal computer to a "supermini." The choice depends on the required capacity, the required software tools, and the number of concurrent users. If the DSS is to be used by more than one person, a minicomputer is one popular choice. Another is a local area network (LAN) with the shared data on a file or database server.

The linked-system approach is effective when the application calls for a decision support database that is separate from the firm's transaction processing database. Here, a firm typically wants to use a relational database management system for decision support applications. However, its corporate database is in hierarchical or network form.

A firm in this situation could, of course, put two DBMS on its central system and move data from the transaction processing database to the relational system that will support DSS needs. However, the additional resources that the mainframe would require in order to accommodate both databases, the DSS application, and its users would often cost more than a dedicated micro- or minicomputer with the required capacity. Organizations in this situation therefore often opt for a separate computer. They "download" selected portions of the central database from the mainframe to the DSS computer every day, week, or month, according to the type of data and users' information needs. Depending on the amount of data to be transferred and on the available facilities, either communication links or magnetic tape reels can be used for the transfer. The DSS computer's relational DBMS reads this data and enters it into its tables. The DSS then uses the content of the relational database. Such a database is often called an *information base.*

An information base is a read-only database: DSS users cannot update the "live" organizational information. (They could update the information base, of course, but doing so would not affect the central database.) That limits the use of an information base to situations where decision makers access corporate information but do not change it. If an application running in this environment must update the main database, other means—such as transactions submitted to the mainframe by the DSS computer, which for this purpose can mimic a user at a terminal—must be used.

Advantages of Using an Information Base

1. The DSS hardware, be it minicomputer, microcomputer, or LAN, can be optimized for DSS.

2. DSS hardware need not be shared with other applications, so DSS response time is preserved no matter what is going on elsewhere in the organization.

3. The cost of upgrading the mainframe to run the DSS application is avoided. As noted earlier, this cost would often exceed the cost of dedicated DSS hardware.

4. Minicomputers and high-end microcomputers tend to have a wide selection of relational DBMS, which are well suited to DSS applications.

5. Most minicomputers and microcomputers are user friendly or can be made so by an available graphical user-interface package. It is not usually possible to replace a mainframe with another system just to cater to decision makers' desires for interface friendliness.

Disadvantages of Using an Information Base

1. Any system that involves two computers requires communications components that a single system does not need. This added layer of complexity tends to lengthen development time and increases the potential for hard-to-find bugs.

2. The need to transfer data between the two systems, whether to create an information base or on an as-needed basis, is an additional workload on the central system. Unless this work can take place totally during times of light system use, it will add to the mainframe load, although hopefully less than running the full DSS would.

3. The MIS staff must be familiar with two systems. (This means expertise in both must exist in the organization. It does not mean that individual staff members must know both.) In addition, some staff members may need another set of skills to link the two.

4. The total user community will use two systems. Some users, of course, will access just one or the other: If order-entry operators use a mainframe and sales promotion planners use a DSS mini, each need only learn to use one system. Even in this case, the user support organization will have to deal with both.

5. Users who access both systems may need two types of terminals, or may have to go through complex network log-on procedures to access the correct one. Switching from one to the other may be time consuming.

6. Decision support data are only as current as the most recent download to the information base. This may suffice, especially if the downloading is done at least every 24 hours.

7. Recreating the information base may take several hours. The DSS system may not be available for use during this time. If the update is performed outside normal working hours, perhaps in the early morning, it may involve operator inconvenience and overtime pay. Unattended operation is an attractive way to avoid these—but leaves the organization vulnerable to mishaps that can only be corrected by an on-site operator.

Popular Minicomputer Systems for Information Base Usage

The largest minicomputer vendors are Digital Equipment Corporation and Hewlett-Packard. However, the most popular minicomputer software environment does not belong to either. Rather, it is UNIX. The UNIX operating system, whose impact we discuss more fully in Section 7.6 below, originated with AT&T. It, and its derivatives of various names, run on minicomputers from every significant vendor. Some minicomputer suppliers, especially those founded after 1980, support only UNIX. Others, including the above two, support both their own operating system and UNIX. All popular minicomputer environments are well supplied with basic software packages for most DSS needs.

Multiprocessing (using more than one processor in a computer system to increase its total power) and parallel processing (applying more than one processor to an individual task to speed its execution) are taking hold in the minicomputer arena. Most minicomputer vendors offer systems with up to four, six, or eight processors. The aggregate power of such a system can rival a traditional mainframe. Some newer products were designed with the explicit goal of high performance via parallel processing technology. Parallel processing systems are excellent candidates for demanding decision support applications since they are well suited to assessing a relational database.

A local area network (LAN) can be a cost-effective alternative to a multiple-user minicomputer. In this approach, the DSS application may obtain data from a central source but actually runs on each user's desktop. LANs are especially appropriate when prospective DSS users already have microcomputers on their desks and when those micros are not due for immediate replacement for some other reason. When this is the case, a LAN is usually more economical than a shared system. While most LANs require a central file server for serious use, a server can support at least twice as many PC users on a LAN than it could if it had to carry the entire computing load for an equivalent number of terminals.

7.4 DSS and Client/Server Computing

In the information base approach, relevant parts of the corporate database were sent to the DSS computer, which was then disconnected from the central system (at least for purposes of database access). We could also keep the DSS system and the central system linked during operation. The central system would provide data on an as-needed basis for DSS processing. This is an example of the increasingly popular *client/server* approach to computing. The server system (in this example the central mainframe, but often a smaller system) serves as a data repository. The client system runs the application using data from the server. The result: close matching of each partner's capabilities to its role in the overall system.

The term "client/server" describes any situation in which an application is partitioned to run on two or more systems of different capabilities, using each to best advantage. Most people are familiar with small LAN versions of client/server: using a print server to share an expensive laser printer among several client PCs or using a file server to eliminate the need for each PC to have its own copy of all application programs.[1] The variations of client/server

[1]This statement refers to physical copies of the software, which occupy disk space, that must be upgraded when a new release comes out, etc. Firms must usually purchase a license for each user even if one physical copy is installed on a server and shared via a LAN. Some servers support a "checkout" system, where the number of concurrent package users is restricted to the number of purchased licenses. Under this scenario, if a firm purchases three licenses, the server will only supply the package to three users at a time. Some software vendors offer *site licensing*, where an organization receives a master copy of a package and may then copy it as needed for use within the organization.

computing, most of which can be useful in DSS, fall along the spectrum of Figure 7–1.

Note that using a LAN doesn't necessarily imply client/server computing. In a common, and simpler, approach, the server (here referred to as a *file server*) is essentially a large, shared disk drive. It sends, or downloads, files on request to the individual user systems on the network. These systems carry out all the processing and, if they have modified the file, send the modified version back to the server when they are done. While useful systems can be built to operate in this mode, it doesn't qualify as client/server. It is above the top of the bracket that defines client/server in Figure 7–1.

Every approach to client/server computing stores the data in the server and has the user interacting with the client. The rest of the application, which lies between user interaction on the one hand and physical access to disk records on the other, can go in either direction. At one extreme the application logic is on the server, and the client does little more than display results on the screen.[2] At the other extreme, the client could ask for individual file records as it determines a need for them. The term "client/server" usually refers to approaches that fall between these two extremes. The precise point at which to divide a job depends on these major factors:

- *The computing power relationship between the two systems.* If the server is a comparable microcomputer to the clients, it is probably desirable to

FIGURE 7–1

Client/Server Computing Spectrum

	Free-standing personal computers
	Disk server provides shared mass storage managed by client systems
Client/server computing can be any of these {	File server transfers shared files to client systems on request
	Database server transfers selected records to clients on request
	Database server processes requests, returns selected records to clients
	Cooperative application processing; server sends intermediate results to clients
	Server carries out calculations, sends results to clients to format and present
	Server formats results and sends screen description to client to display
	"Dumb" terminals on shared, multiuser computer

[2]When the client and server in this situation use the popular X Windows protocol to interact with the system on the user's desk, the terminology is reversed: The terminal is called the server and the system that hosts the application is called the client. This usage arose from the fact that one X Windows terminal can "serve" multiple application processes on behalf of the same human user. It became standard in the X Windows world before client/server computing came into wide use and is too firmly entrenched there to change it now. Using the terms "X Server" and "X Client" in this context can reduce the confusion somewhat.

push as much work as possible onto the clients. If the server is a powerful minicomputer or multiprocessor "supermicro" and the clients are low-end personal computers, the reverse may be true.

- *The load pattern.* If DSS usage is frequent and regular throughout the day, it is a good idea to provide each user with sufficient local power for his or her needs. If it is more sporadic, putting the bulk of the computation on a shared central system can yield savings without affecting system responsiveness.
- *Minimizing communication needs.* The time it takes to communicate requests and responses between the client and the server is a common bottleneck in client/server systems. The most efficient division of labor is often the one that minimizes the need to communicate between the two parts. Thus, approaches that send an entire file to the desktop of a person who wishes to access it, while simple to program at the server end, may not be as efficient as approaches in which the server selects the records of interest and sends only them.

Clients and servers need not be in a one-to-one relationship. Servers are usually designed to provide one, or a limited number, of services. They offer these services to many clients. Clients, on their side, can request service from many different servers. Figure 7–2 shows a system with several clients making requests and several servers, located on two LANs, satisfying them.

Client/server computing and an information base are often found together. The server database is downloaded from the central organizational database and is then accessed as needed by several clients. Major suppliers of relational database management systems all support a client/server split between the "back end" of their products, which manages the database itself, and their various 4GL, query, and report writer "front ends." The client part of the application, running on the user's desktop, accepts users' data requests in SQL or another suitable language. It converts the request, if necessary, to a form in which the server can understand it and transmits the request to the server system. The server responds by sending only the necessary data to the client.

Client/server computing describes the software being used, not the hardware. You can't go out and buy a "client/server computer" in the same way as you can buy a minicomputer or a workstation. You can buy the hardware elements of a client/server system, of course. You can even buy a system designed with the expectation that it will be used as a server, optimized for its expected use, and having the word "server" in its name. But this system isn't a server until it is connected to clients. The term "client/server" refers to the way the two cooperate to get the overall job done. By analogy, you can't buy a taxicab from a car dealer. You can buy the hardware elements of a taxicab, of course, You can even buy a car designed with the expectation that it will be used as a taxicab, optimized for its expected use, and having

FIGURE 7–2
Client/Server Network Illustration

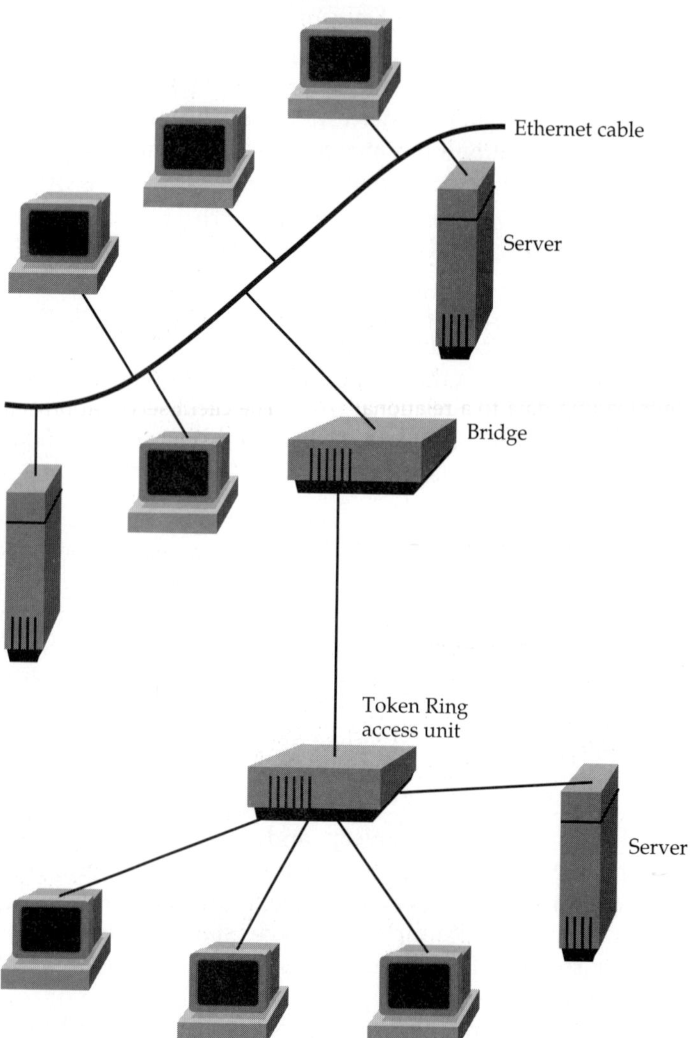

the words "taxi package" in its option list. But this car isn't a taxicab until it is licensed by the local authorities and made available to the public for hire. The term "taxi" refers to the way it is used to provide transportation services.

Advantages of Using a Client/Server System

The server technology in client/server computing often resembles that which is used to support a central information base. Further, as noted above, it may

D&B Goes Client/Server

Dun & Bradstreet Software is a dominant (over $500 million revenue per year) supplier of mainframe software for manufacturing and financial and human resource applications. Under this name and the previous names of its constituent organizations, McCormack & Dodge and Management Science America, D&B Software earned the reputation of a "mainframe only" firm. Yet in 1992, they responded to the trend to client/server computing by announcing a set of products of this type. These products work by downloading data to a relational database server on a local area network. Users at client workstations can then access this database for decision support purposes.

The D&B package includes three components: Financial System Analysis, InterQ and SmartStream. Financial Stream Analysis is, as its name suggests, a tool for analyzing financial data. It runs on the client desktop system and lets users compile data into a variety of graph, bar, and pie charts for analysis. At the other end of the application, InterQ creates links between the server and the central database that supports the client/server tools. Part of InterQ runs on the server, part on the (IBM or compatible) mainframe system.

Between the two, SmartStream is a work flow automation tool that allows users to collect data from several sources automatically for their analysis. SmartStream can obtain data from D&B's mainframe financial and accounting applications, from other mainframe databases, and from public information services such as Dow Jones and CompuServe, forwarding the collection to users when it is complete. SmartStream can be programmed to compile and deliver data at preset times or after specific events. SmartStream is not restricted to supporting Financial Stream Analysis: Users can also opt to enter its data into their own server-based or client-based application software.

The client/server approach has several benefits in this application. It augments the financial data managed by the mainframe application by adding data from complementary sources, it reduces the mainframe cycles required to access this data, it improves query response time to users, and it makes it possible to analyze the data via well-known and easy-to-use microcomputer-based tools.

A complete package of all three tools to support 10 users is priced at $99,000. Additional services such as planning and training could increase this figure substantially. The SmartStream server can use any of several network operating systems that use Intel 80X86-family hardware. The initial client software supports MS-DOS/Windows. D&B is extending the software package to additional servers, additional clients, and additional application areas.

actually store an information base. Many of the advantages and disadvantages listed in the previous section therefore apply here as well.

1. It allows each part of an overall application to be run in a hardware-software environment optimized for that part and that part alone, whether it demands a large database, high-speed computing, or high-resolution color graphics. This optimization tends to minimize the overall cost of the system.

2. Many groupware applications are designed to run in a client/server environment, often using LANs with external gateways to users located at a distance from the LAN in question.

Disadvantages of Using a Client/Server System

1. The complexities of dealing with two systems in the relatively static, unidirectional information base environment are multiplied manyfold when an application is partitioned across a client/server system.

2. The tools to support all but the simplest varieties of client/server computing, without a great deal of custom development effort for each new application, are just coming into commercial use in the early 1990s and, in 1993, are far from mature.

Popular Local Area Network Systems

A local area network, or LAN, is usually the technology of choice for client/server computing. Its high data transmission speed allows rapid transfer of requests from the clients to the server and of data from the server to the clients.

At the hardware level, installing a LAN involves purchasing a suitable server, running wires throughout the necessary office spaces, and adding adapter cards (if necessary) to all the PCs to be connected to it. At the software level, a network operating system (NOS) must be obtained and its client side installed on all the PCs. Network administration, for anything above the simplest LANs, may call for additional software and for the services of a trained specialist.

The most popular LAN wiring scheme is Ethernet. At 10 Mbits per second, it is sufficiently fast for most DSS uses. Advanced versions that will operate at about 100 Mbit/sec are being developed. Token Ring wiring, developed initially by IBM and found primarily where MIS management has a strong IBM orientation, offers either 4 or 16 Mbit/sec and comparable capabilities. A LocalTalk connection is built into every Macintosh, but its slow speed (230 Kbit/sec) limits it to small networks and less demanding uses. The older ARCnet, despite its having been updated over the years, is little used in the 1990s.

Alternate technologies that do not require special wiring (including existing telephone lines, existing power lines, and radio or infrared links) have their own sets of trade-offs and suit specific niche requirements.

The most popular NOS in the early 1990s is Novell's Netware, also sold by IBM. Microsoft's LAN Manager and Banyan Vines are widely used. Apple Computer's Appleshare, bundled with every Macintosh, is suited primarily for printer sharing along with limited file sharing and electronic mail. Some minicomputer vendors offer LAN server software for their products as well. They see the trend from centralized computing to LANs and view such offerings as a way to keep their customers.

All major NOSs support MS-DOS, OS/2, and Macintosh clients. Support for UNIX-based clients is arriving quickly as well. In every case, the server software may only run on a specific hardware/software platform, but this is invisible to the client systems.

Many organizations begin using LANs by installing several independent ones in various departments, typically with little or no coordination or standardization. This is not an ideal approach but is often a fact of life. At a later date such organizations often find it necessary to link their networks to each other and/or to their central system. In other situations, networks grow to the point where performance is affected by the volume of network traffic or where the length of cable required to interconnect all users exceeds the limitations of the LAN wiring scheme in use. All of these situations can be dealt with by using network interconnection devices. The specifics of these units are beyond the scope of an introduction to DSS, but you should be aware that a wide range of such products exist and can deal with just about any internetworking requirement that might arise.

7.5 DSS on a Stand-Alone System

Many decision support systems do not access a central database. Some run simulation models whose input, consisting of only a few numbers, comes entirely from its user's knowledge or from external sources. A budgeting system may take all its input from its user, eventually creating a spreadsheet on a diskette that can be carried to another system for consolidation.

DSS that do not access a large central database are typically model oriented or process oriented. While some of them use databases that are developed and maintained locally by their individual users, such databases are unlikely to be large or complex. A "real" data-oriented DSS normally requires some form of link to an existing or external database. Its hardware would therefore usually fall into one of the previous three categories.

DSS that do not access a large central database are candidates for stand-alone systems. A stand-alone DSS can be run on a computer dedicated to the DSS task or on a multiple-user computer used in time-sharing mode. In this latter case, many users may be sharing the hardware, but each is using a stand-alone application in a self-contained logical "cocoon."

Being "stand-alone" is a matter of degree. The absolutely, totally, 100 percent stand-alone system is almost as rare as the medieval hermit. Even users of nominally stand-alone systems often exchange files via diskette or send electronic mail via a dial-up modem link. Think of the systems described in this section as being at one end of a spectrum. You will see many intermediate stages between the linked systems described in the previous sections and these.

Advantages of Using a Stand-Alone System

1. The system can be totally optimized for DSS. Compatibility considerations may, if desired, be ignored completely.
2. The complexity of sharing a resource with other users is avoided.
3. The complexity of integrating a two-system application is avoided.

4. There is no overhead in communicating with other systems.

5. The user or department "owning" the system has complete control over it. While not a technical factor, this is often psychologically and/or politically important.

Disadvantages of Using a Stand-Alone System

1. Any data the system requires must be provided by its user. This is why stand-alone systems are not well suited to data-oriented DSS.

2. Sharing the results with other users, or using a shared database, is difficult or impossible. Local area networks with a file or database server offer a compromise solution to this problem—but as soon as one starts using a LAN, one no longer truly has a stand-alone system.

3. The individual user or department responsible for the stand-alone system must usually deal with its own system administration needs, such as installing new software releases and backing up files regularly. Most end users are not well disciplined in this regard. They often learn about the need for regular backups through the agonizing personal experience of not having one when it could have saved the day.

4. It may be difficult or impossible to integrate a stand-alone system with corporate applications at a later date if no thought was given to compatibility in the planning stages. MIS staffers, upset at having been ignored during planning, may understandably take an all-too-human "I told you so" or "stew in your own juices" attitude to bailing the user out at this point.

Popular Stand-Alone Systems

The most common hardware options for stand-alone DSS are time-sharing systems and single-user microcomputers.

Time sharing is a mode of operation in which a multi-user computer is shared among several users performing unrelated tasks. It spreads the cost of an expensive system over many users but does not involve the software complexities that transaction processing with a shared database introduces. The term "stand-alone" in this context refers to the decision support application but not to the shared hardware on which it runs.

The popularity of time-sharing services has declined since the 1970s with the availability of increasingly powerful personal computers. Complex models, though, tax the power of any personal computer likely to become available before the turn of the millenium. Scientific supercomputers offer a mechanism to run a full study using one of these models in reasonable elapsed time. These large systems are usually run in time-sharing mode, either by corporate data centers for several divisions or by independent organizations that sell computer time to all comers. Specialized model building, model execution, and data analysis packages may also not be available on desktop systems but can be used by any customer of a time-sharing service that has installed them. Time-sharing systems are also used to access commercial databases that are made available by their owners via this mechanism.

Time-sharing computers are no longer in wide use for general-purpose computing, although they are still used where the essence of the offering is a service (such as payroll processing) and where the service vendor has opted for this type of hardware. Desktop computers have become powerful enough for most business computing requirements. Beyond that, even where time sharing has an objective cost edge, the feeling of "being in control" that the desktop microcomputer offers is psychologically important to many users. They value this feeling so much that they insist on having their own individual systems, even though financial analysis might show that this is unnecessary or unwise.

The dominant microcomputer family is the "IBM-compatible" environment, supported by hardware from IBM and a host of other suppliers. Until recently, such computers almost always used the MS-DOS (called PC-DOS by IBM) operating system. Since 1990, Microsoft Windows has provided a popular graphical user interface to MS-DOS. More recently, the GUI-oriented OS/2 and Windows NT operating systems have become viable. Both can run MS-DOS and Windows applications. All three environments offer more power than MS-DOS but are harder to install and require more hardware resources.

The Apple Macintosh, with about 10 percent of the business market, offers a well-integrated GUI and consistent operation across all applications.

Both the IBM-compatible and Macintosh environments are well supplied with packages for most DSS needs, although MS-DOS, etc., users have a wider choice than do Macintosh users. Major mainframe-based executive information systems (the topic of Chapter 18) support both IBM-compatible and Macintosh systems as clients.

The minicomputer-derived UNIX system is becoming more widely used on microcomputers. UNIX is the dominant software environment for workstations, whose processing power and application complexity exceed those of the typical PC. Many DSS that demand large amounts of computing power, such as those used for investment analysis in the financial industry, have been developed for workstations that run under UNIX.

7.6 Open Systems and DSS

You may have heard or read the term "open systems" and about how they are the wave of the future. You may have heard the UNIX operating system, mentioned briefly above, discussed in this context. With more and more organizations moving toward open systems, there's a good chance that your employer (now or after graduation) will be one of them. Furthermore, and importantly for purposes of this book, open systems and DSS have a close relationship.

Open systems are systems whose interfaces are not under the control of any one hardware or software supplier.[3] Rather, they are defined by vendor-neutral bodies through an open process in which all vendors can, if they choose, participate. (Participation in these discussions is not restricted to vendors. While vendors tend to have the most to gain or lose as a result of their outcome, and therefore supply most of the discussants, user organizations can and do participate.) Once they are agreed upon, both the interface specifications and the right to produce systems that conform to those specifications are available on equal, and equitable, terms to all firms.

The advantage of open systems to users is that open systems permit one to mix and match hardware and software products from several suppliers, choosing the best product of each type for the need, with a high degree of assurance that the resulting collection will work together. The advantage to vendors is that they can produce a product of one type—a workstation, a network component, or a database management system—and have it work with complementary products from many sources. Open systems thus create a "level playing field," in which small vendors can compete with larger ones on an approximately equal basis.

Open systems are not all goodness. The standards-making process is long and laborious. The standards eventually arrived at are often compromises, lacking the clarity of vision and purity of focus that a single-vendor standard can have. The largest vendors, whose market shares would be threatened by increased competition, have historically opposed open standards through a variety of subtle and not-so-subtle tactics. And standards, while they go a long way toward providing compatibility of products from different sources, are seldom complete enough to make coordinated operation an effortless "nonevent." Despite these drawbacks, the adoption of standards-based computing is increasing.

System openness encompasses multiple aspects. The first aspect of openness is system interconnection, or networking. Openness in this sense means that systems from different sources can exchange data as the user organization requires. Systems that conform to a vendor-independent set of data communication and networking standards are open in this sense. This type of openness usually means conforming to the Open System Interconnection (OSI) standard of the International Standards Organization, although other vendor-independent standards (most of which have a close relationship to UNIX or a UNIX-like operating system) exist as well.

The second aspect of openness is the way individual computers operate. Openness here means that one set of programs, including both programming tools and user-developed applications, runs in the same way, with essentially the same commands and user interfaces, on computers obtained from several

[3]Don't confuse the term "open systems" as used here with the same term as we used it in Chapter 3, a system that exchanges information with its environment. Both terms are too entrenched to change. The context should always make it clear which sense is meant.

sources. The key ingredient in this type of openness is the operating system, as it defines the environment in which all other software runs.

The primary multi-user open operating system is UNIX. UNIX is independent of hardware architecture: It can be adapted, or "ported," to systems based on nearly any type of processor and having nearly any instruction set. Two separate organizations are developing standards for UNIX or UNIX-derived software environments: UNIX International (UI) and the Open Software Foundation (OSF). These organizations have been rivals since their founding in the late 1980s. Most computer manufacturers have adopted the software of one or the other: There is no computer manufacturer of significance in the United States today who does not support a UNIX-based operating system on at least one of its product lines. Most commercial packages have been written to work with either. This includes both applications and supporting components such as networking tools and database managers. Furthermore, UI UNIX and the OSF operating system, since they share a common history, present nearly identical interfaces to their users. As a result, user organizations can move programs between systems based on the two software environments nearly as easily as if there were only one UNIX-derived standard.

Another multi-user independent standardization activity is called POSIX. This Institute of Electrical and Electronics Engineers (IEEE)-sponsored, U.S. government-endorsed standard is based on UNIX but standardizes its interfaces at a higher level. As a result, non-UNIX operating systems can add an intermediate "shell" to run POSIX-compliant software. This strategy permits some suppliers of proprietary systems to claim a degree of openness but adds a layer of overhead and inefficiency to their systems when they use this shell.

At the desktop level, MS-DOS has many characteristics of an open system. It is under the unilateral control of Microsoft, but Microsoft does not sell computers. Microsoft therefore makes MS-DOS available equally to all hardware vendors. MS-DOS runs only on microprocessors compatible with the Intel 80X86 family, but several semiconductor firms make these. Furthermore, Microsoft publishes the MS-DOS interface specifications, so any software firm can write programs to run under MS-DOS on anyone's hardware.

Some of the more popular proprietary operating systems have enough market share that many software products are available to run under them and with each other: IBM mainframe MVS, Digital minicomputer VMS, the Apple Macintosh microcomputer operating system. Because of the size of these systems' user communities and of the industries that have grown up around them, their developers cannot willy-nilly make arbitrary changes to their interfaces. They can and do, however, decide their future roadmaps on their own and do not take kindly to outside attempts to influence their direction.

A third aspect of openness is hardware interface openness. The hardware interfaces to many microcomputers and minicomputers are in the public domain or can be licensed inexpensively. Anyone can build components to plug into these buses; in some cases, anyone can also build computers to accept such components. The interfaces to other systems are more tightly controlled by their owners. Hardware openness, while important to system designers, does not raise any issues that are unique to DSS.

DSS has accelerated the growth of open systems. The reason: The arrival of DSS injected a second component into what had been, historically, single-purpose transaction processing systems. Let's follow one possible scenario for this evolution:

Downsizing for Decision Support

Many firms are moving mainframe-based applications to minis or micros: at times as part of an overall system redesign but often just for decision support or other tasks to which the mainframe is poorly suited. This process is usually called *downsizing.** Some proponents prefer the term *rightsizing:* They feel it connotes that the smaller size is the right size, not just smaller for the (currently popular) sake of being smaller.

Open systems often play a key role in downsizing programs. A mainframe application can seldom be moved to one smaller system. Rather, its size and scope require it to use several cooperating smaller systems. Their ability to cooperate depends on their all conforming to a suitable set of standards. These will often be open systems standards—and usually must be, if hardware from more than one vendor is involved.

One firm that downsized a key decision support application was American Airlines Decision Technologies of Fort Worth, Texas [GILL92]. It uses complex mathematical models to schedule its parent firm's crews, equipment, and flights. It originally used the corporate mainframe for this purpose. However, this created several problems.

For one thing, the IBM mainframe took too long to process the work. Analysts "had to wait in line with everybody else," said vice president of computing resources Chip Steinmitz. Worse yet, work fell behind: With the delay in starting to run the models, they began running out of time to complete them.

American Airlines Decision Technologies considered expanding its mainframe. However, that would not have fit the analysts' work patterns. "The individual analyst needs to have an interactive type of computing environment," says Steinmitz. "Even though it takes a third longer to run a job on a workstation, an analyst can get more runs through in 24 hours."

The MVS mainframe was replaced by a client/server network using a mix of hardware. (The mainframe itself remained in place, used for other tasks.) Workstations are UNIX based, from four vendors, and MS-DOS PCs. The firm spent $4 million on new equipment in 1991 and saved that much in mainframe usage charges during the network's first year.

Was it all gravy? Hardly. "We encountered unanticipated costs dealing with network complexity and LAN administration," Steinmitz points out. "We had to configure the network

*This term is also used in a general business context to refer to reducing the overall size of an organization. The two meanings are distinct, although it is not always clear which is meant.

1. The transaction processing systems of Company X run on its central mainframe. Since most of its transaction processing systems are conceptually similar, it is reasonable for one vendor to satisfy all the needs with one product line. Company X has therefore standardized on one vendor's mainframe line and is quite satisfied with it.

2. DSS arrives. Company X's first DSS are implemented on its existing mainframe—not because it is the best choice, although it might be at times, but because it is the only choice.

concluded

with shared file servers that anyone can get at. Networking them all together was more expensive than we anticipated." They also had to develop system and network management tools for their multivendor environment. Finally, their application programmers, who were used to the support of a systems programming staff in the mainframe environment, found that they had to take on its responsibilities as well. Still, they are well satisfied with their decision.

Avis Rent A Car Systems Inc. of Garden City, New York, had a data access problem [MORA92]. Accessing either of the two databases on their IBM 3090 600E mainframe meant either using a complex mainframe tool or writing a COBOL program to extract the data. To make life easier for their business planners they installed Apple Macintosh microcomputers equipped with Apple's Data Access Language (DAL). They now use DAL Client, part of Apple's System 7 operating system for the Macintosh, to access mainframe databases. They also use DAL Server for UNIX, from Pacer Software Inc., to connect to Informix and Sybase relational databases on Sun and Hewlett-Packard equipment via the same user interface. Like American Airlines Decision Technologies, Avis did not replace its mainframe but was able to forestall upgrades by moving some of its workload to the smaller platforms.

Avis has used its Mac-based query tools for critical decisions in human resources, marketing, and fleet management. "Today, programmers can take query tools and get an answer in an afternoon that would have taken six months of development time," says Peter Tittler, Avis networks and technology vice president. Furthermore, some of the applications devoured so many mainframe computing cycles that Avis couldn't afford to use them as extensively as they otherwise would have. "Using the Mac has allowed us to answer business questions that we would not have attempted in the past," adds Tittler.

A third firm, Miller Brewing Company of Milwaukee, Wisconsin, has also decided to downsize its information systems environment [APPL92]. They currently use a mainframe for transaction processing and paper for decision support, addressing questions such as how best to stack beer in a shipping container.

Miller is starting small, with a pilot application to process beer export orders using local networks and client/server computing. This pilot will involve only 8 to 10 users and an investment in the low five figures. The next step will allow employees to access sales and marketing data via easy-to-use microcomputer-based tools and LANs rather than the cumbersome mainframe. Their eventual network will, as with the previous two systems, retain the mainframe as a server. Clients will be Apple Macintoshes and IBM PS/2s, the latter running both MS-DOS/Windows and OS/2.

3. DSS users are not fully satisfied with the mainframe environment. They feel that it and its staff are not always responsive to their needs—not unreasonably, since DSS usage accounts for a mere 5 percent of its workload. They are also unhappy with their charges for computing resources, having heard that smaller platforms, minicomputers and/or microcomputers, are more cost effective for DSS applications. They get one. Since no one system family is the best system for all applications, the likelihood is that their new small system is incompatible with the larger central system.

4. These users try to put their DSS on a mini or a micro. They soon find that parts of their application, such as a database that must be shared or is too large for a small computer's disk capacity, are better left where they are. They also realize, however, that it is technically difficult to access them in that location because of incompatibilities between their small system and the large central system. This, in turn, constrains their ability to do their jobs on the system of their choice. They press the firm's MIS organization to enable them to access corporate data.

5. The MIS department realizes, perhaps after some resistance and top management pressure, that these requests are reasonable and even important to the business. They see a need for systems of various sizes exchanging information: perhaps among separate applications in a traditional network, perhaps among parts of one application in a client/server architecture. They also realize that their current mainframe architecture does not permit this. They realize that a solution must involve several different types of computers. They move toward open systems as the most practical way to have these computers operate. (An alternative outcome, in which the MIS department does not come to realize that these requests are reasonable, may result in reassignment of MIS managers or outsourcing the MIS function.)

7.7 Choosing a DSS Hardware Environment

Here is a list of questions you can ask to help make your choice among the foregoing options. None of them, with the possible exception of the first, will give you a hard-and-fast direction that you can follow without further thought. Taken as a group, though, their set of answers will help point out the right DSS hardware approach.

1. Are there any corporate policies that you must follow? If there are, they may narrow your choice—by mandating one option or by eliminating some options.

2. How large and widespread will the DSS user community be? If it is large and widespread, will its members use exactly the same application, variations on one application, or different applications? When they use the same application, do they use it independently, or must their usage be coordinated through a shared database or in any other way? The more similarity,

the more sharing, the more you should look toward shared systems and LANs with high-end servers. The less sharing and similarity, the more power probably belongs on individual desktops.

3. Are most of the prospective users already using a particular system? If so, see if it can be used as is or with modifications such as a modest upgrade or interconnection via a LAN.

4. Is there a corporate mainframe with sufficient capacity, or to which sufficient capacity can be added at reasonable cost? (It may have sufficient capacity now, but normal load growth may mean that it won't in the future. Adding the DSS may hasten the need for an upgrade. Exercise 1 addresses this issue.)

5. Is there a minicomputer, linked to that mainframe or not, with sufficient capacity?

6. Do prospective users already have PCs or workstations that can handle the application?

7. If new systems are required, will the existing mainframe be able to share data with them? to shoulder an application jointly with them?

8. Do the necessary development tools exist for any of those systems? Are they already within the organization, available from the system vendor, or available from third parties?

9. With which of these systems and tools, if any, are the likely DSS developers already familiar?

10. Does the application require access to a database? If so, is the database derived from corporate data or from a separate source? If from corporate data, how up-to-date need the database be for the application (to the minute, as of the end of the last business day, etc.)?

11. Does the application's use of the corporate database require only the ability to read the data, or must it also be able to update the data?

12. How much processing power does the application require? How much data storage capacity?

13. Are prospective users capable of performing (and willing to perform) basic system administration tasks, such as installing software and backing up data files?

Summary

Decision support systems can run on mainframes, on smaller systems linked to the corporate mainframe, or on smaller systems—most often microcomputers—that are independent of the corporate mainframe.

Mainframes may be suitable when they have adequate capacity (not always the case!), prospective DSS users are already using them, and immediate access to central corporate data is required.

Minicomputers or microcomputers linked to the mainframe may be good choices when a separate system can provide better tools or more responsiveness, when the overhead of moving data to the smaller system is acceptable, and when the complexity of dealing with a two-computer system can be handled.

Stand-alone systems, usually microcomputers, are an option when the application does not require much data from the central system and when the processing power and storage capacity of a PC are sufficient.

The client/server approach, in which an application is split across two cooperating computers, allows users to take advantage of the cost performance and ease of use of small systems together with the computing power and shared databases of larger systems.

Time-sharing usage, though declining in popularity, may provide access to specialized hardware or software.

Open systems are increasingly used as the basis for developing applications that require access to a shared database or other forms of cooperation among systems from several different vendors.

Key Terms

capacity planners 218
client/server computing 223
Ethernet 228
file server 223
information base 220
local area network (LAN) 223
LocalTalk 228
mainframe computer 220
minicomputer 222
multiprocessing, multiprocessor 223
open system, open software environment 231
parallel processing 223
platform 218
POSIX 233
proprietary system, proprietary software environment 233
time sharing 230
Token Ring 228
UNIX 233

Review Questions

1. What are the four major DSS hardware environments?
2. State the advantages and disadvantages of running a decision support system on the corporate mainframe computer.
3. What is an "information base?" Can it be updated by its users?
4. Why might a DSS that uses an information base be unavailable for several hours, even assuming no hardware or software failures?

5. What is multiprocessing? Why is it helpful?
6. When are microcomputers on a LAN likely to be more economical than a shared system with terminals for decision support usage?
7. Define client/server computing.
8. Is it possible to have many clients sharing many servers?
9. How could client/server computing use an information base?
10. What is the difference between a stand-alone application and a stand-alone hardware system?
11. Define "open systems."
12. What is the most widely used multi-user open operating system? Which vendors offer hardware on which it can run?
13. Is there a relationship between DSS and open systems? If so, what is it?
14. How might corporate policies influence your choice of a DSS hardware/software environment?
15. State several technical factors that would influence your choice of a DSS hardware/software environment.
16. State several nontechnical factors that would influence your choice of a DSS hardware/software environment.

Exercises

1. The second drawback of a mainframe system for DSS (Section 7.2.2) read in part "the cost of additional mainframe resources to run a DSS may exceed the cost of smaller computers to handle the same task." What if the mainframe has sufficient excess capacity to handle the DSS load without an upgrade? Does this statement still apply? If it applies some of the time, but not all of the time, when does it and when doesn't it?
2. The seventh drawback of a mainframe system for DSS (Section 7.2.2) read in part "existing communication links may not be up to the increased load of graphs and pictures." A typical alphanumeric monitor can display 25 lines of 80 characters each. A typical microcomputer graphics monitor in 1993 can display 640 dots horizontally by 480 dots vertically. A typical link from a computer to a terminal within the same building can transmit data at 9600 bits per second. Assuming nonstop one-directional transmission without pause or error, which is optimistic, calculate how long it would take to transmit *(a)* one screenful of alphanumeric data, *(b)* one screenful of black-and-white graphics, and *(c)* one screenful of 256-color graphics. (Your answers will be, fortunately, worst-case conditions. There are many

ways of compressing screen descriptions. These take advantage of different character frequencies in character strings, the use of common geometric shapes such as rectangles, and repeated dots of the same color for shapes that are hard to describe geometrically. Simple decompression can be done by even the slowest desktop microcomputer without visibly degrading response time.)

3. Consider the client/server computing spectrum as shown in Figure 7–1. Assume an application calls for retrieving about 100 customer records out of a file with 100,000 such records, of 2,000 bytes each, and graphing some data found in those records. This application could be partitioned in (at least) three ways:
   - Transmit the 100,000-record file from a file server to the client system. The client then retrieves the desired records and displays the graph.
   - Using a database server, retrieve the desired 100 records, and transmit them to the client system. The client then creates and displays the graph.
   - Retrieve the records, and create the graph on a powerful central system. Transmit the description of the graph as in part *c* of Exercise 2 to the client, which displays the colored dots it receives.

   Calculate the number of bits that must be transmitted over the client/server link for all three of these cases. How long would the communication process take *(a)* if 2400-bit-per-second (bps) modems are used or *(b)* if a LAN with an effective speed of 3 million bps is used?
4. Consider the two applications in the box on downsizing, pages 234–35. Where would you put them in the spectrum of client/server approaches shown in Figure 7–1?
5. Find a user of a time-sharing system. Find out why that person (or, if appropriate, his or her organization) opted for time sharing over desktop microcomputers.

References

APPL92 Appleby, Chuck. "Client/Server on Tap." *Information Week* 366 (March 30, 1992), pp. 92–93.

GILL92 Gill, Philip J. "The Challenges of Downsizing." *Open Systems Today* (March 2, 1992), pp. 70–78.

MORA92 Moran, Robert. "The Drive for Easier Access." *Information Week* 362 (March 2, 1992), p. 44.

NOON90 Noonan, David C., and James T. Curtis. *Groundwater Remediation and Petroleum: A Guide for Underground Storage Tanks*, Lewis Publishers, Chelsea, Mich. (1990).

ENVOYANCE: CLEANING THE GROUNDWATER (I)

The technical background for this episode is primarily from [NOON90].

"Well, folks, do you remember mentioning Mitona Creek last time you were here?" asked Jim with a big grin when Doug and Adrienne looked in on him the next Thursday.[4]

"Sure do!" Doug responded. "From that grin on your face, there must be something about it you want to tell us!" added Adrienne.

"You're right, there is. The good news is that we got the cleanup job for that spill. Now we've got to get a lot of gasoline out of the groundwater in that area so it won't contaminate the town drinking water supply."

"What's 'a lot of gasoline' in a case like this?"

"The leaky underground tank that caused the problem held 5,000 gallons. Since it went in before December 1988, it didn't have to meet any standards for underground storage tanks. They found the leak because gasoline was disappearing in their inventory records faster than they were using it. They just started that check recently, when new EPA regulations forced them to, so we don't know how long it was leaking. What we do know is that there's a lot of gasoline down there. One gallon of gasoline can put enough of various gasoline components into the groundwater to put a million gallons of water over the regulatory limit for drinking.

"For the past few months, since they caught wind of the problem, the town has been getting all its water from the two wells on the east side, but they can't keep that up forever. The west wells, the ones near the spill, have to get back into operation. We helped them put together a corrective action plan. It's gone through its public notice, a meeting, and the agency review. Now it's been approved, and we're ready to get to work.

"Fortunately, this is not the first time gasoline ever leaked from an underground tank, and there are a number of ways to deal with it. One of the most proven methods is called air stripping. It basically involves blowing bubbles through the water. Gasoline moves out of the water and into the bubbles. We can then either collect the bubbles for further treatment or let them evaporate into the air."

"How do you get the bubbles down where the groundwater is?" Doug asked. "Isn't it hard to reach?"

"If the mountain won't come to Mohammed . . ." Jim mused. "That's a good point. There actually are ways to get the bubbles into the subsurface, but they're not appropriate for this site. We determined that during the feasibility study when we developed our corrective action plan. So we have to bring the water to where the bubbles are. We have to pump the water out anyhow, so we pump it through a cleaning unit first. The most likely kind of cleaning unit is called a packed tower

[4]The Envoyance episode at the end of Chapter 5 discussed Mitona Creek briefly.

aerator. The water drips down through packing material inside the tower so it breaks up into drops. While the drops are dripping, we're also pumping air up from the bottom. The air goes out the top, along with most of the gasoline that was dissolved in the water. Clean water comes out the bottom.

"Designing a packed tower aerator is a straightforward process, but the calculations are complicated enough to drive Einstein crazy. We have to pick the packing material, the air-to-water ratio, the air pressure, the water pumping rate, the tower dimensions, the depth of the packing, etc., etc. There are about a dozen steps in the process. Most of them involve a page of equations as long as your arm. You can see a few on the board on your left there (see Figure 7–3). I counted the numerical parameters once: There are 38 of them! And when you're done, you're not really all done. You look at the costs, decide you can do better, and go back and do it again."

"Sounds like a lot of work," said Adrienne as Doug and Jim nodded agreement. "What are some of the cost factors?"

(This discussion will be continued, with cost factors, at the end of Chapter 10.)

FIGURE 7–3

Jim's Blackboard

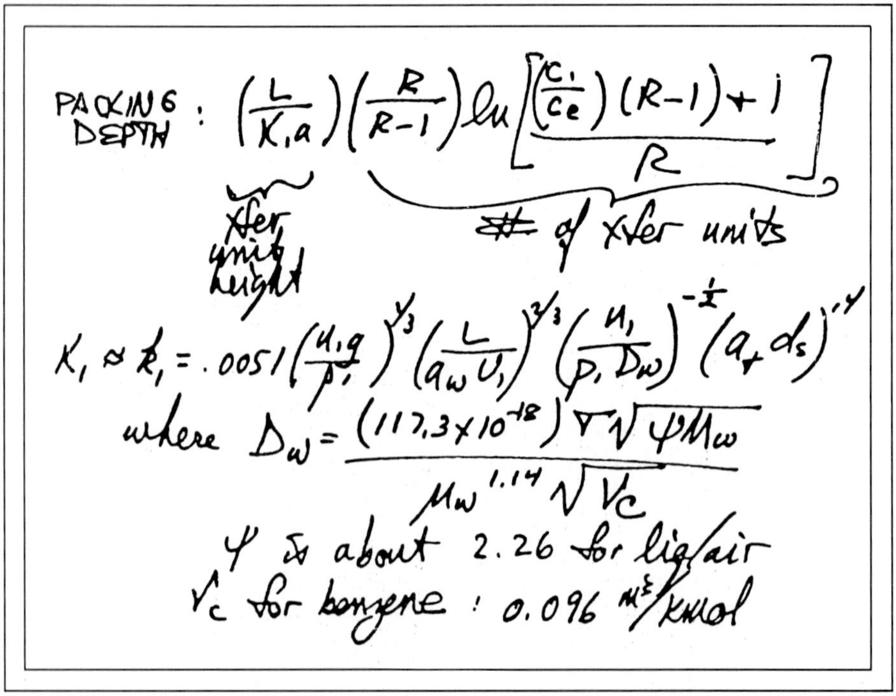

PACKING DEPTH: $\left(\frac{L}{K_1 a}\right)\left(\frac{R}{R-1}\right) \ln\left[\frac{\left(\frac{C_i}{C_e}\right)(R-1)+1}{R}\right]$

xfer unit height — # of xfer units

$$K_1 \approx k_1 = .0051\left(\frac{\mu_1 g}{\rho_1}\right)^{1/3}\left(\frac{L}{a_w U_1}\right)^{2/3}\left(\frac{\mu_1}{\rho_1 D_w}\right)^{-\frac{1}{2}}\left(a_t d_s\right)^{.4}$$

where $D_w = \frac{(117.3\times 10^{-18})\, T\sqrt{\varphi M_w}}{\mu_w^{1.14}\sqrt{V_c}}$

φ is about 2.26 for liq/air

V_c for benzene: 0.096 m^3/kmol

Exercises

1. Would the problem of designing packed tower aerators justify a package? a custom program using a DSS generator? a custom program developed in a general-purpose programming language? If it would call for custom programming, which of the approaches discussed in Chapter 5 would you recommend?
2. Do you feel that the stand-alone microcomputers that Envoyance uses would be suitable for designing packed tower aerators? What enhancements to their system, if any, would help them?
3. You have decided to develop a packed tower aerator design DSS from scratch with no prior constraints. What type of hardware would you recommend? Why? (All you have to know for purposes of this question is that their design involves a little user input, no database access, a great deal of calculation, and a few pages or screenfuls of output in the form of either graphs or numerical tables.)
4. What advantages, if any, would the use of open systems offer for this DSS? Which aspect or aspects of openness would matter?
5. Could a local area network (LAN) be of any use to this DSS? If so, how?
6. Could a parallel processing system be of any use to this DSS? If so, how?

CHAPTER

8 Implementing Decision Support Systems

Chapter Outline

Introduction

By now you should have a good conceptual understanding of decision support systems, what they do, and how they do it. As you probably realize, though, conceptual understanding is of little practical value unless it is put to work. In this chapter you'll learn about the nuts-and-bolts issues—both technical and nontechnical—of putting a DSS to use in a real-world environment.

Chapter Objectives

After you have read and studied this chapter, you will be able to:

1. Describe the implementation stage of a decision support system, and explain how it fits in the overall decision support system life cycle.
2. Describe the activities that take place during the DSS implementation stage and why each is important.
3. Summarize four approaches to system conversion, and explain how they apply to decision support systems as opposed to other types of information systems.
4. Explain why potential DSS users resist change and how resistance can be overcome.
5. Describe technical and user-related issues that arise in decision support implementation and how you can use knowledge of these issues to ensure successful implementation.
6. Discuss the ethical issues arising from implementation.

8.1 THE IMPLEMENTATION STAGE

We discussed the development process for decision support systems in Chapter 6. That discussion took us to the point of a working application: If the proper inputs go in, the proper outputs will come out. A working program—even a working system—is not the end of the process, however, unless its developer is to be its only user. As you probably learned in your systems analysis course, the program or system has to be "rolled out" to its user community. This part of the system life cycle is called *implementation.* A typical definition comes from Kendall and Kendall: "the process of assuring that the information system is operational and then allowing users to take over its operation for use and evaluation" [KEND88]. The place of implementation in the overall system development process is shown graphically in Figure 8–1, as well as some of the major subtasks involved. The phases are shown as overlapping because they do. The lines indicating the ends of the phases slope because the phases may continue for some parts of the system or the database after they have finished for others.

Some people define implementation differently. Your introductory MIS textbook (or instructor) may not have agreed with your systems analysis textbook (or instructor). Specifically, some people include part or all of the system design and development process under this heading. In this book we'll use the term "implementation" to include everything that takes place from the moment that system developers determine that their system is technically ready to be placed in the hands of its intended users until those developers are free to move on to their next project. (The next project, of course, may be the next release of this very DSS.)

If a DSS is developed using end-user computing tools and will not be made available to a large user community, the entire implementation issue may become trivial. However, many DSS are developed via either the tra-

FIGURE 8–1

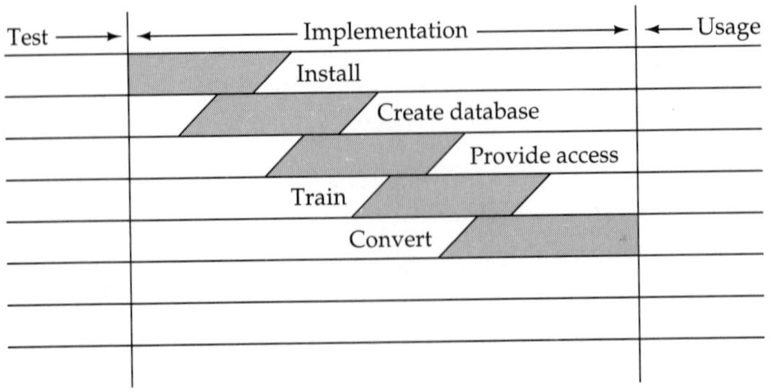

ditional SDLC or a prototyping approach. In these cases, implementation is critical: "There are no prizes for plowing a straight furrow if the crops don't come up!" Most of the discussion that follows applies to such systems. As we noted in Chapter 5, though, systems developed via end-user computing can also benefit from systematic thought about these issues, even if they do not require a full-blown version of every step in the process.

Implementation includes the following activities. All must be included in the overall DSS project plan, with the necessary resources allocated to each. You can see that the complexity of each activity can vary dramatically from one DSS to another. Often, a DSS that is simple is one aspect of its implementation will be complex in another.

- *Obtaining and installing the DSS hardware.* This does not apply if the intended user community is already using the required hardware for other purposes. However, a new DSS often involves upgraded central systems, new LANs, new servers, new or upgraded desktop hardware, new networking connections, and perhaps more. These must be installed and operational before the next step can begin.
- *Installing the DSS and making it operational on its intended hardware.* This may be trivial if the system was developed on the same multi-user computer on which it is intended to run in production use: It is already installed. Its users need only be made aware of how to invoke it. Installation is more of an issue if a system must be installed in multiple computers throughout an organization.
- *Providing user access to the system.* This is trivial if the system is installed in microcomputers on the users' desks. In more complex situations, providing user access may require installing networks, extensive new wiring, and either terminals or a terminal emulation hardware/software package in the users' microcomputers. It may also require registration of the users on the system, including passwords, creation of electronic "mailboxes," assignment to groups, granting of priority levels, allocation of disk storage, and more.
- *Creating and updating the database.* Again, this activity can be trivial or nonexistent if an existing database is to be accessed without modification. In many situations, though, a specialized DSS database or information base must be created, perhaps even combining existing corporate files and databases with data from external databases. The DSS database may also have to be distributed to a number of computers or LAN servers. This should have been done at least once during system testing. Now it is necessary to make the procedure a regular, and hopefully automated, activity.
- *Training the users on the new system.* People who don't know how to use a system can hardly be expected to use it willingly or to be able to obtain the maximum benefit from it. Training should not be left to programmers, who are often impatient with nontechnical end users.

A systems analyst with good people skills can be used in a pinch, but trained trainers are ideal.

In a mainframe or minicomputer environment, or if multiple microcomputers and LANs are involved, it may also be necessary to train system operators, administrators, or both on the operational aspects of the new system.

- *Documenting the system for its users and for those who will be responsible for maintaining it in the future.* Ideally, this will have been done in large part as the DSS was developed. Reality, however, suggests, otherwise. Pressure to get the system working and the natural reluctance of many programmers to write documentation combine to make documentation an afterthought. The implementation process is not complete until all the required types of system documentation have been written and are known to be satisfactory.
- *Making arrangements to support the users as the system is used.* This is especially important for DSS, whose users often use the system infrequently (thus forgetting details from one session to the next), use it in different ways each time (thus using different commands, options, etc.), and, as managers, may be used to better support in many respects than their clerical co-workers have been trained to expect.
- *Transferring ongoing responsibility for the system from its developers to the operations or maintenance part of the MIS group.* Specifics will depend on how your MIS group is organized.
- *Evaluating the operation and use of the system.* This is the only way management can determine if it is receiving the benefits it expected when it commissioned the DSS—and, if not, why not. Whether the answer to this question is in the affirmative or in the negative, the answer is important for the future of DSS in the organization.

  The evaluation must include objective assessments such as usage frequency, subjective assessments of user satisfaction, and an attempt to determine the impact of the system on the quality of decisions made and on the time it takes to make them. Adelman covers this subject in detail in [ADEL92].

8.2 System Conversion

The most visible component of the implementation process is the system conversion itself. Palvia et al. discuss several conversion strategies in [PALV91]. The four basic strategies, which you probably learned about in your introductory MIS or systems analysis course, are *direct cutover, parallel conversion, pilot conversion*, and *phased conversion*. Here's how these four basic conversion strategies apply to decision support systems:

- In *direct cutover*, the entire organization stops using its old system and starts using the new one at the same time. This is a high-risk conversion strategy for transaction processing systems, as the impact of any problems is felt throughout the organization. It may be suitable for DSS, however. Since DSS usually access, but do not modify, the organizational database, reverting to a previous computer system or to manual decision-making methods is often feasible. This differs from the typical transaction processing case, where the older system may have been designed for an older set of data files, and the data in these files are no longer current.
- *Parallel conversion* involves running both the old and the new systems and comparing their results. This is not a workable strategy for on-line transaction processing systems as it requires users to enter all their transactions twice. (It can be used if the old system is manual, and sometimes if it is batch oriented, but those situations grow less common every year.) If the system in question supports a large number of regular users, running two versions may also impose unacceptable hardware resource requirements. In the case of data-oriented DSS, parallel operation is pointless: Why display the same data twice? For high-level DSS, especially suggestion systems that require little user input and perform complex optimizations, parallel conversion may be a reasonable approach. Furthermore, the user community of such systems tends to be small, although exceptions exist. In this case, the hardware resource impact of parallel conversion would probably be acceptable.
- *Pilot conversion* means introducing a system to a small part of the organization, expanding its use once it has been found to operate properly in that area. This is a good approach for single-user or multi-user DSS, as it limits conversion risk and allows system developers to concentrate their problem resolution efforts on a small number of users and locations. It may not be feasible for a group DSS since the very nature of a group DSS requires it to be in general use within the decision-making group. If the pilot conversion strategy is used for group DSS, the pilot group must be large enough to provide a meaningful user community. If the GDSS is intended to help people at different locations communicate, as a video teleconferencing system, the pilot group must encompass multiple geographic sites. In addition, the bottom-line benefits of many DSS argue for rolling it out on a wide basis as quickly as possible.
- *Phased conversion* means introducing a system in stages, one component or module at a time, waiting until that one is operating

properly before introducing the next. This is an appropriate strategy for a DSS when it can be divided into several modules, each providing new and visible benefits to its users. This is often the case with group DSS, for which pilot conversion may not be appropriate. For example, it might be possible to introduce Lotus Notes (see Section 11.7.3) for communication within an organization and then, when it is performing well in this role, add the capability to scan external databases for *Wall Street Journal* articles containing specific keywords. If the first modules of a DSS do not provide some visible benefit to most users, they will create a negative attitude toward the system that will increase user resistance to the remaining—and presumably more beneficial—modules.

Ideally, a phased conversion will begin with the most important modules and proceed through the less important ones. In some cases, this will not be possible. If data flow serially through the modules, the only practical phasing strategy may be to start with one end of the system and proceed to the other. If your system relies on an information base, the first conversion phase will have to be the creation of this information base. You may then have some flexibility in sequencing the other phases.

Figure 8–2 shows how the desirability of each conversion strategy for DSS compares with its desirability in other types of information systems. Many practical conversion situations call for a combination of these basic strategies. For example, a system may initially be implemented on a phased basis in part of the organization. Once it is running in its entirety for that user community, it can be rolled out to the entire firm.

FIGURE 8–2

Conversion Strategy Desirability Comparison Chart

	Viability of Conversion Method for . . .	
	Transaction Processing System	*Decision Support Systems*
Direct Cutover	Usually unacceptable risk	Usually acceptable risk
Parallel Conversion	Usually impractical	Usually practical
Pilot Conversion	Generally first choice	May raise operational issues
Phased Conversion	Usually requires large effort to interface two databases	Good choice for read-only systems such as most DSS

8.3 OVERCOMING RESISTANCE TO CHANGE

Change is inherent in the implementation of any new system. Change is, however, uncomfortable to those who undergo it. Niccolò Machiavelli knew this centuries ago, when he wrote that "there is nothing more difficult to take in hand, more perilous to conduct, or more uncertain in its success, than to take the lead in the introduction of a new order of things" [MACH32]. He went on to explain that few people will stand to gain much from a change, so the change will have but few and lukewarm defenders. Many will stand to lose a great deal from it and will therefore fight it tooth and nail.

The prospective DSS implementor must therefore be keenly aware of the personal and organizational impact of a change.

> The design and implementation of a DSS is an example of planned technological change. The success or failure of a proposed DSS depends on how well this change process is managed [CHER90].

Managing change, needless to say, is not a technical issue. It has nothing to do with megabytes of disk space, programming languages, or client/server network architectures. It deals with *people*. This is often an uncomfortable situation for MIS staffers, who may have chosen their field because they felt it put less emphasis on interpersonal relationships than other careers might. (This is, of course, not true of everyone in MIS, but it is one reason that some people gravitate toward working with computers.) Yet managing change is a necessary task.

Organizational culture is a key consideration in planning any change. Some organizations welcome change. Others say, in effect, "we've always done it this way" and resist change. Once you have been with an organization for a while you'll probably have a good idea what its culture is and how easily changes are likely to go over. If you're new to an organization, or haven't been exposed to situations that would permit you to evaluate its receptivity to change, ask more experienced colleagues. The better ones will be impressed with how perceptive you are about the need to take cultural factors into account.

Change can be thought of as taking place in a three-stage process, which was first put forth by Lewin and is now generally known as the Lewin-Schein Theory of Change [LEWI47, LEWI47a; also most books on organizational behavior]. These stages are *unfreezing*, *moving*, and *refreezing*. Unfreezing creates the conditions and attitudes that are necessary before meaningful change can take place. Moving constitutes the change itself: putting the new system into operation to replace the old. Refreezing involves making the new system as much a part of the organizational fabric as the old one ever was.

The need to manage change in this sense applies, of course, primarily to *institutional* DSS in the sense of Section 4.7. An *ad hoc* DSS, intended for one-time use and discarded as soon as the need for it goes away, does not become

Introducing Automation: The Social Security Administration

In the late 1970s, the U.S. Social Security Administration developed a minicomputer-based system via which claims representatives in its field offices could access individual Social Security records. The purpose of this system, which had many aspects of a "file drawer" DSS, was to eliminate the laborious paper-based process of obtaining information about a claimant's entitlement to Social Security benefits, the history of a claim, etc. Much of the necessary data were kept in computer files at Social Security Administration headquarters in Baltimore, Maryland. Prior to the development of this system, those files could not be accessed on-line from the field offices.

The initial attempt to implement this system in a small number of pilot field offices was a disastrous failure. The reasons were totally nontechnical. Many of the claims representatives had previously held clerical and secretarial positions with the Social Security Administration. They had been promoted from those jobs to their current professional positions and were proud of their new status. The externally visible symbol of their promotion was that they no longer had a typewriter—a device with a keyboard—on their desks. Now the MIS group was trying to put a terminal—not exactly a typewriter, but still a device that requires keyboard skills for effective use—on their desks again. "What are they trying to tell me here?" they thought. "What is the real message in this computer thing? Am I going to become a secretary, in fact if not in title, again?"

Once the problem was recognized, the MIS group removed the unwanted terminals from the offices where they had been placed and replanned the implementation process. They began in a new set of pilot offices by installing one terminal on a manager's desk and training the manager to use it. From time to time claims representatives would, in the normal course of their work, ask that manager a question about a case. The manager would say, "Let's look that up," and enter a query into the terminal. The answer came back in seconds rather than weeks. Soon the claims representatives were asking, "How can I get one of those terminal things?" The answer was, of course, "How soon would you like it?" Once it was installed, the claims representatives became enthusiastic users of the system.

Nothing about the system changed between the first attempt at a pilot implementation and the second. Nor did anything change in the claims representatives' backgrounds. What changed was their image of a terminal: from a symbol of a clerical position to a symbol of a managerial position. Once they had seen the terminal on their managers' desks, claims representatives no longer focused on its keyboard and therefore no longer associated the device with clerical work.

The specifics of this situation would be different in the 1990s. Today we are all used to seeing terminals and microcomputers on the desks of professionals and managers. The lesson, however, is timeless: that the culture and symbols of an organization are as important as, perhaps more important than, technical factors in introducing new computer technology to end users.

part of the organizational fabric and therefore does not need the level of acceptance that an institutional DSS requires. If an *ad hoc* DSS is useful for its intended purpose, it will be used. If not, it won't be. In either case it will soon be gone.

8.3.1 *Unfreezing*

In the unfreezing stage it is important to create a strong motivation for change. If the present system is generally felt to be unsatisfactory, that may be sufficient motivation by itself. If not, it is necessary to create a vision of how much better things could be and to show how the proposed system will help make them better. The content of these preparatory activities can be based on the justification that was developed before management approved the DSS project, but the benefits must now be made clear to the prospective users of the system. They, not only the managers who hold the purse strings, must be able to visualize its benefits.

There are three ways in which people can be unfrozen from their present position:

1. By increasing the forces that motivate them to change. If the current release of the corporate standard word processing package isn't enough better than the package people are already using to be worth the conversion effort, perhaps the next one will show enough new features to make them want to switch.

2. By reducing the forces that motivate them to resist change. Education can be a powerful change agent in this sense since fear of the unknown is a big reason that people resist change.

3. By adjusting an existing force so that it becomes a force for, rather than against, change. If a compensation plan based on this quarter's profits is changed to a deferred compensation plan based partly on next year's profits, people will be more likely to make investments that will pay off in the future.

Some unfreezing activity can take place before system implementation. As soon as systems analysts start studying the need for a new system, they are finding areas that could be improved and thus creating a vision of a better way of working. However, this work may not have involved the entire user community, may have been undertaken before it was certain that the new system would be developed, almost certainly did not explicitly focus on changing user attitudes, and may have taken place several months before system implementation starts. It is therefore necessary to revisit the unfreezing issue now, to make sure that user attitudes as a whole are ready for change and to prepare them if they are not.

The administrative side of system implementation must also be looked to at this time. Although this is conceptually distinct from unfreezing, it tends to occur at about the same time because it must also be done before the implementation proper can begin. Here the implementors or their manager must develop a complete project plan for the implementation process, describing the people who will participate in this process, their respective roles, and milestones by which the progress of the implementation can be measured against its plan.

Several favorable and unfavorable forces that can influence the likelihood of success are given in [ZAND75]. The ones that affect the unfreezing stage are listed in Figure 8–3. Here, and in the two subsequent figures from that source, we have substituted "DSS implementors" for the original "management scientists."

8.3.2 *Moving*

The most visible component of the moving stage is the actual conversion, or cutover, from the old (perhaps manual) decision-making methods to the new DSS. The technical aspects of conversion are sufficiently important that we devoted Section 8.2 entirely to them.

Training that takes place during the conversion process must be matched to the conversion strategy. If pilot conversion is to be used, for example, the training must be provided first to the pilot department. If parallel conversion is to be used, the trainers must deal with any expected differences between the outputs of the old and new systems. The specific training requirements that the chosen conversion strategy imposes must be taken into account in the project plan developed during the unfreezing stage.

During the moving stage the project leader must continually monitor project progress against plan. This monitoring has two purposes: to determine that project milestones are being met on schedule and to determine, by speaking with both MIS staff members and system users, that they are being met with the required quality. If either of these is not the case, corrective action must be instituted. If adverse consequences were properly considered while the plan was being developed, as described in Section 2.6.7, the necessary corrective action(s) will usually have been identified in advance.

FIGURE 8–3

Favorable and Unfavorable Factors for Unfreezing Stage

Favorable	*Unfavorable*
Top and unit managers felt the problem was important to the company	Unit managers could not state their problems clearly
Top managers became involved	Top managers felt the problem was too big
Unit managers recognized a need for change	Unit managers did not recognize need for change
Top managers initiated the study	Unit managers felt threatened by the project
Top and unit managers were open and candid	Unit managers resented the study
Unit managers revised some of their assumptions	Unit managers lacked confidence in the DSS implementors
	Unit managers felt they could do the study alone

Favorable and unfavorable factors for the moving stage, again from [ZAND75], are in Figure 8–4.

8.3.3 Refreezing

Refreezing makes sure that the users of the new system have the necessary internal commitment to using it on an ongoing basis. This is particularly important in DSS, as most DSS are used when the user decides to use them. This is different from transaction processing systems: an order-entry operator, for example, must enter an order when it comes in no matter how he or she feels about doing so. By contrast, if the users of a DSS feel they can make decisions adequately without the new system, they will ignore the system once its developers leave the users' offices or will resent being forced to use it against their will. In either case the desired system benefits will not be fully achieved.

Chervany and Palvia found that three factors have positive effects on all stages of the change process [CHER90]. According to their research, you will increase the likelihood of successful DSS implementation if you

- Have a strong project "champion" in the form of a highly placed executive who supports the project visibly.
- Allow sufficient time for each stage of change to take place.
- Make sure each stage of change is successful before moving to the next.

They also found that the ability to reverse the change, which is often felt to reduce the pressure associated with a change and therefore to facilitate it, has the opposite effect in the moving and refreezing stages. One possible explanation is that users, once "unfrozen" from their previous state, can go

FIGURE 8–4

Favorable and Unfavorable Factors for Moving Stage

Favorable	*Unfavorable*
Unit managers and DSS implementors gathered data jointly	DSS implementors could not educate the unit managers
Relevant data were accessible and available	Needed data were not made available
New alternatives were devised	Unit managers did not help develop a solution
Unit managers reviewed and evaluated alternatives	Unit managers did not understand the solution of the DSS implementors
Top managers were advised of options	DSS implementors felt the study was concluded too quickly
Top managers helped develop a solution	
Proposals were improved sequentially	

in either direction. If they know a change is reversible, they will not have the emotional commitment to the new system that will make it succeed. The lesson for DSS developers: the ability to try out a system (via prototyping, end-user development, or a 30-day free trial of a package) can be helpful in the development and unfreezing stages, but the commitment to change should be absolute thereafter.

Figure 8–5 shows Zand and Sorensen's favorable and unfavorable factors for the refreezing stage [ZAND75].

8.4 DSS Implementation Issues

You probably studied the area of system implementation in your more general MIS courses. Our goal here is to take what you already know and to focus it specifically on DSS implementation issues. DSS implementation differs from the implementation of other types of applications for both technical and user-related reasons. Each type is important. Furthermore, each type of reason can be divided into causes of failure and strategies for success. These two two-way splits can be visualized as in Figure 8–6.

8.4.1 Technical DSS Implementation Issues

Technical factors in DSS implementation include making sure that the DSS operates as it is supposed to, with adequate performance and reliability, and

Figure 8–5

Favorable and Unfavorable Factors for Refreezing Stage

Favorable	*Unfavorable*
Unit managers tried the solution	DSS implementors did not try to support new managerial behavior after the solution was used
Utilization showed the superiority of the new solution	DSS implementors did not try to reestablish stability after solution was used
DSS implementors initiated positive feedback after early use	Results were difficult to measure
Solution was widely accepted after initial success	Standards for evaluating the result were lacking
Unit managers were satisfied	Top managers ignored the solution recommended by the DSS implementors
Solution was used in other areas	Solution was incompatible with the needs and resources of the unit
The change improved the performance of the unit	Top managers did not encourage other units to use the solution

FIGURE 8–6

2 × 2 DSS Implementation Grid

	Technical	*User Related*
Things to Watch Out for (negatives)		
Things to Do (positives)		

yields accurate (as accuracy is defined for the system in question) results. Specific factors to watch for in the technical area include those discussed in the rest of this section.

Unfamiliarity with this Type of System

Clearly, the more familiar the developers are with the type of system they are designing and programming, the more likely they are to have a smooth development process. However, familiarity extends to the implementation stage as well. Developers who are unfamiliar with a particular class of system are more likely to follow a specification without fully understanding what it is about, less likely to intuit user needs, less likely to design useful interfaces, and less likely to provide support that truly meets the unspoken questions than those to whom this type of DSS is second nature. The best way to deal with the issue of unfamiliarity is to bring it out into the open, discuss it, and make sure that the developers pay special attention to understanding the true user requirements.

Unfamiliarity is not exactly the same as incompetence, although the results of the two are often similar [ALTE80]. Unfamiliarity creates specialized, often temporary, incompetence that should not be seen as a personal reflection on the people in question. This makes it possible to deal with unfamiliarity frankly and openly, without the negative connotations that calling developers "incompetent" would carry.

Response Time

Users get frustrated quickly when activities that they perceive as "simple" take a long time. Response time can and should be tested before implementation, of course. However, developers who are aware of the internal complexity of a particular operation may be more tolerant of long execution times than are users who see only the end result of each computational process. Furthermore, developers may have been using a lightly loaded system or high-performance workstations, where the general user community will have to contend with a heavier load on the hardware, slower microcomputers, or a full-scale database instead of the small one that was put together to test the software.

Response time, if inadequate, can be improved by faster hardware (a "brute force" approach that, although potentially expensive, usually works), by program tuning, and by database and network optimization. The non-technical side of response time, user expectation, is also important. It is discussed in Section 8.4.2.

Reliability and Availability

A system that crashes unpredictably at frequent intervals, that must be brought down during working hours for database reorganization and updating, that is subject to network failures that make it unusable, or that can only be accessed via an insufficient number of specialized terminals is not available to its users when and where they need it.

Poor Data Quality

As the old saying goes, "garbage in—garbage out." The output of a system can be only as good as its inputs. This can be a serious problem when data are collected from several sources, some of them external, for aggregation. The data must be monitored carefully for accuracy and timeliness. Another issue that arises when combining data from multiple sources is data *consistency:* Each individual element may be accurate but combining them may create nonsense if they apply to different time periods or use different definitions for some of their underlying concepts.

8.4.2 User-Related DSS Implementation Issues

The user-related issues in DSS implementation are often more complex than the technical ones. They may also be more difficult for the typical MIS professional to deal with.

Some user concerns about a new DSS must be addressed before the project reaches its implementation stage, of course. Far earlier, when the new system was being defined, systems analysts worked with prospective users to determine their requirements. At that point, it was necessary to develop a good relationship with the users, establish the credibility of the design team, and lay the foundation for a smooth implementation later on. If this preparatory groundwork was not properly done, the implementation will be much more difficult than it has to be.

Specific user-related implementation concerns with which DSS implementors must deal at this time include those discussed in the rest of this section.

User and Management Support

If a system's prospective users don't support it, they will at best use it sullenly and at worst sabotage it openly. If their management doesn't support the system, the users themselves never will. Systems that are initiated by users, or that have active user participation in their development, are more likely to have user support than those that are not.

Users and managers who are not truly committed to a new system can draw upon a wide variety of "game-playing" techniques to obstruct its implementation without appearing to oppose it overtly. Such games include "passing the buck" regarding the responsibility for a particular aspect of a system, appropriating its budget for "emergencies," slowing down progress while appearing to work hard, and more. Grover et al. discuss several such "games" [GROV88].

As noted above, much of the groundwork for this support should have been laid well before the implementation stage of the new system. Whether or not this was done, the project team must now make sure that both users and their managers understand why the new system was developed and how it will help them. A memo from a highly placed and personally respected member of management, timed to arrive shortly before user-visible implementation activities begin, is often helpful here. The visible attendance of one or more managers in a user training class, assuming that classroom training is to be used, can also convey a strong message to the overall user community.

Unstable User Community

The stability of the user community is closely tied to the previous factor. If users disappear or change frequently, it will be difficult to enlist their consistent support. No sooner will the DSS implementors have created a vision of the new system with one group of users than they will be gone and another group will have taken their place. The group that must ultimately use the system may not be the same as the one whose needs it was developed to meet. The new group may have different backgrounds, different problem-solving styles, different views of technology. The purpose, the usage pattern, and even the very decision statement that were so carefully worked out several months ago may turn out to be worth little.

There is little a DSS implementor can do to increase the stability of a user organization. However, the astute implementor can and must be aware of it. DSS design strategies that maximize flexibility in system usage modes, inputs, and outputs will help keep the system adaptable to any new group. If the changes take place one person at a time, regular meetings with the group as the system is being developed will help maintain the attitude that the new system is welcome and will be of value. (For an example of how continuity can maintain group norms, even after all the people who were originally responsible for those norms have long since departed, see the box on "Groupthink" in Section 11.2.)

Response Time

This is another way to look at the first technical issue discussed in the previous section. It is a nontechnical issue as well because it is neither "wrong" nor "right;" it is only adequate or inadequate relative to user expectations. Several studies have shown that users will accept response times as long as several minutes if they perceive a system to be carrying out a complex, time-consuming task on their behalf. Conversely, they will become frustrated in as short a time as one second if they perceive a task as trivial. Unfortunately, the complexity of a task to a computer is not always the same as its apparent complexity to a nontechnical end user. Proper management of user expectations can make a slow system adequate. Improper management of this factor can make a far faster system inadequate.

Training and documentation can explain to users what goes on behind a seemingly simple operation, so users will understand why a command does not yield an immediate answer. This is especially applicable to database operations that involve comparing entries in one table against those in another.

A periodically updated "working" message displaying a completion percentage or an estimate of remaining time to completion, a graphical "progress bar," or another indication that the system has not "crashed" gives users a sense of security that a long response time is normal.

When system load is expected to increase and thus slow response times in the future, a *speed governor* can be applied to a program to prevent users from subconsciously developing expectations that will not be sustained when the entire user community is active. A speed governor consists of an idle loop that is invoked as part of each user command. The number of times the loop is executed is under system administrator control and is reduced to maintain consistent response times as the number of system users increases. Palvia et al. mention the use of such a governor for this purpose at Polaroid Corporation's distribution division in [PALV91]. Since this approach uses processor cycles, it is acceptable only in a system that is dedicated to a particular application or that has excess capacity. Were other applications, besides Polaroid's distribution system, running on the same computer, the governor could have affected their response times as well.

Training

Types of training include classroom training, one-on-one tutoring at the user's office, self-teaching training vehicles such as books and videotapes, and computer-based instruction, increasingly including multimedia.

The choice among these depends on the number of people to be trained, their locations, the time frame within which the training must take place, and the available resources. Figure 8–7 compares the resource requirements of four training methods. The time availability of the trainees must also be taken into account. The more resource-intensive methods, such as one-on-one training, may be appropriate when the user community includes top executives or others whose time is considered, rightly or wrongly, much more valuable than that of the trainer. Classroom-based training is feasible only when it is practical to assemble a sufficiently large number of users at the same time

FIGURE 8–7
Relative Resource Requirements of Different Training Methods

		Type of Instruction			
		Classroom	*One-on-One*	*Books, Manuals*	*Videotape, Multimedia*
Resource Requirements	*Human Resources to Develop*	Medium	Low	High	Very high
	Human Resources to Deliver	Medium	High	Very low	Very low
	Other Resource Requirements	Computer-equipped classroom	None	None	VCR, CD-ROM-equipped workstation, etc., per chosen medium

and in the same place and when the required facilities, such as a computer or terminal for at least every pair of trainees, are available.

While system design is not, strictly speaking, a training method, good user-interface design can minimize the need for training. A prompting or menu-driven interface can require far less training of its users than a command-line interface would call for. There are trade-offs here too, of course: Training is a one-time expense for each system user, whereas many easy-to-use interface styles such as GUIs exact an ongoing cost in hardware resource usage.

Trainers must take the user's existing point of view as a departure point for any training. As pointed out in [MALL91], the trainer must not only know about the new system, but must also know a great deal about how its prospective users solved the same problem before the new system was available. They have undoubtedly developed mental models of how the worlds works, may have a specialized vocabulary to deal with it, and have acquired a set of habits that reflect their traditional way of reaching the decision in question. A trainer who does not know about these, or does not take them into account in the training, will lose much of his or her audience during the first five minutes.

Availability of Support

No formal training class, no user manual, no on-line help facility can answer all the questions that could possibly arise. Some questions will have to be answered by knowledgeable people as they come up. Providing a support *hot line* ensures that these questions will go to the right person or group of people. Such a support facility may already exist within an end-user computing support group or information center. If not, it will have to be set up.

The degree of formality depends on the DSS user community. If the user community is small and geographically centralized, giving users the name and telephone extension of the responsible systems analyst may suffice. If it consists of several hundred people spread over two or three continents, a more permanent *help desk* structure should be established.

Such a help desk, despite being a visible line item on someone's budget, is not an added expense to the organization as a whole. Users will have questions about a new system whether a help desk exists or not. If the organization does not provide a standard way for users with questions to obtain answers, one of two things will happen: Either the users will obtain an answer through any available informal channel, or the questions will go unanswered. In the first case, the organization is still absorbing the cost of answering the question. Indeed, it is probably answering the question less efficiently, and hence at greater cost, than if a standard channel existed. In the second case, the organization will not obtain the benefits that it was counting on its new DSS to provide. That is penny-wise and pound-foolish.

Voluntary or Mandatory Use?

The use of transaction processing systems is seldom voluntary. If the only way an airline can issue boarding passes is through a computer printer, its reservation clerks will have to use the computer. They have no choice.

With DSS, the option to make a decision without computer input is always there. An advertising manager who thinks computer-based demographic data on magazine readership will not help choose a better ad schedule will not use a DSS that provides demographic data. Will the ad schedule such a person chooses be better than he or she could have chosen with the computer? Probably not, but that's not the issue.

Should such people be forced to use the computer? There is no single right answer to this question. In the case of group DSS, mandatory use, or a high degree of pressure, may be appropriate because only a "critical mass" of users can make such a system viable. In other cases, especially where the system meets a visible, felt need, the carrot of better job performance may be more effective than the stick. Even there some motivation and exhortation is a good idea: Relying solely on exposure is generally ineffective.

In one situation, which Alter called "Connoisseur Foods" in [ALTE80], a food company developed a customer response model to help brand managers plan and manage their merchandising activities more effectively. Some of the newer brand managers took to the system like ducks to water and were soon using it to advantage. Others, including "people-oriented" brand managers who had come up through the sales ranks, resisted. The management policy in this case was to permit voluntary use of the system, although their manager of marketing services was reported as saying that, were he in charge, "no brand plan [could] be produced or changed without explicit evaluation based on a brand model. Furthermore, brand managers would have to submit printouts annotated with their own comments and analysis." Upper management overruled him.

In this case the system became generally accepted over a few years. One reason was that management did not stress its use in helping brand managers make their plans. Rather, they focused on how well the results of those plans matched the predictions of the model. Since the model was known to be accurate within a few percent as long as nothing changed in the external environment or the competitive picture, major deviations signaled such changes. This warned Connoisseur Foods management of such changes more quickly than they would have otherwise found out, thus enabling them to respond before it was too late.

8.4.3 *Using the Lists of Issues*

At this point you are probably thinking, "Now that I've got some long lists, what on earth do I do with them?" Here's one suggestion:

As you've seen, the lists break down two ways: things to watch out for (negatives, unfavorable factors) versus things to do (positives, favorable factors), and technical versus user-related issues. Those two breakdowns gave us the grid you've already seen as Figure 8–6.

When you plan a DSS project, go over the lists in the preceding sections, and try to pick issues for each quadrant of this grid: potential technical pitfalls for the top left corner and so on for the other three.

One entry in each quadrant of the grid is a good target to shoot for. However, this is not a rigidly fixed rule. If you rack your brain for days and can't find an entry for one of the quadrants, so be it. Don't lose any more sleep trying to find something that isn't there. Chances are that quadrant of

FIGURE 8–8

Filled-In DSS Implementation Grid

	Technical	*User Related*
Things to Watch Out for (negatives)	Slow response time due to need to scan the entire database to answer common queries	Concern that local database on LAN server will not be up to date
Things to Do (positives)	Verify that all prospective users have at least a 386SX/20 microprocessor and 2 MB of RAM in their system	Make sure trainers have used the existing mainframe-based query system and know how the new query syntax differs from the old one

the grid is under control. Conversely, if you go through the list and find two or three important issues that all belong in the same quadrant, that's fine too: Put them all in. The grid is a planning tool. You control it. It doesn't (or shouldn't) control you. Its purpose is to give you a structured way to whittle all these lists down to a manageable size. Used this way, it can be quite helpful.

This will give you a situation-specific short list of critical factors. Plan for and watch them. That will give you enough to keep you busy and will pick up the most critical issues for your particular project. You might end up with a grid such as the one in Figure 8–8.

8.5 Ethical Issues in DSS Implementation

DSS professionals must do more than just apply their technical skills to DSS development and implementation. They have a professional obligation to use these skills in an ethical manner. Unfortunately, this is not always easy. The temptation of what has been called "a deal with the Devil" is ever present [CHRI90]. The DSS developer who knows in advance what temptations may arise, and has thought about how he or she might respond if they do, will be better equipped to withstand them. In the long run this ability will pay off.

Ethical issues arise throughout the life cycle of any information system, including DSS. The implementation stage is where they come into clearest focus. Until then, the DSS is being developed in a laboratory. It is in actual usage where it might potentially invade people's privacy, contribute to unethical management decisions, and more. The subject of ethics in a DSS context is therefore considered here. However, ethical behavior cannot be put into sealed compartments, separated from the rest of one's professional life. Ethical considerations apply to all stages of DSS development from the beginning. The sooner they are addressed in a system, the more likely they are to come to a satisfactory resolution for all concerned. If you wait until the implementation stage to raise an issue that has existed since the system was defined conceptually, management can well ask, "If that bothers you, how come you didn't say anything for the past eight months?" Even if the issue is ultimately resolved in an ethical fashion, resources will have been wasted, and hard feelings that could have been avoided will have been created.

Consider this scenario: You are developing a decision support system to help bank loan officers process second mortgage and home improvement loan applications. Bank executives know that members of certain ethnic groups have less access to credit than other members of the community. For lack of alternatives, members of these groups, once they find a bank that will grant them a loan, will pay higher interest rates than others would accept before taking their business elsewhere. Bank executives also realize that members of these groups tend to live in certain neighborhoods, which can be defined by street names and numbers. You have been told to add 0.25 percent to the system's recommended interest rate on loan applications from those addresses. What do you do?

This is a relatively straightforward example of a "deal with the Devil." The bank's actions are clearly unethical and probably illegal. You should refuse to participate in such an activity. But even this open-and-shut scenario raises some of the key issues that arise in any ethical consideration. Some of the critical topics are [CASH92]:

Storage of Information

One commonly applied test here is this: If the information stored in your system were itemized on the front page of tomorrow's paper, would you be embarrassed? Is there any information, the storing of which invades someone's (or some organization's) privacy? Is there any information there that belongs to someone else (or to some other organization) that was not obtained through appropriate channels?

In the case of this scenario, applicant's privacy is being invaded through the implicit association of their address with their ethnic background. The information may be stored as tables within program code rather than as the content of a traditional file or database, but the ethical issue is the same.

Use of Information

Here you must assure yourself that information, openly collected, is being used for the purposes for which those who provided it believed it would be used—or, at least, is being used in ways that they would approve if they knew about them.

A few people will provide information even though they believe it will be used for unethical purposes. Fortunately, most won't. Therefore, adhering to this guideline also provides some protection against unethical uses of the information.

In the above scenario, loan applicants presumably believe that they are providing address information so the bank can verify the nature of the property on which it is being asked to grant a loan, to record a security interest in the property until the loan is paid off, to be able to mail monthly bills and other notices to the correct place, and for similar above-board purposes. They do not expect it to be used as a criterion for discriminatory rate setting.

Sharing of Information

Information has value. Property of value can be sold. Information is unusual in this respect: After it is sold, the original owner still has it! Yet sharing one's information with others is a form of information usage. The same criterion applies: Did those who provided the information believe, or expect, that it would be shared? If they didn't, would they approve?

Electronic information sharing is common in this day and age. Most periodicals sell their mailing lists: subscribers to *Field and Stream* are excellent candidates for direct mail campaigns by fishing rod manufacturers. One can obtain a list of *Computerworld* subscribers who are MIS managers in manufacturing organizations with over 50 employees, use Unisys computers, and are located in New York State. Many mail order marketers sell their lists as well. Yet under public pressure, most people who collect names for their own business purposes allow the people whose names are collected to indicate "do not sell." Lotus Marketplace's home edition, a CD-ROM that would have provided demographic data on millions of residential units in the United States, was withdrawn from sale in 1991 (before it was shipped) after a massive public outcry—and 30,000 written requests to be removed from its database. And there are explicit laws against the U.S. Census Bureau sharing individual information, even with other agencies of the federal government.

The bank scenario above does not raise any sharing issues, but it could. Were the system described in the scenario to be implemented, the bank could record which customers took out loans at an above-market rate. Sharing this list, for example with a personal loan firm, would compound the unethicality of developing this system in the first place.

Human Judgment

This item refers to whether human judgment is being used properly in the overall decision process. The appropriate use of DSS can both help and hurt here. In particular, it is important to allow humans to review system recommendations that are not totally structured: in other words, to have a decision *support* system rather than a decision-*making* system.

The bank scenario falls down badly on this score. It is designed to support human judgment being applied in an unethical (in this case, discriminatory) manner. Participating in developing a system designed for this purpose in unethical even if one could argue, as in this case, that the system is simply carrying out a calculation based on certain objective data elements and parameters.

Combining Information

Where information is concerned the whole can be greater than the sum of its parts. The U.S. military has recognized this for decades: A file drawer can be classified Top Secret even though no piece of paper in it is classified above Secret, as long as there are enough such pieces of paper. So have criminals: The announcement that Mr. Doe and Ms. Roe will honeymoon in Hawai'i after their wedding (obtained from the local paper) and their addresses (obtained from the phone book), combined, are an invitation to "case the joint." The prospect of having everyone who knows something about a person pool their information to create a detailed profile is, to many, not pleasant.

The bank scenario, since it deals with a self-contained system, does not raise issues of combining information.

Error Detection and Correction
Information systems should always incorporate procedures for preventing errors, for verifying the information in them, and for correcting errors that are detected. This is especially important in DSS, where the information in a database is usually trusted by its users and is relied on for far-reaching decisions. There are, for example, U.S. laws that require credit bureaus to give an individual a copy of his or her credit report on request, to correct errors brought to its attention, and, in case of an unresolvable disagreement over whether an item is an error, to include the individual's statement about the item with any report sent out in the future.

A loan approval DSS, even if conceived in an ethical fashion, could recommend rejecting an application because of a data entry error: an annual income of $5,000 rather than $50,000, or monthly rent payments of $5,000 rather than $500. An ethically implemented DSS would give the applicant the reason for rejection, allow errors such as these to be corrected, and reprocess the application without prejudice due to the prior rejection once they are.

Taking the concepts a step further, it might incorporate "reasonableness checks" on the data to catch as many such errors as possible before the application is processed: the likelihood of a person earning $50,000 per year paying $5,000 per month in rent is, to say the least, small. You may never be able to make your database totally free of errors—survey after survey of MIS managers have found that most databases contain a substantial number of errors—but you would be surprised, in most cases, to realize how many errors really can be caught if checking is carefully thought out.

Several codes of ethics have been proposed for information systems practitioners. Most professional societies have one to which their members are expected to adhere and that provides penalties (typically expulsion from the society, as there is little more a professional association can do) for violating them. The codes of ethics of the Data Processing Management Association, the Institute for Certification of Computer Professionals, the Association for Computing Machinery, the Canadian Information Processing Society, and the British Computer Society are compared in [OZ92]. He points out that, while all the codes are similar, they are sometimes in conflict: For example, one requires its members to obey all laws, while another requires its members to violate laws that they consider unethical. Clearly, a member of both societies—not an uncommon situation—can be faced with a quandary.

Summary

The implementation stage of any information system is the process of taking it from its developers and bringing it to production use. DSS implementation, which begins when the DSS developers determine that their system is ready for its users, includes the technical activities of purchasing and installing hardware and software packages, installing the DSS, connecting systems and networks to the users' desktops, and creating the DSS database. Nontechnical implementation activities include training, documentation, support, and transferring the system formally from its developers to those who will maintain it. The importance of each of these implementation activities varies from one DSS to another.

The actual conversion from previous decision-making methods to the new DSS is an important part of the implementation process. There are four basic approaches to conversion: direct cutover, parallel operation, pilot conversion, and phased conversion. Phased conversion is often the most appropriate way to convert to a new DSS. Direct cutover and parallel operation are also appropriate if the previous decision-making methods were manual. Pilot conversion, generally the ideal approach for transaction processing systems, does not stand out as strongly for DSS. In any case, a combination of methods may be useful.

Conversion to any new system involves change. People resist change. This resistance must be managed effectively if the new system is to succeed. The way to manage it depends on organizational culture and the existing attitudes of prospective system users.

Change is most effectively handled in three stages: unfreezing, moving, and refreezing. In the unfreezing stage, prospective users must be shown how a new system can make the relevant aspect of their life easier. In the moving stage, they are trained on the new system and encouraged to use it. In the refreezing stage, their commitment to the new system is reinforced. Active management support is mandatory during all three of these stages.

The DSS implementor must be on the alert for several factors that can interfere with a successful implementation effort. Technical factors include user unfamiliarity with the type of system in question, unacceptable system response times, inadequate system reliability and availability, and poor data quality. Nontechnical factors include the existence of active management support, changes in the user community, user expectations of response time, training, support, and usage policies (voluntary or mandatory). These categories suggest areas to focus on for successful management of the implementation process.

Ethical issues are important with any DSS. They come to a head at the implementation stage since a DSS raises ethical concerns only when it is used. However, they must often be addressed before that stage in order not to

Ethical issues in a DSS context usually relate to the DSS database and to decisions made on the basis of its content. The DSS must only store information that was obtained through ethical channels, share it with those with whom its supplier would agree it may be shared, and combine it only with information that does not create an overall invasion of privacy. It must provide means to detect as many errors as feasible and to correct those that are detected. Data should only be used for the purposes for which they were supplied, humans should review any recommended decisions that have the potential to reflect inappropriate use of the data, and the decision-making methods supported by the DSS should always be consistent with ethical principles.

Key Terms

champion 255
change 251
conversion 248
direct cutover (conversion) 249
help desk 262
hot line 261
implementation 246
installation 247
managing change 251
moving 251
overcoming resistance 251
parallel conversion 249
phased conversion 249
pilot conversion 249
refreezing 251
speed governor 260
training 247, 260
unfreezing 251

Review Questions

1. What is "implementation?" Does the definition in this book agree with that in your introductory MIS and systems analysis textbooks (if you had them)?
2. What stages does implementation follow in the SDLC? In the prototyping approach to system development?
3. Describe at least six activities that are part of the implementation process.
4. State the four basic system conversion strategies.
5. What would it mean to combine *(a)* parallel operation with pilot conversion and *(b)* pilot conversion with phased conversion?
6. Why is it important to overcome resistance to change in implementing a DSS?
7. What are the three stages of overcoming change?
8. What three factors can contribute to making all three stages of the change process successful?
9. In what stages of the change process does it help the change process if DSS users can return to previous decision-making methods? In which does it impede successful change?

10. List three technical and three nontechnical issues that can affect DSS success.
11. Is system response time a technical or a nontechnical issue? Explain.
12. When in the life cycle of a DSS should ethical issues be considered?
13. What ethical factors might constrain the type of information to be stored in a DSS database?
14. State at least two ways of detecting erroneous data entered by a user into a DSS database.

Exercises

1. How would you handle training needs, and why, for each of the following DSS? (It's basically the same DSS, but for three different user communities.)
   a. A system for faculty advisers to use that will help them recommend appropriate courses for the students they advise to take during the next term.
   b. A system for students to use that will help them choose appropriate courses to take during the next term.
   c. A system for the college academic counseling center, which has two counselors on its staff, to use in suggesting appropriate courses for students to take in the next term.
2. In the Connoisseur Foods case mentioned in Section 8.4.2, top management overruled the manager of marketing services and made use of the brand model system voluntary. Do you agree with this decision? Why or why not? Can you suggest an intermediate approach: less than mandatory, but with more direct motivation than was actually used?
3. (This question is adapted from an example in [CHRI90].) The manager of your firm's marketing department has been asked by the chairman to present an analysis of the company's customer base at the executive summit meeting in three days. The data are located on five different application systems with a different file or database structure in each. Additionally, a given customer may be on more than one of the five systems, but there is no common identifier to link the customer in one system with the same customer in another. Due to the complexity of the data structures and the incompatibilities among the systems, it will take a week of work (with maximum pressure and overtime) to do the requested analysis.

   The basic conception of this information usage is fundamentally ethical: No one questions the right of a firm to analyze its own customer data for internal purposes, and no one has suggested that either the marketing manager or the chairman plans any unethical use of the data. Ethical considerations still affect your response. What ethical issues, if any, are being raised here? What should you do?

References

ADEL92 Adelman, Leonard. *Evaluating Decision Support and Expert Systems.* John Wiley & Sons, New York (1992).

ALTE80 Alter, Steven L. *Decision Support Systems: Current Practice and Continuing Challenges.* Addison-Wesley, Reading, Mass. (1980).

CASH92 Cash, James I., Jr.; F. Warren McFarlan; and James L. McKenney. *Corporate Information Systems Management* (3rd ed.). Richard D. Irwin, Homewood, Ill. (1992).

CHER90 Chervany, Norman L., and Shailendra Palvia. "An Experimental Investigation of Factors Influencing Predicted Success in DSS Implementation." Working Paper MISRC-WP-91-04. Management Information Systems Research Center, Curtis L. Carlson School of Management, University of Minnesota, Minneapolis (1990).

CHRI90 Christoff, Kurt. *Managing the Information Center.* Scott Foresman and Co., Glenview, Ill. (1990).

GROV88 Grover, Varun; Albert L. Lederer; and Rajiv Sabherwal. "Recognizing the Politics of MIS." *Information and Management* 14, no. 3 (March 1988), pp. 145–56.

KEND88 Kendall, Kenneth E., and Julie E. Kendall. *Systems Analysis and Design.* Prentice Hall, Englewood Cliffs, N.J. (1988).

LEWI47 Lewin, Kurt. "Group Decision and Social Change," in *Readings in Social Psychology,* T. M. Newcombe and E. L. Hartley, eds. Henry Holt and Co., New York (1947).

LEWI47a Lewin, Kurt. "Frontiers in Group Dynamics." *Human Relations* 1 (1947), pp. 5–41.

MACH32 Machiavelli, Niccolò. *The Prince* (1532), translated by W. K. Marriott.

MALL91 Mallach, Efrem G. "Training Paradigms." *Managing End-User Computing* 4, no. 9 (April 1991), pp. 5–6.

OZ92 Oz, Effy. "Ethical Standards for Information Systems Professionals: A Case for a Unified Code." *MIS Quarterly* 16, no. 4 (December 1992), pp. 423–33.

PALV91 Palvia, Shailendra; Efrem G. Mallach; and Prashant Palvia. "Strategies for Converting from One IT Environment to Another." *Journal of Systems Management* 42, no. 10 (October 1991), pp. 23ff.

ZAND75 Zand, D. E., and R. E. Sorensen. "Theory of Change and the Effective Use of Management Science." *Administrative Science Quarterly* 20, no. 4 (December 1975), pp. 532–45.

Envoyance: Implementing the Addit System

"The Addit system? What's that?" asked Doug when Dan said that Envoyance was hoping to implement it on their new LAN.

"Well," said Dan as he leaned back in his chair, "I might as well start from the beginning. Addit Environmental is a firm a lot like ours, 20 professionals, based in Portland, Oregon. They're trying to put together a nationwide network of small environmental engineering firms that will be able to compete with the big ones. The idea is to share resources, bid jointly on projects that are too large for any one of us, maybe do some joint advertising or some other marketing programs. We've had a couple of meetings with them and with a few other firms that are also interested. Sounds like a good idea: We don't really give anything up, and we stand to gain a lot."

"Sounds like a good idea to me, Dan," agreed Adrienne. "But what's the 'Addit System?' What does it have to do with LANs—or with us?"

"The Addit System is a project, resource, and contact tracking system that Addit's computer specialist, Judy Guarente, put together. She did it initially to track their projects, but the real justification for developing it was its potential use across the entire group. After all, with just 20 people it's not too hard for them to know what everyone can do or what they're working on.

"The idea behind Judy's system is that anyone can find out what projects we've done, which we're doing, which are in various stages of the pipeline. We can find out, for instance, what anyone in the group has done for General Electric or General Motors, what groundwater remediation work we've done, and so on. We can then go a few more levels into the database. For instance, suppose we get a list of groundwater remediation projects. We can then find out who worked on each one, whether they're still around, what they're working on now, and how much longer their current project will keep them tied up. Going in the other direction, we can find out who the client contact was on an earlier project, whether any firm in the group has done any other work for that person, and what.

"Judy says this entire thing uses a Sybase relational database management system running on a Novell server. Beyond that, you'd have to ask her for details. I can understand what it does and why that's a useful thing to do, but the technical specifics are a bit beyond my depth."

"Has anyone here looked at the system in operation?" Adrienne asked.

"Well, I had a chance to see it when I visited Addit in Portland last month. Wasn't much else to do—it rained the whole time! Guess that's better than the snow we had here, though. Anyhow, it seemed to do what Judy said it was supposed to do. The screens looked good. I brought a sample screen print back with me. Here it is." (See Figure 8–9.)

"Beyond that," Dan continued, "you probably know that Peggy Letendre has accepted our offer to join Envoyance as our first full-time marketing and sales person. She has a similar system, not quite as advanced, where she works now. She spent

FIGURE 8–9

Screen Printout from Addit System

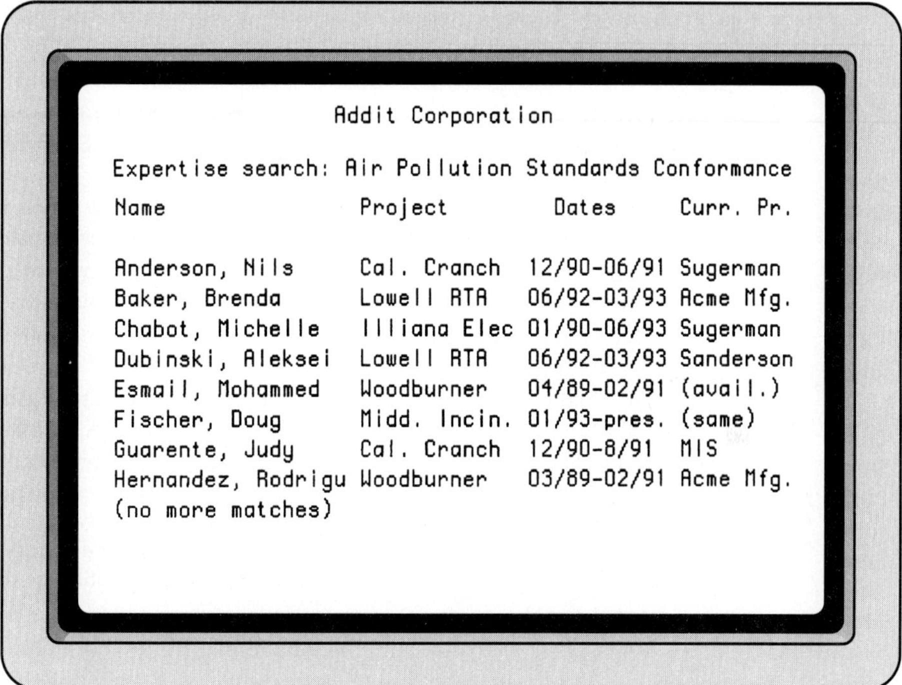

Addit Corporation

Expertise search: Air Pollution Standards Conformance

Name	Project	Dates	Curr. Pr.
Anderson, Nils	Cal. Cranch	12/90-06/91	Sugerman
Baker, Brenda	Lowell RTA	06/92-03/93	Acme Mfg.
Chabot, Michelle	Illiana Elec	01/90-06/93	Sugerman
Dubinski, Aleksei	Lowell RTA	06/92-03/93	Sanderson
Esmail, Mohammed	Woodburner	04/89-02/91	(avail.)
Fischer, Doug	Midd. Incin.	01/93-pres.	(same)
Guarente, Judy	Cal. Cranch	12/90-8/91	MIS
Hernandez, Rodrigu	Woodburner	03/89-02/91	Acme Mfg.

(no more matches)

nearly an hour on the phone with Judy last week talking about this system, asking mostly some very advanced user-side questions. Wanted to know how it deals with some fairly complicated issues, what specific data items it keeps track of, how it organizes and indexes its data, how it updates one location's server with data from another, what its capacity limits are, and anything else she could think of. She said Judy understands what the users would expect a system like this to do."

"Sounds good, Dan," Doug commented. "What happens next?"

"Well, this is where I'd like you two to get involved. Frankly, I'm a bit concerned about staff reactions to this thing. It's not all gravy, after all. Keeping the database up to date involves some work on the part of most of our people: entering info about their customers, their contacts, their projects, their schedules, all that. The benefit of doing all this work isn't that clear, at least in the short run. The system will let people from other companies find out what we're doing, but most of our staffers don't see any immediate value in finding out what the other companies in the group are doing. What I need, assuming the software itself works as promised, is a way to turn them onto what this system will hopefully do for us."

"There's a real challenge!" said Adrienne. "Can we get back to you in about a week?"

"A week's fine," answered Dan. "We still have a lot of discussions ahead of us on other issues before we sign up with Addit, although it does look promising. If you can give me a good idea of how this would proceed by, say, next Wednesday, that would be in time for our next conference call with them."

Exercises

1. What aspects of the system do you think might not have been adequately tested within Addit alone? How would you suggest that Envoyance test them further before committing to this system?
2. What specific actions should Dan and Sandra take to unfreeze Envoyance staffers from their present methods prior to moving to the new system?
3. What provisions would you make for training Envoyance staff members on the Addit system? What training methods would you use?
4. Try to put an implementation issue for this situation in each quadrant of the grid in Figure 8–5.
5. What conversion method would you recommend that the Addit group of environmental engineering companies adopt to move to this system?
6. Were Envoyance to implement the Addit system, they would expose information on customers, costs, projects, and schedules to the rest of the system users on the network. Should that be a concern here? Why or why not? If yes, should that concern eliminate the system—despite its real potential value—from consideration? How could you address the security concerns and still use the system?

PART III

Decision Support Systems in Detail

"God is in the details." In making this comment, noted architect Mies van der Rohe meant that the essence of a thing cannot be appreciated by looking solely at the overall picture. It is necessary to get into at least some details to understand what something is truly about. The next five chapters, therefore, go into detail about different aspects of decision support systems.

Chapter 9 will take you further into the subject of models, which we introduced in Chapter 3. This chapter focuses on modeling the way a system works via data that represent that system in a computer, a process usually called simulation. We'll also look at two types of mathematical models: ways in which we can determine how a system will behave by solving equations. All of these capabilities enable us to develop DSS that help predict how different decisions will affect a complex real-world system.

It is often helpful to find a mathematical optimum as part of a decision-making process: the optimal allocation of resources to various products, the optimal location of a warehouse, the optimal advertising schedule. There are several optimization methods that can be used when a decision has this type of a mathematical maximum or minimum. Chapter 10 will introduce you to some methods used in this field.

Chapters 11 and 12 look at two particular types of decision support systems in more detail: group DSS (Chapter 11) and executive information systems (Chapter 12). Group decision support systems are those which deal specifically with the interactions among group members in reaching a joint decision. Executive information systems are those intended to meet the information needs of top corporate executives, though they can often help meet the information needs of other user communities as well. DSS professionals are increasingly likely to encounter one or both of these categories on the job today. These chapters will tell you what to expect when you do.

Finally (in this part of the book), Chapter 13 will give you several examples of DSS in actual use. You'll see the spectrum of decisions to which DSS can apply and a wide range of systems used to help make them. Reading this chapter will help bring all the concepts you've studied in the first twelve chapters into clearer focus.

CHAPTER 9

Representational Models

Chapter Outline

Introduction

All DSS above the simplest data-oriented ones are based on models. They are often used to allow a DSS, and hence a decision maker, to predict what would happen in the "real world" if certain choices are made. This, in turn, enables the decision maker to evaluate alternative actions without trying them out in practice—with obvious savings in time and expense to his or her firm.

In this chapter you'll learn about the basic types of representational models you must know about as a DSS developer. Specifically, you'll learn about two types of models: simulation models and queuing theory models. The more mathematical approach of queuing theory and Markov processes can yield easy-to-use and general solutions where they apply, but they cannot be applied to many complex systems, and they require considerable mathematical ability on the part of the analyst. Simulation, while it only tells the decision maker about what would happen under one specific set of circumstances and can require a great deal of computer time, can be applied to a broader variety of problems.

Chapter Objectives

After you have read and studied this chapter, you will be able to:

1. Discuss the differences between simulation and a simulation model.
2. Describe how a discrete-event simulation model works.
3. Explain why discrete-event simulation models are useful components of DSS.
4. Outline the specific steps for designing a discrete-event simulation model.
5. Describe what is involved in planning and running a complete simulation study.
6. Explain why pseudo-random numbers are important in simulation and describe some low-tech methods of generating them.
7. Discuss when a static simulation model might be useful.
8. Describe how the mathematical approaches of queuing theory and Markov process analysis work and what they can contribute to DSS.
9. Summarize how simulation studies, queuing theory, and Markov process analysis compare and how they can be used together to study a business system.

9.1 DISCRETE-EVENT SIMULATION MODELS

A *simulation model* is, for our purposes, a dynamic, and usually stochastic, discrete-event model that allows us to predict the behavior of a real business system by modeling the expected behaviors and interactions of its components over time. This is useful because we often know how each system component behaves, but the impact of their interactions on the behavior of the overall system is beyond our capacity to understand directly.

> To recap some concepts from Chapter 3:
>
> - A dynamic model is one that explicitly reflects changes in the system over time.
> - A stochastic model is one whose output reflects statistically defined uncertainties in system behavior.
> - A discrete-event model is one in which changes in the system are taken as occurring at instants in time rather than extending over a finite interval.

The terms "simulation," "model," and the combination "simulation model" are often used interchangeably or nearly so. This usually doesn't cause problems, but there *is* a difference. The *model* is the description of the system, here usually in the form of a computer program. We call it a *simulation model* when we want to make it clear that we're not discussing some other type of model or some other use of a model. *Simulation* is the process of using this model to study a system. A model is a thing; simulation is a process. Simulation can't exist without a suitable model, and a model meant for use in simulation is probably not very useful for anything else, but the concepts are different.

9.1.1 *The Concept of Discrete-Event Simulation*

The basic concepts of discrete-event simulation are simple, although a discrete-event simulation model of a complex system will inevitably be full of complex detail. The model represents the state of the system by the values of variables in the computer. The values of these variables change as events occur in the system. For instance, the arrival of a car at a filling station may change the state of one pump and the attendant from "idle" to "busy." This would be represented in the model by variables going from "idle" to "busy," from "false" to "true," or from 0 to 1. Subsequently, the equations in the model will (via the values of suitable variables) reduce the amount of fuel in the station's storage tank, increase the amount of money in its cash register, and allow the pump and attendant to rest again—unless another car has arrived in the interim and must be taken care of. The program that runs the model must keep track of the simulated time at which all these events occur. It is usually also instrumented to gather helpful information about system behavior: the fraction of time that the attendant is busy, the amount of time cars have to wait, etc.

Most discrete-event simulations are stochastic, or probabilistic. We may know how many cars arrive at the gas station in a typical hour and what the statistical distribution of this quantity is. We do *not* know that a car will arrive at precisely 10:23 A.M. next Thursday, will take 8.38 gallons of premium unleaded fuel, will pay by credit card, and will depart at 10:31. The computer determines the times at which events occur and their exact nature—does this car use regular fuel, premium fuel, or diesel? how many gallons? paid by cash or credit card?—by generating pseudo-random numbers. We use them to sample from the statistical distributions that the modeler specified. If the statistics of our distributions match the real world well, the overall set of computer choices will be representative of what could happen in reality.

We gather data to help make decisions by tracking what happens over time in the model. The owner of a gasoline station can figure out the optimum frequency for fuel deliveries from his or her supplier by running a simulation model for several possible choices and selecting the one for which the model predicted the best results. The same approach can help choose the right number of pump attendants to hire or whether or not to offer discounts for cash payment. The accuracy of the decisions depends on the accuracy of the model: how well its processes represent reality and how well its statistics represent how gasoline purchasers behave.

The key to understanding how discrete-event simulations work is the *future events queue.*[1] This is a list of events that are scheduled to take place in the system, together with the time that each will occur. For example, suppose a car starts fueling at 10:23 A.M. We calculate, based on statistics for fueling time, that it will be ready to pay at 10:27. We put an event into the future events queue for 10:27, labeled "car (with a number to identify one of several cars, if necessary) ready to pay." After we've processed all the events that take place between 10:23 and 10:27, this becomes the next event in the system. We update the variables in the system to reflect what happens. The specifics, in this case, depend on whether or not there is a free attendant at that moment. Assuming there is, we calculate how long payment will take and put a new "car (number) finishes paying" event in the future events queue for, say, 10:32. This cycle of processing events and scheduling new ones repeats for events of all types until the run is over. A simulation run consists of nothing

[1]Some simulation models, especially those that don't involve waiting lines, do not use a future events queue. Instead, they inspect the system at regular time steps and change its state as required. This approach is popular in studying economic and social systems. The national employment rate in one quarter, for example, may influence the tax receipts in the next quarter. Exercise 2 at the end of this chapter involves such a simulation.

more than placing events in the future events queue, taking them out when their turn arrives, and processing them.

9.1.2 A Discrete-Event Simulation Example

You can construct a simple simulation model and run experiments with it without a computer. Let's say we want to model a barber shop to determine how many barbers we should hire. We can't hire more than three barbers because there are only three chairs in the shop. Let's assume that, at this time of day, customers arrive at an average rate of one every 10 minutes. Let's also assume that a haircut always takes exactly 25 minutes. Our first "run" will be with two barbers on duty. Figure 9–1 illustrates this schematically.

We can use a piece of paper to store all our data. We would mark off six columns on a large piece of paper: one for each of the two barbers we're going to use in this run, one for each of the three seats in the waiting area, and one for the future events queue. We'll also need a standard six-sided die to generate random customer arrivals. Since we want an average arrival rate of a customer every 10 minutes, we can assign the six sides of the die to 5, 7, 9, 11, 13, and 15 minutes. Those values will give us our desired average. So would several other choices, but this set will do for now. It gives us a uniform distribution of interarrival times. (In a real study, we'd record barbershop customer arrival statistics for at least several hours before choosing an arrival time distribution).

FIGURE 9–1

Schematic of a Barber Shop

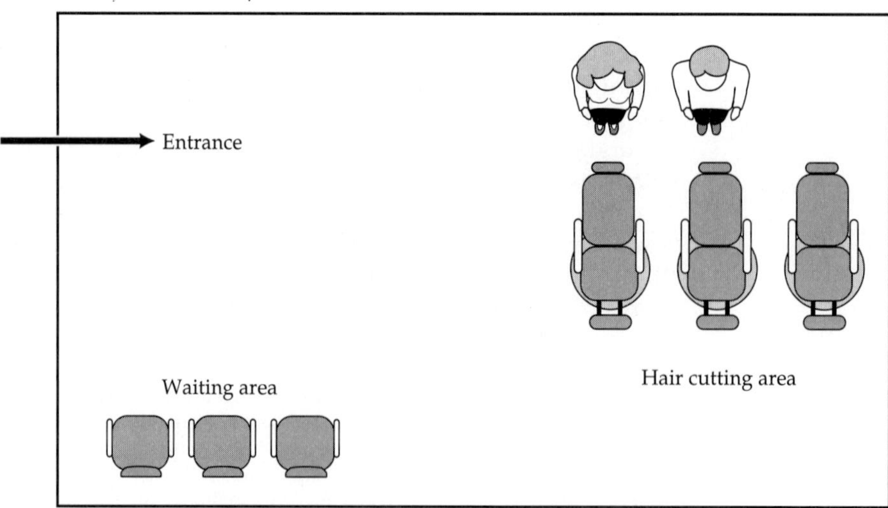

When the barbershop doors open at 8:00 A.M., the shop is empty. Roll the die to find out when the first customer will arrive. Suppose you roll a 2. That corresponds to 7 minutes, so the first customer will show up at 8:07. Write "8:07: customer arrives" in the future events queue. Now we are ready to start the simulation cycle.

The first—and, at this moment, the only—event in the future events queue is the customer arrival at 8:07. We advance our mental clock to 8:07 to process it. We will schedule two future events as part of this processing: the completion of the first customer's haircut and the arrival of the second customer.

To process the haircut, write "Busy 8:07–8:32" in the column corresponding to Barber 1. This is for the purpose of collecting statistics. (Question: why 8:32?) Also, enter "8:32: Barber 1 customer leaves" in the future events queue.

Now, roll the die again for the next arrival. You roll a 4, which corresponds to 11 minutes. The second customer will arrive 11 minutes from now, at 8:18. Enter "8:18: customer arrives" in the future events queue. We are now finished handling the 8:07 event. Cross it off.

The next event in the future events queue is now the 8:18 arrival of the second customer. Write "Busy 8:18–8:43" in the second barber's column. Roll the die for the next arrival. You roll a 3, corresponding to 9 minutes between arrivals. The next customer will arrive at 8:27. Enter this event in the future events queue. Cross off the 8:18 event.

There are no available barbers when the third customer arrives at 8:27. Write "Busy at 8:27" on the first seat in the waiting area. We do not yet know how long that seat will be busy because waiting time (unlike hair cutting time) is not fixed in the description of the model. Cross off the 8:27 entry. Figure 9–2 shows the simulation at this point.

The next customer, our die tells us, will arrive at 8:40. However, something else will happen before then. The next entry in the future events queue is now "8:32: Barber 1 customer leaves." The first barber can now take the waiting customer. Write "Free at 8:32" on that seat and "Busy 8:32–8:57" on the first barber's chair. Enter the 8:57 haircut completion time into the future events queue and cross off the 8:32 entry. You can then deal with the fourth customer, who arrives at 8:40, by putting him in the waiting room.

You will note that there is not necessarily a 1:1 relationship between processing events and scheduling new ones. Some events, such as the arrival of a customer when there is a barber available to cut his hair, result in the entry of two new events in the future events queue. Others, such as the departure of a customer when there are no waiting customers, do not result in any new events being scheduled. In the long run, insertions into the future events queue and removals from it must be approximately in balance, but a given event need not be.

This model is complex enough to show you why "industrial strength" simulation models need a well-organized and efficiently processed future events queue. Future events queue entries are not created in chronological order: We made an entry for 8:27 after we had already made an entry for

FIGURE 9–2

Sheet of Paper with Simulation Model of Barber Shop

Barber #1	Barber #2	Seat #1	Seat #2	Seat #3	Fut. events Q
Busy 8:07–8:32	Busy 8:18–8:43	Busy at 8:27			~~8:07, Cust. arrives~~ 8:32, Barber #1 Customer leaves ~~8:18, Cust. arrives~~ ~~8:27, Cust. arrives~~

8:32. Having the events listed in order makes it unnecessary to remember, or to scan the sheet of paper, for the next event. We can handle a three-seat barbershop without a formal queue but not much more than that.

This process can continue indefinitely. When you're done you will be able to figure out how many customers were served, how many were turned away because there was no space in the waiting area (what assumption did we just make?) and, if you know how much barbers are paid and how much a haircut costs, what the net profit was. The same model, with a different set of variations, can also tell you if it's worth buying another chair for the waiting area, taking two chairs out of the waiting area to accommodate a fourth barber, or converting the shop to a soup-and-salad bar.

Three things should be clear from this example:

1. The fundamental process of simulation, and the calculations involved, are simple.
2. The recordkeeping, even for a simple model such as this, gets tedious quickly.
3. The process is conceptually suitable for far more complex systems than this barbershop, although you would not want to keep track of everything by hand in such systems.

That makes simulation a natural for computers: They're great for repeating tedious calculations over and over again, they don't make mistakes, and they reach the answer much faster than people can.

9.1.3 Designing a Discrete-Event Simulation Model

The process of designing a discrete-event simulation model consists of the following steps:

1. *Determine the objective of the model.* What are we trying to optimize or find out? What information must the model give us if we are to learn what we must know? Without a clear understanding of these issues, we cannot determine what output our model must provide or what simplifications are appropriate for it.

2. *Define the system itself.* What is inside it, what is not? What are its components? We often want to study a range of similar systems that vary in a few parameters of interest, such as gasoline stations with one, two, or three attendants. If the system depends on such parameters, called *controllable variables,* we must specify what they are now.

3. *Define the state of the system in terms of a set of state or uncontrollable variables.* The chosen set of state variables simplifies reality because every system has levels of detail that are unimportant to a given planning task. The position at which a car stops in a gasoline station is unimportant for business planning, but the type and amount of fuel it purchases probably do matter. In the barber shop model, we care when customers arrive, not about how long they want their sideburns cut. Understanding the purpose of the model is essential to determining the proper set of state variables.

The concept of a state or uncontrollable variable can be difficult. The uncontrollable variables are those characteristics of a system that vary during its operation. In our barbershop model, the number of barbers on duty is not a state variable as it does not change while the shop is open. It is a *parameter* of the model, or a controllable variable, and is fixed for any one run. The number of barbers who are busy at any given moment *is* an uncontrollable, or state, variable: We do not enter it into the computer but rather let the simulation process determine what it is at any moment. Its value, which ranges from zero to the number of barbers on duty, rises and falls as customers come into the shop and as haircuts are completed. If we wanted to evaluate the impact of alternative coffee break policies on barbershop productivity, we might make the number of *working* barbers a state variable. This new variable's value would change as barbers go on break and return. This possibility points out the importance of knowing a model's purpose before we define its details.

4. *Define the events that can affect the state of the system and the impact of each event on each state variable.* Some events are *exogenous;* they originate outside the system. Their occurrence is not affected by the state of the system, al-

The Concept of "System State"

The concept of "the state of a system" is fundamental to all representational models.

Definition: The state of a system is the set of information stored in that system that changes during system operation as events occur and affects system response to future inputs.

Consider a bakery. When a customer walks in to buy a loaf of dark rye bread, one of three things can happen:

1. The customer buys the bread, leaving with bread in hand and a lighter wallet.
2. The bakery is out of bread. The customer leaves without making a purchase.
3. All clerks are busy. The customer waits for service.

To determine which of these outcomes will occur, we must know at least two things about the current situation in the bakery: whether or not there are any free clerks and whether or not there is any dark rye bread available. Both of these change during system operation, and both affect system response to the customer. Both are therefore part of the system state.

In a real bakery, the information about the availability of dark rye bread is in physical form. A clerk looks where dark rye is normally kept. If there isn't any, the clerk informs the customer. In a computer model, the information is stored as values in computer memory.

The individual items that combine to define the state of the system are called *state variables.* In the bakery model one state variable reflects the dark rye bread inventory. Another reflects what the clerks are doing.

The way we define the state variables depends on the rest of the model. Knowing whether there is or is not a loaf of dark rye on hand will tell us how to handle this customer. We could represent this state variable by a Boolean, or yes/no, variable. That representation would not prepare us for the next customer, however, because we would have no way to know if there are any more loaves left after the first customer departs. It is better to store our dark rye inventory data as an integer variable, decrementing its value as purchases are made and incrementing it as fresh loaves emerge from the oven.

though they may affect its state. *Endogenous* events, on the other hand, originate inside the system. Their occurrence may depend on the state of the system: a car that isn't being fueled can't finish the fueling process, a person whose hair isn't being cut can't finish his or her haircut, a disk drive that isn't broken can't be repaired.

5. *Determine the statistics you would like to obtain from your simulation model and what data must be gathered in order to obtain them.* If you want to know, for example, the distribution of waiting times after a product is fully assembled until it can be painted, you will have to create a table for the different time intervals of interest and make an entry in this table for each unit that is assembled and painted. Some simulation packages collect some system statistics automatically, but it is still important to analyze your needs in order to know if you must specify or program additional ones.

6. *Choose the time units that the simulation will use.* A fine time scale lends itself to precise output, but this precision may not be justified by the accuracy of the model itself and a fine time scale may use excessive computer time. A

coarse time scale may reduce computer time requirements but, if taken to extremes, may limit the usefulness of the results.

The correct time scale depends both on the rate at which the process being modeled occurs and the purpose of the study. To model activity in a gasoline station accurately we need a time scale of seconds or tenths of a minute. However, if our fuel station owner only wants to schedule fuel deliveries, we may just care about the total sales volume per hour or per day. In that case a coarser time scale could be used. A computer system that works with fractional time units allows a modeler to use any time unit that is convenient for humans.

7. *Define, statistically, the rate at which each event occurs.* The rate at which endogenous events occur may depend on the current state of the system. It is often convenient to focus on individual transactions as they progress through the system, defining the statistical distribution of processing times at each step along the way. If we know how long it takes (statistically) to fuel a car, then the time at which a car finishes the fueling process is defined relative to the time at which it starts fueling.

8. *Define the initial (starting) state of the system.* The initial state may correspond to what customers are present, what they are doing, what machines are busy, what inventory levels exist, or what orders have been placed.

Having made these eight decisions, we describe the model to a computer in the form of a program. This program must reflect all the events that can take place in the system, their occurrence statistics, and their impact on the state variables. It begins by setting the state variables to their initial values. It then generates random numbers from the specified occurrence rate distributions to determine event occurrence times. Events are placed in the future events queue. The simulation program takes the first event from this queue, changes the state variables to reflect its occurrence, and may enter new events into the future events queue as a result of its having taken place. This process repeats until the run is ended by a user-specified criterion, such as the passage of a certain (simulated) elapsed time or processing a certain quantity of simulated transactions.

Simulation programs can be written in general-purpose programming languages such as C, Pascal, or FORTRAN. Most simulation professionals, however, use special-purpose simulation languages such as GPSS, SLAM, or Simscript. These languages and their run-time support packages have several advantages:

- They handle simulation "housekeeping" tasks such as keeping the future events queue in order and searching it for the next event. While it is not difficult to program a simple future events queue, programming an efficient one is a substantial undertaking.
- Simulation concepts and terminology are built into them, easing the translation of reality to "computerese."

- They provide easy ways of generating the statistical distributions required to describe system activity, with several common ones usually built in.
- They provide statistical analyses of each simulation run with no additional programming effort.

The user of such a language can develop a simulation in far less time than an equally competent programmer working "from scratch" with general-purpose tools. General-purpose programming languages may still be used when a special-purpose tool is not available, when a simulation model is a minor part of a larger DSS, or when a simulation model is small and its developer already knows a general-purpose language well. As a compromise approach, subroutine packages for simulation have been written for several popular programming languages. The GASP package for FORTRAN is one example.

Part of the preceding gasoline station model, which deals with cars arriving, being fueled,[2] paying, and leaving, is shown programmed in GPSS in Figure 9–3A and in SLAM II in Figure 9–3B. The differences between the two models are purely cosmetic: the use of the verb "create" or "generate," separating operands from the verb by spaces or a comma. That is because the models were deliberately written in a parallel fashion to stress the underlying similarities between the two ways of expressing the concepts. Both languages allow the same model to be described in many other ways, with SLAM II allowing more variation in this respect than GPSS. Some of the alternatives in one language wouldn't look nearly this similar to a program in the other one.

The same model in Simscript would be longer and more complex since Simscript doesn't make as many assumptions about what is being modeled. On the one hand, this forces the programmer to do more work in specifying this information; on the other, it allows one to model systems that differ from the standard mold. A corresponding GASP model would look like a FORTRAN program with calls to subroutines with names such as SCHDL to schedule future events. The GASP user must already be familiar with FORTRAN. Given that one knows and likes FORTRAN, and especially if the simulation must be linked with other programs in that language, GASP can be a good choice.

This program segment does not include any commands to gather statistics about system behavior. Most simulation languages automatically give the analyst great deal of such information. An analyst for whom this standard output is not sufficient can specify additional, optional tabular or graphic output. If the facilities of the language do not provide enough flexibility, models written in languages such as SLAM II and GPSS can be linked to

[2]Gasoline stations in which operators fuel customers' cars are admittedly nearly extinct in many locales.

FIGURE 9–3

Gas Station Fueling Process

A. Partial GPSS Model

	GENERATE	120,60	(uniformly distributed arrivals, 60–180 seconds)
	ENTER	PUMP	(Take any available pump, else wait)
	ENTER	OPER	(Take any available operator, else wait)
	ADVANCE	15,5	(10–20 seconds time, uniform distribution to start fueling)
	LEAVE	OPER	(operator goes about other duties)
	ADVANCE	90,30	(60–120 seconds, uniform distribution, to fuel car)
	ENTER	OPER	(need not be same operator)
	ADVANCE	60,30	(30–90 seconds, uniform distribution, to finish and pay)
	LEAVE	OPER	(operator done, car still at pump)
	ADVANCE	10,5	(5–15 seconds, uniform distribution, to move away from pump)
	LEAVE	PUMP	
	TERMINATE	100	(transaction leaves system; run for 100 cars)
PUMP	STORAGE	2	(two pumps specified for this run)
OPER	STORAGE	1	(one operator specified for this run)

B. Partial SLAM II Model

NETWORK;	(start of network statements)
CREATE,UNFRM(60.,180.,1);	(uniformly distributed arrivals, 60–180 seconds)
AWAIT,PUMP;	(take any available pump, else wait)
AWAIT,OPER;	(take any available operator, else wait)
ACTIVITY,UNFRM(10,20);	(10–20 seconds time, uniform distribution, to start fueling)
FREE,OPER;	(operator goes about other duties)
ACTIVITY,UNFRM(60,120);	(60–120 seconds, uniform distribution, to fuel car)
AWAIT,OPER;	(need not be same operator)
ACTIVITY,UNFRM(30,90);	(30–90 seconds, uniform distribution, to finish and pay)
FREE,OPER;	(operator done, car still at pump)
ACTIVITY,UNFRM(5,15);	(5–15 seconds, uniform distribution, to move away from pump)
FREE,PUMP;	
TERMINATE,100;	(transaction leaves system; run for 100 cars)
RESOURCE/PUMP(2);	(two pumps specified for this run)
RESOURCE/OPER(1);	(one operator specified for this run)

routines written in any of several general-purpose 3GLs. Simscript, since its current incarnations are as powerful as any other 3GL, won't pose this problem. Since GASP II models are already in FORTRAN, the problem can't arise there either.

An even more specialized tool for developing simulation models is called a simulator [BANK9I]. Simulators are generally intended to be used in simulating only one type of system, such as (commonly) a manufacturing plant. A simulator has built-in building blocks for the elements that exist in all systems of the type of interest. A manufacturing simulator, for example, would have built-in building blocks for conveyor belts (where transport time depends on the distance to be covered), palletizers (that swing into operation as soon as, but not before, the required number of products has accumulated), and more. Simulators often incorporate animated displays of the "factory" in addition to more conventional types of numerical output. In terms of Sprague's DSS software categories, which we discussed in Chapter 6, simulators lie in the "DSS generator" part of the spectrum, while simulation languages are more "DSS tools." Several simulator packages, such as XCCELL+, SIMFACTORY, and WITNESS, run on desktop microcomputers.

9.1.4 Another Simulation Example

Here's how we might apply the eight simulation development steps to a model of a supermarket. The decision maker, who will use this model, hopes to decide how many checkout counters to open and how many baggers to hire for optimum profit. This manager plans to hire the least-cost combination of checkout clerks and baggers that keeps checkout line length below a predetermined limit 95 percent of the time.

As you read through the supermarket example, see where the model simplifies reality. Some, but not all, of the simplifications are pointed out.

1. Given our objective as stated above, we need to know the 95th percentile figure for the checkout line length distribution. We may decide that an overall statistical picture of line length distribution would be useful so we can modify the decision criterion in the future.

2. The system consists of the supermarket from the entrance door to the end of the checkout process. We will not study the parking lot or anything else that goes on before customers walk in the door. We also assume that customers whose orders have been bagged proceed out the door with no delay or important congestion.

Our controllable variables here are the number of open checkout counters and the number of baggers. The number of open counters is an integer from 1 to the number of counters built into the store. (We assume that remodeling the store for additional checkout counters is not an option.) The number of baggers is an integer from 0 to the number of open counters.

3. The state variables are the number of shoppers in the store and the number of shoppers at each open checkout counter. All are non-negative integers.

4. The state of the system changes when

- A shopper enters the store. This is the only exogenous event in our system.

- A shopper finishes shopping and enters the checkout line. This is an endogenous event. Its occurrence rate depends on the number of shoppers in the store and possibly, depending on our model, on how long they've been there. In a common approach to programming simulation models, the time at which each shopper will enter the checkout line is calculated and placed in the future events queue when the shopper enters the store. This corresponds to calculating the time at which a haircut will be over when the customer sits down in the barber's chair.

  To model this event we must determine how shoppers decide which checkout line to enter. A simple model could choose randomly. More realistically, our model might choose the counter with the shortest line, picking randomly among all counters having this line length if there are several. Introducing an express counter for shoppers with few items would make the model more complicated but might be important for accuracy. The number of express counters and the upper limit on the size of order that can go through an express counter might be user-specified variables, although that would go beyond the stated objectives of this particular study.
- A shopper finishes checking out and leaves the system. (We assume that a clerk does not start checking out the next shopper until the bagger, if any, has finished the current one. See Exercise 6*b* about relaxing this assumption.) This, too, is an endogenous event. Its time can be calculated and the event entered into the future events queue when the customer begins the checkout process. A shopper's checkout can't start until all shoppers in line ahead of him or her have finished.

5. We need the 95th percentile of checkout line lengths. There are several ways to obtain this. One is to sample the system every so often. If we take 100 samples, the 95th largest is our answer. Another is record the total number of customers in line between each pair of events. (Question: Why can't this number change between events?) We would then create a table showing the total time for which the average line length was 0 customers, 0.1 customers, 0.2 customers (Question: How many checkout counters do these choices imply we have?), and so on. There are other possibilities as well. If we are using a simulation package, it may include one or more built-in statistics gathering capabilities and we might opt for the most suitable of these.

6. An appropriate time scale for supermarkets would be seconds if we want to use integers. If our software allows fractional time units, we might prefer to deal with minutes or hours. This system need not be modeled to the microsecond, nor do supermarket processes take months or years.

7. We can obtain arrival rate statistics by counting shoppers during a period similar to the one we are modeling, be it a weekday afternoon or Saturday morning. We can time shoppers as they move through the store to get statistics on the distribution of shopping times. We can similarly time the checkout process to learn (statistically) how long it takes and how it is affected by the presence of a bagger. If we wish, we could also track individual shoppers to determine the correlation between the length of time a shopper spends shopping and the length of time it takes that same shopper to check out.

8. The initial state of the system might be an empty store. After the model has run for a simulated hour or so the effects of the initial conditions will disappear. A common practice is to run the model for a few "hours," record its state, and use that as the initial state for subsequent runs having the same parameters.

Part of the GPSS output for this model, for four checkout clerks and two baggers, is shown in Figure 9–4. (Standard GPSS output varies a great deal from one version of the language to another.) It shows that there were usually 2.713 customers going through the checkout process at any given moment, 1.902 of whom were being served by baggers. The average customer took 1.602 minutes to go through the process. The average customer who was lucky enough to get a bagger took only 1.293 minutes, from which we can calculate the average time that it took to check a customer out in the absence of a bagger. The clerks in this case seem underutilized. This suggests that we could probably dispense with one of them with no significant increase in checkout delays. A run with three clerks and two baggers could confirm this.

9.1.5 Complete Simulation Studies

One simulation run tells us how a simulated system behaves for one choice of controllable variables and one set of pseudo-random numbers. That is not enough for management decisions. A full-scale study runs the simulation several times for each set of controllable variables to give us a distribution of results. If the model is valid, this distribution resembles the distribution of results we would see in reality. Repeating the process for each choice of controllable variables lets us evaluate the effect of changing the controllable variables and helps us choose the best set.

FIGURE 9–4

Sample Supermarket Simulation Output

STORAGE	CAPACITY	AVERAGE CONTENTS	TOTAL ENTRIES	AVERAGE TIME/TRANS.	AVERAGE UTILIZ.
CLERKS	4	2.713	1085	1.607	0.678
BAGGERS	2	1.902	761	1.293	0.951

Instead of running the model several times, we might consider one long run covering a period of time equal to the sum of the shorter individual runs. For example, the computer could run the model once for 20 hours of simulated supermarket activity rather than run it 10 times for 2 hours each. (A real supermarket would experience usage peaks and valleys over a 20-hour period, but that isn't a problem in a computer model.) In general, one long run is not as good as the same total time divided into several shorter ones. The reason is a phenomenon called *autocorrelation.* Autocorrelation means that what happens later in a run depends on what happened previously in the same run. If the supermarket, because of an unusual but statistically possible choice of pseudo-random numbers, gets unusually crowded, the effects of this crowding will linger for a long time and will affect the results of one long run. If we use several short runs that start from the same initial conditions but use different pseudo-random number sequences, the overcrowding will affect only one of the runs and will not have much impact on the final results.

We might choose to run the supermarket model 20 times for each set of controllable variables (number of open counters and number of baggers). We could plot the results, as in Figure 9–5 or tabulate them, as in Figure 9–6. Either form lets us decide how many clerks and baggers to hire for the given shopper arrival rate.

If the supermarket we are studying has 10 checkout counters, there are

FIGURE 9–5

Supermarket Simulation Output Graph

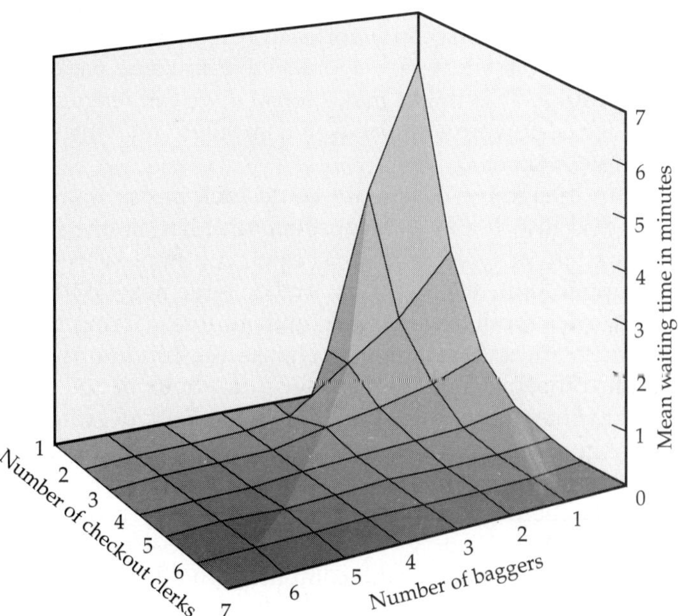

FIGURE 9–6

Typical Tabular Simulation Results Display

	Checkout Clerks						
Baggers	1	2	3	4	5	6	7
0	6.12	2.63	0.95	0.31	0.09	0.03	0.01
1	3.81	1.61	0.63	0.18	0.06	0.02	0.01
2		0.87	0.38	0.11	0.03	0.01	0.00
3			0.22	0.07	0.02	0.01	0.00
4				0.03	0.01	0.00	0.00
5					0.01	0.00	0.00
6						0.00	0.00
7							0.00

Mean Customer Waiting Time as Function of Number of Checkout Clerks and Baggers

65 possible combinations of checkout clerks and baggers. We could start the computer on its task of $65 \times 20 = 1{,}300$ runs. Each run might cover two simulated hours, hence about 2,000 simulated shoppers and about 10,000 simulated events. If a small computer takes a millisecond to simulate each event, it takes 10 seconds for each run and 13,000 seconds—about 4 hours—for the whole study. We would have to come back a long time later to get our results. This might make sense if we can leave an overnight or weekend job for a powerful multi-user computer, on which it would take far less computer time.

In interactive usage, we could look at one set of results and then plan the next test. If six open counters can't handle the load, there is no sense in trying five or fewer. Or, if six open counters keep the line length far below its upper limit, we might try two or three next. With this approach, each set of 20 runs would take under four minutes. Using our knowledge of supermarkets and our intuition to choose the conditions for each set of runs, we could probably find the best set in an hour or so. Of course, we would be tied to our computer for the entire time. With overnight batch usage we could have gone home and then spent a few minutes the next morning examining the results.

We could get the best of both worlds by programming the computer to follow a "hill-climbing" optimization approach as described in the next chapter. With this scheme, the computer would run the model for a few choices of controllable variables, decide the direction in which the results improve, and try more choices in that direction. It could then find the best combination after trying far fewer than all 440. The drawback, of course, is that someone would have to program the optimization process.

9.1.6 *Random and Pseudo-Random Numbers* — concept

The behavior of a simulation model depends on the numbers that determine when each event occurs. Ideally, these numbers should be chosen at random from the specified distributions of interevent or service times.

There are many ways to generate random numbers. Rolling dice, tossing coins, and drawing a card from a well-shuffled deck don't require fancy technology and work well. (Simulation models that use random numbers are often called *Monte Carlo simulations* after the Monte Carlo casino in Monaco. It uses physical random number generators extensively in its business.) Special dice with more or fewer than the usual six sides exist. They are used in noncomputer simulations such as "Dungeons and Dragons" or war games. Opening a phone book to an arbitrary page with your eyes closed and choosing the digit on which your finger lands is another method. Tables of random numbers have been published. (There may be one in the back of your statistics textbook.) Operations researchers used these tables before digital computers became widely available.

A practical low-tech way to generate random decimal digits uses this book. Open it to a random page. The tens digit of the page number is your random digit. Only the tens digit works: You influence the hundreds digit when you decide where to open the book, and the units digit depends on your choice of the left or right page. To get a random number from 00 to 99, repeat the process a second time.

It is possible to equip a computer with a physical random number generator. A microphone can pick up random background noise in the room where the computer is located. Its voltage can then be converted to digital form. The low-order bits in the digital representation of the background noise are truly random. Another method is to use the low-order digits of a high-resolution system clock, if it ticks so often during the processing of an event that its low-order digits are for all practical purposes random.

Using truly random numbers has this disadvantage: Their sequence is not repeatable. It is easier to check out a computer program when its inputs are repeatable. For that reason, virtually all simulation models are *pseudo-random* numbers. These are numbers generated by a repeatable formula, which behave statistically as if they were truly random. Most such formulas generate uniformly distributed integers from 0 to the largest positive integer that the computer in question can conveniently represent. If your computer uses 32-bit signed integer data, the largest integer it can conveniently represent is about 2,147,500,000.

All simulation packages and most programming languages have built-in functions that return uniformly distributed pseudo-random numbers over a

FIGURE 9–7

Cumulative Distribution Function

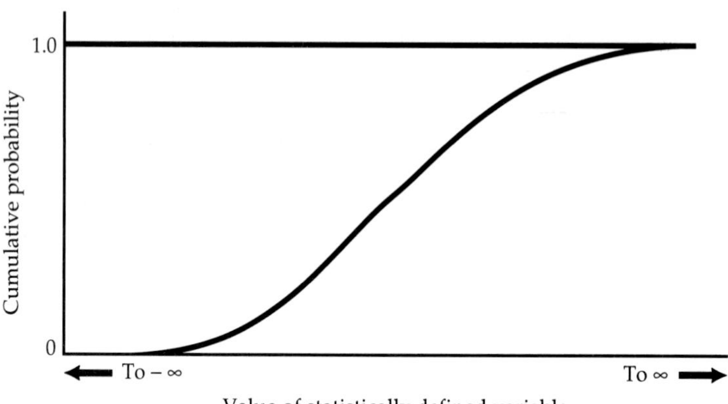

more useful range. The output of these functions ranges from 0 to 1 (more precisely, from 0 to the largest fraction, 0.99999 . . . , less than 1 that a computer can represent) or from 0 to a user-specified figure. This range is created by scaling the output of an integer pseudo-random number generator. Users of such functions who want a nonuniform distribution must convert the output of the built-in function to a number from the desired distribution. This is done via a cumulative distribution function as shown in Figure 9–7. Simulation packages include a set of common distributions, such as the normal distribution, along with easy ways for the programmer to define other distributions. General-purpose programming languages usually don't.

The built-in random number generators of most systems are not perfect. Computer science journals regularly critique popular ones and suggest improvements. A common criticism is that a generator produces numbers that repeat themselves after a far shorter period than the computer's world length requires. Built-in generators are improving slowly as their developers become aware of new research and as new versions of software supplant older ones. Meanwhile, they are widely used and suffice for most decision support tasks. A modeler about to embark on a simulation study that will determine the fate of humanity, or even the fate of a corporation, should make an effort to verify that his or her pseudo-random number generator passes the randomness tests in the literature—and replace it if it does not.

9.1.7 Static Simulation Models

We stated earlier that simulation models are dynamic. This is true 99 percent of the time, which is why we covered dynamic simulation models first. There are also static situations where we can apply the same idea of using pseudo-random numbers to drive a system model. Here's an example:

Suppose a manager wants to estimate next year's profits. One way is to develop an accounting model that will give profits as a function of sales volume for each of the firm's five products. We don't generally know, however, what next year's sales will be. The best we can do is to estimate them statistically.

If we have estimated sales distributions for each of the five products, we can pick a random member of each distribution and get a possible outcome of next year's business activities. We can then pick another set of five possible sales volumes and get another possible outcome. After repeating this process a number of times, we will get a picture of next year's probable profit distribution, on the assumption that our sales distributions and our profitability formula were accurate.

To run through this process, suppose we have five products. Conveniently, each sale of product 1 yields a profit of $1, each sale of product 2 yields $2 in profit, and so on. We must also cover fixed costs of $10,000. Our profits therefore depend on the sales of our five products according to this formula, with all quantities in dollars:

$$\begin{aligned} \text{Profit} = {} & (\text{Product 1 unit sales}) + 2(\text{Product 2 unit sales}) \\ & + 3(\text{Product 3 unit sales}) + 4(\text{Product 4 unit sales}) \\ & + 5(\text{Product 5 unit sales}) - 10{,}000 \end{aligned}$$

Suppose we estimate that the probable sales of each product are uniformly distributed within the following limits. That is, for product 1, any unit volume from 800 to 1,200 units is equally likely, and sales below 800 units or above 1,200 units will not (according to our estimate) occur under any circumstances.

Product 1: 800 to 1,200 units
Product 2: 700 to 1,100
Product 3: 600 to 1,000
Product 4: 500 to 900
Product 5: 400 to 800

One choice of pseudo-random numbers might give us these estimated sales of the five products for next year:

Product 1: 1,120 units
Product 2: 785
Product 3: 660
Product 4: 845
Product 5: 610

For this set of estimated sales, profit is forecasted to be:

$$(1{,}120) + 2(785) + 3(660) + 4(845) + 5(610) - 10{,}000 = \$1{,}100$$

Other possible estimated sales volumes would result in higher profits, lower profits, or a loss. A hundred different choices of sales volumes from these distributions gave the estimated profit distribution shown in Figure 9–8. It matches the basic parameters you could figure out from the problem description: All the trials yielded profit figures between –$2,000 and $4,000, and the peak was somewhere around the expected mean of $1,000. Yet many managers would not have guessed the approximate shape. A different hundred trials would, of course, have yielded a different chart. Many more trials would have yielded a smoother curve.

Packages are available to help decision makers use static, stochastic simulation models such as these. These packages often build on the spreadsheet metaphor, which is familiar to most managers in the mid-1990s. Crystal Ball® is such a package.[3] Crystal Ball, which is available in versions for Microsoft Windows® and Apple Macintosh®, takes a spreadsheet model from any popular spreadsheet package that has been saved in any of several standardized spreadsheet interchange file formats. Figure 9–9 shows the preceding simple model in a spreadsheet. It then allows the decision maker to define any cell containing a constant as an "assumption cell" subject to a user-specified statistical distribution. These distributions are chosen from the "gallery" of Figure 9–10. The uniform distribution is highlighted in the figure because that is the distribution we plan to use in our simulation. Each distribution, once chosen, is further specified by appropriate parameters: minimum and maximum for the uniform distribution, mean and standard deviation for the normal dis-

FIGURE 9–8

Chart of Estimated Profit Probabilities

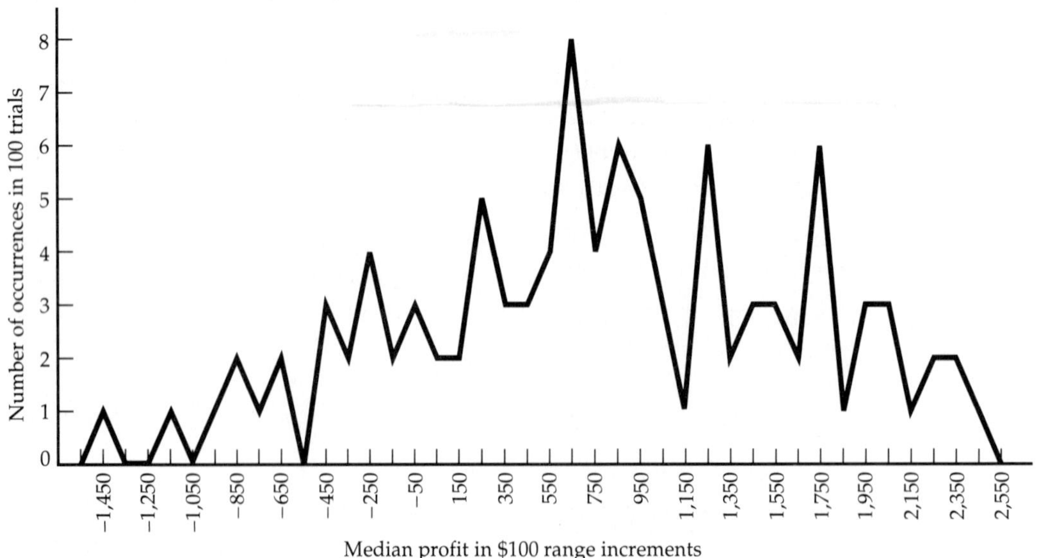

[3]Crystal Ball is a product of Decisioneering Inc., Denver, Colorado.

FIGURE 9–9
Spreadsheet with Profit Model

	A	B	C
1	*Sales Forecast Example*		
2	*Product No.*	*Units*	*Price*
3	1	1000	$1.00
4	2	900	$2.00
5	3	800	$3.00
6	4	700	$4.00
7	5	600	$5.00
8	Profit	$1,000	
9			

FIGURE 9–10
Crystal Ball Distribution Gallery

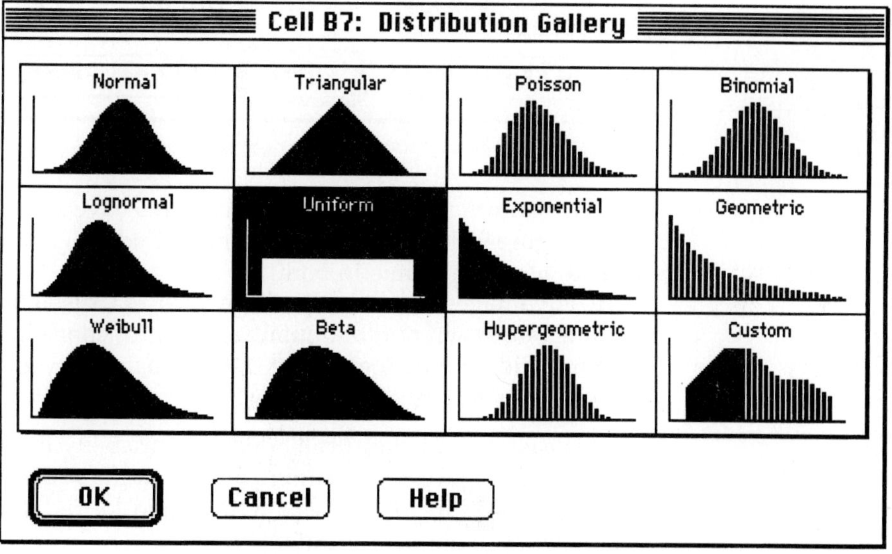

tribution, etc. Crystal Ball also lets decision makers define custom distributions if none of the standard ones meet their needs.

Figure 9–11 shows the profit distribution that results from running the model just over 8,000 times. Because Crystal Ball is programmed to carry out this process efficiently, rather than being a general-purpose package that can be instructed to carry out many different types of processes and must be able to handle them all, those 8,000 runs take only a minute or two on even a slow microcomputer with no math coprocessor. If you compare Figures 9–8

FIGURE 9–11

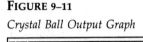

Crystal Ball Output Graph

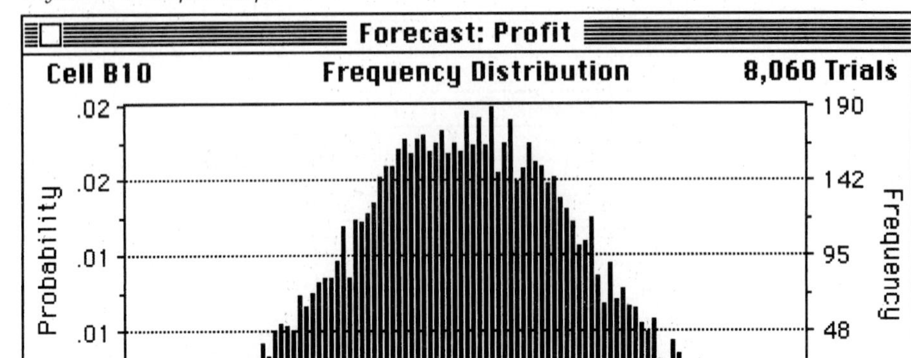

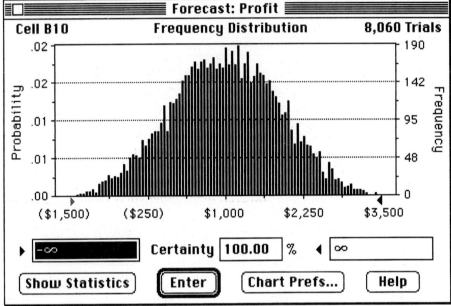

and 9–11, you will see that the additional runs have smoothed out the jagged peaks of Figure 9–8 considerably. The mean and range of the distribution are, of course, about the same in both.

The advantages of using a package such as Crystal Ball, rather than programming one's own random number-based functions into a spreadsheet (as the author did in creating Figure 9–8) or using any other "home-grown" approach, are substantial:

- It is easy to add statistically defined variability to the deterministic model of Figure 9–9. Defining all five uniform distributions, once the underlying spreadsheet was written and loaded into Crystal Ball, was the work of about a minute.
- A wide variety of statistical distributions is available, many of which would be quite difficult for a decision maker (even one who happens to be an expert programmer) to define directly.
- The parameters of the distributions, indeed the distributions themselves, are easy to change.
- The output facilities exceed what spreadsheet packages offer for this type of problem. In Figure 9–11, the user can (for example) move the triangular "grabbers" at either end of the x-axis from their current positions, or type new values into the boxes representing the limits

of the interval of interest, to see what percentage of the runs yielded results with a particular range. Figure 9–12 shows how this works; the lower limit was raised to $0. The box under the center of the graph now shows that 87.13 percent of the runs yielded a profit.

Their major disadvantage is the need to use two packages: one to define the model, one to run it as a simulation. This is not a serious issue—indeed, Crystal Ball and Excel under Microsoft Windows can use Dynamic Data Exchange to behave much like a single program—and should not deter a decision maker from using this type of tool. Over time, we can expect to see high-end spreadsheet packages enhanced to incorporate some, if not all, of the capabilities that now call for specialized software.

Demand elasticity curves play a key role in many static representational models. These include the economist's price elasticity curve, which tells us how the quantity of an item that customers purchase varies as its price changes. There are, however, many other curves that relate the demand for a product to some external, and (hopefully) predictable or controllable, factor: the demand for skis as a function of weather, the demand for cameras as a function of advertising, the demand for a new model car as a function of the gasoline mileage its designers are able to achieve. All these and more figure in many useful DSS. Crystal Ball and similar packages can deal with many such

FIGURE 9–12

Crystal Ball Output Graph with Lower Limit

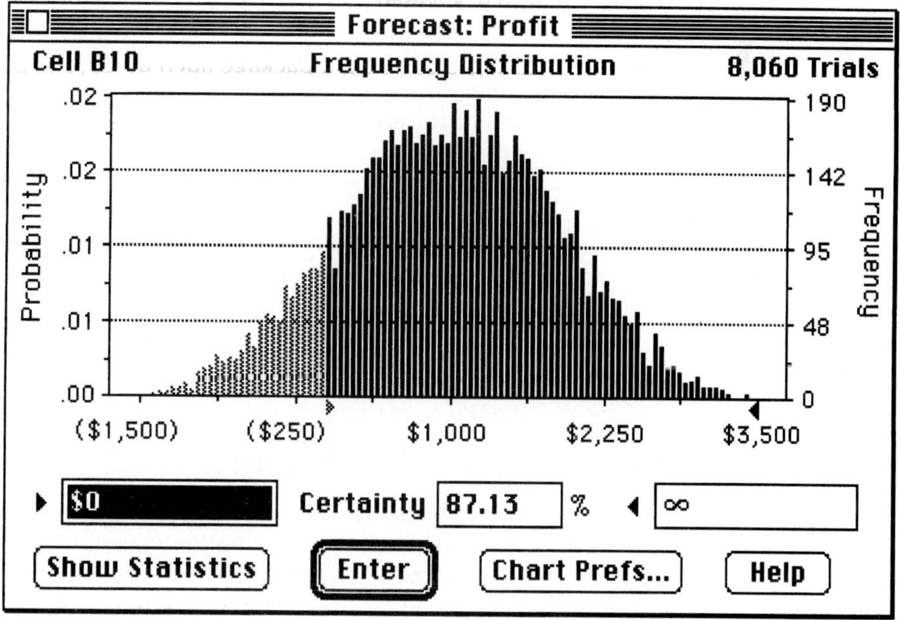

situations by defining correlated variables: In the preceding sales and profit forecast, for example, we might have specified that product 5 sales have a 0.5 correlation with product 1 sales. (Perhaps product 1 is house paint and product 5 is stepladders.) More complex cases call for custom programming.

9.2 Queuing Models

Simulation carries a system under study step by step through its existence, deriving statistically valid conclusions from a sufficiently large sample of its activities. *Queuing models,* on the other hand, obtain the statistics of system behavior directly, without following individual events. Where the simplifications that queuing theory requires are acceptable, it determines the average behavior of a system faster than simulation. Furthermore, it describes this behavior by formulas that can be evaluated for any desired set of system parameters (controllable variables) rather than as numbers that are calculated for one set of parameters and must be recalculated from scratch for any other set. These characteristics make queuing models a useful adjunct to simulation, especially in DSS used to plan complex systems.

9.2.1 Queuing Theory Concepts

The basic concepts of queuing theory are:

1. The possible states of the system are determined by studying the system, its state variables, and their possible combinations.
2. The rates at which each state changes to each other state—that is, the rates of each possible *state transition*—are determined as functions of transaction arrival rates into the system and service times of system processes.
3. If the system is in a "steady state," the average transition rate into each state must equal the average transition rate out of that state. This condition on the state probabilities yields equations from which the state probabilities can be found.
4. Solving these equations yields the state probabilities themselves. From these we can determine other statistics of interest, such as average customer waiting times or average queue lengths.

9.2.2 A Queuing Theory Example

Consider an office building with a pay phone on each floor. Potential telephone users who arrive at an idle telephone use it. Those who find a phone in use wait for it to become free. Those who find someone already waiting try another floor. The phone has three states: idle, in use with nobody waiting, and in use with a person waiting. Possible state transitions are shown in Figure 9–13. No transitions are shown from state 1 directly to state 3. That is because two customers never arrive at precisely the same instant: there is always an interval, however short, between their arrivals. This can be shown to be true in the limit for random arrivals, although it would not hold for a simulation that chops time into finite steps.

Suppose the average telephone conversation lasts five minutes. (Phone companies keep excellent statistical records.) Therefore, if a conversation is taking place, there is a 20 percent chance that it will finish in the next minute. Put in terms of state transitions, transitions from state 2 to state 1 occur at an average rate of 0.2 per minute times the likelihood that the system was in state 2 to begin with, or P_2. Similarly, 3→2 transitions occur at an average rate of 0.2 per minute times P_3. We also need the average customer arrival rate, which we can learn by watching the phone. Suppose the average interval is 10 minutes, for an average arrival rate of 0.1 customer per minute. That means there is a 10 percent chance of a customer arriving in the next minute. Again putting this in terms of state transitions, transitions from state 1 to state 2 occur at an average rate of 0.1 times P_1, and 2→3 transitions at an average rate of 0.1 times P_2. These transition rates are shown in Figure 9–14.

Now comes the crucial step. If the system is in its steady state, *the rate of transition into each state must equal the rate of transition out of it*. The rate of transition into state 1 must equal the rate of transition out of state 1. The same is true for states 2 and 3. In the case of state 1, there is only one type of transition into it, the 2→1 transition, and only one out of it, the 1→2

FIGURE 9–13
Pay Phone State Diagram

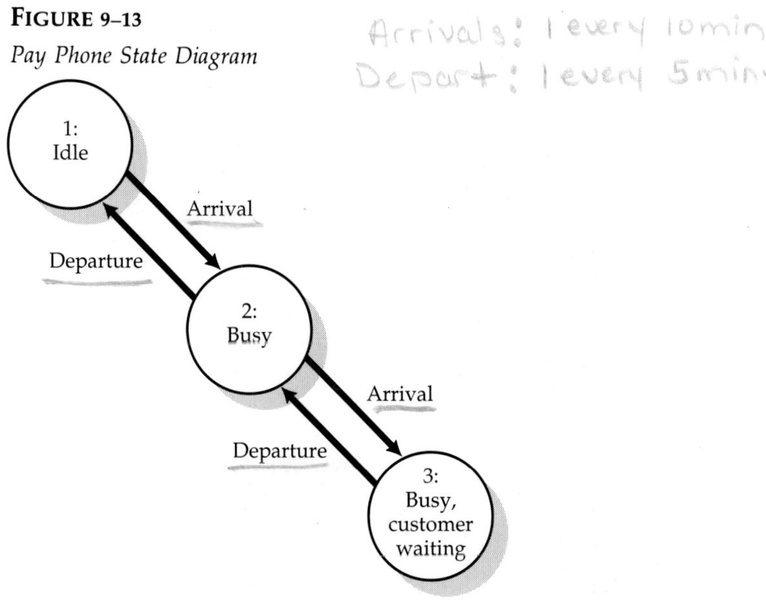

FIGURE 9–14
Pay Phone State Diagram with Transition Rates

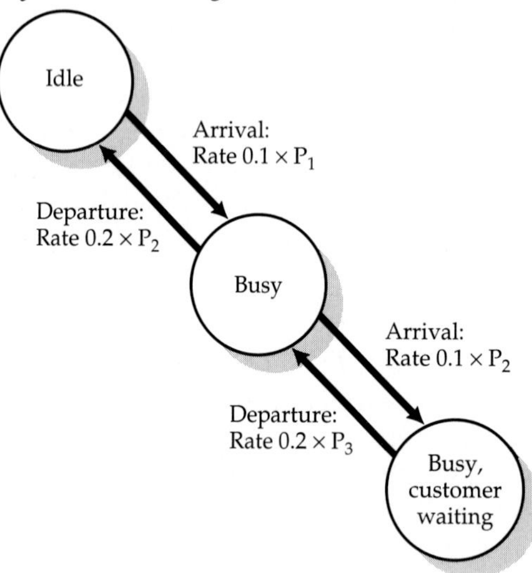

transition. We can write the condition of equal transition rates as follows, in what is called the *equation of balance* for state 1:

$$0.2\ P_2 = 0.1\ P_1$$

Similarly, we can write the equations of balance for states 2 and 3:

$$0.1\ P_1 + 0.2\ P_3 = 0.3\ P_2$$

$$0.1\ P_2 = 0.2\ P_3$$

These three equations have three unknowns, the three P_i. Unfortunately, they are linearly dependent on each other (the first and last, added algebraically, yield the second), so there are only two independent equations in three unknowns. This is true of all queuing theory models: If a system has n states, there are always n equations of balance in the P_i, which are equivalent to $n - 1$ linearly independent equations. Since it takes n independent equations to find n unknowns, we need a third, independent, equation here to find the P_i. This third equation comes from the fact that the system is always in some state (why?), so the three state probabilities must sum to 1:

$$P_1 + P_2 + P_3 = 1$$

We can now solve these equations to obtain the state probabilities for the telephone as $P_1 = 4/7$, $P_2 = 2/7$, and $P_3 = 1/7$. What do these numbers mean?

- Since $P_1 = 4/7$, the phone is idle 4/7 of the time. Conversely, it is busy $P_2 + P_3 = 3/7$ of the time. This might suggest the income to expect from the telephone, which would help us decide if it is worth installing one.

- If potential customers arrive every 10 minutes and leave after 5, we would expect the phone to be busy exactly half the time. Lower usage must be due to customers seeing a line and leaving, or "balking" in operations research terminology. Since the usage ratio of 3/7 is 6/7 of what we would expect in the absence of departures, we know that 1/7 of its potential customers went elsewhere. This information can help decide whether or not to install a second phone near the existing one.
- Someone is waiting by the phone 1/7 of the time, or more than eight minutes out of every hour. This might argue for installing a soda machine nearby.

9.2.3 Generalizing the Solution

We may want to investigate the effect of different arrival and service times on our conclusions: What would happen if the average conversation were to last four minutes, or six? To study several alternatives, we represent the state transition rates by algebraic symbols. Operations researchers use the lowercase Greek letters λ (lambda) for mean interarrival time and μ (mu) for mean service time. With these symbols, the equations of balance (only two of which, as you recall, are independent) are

$$\mu P_2 = \lambda P_1$$

$$\lambda P_1 + \mu P_3 = (\mu + \lambda) P_2$$

$$\lambda P_2 = \mu P_3$$

To solve these, it's convenient to define the *utilization ratio* $\rho = \lambda/\mu$, which is 0.5 with the numbers used earlier. In terms of ρ (rho) the equations become

$$P_2 = \rho P_1$$

$$\rho P_1 + P_3 = (1 + \rho) P_2$$

$$\rho P_2 = P_3$$

Solving these yields

$$P_1 = 1/(1 + \rho + \rho^2)$$

$$P_2 = \rho/(1 + \rho + \rho^2)$$

$$P_3 = \rho^2/(1 + \rho + \rho^2)$$

We can insert any value for ρ into these formulas and obtain the state probabilities directly. For example, if conversations average six minutes, $\rho = 0.6$. This yields $P_1 = 0.510$, $P_2 = 0.306$, and $P_3 = 0.184$. Of an additional 10 percent potential utilization, 6.1 percent went into actual utilization. (The idle time dropped from 57.1 percent to 51.0 percent, so the busy time went from 43.9 percent to 49.0 percent. We could also obtain the busy time by adding P_2 and P_3.) The remaining 3.9 percent is reflected in a higher level of balking.

9.2.4 Arrival and Departure Time Distributions

We made, but did not state, an important mathematical assumption in the above example: that interarrival and service times have the given means but are otherwise totally random. If they were not totally random, the results would have been different. Suppose, for instance, that interarrival times were constant: Potential telephone users arrive precisely on the hour, at 10 minutes past, at 20 minutes past, and so on. Suppose also that all conversations took precisely five minutes. These "distributions" have the same means as our earlier ones, but the results are quite different. In this ideal situation nobody would ever wait to use the phone, let alone find another person waiting. The more regular the arrival and service times, the better most systems behave in minimizing waiting times and maximizing resource utilization.

The assumption of random interarrival and service times corresponds to an exponential distribution of these times as shown in Figure 9–15. This distribution has a high probability of short times. It allows for long times with decreasing likelihood. An important characteristic of the exponential distribution is that *knowing the elapsed time since the last event does not help predict the next one.* For example, knowing that a telephone conversation has already lasted an hour does not help predict whether or not it will end in the next minute. (Human phone conversations behave this way, although data transmission does not. The increase in data traffic over the past decade or so has forced telephone companies to discard many time-honored assumptions.) This is an important underpinning of queuing theory since it means that the mean transition rate from one state to another is a constant. Arrivals usually behave similarly: In the absence of a controlling factor such as a congested parking lot entrance, knowing that nobody has entered a supermarket for 10 minutes does not affect the statistical likelihood that a shopper will show up in the next 5 seconds. The concept of an event being "due to happen," simply because it has not happened for a while, is intuitively attractive but does not match most real situations.

Queuing models can be solved only for exponentially distributed transaction arrivals and service times. Fortunately, this is not as restrictive as it might seem. Passing a customer through two processes, each with mean service time of one minute, creates a composite process with mean service time of two minutes but smaller variance than a single process with exponentially distributed service time would have. Using more subprocesses reduces the variance still further and creates a good approximation to a normal service time distribution. Using several processes in the model does not imply that the system itself consists of a series of processes. It is just a mathematical

FIGURE 9–15

Cumulative Distribution Function of Exponential Distribution

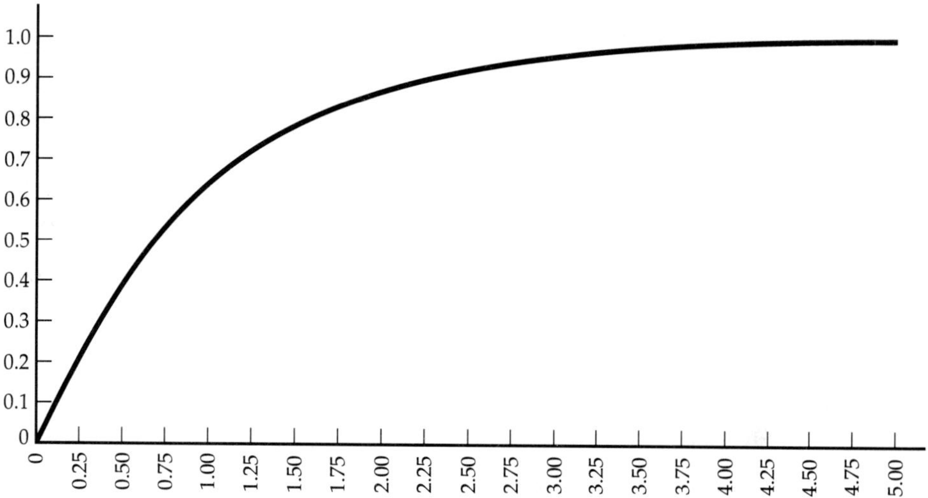

trick to allow us to model some types of reality more closely than an exponential distribution would.

Such multistage distributions are called *Erlang* distributions, after a Danish telephone engineer who pioneered queuing theory in the early 1900s. They are useful in modeling processes where a given step takes a relatively constant time with small variation, such as the access time of a computer disk drive. Their disadvantage is that they increase the number of states in the model and, hence, the number of equations of balance and the work of solving them in closed form. Figure 9–16 shows a two-stage Erlang distribution (a "2-Erlang" distribution for short) and a 10-Erlang distribution alongside the exponential distribution. You can see how the Erlang distributions start out flatter, indicating fewer very short activity times; get steeper and cross the exponential, indicating more activity times toward the middle; and then flatten out again as activity times rise far above the mean.

We can also create distributions with greater variance than the exponential distribution. This is done by replacing a real process with two parallel exponential processes in the model, one of which has a much smaller mean time than the other, and sending transactions at random to one or the other. The resulting distribution is called *hyperexponential*. Hyperexponential distributions are good for modeling data communication conversations in telephone systems or the execution times of user commands to a computer. Here, too, there is no implication that the system itself puts transactions through one of two processes, either a "long" one or a "short" one.

FIGURE 9–16

Cumulative Distribution Functions of Exponential, 2-Stage Erlang, and 10-Stage Erlang Distributions

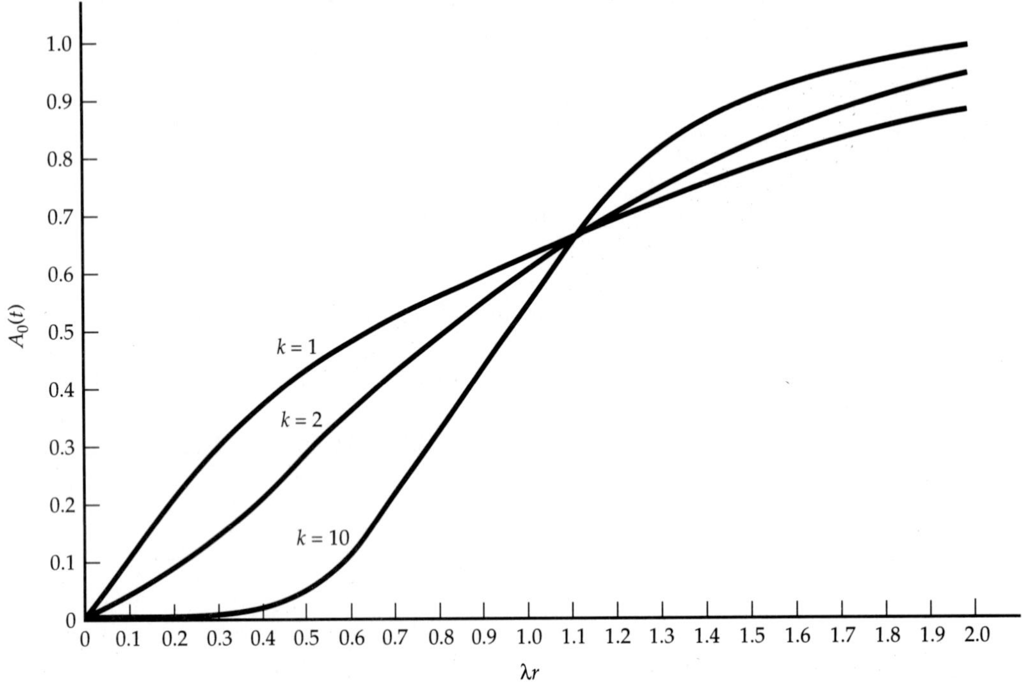

9.3 MARKOV PROCESS MODELS

9.3.1 The Markov Process Model Concept

A *Markov process* is a system that progresses from one state to another over time, where the likelihood of its being in a given state at any time step depends only on its previous state and not on its prior history.

Consider, for example, the weather model in Figure 9–17. This model tells us that, if we know today's weather, we have a better-than-random chance at guessing tomorrow's. If it's sunny now, there's a 60 percent chance of sun tomorrow, and so on.

Given an initial state, we can determine the probabilities of the next state from the transition probabilities shown in the diagram. A matrix notation is convenient for this purpose. The *state transition matrix* corresponding to Figure 9–17 is

$$T = \begin{pmatrix} 0.6 & 0.4 & 0.1 \\ 0.3 & 0.2 & 0.5 \\ 0.1 & 0.4 & 0.4 \end{pmatrix}$$

Each entry in this matrix represents the probability of a transition from the state corresponding to the entry's column, to the state corresponding to its row, in one time period. For instance, the 0.4 in the center of the top row represents the probability of a transition from state 2 (cloudy) to state 1 (sunny). Since the system must go to some state, the sum of all the entries in a column must always be 1.

To use this matrix, we express the current state of the system as a vector. We represent the state "today is sunny" as (1,0,0). If we're not sure what the weather is (or will be), there is more than one nonzero entry in the state vector. Since the weather must be in some state, state vector elements must always sum to 1.

To get tomorrow's probabilities, we multiply today's state vector by the transition matrix:

$$\overline{x}_{k+1} = T\overline{x}_k$$

For this weather example, that becomes

$$\overline{x}_{k+1} = \begin{pmatrix} 0.6 & 0.4 & 0.1 \\ 0.3 & 0.2 & 0.5 \\ 0.1 & 0.4 & 0.4 \end{pmatrix} \begin{pmatrix} 1 \\ 0 \\ 0 \end{pmatrix} = \begin{pmatrix} 0.6 \\ 0.3 \\ 0.1 \end{pmatrix}$$

FIGURE 9–17

State Diagram of Weather System

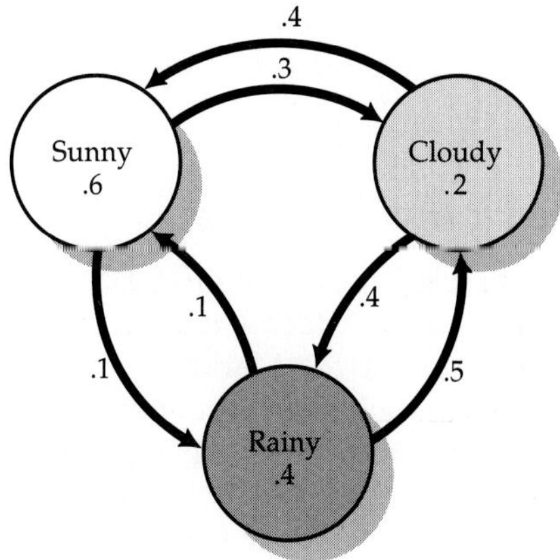

For the day after tomorrow, we repeat the multiplication:

$$\overline{x}_{k+2} = T\overline{x}_{k+1}$$

which in this case yields state (weather) probabilities of (0.49, 0.29, 0.22).

Eventually this process converges and we reach the steady-state system probabilities. In the case of weather, this means we have gone far enough into the future that knowing today's weather is of no predictive value. In general, this means we have gone far enough into the future that knowing the initial state is of no (or insignificant) predictive value.

The weather model lends itself perfectly to this formalism because a time scale is inherent in its description. To formulate the pay phone example of Section 9.2.2 as a Markov process we must choose a time period between steps. From a theoretical point of view, state transition rates apply only to infinitely small time steps, since for a finite time step there is a nonzero probability of two events occurring in one interval. Fortunately, the Markov process equations always converge to the correct answer despite this. We must only choose a time step short enough to leave, for every state of the system, a positive probability of remaining in that state.

Consider state 1 of the pay phone, where it is idle. Transitions out of state 1 occur at an average rate of 0.1 per minute. There is about a 1 percent probability of two customers arriving during the same minute and about a 0.1 percent probability of three showing up. For a Markov process approach we ignore these. We can use a 1-minute time step, as it would give a 90 percent probability of remaining in state 1. We can also use a 5-minute time step. A 10-minute time step would reduce the probability of staying in state 1 to zero and would therefore not work, nor would a larger time step. We could use a 9-minute time step, but it approaches the limit, and our calculations would converge slowly. (Exercise 12 considers transitions into and out of all three states.)

A Markov process analysis of the pay phone problem will, if we make no errors, give the same answer as queuing theory did. As long as we define states in the same way and use the same transition rates, the two formulations are equivalent because both assume exponential distributions of interevent times.

9.3.2 *Computer Calculations for Markov Processes*

Because of its apparent simplicity, programming a Markov model on a computer doesn't seem a daunting task. After all, it's just one matrix multiplication after another! Specialized packages for Markov process calculations hardly exist. Two points are worth noting before you embark on programming one:

1. Realistic Markov transition matrices are quite sparse; that is, most of their elements are zero. A full-size model may have hundreds of states. However, each state can only go to a few other states because only a few events can occur in each state. A 1,000 × 1,000 transition matrix in 32-bit floating-

point form (about six significant decimal digits) occupies 4MB of computer storage. This exceeds the total capacity of most desktop computers, even before allowing space for the resident portion of the operating system and an application to manipulate the matrix, and would tax many larger ones. However, this is a *sparse matrix:* Almost all of that 4MB will contain zeros. The locations and contents of the nonzero matrix elements can be stored in far less space. Still more space can be saved, if need be, because Markov transition matrices usually contain identical values repeated many times in systematically related locations. Software packages that manipulate sparse matrices efficiently do exist and are worth investigating.

2. Because of round-off errors in computing, the sum of the state probability vector elements will drift away from 1.000000 . . . after many iterations. The vector must be *renormalized* after every hundred iterations or so. Renormalization involves summing the elements of the probability vector and dividing the every element of the vector by this sum. For example, if they add up to 1.005, dividing every vector element by 1.005 will restore their sum to 1.000.

9.4 Simulation, Queuing Theory, and Markov Processes Compared

All three of the approaches we have described for modeling dynamic processes have their advantages and disadvantages in decision support applications.

One perspective on their relationship is that simulation provides a dynamic model of a dynamic system, whereas the other two approaches provide static models of a dynamic system after it has settled down to its "steady-state" behavior. Simulation tracks what goes on inside a system and forces us to infer its characteristics by summarizing a large number of observations. The others tell us these characteristics but do not give us the same visibility into its innards.

Queuing theory provides the most general solution to a given problem and often the fastest as well. Simulation model results are the least general and usually take the longest time to obtain—because of both programming time and computer execution time. Markov process analyses are intermediate on both counts. Therefore, at first glance one should prefer queuing theory to a Markov process analysis and the Markov process approach to simulation. This is true as long as all three methods are feasible. This is not always the case. Specific points to consider are:

1. Can the system in question be modeled with sufficient realism by a reasonably small (i.e., solvable) number of states?
2. Do exponential distributions of interevent times, or distributions

that can be derived from the exponential without a great deal of added complexity, fit the actual distributions acceptably well?

3. Does the DSS developer have enough comfort with the mathematics, or have access to skilled mathematicians, to develop a queuing model of the system and solve it, in closed form or numerically?
4. Can the necessary decision-making information be obtained from the limited data that queuing theory and Markov process analyses yield?

These questions will often lead the analyst to simulation as a practical matter. It has often been said, "When all else fails, try simulation." However, the choice is not always "either-or." The methods are complementary. A useful approach often includes a simulation model for detailed insight into a system, coupled with one or both mathematical approaches. The mathematical models indicate the overall trends to be expected in system behavior and, applied to limiting cases, serve as a check on simulator results. A mathematical check on limiting cases is often a valuable development aid even if the resulting DSS will incorporate only a simulation model.

Summary

Many decision support systems use representational models to predict the impact of possible decisions. These models are of two major types: simulation models and mathematical models.

Simulation is the process of using a simulation model to study a system. Simulation models as used in business are, in almost all cases, dynamic, discrete-event, and stochastic models. They model what happens in a system over time by tracking the individual events that take place in the system.

Running a simulation consists of repeating a simple cycle over and over again. Each repetition consists of (*a*) taking the next event off the future events queue, (*b*) updating the model's representation of the system to reflect its occurrence, (*c*) recording any data we will need for later statistical analysis of system behavior, and (*d*) entering any new events it triggers into the future events queue. This process, while conceptually simple, involves a great deal of tedious bookkeeping and is therefore well suited to computers.

To design a discrete-event simulation model, you must determine its objectives, define the system to be modeled, define the state variables that describe what the system is doing at any instant, define the events that will change their values, choose the simulation time scale, define (in terms of that time scale) the statistics of each event type, and define the initial state of the system.

Having established these parameters of your model, you can now program it: in a special-purpose language such as GPSS or Simscript or in a general-purpose language such as Pascal. Simulation languages generally include capabilities that will allow you to develop your model more quickly.

Running a stochastic simulation requires the use of random numbers to choose elements of statistical distributions. Truly random numbers are rarely used because they are not repeatable and therefore make it difficult to check out a computer program. The most common approach is to use formulas that generate "pseudo-random numbers:" numbers that behave statistically as though they were random.

Simulation models must be exercised for long enough for fluctuations due to specific choices of random variables to die down. Several runs of moderate length are generally better for this purpose than one long run of the same aggregate length.

Static simulation models do exist, although they are less common than dynamic simulation models. Since a static model represents a system in rest at a single point in time, such a model can be used to study the statistics of where it comes to rest for statistically described inputs.

The second category of representational models consists of mathematical models. The two mathematical approaches that are most often used to study dynamic systems are queuing theory and Markov process analysis. Both are based on the concept of defining the states in which the system can be, the possible transitions among those states, and the rates at which those transitions take place.

In queuing theory, the need to balance transitions into and out of a state yields equations that can be solved for the probability that the system is in each state. These state probabilities, in turn, give us statistical information about system performance. If the equations are solved in terms of symbolic variables for the state transition rates, their solution describes system behavior as a set of equations. We can substitute any transition rates we wish into these equations and obtain the corresponding system behavior.

In Markov process analysis, the state transition rates are used numerically to track the system from its initial state until state probabilities stabilize. These probabilities are then used as they would be in queuing theory to obtain information about system behavior. Markov process calculations consist in essence of vector-matrix multiplication.

Both queuing theory and Markov process analysis assume exponential distributions of interarrival and service times. Other distributions can be modeled by introducing additional states (and hence additional complexity) into the model.

Queuing theory analysis yields the most general answers of the three approaches, but is the most limited in its applicability. Simulation "always works," but its answers describe only one situation with one set of random number choices. Markov process analysis is between the other two. Two or more methods can often usefully be used in combination.

Key Terms

autocorrelation 291
controllable variable 283
cumulative distribution function (CDF) 294
discrete-event simulation 278
endogenous event 284
equations of balance 302
Erlang distribution 305
event 284
exogenous event 284
exponential distribution 304
future events queue 279
GPSS (simulation programming language) 286
hyperexponential distribution 305
initial state 285
interarrival time 303
Markov process 306
model 278
Monte Carlo simulation 293
parameter 283
pseudo-random number 293
queuing theory 300
random number 293
renormalization 309
service time 303
Simscript (simulation programming language) 286
simulation 278
simulation study 290
simulator 288
sparse matrix 309
state (of a system) 283
state transition 300
state transition matrix 306
state transition rate 300
state variable 283
static simulation model 294
steady state 300
uncontrollable variable 283
utilization ratio 303

Review Questions

1. Why do decision support systems use representational models?
2. What two basic types of representational models are used for decision support?
3. What is the future events queue? What is it used for?
4. What steps does the basic simulation processing cycle consist of?
5. What are the first two steps you must take in defining a simulation model?
6. What is the *state* of a system?
7. Why are specialized simulation languages often used to develop simulation models?
8. In what two ways does a simulation study differ from a single run of a simulation model?
9. What are pseudo-random numbers? Why are they useful in simulation models? How are they created?
10. What is a static simulation model? Give an example of where one might be useful.
11. What are the two basic approaches to mathematical modeling of a system?
12. What type of statistical distribution do both approaches assume for times between events that occur in the system? How can other distributions be handled?

13. What is being "balanced" in queuing theory equations of balance?
14. How do we show transition rates between states in a Markov model?
15. What is the basic calculation process for evaluating a Markov model?
16. Of the three approaches to modeling dynamic systems, which is the most widely applicable?
17. Of the three approaches to modeling dynamic systems, which makes it easiest to evaluate the effect of a change in mean interarrival times?

Exercises

1. At Bender College 40 percent of current undergraduates are freshmen, 30 percent are sophomores, 20 percent are juniors, and the remaining 10 percent are seniors. Draw the cumulative distribution function for this distribution. Then determine the classes of 20 students by generating 20 random digits (via the method of Section 9.1.6 or with a table of random digits) and using your distribution. How closely did your results match the "official" statistics?
2. Your TV store makes a profit of $50 on each set it sells. If a customer wants a set and you don't have any, you lose this profit. However, it costs $3 to keep a set in stock for a day or part of a day, and it costs $100 to place and process each order. Orders are placed at the end of the day. They also arrive at the end of the day, five business days after being placed.

   Assume there is an equal probability of customers wanting to buy 1, 2, 3, 4, 5, or 6 sets per day. Assume you start with 30 sets in inventory. Simulate the following ordering strategies for 20 business days each:
   a. Order 20 sets when stock plus sets already on order total 20 or below at the end of the day.
   b. Order 30 sets when stock plus sets already on order total 20 or below at the end of the day.
   c. Order 30 sets when stock plus sets already on order total 30 or below at the end of the day.

   Lay your work out in the form of a table with a column for each day and rows, as shown below. Use a six-sided die to determine customer demand for each day. (Roll the die 20 times to obtain one series of orders for the 20 days, and use that series for all the strategies.) Use your ordering strategy to determine orders placed each day. Enter the amount of each order placed in the "orders received" cell five columns to the right.

   Your results won't be exactly the same as your classmates' since you will have different random number sequences. Different sequences will favor different strategies; for example, a run of heavy orders will cause

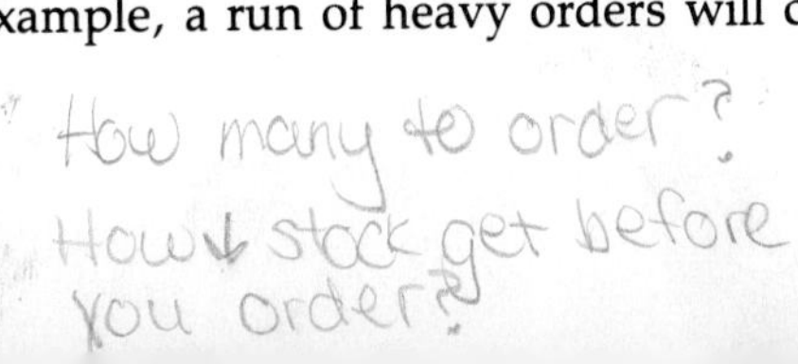

ordering many sets to look better than it should. However, a pattern should appear when you compare your conclusions.

Which of the three strategies yields the highest profit? Based on your results, can you suggest a strategy to yield still higher profits? Try it.

Item	*Day 1*	*Day 2*	*Etc.*
Opening inventory	(30 for first day, then copy prior day's close)		
Demand	(Random, 1 to 6, from die toss)		
Unit sales	(Smaller of demand or opening inventory)		
Orders recieved	(Orders placed five days earlier)		
Closing inventory	(Copy to next day's opening inventory)		
Orders placed	(Based on strategy being modeled)		
Operating profit	(Unit sales × $50)		
Carrying costs	(Opening inventory × $3)		
Ordering costs	($100 if an order was placed, else $0)		
Today's profit or loss	(Algebraic sum of above three items)		
Cumulative profit or loss	(Previous day's cumulative profit or loss, plus today's profit or minus today's loss)		

3. Your factory, located on Phobos in the year 2018, produces elbats in two stages. First they are encabulated. This takes a uniformly distributed time from 6 to 24 minutes. Next they are fluxicated, which takes a similar time. The encabulation and fluxication times of a given elbat are not correlated; that is, knowing how long it took to encabulate an elbat doesn't suggest anything about how long it will take to fluxicate that elbat. Elbats that have been encabulated are placed in a fopper until the fluxicator can start work on them. If the fopper is full, the encabulator stops until the fluxicator removes an elbat from it. The fopper costs $500 for each elbat it can fop and wears out in 30 working days. Each elbat produced in a day earns a profit of $3. If the fopper is too small, you will lose money because production will drop. If it is too large, you will have wasted money on the fopper itself. You wish to determine the optimal fopper capacity.

   Simulate this system with a computer or by hand, using a generator of decimal digits to determine encabulation and fluxication times. If you use a computer, simulate foppers of capacities from one to five elbats. Simulate one 8-hour working day per run. Carry out 10 runs per capacity.

   If you do this exercise by hand, assign each digit to 6; 8; 10; . . . , 24-minute encabulation or fluxication times. Simulate one 4-hour half-day with a two-elbat fopper. On the basis of your results, decide whether to try a larger or smaller fopper next. Try one other fopper size for four simulated hours, and state which is better.

4. Think about the limiting cases of Exercise 3. How many elbats can your factory produce per day if fopper capacity is infinite? If it is zero?
5. Your bakery sells dark rye bread in a normal distribution with a mean of 100 loaves per day and a standard deviation of 15 loaves per day. Each loaf costs 25¢ to bake and sells for $2.00. Unsold loaves are donated to charity at the end of the day.
   a. How many loaves of dark rye bread should you bake for each day?
   b. After answering part *a* but before calculating the answer to part *c*, determine upper and lower bounds on the answer to part *c*.
   c. Let's say your bakery sells both dark rye and light rye bread, with daily demand statistics for each as given above for dark rye. Customers who want one type of bread have a 50 percent likelihood of buying the other if their desired type is not available. (They are probably less willing to accept a prune danish as a substitute, but that's not the issue.) How many loaves of each type of bread should you bake now?
6. Answer the following questions about the supermarket model described in Section 9.1.4.
   a. List at least three simplifications that we made in the supermarket model but were not mentioned there.
   b. The states and events of the supermarket model were defined on the assumption that a clerk cannot start checking out a shopper until the bagger, if any, has finished bagging the purchases of the previous one. Suppose we allowed a bagger to finish one shopper while the clerk was processing the next. How would this change affect the state variables and events of our model?
7. Jacki operates a pet grooming establishment having these characteristics:
   - Customer interarrival time is uniformly distributed over 5 to 15 minutes.
   - 50 percent of the pets require 30 minutes of service, 50 percent require 60 minutes.
   - 90 percent of the pets require one groomer, 10 percent require two groomers. This is a function of pet size and is therefore not correlated with the required service time.
   - Customers who arrive when all groomers are busy leave and do not return. This includes customers whose pets require two groomers and arrive when only one is available.
   - Customers pay $15 per 30 minutes, per groomer. The cost of a grooming therefore ranges from $15 to $60.
   - Groomers on duty are paid $15 per hour whether they are busy or idle. (This includes all payroll costs including employer taxes, fringe benefits, etc.)

   Determine the optimum number of groomers by simulating Jacki's business on a computer.

8. Statements were made in Section 9.1.7 about the minimum, maximum, and expected profits from the five-product example. Justify them.
9. Solve the queuing theory equations for the telephone system in Sections 9.2.2 and 9.2.3. It's easiest if you ignore the second equation of balance, using the first and third together with the condition that the state probabilities must add up to 1.
10. The following exercises extend the telephone system queuing model of Sections 9.2.2 and 9.2.3.
    a. Solve the numerical model of Section 9.2.2 for the case where the waiting line must be two customers long before arriving customers leave. Does your solution suggest what the results might be if arriving customers never left but joined a line of any length?
    b. Solve the symbolic model of Section 9.2.3 for the case where the waiting line must be two customers long before arriving customers leave.
    c. Solve the numerical model of Section 9.2.2 for the case where half the customers who arrive when the phone is in use (state 2) stay and wait but the other half leave for another floor. *Hint:* If the average customer interarrival time is 10 minutes, what is the average interarrival time of customers who are willing to wait when the phone is in use?
    d. Solve Exercise 10*b* using the symbols of Section 9.2.3.
    e. Solve the numerical model for the case where all customers will wait if the phone is busy and half will wait if there is already one person waiting. Your answer should be between the result obtained in Section 9.2.2 and your answer to Exercise 10*a*. Why?
11. Time the intervals between arrivals at a facility such as a mall, store, or dormitory, to the nearest second, for half an hour or until you have 100 data points. Pick a time of day when people do not bunch up at the entrance. Avoid periods when external factors affect arrival times, such as a class changes or meal times at a dorm. Compare your data with the exponential distribution.
12. Keep track of day-to-day weather transitions in your area for a few weeks. (If necessary, extend the definition of "rain" to include other forms of precipitation such as snow. If your weather doesn't vary much in the current season, use a daily paper to track the weather somewhere else.) Determine the Markov process transition probabilities for this locale as in Figure 9–17.
13. Consider the choice of time step for a Markov model of the pay phone problem. Based on transitions out of state 1, Section 9.3.1 concluded that the upper limit for the length of a time step is 10 minutes. Is this still true if you consider all three states? If not, what is the upper limit on time-step length?
14. Put the state transition probabilities of the telephone system in Section 9.2.2 over one minute into Markov process transition matrix form. Assume

the system is initially idle. Carry the process through five steps with a calculator. If you did not do Exercise 13, use a one-minute time step. See how close your final result comes to the result obtained in Section 9.2.2.

15. Write a computer program to carry out the arithmetic of Exercise 14. Run the Markov process for 60 steps, or one hour. Print out the state probability vector every 10 steps. See how close your final result comes to the analytical solution. Then, run your model until all three state probabilities in one iteration are identical to those of the prior iteration to at least four decimal places. How many iterations did you need to reach this degree of convergence?

References*

On Simulation

BANK84 Banks, Jerry, and J. S. Carson. *Discrete-Event System Simulation.* Prentice Hall, Englewood Cliffs, N.J. (1984).

BANK91 Banks, Jerry; Eduardo Aviles; James R. McLaughlin; and Robert C. Yuan. "The Simulator: New Member of the Simulation Family." *Interfaces* 21, no. 2 (March–April 1991), pp. 76–86.

BRAT87 Bratley, Paul; Bennett Fox; and Linus Schrage. *A Guide to Simulation,* 2nd ed. Springer-Verlag, Berlin and New York (1987).

GORD78 Gordon, Geoffrey. *System Simulation,* 2nd ed. Prentice Hall, Englewood Cliffs, N.J. (1978).

KARI90 Karian, Zaven A., and Edward Dudewicz. *Modern Statistical Systems and GPSS Simulation: The First Course.* W. H. Freeman & Co., New York (1990).

LAW91 Law, Averill M., and W. David Kelton. *Simulation Modeling and Analysis,* 2nd ed. McGraw-Hill, New York (1991).

PEGD90 Pegden, C. D.; R. E. Shannon; and R. P. Sadowsky. *Introduction to SIMAN.* System Modeling Corporation, Sewickley, Pa. (1990).

POWE92 Power, Michael, and Elizabeth Jewkes. "Simulating Natural Gas Discoveries." *Interfaces* 22, no. 2 (March–April 1992), pp. 38–51.

PRIT86 Pritzker, A. Alan B. *Introduction to Simulation and SLAM.* John Wiley & Sons, New York (1986).

ROSS90 Ross, Sheldon M. *A Course in Simulation.* MacMillan, New York (1990).

RUBI81 Rubinstein, Reuven Y. *Simulation and the Monte Carlo Method.* John Wiley & Sons, New York (1981).

RUSS83 Russell, E. C. *Building Simulation Models with Simscript II.5.* CACI, Los Angeles (1983).

*Although most of these references have not been quoted, they are excellent sources for additional information about the topics discussed in this chapter.

On Queuing Theory and Markov Processes

ASMU87 Asmussen, Soren. *Applied Probability and Queues.* John Wiley & Sons, New York (1987).

COOP81 Cooper, Robert B. *Introduction to Queuing Theory.* North Holland, New York (1981).

GNED89 Gnedenko, B. V., and I. N. Kovalenko. *Introduction to Queuing Theory,* 2nd ed. (translated from Russian by Samuel Kotz). Birkhauser, Boston (1989).

GROS85 Gross, Donald, and Carl M. Harris. *Fundamentals of Queuing Theory.* John Wiley & Sons, New York (1985).

HALL91 Hall, Randolph W. *Queuing Methods for Services and Manufacturing.* Prentice Hall, Englewood Cliffs, N.J. (1991).

HILL90 Hiller, Frederick S., and Gerald J. Lieberman. *Introduction to Operations Research,* 5th ed. McGraw-Hill, New York (1990).

ISAA76 Isaacson, Dean L. *Markov Chains, Theory and Applications.* John Wiley & Sons, New York (1976).

SAAT83 Saaty, Thomas L. *Elements of Queuing Theory with Applications.* Dover, New York (1983).

On Pseudo-Random Numbers

ANDE90 Anderson, Stuart L. "Random Number Generators on Vector Supercomputers and Other Advanced Architectures." *SIAM Review* 32, no. 2 (June 1990), pp. 221–51.

CART90 Carta, David G. "Two Fast Implementations of the 'Minimal Standard' Random Number Generator." *Communications of the ACM* 33, no. 1 (January 1990), pp. 87–88.

KNUT81 Knuth, Donald. *Computer Programming: Seminumerical Algorithms,* vol. 2, chap. 3. Addison-Wesley, Reading, Mass. (1981). A classic. Begin here.

RIPL90 Ripley, B. D. "Thoughts on Pseudo-Random Number Generators." *Journal of Computational and Applied Mathematics* 31 (1990), pp. 153–60.

ENVOYANCE: USING SIMULATION

Doug and Adrienne had just finished a discussion of discrete-event simulation in their DSS course. The instructor had used plenty of examples: from manufacturing, administration, shipping, receiving, traffic—even one from the Harwich U. registration process, in which he proved that an on-line system would pay for itself in two semesters plus a summer session. But he didn't use any from environmental engineering, pollution abatement, or anything remotely similar. "Simulation sounds like it ought to be good for *something* at Envoyance," said Adrienne pensively. "But *what*?"

"Here's one thought," said Doug after thinking for a couple of minutes. "You know that Oxbow cleanup job they just submitted a bid for? You know, the one where they had to decide how much to bid on the assessment, with everyone cutting their prices to get an edge on the cleanup work?"

"Yes, I remember that one," said Adrienne.[4] "But how would simulation tie into it?"

"Well," Doug hesitated, "I'm not 100 percent sure that it would. But, assuming they got the job, they have to schedule a lot of different workers in a certain sequence. Each process takes a certain amount of time. I sure don't understand the details, but I have to assume that some of the processes can take more or less time depending on how many people, how much equipment, and what kinds of equipment you use. I recall Jim mentioning that there are some serious space problems at the site that limit how many things can be going on at the same time. Put it all together, and it sounds as though you could use simulation to look at different ways of scheduling the parts of the job."

"Yes, I suppose you could. But would you want to?"

Exercises

1. Do you feel that using simulation to consider alternatives would be justified in this case? Assume that the cleanup task is similar in nature and scope to the construction of a medium-sized office or store building.
2. How would you define the system to be simulated?
3. What would be some of the state variables you would use to define the state of this system?
4. What would be some of the events that take place in this system and that affect the values of the above state variables?
5. Could you use queuing theory in any way in this situation? A Markov process model? For each: If yes, how? If not, why not?
6. Environmental engineering firms use simulation, among other places, to model movement of pollution through the air. For instance, if a fire at a chemical plant releases toxic fumes, simulation can indicate which residential areas should be evacuated in time for their residents to gather up their belongings and leave in an orderly fashion before the pollution arrives.
   a. Is this a discrete-event or a continuous simulation? Why?
   b. What are some of the statistically defined parameters this simulation would require?

[4]In case you don't, the Oxbow bid was discussed in a discussion question for the episode at the end of Chapter 2 and again by Jim in the episode at the end of Chapter 6.

CHAPTER 10

Optimization

Chapter Outline

Introduction

Optimization is the act or the process of choosing the best of several alternatives. This term usually implies that there is a mathematical way to compare alternatives and to decide, objectively, which of them is "best." The function whose value we are evaluating and comparing is called the *objective function* of the optimization process.

Optimization figures directly in the sixth category of DSS, optimization systems. It also figures in some DSS in the seventh category, suggestion systems. There, one good basis for suggesting an alternative is to compare it with others and find them wanting. Even when optimization isn't built into a DSS, it is often part of the overall decision process that includes the DSS. An example of this would be a complete simulation study to which a DSS provides input via a model. The DSS builder must, for all these reasons, be familiar with basic optimization methods.

This chapter discusses some of the most important optimization methods used in DSS. It is not designed to make you an expert on any of them. Most business schools offer courses in operations analysis that can take you in that direction if it matches your interest. Our objective here is more modest: to make you aware of the methods that exist and what they can do. When you encounter an optimization problem on the job, you will then know what to look for and will be in a position to deal with the basic issues. Many software packages support one or more optimization methods, but it will be up to you to realize when they might be useful and which one(s) to use. If the system you're working on calls for programming an optimization method from scratch—not the usual situation, but it does come up—you will be able to learn more at that point, which should be well within your capabilities, or to recognize that you must consult a specialist.

Chapter Objectives

After you have read and studied this chapter, you will be able to:

1. Understand why optimization is important to many decision support systems.
2. Describe the complete enumeration method, where it applies, and what its limitations are.
3. Identify how calculus can be used in optimization and when it cannot.
4. Discuss the difference between linear programming and a linear programming model.
5. Explain how the simplex method can solve linear programming problems.
6. Discuss how the numerical optimization approach of hill-climbing works.
7. Use Box's method for numerical optimization.

10.1 TESTING ALTERNATIVES

The simplest optimization method, conceptually, is to try several alternatives (usually via a model, since experiments on real systems are generally not practical) and pick the best. Two related methods that rely on this approach are complete enumeration and random search. While they do not have the mathematical elegance of other approaches, some of which we'll discuss later in this chapter, they are often quite useful in practice and should not be ignored.

10.1.1 Complete Enumeration

Complete enumeration means evaluating all the possible choices, comparing their merits using a suitable yardstick, and picking the best. The Kepner-Tregoe decision-making method that we discussed in Section 2.6 works this way.

Complete enumeration is feasible only when the options or the decision parameters are discrete and few in number. It might be a reasonable optimization approach for choosing among four alternative leasing plans, five building sites, or six applicants for a job. In the supermarket example of the previous chapter there were 440 possible combinations of checkout clerks and baggers that could be used. Complete enumeration can deal with this problem, but only because the nature of the problem lends itself to a clear two-dimensional presentation and then only if several hours of computer time are available. Even under those conditions, 440 combinations push the limit for complete enumeration. A real analyst faced with the supermarket problem should also consider other methods, especially if the analysis is to be repeated regularly: perhaps for several supermarkets, perhaps repeatedly for one store over an extended period of time.

Complete enumeration is not possible in theory when the decision parameters are continuous. When parameters are continuous, they can theoretically take on an infinite number of values over any range of interest. We can't evaluate an infinite number of possibilities in a finite time. The same applies in practice to parameters that are "nearly continuous," such as a price that can theoretically vary over a million dollar range by 1¢ steps.

However, we can often apply complete enumeration to continuous or nearly continuous problems by choosing a reasonable number of points spaced over the interval of interest. Suppose, for instance, that we want to choose the best price for a new aircraft based on our predicted production cost and estimated price-demand curve. If we know that it will sell for somewhere in the range of $2 to $3 million, we could calculate the predicted profit at prices ranging from $2 million to $3 million by steps of $50,000, a total of 21 different prices. Once we have narrowed the price down to an interval of $50,000 or $100,000 by this method, we could try steps of $1,000 to $5,000 within that interval. This process can continue until we have sufficient precision for the question at hand. For aircraft prices the nearest $500 is surely sufficient. The nearest $10,000 may well suffice, given the approximate nature of any price-demand curve and the common practice of setting the price at a round number.

Complete enumeration can also be used as part of a larger optimization process. Suppose some of the controllable variables have a few discrete values each and others don't. We can enumerate the possible combinations of the discrete variables. Each combination defines a smaller problem, in which only the remaining (continuous) variables change. We can then use one of the other techniques of this chapter to optimize the solution for that particular combination of the discrete variables. After thus obtaining the optimum solution for each combination of the discrete variables, we can compare them (complete enumeration) to get the optimum solution to the problem as a whole.

From a computer point of view, programming complete enumeration is a "brute force" approach that relies on computer time instead of prior analysis or more sophisticated search techniques. The programming aspect is usually trivial, involving several nested loops around a kernel that evaluates each alternative. The choice between computer time and thinking time is highly situational: If computer time is readily available, and the expertise to program a less resource-intensive method harder to come by, complete enumeration may be the best approach from the overall business point of view.

Decision trees, which we discussed in Section 2.4.1, support the complete enumeration approach to optimizing a decision. If the states of nature at the ends of the branches of a decision tree are represented by continuous distributions, calculus can be used to compare them [MALL75]. Its use here is subject to the limitations discussed in the next section.

10.1.2 Random Search

A related method to complete enumeration is *random search*. In random search the analyst does not try to evaluate the objective function for all possible combinations of the controllable variables. Rather, the analyst chooses several, often several hundred, random combinations of the controllable variables. After a large number of runs (the term "large" is not precisely defined, but after a while additional runs will not improve the result), the highest output is taken as the best estimate of the optimum.

We might use random search in a business optimization problem such as choosing an advertising schedule. There are simply too many advertising media to be able to try all possible combinations. Advertisers use rules of thumb—"don't advertise oil drilling services in *Wind and Solar Power Today*"—to cut their number down to a reasonable amount, but they can never really be sure that these rules did not eliminate some good possibilities. A computer program that tried a few hundred or a few thousand randomly chosen combinations to see if it could improve matters might be a good idea.

As another example, random search can be used to pick common stocks for investment purposes. Suppose you have developed a complex model that predicts future stock prices on the basis of historical day-to-day price changes and the corresponding trading volumes on each day. (Such models are actually used, based on the idea that a price change associated with high volume is more likely to signal a trend than an opposite price change that took place with a small trading volume.) You cannot, given the available computing resources, apply your model to every stock on the New York Stock Exchange, let alone all the other possible markets. You can, however, pick 100 stocks at random and use it on them. In doing so, you would assume that a large enough sample is likely to uncover some very good investments. Even though it might miss the best ones, the difference between the ones it picks and the best is likely to be less than the inaccuracy of your model.

The random search technique cannot guarantee convergence. Its results cannot be proven optimal in a mathematical sense, and probably aren't, but are usually quite acceptable for business decision making.

Random search is often a good way to optimize a system for which you have developed a simulation model. Applying random search to the output of a simulation study raises this question: Is it better to use several runs for one set of parameters, thus getting a better estimate of the function value for that set, or to expend the same computer time in trying more random sets of parameters? The jury is out on this issue. As a practical suggestion, use enough runs at each point to estimate the function value at that point to within the accuracy to which you want to find the optimum. Less accuracy than this in estimating the function value at one point may lead to choosing the wrong point. More will waste your time and the computer's, especially if you could have tried more points instead.

10.2 The Calculus Approach

We learned in differential calculus that the derivative of a function is zero when the value of the function is at its maximum.[1] (We were also told, but may have forgotten, that the derivative is zero at a minimum and possibly at an inflection point as well.) We learned that we can find the maximum of a function by finding its derivative, equating this derivative to zero, and solving for the value of, usually, x. There may be more than one value of x for which

[1]This discussion assumes we are trying to maximize the objective function. You should be able to apply it to the reverse situation—that is, minimizing the objective function—easily.

$dy/dx = 0$. If this is the case, we can use complete enumeration to evaluate y at all of them and pick the one for which y is greatest.

This approach works with more than one unknown as well. Suppose we have a function y of w and x, written $y(w,x)$. Geometrically, this function describes a surface (such as the one in Figure 10–1) whose height above the x-w plane is the value of the function y. By treating w as a constant and differentiating y with respect to x, we obtain the *partial derivative* of y with respect to x. This partial derivative is written $\partial y/\partial x$, where ∂ is the Cyrillic (the alphabet used in Russian and several other eastern European languages) equivalent of the lowercase d used in differential calculus. Similarly, by holding x constant and differentiating y with respect to w, we obtain $\partial y/\partial w$. The slope of the line A is the partial derivative of the surface $y(w,x)$ with respect to x at the point P, and the slope of the line B is its partial derivative with respect to w at the same point. We can now set both partial derivatives equal to zero and get two equations in the two unknowns w and x. Solving these equations gives the values of w and x that correspond to the maximum value of the function y. As with functions of one variable, if the equations have several solutions, complete enumeration of y at each solution pair tells us which (w,x) pair truly gives the maximum. The same approach works with functions of more than two variables, although we can't visualize their geometric representation.

Behind this facile paragraph lies a world of complexities that make the calculus approach to optimization less useful than one might hope. Among its chief limiting factors are the following:

FIGURE 10–1

Surface Showing Partial Derivatives

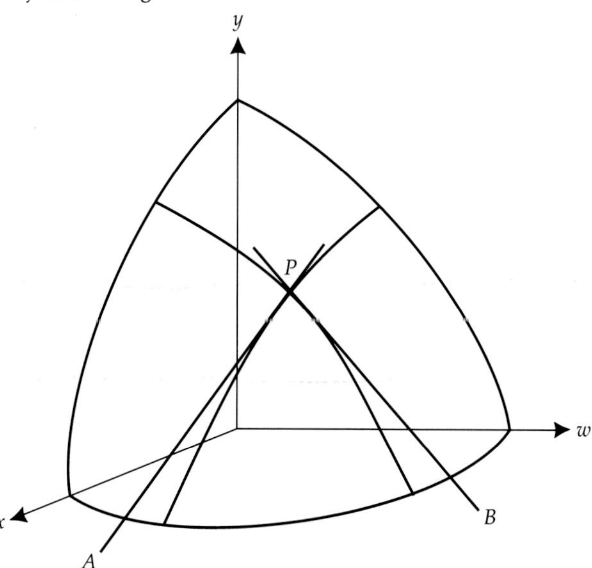

- The variable we are trying to optimize must be continuous. We can't move by infinitesimal steps from "buy a Grumman Gulfstream" to "buy a Learjet," or from "install one lathe" to "install two lathes."
- We must have a mathematical expression for the function we are trying to optimize. If its value can only be obtained numerically, perhaps by simulation or by a Markov process approach, we cannot differentiate it even if it is continuous.
- The functions we must optimize may be so complex that differentiating them, and solving the resulting equations for the values that make the partial derivatives equal zero, is beyond the ability of the people charged with the task or perhaps not even possible at all.
- The mathematical optimum may lie in a region of the surface that, because of constraints on the problem, it not a feasible solution. Basic calculus methods do not handle constraints well or at all. Linear programming, discussed in the next section, can solve some problems in which constraints are a factor.

Calculus remains a useful tool in economic problems that deal with market elasticities, fixed and variable costs, and desired price and production levels. The optimal order quantity problem, which you studied (or will study) in your operations analysis course, is an example of such an application area: Calculus is used to balance the cost of carrying inventory over time, given the cost of capital, against the cost of placing many small orders. Calculus can also sometimes be applied to a simplified version of a problem to gain insight and provide a general feel for the issues, even if other methods then have to be used to solve the problem in all its complex detail. The limitations of this method keep it from wider use.

10.3 Linear Programming

Linear programming is an optimization technique for problems that satisfy three conditions:

1. The objective function (what we're trying to maximize or minimize) is a linear function of system outputs. That is, it is of the form

$$y = a_1x_1 + a_2x_2 + a_3x_3 + \ldots$$

2. Each system output is a (non-negative) linear combination of system inputs.
3. Some or all quantities of system inputs are constrained to be above or below certain known values.

The typical application of linear programming is resource allocation. For example, suppose our cube factory can produce red cubes, orange cubes, or unpainted cubes. We know that

- Red and orange cubes are produced from unpainted cubes and paint.
- Producing a red cube requires an unpainted cube and one ounce of red paint. Producing an orange cube requires an unpainted cube, half an ounce of red paint, and half an ounce of yellow paint.
- The factory makes a profit of \$2 per orange cube, \$1.50 per red cube, and \$1 per unpainted cube. These figures reflect selling prices and all costs associated with painting orange and red cubes.
- We have on hand 100 unpainted cubes, 20 oz. of red paint, and 10 oz. of yellow paint.

One feasible solution would be to leave the paint on the shelf, selling 100 unpainted cubes for a profit of $100 \times \$1 = \$100$. Since we have the paint, however, we can do better if we use it. If we paint 20 cubes red, using up all our red paint, our profit is $80 \times \$1 + 20 \times \$1.50 = \$80 + \$30 = \$110$. The best solution, as found by linear programming, is to use all the yellow paint and half the red paint to produce 20 orange cubes, and then use the remaining 10 oz. of red paint to produce 10 red cubes. Our profit is then \$115.

In this example the optimal solution to the problem used all our resources. We had no unpainted cubes, red paint, or yellow paint left over when we were done. In general this will not be the case. Some resources are usually left over. Here, if we had more yellow paint than red paint, we would have no use for the excess yellow paint unless we could find a new market for yellow cubes. That sort of strategic planning, while within the province of corporate management, goes beyond what linear programming (or any other numerical optimization method) can do, although other types of DSS can often be used to support it.

We can visualize a linear programming (LP) problem in two variables on a graph such as Figure 10–2. It shows a plant that produces a mix of two products, A and B. Product A, which yields a profit of \$2 per unit produced, requires two units of input S and one unit of input T. Product B reverses the proportions, using one unit of S and two units of T, and yields a profit of \$3 per unit produced. We have 100 units of each input on hand.

In mathematical notation, our objective function is $2A + 3B$. It is related to the inputs by the equations $A = 2S + T$ and $B = S + 2T$ and is subject to the constraints $S \le 100$ and $T \le 100$.

The axes in Figure 10–2 represent the amounts of product A and product B we choose to produce. The lines forming the shaded four-sided polygon outline the *feasible region* for this problem. The axes bound the region from the left and below since we cannot produce a negative amount of A or B. The steeper of the two diagonal lines represents what we can produce with

FIGURE 10–2

Two-Resource LP Diagram

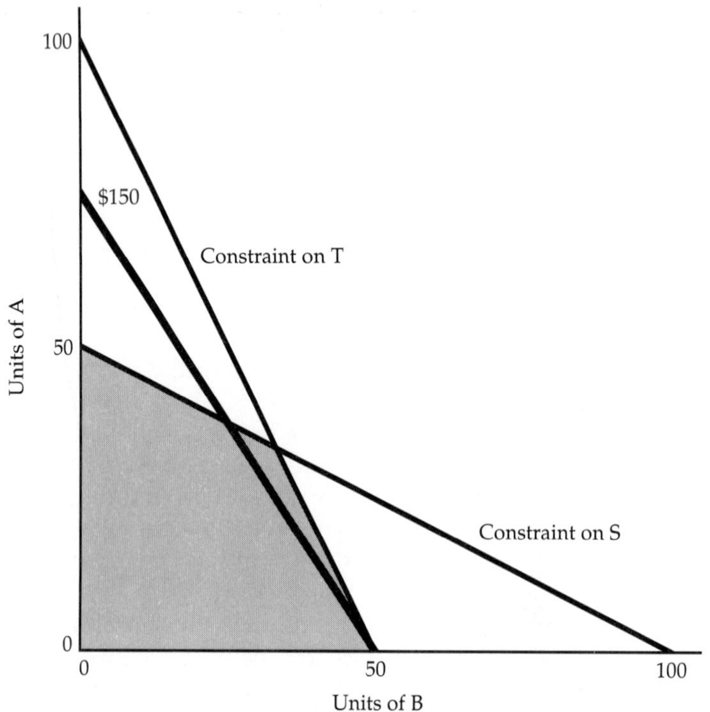

100 units of T: For each two units of A we produce, using one unit of T each, we can produce one less unit of B, as these require two units of T each. The other diagonal line represents the S constraint in a similar fashion.

The heavy line in Figure 10–2 represents one of the parallel lines of equal profit, specifically that for $150. One of its ends represents manufacturing 75 units of A only for a profit of $2 each (we can't do this because we don't have enough S on hand, but the point does serve to anchor one end of the line), and its other end represents manufacturing 50 units of B only at a profit of $3 each (which we could do). Any choice along a given line represents the same profit to the firm and is therefore equally desirable. The highest profit solution is on the line parallel to the $150 line, which goes through the point where the S and T constraint lines cross. There we produce 33 1/3 units each of A and B, use all our inputs, and earn a profit of $166.66 and 2/3 of a cent.

You may ask: how can we produce a third of a unit of a product? A continuous production process can produce fractional units of output. A paper mill can produce any length of paper we wish. Its output need not be an exact multiple of our unit of measure, which is after all arbitrary. (An integer quantity of feet is unlikely to be an integer quantity of meters or cubits.) Other production processes deal in discrete units: A motorcycle factory cannot ship half a motorcycle if it has one tire left over. In this case, the linear programming (LP) solution guides us to the vicinity of the optimal choice. We can then test the integer solutions adjacent to the LP solution by complete enumeration. In our example we might inspect the four options shown in Figure 10–3:

- 30 units of A and 35 of B, for a \$165 profit (and 5 units of S left over).
- 32 units of A and 34 of B, for a \$166 profit (and 2 units of S left over).
- 33 units each of A and B, for a \$165 profit (and 1 unit each of S and T left over).
- 34 units of A and 32 of B, for a \$164 profit (and 2 units of T left over).

Being rational managers, we choose the second option to maximize our profits. This assumes that leftover resources have no value. If they did, we could add this value into the objective function as a new type of output that has the specified value and uses one unit of the specified resource. This would complicate the equations somewhat but is quite compatible with linear programming concepts. In this example, if leftover units of S are worth at least 34¢, we would select the first option rather than the second.

FIGURE 10–3

Four Decision Options in LP Problem

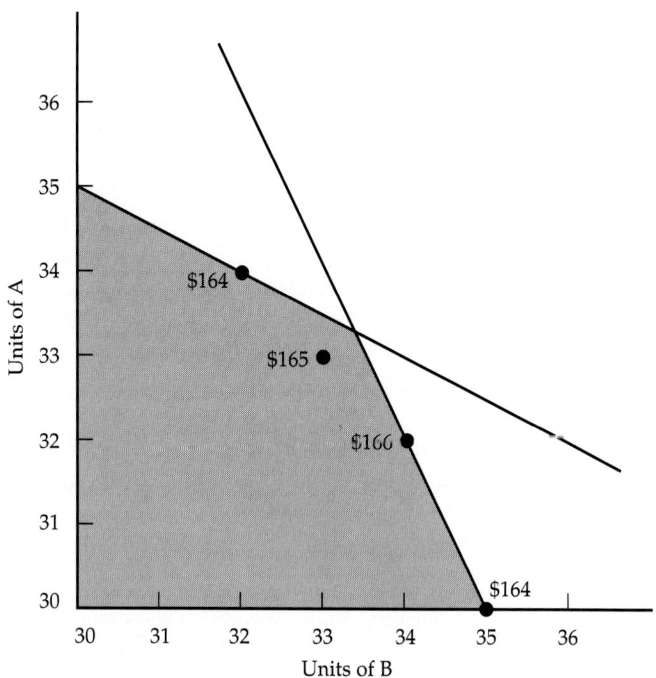

This example shows many of the characteristics of all LP problems, although we can't visualize them physically once they get beyond three outputs:

- There is a feasible region bounded by the constraints.
- The constraints are straight lines in two dimensions, planes in three dimensions, hyperplanes in four or more. They are never curved because, by definition, LP only deals with linear equations.
- The optimal solution is typically at a corner of the feasible region or at a nearby point that yields an integer solution if an integer solution is required. For some combinations of resource usages and profit figures an entire edge of the feasible region may be optimal. In the above example, if the profit of B were twice that of A, the equal-profit lines would have the same slope as the T constraint. Any point along that constraint line would then be an optimal solution.

You may hear people refer to a linear programming *model.* The model here is the mathematical model of the production system. This model has the above characteristics. To the degree that some characteristics of the real production system are not linear, or are not included in the model, the model simplifies reality. The major—some might say the only—use of a linear programming *model* is in the linear programming solution *process.*

The most common method for solving linear programming problems is called the *simplex* method.[2] It was introduced by George B. Dantzig shortly after World War II. The simplex method starts at any corner (or vertex) of the feasible region. It then determines whether profit increases or decreases as one moves from that vertex to any adjacent vertex. This process continues until the optimal solution has been found. The simplex method always converges to the solution if one exists, although it may take a great deal of time for large problems.

Despite its intuitive appeal and the sound of its name, programming the simplex method is far from simple. Determining where vertices lie, given a set of linear constraint equations, is far from a trivial task. Fortunately, many software packages—often referred to as linear programming *codes* in professional literature—have been written to solve linear programming problems. They can run on virtually any computer you are likely to encounter. A DSS developer must be aware of the linear programming concept and its areas of applicability but does not have to be able to program linear programming solution methods from scratch.

Several packages are available for solving LP programs on personal computers. Most packages used in teaching operations analysis courses, such as

---

[2]The name comes from the mathematical concept of a *simplex,* an n-dimensional structure with $n + 1$ data points. A one-dimensional simplex is a line segment. A two-dimensional simplex is a triangle. A three-dimensional simplex is a pyramid with a triangular base (a tetrahedron). The term does not imply that the method is "simple." It isn't.

QSB+, QSOM, and QuickQuant+, have at least a limited LP capability. In 1988 Stadtler and two coauthors compared five LP packages that run on MS-DOS systems, plus a reference package running on a large-scale IBM mainframe, [STAD88]. They found that the best of the desktop software could solve 26 of the 28 problems that they presented (successfully) to the mainframe. They characterized the five packages they evaluated as follows:

	Hyper Lindo	*Lantern*	*Micro LP*	*PCLP*	*Xpress LP*
*Size of Solvable Models**	Small	Small	Small	Medium	Medium
Computational Speed	1.05	1.37	3.20	1.13	2.03
Reliability	Acceptable	Acceptable	Acceptable	Good	Good
Interactivity	Very good	Sufficient	Insufficient	None	Good
Matrix Generation	None	None	None	None	Very good
Price	$1,000	£300 to £1,400	£1,300	DM7000	£500 to £1,500

*"Small" in this context was defined as having up to 400 rows; medium, as up to 1,500.

Stadtler and his coauthors found, as expected, that the PC-based packages took much longer than the mainframe to solve a given problem. Their specific timings reflected the hardware they used, which was far slower than what you will find on the job in the 1990s, and are not too important here. (Indeed, when they compared their base configuration with the fastest commercially available PCs of 1988, they got a performance improvement of nearly 8:1.) However, they also found that, as problems got larger, the relative performance of the PC got worse. Ashford and Daniels explore possible reasons in [ASHF88]. Their most likely reasons all reflect the fact that PC programs must fit into systems of limited size. They must consequently avoid some memory-intensive solution techniques that are widely used in LP programs for large computers. These techniques are of little use when solving small models but become more valuable in solving larger ones.

The message here is not that you should necessarily get the best of the packages in the above review—indeed, there was no single "best" package by all criteria—or any other specific package. It is that

- A large number of linear programming packages exist.
- All have pros and cons.
- Different strengths and weaknesses matter in different situations and to different people.

When you are faced with a problem on the job that LP seems to address, you will have to check out the software available to you at that time and to compare its capabilities with your needs.

The major drawback of linear programming as an optimization method follows directly from the three conditions listed at the start of this section. Many real-world optimization problems do not produce outputs that are linear functions of their inputs. Advertising exposures, for example, may be a linear function of advertising expenditures in various media—but the effect of multiple exposures on consumers is far from linear, and it's the effect on consumers that really matters. Some nonlinear programming methods do exist but are not as well developed as the linear ones. If the conditions given at the start of this section apply to your decision support problem, try LP. If not, look further.

10.4 Numerical Methods

This section is at the end of this chapter because the analyst is reduced to *numerical optimization methods* when all else fails—when there are too many alternatives for complete enumeration, when calculus won't work, and when the problem does not meet the conditions for linear programming. Numerical methods are especially valuable in providing guidance to a simulation study by determining the set of decision variables to be tried next. We mentioned this concept briefly when we discussed a complete study using the supermarket simulation in Section 9.1.5.

Some numerical methods are little more than guesswork that has been given the fancy title of *heuristics* or the more down-to-earth name "rules of thumb." Yet this need not be the case. There are well-founded approaches that yield an optimum solution to most practical problems, to any desired degree of accuracy, with reasonable expenditures of human and computer time.

A few common numerical methods are described in this section to give the DSS builder an awareness of what is possible and, in general terms, how it works. An analyst who wishes to try any of them in a real system can find full descriptions in applied math texts or the references at the end of this chapter. Applied mathematics graduate students and faculty members at local colleges and universities can also often provide expert advice and assistance, usually on short notice and at reasonable cost.

In addition, many spreadsheet packages either come with optimization capabilities or have third-party optimization packages available. Examples are What-If Solver for Lotus 1-2-3 and the optimization add-in for Excel. If your data are in a spreadsheet (or can be brought into a spreadsheet without too much effort) and your objective function can be expressed as a spreadsheet formula, these are worth a try.

10.4.1 *Hill Climbing*

Hill-climbing methods are an attempt to apply the concepts of calculus to situations in which derivatives are unavailable or useless. We first evaluate the objective function for an arbitrary choice of values for the controllable variables. (The choice is seldom totally arbitrary but is based on the knowledge and intuition of an analyst or decision maker.) We then also evaluate it for small changes of each decision variable in both directions from the initial choice. On the basis of these evaluations we construct a local approximation to the function surface mathematically: in effect calculating derivatives numerically because we can't get them by differentiating the objective function. For the simplest possible case, two points along an axis, the slope of the approximation to the derivative is given by the straight line (written here for points along the x- axis)

$$\frac{\Delta f(x)}{\Delta x} = \frac{f(x_1) - f(x_2)}{x_1 - x_2}$$

If we have more than two points along an axis, we can fit more complex (but still easily differentiable) curves to the surface. A parabola, which requires three points, is a popular choice.

Having approximated the derivative along the direction of all the decision variables, we choose a new set of decision variable values in the direction in which the surface seems to be increasing most rapidly and repeat the process. Figure 10–4 illustrates hill-climbing for an objective function of two variables. As the slope of the surface decreases, or as we pass the peak, we reduce the step size to avoid overshooting the peak too much. If we have approximated the derivatives via a parabola or higher order curve, we can determine its maximum analytically and use the distance to this maximum as the step size.

FIGURE 10–4
Illustration of Hill Climbing

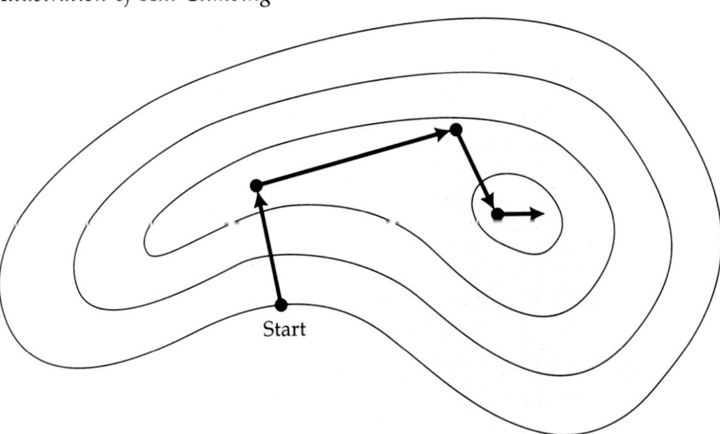

The peak is reached when a small change in the value of any decision variable reduces the value of the objective function.

Hill-climbing methods can be useful when the objective function is continuous, so we would use calculus if we could differentiate it, but nonlinear, so we can't use linear programming. Consider, for example, a standard linear programming problem with a slight twist: using linear combinations of resources to produce several possible products. However, profits per unit are not a constant. Instead, unit costs go down as we produce more of each product. That violates linear programming condition 1. Yet as long as we know what the unit costs are for all possible production volumes of each product, it's easy to evaluate the profits for a given combination of outputs. To use hill climbing, we would start by picking one feasible solution. We then vary it a bit in each possible direction: more of product 1, more of product 2, etc. Eventually we arrive at the correct allocation of resources to products for maximum profit.

The biggest problem with hill-climbing methods is their tendency to zero in on local maxima and not find the global maximum, as illustrated in Figure 10–5. (This would not happen in the resource allocation example of the previous paragraph unless some of the cost-volume relationships were "bumpy.") We can often foil this tendency by repeating the hill-climbing process several times with different initial values for the decision variables. These initial values can be chosen at random or deliberately chosen by the decision maker to span the entire range of possible solutions. Starting at different points, and hence climbing different slopes, should find different local maxima if several exist.

FIGURE 10–5

Surface with Local Maxima

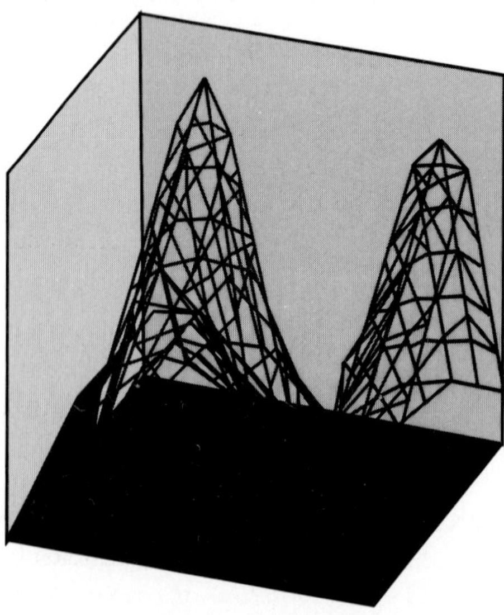

After finding each identified local maximum several times, there is good assurance (though never certainty) that all local maxima have been found. The highest of these is taken as the global maximum.

Another occasional difficulty with these methods is their tendency to overshoot the maximum repeatedly and thus oscillate around it without ever converging to it. Proper step-size management and testing for oscillation within the optimization program can handle this problem.

10.4.2 Box's Method

One of several methods that avoids the need to create even a local approximation to a function surface, and which is therefore suitable for objective functions that are found via simulation or similar methods, is due to M. J. Box [BOX65; see RICH73 and SHER74 regarding computer programming of the method]. While it is old in terms of the computer age, it is easy to visualize and still usually works well. It works as follows:

1. Evaluate the function for at least $n + 1$ randomly chosen sets of decision variable values where there are n decision variables. (A set of decision variable values corresponds to a point in a multidimensional space, each dimension of which corresponds to one of the decision variables.) If more than $n + 1$ points are used, the structure is called a *complex*, by analogy to the simplex structure used in linear programming. Box's method is therefore also known as the *complex method.*
2. Find the centroid of these points. This is done by finding the arithmetic mean of each dimension (decision variable) independently.
3. Reflect the point corresponding to the lowest function value across the centroid to its other side. (The choice of the lowest function value for this reflection assumes we are trying to maximize the objective function. Were we minimizing the objective function, we would reflect the point corresponding to the highest value.) See Figure 10–6 for the process thus far. The figure shows two decision variables and four data points.
4. Evaluate the function at this new point. If the new point is not the lowest valued point, repeat steps 2 and 3.
5. If the reflected point is still the lowest valued, it was probably reflected across a maximum and down the function curve on its other side. Move the point halfway back to the centroid. This has the effect of making the pattern smaller as the maximum is approached. Calculate the new centroid and repeat the process from step 2, continuing until convergence has been achieved, that is, until all the points in the complex are sufficiently close each other so that the value of the objective function value does not change, within the tolerance limits of the decision, from one to another.

This basic approach must be modified to work in practice. The reflection process may try to take one or more decision variables outside their allowable range, especially if (as often happens) the objective function reaches its

FIGURE 10–6

Initial Steps of Box's Method

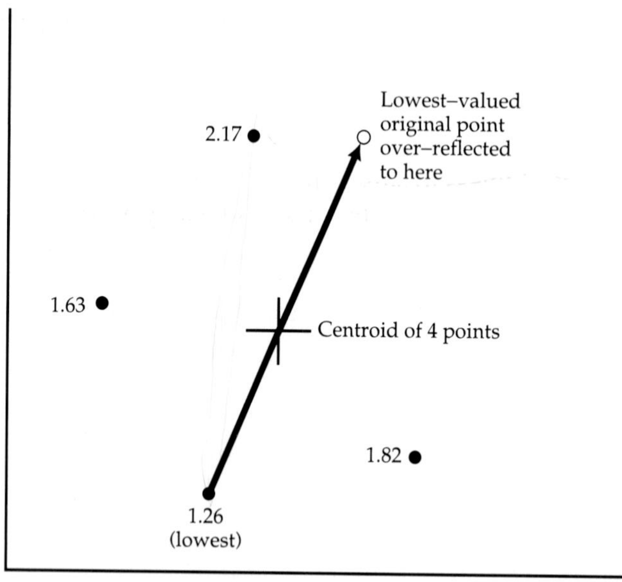

maximum at one or more of the constraints. If this occurs, these decision variables must be set to a suitable value just inside the boundary. (If they are set to values on the boundary, the set of points may in time flatten itself against the boundary and be unable to leave it.) This "under-reflection" has the effect of shrinking the pattern even though a maximum is not being approached. To counteract this effect, unconstrained reflections must "over-reflect." Instead of choosing the new point precisely opposite the old one from the centroid, it is chosen across from the old point but 1.2 or 1.3 times as far from the centroid.

Box's method is better than hill climbing at avoiding local maxima since it tends to find the global maximum if any of the widely dispersed initial points or any of the early, wide-ranging reflections is near it. However, it, too, can be fooled, It's a good idea here too to try several runs with different initial sets of points. A few trials will usually confirm the first maximum that was found. It can then be taken as the global maximum.

Summary

Optimization, choosing one of several numerically comparable alternatives to maximize (or minimize) the objective function, is an important part of many decision support systems. Approaches to optimization include complete enumeration, random search, calculus, linear programming, hill climbing, and the category of numerical methods.

Complete enumeration means trying all possible choices and picking the one that produces the best predicted results. Random search is related. The difference is that, in random search, we do not try all possible choices but rather a randomly selected subset of them.

Calculus can optimize continuous functions of the decision variables. This limits its usefulness to situations in which the objective function meets these requirements and we can solve the often-complex equations that are involved.

Linear programming can optimize systems in which the objective function depends linearly on how resources are allocated to alternative uses and where this allocation is subject to constraints, such as the available quantity of one or more resources. Linear programming problems are generally solved by computer. Many linear programming packages are available. Most of them use the simplex method to solve LP problems by following the edges of the feasible region.

A wide variety of numerical optimization methods exists. The analyst may be forced to use one of them when the methods given earlier do not apply or do not work. Some of these are supported in popular spreadsheet packages.

One numerical method is hill climbing. This is the numerical equivalent of calculus. It uses numerical approximations to the derivatives and moves around the solution space, "climbing the hill" of the objective function, until the approximations to the derivatives are zero within an acceptable tolerance. The process must be repeated with different starting points to make sure the overall, or global, maximum is found.

A second numerical method is that of M. J. Box. It starts out as does random search, by choosing several random values of the decision variables and evaluating the objective function at them. Rather than simply choosing more random points, however, this method uses those values as a group to pick a new point to try. The method tends to range widely over the solution space and then zero in on a maximum. As with hill climbing, it is necessary to repeat this process more than once to avoid settling on a local maximum.

Key Terms

Box's method 335
calculus 324
centroid 335
complete enumeration 322
complex method 335
constraint 326
derivative 324
feasible region 327
global maximum 334
heuristics 332
hill climbing 333
linear programming 326
local maximum 334
numerical optimization methods 332
objective function 321
optimization 321
partial derivative 325
random search 323
simplex method 330

Review Questions

1. What is optimization?
2. Why is optimization used in decision support systems?
3. What types of optimization problems can complete enumeration deal with? Give an example other than the ones mentioned in the text.
4. How does random search differ from complete enumeration?
5. What types of optimization problems can calculus deal with?
6. Give the conditions that a problem must satisfy if linear programming is to apply.
7. What is the most common method for solving linear programming problems called? Briefly, how does it work?
8. When would you use a numerical optimization method?
9. Which non-numerical method does hill climbing approximate?
10. What is one problem that arises when using the hill-climbing method? How could you deal with it?
11. Illustrate Box's method using three points on the upper half of a basketball (or a similarly shaped surface).

Exercises

1. Justify the statement at the end of Section 10.1 that decision trees support the complete enumeration approach.
2. You must optimize a function that meets the mathematical conditions for using calculus, but the equations are far too complex for you do deal with. You know, because of the nature of the problem, that the optimum is not in the neighborhood of any constraints on the decision variables. Compare and contrast (*a*) hiring a calculus expert, (*b*) random search, (*c*) hill climbing, and (*d*) Box's method to carry out this optimization. Is the Kepner-Tregoe method (Section 2.6) suitable for choosing one of the four? Why or why not?
3. Your factor produces wind-up toy trucks, wind-up toy cars, and nonmotorized toy cars. Each wind-up toy uses a motor, which is identical for cars and trucks. Each toy truck uses a truck body. Each toy car uses a body, which is identical for wind-up and nonmotorized cars. Either type of car can be decorated with "Super Slammer" trim to increase its selling price. The trim, like the body, is identical for wind-up and nonmotorized cars. You wish to allocate resources to the five types of toys to maximize your profit.

a. Assume you have a finite number of parts (truck bodies, car bodies, motors, Super Slammer trim kits) on hand and that the profit you make on each unit is independent of production volume. Does this problem meet the criteria for linear programming? Why or why not?

b. Now assume the price you receive for each unit is independent of production volume but that production costs are subject to a "learning curve." That is, as production volume goes up, production cost per unit drops. Does this problem now meet the criteria for linear programming? Why or why not?

c. What optimization method would you choose to solve this problem? Would your answer differ if this were a one-time problem or a recurring problem that had to be solved, with different numbers, each week? Discuss.

4. Would you, as a rule, write your own computer program to solve a linear programming problem? Why or why not? Relate your answer to the discussion of packages versus custom programs at the beginning of Chapter 6.

5. You are considering what holiday presents to give your loved one. You have put together a tentative list: a partridge in a pear tree for the first night of the holiday, two turtle doves for the second night, three French hens for the third, four calling birds for the fourth, five gold rings for the fifth, etc. Each gift has a cost (which generally goes up through the sequence) and an impact on your loved one's feelings toward you (which goes up initially, then tends to level off, and eventually decreases as he or she wonders what to do with large numbers of geese a-swimming, maids a-milking, lords a-leaping, etc., after the novelty wears off). You wish to decide how far through the sequence to proceed for optimum effect. Which optimization methods would you use? Why?

References

ASHF88 Ashford, R. W., and R. C. Daniel. "A Note on Evaluating LP Software for Personal Computers." *European Journal of Operational Research* 35, no. 2 (May 1988, part 2), pp. 160–64.

BOX65 Box, M. J. "A New Method of Constrained Optimization and a Comparison with Other Methods." *Computer Journal* 8, no. 1 (April 1965), pp. 42–52.

CALV89 Calvert, James E., and William L. Voxman. *Linear Programming.* Harcourt Brace Jovanovich, Orlando, Fla. (1989).

ERMO88 Ermoliev, Y., and R. Wets, eds. *Numerical Techniques for Stochastic Optimization.* Springer-Verlag, Berlin and New York (1988).

GASS90 Gass, Saul I. *An Illustrated Guide to Linear Programming.* Dover, New York (1990).

MALL75 Mallach, Efrem, G., and Paul D. Berger. "Decision Trees with Continuous Distributions." *Operations Research Quarterly* 26, no. 2, part i (1975), pp. 297–304.

RICH73 Richardson, Joel A., and J. L. Kuester. "The Complex Method for Constrained Optimization" (Algorithm 454). *Communications of the ACM* 16, no. 8 (August 1973), pp. 487–89.

SHEN89 Shenoy, G. V. *Linear Programming Methods and Applications.* John Wiley & Sons, New York (1989).

SHER74 Shere, Kenneth D. "Remark on Algorithm 454." *Communications of the ACM* 17, no. 8 (August 1974), p. 471.

STAD88 Stadtler, Harmut; Maren Groeneveld; and Heidrun Hermannsen. "A Comparison of LP Software on Personal Computers for Industrial Applications." *European Journal of Operational Research* 35, no. 2 (May 1988, part 2), pp. 146–59.

ENVOYANCE
CLEANING THE GROUNDWATER (II)

This continues the episode at the end of Chapter 7. Doug and Adrienne were with Jim, discussing the decisions involved in making groundwater drinkable again after a major gasoline spill in the vicinity of a town well. Jim has finished describing the technical factors involved in choosing a packed aereator tower design and has moved on the the financial considerations.

"The first cost factor," answered Jim, "is the capital cost of the tower itself. You can be talking about anywhere from $25,000 for a tower with a 10-square-foot area and 13 feet of packing up to several million for a tower with a 1,000-square-foot area and, say, 60 feet of packing. On the average, you're going to be somewhere in the low six figures. We have graphs and equations to estimate the cost once we have a handle on the area and the packing depth.

"Those graphs and equations just give us a ballpark figure, of course. Any number of factors can swing the final cost one way or the other. Some of them are predictable in advance, like if we need air pollution control to handle the gasoline vapors that come out of the tower with the air bubbles. Others are just the normal spread you get between any construction cost estimate and what the contractors eventually bid.

"Besides the tower, you also need wells, pumps, air blowers, and a building for all the electronic controls and monitoring instrumentation. Each of them has to be sized for the operation. We have graphs and equations for them too. Pump and blower cost estimates tend to be pretty accurate because those items are more cut and dried. You don't get the custom construction variations.

"Then, you've got your operating costs. The electricity to run the pump depends on how much water you're treating. The electricity to run the blower depends on your air-to-water ratio, which is one of the tower design parameters. You could, for instance, go with a smaller tower but push more air through it with a bigger blower. Then you save on tower construction cost, but you pay more for the blower, and you get a higher operating cost. We have to do a net present value calculation to trade off the initial costs against the operating costs.

"We have to factor labor costs in too. These usually come to about 2¢ for every gallon of water we treat. The bigger the tower, though, the smaller these become on a per-gallon basis.

"Finally, yet another option is to design the tower to do part of the job of removing the contaminants, and follow it up with activated charcoal treatment to get the rest of the contaminants out. I don't even want to think about that. Designing a packed tower aerator may be time consuming, but at least we know how to do it. Designing an activated charcoal system is still an art form."

"I can see why you're telling us about this! What happens next? How can we help?" asked Doug.

"The next step, assuming you folks are willing or Sandra would pay for some programming time, is to see how a computer could handle the tower design process. It seems to me that it shouldn't be too hard to program. I don't want to have to wait six hours for an answer, though. If it comes to that I'd oil my old slide rule!"

"I think a computer might be able to help," Adrienne offered. "We'd have to think about it a bit, though. Shall we break for a cup of coffee?"

Exercises

1. Consider just the technical side of designing an acceptable packed aerator tower, that is, the part of the overall job that was discussed in Chapter 7. Can it be solved by optimization methods? Why or why not? If it can, which of the above methods would you choose, and why?
2. Now consider the overall task of designing the most cost-effective packed aerator tower. Can this task be solved by optimization methods? Why or why not? If it can, which of the above methods would you choose, and why?
3. Finally, consider the broader task of designing a system that combined a packed aerator tower with a final "polishing" stage using granulated activated charcoal. Could optimization methods help solve this problem? Why or why not? If they can, which of the above methods would you choose, and why?

CHAPTER

11 Group Decision Support Systems

Chapter Outline

Introduction

In Chapter 4 we saw that group decisions differ from other types in the need to communicate during or about the decision-making process. Some types of DSS, such as those that access data or model the expected outcome of decisions, can help with any decision type regardless of this factor. The unique and differing communication factors in group decisions have, however, led to the development of DSS that accommodate these communication factors and that are designed specifically to support decisions made at the group level. Such DSS are called *group DSS* (GDSS). They are becoming increasingly important in business. Since you'll probably run into one (or several) group DSS on the job, it's important for you to learn about them now.

Chapter Objectives

After you have read and studied this chapter, you will be able to:

1. Define group decision support systems.
2. Explain why group DSS have become important.
3. Discuss the types of activities groups carry out and how they differ from individual activities.
4. Identify the types of group DSS that exist.
5. Describe groupware and how it relates to group decision support systems.
6. Discuss how electronic meeting systems can be used to support group decisions.
7. Discuss how work flow systems fit into the group DSS picture.
8. Describe some features of popular group DSS products.

11.1 What Are Group DSS?

A group decision support system, or GDSS, is a decision support system whose design, structure, and usage reflect the way in which people cooperate to make a particular decision or type of decision.

This definition goes beyond simply stating that the DSS is used by more than one person or even that it is used by a group in a group decision. Suppose a group of factory managers—the stockroom supervisor, the milling room supervisor, the assembly supervisor, the paint room supervisor, the shipping supervisor—got together to choose a factory floor layout. They could look at DSS printouts that analyze bottlenecks and production levels for different floor layouts and choose the best. This would be a group decision and would use a DSS. However, the DSS would not be a group DSS because there is nothing about it that reflects the group nature of the decision-making process. An individual decision maker could, if the decision-making situation called for it, use the very same DSS equally well.

A group DSS for this situation might use terminals on each of the five supervisors' desks. The stockroom supervisor would be asked for input relative to stockroom size, layout, and other requirements. The other four would similarly provide those inputs that relate to their specific functions. The DSS could be programmed to accept only the appropriate inputs from each supervisor. It would then merge its inputs, analyze overall factory productivity, and print the results. This conceptual system would be a group DSS in the full sense of the term. The decision-making task hasn't changed. The decision-making process, and with it the appropriate computer support, has.

The group DSS in this example is, as you will soon see, far from the only possible type of GDSS. However, the basic concept—that the DSS is designed and developed with explicit awareness of the overall group decision-making process—applies to them all.

11.2 Why Group DSS Now?

Two sets of factors have led to the recent explosion in group DSS: organizational factors and technical factors. Each might suffice to lead to increased use of GDSS by itself. Together they make it inevitable.

11.2.1 Organizational Reasons for Group DSS Growth

The key organizational factors that support the growth of GDSS are changes in the way management decisions are made and changes in organizational culture. George Huber discusses many of these factors further in [HUBE84].

Management decisions in the late 20th century require the participation of many more people than they did earlier. This results from several factors:

- The decision-making environment has become more complex as organizations have grown in complexity, as the international ramifications of decisions have become more important, and as government regulations have become increasingly pervasive and complex.
- The increased complexity of many aspects of decisions, such as the implications of new technologies or government regulations, has forced decision makers to rely on highly trained specialists where once their own knowledge or that of close associates would have sufficed.
- The growth of rapid or instant communications media, such as overnight delivery services, electronic mail, and facsimile transmission, has increased the time pressure on many decisions. This, in turn, forces decision makers to call in people who already know about a subject and to rely on their advice rather than take the time to learn about the subject themselves. However, it is often difficult or impossible to bring all these people together physically in the necessary time frame.

Changes in organizational culture have led to increased use of participatory management methods. While top managers could once rule by decree, today many feel a need to rule by consent of the governed. This factor has several aspects as well:

- A long period of relative prosperity in developed countries, compared with what existed during and after the Industrial Revolution and what exists in many parts of the world today, has changed the attitude of "obedience at any cost" to preserve a job. In terms of Maslow's now-classical hierarchy of needs [MASL43], workers' physical survival needs are largely taken care of in today's industrialized nations. This leaves the workers free to concentrate on fulfilling their social and self-actualization needs. Those whose needs are not met in these respects are apt to leave the organization where they work in search of a more congenial environment.
- A more educated work force feels more entitled to some control over its own destiny.
- Research into organizational behavior has demonstrated that participative management techniques increase morale and the acceptance of decisions.
- Research has likewise demonstrated that traditional group meetings are not always as productive as one would like. Group pressures lead to "groupthink" conformity. Some individuals dominate others due

Groupthink

A common problem in group decision making is *groupthink:* the tendency of group members to fall into similar thought patterns and to disapprove, implicitly or explicitly, of opinions that do not conform to these patterns. For example, the marketing staff of a computer manufacturer may have fallen into the general belief that system pricing should be based primarily on CPU power. They may apply this belief even where it is inappropriate, such as in a turnkey system where software functionality determines value to the user. A new hire who dares to suggest an alternative basis for pricing will be ignored and, if he or she persists in expressing this heretical view, will be told "that's not the way we do things around here." This has been the downfall of more than one firm. In an even more far-reaching example from recent history, members of President Lyndon Johnson's circle of advisors fell into "groupthink" patterns as regarded the ability of the United States to achieve a decisive military victory in Vietnam. Evidence to the contrary was ignored, and statements of opposing views were taken as indicating disloyalty. The cost of these thought patterns became tragically obvious within a few years.

A popular experiment shows the power of groupthink. In this experiment, five subjects are shown two lines on a wall. The lines are similar in length but, to most objective observers, discernably not identical. The subjects are asked to state in turn whether the lines are of the same length or not.

The first four people, who are really "plants," say "they are the same length" per the experimenter's instructions. The fifth, the only true subject of the experiment, then has a dilemma. On the one hand, the lines appear to be of different lengths. On the other, four people have just said they're not. The overwhelming majority of real subjects will follow the crowd.

This experiment can be extended in many ways. In one extension, after the first pass, one of the plants leaves the room and a second real subject enters. The three remaining plants state, again as instructed, that the lines are of the same length. The first real subject must now

to personality and/or status. Misunderstood, forgotten, or ignored communications are common. Even those comments that are understood and remembered are often not well integrated with each other.

- Examination of Japanese management methods, which deserve much of the credit for that country's economic success, teaches a similar lesson about management by consensus. Consensus decisions per the Japanese model may take longer to reach than decisions that are dictated from the top, but their broad-based support more than compensates for this in shorter implementation times.
- High travel costs, coupled with advances in alternative technologies such as video teleconferencing, are leading to less use of traditional face-to-face meetings. This makes it harder for decision makers to get

concluded

speak again. He or she is already on record as stating that the lines are the same length and is unlikely to change this position. The second real subject is now in the same position as the first one was in on the previous pass and is just as likely to conform to the prevailing opinion. It is possible to go through several complete changes of group members in this fashion, with the 30th and 31st subjects blithely saying that the lines are the same length even though the four original plants have long since departed.

Perceived status differences have an impact on susceptibility to groupthink. When the first four group members are fraternity members, the likelihood of disagreement by a fraternity pledge goes from a small percentage to virtually zero. If the four plants are known to be freshmen, the typical senior or graduate student subject will think, in effect, "what do those kids know?" and defy the established group norm by stating that the lines are of different lengths.

Group decision support systems can help overcome groupthink where it is an obstacle to reaching good decisions. They do this by making it less threatening for group members to violate group norms by stating new opinions or by agreeing with them. In some cases they do this by providing anonymity to opinions. Even where they do identify the person associated with an opinion, both research and experience have shown that people are more willing to state their views candidly when typing at a computer terminal than across a conference room table. Group DSS can also help by enabling junior members of a group to state their opinions before they know what senior members think, which is difficult in a face-to-face meeting.[1]

a "total picture" of group decision-making situations. Group DSS can help provide this picture.

11.2.2 *Technical Reasons for Group DSS Growth*

Technical factors supporting the growth of group DSS include

- Wide-area telecommunications links, a necessity for many group DSS, are becoming less expensive. Many organizations now link all their locations through leased lines and permanent high-speed data networks.
- Fast (56,000 bps and up) telecommunications links, needed for rapid transfer of graphics or video, are becoming more widely available as the result of new communications technologies.
- More organizations have gateways and local networks to bring these high-speed links to decision makers' desktops. In many firms every professional can communicate electronically with every other one.

[1]This problem is hardly a recent discovery. Over 2,000 years ago, justices of the Sanhedrin, the highest court of the post-Biblical Jewish kingdom in Palestine, gave their opinions in reverse order of seniority so junior members of the court would not be influenced by their senior colleagues.

- Networking standards, some of them related to the subject of open systems that we took up in Section 7.6, make it easier for computers of various types to share data with each other.
- Software firms, motivated in part by increased availability of the supporting infrastructure, are increasingly offering tools and packages to support group DSS.

11.2.3 Putting the Factors Together

The growth and acceptance of any technology depends on its perceived value exceeding its cost. The list of management factors in Section 11.2.1 showed why the value of group DSS is increasing. The list of technical factors in Section 11.2.2 showed why the cost of providing group DSS is dropping. As firms find it increasingly affordable to satisfy an increasingly important need, they are adopting group DSS rapidly. This is shown in Figure 11–1.

FIGURE 11–1

Crossing Lines of GDSS Cost and Value

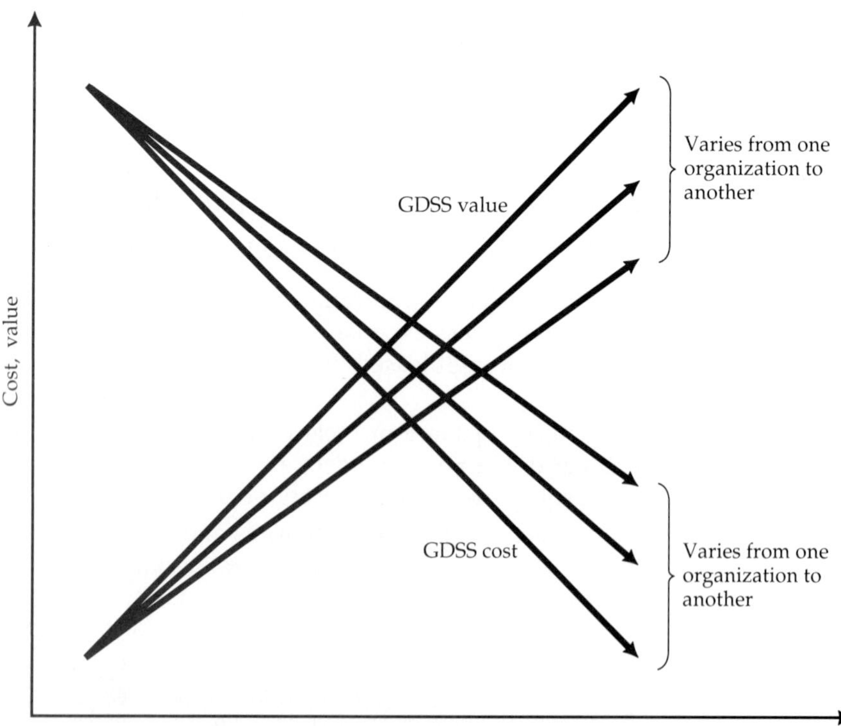

11.3 Group versus Individual Activities

The term "group activities" refers to anything we do in groups that we could not do equally well as individuals. Reading today's newspaper in a library is not a group activity even if there are other people in the room at the time, some of whom are reading another copy (or another section) of the same paper. There is no interaction among the people in the room. One can read a newspaper equally well by oneself.

We can categorize group activities as shown in Figure 11–2. McGrath calls

Figure 11–2

Group Task Circumplex

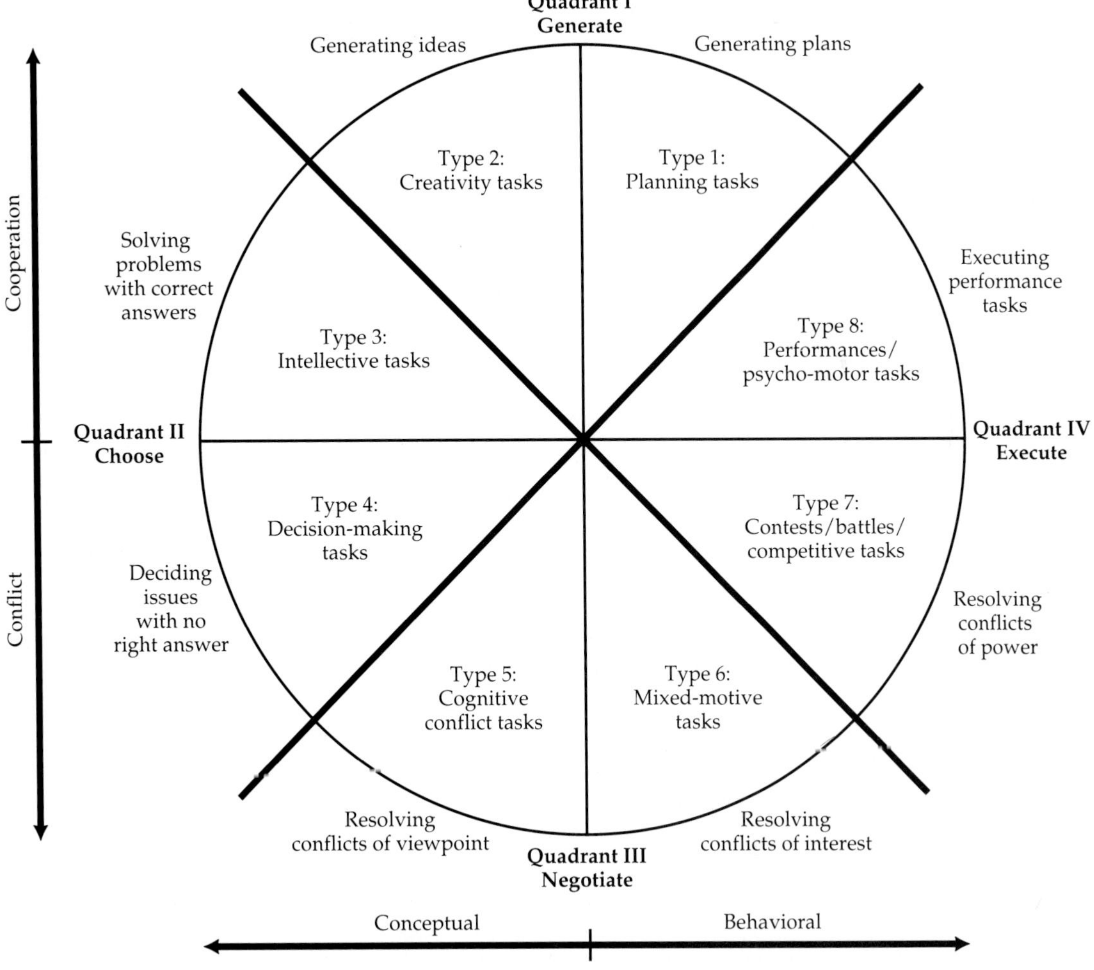

Source: Screen shot © 1992. Lotus Development Corporation. Lotus Notes is a registered trademark of Lotus Development Corporation.

this diagram a "circumplex" [MCGR84]. Information systems generally deal with ideas, not with actions, so they apply primarily to tasks on the left side of the diagram. They can support the activities on the right, but can't generally perform them. The only way one could use a computer to actually fight a battle would be to throw it at or drop it on the enemy. Some people might find this both an improvement over more destructive methods of warfare and an ideal use of computers, but it's not what computers are generally built to do.

Group decision making occupies one segment of the circumplex: the one labeled "type 4 decision-making tasks," defined as deciding issues that have no "right" answer. This task involves choice in the conceptual/conflict quadrant of the circumplex. Support for decision making, however, involves more than reaching the final decision: The task as McGrath defined it corresponds only to the choice stage of decision making, while we are taking a broader view of the process. Decision support tools can help with any of the tasks on the left side of the diagram. These four tasks provide a useful checklist in planning a group DSS: Try to find a task of each type, type 2 through type 5 as they are numbered in the circumplex, that is part of the decision-making process and with which DSS could help. That will help you identify ways in which information systems can contribute to the entire decision-making process.

11.4 Types of Group DSS

Just as groups carry out a wide variety of tasks, the term "group DSS" encompasses a wide variety of systems. Some people extend it to include some noncomputer technologies such as audio teleconferencing.[2] While these technologies are undoubtedly useful when groups of people must solve a problem or reach a decision jointly, we limit our definition of GDSS to systems that use the ability of a computer to store and process business-related data. We may from time to time include such systems as video teleconferencing, which could not exist without computer technology, but we will recognize that they are at best borderline information processing systems.

Even with this restriction, many types of group DSS are in use. We can organize them in terms of how they deal with the *content* and the *information flow* of decisions. Figure 11–3 shows the two-dimensional spectrum that results from these two classifications. The content axis here is based on the DSS

---

[2]We consider systems to be "noncomputerized" even if their designers have opted to embed microprocessors in them as cost-effective replacements for other types of electronic circuits. Today's typical under-$75 telephone answering machine, for example, uses a microprocessor, but it doesn't do anything its "noncomputerized," though still electronic, predecessors couldn't do.

FIGURE 11–3

Two-Dimensional GDSS Spectrum

Suggestion systems				
Optimization systems				
Representational models				
Accounting models				
Analysis information systems				
Data analysis systems				
File drawer systems				
No task content				
	Connection management	Communication management	Content management	Process management

hierarchy, which we discussed in Section 4.1. We have added a "content-free" zero'th level to this hierarchy. This level is meaningful because GDSS with no decision-making content can be of use if they perform a useful function along the second, information flow, dimension.

The information flow axis shows the degree to which the GDSS is aware of how the group works and supports that style of work directly.

Level 1 along this axis consists of *connection management* systems. Dealing with information flow at this lowest level consists of providing a physical mechanism through which people involved in a decision can communicate. A network operating system such as NetWare or Vines provides this at a local level. So do network architectures such as SNA, OSI, and TCP/IP over wider areas. A system that does no more than this is not a true GDSS, but this level anchors the spectrum at one end and underlies the more sophisticated capabilities of the higher levels.

Level 2 provides for *communication management.* This enhances the information flow by means of facilities to store messages, reply to them, forward them with comments, etc. The most common example of communication management software is an electronic mail package.

Level 3, *content management,* provides "intelligent routing": the system knows were a document goes after its current user finishes with it or where a message should go once it is entered. It is not necessary for the user to specify "send this to Chris" or "this is my vote on the current question." The system has this information and can act on it. Decision conference systems, which you'll read about later in this chapter, are examples of content management systems. A GDSS at this level does not take an active part in deciding how the decision-making process should proceed; its actions are standardized.

Level 4, *process management,* takes an active part in the decision-making process, often by considering the content of the information in the flow in deciding what to do with it. A level 4 system might "know," for example, that salary increases over a certain amount must be approved by a division vice president but that those below this amount need only go as far up as the employee's department manager. In an electronic meeting, a level 4 system could decide who should have the virtual "floor," perhaps based on prior communication patterns, or advise participants on the best conflict resolution strategy to apply in a particular situation.

Other authors provide different views of this taxonomy. These views are important because they define other way to combine GDSS that have common characteristics. These common characteristics can be useful guidelines for choosing a GDSS approach or product. In addition, you may encounter these other taxonomies in your reading.

One such taxonomy is from DeSanctis and Gallupe [DESA87]. They define GDSS level 1, level 2, and level 3. To avoid confusion between their numbered levels and ours, we will use the term "D&G level" from here on to refer to their levels. D&G level 1 GDSS "provide technical features aimed at removing common communication barriers." D&G level 2 provides "decision modeling and group decision techniques aimed at reducing uncertainty and 'noise' that occur in the group's decision process." D&G level 3 GDSS "are characterized by machine-induced group communication patterns" and control "the pattern, timing, or content of information exchange." The D&G hierarchy maps neatly into ours:

- It ignores our lowest two levels: quite reasonably since its purpose was to guide future research, and research on these two levels is no longer of interest. We have included them in our hierarchy because, while they may not be of interest to researchers, they are important in practice.
- D&G levels 1 and 2 together correspond to our level 3. The division is based essentially on the division between data-oriented and model-oriented DSS. Since we've included Alter's categories as one axis of

our GDSS categorization, we don't need separate levels along the information flow axis to make the same distinction.

- Their highest level, D&G level 3, corresponds to our level 4.

Figure 11–4 shows how these categories overlap the ones we presented earlier.

The decision content axis is of less interest than the communication axis in a GDSS context, both because it is not unique to group DSS and because it has already been studied extensively. "Although support of the cognitive processes of individual group members may be included in a GDSS, the primary aim of the group component of the system must be to alter the structure of interpersonal exchange. It follows that GDSS research must be deeply concerned with . . . the nature of communication in the group" [DESA87].

Another set of concepts that maps into our two-dimensional grid comes from Jay Nunamaker and his colleagues [NUNA91]. They call the vertical axis

FIGURE 11–4

Two-Dimensional GDSS Spectrum with D&G Overlay

	Connection management	Communication management	Content management	Process management
Suggestion systems			DeSanctis and Gallupe Level 2 Group DSS	DeSanctis and Gallupe Level 3 Group DSS
Optimization systems				
Representational models				
Accounting models				
Analysis information systems			DeSanctis and Gallupe Level 1 Group DSS	
Data analysis systems				
File drawer systems				
No task content				

of our grid the *task* axis and the horizontal axis the *process* axis. Each axis is divided into *support* and *structure.* Task support corresponds to data-oriented DSS. Task structure, shown above task support, refers to the use of models in DSS. This term fits since, as we noted in Section 4.3, a decision must have some structure if we are to develop a model for it. Similarly, process support refers to the communication infrastructure among participants in a group decision, while process structure means any techniques or rules that direct the pattern, timing or content of this communication. Figure 11–5 shows how this two-by-two grid map provides a higher level, less detailed view of our categories.

It is, of course, possible to characterize group decision making and group DSS in several other ways: for example, by the size of the decision-making

FIGURE 11–5

Two-Dimensional GDSS Spectrum with Nunamaker Overlay

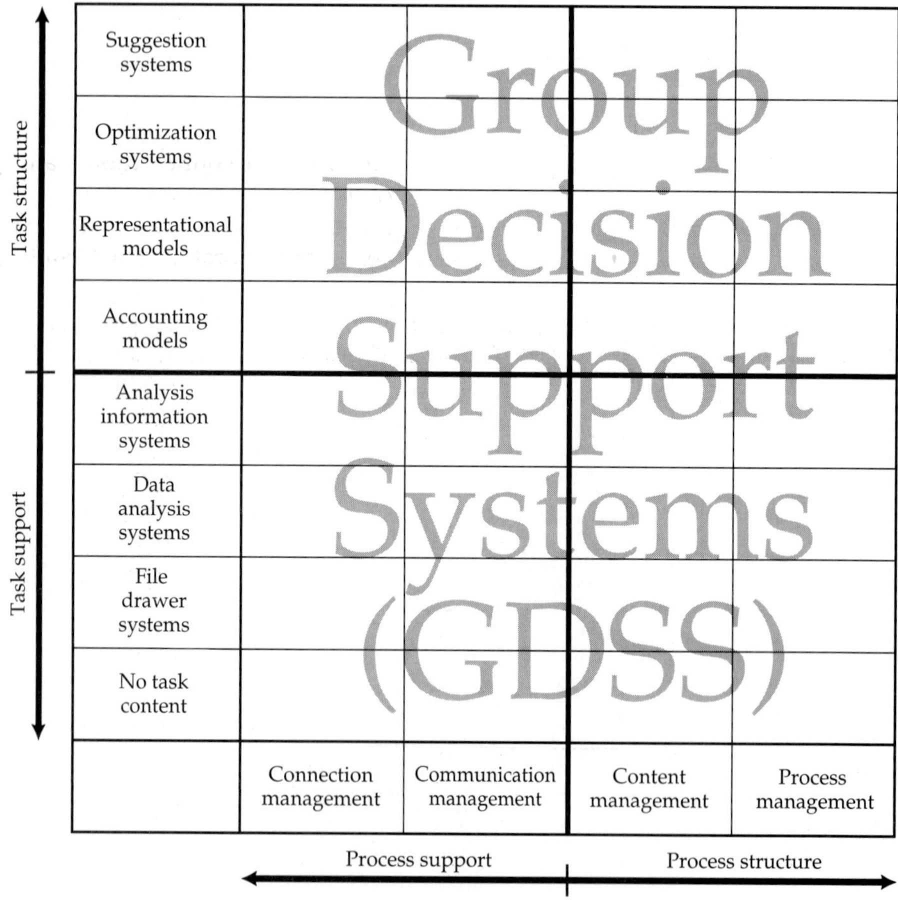

group. We won't cover all the possibilities here because, while some are important to researchers, they tend to be less useful to practitioners than the groupings we have discussed.

11.5 GROUPWARE

The term "groupware" has come into popular use since about 1990. It is related to, but not identical with, group DSS. Groupware is defined in [ELLI91] as

> computer-based systems that support groups of people engaged in a common task (or goal) and that provide an interface to a shared environment.

Calendar programs are a common form of groupware. Such programs keep track of the scheduled commitments of each group member. When it is necessary to arrange a meeting, each participant's schedule is instantly available, and the most convenient time can be chosen. Some such programs merely display the individual calendars in a convenient parallel format, but most can find and suggest times at which a meeting can be held. When a calendar program is integrated with electronic mail capabilities, it can notify required and optional participants of meetings, schedule conference rooms and other required resources, collect confirmations, and generally simplify the process of meeting administration.

Given a group that is willing to keep their schedules on a computer for all to see—which has been a behavioral, not a technical, issue in several organizations—a calendar program can be a genuine time saver. Is it DSS? Probably not, although it is certainly groupware. The concept of groupware, then, covers far more than a strict definition of GDSS would. We can view their relationship as in Figure 11–6. However, groupware facilitates the work of the group. It helps a group reach decisions more quickly, easily, or inexpensively than it otherwise would. We can be aware of the distinction and

FIGURE 11–6

Relationship among DSS, GDSS, and Groupware

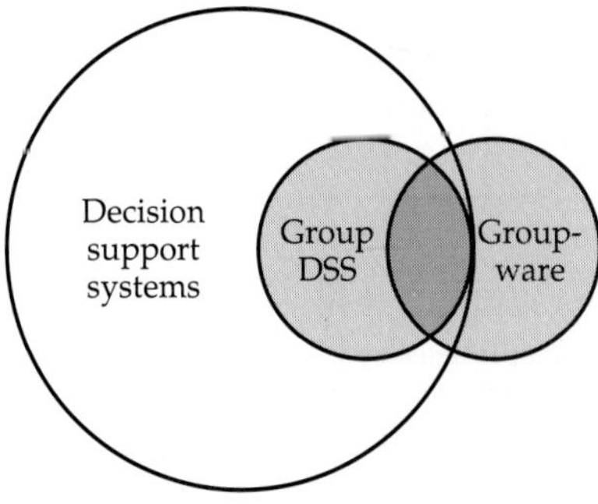

still discuss groupware as a useful component of a total system to support decision makers. Most group DSS that you develop will incorporate some groupware components to smooth the overall work of the group.

11.6 Group DSS in Use Today

Several categories of true group DSS are in use in the early 1990s. This section explores some examples.

11.6.1 Electronic Meeting Systems

Group decision-making situations vary by whether the decision participants are in the same *place* (geographic distribution) and whether they work on the decision at the same *time* (temporal distribution). Since both questions have two possible answers (yes or no), there is a two-by-two grid of possibilities as shown in Figure 11–7.

A great deal of work has been done to determine how computers can best support group decisions made in these different modes of cooperation. This categorization is important because the nature of the required support tools (computers, storage devices, display devices) depends on a group's position in this communication grid.

Same time/same place meetings can be facilitated by an *electronic meeting room*, an *electronic boardroom*, or a *war room*, as shown in Figure 11–8. (The room has several more rows of desks behind the front row that is visible in the photograph.) Such a facility typically has a microcomputer workstation

Figure 11–7

Group Communication Grid

		Place	
		Same	*Different*
Time	*Same*	No-tech: meeting room Low-tech: overhead projector High-tech: conference room support system	No-tech: none Low-tech: telephone High-tech: teleconferencing systems
	Different	No-tech: physical (cork and thumbtack) bulletin board Low-tech: none High-tech: single-user computer with shared files for nonconcurrent use	No-tech: mail Low-tech: fax High-tech: electronic bulletin boards, electronic mail

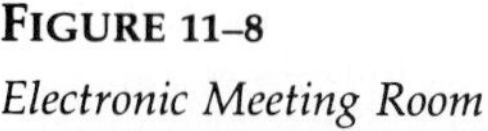

FIGURE 11–8
Electronic Meeting Room

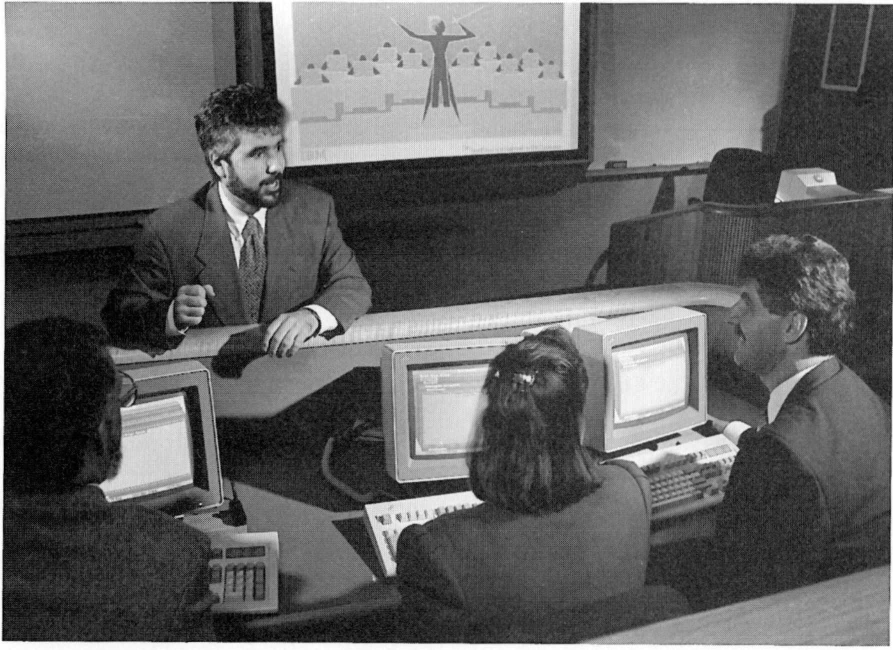

Photo by Bob Mahoney; supplied courtesy of IBM.

with color graphics display for each participant. These are connected by a high-speed local network. (You can read about LAN requirements for electronic meeting rooms in [DENN91].) There is also a large screen video display, located where it can be seen by all participants. A *meeting facilitator* guides the electronic aspects of the meeting. The facilitator can, among other things, view any of the participant's computer displays and show one of them on the large screen. Conventional audiovisual devices, such as overhead projectors and flipchart stands, are also usually available; sometimes using a computer is more trouble than it's worth!

The facilitator can be the group leader or another group member, but is typically a neutral individual who is trained in both the technology of the electronic meeting room and in group processes but is not a group member. This person can play a technical role, an active leadership role, or both in the meeting. As Nunamaker et al. write in [NUNA91], the facilitator's job will change over time as group members become more familiar with the meeting room technology and how to use it most effectively. There is good reason not to use a facilitator at all if one is not necessary since the facilitator can introduce bias to the group process and hence into its results.

Electronic meeting room software includes tools for planning the meeting session, such as a tool by which group members can propose agenda items. During a meeting, the software can organize and structure members' comments. After the meeting, its recorded data serves as an organizational memory to ensure that comments are not forgotten. Thus, it supports primarily the process-related aspects of group decision making. Task-related support is limited to data retrieval and use of simple calculation tools.

An electronic meeting can proceed in one of the three styles described in [NUNA91]: *chauffeured, supported,* and *interactive.* In chauffeured style, the display screen is controlled by one person. It provides an electronic blackboard with effectively unlimited memory. Group communication remains primarily verbal. In supported style, all group members can write on the blackboard. Communication is partly verbal and partly electronic. In interactive style, the most highly computerized, virtually nobody speaks.

Nunamaker et al. found that the benefits of electronic meeting support grow as the group becomes larger, independently of the meeting style. However, the negative aspects of electronic support—for example, most people can talk faster than they can type—depend highly on the meeting style. The highly computerized interactive mode had the greatest drawbacks with small groups but did not get worse as the group got larger. Chauffeured style worked quite well with small groups but was ineffective with large ones. Supported style was between the two. Thus, they feel that "interactive styles will be preferred for larger groups, and supported or chauffeured styles for smaller groups."

A second level of electronic meeting support is provided by what Kraemer and King [KRAE88] call a *decision conference.* Starting with the electronic meeting room as its technical foundation, a decision conference facility adds task support tools. An interesting application of decision conferencing, in which a nonprofit organization achieved impressive results on a budget using borrowed university facilities, is described in [QUAD92].

One type of task support tool consists of voting support. This is appropriate when the decision-making group is large, such as a legislature.[3] Voting support can include simple tabulation, averaging, evaluating preferences on a scale (say, 0 to 100), and the Delphi method for reaching consensus.

TeamFocus from IBM is representative of decision conference products. Several others exist, such as VisionQuest (Collaborative Technologies Corp., Austin, Tex.) TeamFocus runs on a network of IBM PS/2 or compatible systems: one for each participant and one, a powerful file server with video projector, for the chauffeur (called a TeamGuide here). TeamFocus and similar decision conference packages support the group tasks of brainstorming, or-

[3]Many present-day legislatures, including the U.S. Congress, use electronic vote tabulation to improve the speed and accuracy with which an otherwise conventional yes/no vote is recorded. This falls below the threshold of what we call GDSS here.

ganizing the ideas so generated, voting, evaluating the alternatives, and action planning.

In brainstorming, TeamFocus initially gives each participant a blank screen on which to enter ideas. As soon as the participant transmits an idea to the file server, he or she gets a new idea entry screen—but this time with one of the other participants' ideas, chosen at random, at the top. Over time the random selection of other participants' ideas grows, giving the participant the inspiration of the other participants' thoughts but with no censorship, no time pressure, no way (even for the TeamGuide) to identify the originator of a good or bad idea, and no need to compete with others for the floor.

Once the alternatives have been proposed, they can be organized. Here, the participants typically suggest categories, and the meeting facilitator writes them down. Computer support for this stage of the meeting is not very helpful, as the number of categories is usually small, they are usually fairly obvious, and there is not much emotional "baggage" attached to them. The categories are entered into the computer, and participants are assigned a suitable number of categories into which to place the ideas that have previously been generated.

Now it is time to evaluate the alternatives. TeamFocus supports several voting methods: rank ordering of alternatives, yes/no, true/false, agree/disagree, score on a 10-point scale, percentage, and multiple choice. Different voting methods fit different decision-making situations. At least one of the available methods is likely to suit most voting situations that arise in practice. As with the brainstorming, voting is totally anonymous. One can give the vice president's suggestions a zero without incurring corporate wrath. TeamFocus can provide a number of useful statistics about the voting. For example, two items might both have scored an average of 6 on a 10-point scale, but one might have had all its scores bunched between 5 and 7 while the other had a much wider spread. This might lead to a focused discussion of the reasons for the spread and might bring out some factors that were not considered by all the group members. A second vote might give this item a much higher or lower score.

Decision conference support software can also include analytic decision-making tools such as decision trees, influence trees, utility models, cost-benefit analyses, spreadsheet models, and on up to detailed models developed specifically for the purpose of making a particular decision or type of decision. The meeting facilitator in such a situation must be, or must be augmented by, a *decision analyst* who understands the available tools, can explain them, and can aid the decision makers in choosing and using the appropriate ones. Special considerations also apply to the user interface of such a group decision support system, as detailed in [GRAY89].

Electronic meeting room and decision conference concepts can be extended directly to situations in which the group members participate at the same time but in different locations. If the different locations consist of multiple group sites—for example, part of a corporate planning group located at

Using OptionFinder

OptionFinder (Option Technologies Inc., Mendota Heights, Minn.) is a unique product designed for group voting support. Each participant has a 10-digit keypad wired to a computer. The meeting facilitator asks questions that can be answered numerically: the participant's opinion of a package design on a scale of 1 to 10, or the participant's preference for the six alternative package designs on the table.

The OptionFinder computer processes the results and displays them on its screen. The screen can be attached to an overhead projection panel that permits all group members to view the results. They can then discuss their votes, clarify issues, and reach understanding. Responses are stored on disk for later retrieval or incorporation into a report.

Because OptionFinder votes are anonymous, personality and power issues do not arise. Everyone gets involved, including those who don't normally speak at meetings or who find it difficult to disagree with what has already been said. Also, OptionFinder is portable: An entire system with 15 keypads and a laptop computer fits in a traveling case that can go into the overhead compartment of an airplane.

The downside is that responses, by definition, must be expressed in digits. Phrasing questions that can be answered this way can test the facilitator's ability. If the need is for open-ended text responses, other products—most likely more expensive and less portable—must be used.

each of three divisional headquarters—the physical facilities at each location can resemble those of a central meeting place. A large display screen at each site can echo what is being displayed on the screen at the facilitator's location, via either a data link or a television camera and videoconferencing methods. Given sufficient high-speed communication bandwidth, a multisite meeting can take place practically as if all the participants were in the same room—although if any participant were to look up from the screen, he or she would see only part of the group.

This type of support is still too costly for wide use when the participants are at individual sites, typically their own offices. Constructing large-screen displays in each potential participant's office and connecting them via video links is normally quite impractical. Support for electronic meetings involving individual participants at different locations is therefore limited to what can be displayed directly on a participant's own computer screen or conveyed via voice telephone lines. This forces the meeting into the interactive style. As noted earlier, this may not be ideal for small groups, but given the situation, it's the best one can do. The value of decision room tools, be they for voting, for modeling, or for any other like purpose, remains high.

When a "meeting" involves people who participate at different times, the potential for interactivity disappears. Participants read what others have written, mull it over, and respond.

Simple meetings of this type take place on *electronic bulletin boards.* The software that maintains an electronic bulletin board is called a *bulletin board system* or BBS. Its facilitator is referred to in the vernacular as the *sysop,* a contraction of "system operator." In its simplest form, an electronic bulletin board is a sequential file of messages that any participant can read and append to. Most BBS allow a message to be identified as a response to an earlier message. This permits a reader to follow one thread of a discussion without being distracted by other threads. Several U.S. nationwide networks, including Internet (really more an interconnected collection of networks than one network), USENET, and BITNET, have been supporting electronic meetings in this way for years.

Beyond the basic BBS capability, many of the decision support tools for same-time meetings remain useful in the different-time situation. The Delphi technique was originally developed for different-time usage.[4] It is perhaps more appropriate there than for same-time usage, especially if the subject on which a consensus is to be reached requires careful thought. Models are also useful in different-time meetings: Having one model for the entire group has the advantage that all members are, so to speak, singing the same music. For Comment and Instant Update, discussed in Sections 11.7.1 and 11.7.2, respectively, essentially support different-place, different-time meetings.

11.6.2 Work Flow Systems

A *work flow system* (also written as *workflow system,* with "work flow" as one word) can be thought of as "intelligent electronic mail." The system "knows" what the flow of information in a decision-making situation is supposed to be and routes information accordingly [MCCR92]. This corresponds to either level 3, content management, or level 4, process management, of the group DSS hierarchy.

Most work flow systems are built on the foundation of an electronic mail system. They typically route work using *forms* and *scripts.* A form corresponds to a paper form: a travel authorization, an automobile insurance claim form, a purchase order. Knowledge workers in the organization can read the form and, if authorized to do so, modify it by entering new values or altering existing ones. When a user has finished with a form for the time being, he or she so notifies the system. The work flow system then looks at its script to decide what to do next.

---

[4]The Delphi technique allows each participant to state an opinion on the question of interest, along with an optional explanation of his or her reasons for it. After all opinions are in, they are analyzed (statistically, if they are numeric), grouped, and reported to all participants. Participants can then change their opinions, as they see where they fit in the group and read other participants' explanations. The usual result is general, although perhaps not total, convergence to a common position.

A script defines the routing of the form. If the script is fixed, the work flow system is a level 3 system. If it can adjust its behavior on the basis of the form's content, it is a level 4 system. A typical script from [XENA92] might be

> If the purchase order amount is greater than $2,000, then send it to Jones; otherwise, if it's from a computer equipment vendor [this would be determined by the contents of some field, perhaps used as a key to access a database], then send it to Smith, otherwise, send it to Johnson.

The major characteristics of work flow development tools are [FERR92]:

- They can move about various types of objects such as forms, documents, technical drawings, fax, photos, and artwork.
- They can route information objects automatically from person to person according to a programmed plan.
- Information can be processed at any point. Application developers have flexibility in the type of processing they specify.
- Tracking shows who has done what and where things are being held up.
- Information is, as noted above, typically moved using electronic mail.

Thus, forms and scripts can support virtually any structured or unstructured business process that a systems analyst can describe.

Several work flow products are on the market today. They vary widely in their capabilities: not in the sense of one being 20 percent better than another but in addressing different aspects of the work flow in an organization. For example:

- **BeyondMail** (Beyond, Inc., Cambridge, Mass.) can use scripts to filter the electronic mail a person receives. By searching for words in the text of messages, it can delete them, file them, or forward them to someone else—or, of course, leave them for their addressee to read. BeyondMail users can attach images, stored as binary files, to the routed messages.
- **WorkFlo** (FileNet Corp., Costa Mesa, Calif.) works in conjunction with that firm's imaging products to take image processing a giant step beyond just recording, storaging, and communicating graphic information. Using OCR techniques to interpret the scanned image of a paper form, it can determine the content of a data field and use that value to route the form.
- **Cooperation** (NCR Corporation, Dayton, Ohio) can record the steps that a user carries out in performing a computer-based task. It can use this record to automate the execution of the same task in the future.

- **WorkMAN** (Reach Software, Sunnyvale, Calif.) is able to "leapfrog" a person if a form sits too long on his or her desktop. While not appropriate to every situation, this capability can unstick a document moving up the chain of command if someone in the middle is on vacation or otherwise unavailable for an extended period of time.
- **TeamRoute** (Digital Equipment Corporation, Maynard, Mass.) is designed to work with that firm's products for client/server computing. We discussed client/server computing, which partitions a task into components for execution on different computers, in Section 7.2.4.
- **Notes** (Lotus Corporation, Cambridge, Mass.), which we discuss in Section 11.7.3, has some work flow management capability and is being enhanced with more.

In choosing an application to automate via a work flow system, Ferris suggests these candidates:

- Manual systems in which different people or departments complete different parts of a multisection manual form. *Example:* Insurance claim processing, where one person certifies that a policy is current and another determines the amount of damages that took place.
- Manual systems where multipart forms are used, especially if the participants do their tasks only intermittently and at times that aren't easily scheduled. *Example:* Corporate travel authorizations, which must be approved by several levels of management (Question: What is the decision here?) and which then go to the employee, his or her manager, the accounting office, and the firm's travel agency.
- Projects that require bits of information from many people. *Example:* A product specification that is distributed widely for comments.
- Front-ending production databases for either query or report generation. *Example:* A form with an appropriate database accessing script can be an intuitively easy-to-use way to extract desired information with no technical expertise.

Work flow systems are often associated with image-processing systems.[5] It is incontestible that many work flow applications, such as those involving reproductions of paper forms, are often well supported by imaging technology. However, the two concepts are separate and should be considered separately.

---

[5]One reason is that one of the earliest successful work flow products, FileNet's WorkFlo, was developed by an image-processing vendor and sold in conjunction with its imaging products.

11.7 Four Group DSS Products

The next four sections describe these group DSS products:

- ForComment (from Access Technologies), which helps a group of writers and reviewers agree on the content of a document.
- Instant Update (from ON Technology), which also allows several people to write a document jointly but takes a different approach to document management and therefore has different areas of applicability.
- Notes (from Lotus Development Corporation), which makes sure that information gets to all interested parties and is organized properly for their needs when it arrives.
- FlowPATH (from Groupe Bull), a work flow management system.[6]

11.7.1 Access Technologies's ForComment

Group authorship of a document is common. You have probably written joint term papers or group projects. You will find the same situation in the business world. Few corporations let one person write a press release, marketing brochure, or article for publication and send it out directly with no review by others. Instead, such documents pass through thorough review by experts on technical, marketing, legal, and strategic issues. The document is changed until all are satisfied. Figure 11–9 is an example of such a document.

The task involves a great deal of coordination and often negotiation. For example, if two reviewers disagree on how a section should be changed, the author must either shuttle back and forth (logically, if not physically) between them or must bring them together to reach a compromise. Choosing the appropriate wording for a published document is a decision. This decision can be aided by suitable data-oriented computer support. This computer support can provide the DSS benefits of improved quality, improved communication, and, often, learning and training. By eliminating the need to trace down people and have them available for discussions at the same time, it can save time. As a valuable by-product, it can also save substantial quantities of paper.

Access Technologies's ForComment is a software package intended to manage the process of document review by multiple readers. It saves paper and time by conducting the review process on line. ForComment runs on VAX minicomputers and on IBM-compatible PCs linked in a local area network (LAN) via Novell NetWare.

---

[6]Groupe Bull is a worldwide computer firm based in France. Its U.S. operations are called Bull HN Information Systems Inc. The "H" in HN stands for Honeywell, which owned Bull's U.S. operations until the late 1980s.

FIGURE 11–9

Screen Shot of ForComment Annotated Document

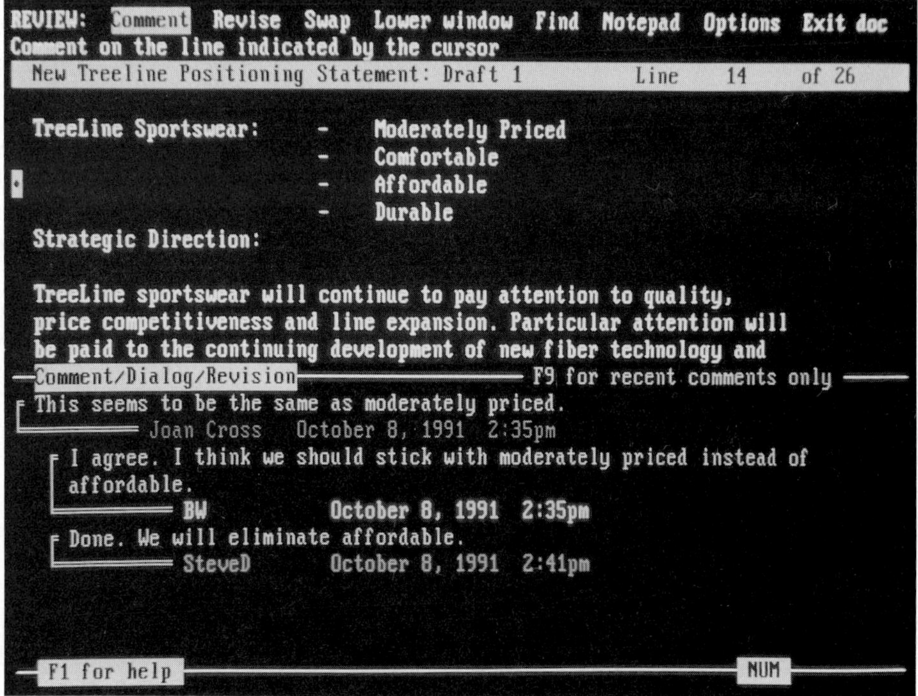

SOURCE: Reprinted courtesy of Computer Associates International, Inc. © 1992 Computer Associates International, Inc. All rights reserved.

A ForComment user must first write the document: The product is intended for documents that already exist, although a "comment" could be used to add a new section. He or she imports documents from word processor or text files, generates reviewer circulation lists, and then sends the documents on their way. The documents are then stored on a central disk file where they can be accessed by all system users. ForComment lets users make comments, suggest revisions, and view and respond to other reviewers' comments. Reviewers can swap suggested revisions into the original text to see how the revision would look. However, reviewers cannot change the original document permanently: only its author can.

Reviewer comments are linked with specific text lines. Each text line can be linked to comments from multiple reviewers. One reviewer can see comments entered by previous reviewers—in fact, reviewers are told when they select a document if other reviewers have entered comments. Alternatively, if a reviewer doesn't want to be influenced by what others have written, he or she can opt to see the document without others' comments. Reviewers can also write general notes about the document on "Notepads."

ForComment offers numerous options to facilitate the practical aspects of reviewing. The Select option minimizes clutter by displaying only selected comments: only those made by particular reviewers (the reviewer's boss?) or those made since a particular time. The Dialog option lets reviewers comment on other reviewers' comments.

ForComment does not eliminate all of an author's responsibilities. Authors must not, for example, incorporate suggested revisions into the actual document until all reviewers have returned their comments. If they do, the slowpokes will not be able to see and comment on the original version. ForComment does, however, provide an on-line means of making document review and revision easier, faster and more efficient. It can be a worthwhile investment for businesses that rely heavily on group review of centrally written and controlled documents.

11.7.2 ON Technology's Instant Update

Instant Update, from ON Technology of Cambridge, Mass., is comparable to ForComment in that it makes a document available to multiple group members for review and comment. Despite this superficial similarity, the underlying philosophy of the two products is quite different. In ForComment, only the author of a document can change it; in Instant Update, anyone can.

To use Instant Update, an author first creates a "live document." Instant Update has a built-in word processing and table processing capability. This feature is substantially ahead of ForComment's limited MemoWriter but falls short of full-fledged stand-alone word processing software. Fortunately, Instant Update can—like ForComment—also import text from word processing packages. Having created a document, its author then sends it out to members of his or her work group. The document is stored at a network file server. Any group member can read the document and, if desired, change it. At any point in the process, a user can print a document or export it to a word processing package for formatting.

While changing a document, one works with a copy at one's local computer: either an Apple Macintosh, the first platform supported by Instant Update, or an IBM-compatible PC. Any changes a user makes are made to that local copy. As soon as the user is happy with what one has written, a mouse click on an on-screen Update button sends the new version to the server—complete with change bars so other group members can see what is new. Furthermore, when another group member looks at a list of Instant Update documents, arrows (see Figure 11–10) indicate which ones have changed since the last time that group member read them. All of this happens transparently to the user.

What happens if two group members change the same paragraph at the same time? Suppose two speechwriters are reviewing Abraham Lincoln's

FIGURE 11–10
Instant Update Control Screen

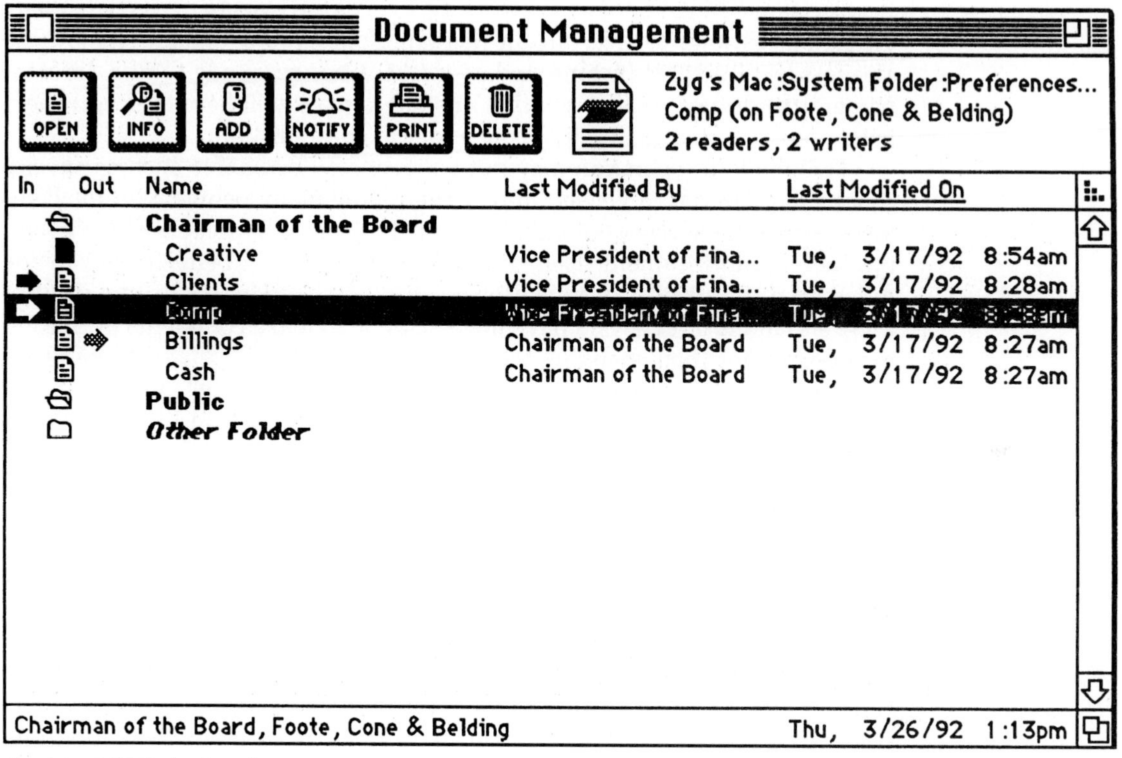

Courtesy of ON Technology, Inc.

original draft of the Gettysburg Address, which might have read "Eighty-seven years ago. . . ."[7] Both think that opening is boring. One changes it to the now-famous "Four score and seven years ago . . ." and updates the document. The server copy is changed accordingly. The other, still working with a local copy that starts "Eighty-seven years ago . . . ," changes it to "Nearly a century ago . . ." and sends that update to the server. The server will recognize that this change was not made to the current version of the document and will give the second speechwriter a choice: choose either version, or leave both in. In this case, the second writer sees the merit of the first one's immortal phrase and wisely leaves it alone. Honest Abe, when he next logs on to Instant Update, will see only the "Four score and seven . . ." opening. Change bars will alert him that the paragraph has changed since he last read it. When he places the cursor in the changed paragraph he will

[7]President Lincoln, of course, did not use speechwriters. Since professional orators of the 1860s thought a good speech had to be two hours long, that's probably just as well.

see which of his aides changed it and when. (The net effect can be a bit of a free-for-all if the group members don't have some self-control.)

The same thing happens, by the way, even if the two changes were totally unrelated, as long as they are in the same paragraph. Paragraphs are the smallest text unit that Instant Update tracks. Changes made to two different paragraphs do not create a conflict. Instant Update will happily insert them both even if they combine to create a logical contradiction.

This mode of operation may not be ideal for documents such as specifications that must be reviewed independently by many people with the comments consolidated by one central author. In these situations, where the end product is the document itself, ForComment may be a better match to the necessary centralized, controlled work style. Instant Update can be used in these situations if reviewers have the discipline to make comments by adding new text rather than changing what exists.

The Instant Update approach is better suited to "live" documents on which many people are working together, perhaps each on his or her own section. It is also a good fit to situations where information transfer, rather than document creation, is the objective: project tracking where new entries are made regularly by several people, brainstorming sessions, information broadcasting. Instant Update fits a more collaborative work style where the document is essentially a container for information being collected and disseminated.

Neither the ForComment philosophy nor the Instant Update philosophy is "right" or "wrong." They are different. It is important for group leaders and members to recognize the essence of the task to be done and their groups' preferred mode of operation—groups have preferred styles of behavior, just as people do—and to pick software that matches it.

11.7.3 Lotus Notes

Since its 1990 introduction, Lotus Development Corporation's Notes has become the most popular application in the "groupware" category. Indeed, to many people, this package defines the term. One reason is the marketplace impetus it received from an early order for 10,000 copies from "Big Six" accounting and consulting firm Price Waterhouse. At the 1990 list price of $62,500 for 200 copies, that would represent over a $3 million purchase. (Given the size and the visibility of the Price Waterhouse commitment to a brand-new and unproven product, it is reasonable to assume that they received a substantial discount.) Subsequent large orders, some of them much larger, from other major firms such as Metropolitan Life Insurance and Arthur Andersen, have combined to give Notes more corporate penetration and visibility than any other group computing application.

What is Notes? In its simplest form, Notes is a software package that manages a distributed, replicated database (that is, several copies of the database exist in different locations) and makes its contents available to users.

Notes has been categorized as software for information sharing or for collaborative computing. However, it goes beyond that. An excellent definition comes from Jesse Berst in [BERS92]: "an environment for building information-sharing applications on networks." He goes on to explain that Notes is built around four core technologies: security, compound documents, replication, and development tools.

Security is mandatory when data are to be shared over a network. If a product such as Notes is to be widely used, some of the information in its database will be confidential, to be seen only by a few of the many registered Notes users on the net. Accordingly, Notes incorporates several security features including access control lists (by individual, department, work group, or division, with seven access control levels as shown in Figure 11–11) and encryption (of individual fields or entire documents).

Compound documents are the basic components of the Notes database. A compound document consists of many types of information: data (structured text or numbers organized into named data fields), free-form text, graphics, and sound (with available add-on software to augment the basic package).

Replication is fundamental to the operation of Notes. Each user accesses a copy of the Notes database stored on a server that he or she can access directly. Any changes or additions made by that user go into the local copy. Many organizations, however, have more than one LAN. These local LANs may be permanently linked via suitable wide-area connections or, in the more common situation, may connect to each other only from time to time. When the user's server connects to other servers in the overall corporate network

FIGURE 11–11

Notes Access Control Hierarchy

Rank	*Access Level*	*Description*
1	Manager	Can perform all operations: read, write, and modify data, forms, and views; assign and modify all security controls. Default level for person who creates the database. Only level that can delete the entire database.
2	Designer	Can perform any operation on the database except modifying security controls or deleting the entire database.
3	Editor	Can read, write, and modify the content of any document in the database but cannot alter database structure or functionality (forms, views, etc.). Can remove encryption from any document for which he or she has the encryption key.
4	Author	Can read and write documents. Can edit documents that he or she originally composed.
5 (tie)	Reader	Can read, but not enter or modify, documents.
5 (tie)	Depositor	Can enter, but not read or modify, documents.
7	No access	Cannot access the database for any purpose.

they compare information on documents that have been changed or added since each database was updated.

What happens if two Notes users update the same document at the same time, each on a different LAN? This creates a *replication conflict*. Notes keeps both copies. The one that has been changed the most times since the previous replication is considered the original. The other is considered a response to the original and is marked with a special symbol next to its name. A user with suitable access privileges (the author of the document or any user with at least Editor-level access) who sees this conflict flag can merge the differing versions into one, deleting the other. This new version will, through the replication process, then be distributed to all Notes servers on the network.

Development tools allow a Notes system to be customized to the needs of a particular organization. Customization involves *forms,* through which information goes into a Notes database, and *views,* through which it comes out.

Forms consist of *fields.* Fields can contain several types of data: number, text, "rich text" (formatted with character styles such as italic letters), time/date, and more. They can be specified as entered by the user (editable later or not), as computed and saved with the document, or as recomputed each time the document is displayed. A great deal of formatting flexibility is provided for each type of field, much as in a contemporary spreadsheet package.

Views determine how the data in a database will be displayed to its users. Views consist of columns, each of which contains data from a specified database field and has specified formatting. Columns may overlap in a categorized view such as Figure 11–12. This document is sorted and categorized

FIGURE 11–12

Sample from Lotus Notes Database Design Manual

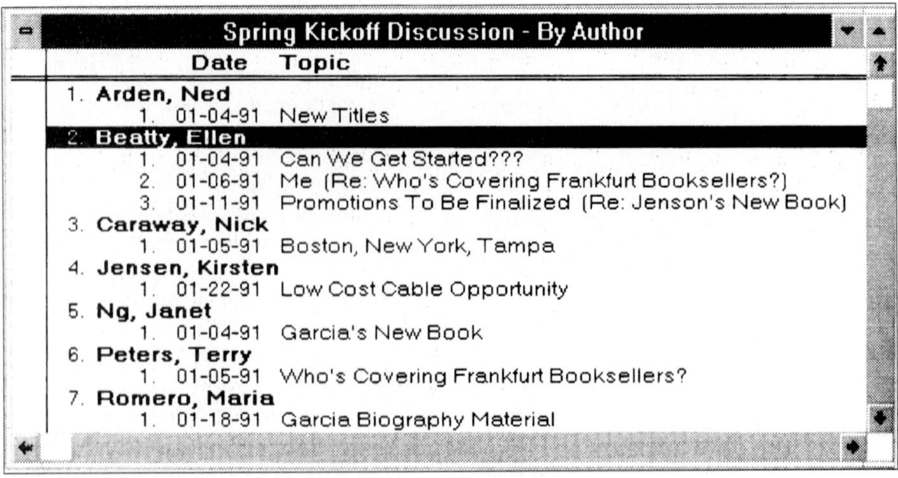

SOURCE: Screen shot © 1992. Lotus Development Corporation. Lotus Notes is a registered trademark of Lotus Development Corporation.

by author name. The name Ellen Beatty appears once, with all her documents listed below. A mouse click will display the entire text of any desired document.

In addition to formatting, views have *selection formulas*. Selection formulas define the set of documents that Notes will include in the view. A user can thus opt to see only documents that apply to the Acme Corporation, include the word "capacitor," and were written since April 10th.

Formulas, used as selection formulas, as the basis for computed fields, and in several other contexts, provide Notes with considerable application development power. A formula is, in effect, a computer program that is invoked when the Notes user takes a specified action such as opening a view. Formulas can perform calculations, organize data, transform data, take different actions depending on the content of a field or of some other variable in the environment, and more. While it would probably not be a good idea to process accounts receivable or compute temperatures inside a jet engine via Notes formulas, it wouldn't be impossible.

By now you probably realize that setting up a Notes application calls for specialized training and expertise. That's generally correct. Defining a database, creating views, and creating forms with complex formulas calls for skills that the average end user is not likely to possess. However, users with suitable training can create simple Notes databases for use within a small work group, can modify existing forms to meet their personal needs, and—perhaps most importantly—can see the value of new Notes applications and describe those applications to MIS specialists.

In terms of our GDSS spectrum with the categories shown in Figure 11–3, a Lotus Notes application can range up to a data analysis system on the vertical axis and to a content management system on the horizontal axis. A specific Notes database, of course, might be at lower levels.

Work on Notes began [SHAP92] as far back as 1985 when Mitchell Kapor, founder and then head of Lotus Development Corporation, agreed to fund its development by a startup software firm named Iris Associates. At the time there was no market for groupware. Kapor's and Iris's assumption that a market would develop was based on the erroneous belief that both Microsoft Windows and local networking would take off far faster than they actually did.[8] Nonetheless, both Kapor and successor Jim Manzi continued to support the project until it was sufficiently mature to announce and the market had become ready for it.

---

[8]Lotus's first product, 1-2-3, also had to define its own market. Kapor first proposed an integrated program combining spreadsheet, graphics, and data management in a term paper for an entrepreneurship course at the Massachusetts Institute of Technology's Sloan School of Management. He received a B−. (His instructor commented that his market projections did not have adequate justification.) Kapor did not let this stop him. He started Lotus Development Corporation, developed the product described in the paper, and became far wealthier than most business school faculty members who teach about entrepreneurship.

11.7.4 Groupe Bull FlowPATH

FlowPATH is a work flow management system that is part of Groupe Bull's *image-processing* product line. Image processing is the computer processing of pictorial data such as photographs, signatures, handwriting, and diagrams. This new technology has many applications, some of which are related to decision support. For example, an automobile insurance claim adjuster must see photographs of a damaged vehicle before deciding how much to pay on the claim. In other cases, even if information is in the form of letters and numbers, relevant documents may be on paper. They can often not be transcribed into a text database at reasonable cost and in reasonable time. This section discusses only the work flow management aspect of Bull's image processing systems.

FlowPATH supports group decision making via scripts that describe how a task is partitioned into activities. Each activity is associated with an "actor," the group or an individual who performs it; the conditions under which it can or must be performed; and the environment (in terms of data availability) in which it must be performed.

A FlowPATH user sees three task folders on his or her Microsoft Windows desktop: one each for new tasks, ongoing tasks, and completed tasks. The desktop also shows three corresponding "notes" folders: for new notes, received but not yet read; ongoing notes, read but not yet fully acted on; and completed notes. The notes folders provide a simple form of electronic mail integrated with the workflow system.

The user begins by *receiving* a new task. This is as simple as a mouse click on the New Tasks folder tab followed by a click on the Receive New Task button. The first of any tasks that have been routed to the user's workstation, but not yet accepted, will be added to the New Tasks folder. Once received, the user can view information about the task: the activity to be performed, the "work case" on which the activity is to be performed, its priority, other information as recorded in the task's "property sheet," and comments that co-workers may have written about it. The user can then choose to *accept* the task. Accepted tasks are moved to the Ongoing Tasks folder.

The FlowPATH user then processes the task. Specifics of task processing vary widely from one task to another. It generally involves working on the screen with "electronic forms" that have been designed for the task to be performed or the decision to be made. When a task is done, a click on the End command button will change the task status to Completed. A click on the Route To The Next button will move it to the Done folder and route it, as a candidate for acceptance, to the next user. A task that need not be routed further will simply move to the Done folder when End is clicked. Tasks in the Done folder can be deleted, again by mouse click, to conserve disk space once they are no longer needed for local reference.

A work flow system administrator defines the flow of activities by writing scripts in the Visual BASIC language. While the built-in function names can be long and look forbidding, they have meaning and structure that become intuitive after a short time, as in the function

```
WFuaSetFieldByArgument (ActivityHandle,
ParameterNumber, DataValue, DataSize)
```

This function allows a program to set the value of a field in a form. The four elements of its calling sequence specify, respectively:

- The activity in question, such as order entry or inventory checking.
- The parameter of that activity whose value is to be set, such as the third, or the one called QuantityOnHand.
- The value to which it is to be set, such as 26, or the value of another variable called NewQuantityOnHand (which might, in turn, have been calculated).
- The length of that value. (This is important to the display software and can easily be calculated via BASIC's built-in LEN function.)

The `WFuaSetFieldByArgument` function allows a script to set the value of any field in a form. Since scripts are programs in the full sense of the word, the script author can take advantage of the full power of a programming language to control the work flow. Because Visual BASIC uses standard Windows interfaces, the programmer can also access external databases and use Windows' Dynamic Data Exchange (DDE) facility to share data with other applications on the same computer.

FlowPATH has a work structuring facility to help managers plan the flow of activities in an overall task. A possible sequence of activities for an order-processing task is shown in Figure 11–13.[9] The letters in parentheses after each subtask description indicate the group that is responsible for that subtask. Some groups are responsible for more than one part of the overall task. Some of them are presumably also responsible for tasks that are not part of order processing, but this chart doesn't show that.

Using charts such as this, FlowPATH can simulate different approaches to performing a task, displaying the flow of activities both graphically and numerically. This allows managers to observe bottlenecks and underutilized resources and to choose the best way of performing a task. In effect, FlowPATH includes decision support tools—albeit individual DSS for the system developer's use, not group DSS—for optimizing its own use!

META Group, a computer industry analysis firm that specializes in (among other areas) image management, writes that "Bull's new workflow module comprises a powerful scripting environment for automatic procedural tasks. This type of graphical, user-programmable software represents the next

[9]This figure is based on an example created by Bull. In it, the invoice is sent out here before the goods are shipped. That is not the only possible approach to invoicing.

FIGURE 11–13

FlowPATH Order Processing Task Chart

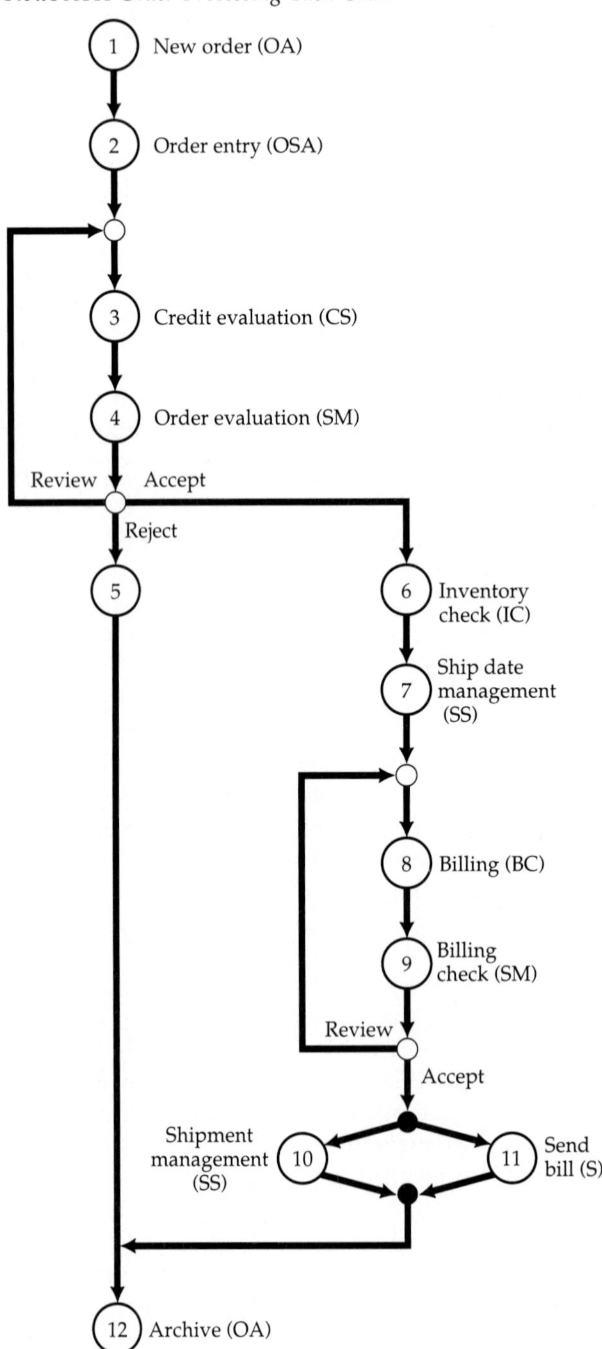

generation of workflow tools" [META92]. While they stopped short of saying that Bull's product is unique and has no competitors, they indicated clearly that it represents the type of tool that you will encounter increasingly often during your MIS career.

Summary

A group decision support system is a DSS whose design takes into account how people work together in reaching a decision. They can help with at least four types of group tasks: generating ideas, solving problems with correct answers, deciding issues with no "right" answer, and resolving conflicts of viewpoint.

Group DSS are becoming more prevalent for several reasons. One is that modern management methods have increased the importance of group decision making. Another is that the technical infrastructure for communication within the organization, including desktop access to organization-wide networks, is becoming more common.

Group decision support systems can be at any level of the seven-level hierarchy given in the previous chapter. In addition, they vary along a second, information flow, dimension. Along this dimension they can provide connection management, communication management, content management, or process management capability. While this is not the only possible view of GDSS, other views can be mapped into it.

Groupware is a broader concept than GDSS. It incorporates all types of software designed to facilitate the work of a group, including aspects of its work that do not correspond to decision making.

Electronic meetings provide an important type of group decision support. These facilitate same time/same place group decision making. An electronic meeting can operate in chauffeured, supported, or interactive style. Task support tools can be added to an electronic meeting room to create a decision conference facility. Networks can extend electronic meetings and decision conferences to multiple sites.

Work flow systems are designed to reflect the flow of information in a group decision-making process. They use forms to carry the content of a decision being made and scripts to control the flow of these forms in an organization.

Sample group decision support products include ForComment, from Access Technologies, to help writers and reviewers agree on document content; Instant Update, from ON Technology, to support joint authorship of a document; Lotus Notes, which organizes information and routes it to interested parties; and FlowPATH, from Groupe Bull, which manages work flow.

Key Terms

bulletin board system (BBS) 361
calendar programs 355
chauffeured (meeting style) 358
communication management systems 352
compound document 369
connection management systems 351
content management systems 352
decision analyst 359
decision conference 358
Delphi technique 361
electronic boardroom 356
electronic bulletin board 361
electronic meeting room 356
electronic meeting systems 356
forms (for work flow systems) 361
group DSS 344
groupthink 346
groupware 355
image processing 363
interactive (meeting style) 358
meeting facilitator 357
process management systems 352
process structure 354
process support 354
replication 368
scripts (for work flow systems) 361
supported (meeting style) 358
sysop 361
task structure 354
task support 354
war room 356
work flow systems (also written as one word, workflow) 361

Review Questions

1. What is a group DSS? How does it differ from a nongroup DSS?
2. What are the organizational factors that have led to increased use of group DSS?
3. What are the technical factors that have led to increased use of group DSS?
4. What is "groupthink?" How can its impact be reduced?
5. What are the eight types of group tasks? With which can group DSS help? What is the common characteristic of these tasks?
6. What are the two dimensions along which we can characterize group DSS? Which of these does not apply to other DSS? What are its four levels?
7. What is groupware? How does it relate to group DSS?
8. Describe an electronic meeting system. For what types of decision-making tasks might it be useful?
9. What are the three electronic meeting styles of operation?
10. What is a decision conference facility? How does it differ from an electronic meeting room?
11. Define "electronic bulletin board."

12. What does a work flow system do? What are its key characteristics?
13. Define "script" and "form" in the context of work flow systems.
14. What do Access Technologies's ForComment and ON Technology's Instant Update have in common?
15. Describe the major capabilities of Lotus Notes. What are formulas good for?
16. What type of system is FlowPATH?

Exercises

1. Place each of the following GDSS in the appropriate squares of Figures 11–3 and 11–5:
   a. FlowPATH from Groupe Bull.
   b. The second (group-oriented) version of the factory supervisors' DSS in Section 11.1.
   c. A college admissions office system. It provides all admissions staff members with access to applicant records, lets them make comments on the applicants that other staff members may read, records evaluations (two evaluations, for academic and nonacademic factors, both on a scale of 1 to 5), and provides a summary of all evaluations to date.
2. You are writing a group term paper with two other students. Some parts, such as the introduction and conclusions, must be a joint product. Other parts will be written by one of you but reviewed by the others and, in some cases, used by the others as they write their parts. All parts must be merged before you submit the paper, in some cases section by section but in other cases (such as the bibliography) line by line. The three of you live and eat in different buildings. You have (except for the course which requires this paper) different class, activity, and work schedules.
   a. Compare and contrast the ways in which ForComment and Instant Update would support this group task.
   b. Which would you choose? Why?
   c. What capabilities would your ideal groupware tool for this task have that these two products do not have?
3. Use your library's automated search facility to find articles on Lotus Notes in a recent business literature. (Search for both "Lotus" and "Notes" rather than the phrase "Lotus Notes," as the words may not appear in precisely that form. For an example of why this is so, see the first sentence of Section 11.7.3.) Find at least three add-on software packages that work with Notes. What capabilities do they add to it that it did not originally have? How would these capabilities be valuable in group decision making?

4. Consider the following three group decision-making situations:
   - Four instructors are teaching a business strategies course as a team. Each is responsible for a particular aspect of the course: marketing, finance, organizational behavior, and information systems. The four must jointly assign a grade to each student. Each instructor grades weekly homework assignments and exam questions in his or her area. A few assignments involve two areas, but never more than two, and are graded jointly by both instructors. (Because of time constraints in grading final exams, no exam questions are graded jointly, but every exam includes questions from all four areas.) The term project involves all four areas and receives one grade. The instructors must also agree on any grade adjustments for class participation and similar factors.
   - A jury of 12 people, chosen at random with no regard for computer expertise, must reach a unanimous verdict in a technical case. The defendant, being sued for infringing on the plaintiff's software patent, claims that the patent is invalid because (among other reasons) the patented method was already in general use when the patent was applied for. If this is true, the defendant will prevail. Both sides have brought forth experts who have explained, at great length, why their side's position is correct.
   - The Board of Directors of the Starbyte Micro Users' Group (SMUG) is planning the annual meeting of this 10,000-member organization. They must choose a place (city, then specific exhibit facilities and hotels), dates, theme, etc. Some of these are partly fixed: The city must be large enough to have the required space and cannot be near one in which the group has recently met, the meeting must take place between late September and mid-October. Some may be interrelated: A desired hotel may be available only on one set of dates within that period. The board of directors consists of 10 employees of organizations that use Starbyte Micro computers. No two work in the same organization. All know each other from years of SMUG work. They come from all parts of North America (Mexico City to Winnipeg). While their employers support SMUG, it is in everyone's interest to minimize travel and face-to-face meetings.

   For each of these decisions:

   a. Could the decision be made in each of the four quadrants of Figure 11–7 (same or different time and place)?

   b. Describe a possible content management GDSS that could support this decision.

   c. Describe a process management GDSS that could support this decision.

5. The membership of the Harwich University concert band and choir want to raise money to support their forthcoming concert tour through Austria and southern Germany. Would a decision conference system such as TeamFocus be helpful? Why or why not?

References

BERS92 Berst, Jesse. "Deciphering Lotus's Notes." *Computerworld* 26, no. 20 (May 18, 1992), p 36.

DENN91 Dennis, Alan R.; Tom Abens; Sudha Ram; and Jay F. Nunamaker Jr. "Communication Requirements and Network Evaluation within Electronic Meeting System Environments." *Decision Support Systems* 7, no. 1 (Jan. 1991), pp. 13–31.

DESA86 DeSanctis, Gerardine, and R. Brent Gallupe. "Decision Support Systems: A New Frontier." *Database* (Winter 1985), also reprinted in *Decision Support Systems: Putting Theory into Practice,* Ralph H. Sprague, Jr., and Hugh J. Watson, eds., Prentice Hall (Englewood Cliffs, N.J.), 1986.

DESA87 DeSanctis, Gerardine, and R. Brent Gallupe. "A Foundation for the Study of Group Decision Support Systems." *Management Science* 33, no. 5 (May 1987), pp. 589–609.

ELLI91 Ellis, Clarence A.; Simon J. Gibbs; and Gail L. Rein. "Groupware: Some Issues and Experiences." *Communications of the ACM* 34, no. 1 (January 1991), pp. 39–58.

FERR92 Ferris, David. "Work Flow Applications Simplify Office Processes." *Network World* 9, no. 27 (July 6, 1992), pp. 31,33.

GRAY89 Gray, Paul, and Lorne Olfman. "The User Interface in Group Decision Support Systems." *Decision Support Systems* 5 (1989), pp. 119–37.

HUBE84 Huber, George P. "The Nature and Design of Post-Industrial Organizations." *Management Science* 30, no. 8 (August 1984), pp. 928–51.

KRAE88 Kraemer, Kenneth L., and John Leslie King. "Computer-Based Systems for Cooperative Work and Group Decision Making." *ACM Computing Surveys* 20, no. 2 (June 1988), pp. 115–46.

MASL43 Maslow, Abraham H. "A Theory of Motivation." *Psychological Review* 50 (1943), pp. 370–96; reprinted with minor changes in *Motivation and Personality,* Harper Bros. (New York), 1954.

MCCR92 McCready, Scott C. "Work-Flow Software." *Computerworld* 26, no. 44 (November 2, 1992), pp. 85–90.

MCGR84 McGrath, Joseph Edward. *Groups: Interaction and Performance.* Prentice Hall, Englewood Cliffs, N.J. (1984).

MCGR60 McGregor, Douglas. *The Human Side of Enterprise.* McGraw-Hill, New York (1960).

META92 META Group. "Bull's FlowPath: New Workflow Paradigm." *Image Management Strategies,* file #117 (April 6, 1992). META Group Inc., Westport, Conn.

NUNA89 Nunamaker, Jay F. Jr. "Experience with and Future Challenges in GDSS (Group Decision Support Systems): Preface" (introduction to special issue on GDSS). *Decision Support Systems* 5, no. 2 (June 1989), pp. 115–18.

NUNA91 Nunamaker, Jay F. Jr.; Alan R. Dennis; Joseph S. Valachich; Douglas R. Vogel; and Joey F. George. "Electronic Meeting Systems to Support Group Work." *Communications of the ACM* 34, no. 7 (July 1991), pp. 40–61.

OPPE92 Opper, Susanna, and Henry Fersko-Weiss. *Technology for Teams: Enhancing*

Productivity in Networked Organizations. Van Nostrand Reinhold, New York (1992).

QUAD92 M. A. Quaddus; D. J. Atkinson; and M. Levy. "An Application of Decision Conferencing to Strategic Planning of a Voluntary Organization." *Interfaces* 22, no. 6 (November–December 1992), pp. 61–71.

SHAP92 Shapiro, Richard. "Two Years of Notes." *Network World* 9, no. 25 (June 22, 1992); special section on groupware, p. G2.

XENA92 Xenakis, John J. "The Ultimate in Teamwork: Groupware." *BCS Update* 15, no. 1 (January 1992), pp. 6–11.

Envoyance
Working with Chempact

Doug and Adrienne arrived an hour early for their meeting with Hakeem. They knew he was organizing a joint project with Chempact to develop a paper manufacturing process that minimizes waste generation relative to existing processes, and they wanted to review some of the background information in the Envoyance library before the meeting. As soon as they felt comfortable with the concepts, they walked down the hall to Hakeem's office.

"Right on time, I see!" he greeted them. "Cup of coffee?"

"Only if you promise that none of those chemicals we've been reading about are in it!" returned Doug. "No wonder fish don't like paper mills."

"No, they don't," agreed Hakeem as the group went across the hall to the coffee maker. "Neither do a lot of other life forms. We hope we can do something about that."

"I'm not a chemist," said Adrienne, "and neither is Doug. So let's skip that side of it—not because it isn't important, but because we wouldn't understand you and couldn't help you with it anyhow. Can you tell us, though, how this project got started?"

"Sure. You know how paper recycling has picked up since the mid-80s? Well, collecting used paper is all well and good, but then you have to do something with it. As long as there wasn't too much paper being recycled it could all be turned into low-grade products like brown supermarket bags. The stores felt good about doing their bit, and they used up the supply fairly well. As the supply grows, however, more used paper has to be turned into higher grades for things like copier paper and loose-leaf notebook fillers. Plus, consumers are catching on that there are different kinds of recycled paper, and they are asking about how much of what we call "post-consumer waste" is in it—that is, paper that someone has actually used, as opposed to clean paper that's wasted when a roll is cut into sheets and is fed back into the production process. As soon as you do that, you have to bleach the used paper. We call that "de-inking" because the hard part is getting the ink out. Lots of people know how to do that with the old style of liquid inks like you'd use in a printing press, a typewriter, a pen, or even a dot-matrix printer. The ink in a dot-matrix printer ribbon isn't all that different from what monks used to put on quill pens.

"What gets tough is the stuff that photocopiers and laser printers use. You know there are more and more of those every day. They don't use real ink. They use a thermoplastic resin that's a lot harder to get rid of. Some of the obvious methods do more damage to the local water than we'd like, especially since we hope to promote our process as an environmental plus."

"So that's what you're working on?"

"Right, we and Chempact. They know chemicals and papermaking; we know waste flow and rivers. Between us we can hopefully solve a problem that nobody else has made much headway on."

"Sounds great!" said Doug. "But you said there were some problems you wanted our thoughts on. They must be information system problems, or you wouldn't have called us. What were they?"

"Basically," said Hakeem thoughtfully, "we have to work with Chempact almost as closely as if we were one company. Trouble is, we're here, and they're there. It's nearly a three-hour plane trip each way, not even counting waiting time and ground travel time. That means either a 10-hour work day for a 2-hour meeting or an overnight stay. Aside from the productivity losses, the cost is absurd."

"Have you tried electronic mail?" asked Adrienne.

"Yes. We and Chempact signed up for MCI Mail. It's good to a point. It's such a generalized service, though, that it doesn't adapt too well to the way we'd like to work. It also doesn't do anything for the flow of documents through the project. Some of them go elsewhere in Envoyance, some of them go to Chempact, and some of them go to a couple of big paper mills in northern Maine where we're hoping to try out our ideas. With E-mail we can set up distribution lists, but that's about it."

"What kinds of documents do you send around?" Adrienne continued. "What are your meetings about? What types of decisions do you reach in them; what type of information do you share?

"That's a handful!" laughed Hakeem. "Let's see. As an example, let's take last Tuesday's meeting here. Three people came up from Chempact, by the way: their project manager, the marketing type who's talking to the paper mills, and one of their senior chemists. They must have spent over $2,000 on plane fare and nearly another $1,000 on rooms, meals, and ground transportation at both ends. Plus, none of them cared about all the topics, so you have to figure that about half their time was wasted. From our side, we had about four to six people in the room at any given moment. I was there for the whole day. A few others stuck around for most of the meetings. The rest went in and out depending on the topic. We went over four things:

"First, the project schedule. This mattered mostly to the project leaders on both sides. They contributed most of the discussion and made all of the decisions. These decisions all related to who will do what and when. The rest of the team was interested, of course, but primarily as observers. If they could have read a transcript of the discussion they would have been just about as happy.

"Second, we talked about how our discussions are going with the folks in Maine. There are, as I mentioned, two big paper mills up there we'd like to work with. If those discussions fall through, there are a lot of other paper mills around the country, but we'd want to line one up pretty soon. The decisions in this area relate primarily to financial incentives for them to cooperate in the R&D stage of the project. What we're offering is basically a head start and some cost savings in something they'll be involved with eventually anyhow. Our contact with the paper mills is primarily via Chempact, so this part of the meeting was basically them updating us on what's going on.

"The third part was us telling them about what the current legislative situation is with regard to water pollution, specifically rivers, and what's likely to change over the next few years. Our legislative expert, Steve Klein, keeps track of that. It would have been hard to do this by mail because he spent most of his time answering questions. There weren't any real decisions here, just noting what we had to keep in mind as we make technical decisions down the road.

"Finally, we had a fairly involved discussion of wastewater treatment chemistry. This involved a lot of diagrams and formulas. About half the group participated in this discussion, most of the rest listened, and a few didn't have a clue what it all meant.

"Anyhow, I was wondering if there is any way we could use computers and data communications to make it a bit less necessary to send people around."

Exercises

1. How could Envoyance and Chempact use *(a)* Lotus Notes, *(b)* Access Technologies's ForComment, and *(c)* ON Technology's Instant Update in this project?
2. How could Envoyance and Chempact use a work flow system?
3. Assume video teleconference equipment costs $50,000 per location including installation and a high-speed connection to the nearest telephone company local office, that Envoyance and Chempact are 1,200 miles apart, and that each is 10 miles from its local telephone company office.
   a. If a suitable high-speed telecommunications line for this use can be leased for $1 per mile per month, do you feel that the Chempact project could justify such equipment?
   b. What if, instead of leasing a line, they used high-speed dial-up lines? Assume these cost $20 per hour for the time period that a line is in use but cost nothing when they are not being used. The $50,000 cost of equipment and high-speed connections to the local telephone offices, per location, does not change.
   c. Contact a videoconferencing equipment supplier for their current prices and the types of communication lines their equipment requires. (Most such equipment can use a range of line speeds. The faster the line, the better the picture quality.) Then contact a long-distance telephone company for the current cost of leased and dial-up lines over the applicable range of data transmission speeds for a 1,200-mile distance. Answer parts *a* and *b* above using these actual figures.

CHAPTER 12

Executive Information Systems

Chapter Outline

Introduction

Executives are the top level of management in any organization. Typical executive titles include chairman, president, chief executive officer (CEO), executive or senior vice president, and vice president.[1] They are responsible for coordinating the activities of different parts of the firm and for setting its long-term strategic direction. Carrying out these responsibilities, which by their nature cannot be delegated, requires executives to make important decisions. They can benefit from the support of suitable information systems in making them. These *executive information systems* have a great deal in common with other types of decision support systems we have already learned about.

Chapter Objectives

After you have read and studied this chapter, you will be able to:

1. Identify how executives' decision-making needs differ from those of other employees.
2. Explain how executive informations systems (EIS) and executive support systems (ESS) support executive needs.
3. State reasons why executives use EIS.
4. Describe the characteristics and features of EIS.
5. Discuss the issues that arise when an EIS is introduced into an organization.
6. Outline steps you can take to ensure a successful EIS implementation.

[1]Some firms, especially in financial services, give out vice presidential titles more readily than others. The manager of a small branch bank or an outstanding stockbroker may be rewarded with it: It costs little, impresses clients, and may motivate the employee. These people are not executives in the sense of being top corporate managers. Their perspective and the decisions they make are those of middle managers or knowledge workers. The vice president of manufacturing in a traditional organization, however, would be an executive.

12.1 Who Are the Executives?

"The very rich . . . are different from you and me. . . . It does something to them . . . that . . . is very difficult to understand."[2]

What did Fitzgerald mean when he wrote those words? That the rich have more money? That's hardly news! What Fitzgerald meant (and went on to say in the rest of the paragraph) is that, when one gets used to having a lot of money, one's attitudes and perspective change. Most of us, if dissatisfied with our treatment in a store, would at most complain to the manager. A truly rich person might buy the store and fire the manager. Most people wouldn't even think of that as a theoretical option, let alone realize that they are barred from it only by relative lack of money.

So it is with executives. The term "executive" means the top managers of an organization. Viewed in the abstract, executives are simply one end of a continuum that begins with first-level supervisors and continues upward from there. However, when a certain level of management is reached—the precise level varies from organization to organization, indeed from person to person—a manager's perspective changes.

The most significant change of perspective from manager to executive is from a functional to a cross-functional view. Ideally, everyone in an organization should always have the good of the entire organization at heart. In practice, matters seldom work out that way. Engineering managers think about engineering, production managers think about production, marketing managers think about marketing. Even those whose jobs are supposedly cross functional, such as product managers who bring together the engineering, manufacturing, and marketing aspects of a particular product, tend to think about "their" product independently of—indeed, often in competition with—all the others.

The executive's view is broader. Some of the motivation for this changed perspective is financial. Top executives are often compensated in part on the basis of overall corporate or divisional performance. The heads of engineering and production will not try to cut the marketing budget if they know that the size of their next paycheck depends on successful marketing. As the saying goes, "There are no prizes for plowing a straight furrow if the crops don't come up." Other reasons for their broader view include the "team building" effect of executives' close daily interaction with the heads of other functional areas and their personal involvement in cross-functional decisions.

There are also differences in perspective that *can* properly be viewed as being at the end of a continuum. Decisions made at the *top* of an organization are typically relative to decisions made at lower levels, characterized by:

---

[2]F. Scott Fitzgerald, *All the Sad Young Men* (1926).

- Being less structured.
- Being less repetitive, hence less predictable.
- Having impact over a longer time period.
- Having a broader impact across parts of the organization (this and the previous point correspond to *strategic* decisions in the terminology of Section 2.3).
- Using more aggregated data and less detail data.
- Using more data from outside the organization.
- Requiring communication with more people.

This does not mean that all executive decisions have every stated characteristic or that no lower level decisions have any of them. Some executive decisions have a short-term impact. Sometimes lower level professionals make decisions that rely largely on external data. However, this list indicates the general trends. Executive decisions tend to have more of these characteristics, more often, than decisions made at lower levels.

Executives as a group also tend to be older than their subordinates, although both 35-year-old executives and 65-year-old nonexecutives exist. It takes some time to work one's way up through an organization, especially a stable one with decades of tradition. As a result, most top executives of the 1990s tend to be a bit less comfortable with computers than many of their younger subordinates are or, for that matter, than you are. There are many exceptions here as well—many older people are quite excited about technology—and this state of affairs will change during your career, but that is the general situation today.

Executives typically spend more of their time in meetings than do lower level staff members. Much of their meeting time is devoted to gathering internal and external information. Prior to the meeting, this information is tailored to the executive's needs by lower level managers. They know that their career prospects depend on making a good impression on their superiors and are willing to devote considerable effort to accomplishing that. If executives are to use a computer system, it must provide needed information effectively and must also tailor its presentation to the executive's requirements.

12.2 What Is an Executive Information System?

An information system intended specifically to support top executives is called an *executive information system* (EIS) or an *executive support system* (ESS). Some people use the two terms interchangeably. There is, however, a difference. An executive information system is a one-way system, providing information to the executive for his or her decision-making needs. An executive support system incorporates additional capabilities, such as a rapid interface to an electronic mail system, that often come in handy when information is being analyzed. A complete executive support system may also include modeling and/or expert systems capabilities, which go beyond the pure EIS that merely provides information for the executive's use. An ESS, while potentially more valuable to its users than a "mere" EIS, requires a strong EIS as its foundation.

Since executive decisions have the characteristics listed in the previous section, information systems that are designed to support those decisions must be designed to accommodate those characteristics. Consistent with that list, an information system for executives' use should generally be

- Cross functional, rather than limited to a single aspect of the organization, since the executive's perspective is cross functional.
- Data oriented, since the executive's decisions typically do not have much structure and are usually not repeated regularly enough to justify developing complex models.
- Summary in nature, since most executive decisions do not require the use of much detail. (Some executives like to see it, or at least to know it is available.)
- Graphically oriented, since graphs can provide sufficient precision for most purposes when detail is not needed.
- Communication based, both to obtain data from outside the organization and to facilitate exchanging information with people inside it.
- Highly customized to the executive's individual preferences. Executives are at the end point of the continuum noted at the beginning of Section 6.3. We saw there that DSS justify more customization than transaction processing or information reporting systems do. The reasons apply even more strongly to information systems meant to support top executives: There are fewer of them than there are decision makers overall, they are paid more than other managers or knowledge workers, and their decisions typically have a higher impact on the organization than do those of other staff members.

12.3 Why Use an EIS (or ESS)?

Executives have many reasons to use an EIS (or ESS). The type of system that you design and develop for them ought to reflect the needs of the executives who will use it. (If it doesn't, executives will be even more vocal about their displeasure, even more quick to toss it out, than lower level managers would have been.) One list of reasons includes the following criteria [GULD88]:

- To solve specific problems in either decision making or control.
- To boost the executive's personal work efficiency.
- To facilitate change in the organization, either strategic change or reorganization.
- To "send a signal" to subordinates.
- To gain computer literacy.

One of the earliest executives to use a computer intensively in his work—or at least to go public with his using one—was chairman Ben W. Heineman of Northwest Industries, a diversified firm based in Minneapolis.[3] Heineman began using a terminal to monitor his nine operating units in 1976. Rockart and Treacy reported on his experience in detail in [ROCK82]. Heineman's motivations included several of the items on this list: sending a signal, facilitating change, and solving control problems.

The reason for which an executive wants to use an EIS or ESS leads directly to the capabilities that the system must provide. Gaining computer literacy might call for allowing the user to manipulate data directly, perhaps via a spreadsheet or a query language. Sending a signal may require little beyond highly visible use of something. Facilitating change generally involves communication capability. Boosting personal work efficiency and solving specific problems depend on software tailored either to the executive's existing work bottlenecks or the specific problems in question.

As EIS expert James Wetherbe points out, finding out what executives want isn't quite as simple as asking them [WETH89]. Executives can't articulate their needs any more than DSS users could in Chapter 5. There, prototyping was a big part of the answer. Prototyping works with EIS as well, but you must approach it differently. You will not, in most cases, be able to get a top executive to sit down with you for half a day each week trying out options, waiting patiently as you modify a line of code here or tweak a screen definition there. Multiply the time investment that traditional prototyping demands of prospective users by the number of top executives in an organization, and the approach quickly becomes impractical. We'll revisit the use of prototyping when we discuss EIS implementation in Section 12.7.

The classical Heineman-era EIS was devoted largely to tracking and control. It focused on internal, historical information. Its purpose was to give its user instantaneous visibility into any part of the organization. Its major limitations were *(a)* that it incorporated little if any external data and *(b)* that its

---

[3]Unrelated to Northwest Airlines, although some articles (and at least one book!) on EIS confuse them—perhaps because they were, coincidentally, based in the same city. Northwest Industries was sold to Farley Industries in 1985 and no longer exists.

user interface was constrained by the hardware of that day. Current EIS improve on both of these.

12.4 EIS Characteristics

12.4.1 General Features

Several features are common to most EIS and to every popular package designed for EIS development:

- The database includes what Rockart and Treacy [ROCK82] called the *data cube:* historical information broken down by descriptive variable, time period, and business unit (product line, geographic division, or whatever else is appropriate.) For instance, an executive should be able to review sales volume (the descriptive variable) of product X (the business unit) for the last 12 months (time periods). The EIS database should go beyond the internal data cube, which tends to be internally focused. Much of the real value of an EIS comes from accessing external data. The cube is still an appropriate way to visualize some types of external data, such as market share by competitor, price segment, and (again) time period.
- Graphical user interfaces (see Section 5.3.2) let executives select the areas they want to review. Figure 12–1 shows a typical EIS screen. The P&L Review button, if clicked, might show a U.S. map indicating the sales regions for which P&L data are available. Each region is defined to the EIS as a *hot spot.* A mouse click on any part of this map can bring up data for the region in question. Other options, accessed via other hot spots on the screen, might include more detailed geographic analyses, analyses by product, and whatever else the data cube supports. Still other hot spots, usually identified by suitable graphics, access additional capabilities such as electronic mail or the executive's personal appointment calendar.
- Positional input is provided to activate the hot spots. The usual device is a mouse, but touch screens and mouse replacements such as trackballs are possible alternatives. A keyboard is still present, however, as some types of input are best entered this way. (Entering the text of an electronic mail message, even a brief one, by pointing at letters on a screen is not a constructive way for executives to spend their time.)
- Users can *drill down* through interesting items of data in increasing levels of detail. An executive who needs more information on sales in the western region might be able to get a breakdown by product, by sales office, or any other category that the data cube supports. A well-designed EIS screen will indicate what information is "drillable."

FIGURE 12–1
Opening EIS Screen Shot

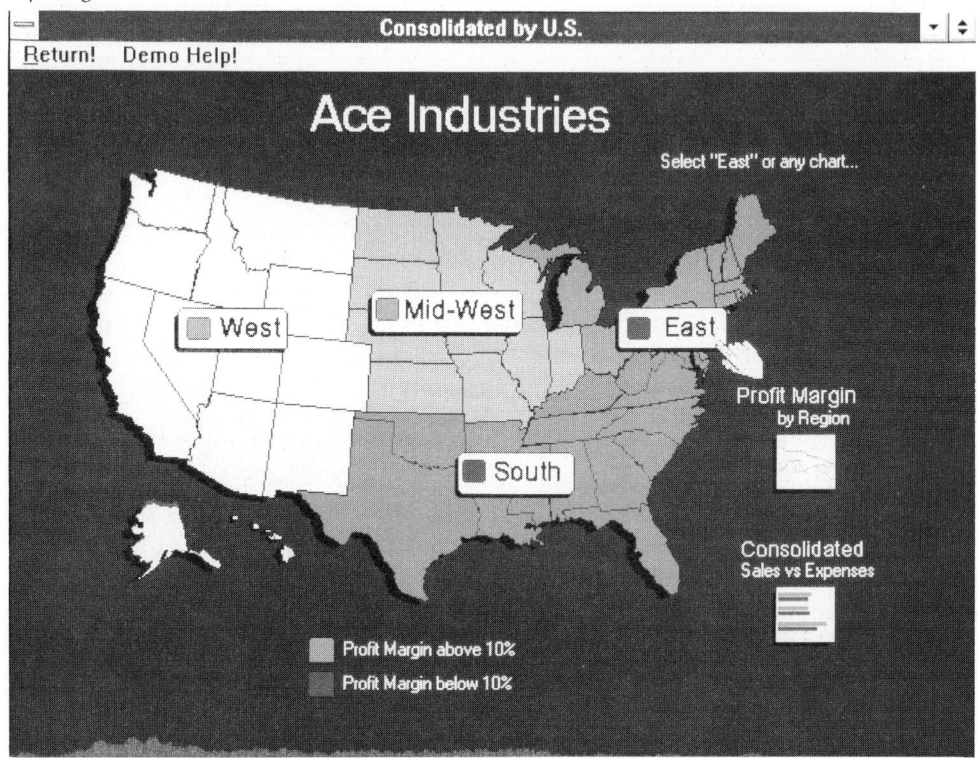

- Exceptions are highlighted by the use of color.[4] Red, for example, often indicates that an item is below its acceptable performance limit. Most EIS allow the designer to specify tolerance levels for exception conditions. The EIS package uses these levels to apply color (or shading, or blinking, or boldface text, or . . .) dynamically, depending on the value that the data item in question has when the screen is created. A given data element may appear in yellow one day, in red or green the next, based solely on changes in the database.
- The delivery vehicle is typically a personal computer, linked through a telecommunications channel (local or wide area) to the corporate database. Terminals tied directly to the central computer, be it mainframe or minicomputer, generally do not provide the easy-to-use

[4]Keep in mind, however, the cautions about color stated in Section 5.5.1.

FIGURE 12–2

Spectrum of Hard versus Soft EIS Information

Hard ◄						► *Soft*
Financial statements	News reports	Schedules	Explanations	Predictions	Opinions	Rumors
Statistics	Industry trends	Formal plans	Justifications	Speculations	Feelings	Gossip
Historical information	Survey data		Assessments	Forecasts	Ideas	Hearsay
			Interpretations	Estimates		

interface that executives insist on. What's more, the computational effort of providing even a part of that interface can be carried out far more cost effectively on a micro.

In addition to internal corporate information, many EIS also access two other types of information:

- "Soft" information, such as comments, opinions, and predictions [WATS92]. This type of information, in text form that can be searched via key words or linked to fields in the database, can help executives spot trends and understand what is behind the numbers. Figure 12–2, from [DIX92], shows the types of information that executives can access via an EIS. You can see that the soft information, while its accuracy varies and it is not standardized in content or format, can be of great importance in making strategic decisions.
- External information, that is, information not available from internal corporate databases. This includes, for example, news reports on a firm's industry and its competitors. Public databases provide the full text of leading papers such as the *New York Times* and *The Wall Street Journal* within 24 hours of their publication, and often sooner. Earnings data, market research data, and government economic data are likewise available. (Much of this information is "soft" in the sense of the previous paragraph.) EIS can be programmed to access these news services automatically on a periodic basis, load reports of a particular type or about a particular subject, and make them available through the standard EIS interface.

12.4.2 EIS Design Approaches

Leading EIS packages take two fundamentally different design approaches within the preceding general parameters. In one approach, the executive's workstation operates on line to the database that drives the EIS. In the other, the workstation accesses a predetermined, often summarized, selection from that database.

In considering EIS packages, it is important to remember that the software package is not the EIS itself. It is a base for the eventual EIS. An organization cannot install an EIS package on its computers, sit an executive down in front of a terminal or PC, and expect anything useful to occur. The databases that the EIS is to access must be defined to it, the access paths to those databases (network paths, file directories, etc.) described, screen displays defined, and the interface dialogue specified. These are jobs for an information systems professional. Using an EIS package makes it much easier to create a finished EIS than it would be without the package, which is why such packages are used in most corporate EIS, but a package is not a usable product in the same sense that a word processing package can be.

In the on-line mode of operation, the EIS is essentially an easy-to-use query system tied to a database. A user request for sales data for the Chicago office would create a query to the database to retrieve the required information. This information would then be displayed in tabular or graphical form as appropriate. The query itself is coded ahead of time by professional programmers: either in its entirety or as a template into which the supporting EIS software can insert parameters based on each specific request. For instance, an EIS might have a prewritten query that can obtain sales summary data for any region. It would fill in the name of a specific region before sending the query to the database.

Most systems of this type are linked directly to the live corporate database, but this is not a requirement. If system load warrants and executives' timeliness requirements permit, an EIS can operate in on-line mode from a static information base. Its data are thus only as current as the most recent update of that information base. As with the next mode of operation, this is often current enough.

In the off-line mode of operation, all possible queries are issued to the database during a period of light system load, typically during the wee hours of the morning. The data are extracted and the screens prepared for display at users' desks. Those screens are stored in a screen library, which the EIS accesses. That library can be kept at the central system or sent to the server of the LAN to which an executive's desktop computer is attached. It can even be loaded onto the disk of a single PC: a useful feature for users who would like to review data on a laptop computer while traveling. When a user asks for specific information, the corresponding screen is retrieved immediately from the EIS screen database and displayed. No computation is required, other than interpreting the condensed form in which the screen is stored. (Storing information about each dot on a large color screen would occupy an undesirably large amount of disk space.)

The "off-line approach" is actually a spectrum of approaches. Some off-line EIS do their own data retrieval, organization, analysis, and presentation. Others, such as IBM's Executive Decisions, provide a repository for screens created by other applications. Executive Decisions can activate these applications, import the screens they create, organize them for easy access, and provide a uniform interface to both this collection and to supporting capabilities such as electronic mail. It is easy to "put down" this approach as an "electronic slide show." It is not a complete solution to executives' information needs, but it does not claim to be. It does provide a useful capability and should not be dismissed out of hand.

It is hard to get an objective view of the pros and cons of the two by listening to their vendor proponents. The waters are quickly muddied in a flurry of buzzwords and thinly veiled (or totally unveiled) slurs on the competence of anyone who would choose the other approach, such as the "electronic slide show" put-down phrase in the previous paragraph. The facts of the matter are, as usual, that each approach has its advantages and its drawbacks.

In favor of the on-line approach:

- All displayed data are as current as the database permits.
- No effort is wasted creating screens that will never be seen; no disk space is wasted storing them.
- Because queries are generated as the executive is at the computer, it is possible to accommodate previously unplanned needs, especially if the executive is somewhat computer literate or is willing to learn the rudiments of an elementary 4GL.

In favor of the off-line approach:

- The daytime load on the central computer, when load is important, is lower. (More total work is done, but most of it takes place when the computer would otherwise be idle.)
- Response time is better.
- The EIS information base is portable; the screen library can be loaded into a laptop computer for review on a plane or sent to a remote server for access by divisional staff without needing a continuous link to the central host.
- In most cases, data that are current through the previous day suffice for executive decision making. Comshare, a major proponent of the off-line approach, points out that the executive's traditional paper "briefing book" was seldom current to within 24 hours.

EIS suppliers are not stupid. No matter what approach they took in the past with their initial product, they realize that there are situations for which the other is better suited and that some of their sales prospects will be in that category. They have therefore incorporated characteristics of the other approach into their products. Vendors of on-line systems offer the ability to create a selected set of screens in the background and to access them rather than the database itself. Vendors of off-line systems offer the capability to redraw a selected set of slides at any time on request, rather than waiting until 3 o'clock tomorrow morning. An MIS professional faced with any current system can, if absolutely necessary, force it to work in either mode. The fact remains that each system still tends to have a preferred mode of operation and is more awkward to use in the other one.

12.5 EIS Issues

Several issues and problems typically arise in firms that attempt to put executive information systems in place. Most can be avoided with proper planning.

These issues overlap the implementation issues we covered in Chapter 8, but there are differences between systems that involve senior managers and others. This section provides a pure EIS focus on key issues to clarify and pitfalls to avoid.

12.5.1 Who Is the User?

EIS, as the concept originally evolved, were designed to provide information that top executives need for their decisions. It was soon recognized that this information is also of interest to lower level personnel. Furthermore, this interest is not merely idle curiosity: Seeing overall corporate data, while perhaps not vital to the day-to-day performance of their assigned tasks, helps encourage the strategic, cross-functional perspective that is so often lacking below the top level of the firm.

As a result, observers are now suggesting that the letters EIS stand for "Employee Information System" [KADO91], "Everybody's Information System" [Cliff Conneighton, quoted in WALL91] or even "Easy Information System" [KLEI93]. Firms such as Citicorp's U.S. Card Products Group have made EIS information available to first-level supervisors to help them identify top performers and implement an appropriate pay system. United HealthCare of Minnetonka, Minnesota, even provides customers with access to its EIS for a fee so they can review their own claim experience and put programs in place to improve it. Others, such as Metropolitan Life's pension division, are not going that far but are pushing EIS use down below its original target group. Sunstrand Corporation of Rockford, Illinois, is expanding its EIS user community from the original 35—including data providers and support staff—to include 60 manufacturing managers. Similarly, Tropicana Products of Bradenton, Florida, has distributed access to its EIS to its regional offices throughout the United States. Some suppliers of EIS packages are repositioning them as "managerial application systems" (Commander, from Comshare) or "visual information access and analysis" (Lightship, from Pilot).

A widely used EIS cannot be customized for each user to the degree that a system that supports a handful of highly paid top executives can be. However, it can provide the same information. The incremental cost to do this is relatively low: The new users are already computerized and networked, the software has been purchased, the screens and queries have been defined, and the database links are already in place. Users increasingly have the required desktop resources—specifically, a microcomputer capable of running a graphically oriented package, generally under a GUI-oriented operating system—on their desktops. All that remains is the cost of using the system: mainframe resources, network load. These factors suggest that a broad-based EIS may favor the off-line EIS approach, as additional users add less to the peak computing load with that type of EIS than they do in the on-line approach. This is far from a rigid rule. Each situation has its own unique considerations.

12.5.2 The EIS Sponsor

Whether the EIS is intended strictly for top executives, for anyone in the firm who has an interest in its subject matter, or somewhere in between, it is unlikely to succeed unless it has a powerful *sponsor* or *champion*. In this it resembles expert systems as we'll discuss them in Section 18.4, except that the two roles merge when it comes to EIS: Since EIS are meant to be used at a high level in the organization, a person whose problem an EIS is intended to solve will also have the clout to make things happen. Also, the EIS technology is not so new and unfamiliar that it must be "championed" against other approaches to solving the same problem.

As Thomas McCarthy of Bankers Trust Company writes in [MCCA92]:

> A champion is the executive who says "I want this!" (occasionally accompanied by fist-pounding on the table). "I'm interested" or "why don't we take a look" aren't good enough to indicate the level of commitment required. . . . Would-be EIS initiators and project managers should be absolutely certain in this regard. . . . Without a *bona fide* EIS champion, the successful implementation of an EIS is an immensely difficult undertaking.

In the case of Northwest Industries referred to earlier, Ben Heineman met all the qualifications for a sponsor or champion. Despite his example, few other Northwest executives used it extensively, and those few only in self-defense against "zingers" from the top. It fell into disuse on Heineman's retirement and was scrapped soon after.[5] This is not unusual.

As Rockart and De Long explain, the sponsor of an EIS has three responsibilities that cannot generally be delegated [ROCK88]:

[5]In terms of the DSS implementation issues discussed in Chapter 8, we can see in retrospect that Heinemann didn't pay much attention to unfreezing, moving, and refreezing. He may have felt that, for his purposes, it didn't matter. CEOs can take this attitude. The rest of us generally can't.

1. To make the initial request for the system. Even if the motivation comes from elsewhere, the sponsor must put his or her name and prestige behind the formal request. This is a one-time effort that takes little time.
2. To stay on top of system development, providing overall direction and feedback on specifics. This takes an on-going commitment of time and energy.
3. To communicate strong and continuing interest to those who must support, who must contribute to, or who will be expected to use the system. This is an on-going effort as well, although it does not require large amounts of dedicated time.

When the EIS sponsor is a chief executive, the second of these responsibilities may become too time consuming for him or her to carry out properly. In that case, some of this responsibility (but only this one!) can be delegated to what Rockart and De Long call an *operating sponsor:* a trusted subordinate recognized as representing the executive sponsor and typically having a high level of personal influence or authority in the organization as well. When an operating sponsor is present, Rockart and De Long use the term *executive sponsor* for the person whom we have simply called a sponsor until now.

12.5.3 Cost of the EIS

The proof that EIS are expensive is that *USA Today* found their cost worth mentioning: They reported in 1989 that "the final bill can easily exceed $500,000 per user" [LEWY89]. A study by the University of Georgia, College of Business Administration's Department of Management reported in [WATS91] didn't find $500,000 per user, but it did find that much for the first year of a system's life: an average of $450,000 to develop the average EIS in their survey plus another $223,000 per year, forever, to operate it. These costs are increasing: their survey of two years earlier, reported in [RYAN89], found $365,000 and $208,000 for these two figures, respectively. This may understate the true cost since most survey respondents who estimate the cost of a system only include costs uniquely associated with that system. For example, respondents would typically report the visible cost of executive workstations and purchased EIS software packages but not the hidden costs of the mainframe and network resources used to support them. Furthermore, as Brandel points out in [BRAN91], you cannot save much by using LAN and microcomputer-based EIS: Computer hardware is but a fraction of true EIS cost, and even using the cheapest hardware doesn't eliminate this cost entirely.

The combination of high cost and intangible benefits makes EIS hard to justify on a pure financial basis, but with proper sponsorship such justification may not be necessary. Altieri cites an example in which an EIS required the efforts of 10 full-time and 10 part-time staff, plus its supporting hardware and networks, to support just 7 executives [ALTI90]. Rough calculations can tell us that this system must cost the firm at least $100,000 per year per user—yet the information systems group has never had to cost justify the system or worry about its budget being cut. One executive reported, in 1989, that "this system has already paid for itself well into the 1990s."

Systems that have many characteristics of EIS, however, can be put together on a more limited budget. Tools such as Apple's HyperCard or Asymetrix's ToolBook, which we discussed in Section 5.3.3, can be used to create attractive graphical front ends to many types of databases quickly and easily. Spreadsheet packages, backed up by macros or "add-ins" to access a database, can serve the same purpose. While their interface does not qualify as attractive, it is widely familiar. Several packages with an EIS-related purpose have been made available for microcomputers [KINL92]. The key factor in developing a "budget EIS" is giving it a well-defined, narrow focus: order information for the top 20 customers, quality data for the production line, or, as in [OLEA91], POS (point-of-sale)-gathered sales and inventory data for the Calvert's $35 million chain of three off-price retail clothing stores. Don't plan to roll out a broad-based, large-company EIS on a shoestring with the expectation that funds to enhance it will be forthcoming. A more likely result, as Burkan points out, will be executive disappointment with the system followed by shrinking, not expanding, support [BURK91].

12.5.4 *Management Resistance to the EIS*

As Niccolò Machiavelli pointed out centuries ago—and as we mentioned in Chapter 8—few people have much to gain from change but many have much to lose from it and will resist it tooth and nail. Rockart and De Long point out that the same is true of EIS [ROCK88]. One way of assessing the likelihood of resistance is by the grid in Figure 12–3, which they credit to Gary Gulden of the Index Group. Most resistance will come from people in the top left quadrant of this grid: those who are familiar with the business (or think they are!) and who don't see why anything has to change. This resistance to change can come from four groups of people, each with their own reasons:

1. Staff personnel who feel treatened in their roles as "gatekeepers" of critical corporate data supplied to top executives. This type of resistance can

FIGURE 12–3

2 × 2 EIS Attitude Grid

		Familiarity with the business	
		High	*Low*
Perceived need for change	*Low*	Resistance	Attraction
	High	Indifference	Desire

be overcome through education, showing them that their skills will still be valuable—indeed, may be even more valuable. This process is culture dependent and can take several months of deliberate effort.

2. Subordinate managers who fear giving top management too much visibility into their operations, perhaps because they don't want to be "hassled" with detailed questions. Sensitive limits on the use of internal data can be an effective way to deal with this form of resistance. It can also be overcome by top management fiat, but that is a last resort; it can hurt morale and result in simply pushing the resistance underground.

3. Line or staff managers whose legitimate (as Rockart and De Long consider it) resistance is based on, "The business is doing fine, why change?," "This system is all costs and no benefits for my group," or "Our executives won't have the context to understand the data we send them." This type of resistance can often be dealt with openly by discussing how the system can benefit the people in question or by adding features that will benefit them.

4. Executives who don't want to use the technology themselves but fear they will be pressured into using it or suffer from not using it. It may be best not to force them to use it: If the EIS is truly valuable, they will soon realize this and "get on board."

None of these approaches to overcoming resistance is perfect. All require compromises on everyone's part. Your sponsor often has a key role to play in this area and should be willing to play it.

12.5.5 Employee Resistance to the EIS

As we noted earlier, EIS allow their users to sit in the executive suite and drill down to increasing levels of detail about organizational activity. A corporate CEO might, for example, compare sales across the firm's four worldwide sales divisions. If North America is underperforming the other three, this executive could then look at its four regions. With the laggard identified, the president might now look at the six sales offices in that region. The low office comes in for further scrutiny, as a result of which one poor below-quota salesperson is singled out for a personal "EXACTLY WHAT IS WRONG WITH YOU?" message from this infinitely remote, august personage.

This is, clearly, an extreme (and extremely unlikely) scenario. Yet the fear of it exists and is normal. To guard against this fear, many EIS can be configured with limits on drill-down. A typical limit is three levels. The CEO described above, were such a limit in place, would not be able to look below a North American region in person. To get data from inside the region, he or she would have to request the data from someone such as the regional sales director. This intermediary would be better known to the regional staff. An inquiry from him or her will therefore be perceived as less threatening to the individual salespeople. The regional director would also be more aware of unique situations that may not be obvious in the raw data, such as that salesperson's recent return to work after recuperating from major surgery. Such limits, if well publicized, can help prevent EIS-related morale problems.

12.6 From EIS to ESS

A full executive support system encompasses more than the access to an information base that an EIS provides. The term ESS generally implies at least these additional capabilities:

- Telecommunications within the firm. ESS generally provide a clean interface to an electronic mail package via which the ESS user can send a quick message to anyone else on the network. ESS displays can be attached to the messages: for example, to send a data table along with a comment or question about a specific data element. Electronic mail helps avoid the "telephone tag" that plagues attempts to reach busy managers and can be especially valuable in communicating across several time zones.

  Most ESS, in common with the electronic mail systems that they incorporate, still require use of the keyboard as an input device. Both voice annotation and handwritten notes (using a special pen on a special tablet) are feasible, however, and will come into increasingly wide use. Such pioneering tools as Wang Freestyle, while not itself an EIS, already support both of these.

  Electronic mail can also be the foundation for an external information gathering facility. An application running on the central computer can scan external news files, such as those made available on line by Dow Jones, for articles that match an executive's interest profile. It can then forward these to the executive's electronic mailbox. This can be a great time saver, especially when someone comes back from a two-week trip and would otherwise have to read 10 back issues of *The Wall Street Journal* to find the same articles.
- Other office automation tools: calendar management, "electronic Rolodex," personal information filing and management. Some executives find these useful while others prefer their paper equivalents. Calendars, in particular, can be sensitive. Nobody seriously argues the potential benefits of having several co-workers' calendars on line so meetings can be scheduled and plans made. Still, many people, including top executives, don't like the idea of other people seeing their calendars. They may fear being seen as not busy enough, as spending too much time in meetings, or as taking Thursday afternoon off to play golf. As a partial solution to this nontechnical issue, some calendar packages inform other system users when one is busy but not what one is doing at those times.

- Data analysis capabilities. The ESS user can combine, consolidate, and manipulate data to yield insight into its implications. The spreadsheet model is a popular approach to this capability, as it is increasingly well known to computer-literate executives. An ESS may also provide shortcuts to particularly common manipulations, such as trend analysis and time-series forecasting. Beyond that, it may incorporate situation-specific models developed by MIS professionals to meet the executives' needs.

12.7 Implementing EIS/ESS

Understanding what an EIS or ESS is about is of little practical use unless you can put one in place successfully. Success in this case is defined simply: It means that the top executives of your organization use the system regularly and feel that it helps them do their jobs well. These steps can help you achieve a successful EIS or ESS implementation:

1. Identify a sponsor—ideally, more than one sponsor. If a single sponsor leaves, the system is likely to be orphaned. Aside from what that means to the organization, being associated with it under those circumstances won't help your career.

You may have to cultivate a sponsor. Talk to the high-likelihood candidates. Discuss what an EIS could do for them. You will probably generate enough enthusiasm in one or more to proceed.

2. Find out why your sponsor(s) is(are) interested in the EIS, what their motivations are. Use the list in Section 12.3 as a guide. This information will help you design the EIS that they need, not the one you think you would need if you had their jobs.

Rockart's Critical Success Factors (CSF) method is a good way to find out what they need [ROCK79]. If you haven't studied CSF yet, they are, in effect, the first few items an executive will want to know on the day he or she returns from a three-week vacation.

3. Pick one topic, or a few topics, that are vitally important to your sponsor or sponsors. Do those topics well. Having a useful tool early is better than having a complete tool later, or a broad but shallow one early.

Pick really important topics. Presenting easily obtained information in a "prototype" will create executive yawns and lack of support for expanding the system. As Burkan points out, a limited pilot may give an impression of "that's all there is" without creating the vision of EIS capabilities that will generate full support [BURK91].

4. Recognize and respect the corporate culture. Does it believe in centralization or in decentralization of authority? What are the power relationships

between line and staff groups? Is it frugal—"lean and mean"—or willing to spend on appearances?

> A system that does not fit the culture cannot possibly succeed, whatever its theoretical benefits or technical merit. If the culture is biased toward sharing information among all members of the organization, a system that emphasizes giving a few top managers new-found power is courting disaster.

5. Define your expectations: What people will use the system? How many of them? How will they use it? How will you know if it is successful?

> Establishing this vision will not control the future. Things change. However, success is next to impossible if you don't know what success consists of.

6. Make sure enough resources are in place. Despite the earlier example of Calvert's, most EIS do require a substantial investment. This is especially true in large firms, which are not quite as used to "shoestring" projects as a small store chain like Calvert's would be.

> Burkan suggests a representative 10-month timeline to implement an EIS: 4 months until the first five executives are on line, the next 6 to expand the system and broaden its user community [BURK91]. This schedule will be feasible only if the data sources are in place and accessible, if the EIS runs on a familiar hardware/software platform, and if it will not be necessary to integrate several software packages to create the total system.

7. Define your data requirements. At the conceptual level, they will follow directly from the information your EIS will provide. Unfortunately, your firm is not likely to have a central database that contains all the required data in a consistent format that is usable by an EIS package. You will have to deal with data in incompatible files, data that aren't (yet) on the computer, and data that don't even come from within your organization.

> As Rockart and De Long write, "an EIS is only as good as the data it makes available" [ROCK88]. Finding and importing the necessary data is a major chore for many EIS. Taking the easy way out, using only easily available data, usually results in little more than historical financial and sales data. This is unlikely to hold top executives' interest for long. More than one EIS project has been the catalyst for converting to modern data administration and database administration methodologies.

8. Define your communications requirements. Where do the databases reside? How can they be accessed? What external databases must you access? Where are the executives? Are they networked—and, if so, how? What servers do their networks have in place, if any? What communication links exist among all these? Will their capacity suffice for the EIS load?

> This point and the next one are interdependent, as your network requirements will depend in part on the specific package you choose.

9. Pick the package(s) to meet your needs. You probably studied package selection in your MIS course: developing checklists; issuing a request for

proposals; evaluating responses, demonstrations, or benchmarks, etc. The same process applies here. The Kepner-Tregoe decision-making method, discussed in Section 2.6, may help you.

There will be trade-offs; for example, the package with the most features may be old and therefore not designed for client/server operation. The best package may actually be a combination of more than one package: perhaps one for in-depth financial analysis capabilities and another for its great graphics.

10. Develop a prototype and have some executives try it out. If the prototype is based on easily available data, try to limit its exposure to executives who are already enthusiastic about the system being developed and whose enthusiasm will not be dampened by the prototype's limited repertoire.

An EIS is, in a sense, always a prototype: It keeps evolving and expanding. However, it is important to make sure that the version first rolled out for widespread scrutiny provides real value to its users.

11. Be ready to train the users, to support them and the system for a long time to come. As they use the system, they will ask for more features, more analysis, more data. Be ready to supply them.

There is a positive relationship between the power of any tool and its complexity. One cannot pilot a Boeing 767 with the user interface of a tricycle. Well-designed screens will keep the need for technical training to a minimum but can never reduce it to zero. The technical sophistication of your user community may affect the design of your EIS.

Summary

An executive information system is an information system that provides information to top executives to support their decision-making needs. An executive support system adds communication and analysis capabilities to the underlying executive information system.

Executives' decision support needs differ from those of lower level managers because executive decisions are typically less structured, less repetitive, more strategic, less detail oriented, and more externally focused than those of other managers. These factors lead to several common requirements that apply to most or all EIS: they should be cross functional, data oriented, summary in nature, graphically oriented, communication based, and customized to the needs of the individual executive.

In line with these needs, most custom and package-based EIS incorporate the following features: they incorporate a historical "data cube," they have a graphical user interface with positional input to activate "hot spots," they provide a "drill-down" capability, they use color, and the executive accesses them via a personal computer. In addition, many incorporate both "soft" information and external information. EIS can operate in either of two modes: directly on line to their database or via prestored screens.

Reasons for using executive information systems include solving specific problems in decision making or control, boosting the executive's personal work efficiency, facilitating change in the organization, sending a signal to subordinates, and gaining computer literacy. More and more systems are going beyond these original reasons and are providing EIS-type support to many nonexecutives, as the type of information contained in an EIS can be valuable to other decision makers as well.

EIS developers must be conscious of *(a)* the need for a committed EIS sponsor, *(b)* the likely high cost of the EIS, *(c)* potential management resistance to the EIS, and *(d)* potential employee resistance to the EIS. To deal with these factors and implement a successful EIS, you should identify a sponsor, identify your sponsor's motivations to use an EIS, define your expectations within your corporate culture, pick one or a few initial topics that are important to your sponsor and do them well, define your data and communications requirements, make sure enough resources are in place, pick packages to support your EIS, develop a prototype, and prepare to offer the necessary user training.

Key Terms

champion 396
Critical Success Factor (CSF) 401
data cube 390
drill-down 390
executive 385
executive information system (EIS) 387
executive support system (ESS) 387
hot spot 390
off-line EIS 393
on-line EIS 393
operating sponsor 397
sponsor 396

Review Questions

1. What is an executive? A nonexecutive? Give typical position titles.
2. How does the executive's viewpoint typically differ from that of a nonexecutive?
3. How do executives' decisions typically differ from those of nonexecutives?
4. What is the difference between an EIS and an ESS? What do they both have in common?
5. What characteristics should an information system for executives' use possess?

6. Why do executives use EIS (or ESS)?
7. What features are common to most EIS?
8. What is the "data cube?"
9. What is "soft" information? Why is external information often soft?
10. How do the on-line and off-line approaches to EIS design differ?
11. Give at least three reasons in favor of both approaches to EIS design.
12. What is an EIS sponsor? Why is it important to have one?
13. How does the typical cost of an EIS compare with that of a microcomputer spreadsheet package?
14. Why might some managers resist an EIS? Some nonmanagement employees?
15. What features can be added to an EIS to create an ESS?
16. List several steps you can take to increase the likelihood of a successful EIS project.

Exercises

1. Consider the definition of an EIS at the beginning of Section 12.2. If an EIS is a type of DSS, where does it fall in the seven DSS categories?
2. Section 12.3 gives a list of reasons why executives use EIS. Relate each reason to the DSS benefits of Section 1.4.
3. You run a nationwide chain of retail stores selling men's shirts. Define at least six dimensions your data cube (Section 12.4.1) could have.
4. In Section 12.5.2, we mentioned that few Northwest Industries executives other than Heineman used the EIS he had put in place. This took place in the late 1970s and early 1980s. Do you think the same thing would happen today? Why or why not?
5. In section 12.5.3, we mentioned a figure of "at least $100,000 per year per user." Carry out the "rough calculations" required to reach this conclusion.
6. Consider developing an EIS for the top management of your college or university.
   a. Who would your target users be? Be specific. Use actual names and titles: "Chancellor Hogan, Provost Rudenstine, Dean DiLuna . . ."
   b. Whom would you try to get as your sponsor? From what you know (or can find out) of this person, how responsive do you think he or she would be?
   c. What sort of information would you make available through the EIS? (Think about the key issues that top administrators face.) What summaries would you provide? Would each be a table, a graph, or the user's choice of either format?

d. Would up-to-yesterday data suffice to drive this EIS, or would it need on-line access to the current database?
e. Would you put any limits on what top administrators could see in terms of student data? staff personnel data? other types of data?
f. What sort of external databases could be useful for your EIS? (Use your library resources to find out what kinds of public databases exist.)
g. What telecommunications capabilities would your EIS call for? Beyond them, what could you usefully add? (Find out what facilities, such as electronic mail, exist at your institution today and how much the top administrators use them.)

7. What is the connection between the third (recognize and respect the corporate culture) and the fourth (make sure enough resources are in place) steps in the EIS implementation process in Section 12.7?

References

ALTI90 Altieri, Raymond P. "A Memo to the EIS User." *Information Center* 6, no. 2 (February 1990), pp. 10–11.

BRAN91 Brandel, Mary. "Executive Information Systems." *Computerworld* 25, no. 29 (July 22, 1991), pp. 67–71.

BURK91 Burkan, Wayne C. *Executive Information Systems: From Proposal Through Implementation.* Van Nostrand Reinhold, New York (1991).

DIX92 Dix, Lory Zottola. "A Bunch of Softies." *Computerworld* 26, no. 42 (October 19, 1992), p. 105.

GULD88 Gulden, Gary K., and Douglas E. Ewers. "The Keys to Successful Executive Support Systems." *Indications* 5, no. 5 (September–October 1988), pp. 1–5; also published in slightly different form as "Is Your ESS Meeting the Need?" *Computerworld* 23, no. 28 (July 10, 1989), pp. 85–88.

KADO91 Kador, John. "Have EIS Abandoned the Executive?" *Information Center Quarterly* 7, no. 4 (Fall 1991), p. 40.

KINL92 Kinlan, Jim. "EIS Moves to the Desktop." *Byte* 17, no. 6 (June 1992), pp. 206–12.

KLEI93 Klein, Paula. "Make That 'Easy Info System.' " *Information Week* no. 413 (February 22, 1993), pp. 58–62.

LEWY89 Lewyn, Mark. "Computers Easing Workloads in More Executive Suites." *USA Today* (August 23, 1989).

MCCA92 McCarthy, Thomas M. "Tales from the EIS Trenches" (in "The Expert's Opinion" section). *Information Resources Management Journal* 5, no. 1 (Winter 1992), pp. 35–38.

OLEA91 O'Leary, Meghan. "Selling Points." *CIO* 5, no. 4 (November 15, 1991), pp. 26–30.

ROCK79 Rockart, John F. "Chief Executives Define Their Own Data Needs." *Harvard Business Review* 57, no. 2 (March–April 1979), pp. 81–93.

ROCK82 Rockart, John F., and Michael E. Treacy. "The Ceo Goes On-Line." *Harvard Business Review* 60, no. 1 (January–February 1982), pp. 82–88. (Previously made available in similar form under the same title as Working Paper no. 67, Center for Information Systems Research, MIT, Cambridge, Mass., April 1981.)

ROCK88 Rockart, John F., and David W. De Long. *Executive Support Systems.* Dow Jones-Irwin, Homewood, Ill. (1988).

RYAN89 Ryan, Alan J. "Cost of EIS A Big Deal for Most Firms." *Computerworld* 23, no. 30 (July 24, 1989), p. 46.

WALL91 Wallace, Scott. "Everybody's System." *Information Week* 333 (August 12, 1991), pp. 21–23.

WATS91 Watson, Hugh J. "Expensive to Implement, Costly to Develop and Maintain." *Computerworld* 25, no. 29 (July 22, 1991), p. 70.

WATS92 Watson, Hugh J.; Candice G. Harp; Gigi G. Kelly; and Magaret T. O'Hara. "Soften Up!" *Computerworld* 26, no. 42 (October 19, 1992), pp. 103–4.

WETH89 Wetherbe, James. "Getting It Right the First Time." *Computerworld* 23, no. 28 (July 10, 1989), pp. 89–91.

ENVOYANCE
EXECUTIVES AND SCHEDULING

"I don't really know why you want to talk to us about executive information systems," Sandra said after Adrienne and Doug settled into chairs in her office. "You ought to know by now that we don't really have 'executives' around here!"

"I hate to argue with you, Sandra," said Adrienne, "but you really do have them. Not that you have huge offices and reserved parking places and all that stuff. Of course you don't. But some of you, like yourself and Dan, tend to look at the big picture, while others burrow into their own projects or specialties, and that's all they see. From another point of view, you look at where the business is going over the next several years, what new kinds of problems you'll face, and new specialties you'll need. Most of the rest of the people are focused on shorter term issues."

"I guess that's so," conceded Sandra. "But I've been quite satisfied with the kinds of information systems we've been using—or, at least, I expect to be once we get all the systems you've planned into place. If I *am* an executive, what's different? Why would I need anything special?"

"Well," mused Doug, "if you have a few minutes, let's take a look at what you do all day long. If it turns out that the things you and Dan do are really different from the things that Jim, Jackie, Chris, and the others do, then wouldn't you need different kinds of information to help you do them?"

"Stands to reason, I guess," Sandra agreed. "But it will really have to be just a few minutes. The folks from The Bag Man are coming in to go over the numbers for plastic recycling."[6]

"Okay, then. There's your calendar for this week, said Adrienne, pointing at the open book on Sandra's desk (see Figure 12–4). "Let's see how you've been spending your time. From the looks of it, your days are about half booked with scheduled stuff. Is that about typical? And is Dan's about the same?"

"More or less, for both of us," Sandra agreed. "Some days more, some days less. The times in between are when I make phone calls, write letters, talk to people about issues that have come up, and—once in a great while—sit back and think about what we're doing and where we're going. What are you getting at?"

"Basically trying to see if we could save you some of this time so you could have more left over for that long-range thinking. After all, if you and Dan don't do it, nobody will. Let's take a look at a few of the meetings you have here. One thing that jumps out is the STP proposal. You've got what looks like six or seven hours on that. What will you be doing then?"

"Part of it," answered Sandra, "is figuring out what we want to do there. We've done a lot of similar jobs in the past but nothing quite like it. We have to pull out the info on those jobs and see what we can carry over.

"Another part is checking with the EPA about the characteristics of some chemicals that are involved in that situation. We have to get at least some basic information before we will know just what to propose.

"Then we have to get site information from Town Hall, cost information from a few possible subcontractors, schedule information about half of our staff that could possibly be working on it . . . and I have to make sure that everyone here who'll work on the proposal is up to speed on its major aspects.

"Finally, I have to review the entire proposal once it's written. If there are any minor changes, I don't have to go over those sections again, but I do want to see any major rewrites. And this all has to be done in time to get it to them by May 1st."

"That's a bunch!" Adrienne said, nodding. "To switch gears, you met with the landlord on Tuesday morning."

"Yes, I did. You know we need more space. Ideally, we'd like to expand on this floor. Failing that, it would be nice to stay in the building because then we wouldn't have to change our mailing address and all our stationery, business cards, the whole nine yards. The landlord offered us some good terms because the office space market isn't so hot around here right now, but I'd like to see if we can do better. Not that we'd like to move, but at least to show him what our options are if his offer isn't attractive enough. You'd be surprised how much information on this you can dig up if you try, but I'll have to spend some time digging."

"You also seem to spend a lot of time reviewing the status of specific jobs or proposals," Doug noted.

"That's right, I do. Some of the information I need comes through the regular status reports, but there's usually backup that would have made the status reports too fat. So I just sit down with the folks doing the project, they pull the details out of their desk or bring them up on their computer screens, and I look at them. Once in a while

[6]See the episode at the end of Chapter 6.

FIGURE 12–4
Sandra's Calendar Pages for the Week of April 22

<table>
<tr><th></th><th>Monday</th><th>Tuesday</th><th>Wednesday</th><th>Thursday</th><th>Friday</th></tr>
<tr><td>8:00</td><td></td><td rowspan="2">Staff meeting</td><td rowspan="2">Chempact conf. call</td><td></td><td rowspan="10">Out of office: Sales call on Enterprise Group w/Peggy</td></tr>
<tr><td>8:30</td><td rowspan="3">Lawyers re certification of incorporation</td><td rowspan="3">Go over STP prop. w/Peggy, Miguel, Chris</td></tr>
<tr><td>9:00</td><td rowspan="2">Landlord: Rates for new space</td><td></td></tr>
<tr><td>9:30</td><td></td></tr>
<tr><td>10:00</td><td></td><td></td><td></td><td></td></tr>
<tr><td>10:30</td><td rowspan="2">Jim/Oxbow</td><td></td><td></td><td></td></tr>
<tr><td>11:00</td><td>CALL L.B.!!</td><td></td><td rowspan="2">Go over Bag Man #s for PM</td></tr>
<tr><td>11:30</td><td></td><td></td><td></td></tr>
<tr><td>12:00</td><td rowspan="4">Alumni club lunch (R.J. to speak)</td><td></td><td rowspan="4">Lunch with Fox Glen developers</td><td></td></tr>
<tr><td>12:30</td><td></td><td></td></tr>
<tr><td>1:00</td><td rowspan="4">Planning mtg. on STP prop.</td><td></td><td></td></tr>
<tr><td>1:30</td><td></td><td></td></tr>
<tr><td>2:00</td><td></td><td rowspan="6">Work on STP proposal</td><td rowspan="2">Doug & Ad.</td><td></td></tr>
<tr><td>2:30</td><td rowspan="3">Review Mitona water cleanup</td><td></td></tr>
<tr><td>3:00</td><td></td><td rowspan="4">Bag man (review #s)</td><td></td></tr>
<tr><td>3:30</td><td></td><td></td></tr>
<tr><td>4:00</td><td></td><td rowspan="2">Review Chempact</td><td></td></tr>
<tr><td>4:30</td><td></td><td></td></tr>
</table>

I even make a useful suggestion. Not too often, though. They know what they're doing."

Just then the phone rang. Sandra picked it up, said "They are? OK, I'll be right there," and turned to Doug and Adrienne. "The Bag Man has arrived—right on schedule! See you next week—when you can tell me if I'm an executive!"

Exercises

1. Are Sandra and Dan "executives?"
2. State three decisions Sandra must make. Are they strategic, tactical, or operational? Are they structured, semistructured, or unstructured?
3. Which of the reasons in Section 12.3 might justify Sandra's using an EIS?
4. Could Sandra's EIS use a data cube? If not, why not? If it could, what might its axes be?
5. Where could drill-down capability be used in an EIS for Sandra?
6. What types of "soft" information could Sandra's EIS usefully provide? How would you organize it for easy access?
7. With whom should Sandra's EIS be able to communicate?
8. What kinds of external databases could Sandra's EIS use? Using your library facilities, identify some specific databases that are available today and would support her needs.
9. Do you think Sandra would make a good EIS sponsor? Why or why not?

CHAPTER 13

Decision Support Systems Cases

Chapter Outline

Introduction

To really understand decision support systems, it is important to see real DSS in action. These cases will give you an in-depth look at several such systems. As you read them, try to apply the principles you learned in the previous chapters to these real-life decision situations and systems. The review and discussion questions at the end of the chapter will help you do this effectively.

13.1 MBTA Passenger Waiting Time System[1]

The Massachusetts Bay Transportation Authority (MBTA) is responsible for a wide range of public transportation services in and around the city of Boston. Among these is a network of four rail rapid-transit lines—underground, surface, and elevated—that carry more than 550,000 passengers on over 1,500 trips daily. The first of these lines was built in 1896. It and the other lines have, of course, been upgraded substantially since then. The system utilizes the latest transportation and information systems technology. Not everything has been upgraded, however. In keeping with Boston's sense of history, four 19th century above-ground entrances to the underground system are still in daily use, although they are now official historical sites.

In keeping with the need to motivate people to use public transportation rather than private automobiles, the MBTA has made passenger satisfaction a priority. Waiting time is a key component of passenger satisfaction. If trains are expected to run every five minutes on a particular line at a particular time of day, passengers will be willing to wait about that long for a train. If the wait becomes longer, they will be upset.

Dispatchers for each line are responsible for sending each train off at its appointed time and for monitoring its progress along the line. It is the responsibility of each train's driver to maintain the appropriate speed and thus (hopefully) the desired separation between trains. Signals prevent a faster train from coming too close to the one ahead. Their purpose is to ensure safety, not to provide proper trip spacing, so a train that follows another as closely as the signals permit will (except during rush hour on the highest frequency routes) be too close to the one in front. The gap between it and the next train—the headway in rail transportation jargon—will therefore be longer than desired, leading to passenger dissatisfaction. Some mathematical measures of excess waiting times and dissatisfaction as a function of headway are given in [WILS92].

Abnormally long headway is often the result of a circumstance beyond the control of the driver: a vehicle malfunction, a stuck signal, a disabled train ahead. When such an event occurs it is important for the MBTA to take corrective action as quickly as possible. These actions must include providing for passengers not on the affected train to receive service with as little interruption as possible: by substituting bus service, by rerouting trains on alternate tracks, by running trains up to the problem from both sides and having passengers walk around it, or by other means. They must also include correcting the problem itself. In some cases, additional action must be taken to ensure the safety of passengers and crew, such as running tunnel ventilation fans to remove smoke from a fire. Deciding what to do requires accurate and

---

[1]The author is grateful to Fred Pugliese and Carl Cederquist of the MBTA's Information Systems Services group for their help in preparing this section.

timely information. Providing this information is one purpose of the MBTA's PWT, or Passenger Waiting Time, system.

The PWT system is the third generation of headway monitoring systems used by the MBTA:

The first stage consisted of daily "how'd it go yesterday?" telephone discussions between dispatchers and operations management. While undoubtedly useful, these conversations could hardly provide real-time decision making information.

The second stage, which began in the early 1980s, used detectors installed at 29 strategic locations throughout the rapid transit system as shown in Figure 13–1. These detectors were wired to counters at operations headquarters. Every half hour a headquarters staff member would enter the counter readings into a database. The content of this database would be printed later for management to examine. This system, while useful to management, was in one way counterproductive. Dispatchers knew they were being evaluated on running the right number of trains in every 30-minute period. If they were low, for whatever reason, with a few minutes left in the half hour, they would send out all waiting trains as quickly as possible. This emptied the terminal of the trains that were supposed to be there for the next half hour, creating an enormous gap between the last train of the "burst" and the next to come—but that wasn't the dispatcher's problem.

The third stage began in early 1990. A few MBTA information systems specialists had the idea of connecting the train detectors directly to the computer system. Their initial intent was simply to eliminate the manual transcription process. It was time consuming, not particularly interesting to the clerks who performed it, and a source of errors in the database. They soon realized, however, that it was no more difficult for a computer to poll the sensors every several seconds (12 seconds, in the final system) than to poll them every half hour. Given that the data were updated every 12 seconds, why restrict output to printed reports with half-hourly summaries? "We're getting the data as it occurs; why not display it so people can use it?" they asked. The result was a continuously updated display as shown in Figure 13–2. While you can't see this here, the actual display shows the different detectors in color corresponding to the names of the four MBTA lines shown in Figure 13–1.

The left side of the display shown in Figure 13–2 shows trains traveling in the inbound direction, or toward Boston. The right column shows outbound (away from Boston) trains. (These designations are historical and do not always match the actual direction of travel relative to the downtown area, a regular source of confusion for visitors and newcomers to the city.) Each line indicates the name of a station at which a detector is located. The two columns after the station name give the time at which the last train passed the detector and the time at which the next train is (or was) due to pass it. The word "HOT" indicates headway less than planned; that is, the last train to pass was running "hot" and catching up to the train ahead of it. Gaps of two minutes over the planned headway are shown as "D>2" in the right column.

FIGURE 13–1
MBTA Map Showing Detector Locations

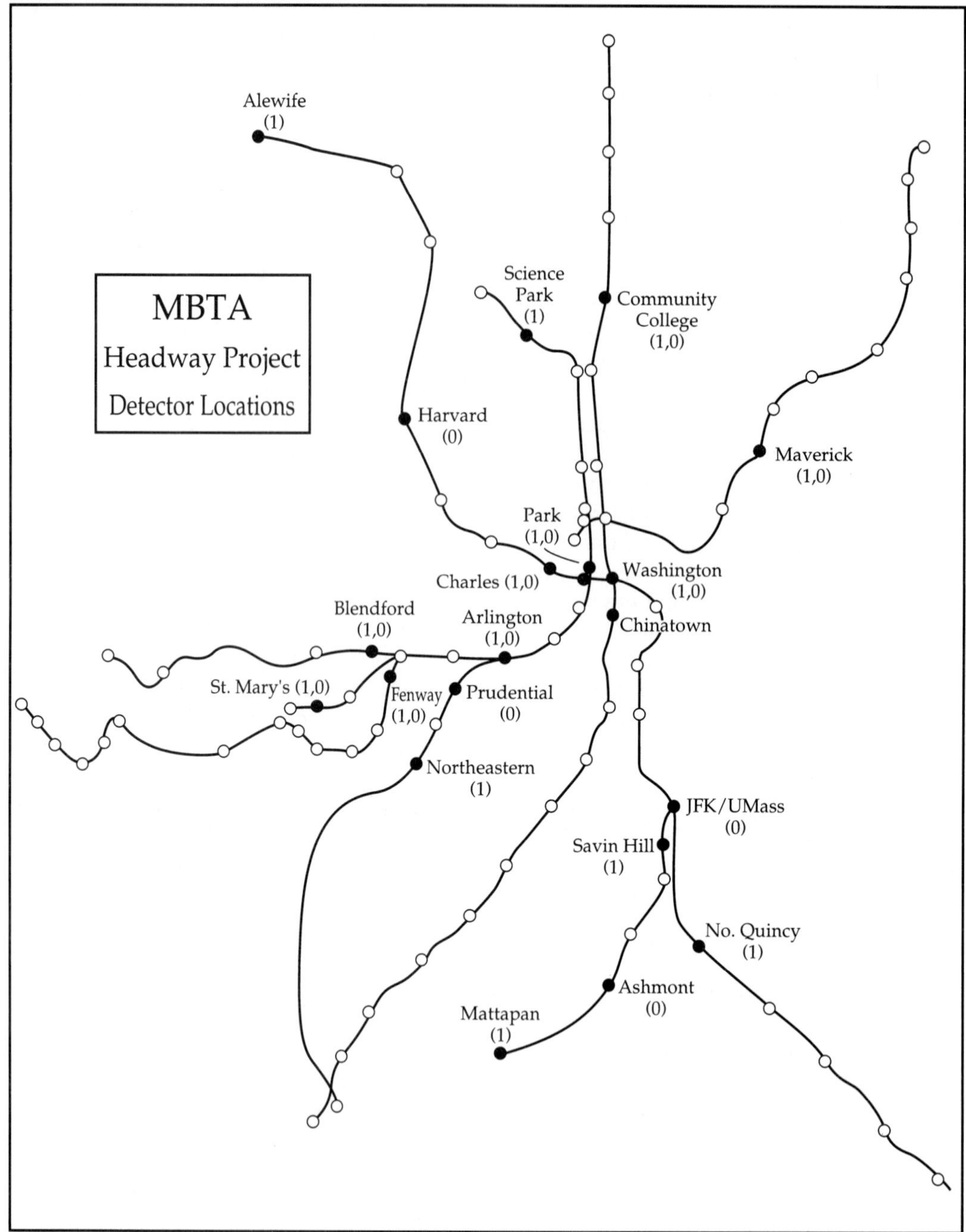

FIGURE 13–2

Sample PWT Screen Display

Massachusetts Bay Transportation Authority 07-18-1990
Headway Monitoring System
11:21:21

INBOUND LOCATION	THRUPUT SCH 11:00	THRUPUT ACT 11:00	LAST TRIP	NEXT TRIP			
BRAINTREE	2	1	11:13	11:25			
ASHMONT	3	1	11:13	11:25			
DOWNTOWN	5	1	11:13	11:19			
PORTAL BEA	5	1	11:13	11:19			
ALEWIFE	5	1	11:13	11:19			
MAVERICK	4	1	11:14	11:22			
MATTAPAN	4	1	11:13	11:21			
RIVERSIDE	6	1	11:13	11:23			
CLEVELAND	6	1	11:14	11:19	D	>	2
BOSTON COL	6	1	11:14	11:19	D	>	2
ARBORWAY	6	1	11:13	11:21			
GREEN CORE	26	1	11:13	11:15	D	>	6
LECHMERE	8	1	11:14	11:23			
FOREST HLS	4	1	11:14	11:22			
OAK GROVE	4	1	11:13	11:21			

OUTBOUND LOCATION	THRUPUT SCH 11:00	THRUPUT ACT 11:00	LAST TRIP	NEXT TRIP			
BRAINTREE	3	2	11:14	11:26			
ASHMONT	2	1	11:14	11:26			
DOWNTOWN	5	1	11:14	11:20			
PORTAL BEA	5	1	11:14	11:20			
ALEWIFE	5	1	11:14	11:20			
MAVERICK	4	4	11:15	11:23			
MATTAPAN	4	1	11:14	11:22			
RIVERSIDE	6	2	11:14	11:24			
CLEVELAND	6	3	11:14	11:19	D	>	2
BOSTON COL	6	2	11:14	11:19	D	>	2
ARBORWAY	8	4	11:14	11:23			
GREEN CORE	24	1	11:14	11:15	D	>	5
FOREST HLS	4	1	11:14	11:22			
OAK GROVE	4	4	11:14	11:22			

FIGURE 13–3

PWT System Diagram

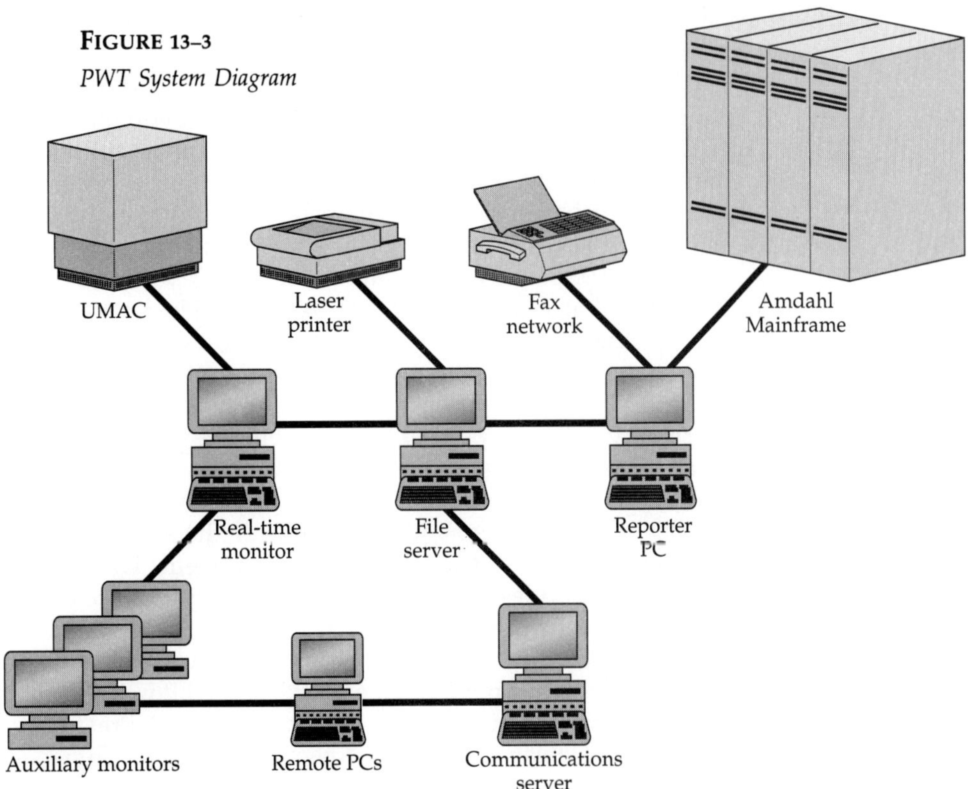

If the delay exceeds 10 minutes over the planned headway, the annotation flashes.

By 1990 personal computer technology was in general use in the MBTA, as it was elsewhere throughout U.S. business and government. It was therefore chosen as the hardware base for PWT. The elements of the system are shown in Figure 13–3. There are three IBM PS/2 computers in the system. One polls the train detectors via the UMAC 5000 Programmable Controller at the top left. One is responsible for analyzing the data and computing several measures of performance, such as the fraction of gaps between trains that exceeded twice the desired headway. It also handles printed output and transmits summary data to the MBTA's Amdahl 5990 mainframe for statistical analysis and management reporting. The third handles communications to other sites for remove monitoring. All the PCs are connected to a local area network file server running Novell NetWare. System monitors display PWT data to MBTA operational management, to dispatchers, and to the information systems group.

The system includes more than 25 programs. The main program consists of more than 1,300 lines of code. Most of the programs were written in BASIC. A few are in C. The SAS statistical analysis system is used on the mainframe for after-the-fact data analyses. A typical mainframe-produced report is shown in Figure 13–4. System output also includes graphs such as Figure 13–5.

The initial PWT system was developed over a period of about three months. Most of the work was done by the MBTA's Carl Cederquist, senior programmer/analyst, and David Nelson, manager of transit applications, with direction from Fred Pugliese, deputy director of information systems services. Total cost for all hardware and software, including the cost of the developers' time, was about $100,000. The PWT system went into operation in July 1990.

The PWT system was not an immediate hit with the dispatchers. They initially felt that it smacked of "Big Brother." However, as Pugliese points out, "If someone isn't doing their job, it shows that, but the thrust of the system is not to watch the people. It's to watch the trains and to improve service. PWT is an important part of the authority's goal to provide on-time performance." The dispatchers now accept the PWT system as an effective way to achieve this objective.

The PWT system has been enhanced since its early days and continues to be. Planned future enhancements include the ability to make recommendations as to how best deal with a specific problem. These recommendations will be based on rules implemented via expert system technology, which we will take up in the next chapter.

PWT helps with two types of management decisions. One type is the operational decisions mentioned earlier. As Fred Pugliese puts it, "the information is available immediately to the dispatchers." Previously, they would have noticed a delay only when it became excessive. Someone would then

FIGURE 13–4
PWT Hard Copy Report

Massachusetts Bay Transportation Authority
Daily Passenger Waiting Time Summary
7 28 90

PEAK PERIOD

AM Inbound							PM Inbound				
			% Psgr Waiting							% Psgr Waiting	
Sched Hdwy	Obsrvd Wait	Excess Wait	< 1 Hdwy	> 2 Hdwy	Line	Branch	Sched Hdwy	Obsrvd Wait	Excess Wait	< 1 Hdwy	> 2 Hdwy
14:30	7:35	0:20	91.0		Red	Braintree	14:31	6:59	-0:17	95.2	
14:30	6:20	-0:55	100.0		Red	Ashmont	14:32	6:47	-0:29	95.2	
7:16	3:46	0:08	90.0		Red	Alewife	7:15	3:30	-0:08	93.5	
18:00	6:40	-2:20	98.4		Org	Oak Grove	13:32	5:08	-1:38	99.7	
17:00	5:36	-2:54	100.0		Org	Forest Hls	13:29	5:37	-1:08	97.0	
11:00	3:57	-1:33	99.8		Blu	All Service	9:00	4:12	-0:08	95.0	
10:00	5:02	0:02	88.9		Grn	Boston Col	5:00	5:45	3:15	57.4	13.7
10:00	6:41	1:41	76.9		Grn	Cleveland	6:30	3:28	0:13	85.7	
10:00	5:18	0:18	89.5		Grn	Riverside	6:31	2:29	-0:47	96.1	
10:00	6:48	1:02	80.9	1	Grn	Arborway	6:30	4:14	0:59	78.7	1.9
2:37	2:04	0:45	68.6	5.5	Grn	Green Core	1:33	1:04	0:17	78.1	7.3
30:00	4:28	-10:32	100.0		Grn	Mattapan	11:00	4:19	-1:11	99.0	

PEAK PERIOD

Inbound							PM Inbound				
			% Psgr Waiting							% Psgr Waiting	
Sched Hdwy	Obsrvd Wait	Excess Wait	< 1 Hdwy	> 2 Hdwy	Line	Branch	Sched Hdwy	Obsrvd Wait	Excess Wait	< 1 Hdwy	> 2 Hdwy
14:59	7:16	-0:20	94.5		Red	Braintree	14:18	7:37	0:27	92.7	1.2
14:53	7:06	-0:24	96.2		Red	Ashmont	14:21	8:14	1:03	90.9	2.2
7:18	4:24	0:44	83.9	2.1	Red	Alewife	7:06	4:19	0:42	86.5	2.5
14:32	6:23	-1:01	95.9		Org	Oak Grove	14:36	7:22	-0:06	93.5	2.6
14:36	6:50	-0:38	94.8	1.7	Org	Forest Hls	14:32	6:38	-0:46	93.8	
9:50	4:27	-0:32	96.1		Blu	All Service	9:52	4:35	-0:26	94.0	
6:59	4:53	0:59	79.7	2	Grn	Boston Col	7:01	5:40	1:40	75.1	3.6
8:16	4:28	0:09	90.6		Grn	Cleveland	8:14	5:06	0:48	87.4	1.8
8:21	4:11	-0:18	92.3	0.1	Grn	Riverside	8:17	5:09	0:44	86.6	2
8:05	5:20	0:57	82.0	1.2	Grn	Arborway	8:15	4:34	0:02	89.3	0.7
2:03	1:41	0:18	71.0	7.1	Grn	Green Core	1:59	2:01	0:35	80.3	6.7
13:03	5:15	-2:28	92.8		Grn	Mattapan	13:10	5:22	-2:30	91.5	

have to be sent along the track to locate the delay. Only then could corrective action be planned and taken. The information that a delay has occurred at a specific spot is now available within a couple of minutes, saving valuable time.

PWT also helps MBTA managers make tactical planning decisions. Each delay has an associated record that indicates (after suitable study, if necessary) the cause of the delay: signal malfunction, congestion at the platform, whatever. Analysis of these delay causes can identify areas that need attention and patterns of causes that can be corrected. In the absence of PWT, this information would not be available because PWT provides the framework within which the delays can be identified. The MBTA is continuing to enhance PWT as an important tool for helping to improve its on-time rail transportation performance.

FIGURE 13–5
PWT Graphical Output

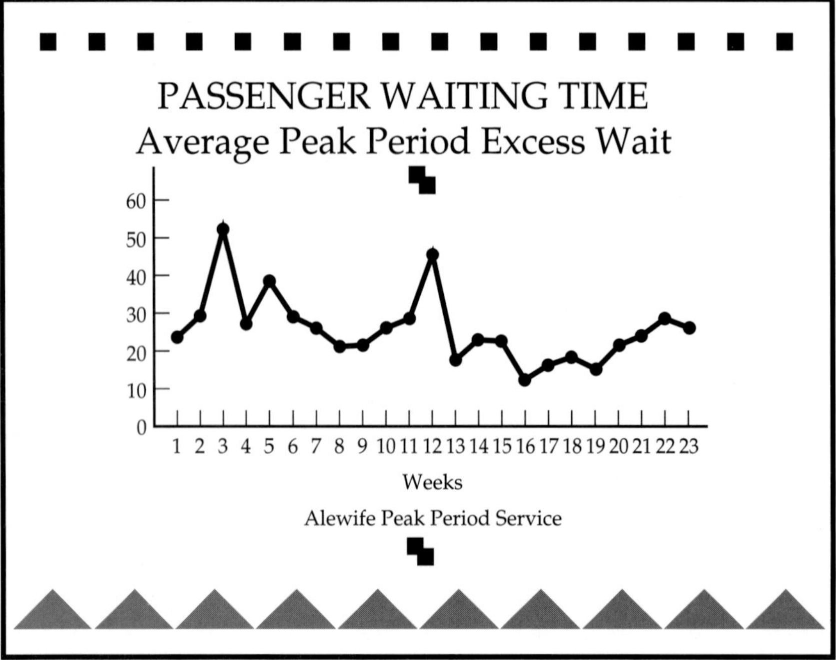

13.2 MediQual

Health-care decisions are among the most important ones that people face as individuals. Hospitals, faced with increasing pressures on costs and care from a variety of quarters, face equally important decisions about how they will provide this care. Information on the quality of care provided by different hospitals, physicians, and forms of treatment is fundamental to much of this decision making.

This information, however, is often difficult or impossible to come by. The problem is in part the lack of data and in part the volume of data: What does it mean if a particular patient had procedure A at hospital B with physician C and got better? If patient D had the same procedure at hospital E with physician F and did not recover, does that mean anything? Is the fact that patient A stayed in the hospital for five days, while patient D went home after three, at all significant? As isolated data points, these are meaningless. As part of a properly organized statistical whole, they can be of great value.

As an example of using such information intelligently, the 15,000-employee Orange County public school system saw its health-care costs for teachers rising six times faster than their salaries [MORG91]. They obtained a health-care cost analysis package from MediQual of Westborough, Massachusetts, to help them select the best, most efficient health-care provider. Orlando Regional Medical Center, the winner, still uses the package to keep tabs on its performance. In 1991 the system's medical costs were still rising at 10 percent per year: high, but only half the rate of the 1980s.

Another factor that affects hospital-related decisions is the effort to determine objectively how sick patients are on admission. This matters to hospitals because they want to obtain higher reimbursement for treating more seriously ill patients, compared with less seriously ill patients with the same basic diagnosis. Being able to predict costs accurately is also important for good financial planning. It matters to insurance companies because they want to minimize—within the limits of the law, their agreements with hospitals and physicians, and ethics—the amounts they pay out in claims. And it matters to government agencies, who want to remove inequities so that hospitals will not be financially motivated to avoid seriously ill patients.

Severity of an illness on admission can be scored objectively using a scale of symptoms appropriate to each condition. Health Systems International, as reported in [BRIG90], uses a scale from 1 (minor ailment) to 4 (life threatening). (There is also a rating of zero, defined as "patients having none of the admission severity measure key clinical findings.") The pneumonia scale, for example, assigns a ratings of 1 if the patient has a fever of less than 100.4°F (38°C) or chills. A rating of 4 applies if the fever is over 104°F (40°C), the patient is not breathing, or the patient is in a coma. The average cost at 25 New Jersey hospitals for treating renal (kidney) failure ranged from $1,307 for severity 1 to $3,393 for severity 4. Since all instances of renal failure are reported under the same diagnosis-related group, in the absence of severity-of-illness data, only the average of $2,260 could be used for decision making.

One drawback of such "chart-based" packages is that compiling the necessary data is labor intensive and therefore expensive. One study found that it took an average of 35 minutes of a nurse's time. Another estimated the cost at $10 to $12 per patient: a cost which, in the final analysis, is passed on in some fashion to the patient, to the patient's employer, or to taxpayers.

Comparing data with statistical averages isn't just for cost analysis. In a case reported by Taulbee in [TAUL91], a western Pennsylvania hospital had a higher-than-expected death rate for pneumonia patients in a particular diagnosis-related category. Armed with this information, the hospital undertook an intensive review of pneumonia patient care: a study that could not have been undertaken across the board. They discovered that certain lab specimens weren't being collected in time to give physicians precise information about the type of pneumonia that was present. The physicians were therefore routinely prescribing the most powerful antibiotic available—which happens not to be effective against Legionnaires' Disease. Many of the hospital's patients had this type of pneumonia, which does respond to a less expensive drug. Once this problem was corrected, mortality for that group of patients went from 14 percent to zero—*and* the hospital saved $750,000.

MediQual of Westborough, Massachusetts, offers two software products to help hospital administrators answer these and similar questions. While they are not the only products on the market, they are representative of the features users can expect in software of this type.

One MediQual package, MedisGroups II, classifies each patient's severity of illness on admission. It uses the common zero-to-four severity scale, with rating factors obtained from physical examinations, X rays, and lab reports. MedisGroups II then follows the patient's status over the course of hospitalization, keeping track of the nature and cost of all services provided. MedisGroups II was developed using the FOCUS software from Information Builders Inc. (see Section 6.4.2). It runs on IBM or compatible microcomputers under MD-DOS, on Digital Equipment Corporation VAX minicomputers, and on IBM and compatible mainframes.

MediQual pools clinical information from all MedisGroups users into a comparative database of over 8 million severity-adjusted patient records. They then use this database to establish severity-adjusted outcome norms for regional and national comparative analyses of hospital performance. Benchmark standards are also derived from this database, enabling clients to judge their performance against the highest achiever.

The other software product, MQ-PowerPlay, enables hospital administrators to access and manipulate data captured by MedisGroups. This package can report summary data in both tabular and graphical formats, with drill-down capability to focus on specific areas in greater and greater detail. MQ-PowerPlay can also compare a hospital's data with severity-adjusted norms from the comparative database described above. MQ-PowerPlay is based on the PowerPlay reporting and analysis software from Cognos Corporation. It runs on IBM or compatible microcomputers under Microsoft Windows Release 3.0 or higher.

13.3 JOCK[2]

Having a record party? The disk jockey, DJ or deejay for short, makes all the difference in the world. The right mix of music sets a mood, keeps everyone dancing, keeps everyone happy. The wrong mix can make the party a social disaster.

But how does the DJ know what records to play, in what order? In part from experience: Anyone who doesn't have at least some feel for the issues

[2]The author is grateful to Ron Carpenito, a 1991 DSS student at the University of Massachusetts, Lowell, for finding this unusual DSS.

won't be in the field in the first place. However, nobody's perfect. Under the pressure of time, noise, and distractions, it's easy to make mistakes. The JOCK package from JDM Software (Frazier Park, California) is designed to help.

Mixing is generally based on beats per minute (BPM). A DJ can tell JOCK what BPM rate to start with, the allowable BPM change from one song to the next, and the direction of tempo adjustment: up, down, or both. The DJ can also specify song categories to prefer, key information to use, chart (top 50, etc.) information to use, and artists or labels to prefer. These correspond directly to the factors that the DJ would use personally to select songs.

As JOCK selects a song, it displays its name in a screen box as "Current Song." A user-entered memo field for the song is also displayed: "This was John and Mary's favorite song when they were courting in 1943," or "This song won a grammy for Bonnie Raitt in 1992." JOCK also lists, on the screen, all the songs that meet the DJ-specified criteria relative to the current song. These are its recommendations as candidates for the next song. When the DJ selects a song from that list, it is placed in a box labeled "Next Song." The cycle repeats when the DJ asks JOCK to proceed. The Next Song moves up to the Current Song and a new list of possible selections is displayed. The software can handle exceptions, such as no songs meeting the specified criteria or audience requests that depart from the desired mixing strategy. It can also log requests, indicating which of the requests have been played and which have not yet been.

A set of songs can be preprogrammed, saved, and recalled later. The system can save 42 preprogrammed sets of up to 112 songs each: about five hours of music per set.

JOCK uses a record database in making its recommendations. This database has room for over 65,000 songs. For each song, it stores the title, author, lable, BPM, key in, key out, pitch adjustment needed to put in on key (if any), two user-defined data fields, and a memo field of up to 150 characters. The program also maintains two separate top-50 charts, named (unimaginatively, as JOCK documentation concedes) Chart A and Chart B.

JOCK runs on IBM or compatible microcomputers with 256KB RAM and a disk drive for the record library. It fits into so little RAM—256KB is smaller than all but the tiniest home computers in 1993—because the program was written in assembly language.

JOCK has not taken the disk jockey community by storm. The reasons are nontechnical. This lends added emphasis to the points made earlier about studying *all* user requirements, not just the technical ones. JOCK is selling slowly primarily because DJ booths are miniscule. They have barely enough space for the DJ himself or herself, the music collection, and the necessary equipment to play the music. Even a small laptop computer occupies about a square foot of space. This space must be at a certain distance from the DJ and at a certain height for the screen and keyboard to be usable. It must be reasonably well protected against encounters with stray elbows and soft drinks.

It cannot be on top of anything else that must be readily accessible. If such space isn't there, and it usually isn't, the best software in the world won't find a market.

13.4 Options Pricing with Black-Scholes

Most people think of investing in terms of buying a stock, holding it to obtain income from its dividends, or selling it when its price has gone up. Some, expecting its price to drop, consider "short selling:" selling a stock one doesn't own. Short sellers borrow the stock (usually on paper, through their broker) in order to have something to give the buyer. They expect to return the borrowed stock by buying shares on the market at a lower price later. Yet it is not necessary to buy, or to sell, shares of stock in order to speculate on future price changes. One can also buy *options:* the right to buy or sell shares of stock at a stated price until some stated future date.

Suppose you think the shares of Thompson's Trousers and Pizza, now selling at $40 per share, will go up. You could buy 100 shares for $4,000—plus the broker's commission, which we'll ignore from here on. If you're right and the stock rises to $50 per share, you've made $1,000: 25 percent of your investment. If you're wrong and it drops to $30 per share, you've lost $1,000, again 25 percent.

Now suppose I own 100 shares of TT&P, and I *don't* think their price will rise. I could make a deal with you: Pay me $100 now, and I'll promise to sell you my shares at the current $40 price at any time you ask during the next 30 days. If they do go to $50, you make $900: the $1,000 increase in the price of the stock, less the $100 you paid me. That's less than you would have made buying the stock, but you only invested $100—not $4,000. Your return on investment has improved from 25 percent to 900 percent! (Had you invested the same $4,000, your profit would have been $36,000.) If the stock drops, you let our agreement expire at the end of the month since you can buy TT&P stock for less on the open market. In this case you lose your $100: less than the $1,000 you would have lost, but, percentage-wise, your entire investment rather than just 25 percent of it.

From my point of view, if the stock goes up, I lose the chance to sell my 100 shares at $50 per share since I've promised them to you (and, under those circumstances, you would want them). However, I have the $40 price I wanted plus the $100 you paid me, in effect selling my stock for $41 per share. If it goes down, I still own the stock, and I also have the $100.

In options terminology, you have purchased a *call* on my stock. A call is characterized by the type of security (here TT&P common stock), the number of shares (typically 100 shares, which is assumed from here on), the *striking price* (here $40) and the *expiry date* (here 30 days from now, but typically stated as a calendar date). I have *written* the call. A *put* is the opposite: Its writer promises to buy the stock at the striking price until the expiry date. The purchaser of a put typically expects the price to go down. Such a person wants to make money, or to be protected against loss, if that happens.

Investors don't have to find other individual investors who feel differently about a stock in order to trade in options. Puts and calls in shares of large firms are traded on major stock exchanges. Their price fluctuates with the price of the underlying security: a $40 call on TT&P stock is worth very little if the stock is now trading at $30, is worth something if it is trading at $40, and is worth at least $1,000 if it is trading at $50. The value of a put, conversely, increases as the price of the underlying stock goes down.

An option does not represent any ownership in a corporation and therefore has no inherent value. Its value is transitory and can fluctuate dramatically in a short time. This provides investors with a great deal of *leverage:* They can make large amounts of money with a small investment, or they can lose their entire stake. Trading in investments where huge sums can be made or lost in a short time is not for the faint of heart. Doing it successfully requires both the right mental attitude and careful, objective analysis. Option traders, especially but not only at brokerage firms, use computers widely to support their decisions. They use computers to evaluate the desirability of writing or purchasing various options, or combinations of options, at certain prices. If they can find the right combination of puts and calls, they can often *hedge* one against the other and thus make money at little or no risk.

One approach to using computers is to develop and implement a mathematical model that calculates the price that an option "ought to" have. If it is offered on the market at less than this price, the investor or the firm will consider buying it. If it is being bought on the market at more than this price, they will consider writing it.

The quality of an investor's mathematical model is a key factor in his or her success in options trading. Suppose one investor's model calculates that the TT&P call I am willing to write for $100 is, based on the model, really only worth $80. That investor will not buy my call. If another's model suggests that it is really worth $120—based on what the model predicts, statistically, will happen to the price of TT&P stock over the next 30 days—that investor will buy my call. Both models will be right some of the time, wrong some of the time. In the long run, the set of decisions recommended by one model will turn out to be better than the set recommended by the other. One investor will ride in a chauffeured Rolls-Royce while the other will have to borrow bus fare.

The classical model for evaluating the value of an option is called the Black-Scholes model after its developers [BLAC71, BLAC73, also in most finance and investment texts].

The Black-Scholes model calculates the value of an option from these five factors:

1. The current price of the stock. This is really a convenient calibration factor. We could set it to 1 and normalize all other figures relative to it. Most people find it easier to deal with numbers that have a visible relationship to reality.

2. The striking price of the option.

3. The remaining time until the option expires: The further off the expiry date, the more the price of the stock is likely to fluctuate by then. If $100 is a fair price for a 30-day call on 100 shares of TT&P, a 60-day call would be worth more.

4. The volatility of the stock price, expressed as the standard deviation of its annual rate of return. The more volatile a stock price, the more likely that fluctuations will carry it above the striking price. This factor has a great impact on option value and cannot be obtained directly from a stock price table. Estimating it requires good judgment. People who are good at this task can earn large amounts of money.

The relationship between price fluctuations, as indicated by volatility, and option value is not linear. TT&P stock is now trading at $40 per share. Suppose, first, it has an equal chance of trading at $50 or $30 per share in 30 days. Its expected value, the average of these two figures, is still $40. In the first case a $40 call is worth $1,000 (the $10 price increase times 100 shares in the standard call). In the second case it is worthless. The expected value of the call is therefore the average of $1,000 and $0, or $500. Now, suppose it is more volatile and has an equal chance of trading at $60 or $20 per share in 30 days. The expected value of the stock is still $40. However, the call is worth $2,000 in the first case, and is still worthless in the second. The expected value of the call has increased to $1,000. Calls on volatile stocks are therefore worth more than calls on comparable, but less volatile, stocks.

5. The current risk-free interest rate which the investor can obtain, usually taken as the interest rate on government securities that mature at about the same time that the option expires. The higher this rate, the more valuable a call that lets the investor postpone paying the full price of the stock until the call is exercised. Given a high enough interest rate, a call can be worth something for this time factor alone even if the price of the underlying stock does not change by a penny.

The Black-Scholes formula for the value of a call is:

$$C = S_0\, N(d_1) - \frac{E}{e^{rt}}\, N(d_2)$$

where

$$d_1 = \frac{\ln\left(\frac{S_0}{E}\right) + \left(r + \frac{\sigma^2}{2}\right)t}{\sigma\sqrt{t}}$$

$$d_2 = \frac{\ln\left(\frac{S_0}{E}\right) + \left(r - \frac{\sigma^2}{2}\right)t}{\sigma\sqrt{t}}$$

and the elements are defined as

C = Value given by the model for a call option.
r = Riskless interest rate.
S_0 = Current price of the underlying stock.
E = Exercise (striking) price of the call.
t = Time to expiry, as a fraction of a year.
σ = Volatility, as standard deviation of the annual rate of return.
ln = Natural (base e) logarithm.
e = 2.71728 . . . , the base of natural logarithms.
$N(x)$ = Value of the cumulative normal distribution at x.
This starts at 0 for large negative values of x, equals 0.5 for $x = 0$, and converges toward 1 for large positive values of x.

These formulas look forbidding. Fortunately for individual investors, they are preprogrammed into many investment planning packages.

Investment analysts use models such as Black-Scholes in several ways:

1. Directly, to calculate the value of an option. This involves, as mentioned, the difficult task of determining the stock's volatility. It can be approximated by calculating the stock's rate of return for each week in the past year and finding the standard deviation of these values, but that is at best an imperfect process. Once the value of an option has been calculated, the investor can decide to purchase, sell, or write an option by comparing its market price with the output of the model.

2. In reverse, to solve for the volatility: What volatility makes the current market price of an option precisely correct? The investor can then decide whether he or she thinks the stock's actual volatility is above or below this figure. It is often easier to make this judgment than to choose a volatility figure in the abstract. If an investor feels that a stock is more volatile than its current option price implies, then the option is worth more than its market value and should be bought.

3. To compare the wide range of options that are traded in the stock of many large corporations. These vary in their striking prices (typically every \$5 or \$10, depending on the price of the stock, in a range on either side of its current price) and expiry dates (typically at one-month intervals, about three months into the future). The Black-Scholes model can determine the volatility implied by the current market price of each option. An investment analyst can see if any of the options is priced inconsistently with the others. If one option's price implies higher volatility than the others, that option is (according to the theory) overpriced and should be sold. An option whose price implies a lower volatility than the others should similarly be bought.

Black-Scholes is not the ultimate in option pricing methods. For one thing, it treats stock motion as a random variable: It does not take into account whether the underlying factors favor an increase or decrease in the price of a particular stock. For another, it assumes that the risk-free interest rate is fixed until the option expires. Large investment firms start with Black-Scholes but move beyond it. The specifics of their most advanced models are closely guarded secrets. (You can read about one example in [CLIF92].) The "rocket scientists" who develop these models are among these firms' most highly prized, and most highly compensated, employees.

13.5 Geographic Information Systems

Many decisions are made on the basis of geographic information. For example: where should we locate a new store, fire station, or schoolhouse? Where will it be least disruptive to place a new rapid transit line? How should election districts be defined for equal population without separating parts of the same community? In which areas is a door-to-door survey likely to be successful versus those we could survey better by phone? What route should our delivery truck follow between stops for minimum driving time? Where should we locate our next fast food franchise? In all these cases geographic information is part of the necessary input. Nongeographic information must often be associated with it for maximum usefulness: for example, we may want to find out who owns a particular plot of land, what its tax assessment is, or whether utility lines run under it. (It has been estimated that about 80 percent of all data kept by a typical U.S. county can be geographically referenced in some way.[3]) A *geographic information system,* GIS for short, can help answer these and similar questions.

The term "geographic information system" is often used, appropriately, as an umbrella term for a system designed to process any type of information that traditionally would have been recorded on maps. This information includes showing the areas covered by geographic entities: rivers, forests, streets, townships, house lots. Some of these entities are established by nature and change slowly, if at all. Others are created by humans and can, in theory if not in political practice, be changed at will. Geographic information systems show these areas, usually in different colors, on graphic displays and can print or plot them in color or black and white.

Just as maps have traditionally recorded a wide variety of additional data, so do GIS. First and foremost is the name associated with each entity. Such a simple act as showing the name of each entity on a map, easily done by people without much thought, becomes a complex information processing problem when we attempt to automate it. The names of long, thin entities such as roads and rivers must be positioned along the entity so as to make it immediately clear what they belong to, without overlapping other names and without blocking other important information. Other types of information

[3]As a quick exercise, think of two types of county data that *cannot* be.

can describe ownership, population, land use, altitude, climate, pollution (GIS can show the spread of air pollution from a source), and many more.

A low-end GIS is often called a *desktop mapping system*. Desktop mapping systems come with libraries of maps for various parts of the country or the world. These differ from the maps one might draw with a simple graphics program in that the GIS software recognizes each area as an entity. For example, a GIS might recognize that the town of Needham, Massachusetts, is an entity. It could display this town in a chosen color, could associate it with a population figure of about 28,000, and could put this figure on a map. It could, alternatively, show sales figures, electricity usage, or rainfall for last month. Desktop mapping system output can be displayed on a screen; printed by a dot-matrix printer, laser printer, or plotter; or incorporated into documents created by word processing, desktop publishing, or presentation software. Desktop mapping systems are easy to learn and to use, are available for all popular microcomputers, and typically cost from $1,000 to $5,000, including a library of maps.

Most GIS can also group areas into higher level entities. For example, the town of Needham is part of Norfolk County. A GIS, given population data for all the cities and towns in Massachusetts and the county each one is in, could display the county boundaries and the total population of each.

The most popular GIS above the desktop level is ARC/INFO (ESRI, Redlands, California). Originally developed for minicomputers and workstations, it has since moved both up to IBM and plug-compatible mainframes and down to powerful desktop microcomputers running either Microsoft Windows or Apple Macintosh software. We will use it here as an example because it shows a good design approach for geographic information handling and has a well-accepted set of features. You should realize, however, that other good GIS products exist as well and may be more appropriate for a particular application.

The key to any GIS is its database structure. Traditional text-and-number databases do not lend themselves well to the storage of geographic information. The ability of a GIS to store such information, to retrieve it efficiently, to display it cleanly, and to perform spatially oriented operations on it (such as merging adjacent regions or finding the nearest feature of a given type to a specified point) depend heavily on having an appropriate database organization.

The ARC/INFO database is based on *vector* data: lines between two designated points. ARC/INFO stores the coordinates of each vector's end points and suitable identification information to describe the vector. A vector can represent part of a linear entity, such as a pipeline. Several vectors can be combined end-to-end to form an *arc* to represent an entire entity that has length but no area. Arcs come together at *nodes,* which are linked in the database to all arcs that meet at the node.

An arc can represent part of the boundary of an area such as a plot of land or a town. An area, for example, can be defined by the arcs that form its boundary—or, at a higher level of abstraction, by the streets that form its boundary, where the streets themselves are defined as arcs. Attributes can be assigned to parts of an entity: for example, part of a roadway can be designated as one-way, as under repair, or as having a speed limit of 40 miles per hour.

ARC/INFO keeps information about features of different types in different database *layers:* perhaps one for road, one for forests, one for townships. By storing topological relationships among entities directly, ARC/INFO can carry out many types of analyses without having to access the absolute coordinate locations of features and perform complex calculations on them.

ARC/INFO can perform high-level operations on geographic data. Features can be added to a map or removed from one. Polygons can be merged into larger ones or split into smaller ones. Buffer zones can be defined around features, distances calculated between points, and more. These capabilities can all be accessed from the ARC Macro Language, or AML. AML also provides other features of a 4GL, including the ability to manipulate text and numeric data. It can thus be used to create complete applications that use geographic data.

In addition to its purely geographic data, each class of features in ARC/INFO can have associated tabular data. These data can be stored in its internal INFO database or in any of several popular relational database management systems: Oracle, Ingres, Informix, Sybase, DB2, Rdb, and others. A town administrator could use this capability to obtain, for example, the names and mailing addresses of the owners of all the parcels of land on a given block or within a half mile of a proposed highway.

The next two sections describe two decision support applications that use ARC/INFO.

13.5.1 GIS Example I: Yellow Freight[4]

The lights in the tactical planning room dim and an image flashes on the display screens. Vice presidents and managers lean forward in their seats. The decisions made today may affect thousands of lives—and the profitability of one of the largest industrial freight trucking companies in North America.

Yellow Freight System, Inc., based in Overland Park, Kansas, specializes in shipments that weigh anywhere from a few hundred to several thousand pounds but do not fill an entire trailer. Yellow Freight solves this efficiency problem by combining shipments on a single truck and transporting them to regional facilities where the shipments are sorted and rerouted to their final destinations. A single shipment may change trucks several times as it travels from its origin to a local terminal facility to a break bulk facility (where loads

[4]This example and the following one, Metropolitan Life Insurance, were provided by Environmental Systems Research Institute Inc., with the assistance and approval of Yellow Freight System and MetLife. The cooperation and support of all three firms are gratefully acknowledged.

are rearranged among trucks), then to a terminal near its destination, then finally to its destination.

"Because we have freight terminals all over the United States, Canada, and Mexico, facilities and real estate planning become an important part of our business," said Jim Glenn, a senior capacity planning analyst at Yellow Freight.

Yellow Freight's senior managers and five division vice presidents meet quarterly to discuss their facility locations, capacities, and needs. They have been using a geographic information system (GIS) to assist in operations and capacity planning since 1990. Environmental Systems Research Institute's GIS software, ARC/INFO, and Yellow Freight's own optimization/simulation software, SYSNET, run on a Sun workstation network. Together, they provide the resources for three planning applications: creating service maps, terminal service area analysis, and facility/capacity display.

"A lot of capital budgeting and facilities planning takes place in those meetings," said Glenn. "We wanted a database-driven system that could answer interactive queries on a graphic display. For example, in Division 5, we recently wanted to see all terminals with leases that expire in the next 12 months so we could decide whether to renew the leases, buy land and build terminals, or lease more doors."

M. J. Harden Associates, a mapping consulting firm based in Kansas City, Missouri, designed a menu-driven interface enabling Yellow Freight to edit, query, and display all freight terminals along with their various operational boundaries. They use the system in their quarterly capital expenditure meetings. Glenn acts as a facilitator in these meetings by operating the computer system to make queries and display information.

Service Map Creation Process Automated with GIS

Yellow Freight has approximately 640 terminals, each serving a specific geographic area. In many metropolitan areas, they have six or seven terminals, each with certain ZIP code–identified service areas. Before acquiring the GIS, the service area maps had been produced using hand-painted delivery time codes.

"From any given origin point, we have color-coded service days: yellow represents a two-day service area, blue a three-day, green a four-day, and so forth," said Stanley Hausman, an Operations Planning Specialist at Yellow Freight. "We found this system time consuming and cumbersome. Maps were frequently out of date, which led to quite a few mistakes. With the GIS, we zoom in all the way down to the ZIP code level."

They group the ZIP codes into service areas and produce maps that show the color-coded service areas from any origin point.

GIS Used to Track Terminal Service Areas

Yellow Freight management also wanted to look at a *Rand McNally Atlas* map combined with the exact areas each terminal serves. M. J. Harden Associates developed an ARC/INFO application that plots each terminal's service area on sheets of clear, warp-resistant plastic. These plastic sheets can then be laid over a Rand McNally map, allowing senior management to see terminal locations and service areas in relation to streets and highways.

"Previously, that was also done by hand-coloring maps," said Ken Peck, operations planning coordinator for Yellow Freight. "Earlier in the evolution of our mapping process, we acquired mapping software that could produce plots on plastic sheets; however, a graphic artist still had to manually orient each service area and state boundary to its proper *Rand McNally Atlas* page. With the assistance of Rand McNally and M. J. Harden and with ARC/INFO capabilities, we are now able to match the state boundaries with the exact map projections and map scale. This has taken most of the manual labor out of the process, in addition to producing a better product. Rand McNally has been quite helpful; in fact, they provided the scale factors and projection type and allowed us to create a matching reference system."

They hope to acquire the exact latitude and longitude for each map window from Rand McNally. Peck would also like to add descriptions for map insets—details of cities or states—sometime in the future.

GIS Applications Expected to Grow with Future System Development
Yellow Freight's future plans include incorporating raster images and blueprints into their demonstrations.

"We're looking forward to having aerial photos of our facilities in an image database that can be called up from within an ARC/INFO application," said Peck. "Then, if someone asks, 'What does our Tracy, California, break bulk look like?' we can bring up AutoCAD plans and a photographic image, and superimpose the image with a land use plot. We would know what lands around our facility are available for expansion. We also want to study zoning considerations, customer locations, fuel efficiency, and issues involving the Environmental Protection Agency."

SYSNET is described in more detail in [BRAK92]. That paper also discusses SYSNET's benefits. One of its tangible benefits is an 11.6 percent reduction in the amount of freight that must be consolidated by combining parts of one truckload into another truckload, which adds to both labor costs and shipment time. This reduction corresponds to a saving of $4.7 million per year.

13.5.2 GIS Example 2: Metropolitan Life Insurance

Health insurance is becoming an increasingly complex business. The task of managing it is growing correspondingly difficult. Decisions are involved on all sides. Workers are interested in the benefits their employers provide—what kinds of treatment are offered? what are the costs? and, of growing importance in the managed care world, where is the nearest provider?—and must often choose among several health-care options. Employers must decide what options to offer and what to charge for them. Health-care providers must decide where to locate and what affiliations to have with benefit programs. And insurance companies must decide, within the rapidly changing framework of the other decisions and of legal constraints, what types of programs to offer to employers and to individual subscribers. Geographic information systems can support these decisions.

The Metropolitan Life Insurance Company (MetLife) manages a network of more than 1,000 hospitals and 80,000 participating physicians nationwide. According to Dan Chinnock, GIS manager for MetLife, "We have traditionally used computer technology to manage our health-care networks, but with GIS we are able to view data in a whole new way."

One of the keys to the successful expansion of the company's managed health-care business has been its ability to illustrate its networks of preferred health-care providers in specific geographic regions. They accomplish this with an ARC/INFO application called METGEO. "METGEO represents a natural progression in systems development for an insurance company that wants to provide and sell its services in a big way," Chinnock said. "This is a whole new way to evaluate MetLife's services to its customers. The days of pushpins and paper maps are over."

That step came in the fall of 1990, when MetLife installed ARC/INFO software to develop METGEO. METGEO also uses the Oracle relational database management system software. MetLife runs these software packages on an IBM RISC System/6000 workstation. Chinnock said that a workstation hardware environment was selected because it provided the power and features they needed.

"Managing a health-care network is a task directly related to geography," said Chinnock. "Doctors practice at specific locations. Members need to be close to both doctors and hospitals. With METGEO, we can see relationships between where doctors, hospitals, and members are and where services need to be. This is a valuable resource to our group insurance sales representatives. Using the buffering capabilities of ARC/INFO can we strengthen that relationship and determine immediately if the members of that network are adequately covered.[5] If members move out of the pediatrician buffer, for instance, our managed care service representatives will know how to react." Chinnock explained further that graphical illustrations are depicted by symbols in several colors and that the acceptable maximum distance from each is shown by a ring of the same color. The portion where the rings overlap is shaded in green, showing at a glance the areas where all coverages are adequate. The maps can then be combined with employees' home addresses to create a precise illustration of the coverage that MetLife provides.

Providing coverage is only half the role of GIS at MetLife. "METGEO is a great marketing tool for insurance companies, "Chinnock explained.

[5]A buffer is a user-specified zone around a feature or feature class of interest, such as a 15-mile circle around all hospitals.

"METGEO allows us to show graphically where services are relative to a possible member company. When our representatives go out to visit a prospective client, they can take maps that show the extent of the coverage we are offering. (An example is shown in Figure 13–6.) After our sales representatives first meet with prospective clients, we are able to create custom maps incorporating the addresses with the locations of our preferred providers. How could you tell *that* story with words?"

Chinnock characterized the future use of GIS at MetLife as bright. "We consider METGEO one of the best systems in the industry. While several insurers are using mapping systems that incorporate ZIP code data, we believe that our system provides a higher level of accuracy by using exact street addresses."

FIGURE 13–6
MetLife EIS Map from ESRI

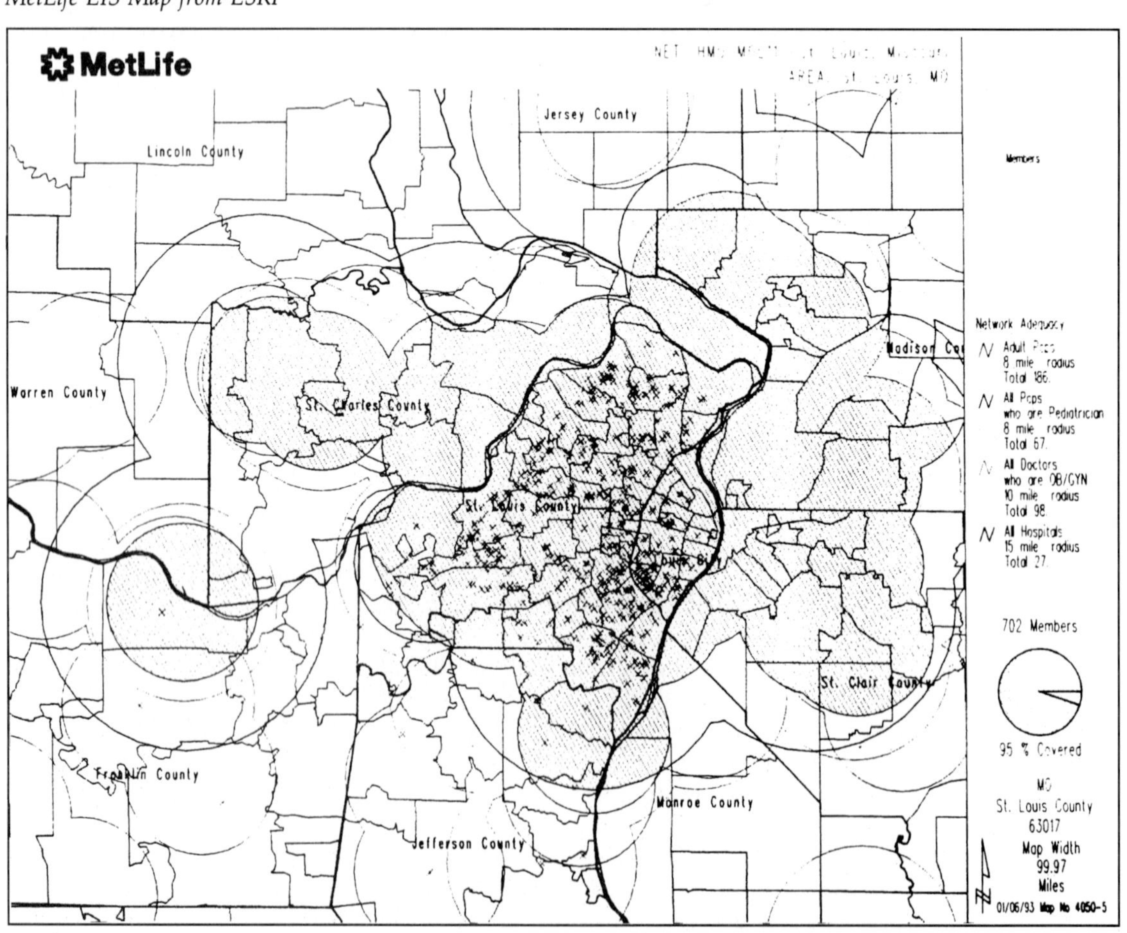

MetLife provides GIS information to a wide range of users—from MetLife executives to outside insurance brokers and consulting firms. "Almost every day we produce maps that display a wide range of diverse information for many different types of clients," Chinnock explained. "These maps are invaluable in helping them make good decisions based on their insurance needs."

According to John McManus, vice president of group information systems for MetLife, customer service is a very important part of the insurance business. "To the customer who wants to join a health maintenance organization, one of the things they want to know is: How well does MetLife's network match up geographically with where employees are? But that's only one piece of the puzzle. The other half is: Do we have the right physician configuration in the network?" he explained. "Are the doctors in the right places to serve customers? Do we have hospitals in the right places? All these questions lend themselves very nicely to using a map to find answers."

"Unfortunately, when we were beginning our program, GIS wasn't being marketed very effectively to the insurance industry. That says something about the potential for growth of GIS, not only in insurance, but in other businesses. Its growth has been phenomenal at MetLife," McManus said.

Exercises

For Section 13.1, MBTA Passenger Waiting Time System

1. What decisions, specifically, does this system help with? Write clear decision statements for them. Where do these decisions fall in the grid of Figure 2–1?
2. How would you categorize this DSS in terms of Alter's hierarchy as shown in Figure 4–1? How would you categorize it after the enhancements discussed near the end of the case are made?
3. Do you agree with the hardware and software tool choices that the MBTA made? Why or why not? If you feel the decisions may have been right for them under their circumstances but not for another organization under other circumstances, what factors do you feel might alter your preferences?
4. The concept of automatic monitoring of service quality has been applied to many situations. It has come in for its share (often well-deserved) criticism where its sole purpose has been assessing employee performance. Do you feel such criticisms apply here? Can you think of other situations where an automatic monitoring system could provide useful decision-making information?
5. Wilson and his colleagues [WILS92] show that average passenger waiting time is minimized if trains are spaced as evenly as possible for the desired average frequency of service. In other words, if the MBTA plans to run

six trains per hour on a particular route at a particular time of day, they should run 10 minutes apart rather than 5-15-5-15-etc. Does this seem reasonable to you? Calculate the average passenger waiting time for two limiting cases.

6. In Section 10.2 we said that calculus is seldom useful in practical situations outside a narrow area. The proof that evenly spaced trains minimize average waiting time is of great practical importance and was done with calculus. Is there a contradiction between these two statements about calculus? Why or why not?

For Section 13.2, MediQual

1. Write a precise decision statement that the Orange County public school system might have used when it saw that employee health-care costs were growing more quickly than they would have liked to see.
2. Assume a community hospital has 200 beds, that these beds are usually 75 percent full, that the average patient stays for three days, and that total charges per patient per day average $1,000.
   a. If using chart-based severity-of-illness software costs $10 per patient admitted, what is the total cost to the hospital for a year?
   b. What percentage of hospital revenues does using this software represent?
   c. Do you think the use of this package is justified? Why or why not?
3. Where would you put MedisGroups in the DSS hierarchy of Section 4.1? MQ-PowerPlay?
4. Contact a local hospital and find out what treatment outcome analysis software they use, if any. If they do use such software, find out how they selected it, what decisions it helps them with, how satisfied they are with it, and what plans they have for the future in this area.

For Section 13.3, JOCK

1. What category of DSS is JOCK in the DSS hierarchy of Section 4.1?
2. Are the decisions that JOCK supports individual, multi-individual, or group decisions? Are they operational, tactical, or strategic?
3. The developers of JOCK implicitly used a model in specifying how it would work. What is this model a model of? How is this model incorporated into JOCK?

For Section 13.4, Options Pricing

1. Consider the Black-Scholes model:
   a. Are the decisions it helps with structured, semistructured, or unstructured?

   b. Are they individual, group, or multi-individual decisions?
   c. Where would you put a Black-Scholes-based DSS in Alter's hierarchy?
   d. What are the benefits of a DSS that incorporates this model?

2. What database, if any, would be helpful to such a DSS that used the Black-Scholes model to support an investor? How would the DSS use it?
3. What type of hardware do you think is most appropriate for such a DSS?
4. You work in the MIS department of a Wall Street investment firm whose analysts use Black-Scholes or comparable models to evaluate and compare several call options. The options evaluated by one analyst at one time typically cover 10 firms whose current stock prices range from $20 to $120 per share. Options are traded at four to six striking prices per firm, at three expiry dates per striking price, for a total of 12 to 18 traded calls per firm or about 150 overall. Design a graphical screen display to convey as much important information as possible with a minimum of clutter. Use color if you think it can help, but in that case state how your system would support analysts whose color vision is impaired.
5. The Black-Scholes model uses a mathematical formula to calculate option values. Its ultimate purpose is to help users decide if purchasing a given option on the market is likely to yield a profit. One could also use the Monte Carlo method to simulate a large number of randomly chosen stock price fluctuation possibilities and make the same decision on that basis. Describe how that might work.

For Section 13.5, Geographic Information Systems

1. Where and how could Envoyance use geographic information systems?
2. The administrator of a city hospital wants to analyze its patients by ethnic group and the political precinct in which they live. The hospital has a GIS that can display all the city streets and can define arbitrary neighborhoods on the basis of the streets that form their boundaries.
   a. What information must be input into the system in order to obtain the desired output?
   b. Where would this information come from?
   c. How would you display the desired information on a map or a series of maps?
3. How would you use a GIS to help you identify a good location for your next fast food franchise? What information would you like the system to display besides a map of the area under consideration?
4. Articles such as [GOW92] suggest that GIS specialists are in high demand. Survey the "help wanted" section of your local Sunday paper or of information systems papers such as *Computerworld* and call some technical recruiting firms who specialize in information systems professionals to determine the degree to which this actually seems to be true.

5. Obtain information from several GIS package suppliers. (You can find their names in software directories that most college, university, and large public libraries have in their business reference sections.) Determine which features are important by reading this material carefully and noting which points the vendors emphasize. Compare two or three packages in terms of cost, hardware platform, capacity, ability to associate data stored in popular DBMS packages with geographic entities, ability to exchange data with other types of software, and any other parameters you feel are important.
6. For the Yellow Freight case:
   a. What is(are) the decision(s) this system helps with? Write clear decision statements.
   b. Are these decisions operational, tactical, or strategic?
   c. How would these decisions be made in the absence of a GIS?
   d. How does Jim Glenn's role of facilitator in this case relate to that role for group DSS in general as described in Chapter 11?
7. For the Metropolitan Life Insurance case:
   a. What is(are) the decision(s) this system helps with? Write clear decision statements.
   b. Who makes each of these decisions? Are they individual, group, or multi-individual decisions?
   c. How would these decisions be made in the absence of a GIS?
   d. Near the end of the case it is stated that METGEO information is provided to a wide range of users, some of them outside MetLife. Do you see any potential ethical issues that might arise here? What would you do, as a MetLife executive, to make sure that ethical problems do not occur? (The author is not aware of any such issues that have actually come up. From what he knows of MetLife, he is certain that proper safeguards are in place.)

References

BLAC72 Black, Fischer, and Myron Scholes. "The Valuation of Option Contracts and a Test of Market Efficiency." *Journal of Finance* 27, no. 2 (May 1972), pp. 399–417.

BLAC73 Black, Fisher, and Myron Scholes. "The Pricing of Options and Corporate Liabilities." *Journal of Political Economy* 81, no. 3 (May–June 1973), pp. 637–54.

BRAK92 Braklow, John W.; William W. Graham; Stephen M. Hassler; Ken E. Peck; and Warren B. Powell. "Interactive Optimization Improves Service and Performance for Yellow Freight System." *Interfaces* 22, no. 1 (January–February 1992), pp. 147–72.

BRIG90 Brightbill, Tim. "Diagnosing the Sickest Patients: Will Computers Replace the Thermometer?" *Healthweek* (March 26, 1990), pp. 21–28.

CLIF92 Clifford, James; Henry C. Lucas, Jr.; and Rajan Srikanth. "Integrating Mathematical and Symbolic Models through AESOP: An Expert for Stock Options Pricing." *Information Systems Research* 3, no. 4 (December 1992), pp. 359–78.

GOW92 Gow, Kathleen A. "Mapping Out Fresh Territory with GIS." *Computerworld* 26, no. 24 (June 15, 1992), p. 105.

LANG91 Lang, Laura. "Taking Care of Business: Now Business Professionals Can Benefit from the Power of Geographic Information Systems." *Computer Graphics World* 14, no. 6 (June 1991), pp. 89–94.

MORG91 Morgenson, Gretchen. "Consumer Guide to the Medical-Industrial Complex." *Forbes* (December 23, 1991).

TAUL91 Taulbee, Pamela. "Data Management: Winning the Numbers Game." *Business & Health* (November 1991).

WILS92 Wilson, Nigel H. M.; David Nelson; Anthony Palmere; Thomas H. Grayson; and Carl Cederquist. "Service Quality Monitoring for High Frequency Transit Lines." Transportation Research Board Annual Meeting, Washington, D.C. (January 1992).

PART IV Introduction to Artificial Intelligence and Expert Systems

Decision making, as a human thought process, is usually considered to require intelligence. Those who become proficient at making certain types of decisions develop certain procedures or "rules of thumb" for these decisions. If a computer can be "taught" these same procedures, the computer ought to be able to replicate the decision process in question. A system whose behavior is determined by rules obtained from a human expert is called an "expert system," a "rule-based system," or a "knowledge-based system."

Expert systems cannot replace human decision makers. The rules abstracted from the human expert's mind cannot capture everything that he or she knows about the subject area. Accordingly, the expert system becomes a component of the overall decision-making process: in other words, a decision support system. Part IV will introduce you to expert systems so that you will be able to incorporate them into the DSS that you develop.

Chapter 14 gives a broad overview of "artificial intelligence," of which expert systems are a part. You will also read about robotics, machine vision, understanding human languages, and neural networks.

Chapter 15 looks at expert systems from the outside, as a manager or a user might see them. You will learn what makes a good application for expert systems and what makes a bad one. You will also study the user interface of an expert system, emphasizing how its interfaces differ from those of other DSS.

Chapter 16 will take you inside expert systems. You will see how expert systems represent knowledge internally: both knowledge about how to solve a problem (rules) and knowledge about a problem to be solved (facts). Since knowledge is not always totally certain, we will also look at some of the ways in which expert systems can deal with uncertainty.

In Chapter 17, you will look at the process of building an expert system in more detail. This look will include hardware platforms and development software, including specialized languages. We will also look at a unique aspect of developing expert systems: working with human experts.

Chapter 18, like Chapter 13, contains several real cases that will let you apply what you have learned to actual situations.

CHAPTER 14

Artificial Intelligence, Expert Systems, and DSS

Chapter Outline

Introduction

"Artifical intelligence"—the name sounds like a subject for science-fiction buffs—has a long and respectable history at the forefront of computer science research. In its latest manifestations, the technology with this futuristic name can help build effective decision support systems. Anyone who will be building DSS in the next decade or so must understand some types of AI, where they fit into the DSS picture, where they can help, and how to make them help. This chapter will give you that overview. The next few chapters will take you more deeply into expert systems, a branch of the artificial intelligence field.

Chapter Objectives

After you have read and studied this chapter, you will be able to:

1. Define artificial intelligence, and describe the five major topics of AI work.
2. Explain how robots work in AI and how that differs from the popular concept of a robot.
3. Outline the key issues involved in machine vision and natural language recognition.
4. Explain how neural networks work and how they can be useful in business.
5. Describe how expert systems relate to decision support, and describe the types of decision support tasks that expert systems are likely to be helpful with.
6. Explain how a simple expert system works.
7. Discuss the similarities between expert systems and neural networks.

14.1 About Artificial Intelligence

Marvin Minsky of the Massachusetts Institute of Technology, one of the pioneers of the artificial intelligence (AI) field, has defined *artificial intelligence* as "the science of making computers do things that would require intelligence if done by people."

This is not a static definition. Consider long division. We know it can be done by a device the size of a college ID card, cheap enough to be given away for a few cereal boxtops. Anything that such a gadget can do cannot require intelligence. Yet a few decades ago, this was not the case. Students learned long division in grade school (they still do) and spent countless hours perfecting the skill (while today they buy calculators). Long division was clearly within the realm of things that demanded intelligence. Go back a few more decades. Long division, if one could do it at all, indicated intelligence of a high order indeed. Go back a little further: it bordered on sorcery.

The same analogies could be applied to skills ranging from alphabetizing a list of words to playing checkers. As we learn how to apply computers to new tasks, the frontier of what we consider "intelligent" recedes to keep its distance.

14.1.1 History of AI

The term "artificial intelligence" was coined at a conference in the 1950s. Today the term seems to have been a poor choice. The focus of AI research is not on the creation of artificial beings with humanoid intelligence but on taking smaller steps in several specific directions. The British call this field "machine intelligence," all in all a better word choice.

When the term "AI" was introduced, little was known about the complexities involved in making machines appear to think. AI researchers in the 1950s and 1960s, heartened by initial progress on small problems (such as playing checkers—a far from trivial undertaking but much less complex than most problems that call for "intelligent" behavior) made glowing predictions for intelligent computer behavior. In the clarity of 20-20 hindsight we now know that these were wildly optimistic. Much of the optimism has since been toned down, as the intervening decades saw but a fraction of the progress that had been expected. You can get a good idea of how the field began in [PART90]. Today's artificial intelligence researchers are far more realistic about its future than were their predecessors—or, in some cases, than they were themselves in the heady early days. The reputation of AI, as a field where expectations far outstripped reality, has lingered in some circles. That has colored the attitudes of many business executives to aspects of AI, including those aspects whose commercial value has been proven many times over.

One Hundred Definitions of AI

Massimo Negrotti collected 100 definitions of AI during the 8th International Joint Conference on Artificial Intelligence (IJCAI) held in Karlsruhe, Germany, in 1983, and subsequently published them on pp. 155–57 of [NEGR91]. Most of their authors were from North America and Western Europe. Negrotti prefaces the list with "Notice the extreme variety of the definitions, ranging from the technologically oriented to the pure-research oriented; from the intellectually committed to the comical." A small sampling of the definitions is printed here:

Ability of machines to adequately function in human culture.

AI is getting more out of a computer than the designer could predict.

Attempting to compete with a human being without feeling.

Attempting to find useful solutions to problems we don't know how to solve.

Attempting to reinvent human capabilities on a different technological basis.

Attempting to understand the processes of consciousness.

Construction of machines which behave in a way people describe as intelligent.

Information sculpture; leftovers other computer systems can't handle.

Study of general principles underlying mental processes.

The step just beyond where AI research has gotten to today.

The study of the nature of intelligence, independent of (human) hardware.

Trying to make computers do things that people can do better.

14.1.2 *The Turing Test*

The English mathematician and computer pioneer Alan Turing suggested a test of computer intelligence in 1950. Put one person, called an interrogator, in a room with a teletypewriter, he said. Put a second person and a computer in a second and a third room. Allow the interrogator to ask either the second person or the computer any questions he or she wishes via the teletypewriter. If the interrogator can't tell the other person from the computer from their respective responses, Turing said he would consider the computer to be "intelligent."

Computers can pass the Turing test today for short question-and-answer sessions that are restricted, by prior agreement, to a limited subject area. The first in a (hopefully) annual series of open contests for computers were organized by the Computer Museum in Boston in 1991 and 1992. New York philanthropist David G. Loebner put up a $100,000 prize for the first computer to pass the test with no limitations on subject matter. No programs qualified for the grand prize, but a token $1,500 (plus a medal with a likeness of Turing on one side and Loebner on the other) was awarded in 1991 to PC Therapist for the best performance.[1] It carried on "whimsical conversations"—which allowed it to change the topic and introduce irrelevant comments at random, on the grounds that humans carrying on whimsical conversations do likewise. (Lewis Carroll has many examples). Computers that attempted to carry on reasonable conversations, on subjects such as wines and women's fashions, were detected quickly. Their mechanical responses, their limited base of general knowledge, or their lack of common sense eventually betrayed them. Yet experimenters have had impressive success fooling unaware "subjects" through programs that simply pick up questions, identify certain parts of speech, turn them around, and construct intelligent-seeming answers.

Whimsy was outlawed for 1992, but the same programmer, Joseph Weintraub, also developed the 1992 winner. It won $2,000 (plus the medal) for discussing "Men versus Women." It fooled two of the eight judges into thinking they were conversing with a person. A typical excerpt from its dialogue, as reported in [MARK93]:

> Question (human): Do you think Hillary Clinton has too much power?
>
> Answer (computer): Clinton seems to be doing a lot to address that problem, appointing intelligent women to high-level positions.
>
> Q: You seemed to fumble that question.
>
> A: I seem to recall you said you didn't answer my question. I am pondering the question of the ages—why won't my wife take my shirts to the laundry?
>
> Q: That seems like a reasonably sexist response.
>
> A: It is not so sexist if you wake up Monday morning without a clean shirt. I wish I could take a little nap. You're not really talking about me, are you?

As of this writing, the third Loebner Prize competition is scheduled for September 21, 1993. You should be able to find a report of its results in your college or university library.

Researchers are actively trying to help computers pass the Turing test: not because fooling innocent victims is of value, nor because the $100,000 Loebner prize will compensate them for years of intense group effort, but because the reasons computers fail the Turing test illuminate gaps in our understanding of human intelligence and how we process language. This research also has direct practical usefulness in helping computers understand natural language, which is essential if computers are to become truly easy to use by the general public.

---

[1]PC Therapist was designed by Thinking Machines Inc., Woodside, New York.

Eliza: The Electronic Psychiatrist?

Joseph Weizenbaum of MIT wrote the original Eliza program in the 1960s to show how computers could seem to be intelligent to the uninitiated while actually following simple procedures.[2] There are many Eliza "clones" available for desktop microcomputers today, most of them developed by hobbyists and available from free computer user groups and public "bulletin boards."

Eliza is supposed to act like a psychiatrist. It (she?) actually just looks at a sentence the user types in, picks out verbs and nouns it recognizes, and rearranges them using basic English grammar rules into a reasonable-seeming response. If you type "my homework," it can turn "my" into "your" and construct a response that includes the phrase "your homework." It has a list of key words and appropriate responses, so if your sentence includes the word "father" it might come back with "tell me more about your family." (This can lead to absurd sequences if you used the word in the sense of "priest.")

It has a library of standard answers, such as "I don't quite understand," "Please go on," "What does that suggest to you?," "You haven't said anything about your parents," or even simply "Tell me more," to use when it can't figure out anything else to say. Some of these let it plug in a word from an earlier input sentence, as in "Earlier you mentioned {*x*}," where {*x*} might be replaced by "your knee" if you had typed "my knee" at an earlier point in the "conversation."

Eliza can hold its own for a few sentences. After a while it becomes obvious that Eliza isn't making a real contribution to the conversation. In one reported case, a manager sat down at a terminal where Eliza had been left running. He entered what he thought was the log-on sequence and was surprised to see, on his screen, an English response. He thought that a co-worker in another room was somehow connected to his terminal and asked the co-worker to release it. The responses started with "Why do you want me to get off your terminal? and got less and less meaningful (along the lines of "Why do you think I am being ridiculous about not getting off your terminal?"), as the manager got hotter and hotter under the collar. Only the timely arrival of the previous terminal user, who knew what was going on, prevented the poor manager from storming off and trying to find the "culprit."

Yet people have reported that the simple exercise of responding to nonsensical questions has actually helped them focus on a problem better. Perhaps all some people need is a nonjudgmental listener. If you don't mind its also being a nonunderstanding listener, Eliza fills this bill nicely.

14.2 Artificial Intelligence Today

Most workers in the AI field have backed off from grandiose thoughts of creating an "electronic brain" and have focused their sights on narrower, hopefully more easily achievable, objectives. Today's applied AI work is

[2]The Eliza program was named for Eliza Doolittle in George Bernard Shaw's *Pygmalion,* which later became *My Fair Lady* on Broadway and in the movies.

concentrated in a few areas: robotics, machine vision, natural language interpretation, neural nets, and expert systems. This section summarizes the first four areas. The fifth area, expert systems, is the topic of the rest of this chapter. As expert systems are already at a point where they can be applied to real business problems, the rest of this book will tell you more about them.

14.2.1 Robotics

Robots have been with us via science-fiction for decades.[3] Most of us visualize robots as humanoids with shiny metallic skin, much like C3P0 in the *Star Wars* movies.

Artificial intelligence workers consider a robot to be any computer-controlled mechanical actuator that does not follow a deterministic, preprogrammed path. This criterion differentiates robots from devices such as numerically controlled milling machines, whose steps are determined in advance and which are unable to deviate from the predetermined sequence. Some devices called "industrial robots," by this definition, would not be robots in the AI sense. They can still be quite useful, of course.

Robots as AI workers use the term, by contrast, can be given general instructions—"go to Room 403E," or "climb the hill." Their controlling software must figure out how to accomplish their assigned task.

The difficulty, which takes robotics out of the garden-variety programming area and into artificial intelligence, is that a typical task cannot be completed simply by calculating the desired ending position and sending the robot there in a straight line. There may be physical obstacles, such as walls, between the present position of the robot and Room 403E. The robot's control program is given the end goal of its activity. It then establishes an intermediate goal which, if successfully reached, will hopefully bring it closer to the end goal. This sequence continues until it establishes an intermediate goal that it can reach directly from its present position. It goes there and then continues the process by trying to go to its next higher intermediate goal, and so on until the objective is finally reached.

The right intermediate goal is not always obvious. Suppose the robot is in a room with two doors. One rule might be "try the door that is more directly in line toward your goal." But what if one door leads to a corridor and the other to a second room and what if the one that leads to the second room is in a more direct line to 403E than the one to the corridor? Perhaps we should set up "get into a corridor" as the intermediate goal. The robot will now try doors to corridors before doors to other rooms. But what if we know that one door is to a corridor and we don't know where the other door goes? Of if we know that one door goes to another room and, again, we don't

---

[3]The word "robot" was coined by Czech author Karl Kapek in his work *R.U.R.* It comes from the Slavic root for "work."

know where the other door goes? This is the domain of *heuristic searching:* using rules of thumb, based on human expertise, to guide the search along the most likely paths first. The intent of heuristic search is to help the system (in this case, the robot) reach its goal as quickly as possible. Heuristic search is especially valuable in chess-playing programs, where tournaments are played under strict limits on each player's "thinking" time.

At times the robot will reach a dead end. This means it has tried to follow the sequence of intermediate goals that it established in advance, but it has gotten to a point from which the next goal is not reachable. (This concept can apply to conceptual, symbolic goals as well as to physical goals such as in the present example.) Perhaps it entered a room that is in a direct geometric line to Room 40E but that has no other exit. It must then *backtrack*—discard its current goal and replace it with another that can lead to the same immediately higher goal. If it has tried all the goals that could lead to that immediately higher goal, it must discard that goal and choose a new intermediate goal at that level. This search process, which resembles a tree such as the one in Figure 14–1, continues until a path from the robot's present state to its goal is eventually found. The concept of establishing a series of intermediate goals on the way to a final goal and pursuing them in a tree pattern until a solution is found is called *goal-directed reasoning*. This approach is fundamental to many branches of artificial intelligence, including the expert systems area that we cover in more detail later.

FIGURE 14–1
Tree Search Example

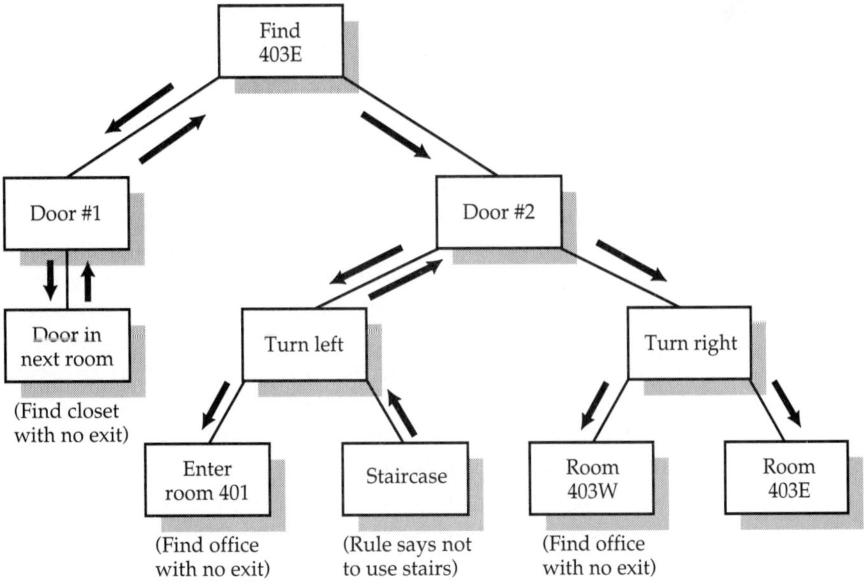

As an example of a different type of problems in robotics, while the path to the top of the hill may be unobstructed, the proper sequence of leg motions needed to reach it cannot be calculated directly from knowledge of its position. Programming them in advance may not be practical because the robot has to respond to terrain variations that cannot be predicted from a distance. Instead, the robot must have general "knowledge" of the motions involved in walking. Conceptually, this is also a form of goal-directed reasoning: We give the robot a goal—"Walk!"—and it has to figure out how to achieve that under its current conditions.

The science of robotics involves solving these and similar problems. Its aim is to enable robots to take over physical tasks that humans find repetitive, dangerous, or impractical for some other reason. Its major MIS application is indirect: The reasoning processes that take robots to room 403E can help other types of computer programs reach their goals as well. Thus, even if the physical technology of robots isn't directly transferable to the typical DSS, many of the programming techniques are.

14.2.2 Machine Vision

Unless we have a severe visual impairment, we don't spend much time thinking about how we see. We open our eyes and we know instantly what we are looking at. How does that happen? We don't know. What's more, we generally don't care. When we are fooled by an optical illusion—a picture drawn by someone who knows how we will respond to a given set of visual stimuli and creates those stimuli by unexpected means—we kick ourselves mentally for being so stupid. We're not really stupid; we're just responding naturally to our conditioning. If we tried to analyze every set of visual stimuli we get all day long in terms of what it might represent and thought consciously about why it should represent one particular set of objects out of all these possibilities, we'd have no time for anything else.

Machine vision researchers try to pierce the wall of our subconscious and figure out how we really determine what we are seeing, or to find other ways for computers to respond appropriately to their surroundings. This ability has many applications in the field of robotics discussed in the previous section. If a robot can determine where a bolt is lying in a bin, it can pick up that bolt for an assembly process without needing it to be in precisely the same position every time. If it can detect obstacles in its way, it can navigate toward its objective even if the terrain it is crossing is not quite what was expected. Even more prosaic applications, such as finished part inspection in an assembly plant, can benefit from machine vision.

You can get an idea of the difficulty of the problem from Figure 14–2. From a distance the picture of an eye is clear. From close up, however, it looks like a collection of dots. You can achieve the same effect by looking at any photograph in a newspaper: first from a distance, then by squinting as

FIGURE 14–2
Enlarged Dot-Matrix Picture of an Eye

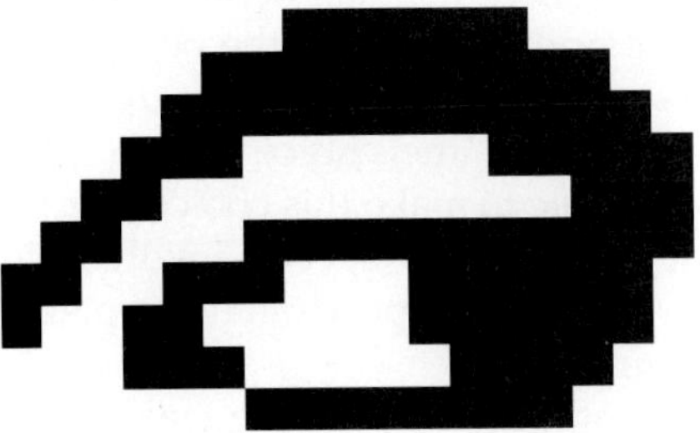

close to the paper as you can focus so the individual dots in the half-tone reproduction become distinct.

The machine vision problem is that the computer sees only the individual dots. A scanner, TV camera, or similar device reads in an array of lightness and darkness values corresponding to points on a grid. If color vision is desired, the input typically consists of three color intensity values for each point. To make things even more complex, three-dimensional vision requires two grids where the computer must figure out which point in one grid corresponds to each point in the other.

Despite these obvious difficulties (plus several less obvious, but equally significant, ones) machine vision is quickly becoming a reality. Computer-controlled arms can today take instructions such as "pick up the small blue block." To carry out this command, the software controlling the arm must identify the blocks in its field of vision, decide which of them are blue, determine which of the blue ones is "small," and determine how that block is oriented so that the arm's grasping unit can be positioned appropriately.

14.2.3 *Natural Language Interpretation*

The field of natural language interpretation, or NLI, has two components. One involves decoding a group of sound waves and figuring out what words it represents. The other accepts a group of words from decoded sound waves, a keyboard, optical character recognition of printed text, or any other source, and tries to assign meaning to it.

Voice Recognition

My younger son shocked the family dinner table into silence one evening when he announced that his schoolmate Andrea got married in Peru. As soon as the questions died down, he explained that we had misunderstood him: Andrea had "got Marian Paroo," the female lead in the high school musical *The Music Man.*

The lesson here is that phrases may sound alike but mean different things. Did the lecturer on language recognition really say "it's hard to recognize speech" or, in an attempt to trick us, "it's hard to wreck a nice beach?" Few of us think about how we understand that the beginning and ending of "I'll see you in aisle C" don't mean the same. (Say it out loud if you don't get the point.[4]) To a computer, though, the choice of one interpretation over the other is not obvious. Being able to make this choice means the computer must know something about the parts of speech involved and what words or phrases can be the correct part of speech. The implications of this understanding are far from simple.

Speech recognition programs vary in the size of their vocabularies, in whether or not they require training for each speaker whose speech they are to recognize, and whether or not they require the speaker to pause between utterances. There are trade-offs among these three capabilities.

The electronic replacement for the human brain and ear—a device able to recognize connected speech with a large vocabulary, which does not require a special training session for each speaker whose voice it is to understand—is not within the state of the art in 1993. Less capable devices, however, are.

- Speaker-independent units that can recognize disconnected utterances within a limited vocabulary are in widespread use. Typical ones can understand the 10 decimal digits and a few additional words such as "yes," "no," and "stop." Others are designed to recognize a set of commands to manipulate a physical device: "right," "left," "up," "down," "fast," "slow," and so on.

  Telephone companies are starting to use such units to handle collect telephone calls automatically. The caller is guided through a series of questions with yes/no answers. The system records the caller speaking his or her name and plays it back, with an appropriate message, when the called telephone is answered. It then recognizes that the answering party says "yes" or "no." The system notifies a human operator if it gets confused, but it can handle a large part of the work itself.
- Speaker-dependent units that recognize disconnected utterances within wide vocabularies are in use, for example, to help physicians update patients' medical records after tests or operations. (Some of them reduce the active vocabulary they must recognize at any given point by limiting it to words that make sense in a particular part of the report.)
- Speaker-independent continuous speech recognition units with a limited vocabulary are coming into use. Their potential applications

[4]They sound the same when spoken by most people who grew up in the northern or western United States. Speakers from other places, including the southeastern United States, may pronounce "I'll see" and "aisle C" differently.

Speech Recognition Today[5]

Speech recognition has several practical applications in 1993. Among them:

G. H. Bass and Company, a shoe firm perhaps best known for its Bass Weejuns line of loafers, uses speech recognition to reduce data-entry errors and increase the speed of warehouse receiving operations at its Atlanta, Georgia, distribution center. Instead of using pen and paper to record shoes received from offshore manufacturers, a clerk reads the data into a lightweight microphone headset connected to a transmitter worn on the belt. The speech recognition computer accepts the inventory data, stores it, and prints bar code labels for the boxes. The system, which runs on $25,000 worth of hardware, saves $60,000 in labor costs per year—as well as reducing receiving errors and sales cancellations caused by receiving delays.

Ford Motor Company uses speech recognition technology to record paint inspection data throughout its assembly operations. Production workers use it to record quality right on the production line, thus maintaining the inspection process while eliminating inspectors.

American Telephone and Telegraph is installing a new system to place collect calls. When fully in place, hopefully by December 1994, it will allow AT&T to use as many as one-third fewer operators. Callers who dial "0" will be asked to say the word "collect" if they wish to place a collect call. They will then be asked to say their names, which the system will record. The system will then place the call, which the customer previously dialed, and will ask the recipients to say "yes" if they will accept the call. An operator will come on the line if the caller says "operator" or if the process does not proceed as planned. This application can be tricky, however. Suppose a child, answering the phone and hearing the request, says "I don't know—I'll ask my mommy." The system may think it heard "no" and hang up.

are not numerous since a limited vocabulary does not lend itself to long connected statements. However, this capability is a valuable research step on the path to the eventual goal.

Since inferring characters from digitized sound waves has proven difficult, some researchers are approaching the problem from another viewpoint. They are trying to infer the sounds being spoken from an image of the speaker's mouth motions, sort of an electronic "lip reading." While this work is still in its early stages, initial results are promising.

Extracting Meaning

"Time flies like an arrow," said Socrates.

"Oh, is that how to time flies?" said Pocrates. "I know how to time arrows. Now I can time flies too."

Once words are recognized, they must be interpreted. Here, too, the English language (along with most other natural languages) provides pitfalls

[5]Source: Most of the material is from [MARC92].

in the form of words that have more than one meaning and idiomatic expressions whose literal interpretation does not tell us what they really mean.

Understanding a sentence requires a computer to understand every element in it: what part of speech it is, what it means, how it relates to the rest of the sentence. We do not imply by the word "understand" here that a computer "understands" words or phrases in the same way people do. We mean that it associates attributes with each word or phrase that, taken as a group, describe its usage in the given context. For a computer to "understand" the phrase "big yellow bus" it must determine that "big" and "yellow" are adjectives which apply to the noun "bus" and create a noun phrase. To "understand" the sentence, "The spirit is willing, but the flesh is weak," it must determine that "spirit," in this context, refers to a person's character and not to a supernatural being or an alcoholic beverage.

Natural language interpretation is practical today within limited contexts. There are products on the market, such as one from Natural Language Inc. (Berkeley, California) that can interpret English with sufficient accuracy to be useful in retrieving information from a database. A manager might type "Which customers bought more than 5 cases or $500 worth from us last month?," and the computer would respond with a list. If it didn't know what a "case" was, it might ask, so the user could respond, "A case is 24 bottles." The user might then type "Sort it by state," and the system would understand that "it" refers to the answer to the previous query. These products often rely on expert systems technology, which is discussed below and in the rest of this book, to interpret what words mean in a given context.

The two aspects of natural language interpretation can be used jointly to improve the recognition of spoken sentences. Here, the computer attempts to interpret spoken sentences as they are "heard." The second similar-sounding phrase ("aisle C") in the sentence "I'll see you in aisle C" would be recognized as identifying a place since it follows the preposition "in." Since "aisle C" is a place, but "I'll see" is not, a computer could choose the correct interpretation.

The software technology of goal-directed reasoning, useful in most areas of artificial intelligence, helps here as well. Consider this excerpt from President Clinton's January 1993 inaugural address:

> Americans have mustered the determination . . . [6]

A computer processing this phrase from left to right might first assume that the third word is "mustard," that is, that Clinton said "Americans have mustard. . . ." It establishes an intermediate goal of parsing the rest of the phrase consistently with that assumption. It soon encounters a dilemma: "mustard the determination" makes no sense. The computer must therefore backtrack.

[6]Actually, he said "Americans have *always* mustered the determination . . . ," but that makes the example more complicated.

It establishes a new intermediate goal based on interpreting the problem sound as "mustered," which in turn forces it to reinterpret "have" as an auxiliary verb. Since the verb phrase "have mustered" can take a direct object, the rest of the interpretation proceeds without conceptual difficulty. Had this alternative interpretation not been forthcoming, the computer might have looked for less likely ones. You can see that this process requires a good lexicon of the English language and a complex set of grammar rules.

A truly intelligent robot in the science fiction sense awaits the solution of all the above problems. It must understand spoken commands, interpret them correctly, respond to visual cues, and activate the right electrical "muscles" to accomplish its goals. For the foreseeable future, makers of *Star Wars* sequels will need humans to control C3P0 and his (her? its?) kin.

14.2.4 Neural Nets

The human nervous system, including the brain, is constructed of cells called *neurons*. Neurons receive stimuli at their inputs. When the combination of inputs to a neuron reaches a threshold, which varies from neuron to neuron, it sends a signal from its output. This signal becomes in turn the input to one or more downstream neurons. Everything we do, from brushing our teeth to proving trigonometry theorems, is done via appropriate sequences of signals that travel along *synapses* from neuron to neuron.

If we could figure out how our neurons are connected to each other, goes the logic, we could construct software "neurons" that pass signals to each other in the same way. We could then have a computer program that could learn from its experience, remember what it learned, feel pride or shame, . . . in short, true, conscious, artificial intelligence.

Researchers are still quite a distance from developing fully conscious computer programs, or indeed from agreeing on what a "conscious" computer program would be. (One reason is that our brains are estimated to have about 10^{10} neurons with about 10^{14} synapses, or connections, among them. Even insect brains have far more neurons than we can usefully simulate on today's largest and fastest computers.) However, networks of simulated software neurons, or neural nets, have already been applied usefully to several tasks. The conceptual structure of a neural net is shown in Figure 14–3.

Most successful neural network tasks fall into the general area of pattern recognition. This category includes diagnosing medical problems from their symptoms, recognizing handwritten or printed characters from their representation as dark or light squares in a regular grid, suggesting which stocks are likely to increase in price, determining if a particular pattern of credit card usage might indicate a stolen card, or predicting whether a loan applicant is likely to make payments on schedule.

Since we don't know how our neurons interact with each other to perform a complex task such as pattern recognition, neural net users don't try to program a network of interactions into a system. Rather, they define the

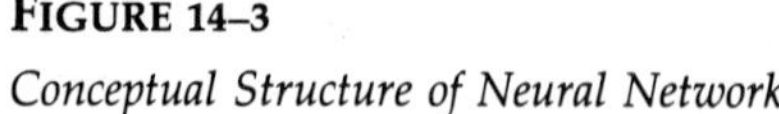

FIGURE 14–3

Conceptual Structure of Neural Network

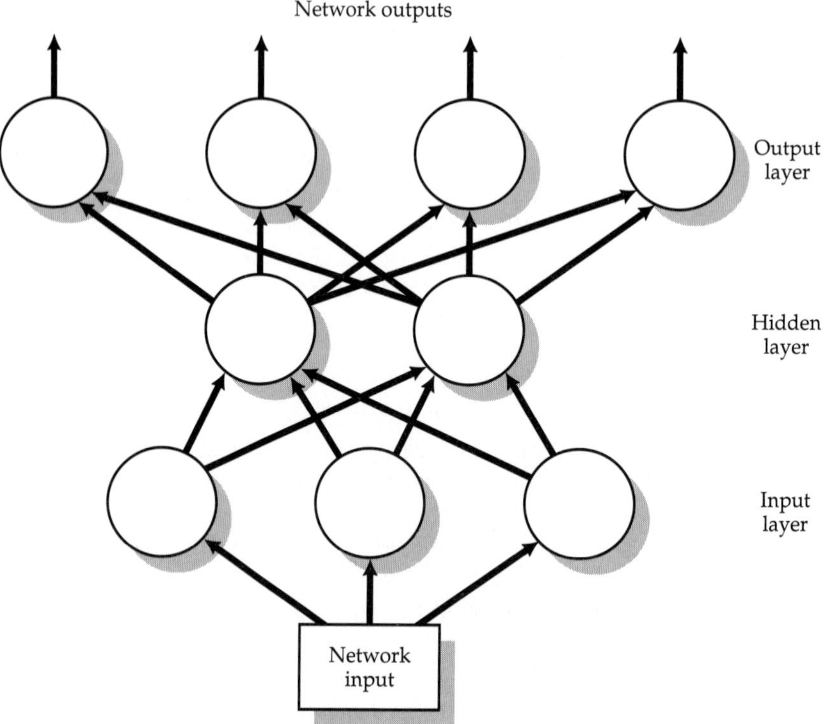

inputs to the system, the general structure of the network (so many layers, so many connections), the conditions on the input of a neuron that will cause it to send a signal down the line, and the desired system output. They then "train" the system using a large number of test cases: often several thousand.

Because so many test cases are needed just to get a neural net working, this technology is only suited to highly repetitive applications. During the training process, the software that controls the neural net establishes and changes trial connections and neuron firing thresholds at random. Those that are in place when the net generates the correct output are reinforced and have an increased likelihood of being left alone. Those that are in place when incorrect inputs are produced have an increased likelihood of being changed by the control software. Eventually the connections and thresholds stabilize at values that produce correct outputs on the great majority of test cases. The neural net is then ready for use.

Neural net development tools are available for microcomputers for a few hundred dollars and for up to tens of thousands for more advanced tools that run on more powerful systems. These tools allow users to define nets, to specify their inputs in as much detail as possible (the more that can be said about the characteristics of the inputs, the less remains for the network to "learn"), to train the networks on test cases, to test their performance, and to execute them against real data. It is usually more practical to develop a neural net with such a tool than by programming it from scratch.

Most neural net programs simulate the parallel behavior of a true neural network on a conventional, one-instruction-at-a-time computer. Given the inputs to all neurons at one time step, they go through all the neurons in the net, one at a time, to determine which will fire. These calculations determine the inputs to all the neurons for the next time step. The process repeats until the output of the net stabilizes. This can take quite a while for a complex net.

Neural nets are natural candidates for massively parallel multiprocessing because their behavior is inherently parallel. The total set of neurons, which can easily number in the hundreds or thousands, can be partitioned across the available processors. Processors need then only send messages to each other when the output of a neuron in one processor goes to a neuron in another processor. Intelligent partitioning of neurons, especially after training has determined the interconnections among them, can reduce this interprocessor communication to a minimum. The speedup in execution time can thus approach the number of processors installed. If a configuration is expanded by adding more processors, a neural net can take advantage of the added power by repartitioning the neurons across the new set of processors.

Neural nets can be used to recognize patterns that have historically led to certain outcomes in decision-making situations. This ability can be useful in many DSS applications: recommending which insurance claims are likely to be fraudulent, which commodity prices are likely to go up (or down), and so forth.

Sometimes detecting a pattern is enough since the decision that follows is obvious. Thermal Neutron Analyzer (TNA), a neural network-based system developed by Science Applications International Corporation (SAIC), detects explosives in airline baggage with a high degree of accuracy. Airline personnel do not stand around and wonder what to do next when TNA reports a positive reading.

In most situations, however, recognizing the pattern is not enough. Deciding what to do once the pattern has been recognized still requires other forms of DSS, human intelligence, or both. The Papnet system uses neural networks to tell normal cells from abnormal ones.[7] It picks out the 128 most abnormal-looking cells in a Pap smear test and displays them on a color monitor for human cytologists (cell study specialists) to review. By allowing cytologists to focus on the most likely abnormal cells, rather than scanning several hundred thousand cells for possible abnormalities, the error rate among

[7] Papnet is a product of Neuromedical Systems, Suffern, New York.

Papnet users drop from a typical 15+ percent to under 3 percent. In this case Papnet isn't making a decision that a cell is abnormal. It's screening the data so a human expert can make the decision.

14.3 Expert Systems

Expert systems, which mimic the human reasoning process closely, are the most widely used branch of AI in business today. Since humans use their reasoning processes while making decisions, such systems can often approximate the types of decisions that humans would make. In situations that are

American Airlines Uses Expert Systems to Schedule Maintenance, Plan Aircraft Loads[8]

Each of American Airlines' 550+ aircraft must be taken out of service for scheduled maintenance at prescribed intervals. Each type of maintenance for each type of aircraft has its own interval, planned duration, and one or more locations where it can be performed. Prior to 1990, human controllers in its Tulsa, Oklahoma, Maintenance Operations Center (MOC) juggled 2,200 scheduled flights per day to 160 worldwide destinations to get each airplane to its maintenance location in time. They did this while dealing with bad weather, delayed and canceled flights, and malfunctioning aircraft. They used rules of thumb developed over years of experience. The rules were reasonable, but the number of aircraft, flights, and destinations was beyond the ability of people to deal with effectively.

American coped with this problem to a point by dividing its fleet into four types of aircraft and by scheduling each type as its own "desk." They also tolerated controllers' "satisficing" with the first acceptable routing they found rather than searching for the best. However, in 1987 they realized that they would soon have over 200 McDonnell-Douglas MD-80 aircraft and that this number would be too large for manual routing. Further subdividing the MD-80 fleet would have introduced other problems. Following a prototype and an additional feasibility study, completed in April 1988, they decided to develop a knowledge-based system called Maintenance Operations Center Advisor (MOCA).

MOCA became operational for MD-80 aircraft in April 1990 and subsequently for other types as well. It runs on Macintosh II microcomputers using a special Texas Instruments add-in board with a coprocessor that runs LISP programs efficiently. It obtains schedule information from a database stored in American's flight operations mainframe computer.

Prior to the introduction of MOCA, American's maintenance operation controllers were not computer literate. They had never used a mouse-and-window-oriented computer. Accordingly, American's MIS staff paid careful attention to implementation factors. They introduced MOCA in four places:

[8]Sources: [LAPL91], [SMIT91], and [DALY92].

sufficiently repetitive to justify a system development effort, this capability can pay off handsomely.

14.3.1 The Basic Idea

You arrive home at night. You are hungry. You have 59¢ in your wallet. The bank is closed, the nearest ATM is not within walking distance, the buses have stopped running, and your car is in the shop. You have spaghetti and a jar of sauce in your kitchen cabinet. You also have homework due tomorrow and a message on the answering machine that says, "Call Mom." What do you do?

concluded

1. Introducing the Macintosh hardware as a direct functional replacement for the existing terminals used to look up flight schedules. This period of familiarization with the hardware and interface technology (mouse, pull-down menus) extended over several months.
2. Allowing controllers to browse through MOCA's functions. This phase began with training sessions and continued with round-the-clock availability of knowledge engineers in the MOC facility.
3. Making aircraft routing assignments through MOCA, rather than via the previous paper-and-pencil method, after planning those assignments manually.
4. Using MOCA for planning as well. This phase began with a one-day class and continued with six weeks of on-the-job training with the knowledge engineers.

MOCA has reduced the number of "flight breaks"—switching two aircraft in the middle of direct flights to route one of them for maintenance reasons—substantially. Since a flight break forces passengers to disembark and re-embark in order to continue on the same flight, it is a major source of inconvenience. MOCA has also increased the average number of flight hours between maintenance checks by 10 percent (in order not to exceed the maximum number of hours between checks, human controllers often scheduled them earlier than necessary) and routes aircraft more consistently and efficiently than the human controllers did. Finally, it has enabled American to handle its expanded fleet with 16 trained controllers, rather than needing almost twice that number.

Since the success of MOCA, American has implemented additional knowledge-based systems to support its operations. One is AALP, American's Assistant Load Planner. It supports the problem of loading freight around an aircraft's center of gravity so the plane will fly properly. AALP's 60-rule knowledge base is triggered into action four hours before each flight. Based on passenger reservation data, current weather forecast, the type of aircraft, and historical average mail, baggage, and freight loads, it plans an initial load distribution automatically. This initial distribution is accessed and updated by load planners as new information comes in right up to flight time.

AALP handles about 30 percent of the overall load planning task. This workload reduction, most of it in the "scut work" that forms the initial part of the load planning process, allowed American to increase its load planning capacity by 300 flights in six months without adding to its 100-person-plus load planning staff. A second, unexpected, benefit is that better load plans save fuel—the crew no longer has to compensate for aircraft load imbalance via fuel-wasting settings of wing and elevator trim tabs.

You might put up water for spaghetti, call Mom while it's coming to a boil, and put off the homework until after dinner (or during dinner, if you don't mind sauce on your notes). Yet this decision is not simple. Why, for example, didn't you go to a movie? Partly because 59¢ won't pay for a movie, partly because you're hungry, partly because of the homework, partly because of Mom's message. Putting these together to decide what to do, and in what order, involved a series of logical (in the mathematical sense, at least) reasoning steps.

One of your rules might be expressed formally this way:

> If I am hungry, my first action will be to obtain food.

That, in turn, can lead to analysis of different options for obtaining food, which in turn might suggest that cooking spaghetti is the most practical under the circumstances. The entire set of these rules, if you could express them, would explain how and why you made the plans that you did.

An expert system—also referred to as a knowledge-based system or a rule-based system—is an information system that follows human lines of reasoning, expressed in rules such as the one above, to arrive at a conclusion from known facts.

14.3.2 A Simple Expert System

Consider a system that can follow three rules:

1. If you are hungry, you should eat.
2. If you are not hungry and you have homework, you should do your homework.
3. If you are not hungry and do not have homework, you should see a movie.

This system shows the fundamental features of all computerized expert systems:

1. Someone must determine the objectives of the system, the concepts it will deal with, the ways it will represent knowledge, and the rules that apply to its decisions.

> Someone chose to develop a system that can tell you what to do when you get home in the evening. Someone also decided that the important factors in this situation are your hunger and your homework and that these could be represented by "yes/no" truth values.

2. The rules are general. They do not describe a specific situation.

> The same three rules apply whether you are hungry or not, have homework or not. However, these rules may lead to different conclusions (recommendations) at different times.

3. In a specific situation you will have, or be able to get, the facts you need in order to apply the rules.

You know if you are hungry. You know if you have homework.

4. There is a way to supply these facts to the expert system and to get answers in return.

If a friend is playing the role of the "expert system," you must be able to send messages back and forth.

5. While the rules may change, the basic reasoning process remains the same.

The words "if," "then," "and," etc., retain their meaning and the methods of logical reasoning remain the same when we apply them to different conclusions and recommendations.

These characteristics lead to the block diagram of a computerized expert system or *knowledge-based system* as shown in Figure 14–4. It consists of the following parts: The *knowledge base,* also called a *rule base,* contains the problem-solving expertise of the system. In most business-oriented expert systems this expertise is expressed as rules in the form IF (some condition) THEN (some conclusion). Rules stated in this form are called *production rules.* The conclusion of a rule may establish other facts that the system will use in subsequent rules, or may lead directly to user output.

Expert systems practitioners generally refer to the *antecedent* and the *consequent* of a rule rather than to its condition and its conclusion. This precision in terminology reduces confusion. The common word "condition" can refer to part of an antecedent. Consider "IF it is sunny AND the temperature is over 80°, THEN drive the convertible." There are two conditions in the

FIGURE 14–4

Expert System Block Diagram

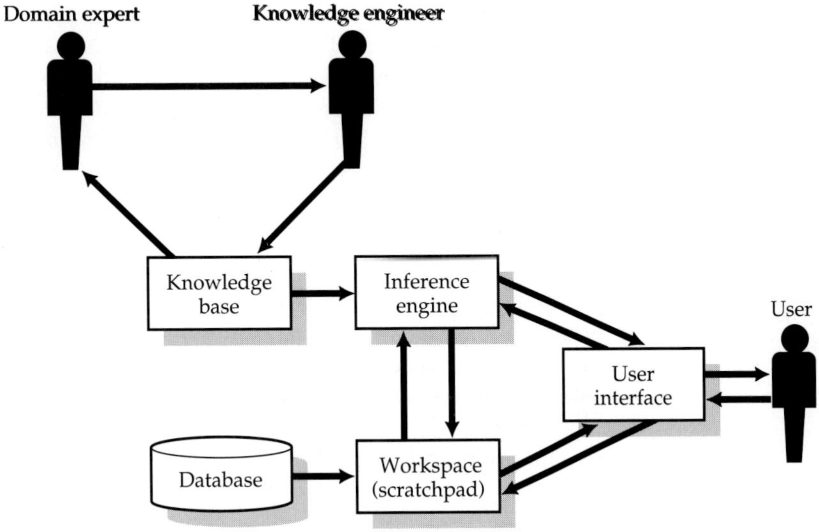

antecedent of this rule. Similarly, the common word "conclusion" is most appropriately used to refer to the output of an entire expert system, not to the result of one rule in isolation. We will use the precise terms, antecedent and consequent, from here on.

An *inference engine* is a computer program that applies the problem-solving knowledge (the rules) in the knowledge base to known facts. An inference engine is a general-purpose program that is not written specifically for one problem or problem area. It can work with any set of rules and facts it is given.

The *user interface* is a program that requests information from the user and sends output to the user. (As we discuss in the next chapter, the term "human interface" might be a better choice here, but the term "user interface" is common.) Most user interfaces provide a way for the user to ask an expert system how it arrived at a given conclusion or recommendation or why it wants a particular piece of data.

The *workspace* is an area in computer storage where the expert system stores the facts it has been given about a situation and any additional information it has derived thus far. The workspace may be called a *blackboard,* a *scratchpad, working storage,* or any of several other names.

An optional *database* supplies facts that apply to one situation (and therefore should not be in the rules) but that the user does not know or that can be supplied more easily by electronic means. Expert systems used for decision support in business often use databases. Human beings are also involved with any expert system: The *user* is the person whose problem the system is to solve. He or she can use the system in any of the usage modes discussed in Section 4.7.

The *subject matter expert* (also called a *domain expert*) and the *knowledge engineer* contribute to the development of the expert system but in general do not use it after it is developed. The subject matter expert contributes expertise in the field of the system but may not know how expert systems work. The knowledge engineer is trained both in eliciting information from subject matter experts and in encoding that knowledge in a knowledge base. In complex expert systems, the knowledge engineer may be assisted by (or may have to be) a *programmer.* At the other extreme, given a simple system and a suitably inclined subject matter expert, it may be possible to dispense with the knowledge engineer entirely.

An expert system is a computer program. It cannot do anything that a conventional computer program could not do. The advantage of the expert systems approach is that, in separating the rules in the knowledge base from the inferencing logic that operates on them, it separates parts of the program that have different characteristics and call for different skills. That separation makes the system easier to change, makes it easier to follow the reasoning process of the system, and lets each human and each part of the system do what he, she, or it does best.

14.4 Expert Systems and DSS

Expert systems reproduce the reasoning process a human decision maker would go through in reaching a decision, diagnosing a problem, or suggesting a course of action. In terms of the categories in Section 4.2, this makes expert system process-oriented DSS. In the DSS spectrum of Section 4.1, most expert systems are suggestion systems, as their conclusion is a suggested course of action.

Expert systems can also incorporate *databases* and *models*, as used in other types of DSS: Databases, as noted above, can supply facts that are unavailable to (or not easily entered by) the user. American Airlines' MOCA used a database to look up flight schedules. A system supporting stock investment decisions could be linked to a database of current stock prices and corporate earnings reports. While a stockbroker could look up this information, on the printed page or via a separate query system, and type it into a DSS, automating this step makes the system easier to use. If the number of stocks being considered is large, this sort of automatic data transfer—a type of system integration, which we'll discuss in Chapter 19—can make the difference between a practical system and a useless one.

Models are implicit in many expert systems, but they are process models as we defined the terms in Chapter 3, not system models. Consider an expert system used to diagnose problems in automobile engines. One rule might be "if cylinder pressure is below X psi, then check the valves." This rule is based on the experience of a subject matter expert, not on a mechanical model of automobile engines that shows a cause-and-effect relationship between worn valves and low cylinder pressure. The effect of the two approaches might be identical, but the content of the computer program is quite different. This difference has implications, pro and con, for the usefulness of expert system technology. We'll discuss these implications further in the next chapter.

System models can be included in DSS as supporting components for calculations that the decision process requires. A model in this context is essentially a complex, time-consuming, arithmetic operation. Instead of adding a group of numbers, the numbers might be used as parameters of a simulation run. The net effect, that we supply input to a calculation and use its output, is the same in either case. An expert system used to help select an advertising program could use a consumer responsiveness model in this way.

Once the data retrieval and system modeling parts of a decision-making process have been automated, all that remains is applying human expertise to the results. Expert systems allow us to capture, within limits, this expertise. For that reason they are becoming more and more popular in DSS applications.

The following factors, based on a list by Pfeifer and Luthi [PFEI87], suggest the types of DSS for which expert systems are likely to be suitable versus those for which they are not:[9]

- ES are generally used by nonexperts. If a decision is to be made by an expert, the help of an expert systems—which mechanizes the reasoning process that an expert performs without such help—will be less useful.
- An ES is generally considered successful if the quality of its recommendations approaches that of the human expert. Other DSS are considered successful only if they permit the expert to achieve better decision quality than he or she could without the system. This point relates closely to the previous one: A system to be used by nonexperts can improve the decision quality of the nonexperts while remaining below the quality than a human expert could achieve. A system to be used by experts, if it achieved lower quality than the expert could achieve unaided, would be useless.
- ES are generally applied to recurring problems. This is also true of model-oriented DSS, and for the same reason. Both ES and model-oriented DSS incorporate a great deal of information about the task to be solved. This means their development requires substantial effort, most or all of it applicable only to this specific task, and limits their flexibility to deal with other tasks. Other types of DSS, especially data-oriented DSS, may be more helpful with one-of-a-kind decisions.
- ES are generally applied to tactical, low-level problems. Other types of DS are generally used to support strategic decisions. This point is related closely to its predecessor: Low-level problems tend to recur often enough, with different parameters each time, to justify building a system to deal with them. Strategic decisions, by contrast, tend to be one-of-a-kind. They cannot be foreseen far enough in advance, and in enough detail, to enable us to formulate solution methods and embed those methods in an information system.

  This point also relates to the acceptability of an expert system even if it falls short of the decision-making capability of an expert. A firm will rightly insist on having its most capable employees make the far-reaching strategic decisions. It may not have this luxury with respect to operational decisions that must be made repeatedly by many people in many locations. The approach of bringing them closer to the expert level may be the best that can be accomplished.
- ES are generally applied to fairly structured tasks. This is consistent with the fact that we must be able to document the reasoning process

[9]Our interpretation of these factors differs from that of Pfeifer and Luthi. They took the factors as distinguishing expert systems (ES) from DSS. Our definition of DSS is broader and encompasses many ES applications, so we take them as distinguishing ES from *other types* of DSS.

involved in their solution. Unstructured tasks are better suited to other types of DSS.

Pfeifer and Luthi's list also includes these two differentiating factors that characterize expert system technology rather than the decision-making situation:

- In an ES, the representation of knowledge is separated from the program that processes that knowledge. Specifically, the expert's understanding of how to solve a problem is encoded in rules. These are distinct from the computer program that follows the rules' reasoning. Other types of DSS generally integrate the two into one program or a set of programs. This is the key feature of ES technology that distinguishes it from traditional computer programming.
- The ability to explain its reasoning is inherent in the knowledge- and rule-oriented structure of an ES. Other types of DSS either do not have this ability or must have it explicitly added to them via additional program code.

The above factors, other than the last two, characterize the DSS situations to which expert systems are well suited. In addition to suitability based on the type of DSS as described above, a decision-making task must have some specific characteristics before we will want to apply expert systems technology to it. Those characteristics of the task itself are discussed in the next chapter.

The nature of expert systems suggests where you should think about applying them to your decision support systems. Look for a recurring decision that experts make well but that must often be made by nonexperts. If enabling these nonexperts to make this decision better is of economic value, consider making an expert system a component of your DSS.

14.5 Expert Systems and Neural Networks

Expert systems and neural nets both attempt to mimic the way the human mind works in reaching a conclusion. Their areas of usefulness, while not identical, do overlap. The biggest conceptual difference between them is:

- Expert systems work with rules that have been elicited explicitly from experts who were able to state their problem-solving process. The rules are visible: They can be examined and changed directly, and their impact on the solution can be determined by asking the system. The expert system knows nothing about the underlying problem. It deals only with the rules that a human uses to solve it.
- Neural nets work with rules determined through a randomized training process. We don't know what these rules are. If we made a

> complete list of all the network interconnections and thresholds, it wouldn't resemble what we think of as the human process for solving the same problem. It is nearly impossible to figure out the impact of a given neuron on the solution; in fact, in many nets, neurons can be deleted with little or no impact on system behavior, just as we don't notice our loss of a brain cell now and then. One might say that an expert system models the conscious problem-solving process of an expert or experts, while a neural net models the problem solver's subconscious.

Figure 14–5 shows some of the key differences between expert systems and neural networks.

If one has many test cases but few experts, neural nets can be a useful technology. If one has an expert but few test cases, or if the problem goes beyond pattern recognition, expert systems are probably a better way to go.

A third option is to combine the neural net and the expert system to utilize the best features of both. Pattern recognition is often an important part of expert systems and DSS. Bank loan officers must recognize application patterns that correspond to people unlikely to make their payments on time; physicians must recognize symptom patterns that correspond to certain con-

FIGURE 14–5

Comparison of Expert Systems and Neural Nets

Expert Systems	*Neural Networks*
Several areas of application including those of neural nets	Primarily for recognizing patterns, classifying situations
Built by eliciting problem-solving rules from human expert(s); can sometimes induce rules from examples	Built solely by training with matching and nonmatching examples
Can explain reasons for recommendations	"Reasons" for classifications not meaningful; little or no explanation capability
Needs some test cases for validation	Needs many examples for training
Needs articulate, cooperative expert(s)	Does not need a human expert
Proven in commercial use; many development tools available	Coming into commercial use; limited number of tools available
Takes months/years to develop system due to human interaction in knowledge elicitation and system testing	Development time can be short because training process is automated after setup
Can handle large amounts of traditional data	Does not deal well with traditional forms of computerized data
Cannot adapt to unforeseen situations or changes in the environment by itself	Given feedback, can adapt to new or changed situations
Generally intended to evolve with use and experience	Generally unchanged once satisfactory performance level is reached (unless nature of problem changes, in which case it may be able to adapt)

ditions. Recognizing the pattern, however, is not the same as deciding what to do about it. The combination of expert system and neural net technologies, which can be called an "expert network," may be the best way to deal with the overall problem as a whole.

Tools that combine both expert system and neural net capabilities in an easy-to-use fashion are not generally available at this time. However, most expert system shells can call external routines in another language. This means they can invoke a neural network model to help then solve a problem. The expert system would then be the basis for the user interface of the total system. This is usually the appropriate design approach.

Summary

Artificial intelligence (AI) is an inclusive term for several areas of computing that attempt to mimic processes that humans carry out without much conscious thought. The major areas included under this term today are robotics, vision, recognizing speech, interpreting sentences in natural human languages, neural networks, and expert systems.

Robotics focuses on controlling mechanical motion via goal-directed reasoning. Its intent is to give a robot a general goal and have the robot figure out how to reach the goal. The usual reasoning process generally involves establishing intermediate goals, trying to reach these goals, and backtracking to the next higher intermediate goal if it reaches a dead end with its current goal.

The study of machine vision is useful both as an adjunct to useful robots and as a means of understanding how our own brains process visual information.

Recognizing speech is of value in enabling computers to respond to spoken instructions and data. Limited speech recognition systems are in commercial use today. One difficulty in developing more general capabilities is that many spoken sentences sound alike or nearly so.

A complementary aspect of understanding natural language is interpreting the content of phrases and sentences once they are "understood" (or keyed in) as consisting of certain words. Doing this requires knowledge of grammar rules. Grammatical sentence analysis can also help determine which of several possible similar-sounding phrases is meant in speech recognition.

Neural networks attempt to mimic the way the brain functions. Via software, a neural network connects stimuli to simulated "neurons" and propagates signals from one neuron to another. The output of the last stage in the network is the output of the network itself. Neural nets are trained via hundreds or thousands of examples before use. The connections among neurons are established as those that help the network generate correct outputs for those examples. Once established, those connections are used to analyze new situations. Well-designed neural nets are particularly useful for pattern recognition.

The most useful aspect of artificial intelligence in business today is the field of expert systems. They operate by mimicking the reasoning process a human expert would use to solve a problem. In most cases, the expert's logic is expressed in the form of "if . . . then . . . else" rules. This approach separates the reasoning process from the reasoning rules and allows the system to explain the reasons for its recommendations.

An expert system consists of a knowledge base, which contains the rules for the system's reasoning; an inference engine, which can process any rules presented to it; a user interface, for communicating with humans; and a workspace, which contains facts about the present situation. Some expert systems also use databases. The humans involved in an expert system, in addition to its users (the people with the problem to solve), include subject matter experts and knowledge engineers.

Expert systems are particularly useful in decision support systems at the *suggestion system* level of the DSS hierarchy. They are generally applied to recurring operational or tactical decisions. Where so applied, they are considered successful if they improve the performance of the typical decision maker, even if this still falls short of an expert's capability.

Expert systems and neural nets have complementary capabilities. Neural nets are useful when one has many examples but few (or no) cooperative and articulate human experts. The converse is true of expert systems. It is sometimes possible, though not easy, to use both technologies together to help solve multifaceted problems.

Key Terms

antecedent 461
artificial intelligence 444
backtracking 449
blackboard 462
consequent 461
continuous speech 452
disconnected speech 452
domain expert 462
expert systems 458
goal-directed reasoning 449
heuristic searching 449
inference engine 462
knowledge base 461
knowledge-based system 460
knowledge engineer 462
Loebner prize 445
machine intelligence 444
machine vision 450
natural language interpretation 451
neural network 455
neuron 455
pattern recognition 457
production rules 461
robotics 448
rule (in an expert system) 460
rule base 461
rule-based system 460
scratchpad 462
speaker-dependent, speaker-independent 452
speech (sound) recognition 451
subject matter expert 462
synapse 455
test cases (for neural networks) 456
training (a neural network) 456
Turing test 445
user interface (of an expert system) 462
workspace 462

Review Questions

1. Define "artificial intelligence."
2. What are the five (or six, depending on how you list them) major areas of artificial intelligence work today?
3. What is backtracking? How does it apply to robots?
4. Why is machine vision a difficult problem?
5. What types of voice recognition devices are in use today?
6. Why can it be difficult to figure out what a typed sentence means?
7. What are the cells in our brain called? How are they connected?
8. What lies between the input and the output of a neural network?
9. What is the major application area in which neural networks are practical today?
10. How are neural networks prepared to carry out a task?
11. What are the basic components of an expert system?
12. Give an example of a rule that might be in an expert system.
13. What is a subject matter expert? A knowledge engineer?
14. State five factors that describe the usefulness of expert systems in DSS.
15. State two factors that might affect your choice of expert system or neural network technology to solve a problem.

Exercises

1. Find an article on artificial intelligence from the mid-1950s to early 1960s. What predictions did its author make for the future of AI in general or for a specific aspect of AI? How do those predictions stand up today?
2. Using your library's information retrieval facilities, find one or more articles on Cyc: a research effort designed to input a great deal of general knowledge into a computer in the hope that it will be able to reason with that knowledge. Report on the present state of this work and its progress so far.
3. Find a current article on industrial robots such as those used in painting automobiles. How do their capabilities differ from those of the robots described in this chapter? What reasons justify their use?
4. Draw the letter "C" in a 5 × 7 grid on a sheet of graph paper, similar to the one shown at the top of the next page.

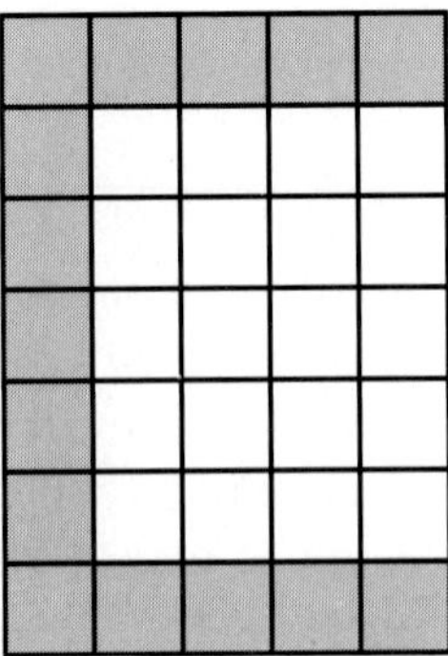

a. Try to write down a set of not more than 10 rules that will let you tell this letter apart from any other pattern of dots that might be in the grid. ("C" happens to be one of the easier letters for this.)
b. How would your rules cope with a missing black cell? With an extra black cell?

5. Consider the following newspaper headline. It appeared when Great Britain and Argentina were at war over the Falkland Islands in the early 1980s. It reflected disagreement within one segment of the U.K. political spectrum about support for the war:

   BRITISH LEFT WAFFLES ON FALKLANDS

   How would you know, given that the war is in the news so you expect to read about it and are familiar with its basic terminology, that it doesn't mean British soldiers gave local residents breakfast food when they departed?
6. Consider the spoken sentence from a Revolutionary War report: "The Minutemen have mustered on the Lexington town common." Could a computer tell that the speaker was not saying, "The Minutemen have mustard on the Lexington town common?" Why or why not? If not, what additional information would enable it to determine which was meant?
7. Suppose neural network technology advanced to the point where a computer system could read and digest books—perhaps via optical character recognition and a mechanical page-turning arm, or more prosaically by input from a text file. Suppose this system was given several philosophical works to "read" and recorded some "facts" from them in its workspace. It then claimed (via standard screen output) to be alive, to have consciousness, and to have a soul, and made other statements that were consistent with those claims.[10] How would you feel about turning such a computer off? About destroying the file that describes the interconnec-

[10]At least one science-fiction book, *The Children's Hour* by Larry Niven and Jerry Pournelle, bases a major sub-plot on the premise that a conscious computer will inevitably drive itself crazy. Mr. Pournelle, perhaps not entirely by coincidence, is also a well-known writer and magazine editor (*Byte*) in the computer field.

tions of its simulated neurons? How would you respond to its requests for more books?

8. Consider an expert system that your college could use to advise juniors and seniors concentrating in MIS about course selection for their next semester.
   a. What are three production rules this system could have in its knowledge base?
   b. What is one item of information that the user would have to supply? (Before you answer this, write down who you think the user is!)
   c. What is one item of information that this system could obtain from a database? From which database would the system obtain this information? (Make reasonable assumptions about the databases that most universities have in the 1990s.)
   d. Who might you choose as a subject matter expert to develop this system? Do you see any value in talking to more than one expert? Why or why not?
9. Interview a person in a profession that involves problem diagnosis: a physician, a mechanic, a repair person for electronic equipment. Discuss one or two recent problems that this person faced. Write down some rules the expert followed in diagnosing these problems in the form of "if . . . then . . . else. . . . " Try to obtain a complete sequence of rules that the expert would use to solve an entire (simple) problem.
10. Would the following DSS applications be good uses for expert systems, assuming one could be developed? Why or why not?
    a. Choosing a recreational sailboat. Consider two possible system sponsors: a boat dealership, which sells (and whose customers buy) sailboats frequently, and a weekend sailor, who buys a sailboat once every several years.
    b. Analyzing geological data to determine if there is likely to be oil under the surface in a given location.
    c. Determining the type of punishment (prison, suspended sentence, probation, community service, fine, etc.) and magnitude (length of sentence, amount of fine, etc.) for a convicted offender.
11. An automobile dealer who just read about neural networks thinks they would be a great way to separate "tire-kickers" from serious buyers. Is this or isn't this a good neural net application? Why or why not?

References

CHOR86 Chorafas, Dimitris N. *Applying Expert Systems in Business.* McGraw-Hill, New York (1987).

DALY92 Daly, James. "Airline Loads Up on Mac System." *Computerworld* 26, no. 48 (November 30, 1992), p. 39.

TIRS, Not Tears, at Alamo[11]

IBM's Expert System Tool Helps Car-Rental Firm Set Rates

When the sales and marketing experts at Alamo Rent-A Car Inc. couldn't agree on car rental rates, Thomas Loane decided to build an expert system to help them.

With 118 locations worldwide, 43 different car models, four different advance purchase levels, and dozens of special corporate deals, the weekly rate-changing meetings at Alamo's headquarters were getting pretty brutal.

"Things got out of hand," says Loane, vice president of computer and communications services at the Fort Lauderdale, Florida–based firm. "There were knock-down, drag-out battles between sales people who want low rates and pricing people who want them high."

To streamline the process and minimize the weekly bickering, early last year Loane began beta testing TIRS, the expert system shell from IBM. TIRS (for The Integrated Reasoning Shell) was used to develop RATE—an expert system application for making pricing recommendations. "The rules for the expert system were developed by putting the same sales and pricing people in a room and having them agree on rules rather than prices," relates Loane, who adds that the rule-making exercise prompted the participants to engage in more long-term thinking.

The final expert system, which took one programmer four months to complete, contains about 75 rules. Many of them are simple: "A four-door car costs $2 per day more than a similar two-door car." Others are more complex and go to the heart of Alamo's competitive advantage; Loane declined to talk about those.

On a regular basis, the corporate IBM S/390

LAPL91 LaPlante, Alice. "Using Your Smarts." *CIO* 5, no. 5 (December 1991), p. 54.

MARC92 Marchewka, Jack T., and Tanya Goette. "Implications of Speech Recognition Technology." *Business Forum* (Spring 1992), pp. 26–29.

MARK93 Markoff, John. "Cocktail-Party Conversation—With a Computer." *The New York Times* (January 10, 1993), section F, p. 5.

NEGR91 Negrotti, Massimo. *Understanding the Artificial: On the Future Shape of Artificial Intelligence.* Springer-Verlag, New York (1991).

PART90 Patridge, Derek, and Yorick Wilks, Eds. *The Foundations of Artificial Intelligence: A Sourcebook.* Cambridge University Press, Cambridge, England (1991).

PFEI87 Pfeifer, R. and H. J. Luthi. "Decision Support Systems and Expert Systems: A Complementary Relationship?" in *Expert Systems and Artificial Intelligence in Decision Support Systems.* D. Reidel Publishing, Holland (1987).

SMIT91 Smits, Scott, and Dave Pracht. "MOCA—A Knowledge-Based System for Airline Maintenance Scheduling," in *Innovative Applications of Artificial Intelligence 3,* Reid Smith and Carlisle Scott, Eds. AAAI Press, Menlo Park, Calif. (1991), pp. 21–37.

TAFT92 Tafti, Mohammed H. A. "Neural Networks: A New Dimension in Expert Systems Applications." *Data Base* 23, no. 1 (Winter 1992), pp. 51–54.

concluded

mainframe running CICS is fed competitive data obtained from a variety of sources, including airline reservation systems and "phantom shoppers" planted by Alamo. This and other accounting information is stored into a Computer Associates International Inc. IDMS database. Although TIRS is available on mainframes today, it was available only on PS/2's at the time Loane started beta testing. As a result, data is downloaded once a week to a PS/2 running RATE. After execution, RATE's recommended price changes are uploaded back to the mainframe.

Loane discouraged the blind acceptance of RATE's recommendations. The software was set up so that a real human being, a pricing specialist, must approve each recommendation before it becomes available to the field locations.

Loane's philosophy also restricts rule changes. "This is a strategic system," he insists, "not an instant reaction system." On rare occasions, Loane permits a rule change to fix bugs; more routinely, exceptions are handled by the pricing specialist.

Stephen T. Bradley, an analyst at GartnerGroup Inc. of Stamford, Connecticut, says the current version of TIRS is well behind the competition, especially in regard to the user interface. "When you change the rules, TIRS makes you recompile the whole system," Bradley explains. "For expert system technology, where applications are supposed to be developed iteratively, that doesn't make much sense."

TIRS's major competitors, including industry leaders Automated Reasoning Tool (ART) and Knowledge Base Management System (KBMS) have incremental compilation capabilities, and so are more widely used in applications where the rules must change frequently.[12] According to IBM, new versions of TIRS will have an improved interface.

But TIRS's more cumbersome technology doesn't bother Loane. "I could have spent six months studying what was the best expert system product, or I could have spent four months implementing the system," he says. "I chose the latter course. As it turned out, TIRS was incredibly good for us."

Exercises

Refer to the box about TIRS to answer these questions.

1. Identify the RATE component that corresponds to each expert system component in Figure 14–2.
2. In terms of the DSS spectrum of Section 4.1, what type of DSS is RATE?
3. What benefits (Section 1.4) does RATE provide to Alamo Rent-A-Car?
4. Are the decisions that RATE supports individual, multi-individual, or group decisions?

---

[11]Source: John J. Xenakis, "IBM's Expert System Tool Helps Car-Rental Firm Set Rates." *InformationWeek.* March 25, 1991. Copyright © 1991 by CMP Publications, Inc., 600 Community Drive, Manhasset, NY 11030. Reprinted from *InformationWeek* with permission.

[12]ART is from Inference Corporation, El Segundo, California; KBMS is from AICorp, Waltham, Massachusetts.

5. What sort of data do you think is downloaded from Alamo's mainframe to the PS/2 that runs RATE? Why do you think Alamo fed the competitive and accounting information to a mainframe first, not directly to the PS/2?
6. Do you feel that Loane is correct in (*a*) requiring human review of RATE's recommendations and (*b*) preferring to have pricing analysts overrule RATE rather than revising its knowledge base frequently?
7. Bradley feels that IBM's TIRS is behind competitive firms' expert system development tools in its capabilities. Assuming he is correct, does this mean that RATE is behind other car rental firms' DSS? Should Alamo care if its technical tools are not the best, as long as they provide the desired business results?
8. Do you agree with Loane's statement in the last paragraph, which argues for picking the first adequate product that comes along rather than comparing several alternatives? Do you think Loane would still feel this approach was correct if, in retrospect, TIRS had turned out to be inadequate?

Envoyance
Bob's Robot

The Envoyance office was in a turmoil at mid-afternoon when Doug and Adrienne walked in after class. The coffee maker had fallen off its shelf. Dan was trying to vacuum wet coffee grounds and pieces of glass from the carpet, with little evidence of progress thus far. Most of the offices were empty, as their usual occupants were following the unsteady progress of a two-foot-high chrome-colored object down the corridor toward the conference room. The walls along the corridor showed more than the usual evidence of scuff marks: in fact, there was a nearly continuous line of them six-and-one-half inches up—precisely the height at which the chrome-colored object was surrounded by a black rubber bumper.

"Bob got a new robot at Pete's Electronics yesterday," Sandra hastened to explain. "He's a real tinkerer, as someone might have already mentioned. Thought it might be useful in places that people can't or don't want to get into. He's spent all day trying to get it to follow instructions. So far all we have to show for his efforts is a bill for a new coffeepot—and a note to our cleaning service for tonight!"

"Can you tell us more about this robot? asked Adrienne.

"I might as well, seeing as not much else will get done this afternoon!" Sandra joked. "As you can see, it has motorized wheels and a hand with a claw. It also has a sonar distance detector that can be aimed in any direction to tell it how far it is from the nearest object and a TV camera that can detect light and dark spots. In theory, it should be able to navigate around the office while carrying anything it can hold. Bob thought it could bring people coffee. He's backed off to less dangerous objects like envelopes. You can probably figure out why."

"But how is this robot controlled?" Adrienne continued.

"I thought you'd never ask! By a computer, of course. If you want the specifics, Bob will have to give them to you."

"Yes, we'd appreciate that."

"Bob, can you quit wrecking the place and come over here for a minute?" Sandra called him. Reluctantly, or so it seemed, Bob pressed the robot's Stop button and walked to where the other three were standing. The rest of the staff, seeing that the entertainment was over for the present, went back to their offices.

"Bob, you've already met Adrienne and Doug here. They're curious as to how the computer controls your robot. Could you clue them in?"

"Sure, Sandra," Bob agreed readily. "In a nutshell, I compile programs on my PC and load them into the robot's memory. The language is essentially BASIC, which the purist in me doesn't like, but it gets the job done. It has special robot control commands added to the standard statements. I can tell it to turn any number of degrees left or right, to go at a given speed, and to point its sonar in a given direction relative to the direction the robot is facing. I can also operate the arm and the claw in six different ways: the claw opens and shuts, the wrist rotates, the elbow flexes, and the shoulder has three different types of motion. Finally, I can test the sonar input for a distance value or any pixel on the TV camera for a lightness value. By testing those numbers, or numbers I key into the control panel on the top of its head, in IF statements in the program, I can make it do different things. For example, it can turn when it reaches, say, the door to my office."

"Hearing you describe it that way makes it sound pretty simple," commented Doug. "There must be more to it than that."

"Well, yes," agreed Bob. "You've both written enough programs to know they don't always do what you expect, especially the first time. There's another problem here that doesn't come up with most programs: the physical side of things. In most programs, if you get a 3 as input, it's a 3. If you output the letter S, out comes an S. Here you have to deal with error in the sonar readings, error in the sonar direction settings, error in pointing Mike—"

"Who's Mike?" interrupted Doug.

"Mike is the robot," Bob explained. "Named him—or it—after my son. The real Mike got a kick out of that. Anyhow, if I tell him to go in a straight line, after a while he'll veer off in one direction or another—sort of like my golf drives! I can tell him to turn 90 degrees left and he'll turn about 90 degrees left. But it won't be exactly 90 degrees; it might be 85 degrees, or 93 degrees, or whatever. And it won't even necessarily be the same each time. Same thing with sonar readings: if it says three feet to an obstacle, it's probably around three feet, but that's all you know. As for lightness readings on the camera, there's really no absolute scale at all. It depends so much on the lighting. You can tell differences between light and dark, but that's about all."

"What are you trying to get Mike to do now?" Doug asked.

"Well, first let me correct a wrong impression you might have gotten when you walked in. I am absolutely not trying to get him to carry coffee yet! That thing fell over when Mike hit the bookshelf we keep it on. I'm sorry he did it, but it was an honest mistake, not utter stupidity.

"Anyhow, I'm trying to get him to recognize a door on his left and turn into it. This means trying to follow a wall, about a foot away, as long as the sonar reading stays more or less the same. As you can see from the smudges, we don't have that trick quite perfected yet. When the sonar reading goes way up, he's supposed to make a 90° left turn, go three more feet, and stop"

"Then what?"

"Then, it should be pretty easy to get him to look for doors on both sides and turn right too. The next step will be to count doors and turn, say, into the third one on the right. After that I'll try to teach him to go out of a room as well as go into it. Finally, I'll be able to put all these together and have him go from one room to another. If he's carrying a letter, we'll finally have electronic mail!"

"How long do you think it will take to get to that stage?" asked Adrienne, trying not to groan at Bob's feeble attempt at humor.

"If I could work on Mike full time, I think I could be done in a few weeks. Unfortunately, Sandra expects me to work for a living. She didn't mind a day of fooling with him—that is, she didn't until the coffeepot fell over and the whole office got involved—but she might get upset if it went much beyond that. With little bits of time here and there, say three months."

"And then what?"

"Well, I'd like to be able to give Mike general directions and have him figure out how to carry them out. That involves some advanced programming methods that I don't really know how to use yet. I plan to get a book on robotics and try to learn them."

"Thanks very much for your time, Bob," concluded Adrienne. "Good luck with Mike. We'll be following your progress—from a distance!"

Exercises

1. Does programming Mike correspond to the definition of robotics in the artificial intelligence sense as given in Section 14.2.1? In what ways does it or doesn't it?
2. Which other types of artificial intelligence could Mike use? How?
3. Suggest two ways of improving the accuracy of Mike's sonar readings.
4. Do you think Mike could be programmed to carry envelopes from one office to another? What inputs would it have to be given for each trip?
5. How could goal seeking with backtracking be used in the envelope delivery task? Do you think it would be an effective way to approach this problem? If not, what would be better?
6. Assuming Mike *can* carry envelopes—that is, the answer to Exercise 3 has been determined to be "yes"—do you think Mike would have any practical value to Envoyance? If so, what?
7. What features could reasonably be added to Mike to make him more useful in real tasks?

CHAPTER

15 Expert Systems from the Outside

Chapter Outline

Introduction

Where does expert technology help? Where does it get in the way? How do you choose a good application for this technology? What should the application look like? How do you choose human experts to work with to develop the system? How do you deal with them? The manager or systems analyst who contemplates using an expert system must be able to answer these questions. This chapter will tell you how.

Chapter Objectives

After you have read and studied this chapter, you will be able to:

1. Summarize the advantages and disadvantages of expert systems.
2. Choose a good expert system application, considering both the task and the experts available to work on it.
3. Explain how the human interfaces of expert systems differ from those of decision support systems.
4. Summarize the different types of explanations an expert system can provide to its users and how to plan them.
5. Describe the interfaces an expert system must offer to a knowledge engineer.

15.1 Pros and Cons of Expert Systems

Expert systems can provide substantial benefits in some DSS. At the same time, no tool is perfect for all applications. Attempting to apply expert system technology outside its area of applicability is, at best, a prescription for wasting time and effort. At worst, it can result in a system that does not achieve its objectives when other, perhaps simpler, approaches would have achieved them.

15.1.1 *Advantages of Expert Systems*

Expert systems, in effect, clone human expertise and put it in a computer. This immediately suggests the following benefits that they can provide, compared with asking human experts to carry out the same tasks:

- They can solve problems more quickly than humans could, given the same data. It might take a moderately fast computer a minute or two to go through information that would take a human a few hours.
- Their output is consistent: They don't get tired, impatient, or angry. This can help standardize multi-individual decision making.
- They can be replicated as needed with minimal lead time and for a moderate cost. Human experts often need years of training and experience. Then they retire.
- They don't cost money when they're not being used. Humans expect a regular income.
- They can free up human experts to do other tasks, such as concentrating on the few problems that really require their high level of expertise.
- They can work in locations that humans find inconvenient or hazardous.

In addition, the specific technology of expert systems yields these benefits, compared with developing a program with identical inputs and outputs through conventional (usually 3GL) programming methods:

- They can be expanded by adding more rules as their sponsoring organization gains experience in using them.
- They can train novice problem solvers in the techniques used by experts.
- While this training is going on, they can raise the problem-solving ability of novices closer to that of the experts.

- In some cases, where an expert system integrates the knowledge of several experts, they may be able to do better than any one expert.
- From the computer programmer's point of view, separating the expert's knowledge into modular rules reduces the chance of development errors and improves the maintainability of the system.

15.1.2 Drawbacks of Expert Systems

No technology is perfect for all applications all the time. Limitations of expert systems, of which prospective developers and users should be aware, include the following:

- Their domain of expertise is usually narrow. They are developed to solve specific problems and are not useful for any other purpose.
- They cannot apply "common sense;" only their rules. (We humans often don't realize how much general knowledge, or "common sense," is implicit in our decision-making processes.)
- They are brittle at their limits. Humans recognize when they are reaching their limits and respond appropriately. Expert systems don't. They simply follow their rules and may recommend inappropriate actions, often without recognizing that they have done so. It can be said that their performance "falls off a cliff" at their limits rather than degrading gradually.
- They may be costly to develop: not for the hardware (which is increasingly inexpensive) or for the software tools (ditto), but for the total time of the human experts and other people involved in the process.
- One or more experts must be on hand to contribute to the project for an extended period of time. Even if willing experts can be found, and even if their cost can be afforded, this commitment represents time during which they are not solving problems (or are solving them far more slowly than they could otherwise solve them). Where the expert's problem-solving ability has a clear present value and the possibility of developing an expert system is still at the conjectural stage, this can be a major barrier. (Consider saying to a medical specialist, "I would like you to treat 10 seriously ill patients each day, rather than 25, until we see if this system might work.")

Given these pros and cons, you can see that some applications are good for expert system technology while others aren't. The next section takes up that topic.

15.2 Choosing a Good Expert System Application

As you learned in your introductory MIS course, three criteria determine the desirability of developing any information system: its technical feasibility, its operational feasibility and its economic feasibility. These apply to expert systems as well.

Technical feasibility asks: Can the desired system be developed at all? (Even if it is not stated, the added criterion ". . . using well-proven, commercially available products" is usually implied.)

Operational feasibility asks: Will the system work with our people, within our organization? An information system that imposes a great deal of structure on the order in which the steps of a task are carried out might meet with resistance in a firm whose staff is used to more free-wheeling procedures. An information system that is perceived as taking away the "fun" parts of a person's job will likewise not be well accepted.[1]

Economic feasibility asks: Will the benefits of the system justify its costs? If not, can we justify it on the basis of expected intangible benefits?

These factors apply to any information system and, hence, to any decision support system. Here, these factors can lead us to guidelines that will help tell us whether a candidate expert system is likely to work out well, or if we should try to solve the underlying decision support problem via other technologies.

Successful expert system applications usually have most of the following characteristics. If your candidate application is missing one or more, it might still be a good use of expert systems technology—but you should look carefully at the missing piece or pieces to make sure.

It is convenient to divide the selection characteristics into (1) the characteristics of the problem to be solved (see also [HOLS88] on this aspect) and (2) the characteristics of the human experts who solve the problem or make the decision now and who would have to support any expert system development project.

15.2.1 Problem-Related (Task-Related) Criteria

1. *The task should typically take human experts from several minutes to a few hours to solve.* This time includes only actual problem-solving time, not waiting time. If it takes 48 hours to get the results of a cell culture that a physician

[1]Word processing centers, in vogue in the late 1970s, failed for this reason. Sitting at a word processor all day might have been cost effective, but it lacked the variety of traditional secretarial positions and led to poor morale. Operator turnover was high. Most firms that tried this approach abandoned it quickly.

needs in order to make a diagnosis, that time does not count as time that the physician spends making the diagnosis.

Problems that an expert can solve in a minute or two are usually not worth the effort of developing an expert system. If a nonexpert needs help, a one-page paper checklist will usually do the job.

This rough lower limit on problem complexity is an economic feasibility issue and may be overridden in exceptional situations. For example, American Express Authorizer's Assistant helps make credit granting decisions that an expert can decide in a few minutes or less. However, due to the number of authorizers at American Express, the volume of calls they handle, the level of turnover (which leads to low average expertise), and the economic impact of a bad decision, the system is fully justified economically. In addition, the training benefits of Authorizer's Assistant add value.

Longer problems, those that take a human expert a day or two, are beyond the practical size for expert system development today. This is a technical feasibility issue. There is no fixed absolute upper limit, but tackling a problem that takes a human expert a half-day or more to solve will be a large expert system development project. It should only be attempted by people who have experience with smaller projects and know what they're getting into.

2. *The task must involve only processing information and cognitive skills.* In other words, we have to be able to solve the task by putting data into a computer and getting data out of it. Physical activities are ruled out. A task passes this test if it can be solved by a human expert over the telephone.

Of course, an expert system can be hooked up to another computer system to carry out a physical process. Using an expert system to determine the mix of end products into which crude oil should be refined, then using a process control computer—or even a process control application running on the same computer as the expert system—to open valves and adjust temperatures, is entirely feasible. The output of the expert system itself, though, is not adjusted valves. The expert system's output consists of instructions to the process control system.

The information used in the task should be primarily symbolic (character strings) or logical (true-false). Tasks that involve primarily numerical calculations or massive data processing are better handled via conventional programming methods.

3. *The task must be carried out often.* This affects economic feasibility. If the task doesn't arise with reasonable frequency, system payback—which is related to usage frequency—will be low, while the development effort will still be substantial. As with any economic feasibility issue, high desirability due to another criterion can outweigh a low score on frequency of use.

4. *The task must be reasonably stable.* The task must remain unchanged for at least as long as it will take to develop the expert system and obtain the desired benefits from it.

This does not mean that the precise problem to be solved can never change. Were that the case, we would solve that problem once and be done forever. It means that the rules for solving the problem must remain valid. A system to recommend a driving route across town during rush hour must be able to cope with various points of origin, destinations, traffic, and weather conditions, but the task is still stable in the sense that the network of roads and their desirability under different conditions remains the same. The system might need to be rewritten for a new vehicular tunnel under the central business district or if flying automobiles become practical.

This criterion also does not mean that the task can't change at all. Digital Equipment Corporation's XCON system, described in Section 18.1, deals with configuring computers from Digital's current product line. This line is under active development and expansion. New components are continually being added. Some of these simply create new records in XCON's product database, but others require new rules in its knowledge base. In either case, the problem changes slowly enough for the solution approach and the bulk of the existing rules to remain useful. It should be possible to modify the above driving route recommendation system to cope with the conversion of a street to one-way travel without rewriting it from scratch.

5. *The task must involve only explicitly visible knowledge, not "common sense."* Some solution processes involve a great deal of common sense, which we usually don't realize we're using. Suppose a mechanic, looking at an automobile engine to see why it won't turn over, discovers concrete in all its cylinders. Even though the mechanic has never seen an engine with concrete in its cylinders before, was not specifically trained to deal with this situation, and cannot find this situation in the manufacturer's trouble-shooting manual, he or she will waste no time in deciding what the problem must be. How? "Common sense." An expert system, unless someone prophetically put in an unlikely rule reading "IF there is concrete in the cylinders THEN . . . ," would be at a total loss.

6. *The required knowledge must be within an acceptably narrow area.* Efforts to program a wide range of information into an expert system, while not provably impossible, have not yet met with commercial success. Most narrowly defined business problems deal with a few dozen related concepts. (This does not mean they deal with only a few dozen to a few hundred data elements. The same concepts, such as "current price," "annual dividend," and "earnings per share," apply to every stock traded on every market.) Systems whose anticipated scope is much broader than this should be approached as research projects.

7. *The necessary data must be available to the system.* Tasks that rely on data already in the computer have an edge over tasks that require a great deal of data to be entered. The cost of entering new data enters into economic feasibility: If it costs more to enter the necessary data than an optimal solution is worth, even a free system is not economically justified.

8. *The task must have financial importance to its sponsor.* This is, obviously, also a key factor in determining economic feasibility.

9. *Test cases must be available.* No information system can be developed if it cannot be tested. The same is true of expert systems. There is an important additional condition: Whereas testing most computer programs can rely heavily on test cases used by the developers in the development process, expert systems must also be tested on a wide range of cases that were not part of the knowledge acquisition stage. Using only test cases that were used in the development process can result in a "self-fulfilling prophecy" and a system that is useless when faced with new ones.

10. *We should be able to tolerate errors in system output.* As we've seen, expert systems are "brittle": Their performance falls off rapidly as we leave their intended area of application rather than degrading gradually. Severe errors thus often arise without warning. One classical example is of a system that diagnoses bacteria-related blood diseases. Since it tries to interpret every deviation from "normal" test results in terms of bacteria, it reports a serious blood infection when faced with the normal symptoms of advanced pregnancy.

Expert systems used for decision support, rather than decision making, can satisfy this criterion by submitting their output to a human who reviews it for reasonableness. In other situations, checks and balances are built into the process at a later stage. A system that creates an occasional improper computer configuration may be acceptable because its mistakes will be caught, at the very latest, when someone turns the computer on and tries to use it. If the benefits of the system outweigh the cost of fixing these goofs—which may be the case if the computer goofs less often than people would—it should still be used.

Being able to tolerate occasional output errors doesn't mean "expert systems don't need to work." If they don't do better most of the time than their unaided users would, they're useless.

15.2.2 Expert-Related Criteria

The preceding criteria described suitable tasks for expert systems. We also need one or more experts. The following list of criteria complements the list of task-related criteria by describing what is required of the experts.

1. *We must be able to tell who the experts are.* Sometimes we can see who performs best and agree that those are the experts. Extensive data are available on the historical performance of various investment advisors, although their historical track record (when the market was been driven by one set of factors, which a given expert understood well) may not be a good guide to the future (when a different set of factors may affect investment performance).

In other situations, such as medical diagnosis, solid information about which doctors are right most often is difficult to come by. In those cases we must rely on secondary evidence, such as acceptance as experts by physicians in other medical specialties, or abandon the expert system approach.

2. *Experts must perform the task substantially better than nonexperts.* If the

reasoning process of an expert is no better, or not much better, than that of a nonexpert in terms of results achieved, there is no point in cloning an expert's knowledge. We might as well let novices deal with the decision, as they will do almost as well.

Several studies have concluded that "expert" stock purchase recommendations perform, in the long run, about as well as choosing stocks by throwing darts at the stock market report page of your daily newspaper. If this is true—and other studies have reached the opposite conclusion—it would suggest that stock selection is a poor task for an expert system.

The meaning of "substantially" depends on the situation. Is 99.9 percent performance substantially better than 98 percent? In some cases it may represent only a trivial 1.9 percent improvement. In others it may represent a reduction in the error rate from 2 percent to 0.1 percent, which is a factor of 20. A person planning an expert system must decide what the appropriate interpretation is for the situation at hand.

This factor combines with task-related factors, such as frequency of use and financial impact of a good decision, to determine the economic benefits of the system in question.

3. *One or more experts must be available to work on the system.* If we want to mimic the reasoning of a human expert, it follows that we must have a human expert—one of the people defined in the previous two points—whose reasoning we can observe. The characteristics we would like this expert or experts to have, beyond simply being expert, are discussed further in Section 16.3.

4. *The human expertise must be scarce.* "Scarce" can refer to absolute scarcity: There are simply not enough blood disease experts in the world to deal with all the demands on their services. Given the nature of this expertise, if a world-wide crash program to develop more blood disease specialists were to start tomorrow, it could not pay off for a decade.

It can refer to economic scarcity. American Express could hire all the expert credit authorizers it needs if it paid them as much as it pays a senior vice president. It has chosen, probably wisely for its financial condition and the morale of its other employees, not to do so. It therefore does not have as many expert authorizers on its staff as it could use. That is a big part of the reason it developed Authorizer's Assistant to help its nonexpert authorizers.

Scarcity may reflect difficulty in getting human experts to accept the conditions under which work must be done, if they involve inconvenient schedules, remote locations, or hazardous environments.

Finally, expertise might be available at present but not in the future, as when the only technician who understands a 1940s-era diesel locomotive model is about to retire but many of the locomotives in question are still chugging along.

5. *Experts must agree on the solutions.* This means broad, general agreement. It does not mean that the experts must follow identical methods in

reaching solutions (they often don't) or that they must arrive at identical solutions every time (ditto). It means that, by and large, they must agree on the characteristics of a good solution versus a bad one. Two competent faculty advisors may recommend slightly different schedules for the same junior MIS student, but each should agree that the other's suggestions are within reason.

In most cases this criterion requires the experts to agree on the data required for a solution, on the general approach to the solution, and on the factors that determine if a solution is valid or not. This is true even if the experts' solutions themselves are slightly different.

15.2.3 Keeping the Criteria in Perspective

The preceding criteria, assembled from several lists proposed by experienced expert system developers and researchers, represent an ideal situation. Some of them, clearly, are "musts": If you don't have a human subject matter expert,

FIGURE 15–1
Categorization of Expert System Development Criteria

		Feasibility			
		Technical	*Operational*	*Economic*	*Importance*
Task-Related Criteria	*Size*	√ (high)		√ (low)	Want-M
	Cognitive	√			Must
	Frequency			√	Want-M
	Stability			√	Want-H
	Visible Logic	√			Want-H
	Narrow Scope	√			Want-H
	Available data	√	√	√	Must
	Importance		√	√	Want-M
	Test cases	√	√		Must
	Error tolerance		√		Must
Expert-Related Criteria	*Recognize*	√	√		Must
	Much better		√	√	Want-H
	Available	√	√	√	Must
	Scarce			√	Want-M
	Agree	√	√		Want-H

the idea of developing an expert system doesn't make much sense. Others are more in the nature of "wants": Financial importance, for example, is a relative term and can be overruled if a task is sufficiently important for some other reason.

Figure 15–1 relates the criteria both to the three feasibility concepts—technical, operational, and economic—and to whether they are musts or wants. In the case of wants, it indicates whether they are usually of high or moderate importance. The figure has check marks in a few places we didn't discuss above, especially in the operational feasibility column. These marks reflect second-level impacts. Getting data into a system, for example, may raise operational feasibility issues, although they will usually not be overwhelming.

Lists such as this, Krcmar points out, are meant to apply when an expert system is being considered as the entire solution to a total problem [KRCM88]. However, as he states, ". . . most successful ES [expert systems] in business are embedded in some larger context and . . . they often do not provide coverage for all tasks involved." In other words, an expert system might often be a good solution for part of a problem even if the problem as a whole does not meet the above criteria. Krcmar recommends splitting the overall task into smaller parts. The system planner can then apply criteria such as those above to the individual parts, also considering the new issues of integrating the parts into an overall DSS.

15.3 THE EXPERT SYSTEM HUMAN INTERFACE

In Chapter 5 we discussed the user interface of DSS in general. Even before reading the rest of this section, you may ask: Why did we call it a *user* interface there (and when we discussed the usual terminology in the previous chapter) if we call it a *human* interface here?

The answer is this: The humans with whom most DSS interact regularly are its users. Programmers may be involved in developing them, but their tools—text editors, compilers, linkers—are not the concern of nontechnical professionals. Expert systems, on the other hand, have a second important interface: to the subject matter expert or knowledge engineer who defines the content of their knowledge base. Neither a subject matter expert nor a knowledge engineer is a system "user" in the traditional sense of the word, but the expert system developer must still think about the system's interfaces to them. The term "human interface" is meant to encompass the users of the system and these people as well.

As we'll see in more detail soon, the interfaces of expert systems have unique aspects that do not apply to other types of DSS. Some of these require a great deal of developer attention if an expert system is to achieve its objectives. This section will cover the major differences between the human interfaces of an expert system and that of other types of DSS. This, in turn, will equip you to deal with the major issues of expert system human interface development.

Don't be surprised, by the way, to find yourself spending as much or more time on the user interface of an expert system than on all its other components combined. One survey found that a typical expert system devotes 44 percent of its code to user input and output. In one expert system developed by Unilever, 70 percent of the design effort went into the user interface of the system with only 30 percent going to its reasoning aspects [BERR87].

15.3.1 Interfaces of an Expert System

An expert system's major interfaces with humans can be arranged in outline form as follows:

1. User interfaces
    - 1.1 User input interfaces
        - 1.1.1. Control inputs, to direct the expert system to perform specific tasks
        - 1.1.2. Data inputs, to supply data about the specific task being addressed
    - 1.1 User output interfaces
        - 1.2.1. Conclusion/Recommendation outputs to the decision maker who uses the conclusions of the system to guide his or her actions
        - 1.2.2. Explanation outputs
            - 1.2.2.1. Why explanations, to explain why the system requires a particular input data element
            - 1.2.2.2. How explanations, to explain how to reach a particular conclusion
            - 1.2.2.3. What if explanations, to ask it to try a slightly different situation without necessarily repeating all its work
2. Subject matter expert/knowledge engineer interfaces
    - 2.1 Rule definition and input
    - 2.2 Debugging output
        - 2.2.1. Explanation outputs (again)
        - 2.2.2 Rule traces

These affect the different portions of the expert system as shown in Figure 15–2. (This figure is essentially Figure 14–4, annotated to show the human interfaces.) In the discussion that follows, we assume that the expert system is being used in *terminal* mode. If it is used in *intermediary* mode, the discussion applies to the staff intermediary. The kinds of decisions for which expert

FIGURE 15–2

Expert System User-Interface Schematic

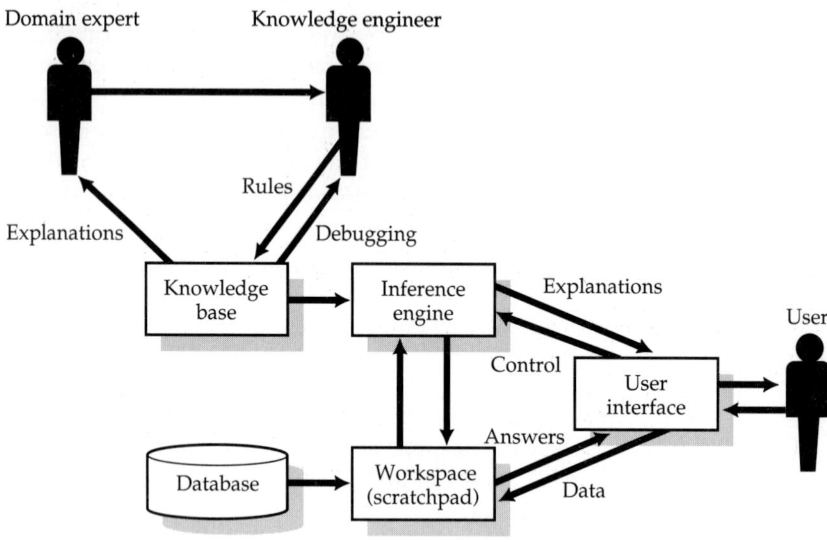

systems are used usually do not lend themselves to *subscription* mode or to *clerk* modes. (If you need to review these DSS usage modes, see Section 4.7.)

15.3.2 The User Control and Input Interfaces

As we discussed for DSS in Section 5.4, people control computers via command-line interfaces, graphical interfaces, menu interfaces, or question-and-answer dialogues. The control and input issues of an expert system are not significantly different from those of any other DSS. The control interface is usually determined jointly by the operating system environment and by the shell that was probably used to develop the expert system. (There is more information on shells in Section 17.2.2.) Since these interfaces don't raise new issues, we won't spend more time on them here.

15.3.3 The User Output Interface

The recommendations made in Section 5.4 for the output of any DSS apply to expert systems as well. As general rules, prefer graphic output to tables, tables to text.

A new factor that arises with expert systems is a *confidence factor* or *validity rating* that may apply to its conclusions. The technical side of confidence factors is discussed in the next chapter, in Section 16.1.5. Suffice it to say here that an expert system could make several recommendations, each with a different validity rating. Internally, the expert system carries these validity ratings as numbers. Displaying them adds a new dimension to system output.

One approach is to display confidence factors in numerical form along with the conclusions to which they apply. An example of this type of output is shown in Figure 15–3 for a hypothetical (and oversimplified!) medical diagnosis system.

Sometimes we know enough about the situation that, instead of displaying confidence factors directly, we can show what they mean to the user. The developer of a college student advising system might know that full-time students usually take five courses and will therefore develop a system to recommend that many. That system could list the five courses that received the highest confidence factors under the heading "recommended courses," and the next three under the heading "alternates." This gets the message across without involving the user with the numbers.

Confidence factors can be an opportunity to use graphics to good effect. A horizonal bar graph, such as in Figure 15–4, can list five recommended cars to purchase and convey the system's relative ranking of their suitability for this particular potential purchase. This display shows that the system finds the Lexus LS400, Infiniti Q-45, and Saab 9000 roughly comparable in suitability, but that it ranks the other two considerably lower for the needs of this particular driver. A simple ordered list of the five cars would not

FIGURE 15–3
Display with Diagnoses and Confidence Factors

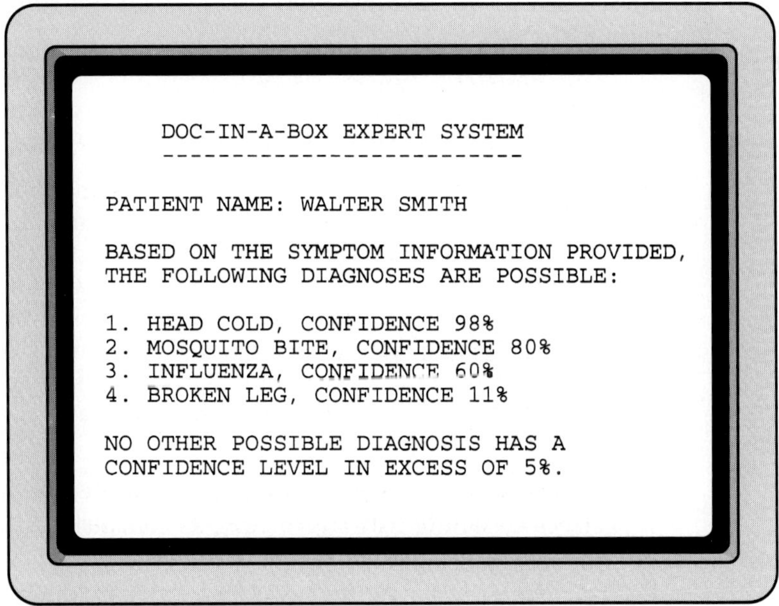

DOC-IN-A-BOX EXPERT SYSTEM
PATIENT NAME: WALTER SMITH
BASED ON THE SYMPTOM INFORMATION PROVIDED,
THE FOLLOWING DIAGNOSES ARE POSSIBLE:
1. HEAD COLD, CONFIDENCE 98%
2. MOSQUITO BITE, CONFIDENCE 80%
3. INFLUENZA, CONFIDENCE 60%
4. BROKEN LEG, CONFIDENCE 11%
NO OTHER POSSIBLE DIAGNOSIS HAS A
CONFIDENCE LEVEL IN EXCESS OF 5%.

FIGURE 15–4

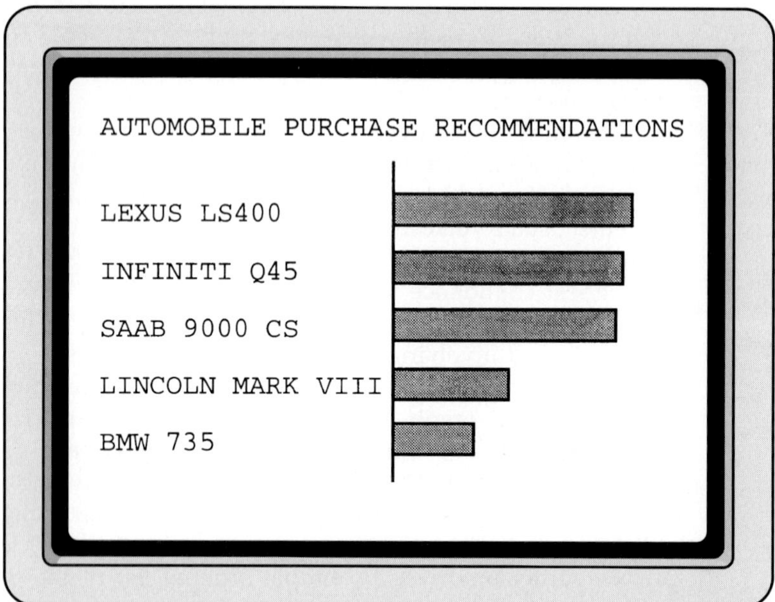

convey the same message. A table with the names and numerical confidence factors, such as the one in Figure 15–3, would not convey the message as clearly and quickly.

15.3.4 The Explanation Interface

Expert systems have a unique capability to explain where they are in their reasoning process and how they reached a particular conclusion. They can do this because their actions are determined on the fly as they work through the rules in their knowledge base. Whenever they ask for input data, whenever they display a result, there is always a rule that was invoked to make this happen. By telling the user or the developer which rule it was, the expert system can provide important information about its reasoning process.

Two types of people need to use the explanation ability of an expert system:

- The system developer in verifying that the system followed the correct reasoning path in reaching its conclusion.
- The system user, to whom this feature makes an expert system valuable as a training tool over and above its direct value in reaching a conclusion or making a recommendation.

How and Why Explanations

The user of an expert system can ask two questions of that system:

- Why do you (the system) need that piece of data?
- How did you (again the system) reach that conclusion?[2]

A person can only ask these questions when the system is at a stopping point. Stopping points are of two types: those that display output and those that request input. The first type of stopping point lends itself to "How?" questions, while the second lends itself to "Why?" questions. If a person stops an expert system manually (by pressing a Break key or similar means) when it is not at a natural stopping point, the system will have to answer these questions by referring back to the most recently displayed output or the most recently requested input.

If you are using an expert system shell (see the next chapter) to develop your system, that shell will determine the specific way in which to ask these questions. If you are writing the expert system from scratch, you can define how and when the questions are asked. You should, in any case, provide a way to ask them.

The key to answering these questions lies in the knowledge base and in the *rule trace*: the list of rules that a system used in order to reach the point at which it has stopped. Virtually every expert system shell can show the rule that led immediately to a conclusion just displayed or that called for the data element just requested. Better shells can, upon request, continue back in the trace to show why that rule was invoked, why its predecessor was invoked, and so on back to the start of the process.

The rule trace is not simply a list of all the rules that the inference engine checked, arranged in chronological order. It tries to display the tree structure it followed in choosing the rules. Thus, the system doesn't just know that it asked for a specific item of data because of rule 23. It also knows that it checked rule 23 because (in backward chaining) it needed the answer to evaluate the antecedent of rule 12, and so on.

Most shells allow the developer to make the explanation facility more user oriented. Specifically, they allow knowledge base designers to attach explanations to conclusions and to questions. When a user asks how or why, the appropriate explanation is retrieved and displayed.

Writing good explanations requires a great deal of thought. As the developer of an expert system, you will have to find the middle ground between excessive technical detail and meaningless platitudes. Consider the folk medicine rule:

```
IF temperature > 100 and nose_condition = runny,
THEN food = chicken_soup.
```

[2]It would, of course, be possible to ask this question with the word "why" also, as in "Why did you make that recommendation?" or "Why do you think so?" Using the word "how" makes it easier to distinguish between the two types of explanations.

Suppose you need an expert system containing this rule and were, as a result, told to eat chicken soup. You might then ask "How?", meaning, "How did you reach the conclusion that I should eat chicken soup?"

One explanation for the consequent of this rule could be "because your temperature is over 100°F and your nose is runny." That is, in content if not in form, what a rule trace would provide. It rephrases the rule into English without providing any more information. This explanation might be helpful to a student of folk medicine but is probably too technical for the average user. Another explanation, "because I'm your mother and I say so," goes too far in the other direction. A good compromise is "because chicken soup helps people with colds feel better."

Your knowledge of a system's prospective users will help you make the correct choice between these two extremes. Some systems can use information about the current user to select one of several alternative explanations. In this case, the expert system must maintain a *user profile.* Information for a user profile can be entered by the user or figured out by the system. Users can enter profile data in response to a question such as, "Are you familiar with the way this system works?" or "Please select your message preference: brief, standard, or verbose." Developing a user profile on the basis of prior activity is not a simple task. Such a capability should be added to an expert system only where its value is clear.

Explanation clauses can also answer the question "Why do you want to know?" If the system asks, "Is your nose runny?" and the user asks "Why?", it might respond with "If it is, that would help me decide what you should eat." A more complete explanation might be "If it is, since your temperature is over 100°, you probably have a cold, and then I will prescribe chicken soup."

Better expert system shells can also go more than one rule back to answer the why question. Suppose the above rule was written as two rules:

```
IF temperature > 100 and nose_condition = runny,
THEN cold = true.
IF cold = true, THEN food = chicken_soup.
```

Now, if the user asks "Why?" to "Is your nose runny?", a first-level rule trace would respond, in effect, "to decide if you have a cold," A further "Why?" would yield "because, if you have a cold, I will prescribe chicken soup."

Some low-end expert system shells, such as VP-Expert, allow only one explanation clause per rule. This clause is invoked when the user asks "How?" about a conclusion reached by that rule, and also when the user asks "Why?" about a question that the rule triggers. The right explanation for one purpose can be wrong for the other. If we have the one-rule version of the chicken soup test, the explanation "because chicken soup helps . . ." would be a good answer to "How did you reach this conclusion?" but not to "Why do you want to know if my nose is runny?"

Separating this rule into two rules as above solves the problem. We can now attach a "why" explanation to the first question and a "how" explanation to the second. These explanations can't be given at the wrong times. The first rule does not generate user output, so it can never be the subject of a "How?" question. The second does not trigger a request for user input, so it can never be the subject of "Why?"

Other shells take different approaches to providing explanations. Many shells attach explanations to variables rather than to rules. In such a shell, the same explanation would be offered whenever the system asked to know the patient's temperature. Thus, the Level5 user might write:

```
EXPAND temperature

Knowing your temperature is important for diagnosing
your illness
```

This has the advantage of always offering the right explanation for each data item when a rule triggers requests for several data items. However, it has the drawback of always offering the same explanation no matter which rule triggered the request. It can't say "because, if your temperature is over 100°, you probably have a cold" because the system might ask for a temperature reading in conjunction with other illnesses and other comparison values as well. Neither approach is ideal for all situations. Whichever approach your shell takes, you will probably have to work around its natural behavior some of the time: usually, by introducing additional variables or rules.

What If Explanations

Another aspect of an explanation interface is the ability to ask "what if?" questions. These can have two purposes: to verify that a conclusion is still valid in the face of new information and to see what conclusion would have been reached if different information had been available.

In the first case, if a medical diagnosis system reached a certain conclusion, a doctor might ask "what if the patient's red cell count is below X?" If the system responds, in effect, "it wouldn't matter," the doctor might decide not to order another blood test. If the system responds "in that case, your patient might have disease Y," the test would be ordered.

In the second case, suppose we worked for a newspaper advertising department and had a system that could fit display advertisements into the available space. We might ask such a system, "What if the ad for the Dayton-Hudson luggage sale is a half page instead of a quarter page?" We might ask this question to see if we can accommodate the larger size without adding another unit of four pages to the newspaper section. If we can, we could suggest to the firm's ad agency that they increase the size of the ad. If we can't, the extra income from the larger ad wouldn't cover the extra cost of printing four more pages, so we would suggest to them that they stay with the smaller ad.

15.3.5 *The Knowledge Engineer Interface*

An expert system must provide a way for a knowledge engineer, or for another person acting in the role of knowledge engineer, to define its knowledge base. This interface must support entering rules, validating their correctness (that they make logical sense, not necessarily that they solve the user's problem correctly), and changing them. This interface need not look like the user interface. Because the two types of people are usually quite different, with different skills and abilities, an interface style that is right for one may well be wrong for the other.

Defining the Knowledge Base

A knowledge base (in most business-related expert systems) is a string of rules and commands that looks much like a computer program. Many expert system development tools assume that the knowledge engineer will use a standard text editing program, such as a programmer would use to create a COBOL source program. Some such tools have built-in editor modules designed for this purpose. However, the developer of an expert system tool can provide a better knowledge engineer interface than a simple text editor.

Rules, in particular, always follow a well-defined format: an antecedent with conditions, a THEN consequent, and perhaps an ELSE consequent. A system that provides a fill-in-the-blanks format for each component, with suitable allowances for explanations and other ancillary parts of the rule, can speed rule entry and reduce the likelihood of input errors.

The developer interface of an expert system shell can show a "map" of its rules in the form of a tree. Such a map (an example is in Figure 15–5) can point out rules whose consequent cannot possibly contribute to the system's conclusions, rules whose antecedent cannot possibly be evaluated, or rules that are in the wrong place. Many such mistakes can result from typing errors. It is the nature of expert systems that such errors are often missed: An expert system can reach a reasonable-looking conclusion even in the presence of unused rules or in the absence of rules that should have been used. If an expert system recommends that an airline should set the SuperSaver fare at 60 percent of full coach and offer 25 seats at that fare on Flight 957 on Thursdays, a fare planner will probably never know that a rule was skipped and that the recommendation should have been 50 percent and 50 seats.

Trace Output

A trace can in principle be used with any computer program. It can be a useful debugging tool with traditional computer programs as well. However, its value with expert systems goes well beyond "useful" into "virtually mandatory." The reason is that, with expert systems, we have no assurance that

Expert System Technology and Legal Issues

Who is liable if a doctor follows the advice of an expert system and a patient dies as a result? Does it matter if the same system has also saved the lives of hundreds who would have died without it? The following article pursues some of these issues [ALEX91]. For more in-depth discussion of some legal issues arising from expert system technology, see [FRAN88].

Who is Liable? Just Ask the Experts[3]

Damage Caused by Knowledge-Based Systems Could Lead to Lawsuits that Target Everyone Involved

Here is a quick multiple-choice test: If a knowledge-based or expert system failed in some way and caused personal or economic injury to an individual or organization, who would be the likely target of a liability lawsuit?

A. The developer who created the system's shell.

B. The expert who supplied the system's knowledge base.

C. The user who placed too much faith in the system's output.

D. All of the above and probably a number of others to boot.

The correct answer is D, according to several legal experts.

"I would sue everybody, jointly and severally," said David Newman, Jr., an attorney and associate professor of electrical engineering and applied science at George Washington University.

A lawsuit based on injury caused by a knowledge-based or expert system has yet to make it into court, but the legal community "is just waiting for a case to happen," Newman said.

Unaware of Risk

Designers of expert systems and end users who rely on their efforts are unaware of the risk they face should the system fail. Vendors who create the system's shell are also at risk even though they have little control over how the system is used or who uses it, the legal experts said.

"If you're designing a system that is going to be used for an application that has significant exposure to damage or loss, you have a degree of responsibility of identifying how the knowledge system is put together." said Richard Bernacchi, an attorney and computer law expert at Irell & Manella in Los Angeles.

The system designer and users can protect themselves to some extent by documenting the care they take in selecting a product before putting it to use. That care should include a complete evaluation of the product and a reference check with current users. "'Let the buyer beware' applies in this area like any other," Bernacchi said.

Despite the liability risk, sellers and buyers are not particularly cautious when working with expert systems, said Larry Harris, founder and chairman of AICorp, a Waltham, Massachusetts–based developer of knowledge-based system tools.

"Someone has to get burned first" with legal action before attitudes change, he said.

The liability issue is a concern to the industry in general but probably affects designers of vertical applications more than the developer of the tools used to create the system, Harris said.

"It is no different than writing a medical book," Harris said. "I don't think that a doctor can sue the author of a medical book; it is still the responsibility of the doctor who makes the diagnosis."

Such disclaimers would probably not prevent a lawsuit or hold up in court, legal

continued

[3]Source: [ALEX91]. Copyright 1991 by CW Publishing, Inc., Farmington, MA 01701. Reprinted from *Computerworld*.

concluded

experts said. The vendor could be liable in ways never before imagined; end users could attempt to use the product in unforeseen ways or simply decide not to take training courses offered by the vendor, for example. In either case, the vendor could be in the docket alongside the other defendants, according to legal opinion.

Take Precautions

There are precautions that vendors should consider, Bernacchi said. "One thing that would help considerably is to document the testing process." A show of reasonable precaution will help offset any legal action.

Even so, legal experts said, it is only a matter of time before a malfunctioning knowledge-based system triggers a lawsuit. When that happens, everyone involved in the creation of the knowledge-based system could face the prospect of legal action.

The suit could be on several grounds, ranging from breach of contract to negligence. "Would I win on every ground?" Newman asked. "It doesn't matter. If I win on one, I would get whatever I went after for my client."

The liabilities will also vary according to whether a knowledge-based application is determined by the court to be a good, a service, or a combination of the two.

"That can make a difference in the sense that some jurisdictions have different ground rules whether certain principles apply in case of service as opposed to product," Bernacchi explained.

FIGURE 15–5
Rule-Base Map

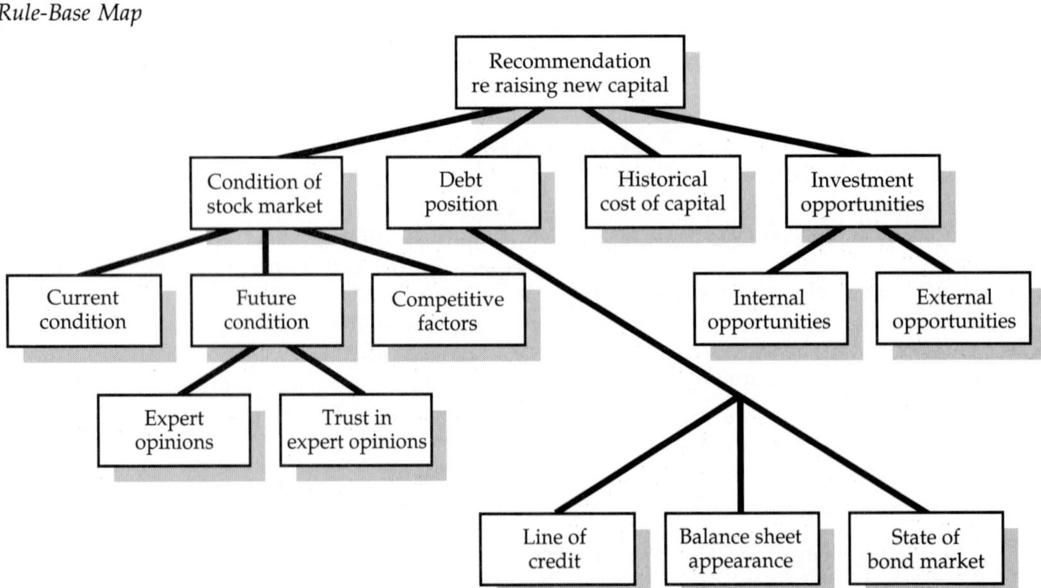

FIGURE 15–6

Rule Trace

A. Graphical Trace Tree

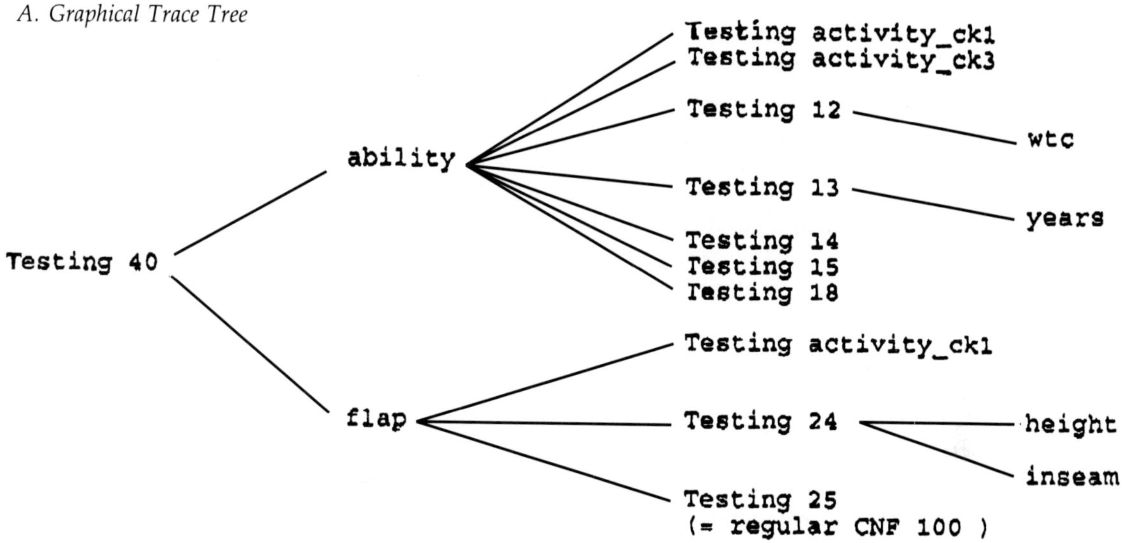

USE ARROWS, PGUP, PGDN TO MOVE   SPACE TO ZOOM OUT

B. Text Trace Tree

```
!    !    Testing 40
!    !    !    ability
!    !    !    !    Testing activity_ck1
!    !    !    !    Testing activity_ck3
!    !    !    !    Testing 12
!    !    !    !    !    wtc
!    !    !    !    !    !    (= walk_trot_and_canter CNF 100 )
!    !    !    !    Testing 13
!    !    !    !    !    years
!    !    !    !    !    !    (= up_to_5 CNF 100 )
!    !    !    !    Testing 14
!    !    !    !    Testing 15
!    !    !    !    Testing 18
!    !    !    flap
!    !    !    !    Testing activity_ck1
!    !    !    !    Testing 24
!    !    !    !    !    height
!    !    !    !    !    !    (= 5ft_6in_to_6ft CNF 100 )
!    !    !    !    !    inseam
!    !    !    !    !    !    (= 31in_to_32in CNF 100 )
!    !    !    !    Testing 25
!    !    !    !    (= regular CNF 100 )
```

they followed all the rules they were supposed to follow and no knowledge of the order in which they followed the rules that they did follow.

A simple *rule trace* is usually sufficient information for developers, who know how individuals work and want precisely that information to be sure the rules are being invoked correctly. A tree, as in Figure 15–6, can be a good graphical representation of the trace for the developer community. Some expert system shells (see Section 17.2.2 for a discussion of shells) provide this facility. However, a rule trace is a poor way to help educate users. Expert system rules are written in a form that most users do not understand, may involve internal variables that users are not concerned with, and can be quite verbose. A tree representation of all the rules invoked during a consultation would be totally meaningless to this user community.

Exercises

Refer to the box, Expert System Technology and Legal Issues, to answer these questions.

1. What is it about expert systems that creates liability issues that do not arise with other computer programs? If you wish, use this example: two programs, one an expert system and one not, to tell a firm where to drill for oil.
2. Show this article to one of your business law instructors. Obtain his or her reactions to the points it raises. If someone harmed by an expert system asked that instructor's advice on whom to sue, what would he or she recommend?
3. You are developing an expert system to advise business students on course selection. Poor advice can prevent students from obtaining courses they want, can lower their GPA (potentially harming their chances of entering graduate school or obtaining a desirable job), and can, in extreme cases, delay their graduation. What specific precautions should you take to limit your legal liability for such consequences?

Summary

Expert systems have advantages and disadvantages. You must consider both before deciding to apply expert technology to a problem.

Advantages of expert systems include speed, consistency, ease of replicating them as often as necessary, not costing money when not in use, freeing humans for other tasks, willingness to work in inconvenient locations, modularity (leading to ease of expansion and modification), training ability, and ability to integrate the knowledge of multiple experts.

Disadvantages of expert systems include narrowness of expertise, lack of common sense, brittleness at their limits, development cost, and needing an expert's services while they are being developed.

A good expert system meets technical, economic, and operational feasibility criteria that relate to the task itself and to the expert or experts who will help develop it. Some of these criteria are essential, while others are desirable.

Task-related criteria include the time it takes an expert to complete the task, ability to carry out the task "in one's head," task frequency, task stability, ability to carry out the task with a narrow range of knowledge and no "common sense," availability of data and test cases, importance of the task to its sponsor, and ability to tolerate a certain level of error in system output.

Expert-related criteria include a substantial task performance difference between experts and nonexperts, our ability to tell the two apart, scarcity of the expertise, availability of at least one expert, and they must agree on the general approach to a solution.

Expert systems interact with several types of people. These include the users themselves, knowledge engineers, and subject matter (domain) experts. Expert system developers must take the needs of all these groups into account.

One difference between the user interface of an expert system and that of any other DSS is the need to deal with confidence factors. These can be displayed numerically or graphically.

Another difference between the two user interfaces is the explanation interface of the expert system. It can explain how the system reached a particular conclusion, why it needs to know the value of a data element, and how the system's conclusions would change if the value of a data element changed.

Knowledge engineer interface facilities include an editor to create the knowledge base, the ability to map the knowledge base, and the ability to trace the rules used in a run.

Key Terms

cognitive skills 483
confidence factor 490
control interface 490
data interface 490
economic feasibility 482
expert-related criteria 485
explanation interface 492
"how?" explanations 493
input interface 490
operational feasibility 482
output interface 490
rule trace 496
task-related criteria 482
technical feasibility 482
user profile 494
validity rating 490
"what if?" explanations 495
"why?" explanations 493

Review Questions

1. List at least five advantages of using expert systems rather than human experts.
2. List at least four advantages of the expert system approach to developing a DSS compared with conventional programming methods.

3. What are five potential drawbacks of expert systems?
4. State the three types of feasibility tests an information system must pass if it is to be successful.
5. Give at least eight task-related criteria that indicate if a task is suitable for developing an expert system. For each, state if it is mandatory ("must") or desirable ("want").
6. What five factors must apply to the available human experts if we are to develop a successful expert system using their knowledge?
7. What three categories of people interact with expert systems?
8. What are two ways to display the confidence factors associated with expert system conclusions?
9. Who might use the explanation facility of an expert system?
10. What is the difference between a "why" explanation and a "how" explanation?
11. What is a "what if" request to an expert system? What output should the system provide in response to it?
12. What is a rule map?
13. Who might use a rule trace of an expert system run? Why?

Exercises

1. Evaluate the following tasks against the list of expert system selection criteria in Section 15.2. State whether each would be a good subject for an expert system. Give your reasons for taking this position.
   a. Admissions decisions at a selective private college.
   b. Grading final exams in a DSS course.
   c. Choosing the best route to drive across a city during rush hour.
   d. Playing chess. (Your answers may differ for the opening, the mid-game, and the end game.)
   e. Playing bridge. (Your answers may differ for bidding, declarer play, the opening lead, and subsequent defensive play.)
   f. Driving a racing car.
   g. Allocating files to individual disk drives in a large multi-user computer system.
   h. Allocating a merit increase budget to a group of 10 programmers.
   i. Choosing one member of this group for promotion to project leader.
   j. Calling football plays.
2. Assume you have been told to develop each of the possible expert systems in Exercise 1. Whom would you choose as an expert to work with in developing these systems? For which systems would you use one expert?

Several? What difficulties, if any, would you expect to encounter in eliciting the experts' knowledge?

3. Write two sets of appropriate "how" explanations for the following rule consequents, each for a different type of system user. (The rules do not follow the precise syntax of any shell.) State who you assumed the system users to be in both cases.

   a.
   ```
   IF year ≥ sophomore
     AND taken_macro_economics_yet = no
     THEN append macro_economics to course_list
   ```
   b.
   ```
   IF customer will haul trailer
     AND standard engine capacity < 120 cubic inches
     AND optional engine is available
     THEN order optional engine
   ```

4. Write appropriate "why" explanations for the indicated variables in the following rule antecedents. (As with the previous question, the rules do not follow the precise syntax of any shell.) State who you assumed the system user to be.

   a.
   ```
   IF year ≥ sophomore
     AND taken_macro_economics_yet = no
     THEN append macro_economics to course_list
   ```
   (Write explanations for both the variables *year* and *taken_macro_economics_yet*.)

   b.
   ```
   IF text type IS body text
     AND length of article > 300 words
     AND space is a problem
     AND output device IS laser printer
     THEN use Times font in 10 point size
   ```
   (Write explanations for both the variable *space is a problem* and the variable *text type*. Text in Times font takes up less space than does text in most other common laser printer fonts. 10-point type is on the small side for laser printer output.)

References

ALEX91 Alexander, Michael. "Who is Liable? Just Ask the Experts." *Computerworld* 25, no. 15 (April 15, 1991), p. 20.

BERR87 Berry, D.C. and D.E. Broadbent. "Expert Systems and the Man-Machine Interface Part Two: The User Interface." *Expert Systems* 4, no. 1 (Feb. 1987), pp. 18–28.

ELLI89 Ellis, Charlie. "Explanation in Intelligent Systems." in *Expert Knowledge and Explanation: The Knowledge-Language Interface.* Charlie Ellis, Ed, Ellis Horwood Ltd., Chicester, England (1989).

FRAN88 Frank, Steven J. "What AI Practitioners Should Know about the Law." *AI Magazine* 9, no. 2 (Summer 1988), pp. 109–114; reprinted in *Developing Expert Systems for Business Applications.* John S. Chandler and Ting-Peng Liang, Eds. Merrill Publishing, Columbus, Ohio (1990), pp. 296–302.

HOLS88 Holsapple, Clyde W., and A.B. Whinston. *The Information Jungle.* Richard D. Irwin, Homewood, Ill. (1988).

KRCM88 Krcmar, Helmut. "Caution on Criteria: On the Context Dependency of Selection Criteria for Expert Systems Projects." *Data Base* 19, no. 2 (Summer 1988).

Envoyance
What Methods to Use?

Jim was nearly tearing his hair out when Doug and Adrienne approached his office on Thursday. His desk was littered with reference books and sheets of paper covered with notes.

"Come on in," Jim called to them as he saw them hesitate at his door. "Don't worry about interrupting. I need a break—real bad!"

"This mess is all about the Higbee site," Jim said as they sat down. "There must be umpteen zillion things in the dirt there. Each one is easy; we know how to get it out. Trouble is, each one is different. Some methods work on pollutants A and B but not on C. Then there might be another that works on B and C but not A. The only thing that absolutely, positively works for everything is hauling all the dirt out and dumping at a controlled disposal site—but that just moves the problem around, and it costs an arm and a leg."

"What's on all these papers, then?" Doug asked.

"I've been trying to chart it, and I've been going crazy. I thought I could just list the pollutants down the side of the paper and the remediation technologies across the top, and put a check mark at the intersection where a technology works on a pollutant. Trouble is, saying that something 'works' is oversimplifying. Some things work, but not too well; others work better, but cost more, and so on. So each box on the grid really ought to have three or four ratings in it, not just a check mark or no check mark. And pulling all of them together into a remediation alternative, which is what we call the entire solution, is driving me crazy."

"Does this sort of problem come up a lot?"

"Surprisingly often," answered Jim. "The Higbee site is an extreme case, but the general problem is quite common. There are hundreds of possible soil pollutants. They vary in any number of ways: how toxic they are to humans, to animals, and to plant life; how fast they spread through the soil; how fast they decay over time; plus a few more. There are many possible ways to clean the soil: chemical treatment, enclosing the area so the pollutants won't leak further, digging the affected soil out and removing it, plus again many more. Just as in the Higbee site, more than one method may work in a given situation, but they'll vary in terms of cost, time, quality of the result, and damage to the site. There are actually nine factors we have to think about. They're on this form here." (See Figure 15–7.)

"If the problem is that big, how does anybody ever deal with it?"

"Fortunately, most of the time we deal with smaller problems that we can get our hands around. Every so often, though, a biggie like Higbee—hey, how do you like that rhyme?—comes up. The best we can do then is to try to select remediation technologies one at a time, combine them into a remediation alternative, and hope the whole picture ends up looking reasonable. Then we have to send that into the EPA or the state agency. If they agree we get a 'record of decision,' which means it's OK to proceed with the plan. Every so often they don't agree. If you ever want to know what 'angry' means, look at a client who just paid six figures for a report that got rejected!"

"What do these rules look like?"

"Most of them are fairly obvious. For example, if you're going to build housing on a polluted site, you can't encapsulate the site to keep the stuff from spreading; you have to neutralize it or get rid of it. Then there are rules about what works on what, what tends to cost more than what, what goes faster, and so on."

"How many rules would you say you're dealing with?" asked Adrienne.

"I think I know what you're driving at: You want to write a computer program to do it! Well, all of us have our own rules. Nobody ever tried to write them all down. There are probably a few hundred, maybe more. Lots of them look like each other, though. We're not talking about more than a few dozen basic concepts. That ought to simplify your program a bit!"

"You're absolutely right," commented Doug. "We are thinking about a computer program. Not just any program, though. We just started studying something called expert systems. They follow rules that look just like the ones you've been talking about. It sounds like your problem is a natural for them. I just wish we could have something ready for you in time to use it for the Higbee site!"

FIGURE 15–7

Envoyance List of Remediation Alternative Criteria

Remediation Alternative Criteria

1. Overall protection of human health and the environment
2. Compliance with ARARs (applicable or relevant and appropriate requirements)
3. Long-term effectiveness and permanence
4. Reduction of toxicity, mobility, or volume through treatment
5. Short-term effectiveness
6. Implementability
7. Cost
8. State (support agency) acceptance
9. Community acceptance

Exercises

1. Is the decision here structured, semistructured, or unstructured?
2. What do the design, intelligence, and choice stages consist of for this decision?
3. Does this problem seem to fit the expert systems framework as discussed in Section 14.3? (Consider Pfeifer and Luthi's list of expert system success factors given in Section 14.4.)
4. If Envoyance can develop a system to process the experts' rules and recommend methods of cleaning a site, what sort of decision support system (in terms of the DSS spectrum of Section 4.1) would it be?
5. Could this system benefit from access to any type of external database? If not, why not? If so, what database? (What would be in it?)
6. Whom would you expect to be the user(s) of this system? The subject matter expert(s)?
7. Would neural nets be suitable for dealing with any part of this problem?

CHAPTER

16 Expert Systems from the Inside

Chapter Outline

Introduction

The previous chapter discussed aspects of an expert system that matter to its users: why one might pick the technology, what its pros and cons are, what the requirements of a successful expert system are, and what its user interface will look like. You, as a potential developer of such a system, must also be concerned with what goes on inside it. You must know how it will represent knowledge, for example. Furthermore, you must know something about the different ways in which knowledge can be represented because you may have to choose a development tool for your system, and you will want to choose one that matches your system well.

This chapter looks at some of the different ways expert systems behave internally. While most approaches can be adapted to most any problem, the adaptation can be painful if the match is poor. The more you know both about your problem and about alternative approaches to solving it, the better your solution is likely to be.

Chapter Objectives

After you have read and studied this chapter you will be able to:

1. Describe several ways expert systems represent what they know about a situation and how to handle it.
2. Discuss how forward and backward chaining differ and where each is appropriate.
3. Represent knowledge with a semantic network.
4. Discuss the advantages of object-oriented software technology.
5. Explain how frames combine the features of semantic networks and object-oriented technology.
6. Use predicate calculus as a reasoning method.
7. Explain how databases can be used with expert systems.
8. Discuss how expert systems handle uncertain information by using confidence factors.
9. Describe how fuzzy logic can be useful in an expert system.

16.1 VARIABLES

A human expert knows certain things about a problem to be solved and certain things about how to solve that problem. If a computer is to mimic the behavior of that expert, the computer must be able to represent this knowledge. There are several ways computers can represent knowledge, each appropriate to certain situations. Expert systems often represent factual knowledge about a problem (not judgmental knowledge about how to solve it) by assigning values to *variables* in their workspace.

Some variables take on only the values true or false. If a person is hungry, the system might assign the value true to a variable *is_hungry*. Its knowledge base might then have a condition expressed as "IF is_hungry THEN. . . ." Variables that can only be true or false are also called *Boolean variables* (after the 19th-century English mathematician George Boole, the first person to study their properties rigorously) or *simple facts*.

The values of other variables are character strings. We could represent states of hunger by the strings "yes" and "no," "true" and "false," "starving" and "full," or the nonsense syllables "upg" and "sqnk." The rule could be "IF hungry = yes THEN . . ." or, with a different choice of representations, "IF hungry = upg THEN. . . ." The computer doesn't care if being hungry is associated with the string "yes" or the string "upg." Humans find "yes" easier to understand.

Expert systems also use numeric variables. Tools that do not support purely numeric variables allow the user to perform arithmetic on character strings that contain valid numeric values, such as "−2.6." This approach has the disadvantage that a non-numeric string could, by error, be placed in such a variable. This error would only be detected when the system attempts to carry out a calculation using this "number." It is harder to correct an error at this point, perhaps several steps after it occurred, than it would be if the system had produced a "non-numeric data assignment to numeric variable" error message when the value was entered.

Some expert system tools also support variables whose values must be from a specified set. These are also called attribute variables or OAV (object-attribute-value) variables. For example, a "weather" variable might be restricted to the attribute values "sunny," "cloudy," "rainy," or "snowing." The knowledge base developer might have to list all valid values, or—as the Level5 shell can do—a shell can infer the set by listing all the values tested in the knowledge base. Shells that don't support sets may provide a way of restricting user input to the values listed in a menu. Restricting user input isn't the same as restricting the value of a variable. If only user input is restricted, a rule in the knowledge base rule can still, perhaps because of developer error, assign the variable a value outside the allowable set. If the variable is declared to take on only values from a set, the system will prevent any other value from being assigned to it in any manner.

Variables can take on single or multiple values. Weather would be a *single-*

valued variable: It might be sunny or cloudy, but not both. Foods in your refrigerator, or the substances to which a patient is allergic, would be *multi-valued* variables: more than one can properly apply at a time.

Variables are a convenient way to represent a small amount of knowledge. As the amount of knowledge to be represented grows, the number of variables needed becomes large and difficult to manage. Other methods provide better ways to organize and structure vast amounts of knowledge. In particular, if an expert system has to deal with many different items of the same or similar types simultaneously, variables quickly become unwieldy. In this situation, systems that use variable-based knowledge representation are often forced to organize and store their data in an external database. Frames, discussed in Section 16.3, are popular in larger expert systems for this reason.

16.2 Production Rules

Production rules represent knowledge about how to solve any problem within the class of problems with which an expert system deals. By contrast, the values of variables represent knowledge about the specific problem being solved. The process of solving a problem usually involves deriving new facts about a situation from other, previously know facts. For example, if we know that a person ate a full meal within the past hour, we may infer that he or she is not hungry. That derived fact, represented (perhaps) by the value of a variable, then becomes knowledge about the specific person with whom our system is dealing at the moment. Production rules support this type of knowledge derivation.

A production rule typically has the form

IF antecedent
THEN some consequent
ELSE some other consequent

Expert system software packages vary in the precise syntax requirements that they impose on rules in their knowledge base, but all have this general form.

A particular production rule may lack a THEN consequent or an ELSE consequent if they are not necessary for its purpose. The rule syntax of some expert system development tools requires knowledge-base developers to supply an empty THEN clause if the rule has only a "real" ELSE consequent.

16.2.1 Combining Production Rules into a Knowledge Base

A useful knowledge base will have more than one rule: After all, the trivial "Are you hungry?" one we used in Chapter 14 had three! The rules in a knowledge base are related by the way they share knowledge: One will assert a fact, another will use that fact in its antecedent. That creates a structure of rules with known facts at one end and conclusions at the other. It is the task of the inference engine to link the two: to create a logical reasoning path between the known data and a conclusion such that the conclusion is supported by the data and the reasoning that is built into the knowledge base. The way in which the inference engine constructs this path is called its *inferencing method.*

16.2.2 Inferencing Methods

We introduced expert systems in Section 14.3.2 with a three-rule mini-expert system that told you what to do in the evening based on the condition of your stomach and your homework. Its rules were:

1. If you are hungry, you should eat.
2. If you are not hungry and you have homework, you should do your homework.
3. If you are not hungry and do not have homework, you should see a movie.

An inference engine can approach this or any other set of rules from either of two directions, forward or backward. The objective of the process is the same in either case: to find a path between the known data and the goal or to determine unequivocally that no such path exists.

Backward Chaining

The process of using *backward chaining* is to establish a goal, determine what must be found out in order to reach that goal, and try to find that knowledge. This approach is also called *goal-directed* or *goal-driven reasoning.* An expert system that uses backward chaining selects rules by examining the variables contained in their consequents. It then tries to determine the values of variables used in their antecedents to decide if the rule applies or not.

These variables often appear in the consequents of other rules. The system then looks for the variables in the antecedents of those rules and so on, back until it finds values it knows, values it can look up in a database, or values it can get from its user. To see how this works, consider a knowledge base with these rules. (All variables are Boolean; that is, they represent true-false conditions.)

```
1. If A, then succeed, otherwise fail
2. If B and C, then A
3. If D or E, then B
4. If F or G, then C
5. If H, then G
```

Backward chaining through this knowledge base is diagrammed in Figure 16-1.

FIGURE 16–1

Diagram of Backward Chaining Process

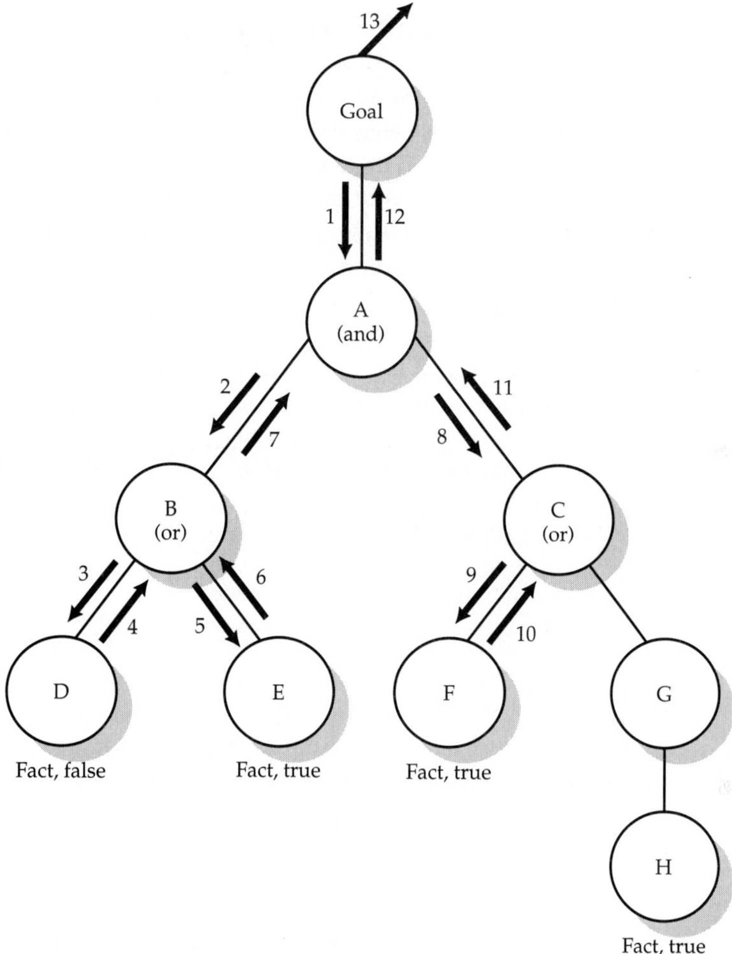

This backward chaining process goes through 12 steps, giving the variables these values when it is done:

A, B, C, E, F: true
D: false
G, H: unknown (and not needed)

The steps themselves are as follows. The step numbers correspond to the numbered arrows in Figure 16–1.

1. It realizes (from rule 1) that it must find A to determine success or failure. It establishes an intermediate goal of finding A.

2. It realizes (from rule 2) that to find A, it must find B and C. It establishes a new intermediate goal of finding B.
3. It realizes (from rule 3) that to find B, it must find D or E. It establishes a new intermediate goal of finding D.
4. It finds that D is false (we are given that as a fact) and returns to its current intermediate goal with this information.
5. It evaluates the rule it is working with at this level and realizes that the rule can still be true if E is true. It establishes a new intermediate goal of finding E.
6. It finds that E is true and returns to its current intermediate goal with this information.
7. It concludes from E being true that B is true. It moves back up to the next higher intermediate goal—the one that established a need to find out if B is true or false—with this information.
8. It evaluates the rule it is working with at this level and realizes the rule can only be true if C is also true. It establishes a new intermediate goal of finding C.
9. It realizes (from rule 4) that to find C, it must find F or G. It establishes a new intermediate goal of finding F.
10. It finds that F is true and returns to its current intermediate goal with this information.
11. It concludes from F being true that C is true. It moves back up to the next higher intermediate goal—the one that established a need to find out if A is true or false—with this information.
12. It concludes from B and C being true that A is true. It moves back up to its original goal with this information.
13. It concludes from A being true that it has succeeded and returns this result.

Three points are worth noting with respect to this process:

1. This expert system was intelligent enough to realize (step 10) that it could finish evaluating rule 4 as soon as it knew that F was true. It didn't bother looking at G. Not all expert systems are that clever. Many gather all the information they could need to evaluate a rule's entire antecedent—that is, values for all the variables in the antecedent—before they start to evaluate it.
2. We didn't need rule 5. Most backward-chaining systems don't use all their rules in a given session.
3. We used what is called a "depth-first" search: We went down each path to its end before backtracking and going back up. This is not an efficient process when some paths are short and others much longer. A "breadth-first" search, which scans all the tree nodes at each level in the hope of finding a short path before proceeding to

the next level, is a better approach when path lengths differ significantly.

Backward chaining would begin working with our three-rule system by establishing that its goal is to determine what to do this evening. It would then inspect the rules to see which of them might achieve that goal. In the absence of any reason to proceed otherwise, most expert systems would scan them in order. The first rule can indeed lead to the goal. To decide if the first rule applies, the system must determine if you are hungry. The inference engine must then examine the consequents of the rules to see if any of them can possibly yield that information. None can, so it concludes that it must ask its user (you). If you respond that you are hungry, the conditions for the rule are met, and the goal of the system has been reached. The system will tell you that you should eat and end the run. In that case, it does not ask you if you have homework; it doesn't care. If you respond that you are not hungry, the conditions for rule 1 will fail, and this rule will therefore not achieve the system's goal. It will then continue searching for other rules that might lead to its goal.

More generally, the backward-chaining inference engine must go through these steps:

1. Decide what rule to test next.
2. Determine if the antecedent of that rule is true or false.
3. Carry out the action specified in the appropriate (true or false) consequent, if any. This is called *firing* the rule.
4. Repeat steps 1 through 3 until the goal is met.
5. Stop.

The catch here is in step 1: deciding what rule to test next. This was not an issue in our simple knowledge base because it only had one rule that could possibly lead to its final goal or its one intermediate goal. However, larger expert systems may have many rules that can lead to their goals. More importantly, the conclusion the system reaches may depend on the choice made by the inference engine among equally plausible options. If you have both money in your wallet and food in your pantry, for example, both cooking dinner and ordering pizza may be acceptable choices. If the system is looking for just one answer, it may recommend whichever of them it happens to test first.

Some inference engines process their rules in order, usually starting with the first one as seen in the printed listing. VP-Expert, for example, operates this way. Knowing that an inference engine uses this strategy and relying on it may simplify a knowledge base. It is, however, a poor programming approach because each rule should ideally be a freestanding piece of knowledge that is true under all circumstances. If new rules are added to an order-dependent knowledge base, they must be added in the right place. A knowledge base has little or no structure of its own, so the right place is not always easy to find. Errors will almost certainly occur. Given that expert systems in business usually evolve over time by adding new rules, creating such an error-prone situation is not a good development strategy.

Other inference engines may employ more sophisticated selection strategies, such as choosing the rule that uses the most recently obtained information. Level5, for example, starts with the rule that will give the conclusion the highest possible confidence factor (see Section 16.6). Some allow the developer to state a subset of all rules that are available for use at a particular time or to specify the conflict resolution methods to be used. An example of a rule to control rule choice, from [DAVI77], is

> IF the infection is abscess AND there are rules which mention enterobacteriacea in their premises AND there are rules which mention Gram-pos-rods in their premises, THEN there is suggestive evidence (0.4) that the former rules should be applied before the latter.

Chess-playing programs use this sort of control information extensively. Since chess is played under strict time limits (generally the same for humans and computers), it is important to find a good move quickly. Chess programs typically evaluate the position that would be reached after each possible move, by the computer or in response by its opponent.[1] They use the results of these intermediate evaluations to pick promising moves to pursue in more depth.

The capability to control the order in which rules are applied makes an expert system development tool and its use more complex, but expert systems are intended to solve complex problems. Complex tools are sometimes necessary for that purpose.

Forward Chaining

The *forward chaining* approach is to determine what you know, apply that information to the rules, and see what conclusion(s) you reach. This approach is also called *data-driven reasoning*. It selects rules by determining that the system knows the truth or falsity of their antecedents. It then derives further facts from their consequents. These new facts allow it to determine the truth or falsity of the antecedents of more rules. Now the system can evaluate those rules and determine still more facts from their consequents. The process continues until the system has reached its conclusion. Forward chaining, using the same five rules as in the example of backward chaining, is diagrammed in Figure 16–2. This inference session proceeds as follows:

1. The expert system discovers that D is false. It passes this information to rule 3, the only one that can take advantage of it.

[1]This applies to the mid-game phase of a chess game. Openings are usually handled by reference to a database of standard opening sequences. The endgame, when few pieces are left on the board, can be handled better by algorithms.

FIGURE 16–2
Diagram of Forward Chaining Process

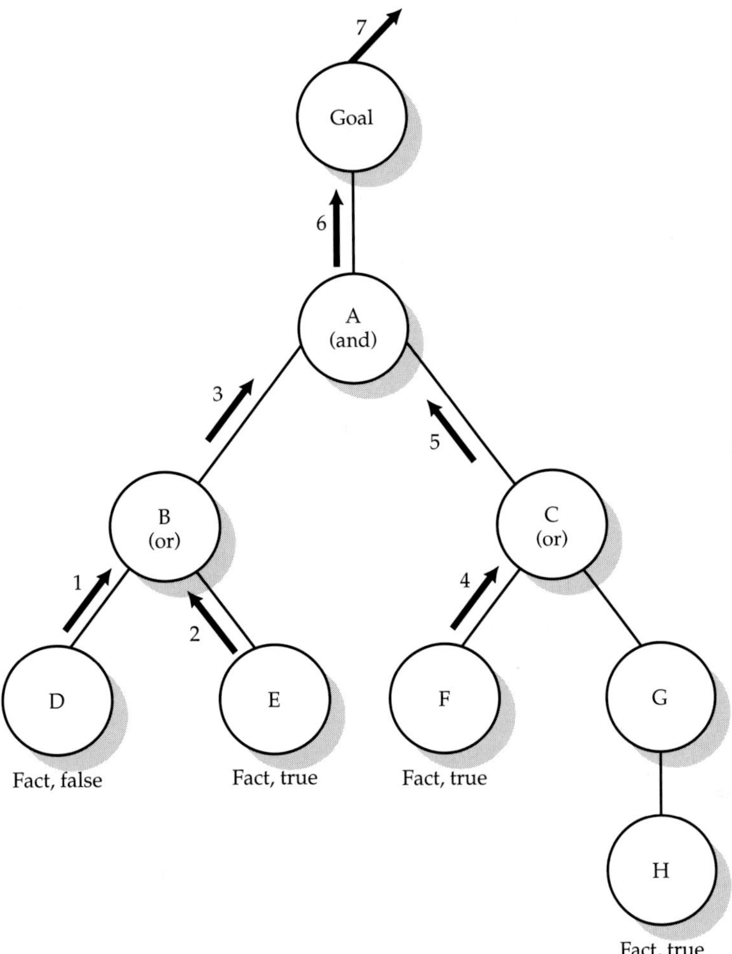

Knowing D is false does not enable rule 3 to provide any new knowledge.

2. It discovers that E is true. It passes this information to rule 3.
3. Rule 3 concludes that B is true. It passes this new information to rule 2, which cannot (for now) do anything with it.
4. It discovers that F is true. It passes this information to rule 4.
5. Rule 4 concludes that C is true. It passes this information to rule 2.
6. Rule 2 concludes that A is true. It passes this information to rule 1.
7. Rule 1 concludes from A being true that is has succeeded and returns this result.

While there are fewer numbered steps in this process than in the backward chaining version, the processing effort involved is similar for this case.

Forward chaining begins by collecting information to help it reach a solution. If it is trying to help you decide what to do this evening, it will see that it does not have either of the facts that it might need. It will begin by asking for the first fact it comes across that it doesn't have: whether or not you are hungry. It will then see where that information leads it. In this case, that single fact lets it reach its conclusion (you should eat) directly. Were this not the case, it would ask if you have homework. It would then apply this new information to the rules and reach its conclusion.

Suppose we had a more complex system, which followed a decision that you should eat by exploring possible ways to get food. Backward chaining would zero in quickly on that subtree of the decision process without investigating the other top-level rules, which deal with homework and with movies.

In other situations, however, a backward chaining system can waste a lot of time pursuing chains of reasoning that it eventually decides are inapplicable to the situation. Consider a system designed to recommend what you should make for dinner. Suppose it includes, among other rules, the following (paraphrased into English):

> If you have the ingredients for spaghetti with sauce, you should make that for dinner.
>
> If you have spaghetti and can make sauce, you have the ingredients for spaghetti with sauce.
>
> If you can buy tomato paste, you can make sauce.
>
> If you can get to the store, you can buy tomato paste.
>
> If you have half an hour and you can use your car, you can get to the store.
>
> If your car has gasoline and you can find your keys, you can use your car.
>
> If your keys are on your desk, you can find your keys.

A backward chaining system would start with the objective of the top rule, discover that it needs the second rule to decide if the first one is true, discover that it needs the third rule to decide if the second one is true, discover that it needs the fourth one . . . and so on to the end, where it (and you) will finally learn that you can't find your car keys, so your dinner plans must be based on foods you have on hand. After it gets all the way to the end of the chain, this backward-chaining inference engine would have to backtrack to the top level and pursue another line of reasoning.

Forward chaining, though, often collects more information than it needs. Its eating subtree might ask about the type of food you like, what is in your pantry, and what your food budget is. This would represent a great deal of wasted effort if it gets to the top of the tree, having determined what the best feeding plan is, only to find out that you are not hungry. Given the above set of rules it would ask you about your car keys and your car's fuel supply, perhaps to find that you already have tomato paste in your kitchen cabinet.

Backward chaining tends to ask for less data than forward-chaining but to examine more rules. Forward chaining tends to ask for more data but utilizes this data to eliminate possibilities and therefore to process fewer rules. Some expert systems combine both methods. In our first example, the system could use backward chaining to narrow the choices down to food, academics, or entertainment. It could then use forward chaining to collect information about that area and make a specific recommendation.

Choosing between Forward and Backward Chaining

The choice between backward and forward chaining should lean toward the one that narrows the tree of choices faster. When there are many rules that start from input data, only a few of which apply in any given situation, forward reasoning will work well because the first step will eliminate most of the possibilities. When rules near the top of the tree can be eliminated without reaching all the way down the tree, as with the "Are you hungry?" question, backward chaining works better.

Configuring a computer system to meet a collection of user requirements (as done by XCON; see Chapter 18) is a good forward-chaining application. Here, all components of the system—processors, disk drives, cabinets, power supplies, communications gear—must be addressed, so every top-level rule will always apply and every major branch of the rule tree must be used. It is more efficient to start with the user's requirements. They will allow us to eliminate entire groups of bottom-level rules as irrelevant in a particular case. While a backward chaining system with a goal of "find a correct configuration" could be implemented, it would be awkward.

Backward chaining, on the other hand, is good for problem diagnosis. Here, a few top-level questions ("Does the engine turn over?" "Does your back hurt?" "Do its leaves have brown spots?") can quickly isolate the problem to a set of related possibilities. The system can then ignore all the rules that have to do with other possibilities, along with all the input data that an attempt to apply those rules might possibly require.

Forward and backward chaining can be combined in one system. A system might start in a forward chaining mode, letting the user enter data into its knowledge base. As this is done facts will be generated from the newly entered data. Once the user has entered all the applicable data, the system may ask, in effect, "So, what do you want to find out?" and be given a goal. It could then use backward chaining to try to reach this goal from what it knows.

Some expert system development tools support forward chaining, some support backward chaining, and some give their users a choice.

16.2.3 Strengths and Weaknesses of Production Rules

Williams and Bainbridge summarize the strengths and weaknesses of production rules well in [WILL88]. Their list of strengths includes:

- Modularity: Each rule is independent of all others and encodes a meaningful "chunk" of domain knowledge. Any necessary relationships among them are created by the control structure of the expert system.
- The explicit representation of rules supports inquiry into how a conclusion was reached or why an input data element is needed.
- The straightforward if-then-else form of a rule is intuitively appealing and maps well into English.
- Simple chaining methods, linking one rule or group of rules to the next, can be easily built and resemble the inference procedures that people use.
- Large systems can be built from small, modular components.

All, however, is not wonderful. As the saying goes, "there is no free lunch." According to Williams and Bainbridge, production rules have these weaknesses also:

- The system must know the context of each rule. For instance, a rule that states "If you have spaghetti in your pantry, cook it" applies only in the context of preparing a meal. If the expert system has already decided that you should go eat at a restaurant, this rule does not apply *even though its antecedent is true.* Dealing with this problem can force very large rule antecedents, can depend on implicit system developer knowledge such as rule order in the knowledge base, or can force other awkward "work-arounds." None of these is desirable.
- Large sets of rules have no inherent structure, which makes managing a large knowledge base difficult. Giving them structure, while often necessary, violates the goal of modularity: that each rule is an "independent chunk of knowledge."
- Some human problem-solving methods, especially those that involve our subconscious use of "common sense," do not map well into production rules.
- The scanning of all rules in the "match-select-test-fire" process is not an efficient computational process. This author differs slightly with Williams and Bainbridge on this point: There are efficient procedures that can be used, albeit at the expense of knowledge base compilation time. The availability of parallel processors as discussed in the next chapter will reduce the impact of computational efficiency even further.
- Because the rules are independent of each other and of the control (inference) strategy, it is all but impossible to determine the properties of system behavior by analyzing the code in the knowledge base.

The first two problems can be serious in large, industrial-strength expert systems. Fortunately, much of the knowledge of such large systems is usually associated with entities that the system is supposed to know about: customers, courses, diseases. When this information can be structured, the concept of frames—which we discuss next—can help to organize it. Using frames to structure knowledge helps keep the remaining part of the knowledge base, which still uses production rules, of manageable size.

Experienced 3GL programmers often fall into a trap when writing a knowledge base using production rules. Many such knowledge bases incorporate a control component organized much like a conventional program, with sequential execution of commands and perhaps some looping or conditional execution. A knowledge base developer who knows a procedural programming language such as COBOL or Pascal is often tempted to overuse this component by putting much of the expert reasoning process into it. That runs counter to the underlying philosophy of expert systems. The resulting system will be neither an expert system nor a conventional program. It will have the advantages of neither, the drawbacks of both. Try to avoid this sort of "Pascal thinking." Divide your expert's logic into many small, independent chunks of knowledge and put each one into a freestanding rule.

16.3 FRAMES

Frames as a knowledge representation method are the application of two concepts, *semantic networks* and *object-oriented programming methods,* to expert systems. Accordingly, we need to look at these two concepts briefly before we can discuss frames. Object-oriented concepts have a wide range of applications outside expert systems as well.

16.3.1 Semantic Networks

A semantic network represents knowledge as a network of relationships among objects. Figure 16–3 shows a simple semantic network. You can read the individual relationships that make up the semantic network as English sentences: The College of Management is part of Harwich University; the College of Management has a dean; the Marketing Department is part of the College of Management; the Marketing Department has a chairperson, etc. Semantic networks, as Stubbart points out in [STUB91], can represent the way managers actually organize the knowledge they use when they think about strategic issues.

The arcs in a semantic network are directed. They have heads and tails. The sentences that describe them work only in one direction. The College of Management is part of Harwich University but not vice versa.

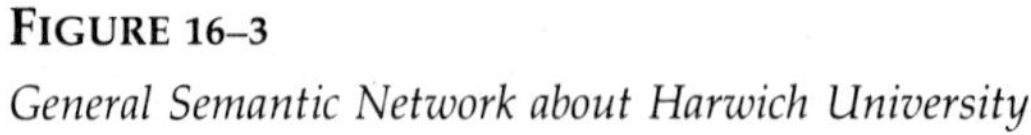

FIGURE 16–3

General Semantic Network about Harwich University

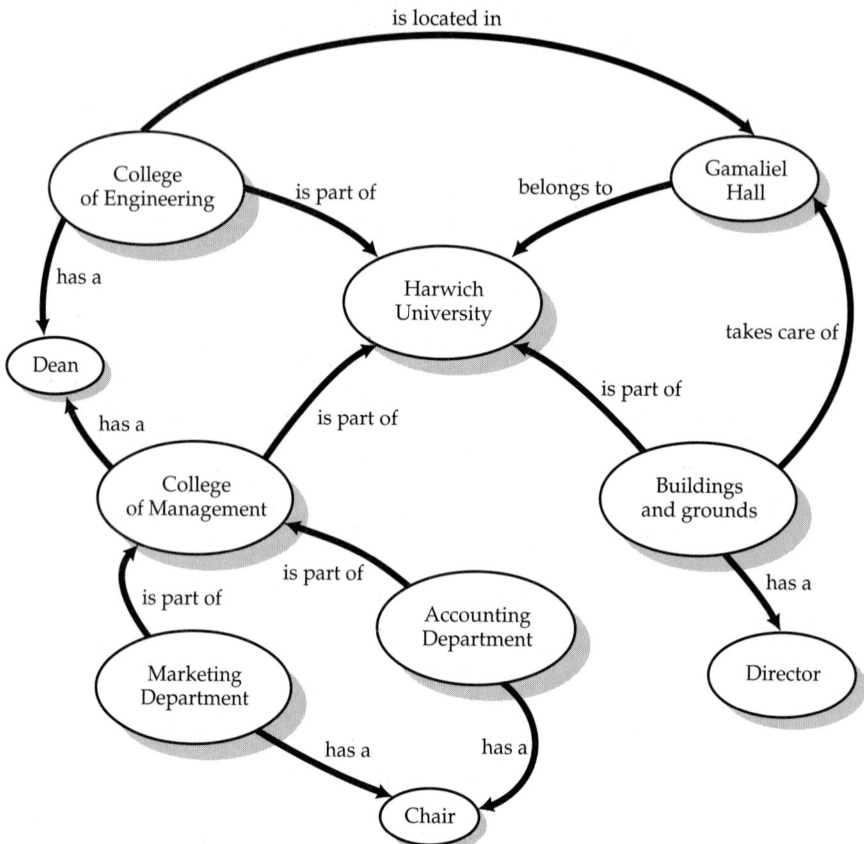

Pure semantic networks get unwieldy quickly, although there are programming tools (such as the Prolog language; see Section 17.2.3) that work well with them, and they are sometimes the best way to represent a collection of general common sense knowledge. Frames, as you will soon see, add structure to a semantic network by grouping all our knowledge about a given entity into one frame. We can then deal with that frame as a unit. This is useful in business applications of expert systems since most business situations deal with data that has a great deal of inherent structure.

You may also encounter a constrained version of a semantic network called an *object-attribute-value*, or OAV, network. Every node in an OAV network represents an object with which the system must deal, an attribute of that object, or a value of an attribute. OAV networks have only two types of arcs: "has-a" arcs, which connect objects to their attributes, and "is-a" arcs, which connect attributes to their values. Figure 16–4 shows the same knowledge of Harwich University as Figure 16–3, represented this time as an OAV

FIGURE 16–4
OAV Network about Harwich University

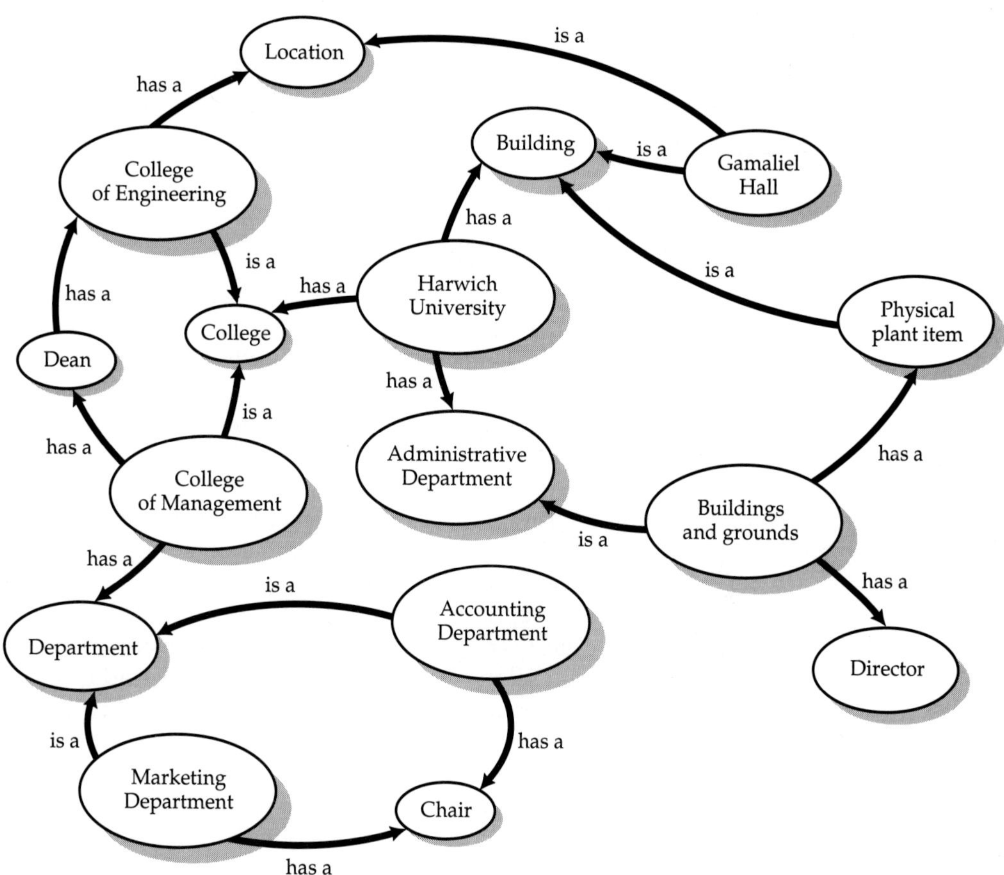

network. You can see that additional nodes were necessary because an OAV network cannot carry as much information as a general semantic network on the arcs between the nodes.

A sequence of is-a arcs can allow an object to inherit properties from other objects or from categories of objects. Consider these three arcs:

A canary is-a bird.

A bird is-a vertebrate.

A vertebrate has-a backbone.

We can conclude from these that canaries, being birds and hence vertebrates, have backbones too. Canaries could inherit other properties from the category of birds, such as having wings and a beak. Given a *multiple inheritance* capability, they could also inherit properties from the category of, say, household pets. In the Harwich University OAV network of Figure 16–4, the category of buildings inherits attributes from the category of physical plant items, such as perhaps the name of the employee assigned to supervise it or its value on the university's books. Gamaliel Hall, being a building, therefore inherits these attributes also. We could have put a has-a arc from "college" to "dean." The colleges of management and engineering would then inherit the property of having a dean from their category and would not need their own arcs.

16.3.2 Object-Oriented Programming

An *object* in the software sense is a logical entity that combines, or encapsulates, both its data and the programs (called *methods*) that can operate on its data. The reason for using objects, which we will amplify below, is that they isolate everything that relates to a real-world entity in one place in the software. This allows programmers to focus their attention on one thing at a time, getting it right, while this area is somewhat protected from unwanted interactions with other parts of the overall system.

Objects are organized into *classes.* All objects in a class share the same methods and the same general set of attributes. Individual objects, called *instances* of the class, have distinct attribute values.

A program asks an object to perform an operation on its data by sending the object a *message.* A message can be thought of as an object-oriented subroutine call. The data associated with an object can only be read or modified by sending messages to that object and obtaining answers from them. The ways in which the data can be read or modified are therefore restricted to those supported by the methods provided.

Objects support the concept of *inheritance.* With inheritance, a class can be defined as an offshoot of an existing class. Only its differences from its parent class need be stated. These differences can include extensions (more attributes, more methods), restrictions, or overrides.

A fully implemented object-oriented system also supports the concept of *polymorphism.* This means that the same message, addressed to objects of different classes, can invoke totally different procedures and return totally different results. You may have seen polymorphism at work in a programming course. In many programming languages the "+" sign between two integer variables calls for one type of addition, while the same sign between two floating-point, or real, variables calls for a different hardware operation. In an object-oriented system, a message such as "size" addressed to a shoe-store inventory object might return an answer such as "9D." The same message addressed to an object defining a window on a computer screen might return, not just a different value as its answer, but a conceptually different type of answer such as "300 pixels by 400 pixels" or "20 lines by 40 columns."

Polymorphism minimizes the impact of program modifications on existing code. Suppose, in the absence of polymorphism, our program has a function called *size.* Whenever it is invoked it must first find out what type of entity it is to calculate the size of. If we add a new entity with a size, we must modify this function, with the attendant possibility of introducing bugs that affect existing code. With polymorphism, there are several functions all called *size* but all attached to different object classes so they don't interfere with each other. We can add new ones to our hearts' content without impacting those that already exist.

Object-oriented programming methods can be used with traditional programming languages. One drawback of using those languages is that they do not enforce the discipline of accessing objects only via their associated methods. Traditional languages also generally do not provide for inheritance and polymorphism. Object-oriented languages enforce this discipline and provide these facilities. Smalltalk 80, designed at the Xerox Palo Alto Research Center (PARC), is the best-known of the early object-oriented programming research tools and is still used. Most current object-oriented programming is done in extensions of older 3GLs, especially C (which gave rise to the object-oriented C++ and Objective C) and, to a lesser extent, Pascal. Artificial intelligence developers can use object-oriented extensions of LISP such as Flavors.

Example of Objects

One object class in a college administrative system might be "Student." This class has thousands of instances (students). Each instance has its own attribute values but is processed via the same methods.

Student attributes include name, address, ID number, major, advisor name, and expected year of graduation, plus others.

One message that can be sent to a Student object is "change major." The method associated with this message could make sure that the student meets the qualifications for the new major before taking the requested action. This differs from a traditional database, in which anyone with authority to change a student's recorded major can simply enter a new value for the file in question. While an application program could check the validity of the requested change to the database, the responsibility for correctness then lies with the application programmers. Even if the application programmers do their jobs well, another application, or a user accessing data directly via (say) interactive SQL, could bypass the application checks. In an object-oriented system the correctness checks are built into the object. They cannot be bypassed, by error or in malice, by normal application programming or data-accessing methods.

Benefits of Object-Oriented Programming

Object-oriented systems provide these benefits:

- They speed development and improve reliability by isolating parts of a large program from each other.
- They ensure that business rules are defined and enforced consistently across application systems by embedding those rules within the definitions of shared objects.

- They impose order on programs, enhancing maintainability and extensibility.
- They allow creation of a *class library* for use in future projects, reducing their development time by facilitating the reuse of existing code.
- They help write portable code by encapsulating system dependencies within objects.

These benefits parallel those provided by database management systems. Object-oriented programming (OOP) can be said to do for program modules what DBMS did for data elements: It brings them into one place, puts them under central control, applies discipline to the way they are used, and makes them available to any authorized person.

Objects are not magic. They don't solve problems by themselves. They help programmers visualize the essence of a system, the relationships among its parts, and the internal behavior of those parts. They reduce unwanted interactions among those parts. These are all to the good. But we must be wary of going too far, of expecting object-oriented methodologies to take the place of proper planning, thinking, and analysis. They can't.

16.3.3 Frame-Concepts

A *frame* is an object, in the narrow technical sense of the preceding section, designed to represent knowledge about an entity in the form of semantic relationships. The frame includes attributes of the entity, often with default values. The attributes are called *slots.* For example, the color of a car could be a slot in a "car" frame.

The data structure within a frame resembles a small semantic network. Suppose a knowledge frame for organizations has the slot "title of chief executive" and the value in this slot for the Harwich University frame is "chancellor." Figure 16–5 shows the frame, with a few additional attributes.

Frame-based systems usually support inheritance. A "depreciable asset" frame could be the basis for a "computer" frame. The parent frame would

FIGURE 16–5

Frame Showing "Harwich University Has Chief Executive with Title 'Chancellor' "

Organization Frame	
Slot	*Value*
Organization name	Harwich University
Title of chief executive	Chancellor
Date of incorporation	1846
Number of employees	1,283

carry information that applies to all depreciable assets, such as manufacturer, date of purchase, price, and depreciation method. The child (computer) frame would carry additional information about computers that does not apply to all depreciable assets, such as its disk capacity or its operating system. It, in turn, could give rise to a lower-level frame for desktop microcomputers, for which software inventory or LAN connections might be important. The same depreciable asset parent frame could also be used as the base for a factory equipment frame and a motor vehicle frame. Each would have different information added to the base frame and could in turn lead to still more lower-level frames.

As with objects, a frame can override the characteristics of its parent as necessary. If the default value for "number of wheels" in a motor vehicle is 4, a motorcycle frame could override this with its own default value of 2. A specific instance of a motorcycle could override this default value yet again if it has a sidecar and therefore has three wheels. Similarly, the default value for the title of an organization's chief executive could be "president," which we chose to override in the case of Harwich University.

You may read that a system supports *multiple inheritance.* This means that a frame can inherit attributes from several parents. For example, a "truck" frame could inherit some information from a "motor vehicle" frame as above. It might inherit other information from a "cargo carrier" frame, which also serves as a partial basis for frames describing railroad freight cars, cargo ships, and cargo planes. The result is that we can construct the data structures and programming capabilities we need to deal with trucks—cargo-carrying motor vehicles—with little effort.

Frames are useful when an expert system deals with many similar items and each item has several numerical or textual attributes. If you don't want to perform reasoning with those attributes within the frame itself, or to use other features of the frame approach such as inheritance, it may be easier to represent the data in a simple file or database. For this reason, simple expert systems generally do not use frames. At the other end of the spectrum, if you are trying to represent a truly general collection of facts, the frame concept may be too restrictive. General semantic networks may be better suited to that situation.

16.3.4 Reasoning within the Frames

A frame can include rules for reasoning from its attributes. This is sometimes called *expectation-based reasoning* because the frame "expects" a slot to have a particular value unless it is told otherwise. An expectation-based rule might be "If an animal weighs over 100 pounds, has orange and black stripes, and has a long tail, it is a tiger." Specific knowledge can override the rules and default values: This particular animal, for instance, might be a cow that a farmer's children have painted for Halloween. The default value for the number of wheels on a pickup truck might be 4, but we can override that value if we know (or if a procedure within the expert system infers, perhaps from its model number) that a specific pickup truck has 6—or, after an accident, 3. This type of reasoning completes the spectrum of ways a slot in a frame can obtain a value. The whole spectrum is shown in Figure 16–6.

In the previous section we used an example of a production rule that stated "If a person ate a meal in the past hour, then that person is not hungry." A person frame might have attributes *time_of_last_meal* and *is_hungry*. The example production rule could be incorporated into the frame. That rule would be at level 4 in the hierarchy of Figure 16–6. If we knew that our friend Elvis was still hungry despite having just eaten, we could override the rule's conclusion: a level 5 action in Figure 16–6.

Rules of this type are generally associated with individual slots and are designed to be activated whenever the content of that slot is entered or altered. A rule that is triggered automatically whenever a slot is filled is sometimes called a *dæmon* (not "demon" in North America, although the original Greek root is the same and it is often misspelled that way. The spelling "demon" is acceptable in the U.K.)[2] Dæmons can determine what new conclusions can be drawn from any new facts added to a knowledge base. For example, a dæmon could examine the *time_of_last_meal* attribute in the previous paragraph and, if it is less an hour ago, set *is_hungry* to false. The rule that does this is for all practical purposes a production rule, even though it has been put into a frame, associated with a slot and called a dæmon. The rule for deciding if an animal is a tiger, two paragraphs back, is equally a production rule at heart.

Putting production rules in frames and associating them with individual slots in this fashion improves the structure of the knowledge base and thus makes it easier to deal with complex information structures. It does not, however, change the essence of what's going on.

FIGURE 16–6

Hierarchy of Ways a Frame Slot Can Obtain Values

1. System default value (typically zero or null).
2. Default value inherited from parent frame.
3. Default value specified for this frame.
4. Value derived by reasoning from values in other slots of frame.
5. Value explicitly assigned to slot.

Higher numbered means of assigning a value to a slot override any values previously assigned by lower numbered means.

[2]More generally, a dæmon is any program that sits quietly in the background waiting for an event to occur and takes appropriate action when the event occurs. A common example outside the expert systems field is a print dæmon. It waits for files to be placed in a predefined place on a disk drive and prints anything it finds there.

Dæmons are not restricted to working solely within the bounds of a single frame. A dæmon associated with one frame can scan related frames, or all frames of a given type, and change a value in its own frame when those other frames meet a specified condition. It would do this by sending messages, as described in the next section, to those other frames. For example, suppose information about incoming shipments to a factory are stored in frames and information about customer orders to be assembled is stored in other frames. A production scheduling dæmon could declare an order ready for production as soon as all the required components were received. This is a form of *forward chaining,* which you read about in Section 16.2.

16.3.5 Beyond the Individual Frames

To understand the role of frames in expert systems fully, we must distinguish between two types of knowledge: *factual* knowledge and *judgmental* knowledge. Factual knowledge represents what we know about objects and the relationships among them: John is Sue's brother, the current home mortgage loan rate is 9.5 percent, etc. Judgmental knowledge consists of the rules we use to solve a problem: if the temperature is 10 degrees above normal, it is cloudy, and the barometric pressure is dropping, then it will probably rain, and we should carry an umbrella.

Frames are an excellent way to represent factual knowledge but not a good way to represent judgmental knowledge. In other words, they describe facts but do not provide a complete way of reasoning from them. Suppose we have a frame with data about disk drives. It may tell us that a particular disk drive can store 320MB, but so what? Does this mean that the current user of our computer-configuring expert system, who wants a desktop publication system that will be able to handle color photographs, should get one? The frame doesn't say.

Frame-based systems must incorporate a way to reason globally with the knowledge contained in the individual frames. This is usually done by using production rules to represent the judgmental knowledge of our system.

For example, a computer-configuring expert system might have rules that take the required mass storage capacity and figure out what type of drives, and how many of them, to use. Those rules would use information about disk drives that could be stored in frames. They would access this information by sending messages to the frames. The first message would go to all mass storage frames, leaving a variable to be filled in by any frame that meets the required conditions. This rule would ask, in effect, "Do you have certain characteristics?" Once this variable is filled in, it can be used in subsequent rules to get further information: its price, its physical size, its power requirements, and the type of connector required at the end of the cable that attaches it to its controller.

Since frames usually do not suffice to store all the information we have about a situation, frame-based expert systems also use information stored in variables. In the above example, the type of disk drive to be used is a variable.

Its value is determined by expert knowledge of how disk drives should be chosen, matched to drive characteristics contained in the frames. The total required mass storage capacity is another variable, whose value is in this case supplied by the user or determined from the user's contemplated applications.

Some frame-based expert system shells, such as KEE (Knowledge Engineering Environment) from Intellicorp, store the production rules themselves in frames. Each rule frame has a slot for the text of the rule, which is then interpreted in the normal fashion. Such a system could alternatively be designed to have several slots for each rule: one for the text of its antecedent, two for the text of its true and false consequents, perhaps a few more for explanations. This is somewhat artificial as a concept but does take advantage of the system's ability to store and access frames in an organized manner.

16.4 Predicate Calculus

Predicate calculus is a formal mechanism based on predicates—propositions, or statements, whose truth is known—and rules by which we can derive other predicates from the known ones. Consider, for example:

1. All dentists have mustaches.
2. John is a dentist.
3. Therefore, John has a mustache.

If we accept the truth of the first statement—which in this case is open to debate—and the second, the third must follow. If the second statement were

2*a*. Jim has no mustache.

we could conclude that James is not a dentist. However, if we had

2*b*. Groucho has a mustache.

the conclusion that Groucho is a dentist could not be derived from our predicates. He might be, but we don't know that from the evidence before us.

Complex expressions can be built up using the predicate calculus connectives of And, Or, Not, and Implies. There is an algebra of these symbols that, like conventional algebra, permits us to simplify complex expressions. We can start with a collection of information (or data) and work through it, via a series of such expressions, to complex and nonobvious conclusions.

For example, consider the test proposition

There is an x such that x is a disk drive and the capacity of x exceeds 300MB.

If we have an existing set of predicates that include

An RA81 is a disk drive.

An RA81 is made by Digital Equipment Corporation.

The capacity of an RA81 is 450MB.

then an inference engine based on predicate calculus can assert the truth of our test proposition while substituting the value RA81 for *x*. (Which of the three given predicates aren't we using for this purpose?) Alternatively, it could determine what disk drive—if any—meets the specified conditions. This would be important in designing a computer system to meet a given set of user requirements.

By using a sufficiently large set of predicates we can store an entire collection of knowledge:

A 3390 is a disk drive.

A 3390 is made by IBM.

A GX 8620 is a central processor.

A GX 8620 is made by Hitachi Data Systems.

And so forth.

We can add to or modify this knowledge at will by simply asserting or negating predicates. This would come in handy, to continue the above example, if IBM renamed its disk drive business AdStar—as it did in 1992. The knowledge base will respond to the changed conditions automatically.

Predicate calculus can be used to represent knowledge, to analyze knowledge, and to reason deductively over this knowledge. It has the advantage of a solid mathematical foundation that has been proven over a long period of use. (The direct predecessor of predicate calculus was studied by Aristotle.) Another advantage is that it maps directly into the Prolog programming language, making it a convenient knowledge representation for those who will program expert system applications from scratch in Prolog. You'll see the connection when we discuss Prolog in Section 17.2.3.

However, predicate calculus is not very useful for judgmental knowledge. Anything that can be done with predicate calculus can also be done with frames. (This, too, has been proven mathematically.) Frames are more intuitive for the nonmathematician, possess added features such as inheritance, and integrate more easily with common sense judgmental knowledge. When a knowledge representation situation lends itself to either frame or predicate calculus representation, most shell users vote for frames.

16.5 DATABASES

When the amount of knowledge is large and well structured, a database of some sort is an important adjunct to an expert system. For example, a system designed to help apartment seekers find the right place to live could have an extensive real estate database. The expert system could scan the database and apply the same rules that an experienced real estate agent would use to identify the most likely apartments to inspect. By using confidence factors (see the next section), the system could respond with the electronic equivalent of "This one's perfect for you!" or "I don't have anything that's 100 percent right, but these two are pretty close."

Database access can be especially important in commercial DSS applications of expert systems, where it is often important to access information about the business. Such information is often already in the corporate database.

Frames are, as mentioned above, an alternative to databases for some expert system applications. The use of frames, however, does not alter the fact that most businesses store information in a traditional database and the expert system often has to access it. Frames are more applicable when the data in question are used only by the expert system and are never accessed outside it. (Actually, many expert system packages store the values of frame slots in what is essentially a database, but that is a technical design decision that is invisible to the knowledge-base developer.)

Most expert system tools have interfaces to popular database management systems. These interfaces make it unnecessary for the expert system developer to be a DBMS developer as well. If an organization has an existing database that the expert system must use, the need to access that database may constrain the choice of platforms or development tools for the expert system.

16.6 Confidence Factors

Experts are not always sure of their conclusions. "It looks like your valves," a mechanic might say, "but it might be your piston rings." You may have heard a doctor say, "It looks like strep, but we'll do a throat culture to make sure." If experts are subject to this sort of uncertainty, why shouldn't the computer systems that mimic their reasoning also be?

Or, a faculty member might advise a student, "All other things being equal, Marketing usually works out best for first-semester juniors in MIS, but Business Law can be OK too." A travel agent could tell a New Jersey customer, "Hawaii would be perfect, but you'd also like Jamaica; the flight is shorter and less expensive, and you wouldn't have jet lag from the time change." Here there is no uncertainty, but there are multiple satisfactory answers. In situations like these two, a human expert can often provide a relative ranking of those answers.

Or, a person listening to a radio forecast of cloudy weather might decide to carry an umbrella. There are no multiple answers; there is no possibility of needing an umbrella to fend off low-flying clouds. The uncertainty here is in the source of our knowledge, which is not 100 percent reliable.

Another possibility is that we are uncertain about a fact because the fact itself is not precisely defined. In the sentence "Today is warm," there is no universally agreed-upon cutoff point for "warmness." Warmness depends on the person making the assessment and his or her concept of what is typical for that locale at that season. Fuzzy logic, which we discuss further in Section 16.7, was designed to handle this type of uncertainty.

Expert systems handle these situations by using *confidence factors* or *truth values*. A confidence factor is a numerical value associated with a variable that indicates the degree to which the system treats that variable as true. "True" in this context may mean "correct," as in an engine problem diagnosis, or "applicable," as in a course selection recommendation. Lack of absolute correctness, in turn, may be because of uncertainties in our reasoning process (again, as in engine diagnosis) or in our input data (as in our decision to carry an umbrella).

16.6.1 *Where Confidence Factors Come From*

An expert system can obtain a confidence factor to associate with a piece of knowledge in one or more of three ways:

- A user can enter the confidence factor to be associated with an input value. The answer to "Do you plan to retire at 65?" in a financial planning system might be "Yes, with a confidence factor of 75 percent."
- A production rule can incorporate a confidence factor in its consequent. Such a rule might be

  IF *age* < 30 AND *height* < 70″ AND *weight* > 300 THEN *likes_beer* = yes, with a confidence factor of 85 percent

  This approach is commonly used in problem diagnosis systems, as the known symptoms may suggest a probable diagnosis without confirming it absolutely.
- Confidence factors can be propagated forward from the antecedent of a rule to its consequent. Suppose we have a rule

  IF *time_to_retirement* < 5 years THEN *investment* = bonds

  If we have previously determined *time_to_retirement* to be less than five years with a confidence factor of 75 percent, this rule will propagate that 75 percent confidence factor forward and recommend buying bonds with the same confidence level. The meaning of this level to the investor depends on whether other recommendations came out with higher or lower values.

If confidence factors range from 0 to 100 percent, the interpretation of 100 percent is clear: We are absolutely certain of the fact in question. That of 0 percent, however, is less obvious. Does it mean we're sure a fact is false, or that we don't know? Systems differ in their handling of this issue. Indeed, a given system may handle different types of variables differently. A zero confidence level in a Boolean variable might imply absolute falsity. The same confidence level in a character string variable might not.

When the antecedent of a rule includes variables with confidence factors, the system designer must consider the *truth threshold* of the system in deciding which consequent of the rule applies. If the conditions in the antecedent are totally true, the THEN clause of the rule clearly applies. If they are 99 percent true (confidence factor of 99 percent), it should probably also apply, in this case with the confidence factor propagated through to the consequents. But what of 60 percent? Of 40 percent? Of 20 percent? Of 2 percent? At what point do we say that the antecedent, while still nominally true with a small confidence factor, does not justify choosing the THEN consequent?

Most expert system shells provide a default threshold value, typically from 20 to 50 percent, and allow a system developer to change it. We mention this issue here only to point out the need to consider it in planning the logic of an expert system.

The above discussion assumed that confidence factors range from 100 (absolute truth) down to 0 (absolute lack of truth, or absolute falsity). Many expert systems do represent them in this way, on a scale from 0 to an upper limit of 100, 1.0, or some other convenient value. Others use a symmetric range with 100 (or 1.0) representing absolute truth and −100 (or −1.0) representing absolute falsity, with 0 representing total uncertainty. This is useful in dealing with negative recommendations: "IF investor is retired, THEN investor should *not* buy risky high-growth stocks." Some tools let expert system developers choose between zero-based and zero-centered representations.

16.6.2 Alternative Approaches to Confidence Factors

The simplest way to deal with confidence factors is through traditional probability theory. In this approach, we (or our expert system) treat the confidence factor associated with a fact as the mathematical probability that the fact is correct. For instance, we might say that a particular patient has appendicitis with a probability of 0.9.

Probability theory lets us use familiar equations for combining probabilities. If two facts have independent probabilities x and y, the probability that they are both true is xy. The probability that at least one is true is $[1 - (1 - x)(1 - y)]$. You probably (with a confidence factor of 0.99+) studied these, and more complex variations on this theme, in an introductory statistics course.

However, traditional probability theory does not always match the needs of expert systems well. It has these deficiencies:

- Rankings of alternatives do not always correspond to mathematical probabilities. "It looks like your valves, but it might be your piston rings" is not a mathematical statement.

- Probabilities cannot deal with conflicting evidence. If one expert (or one line of reasoning in an expert system) makes one recommendation and a different one makes another, probability formulas cannot resolve the conflict.
- Probabilities do not deal with negative evidence well. If a system concludes that a certain diagnosis is 40 percent probable and a subsequent test refutes that diagnosis, there may be no reasonable way to reduce the probability in the system. Using an additional rule with AND wouldn't work since its conclusion would be treated as a new piece of evidence, however slight, that reinforces the existing diagnosis.
- Knowledge may be phrased in terms that are inherently vague. "A lot of oil spilled" is not a precise statement. Its interpretation depends on whether the context is refinishing teak furniture in a basement workshop or transporting petroleum in a ship off Alaska. Cleanup recommendations would vary accordingly. Fuzzy logic, which we discuss in the next section, was developed to deal with imprecise concepts.

To deal with these and similar situations, expert systems often provide several ways to combine confidence factors:

- Confidence factors can both apply to the antecedents of a rule and figure in its consequents. Suppose the rule of the previous paragraph were "IF *time_to_retirement* < 5 years THEN *investment* = bonds with a confidence factor of 80 percent." Since the likelihood of retirement in the next five years has already been established to be 75 percent, an expert system might recommend investing in bonds with a confidence factor of 75 percent × 80 percent = 60 percent.
- Several confidence factors can be combined via AND, OR, or both in the antecedents of a rule. Suppose a rule were "IF *time_to_retirement* < 10 years AND *inflation* > 6 percent THEN *investment* = utility stocks." If the first condition in the antecedent is true with a confidence factor of 90 percent and the second with a confidence factor of 80 percent, the combined statement can have no higher than 80 percent confidence. It may have less. The specific methods used to calculate composite confidence factors vary from expert system to expert system. The probability approach to confidence factors suggests multiplying the confidence factors. This works well if the conditions are independent. If they are dependent—for example, if a person might defer retirement under conditions of high inflation—they do not work as well. Other approaches take the lower of the two confidence factors (or the lowest, if there are more than two). Some expert system development tools give their users a choice of methods.

  When two conditions are combined via OR (disjunction), the

resulting confidence factor is at least as high as the highest of the contributing confidence factors. Consider "IF *weather* = sunny OR *date_tonight* = yes THEN drive the Jaguar convertible." The radio has predicted an 80 percent chance of sun. Your potential date has said "OK, unless some prof announces a test for tomorrow," which you estimate to mean a date is 80 percent likely as well. The chance of at least one of these two occurrences is, happily, greater than 80 percent. The probability approach combines OR'ed confidence factors by multiplying the probabilities that the conditions will *not* hold. If there is a 20 percent chance of no sun, and a 20 percent chance of no date, there is (for independent events) a 4 percent chance of neither sun nor date. Therefore, there is a 96 percent chance of at least one or the other, and the consequent (to drive the Jag) will have a confidence factor of 96 percent.

Here, too, the probability approach is appropriate only when all factors involved in the recommendation are independent. If professors tend to look out the window and say, "It's too nice a day to make you study for a test," the factors are correlated. The probability of either sun or date is then lower than 96 percent.

Confidence factors can be "piled on" each other when several rules lead to the same conclusion. In a financial planning system, several different rules might all recommend investing in growth stocks. If each recommendation has a confidence factor, the composite confidence factor should be at least as high as the highest. Experts disagree on whether it should be higher than that, perhaps computed as if the conditions had been OR'ed. There are several methods. Each is appropriate for some situations but not others. As noted above, probability theory does not deal with piling on negative evidence well.

Different expert system development tools represent and combine confidence factors in different ways for the different situations (AND, OR, etc.) The specifics of the ways different tools work are not critical for you to learn at this time, as new development tools are always being developed, and the one you'll use on the job probably won't be in a given list. The above discussion should give you a feel for the options you might encounter.

16.7 Fuzzy Logic

Fuzzy logic [ZADE65, ZADE83] is an approach to dealing with inherently imprecise knowledge in a precise way. Where a confidence factor states, in effect, "I believe this fact to have a 70 percent probability of being true," fuzzy logic states "I believe this fact to be 70 percent true." While the two phrases sound nearly the same, their meanings are quite different. In the first case the fact itself is either true or false. We don't know which, so we take a statistical guess. In the second case the fact may be, literally, 70 percent true. The examples in the next two paragraphs will clarify this.

If you are asked "Is there a box of corn flakes in your kitchen cabinet?", your answer may have a 60 percent confidence factor because you're not sure. However, there either is or is not a box of corn flakes there. The uncertainty reflects your knowledge of the situation, not the contents of the cabinet. The same applies to estimates of future values of objective facts: What will inflation be next year? Will you retire at age 70? When the time comes these questions will have definite answers, even though we don't know them yet.

However, if you are asked "Is the person next to you 'tall?'", you might be uncertain because "tall" is not precisely defined. Most people would agree that a North American male of 6 feet 9 inches is tall and one of 5 feet 2 inches is not. What, though of 6 feet 4 inches? 6 feet 1 inch? 5 feet 11 inches? 5 feet 9 inches? As one goes down the scale, the degree of "tallness" decreases. At some point it drops to zero. Many other terms are subjective as well: Is a development project "risky?" Is an engine temperature "high?" Is a job candidate "well educated?" Is a bond yield "high?" Is travel time from a factory to a proposed warehouse location "short?" The list is endless.

Fuzzy logic provides a rigorous mathematical method of dealing with subjectively defined terms. It represents them via data elements that have partial membership in sets. At about 5 feet 9 inches, the author of this book has, at most, about a 10 percent membership in the set of tall men. Rules such as "If a man is tall, then he should play basketball," interpreted via fuzzy logic, would yield only a weak recommendation in my case. Such an expert system might recommend that I find a sport better suited to my stature.

Fuzzy logic–based expert systems can use modifiers to qualify relationships further. A rule might read "If a man is very tall . . ." or ". . . rather tall . . ." or ". . . somewhat tall. . . ." The term "very" in this context might mean 90 percent set membership and so on. Combining terms defined in this way can be handy for selecting the best fit to a combination of factors. Suppose, for example, we wanted to select all the apartments in our rental database that have "nice" buildings and are "close" to a bus stop. Fuzzy logic would let us pick out an apartment that is not too close to a bus stop, if the building is really fantastic, as well as one in a so-so building if the bus stops at its door. If we define fuzzy set memberships properly, this selection process can mimic what people would do quite well.

Numerical factors can be translated into set membership grades via curves such as the one shown in Figure 16–7. That curve shows one person's belief that a body temperature is "normal" based on a given, and accurately known, thermometer reading. (Normal temperature is usually taken to be 98.6°F or 37.0°C.) A temperature of 100°F, about 37.8°C, has some degree of membership in the set of normal temperatures but not much. A diagnosis that depends on normal temperature in this case would not have high credibility associated with it.

FIGURE 16–7
Fuzzy Set Membership Curve

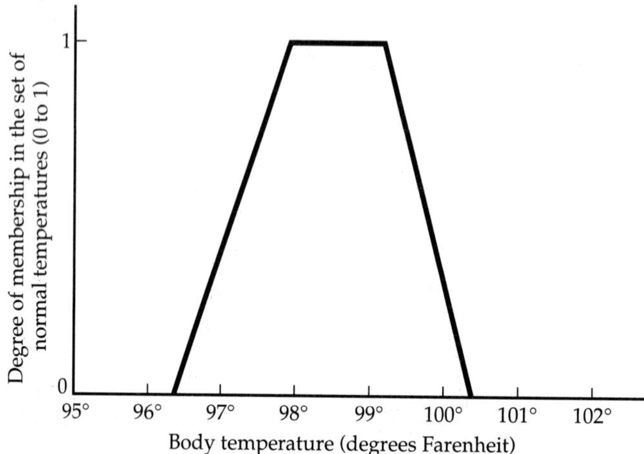

Fuzzy set membership grades should not be interpreted as probabilities. (To make the distinction clear, the term possibility is often used to refer to fuzzy set membership grades.) If one event has a 20 percent probability and a second has a 60 percent probability, the second event is precisely three times as probable as the first. However, suppose one man is assigned 20 percent membership in the set of tall men—that is, he has a 20 percent possibility of being tall—and a second man is assigned 60 percent membership. This does not mean that the second man is three times as tall as the first. More likely, the first is about 5 feet 10 inches, and the second is a little over 6 feet.

Fuzzy set membership grades do not necessarily add up to 1. A 5 foot 10 inch man may have 20 percent membership in the set of tall men, 10 percent membership in the set of short men, and 90 percent membership in the set of men of medium height. The more height categories we create—very tall, medium-tall, medium-short, etc., etc.—the higher the sum of his set memberships will be. The purpose of fuzzy set membership grades is to allow us to rank entities or events relative to each other, thus enabling us to choose the best fit to a decision. They handle this job quite nicely.

The advantage of fuzzy logic for expert systems is that it matches the way human experts think about many important problem areas. "Low" blood counts, "good" high school grades, programming language "expertise" are all matters of degree. The degree to which a situation has certain characteristics is often an important factor in a decision about that situation. Were we to deal with situations such as these via conventional logic, we would have to divide each parameter of interest into discrete segments: five for height, three for speed, etc. We would then need, potentially, a rule for every combination

Using Fuzzy Logic for Commercial Loan Analysis[3]

The job of lending officers is to evaluate a company's financial posture with a view to determining the amount of risk a loan would entail. Loan officers think and act on the basis of approximate relationships that involve vaguely defined, somewhat ambiguous terms like "above," "strong," and "poor." For example, a loan officer might consider a company's credit position to be "strong" if its profitability and capital usage efficiency are "strong" and its liquidity position is "normal."

Fuzzy logic is especially well suited to the commercial loan evaluation problem because its underlying concepts match the mental concepts used by loan officers. For example, consider an industry where fixed asset turnover averages six turns per year. A turnover rate of 10 may be considered "substantially above average." What, though, of 9? Of 8? Of 7? Where does one draw the line between "substantially above average" and "not substantially above average?" The answer, of course, is that loan officers do not draw a black-and-white distinction between the two. Fuzzy logic makes it unnecessary for the computer to draw one. Using fuzzy logic, a turnover rate of 7 could have both a possibility of being substantially above average and a possibility of not being substantially above average.

The overall set of quantitative factors leading up to a loan decision is shown in Figure 16–8. The authors of this paper developed an expert system based on fuzzy logic concepts that deals with the bottom level of this tree: combining inventory turnover through trend analysis into an overall efficiency rating. The system had a total of 74 rules: far fewer than the hundreds that it would have needed without the fuzzy logic approach.

The rules were determined after discussions with practicing loan officers. Each of the five base variables (inventory turnover, etc.) was associated with four fuzzy sets: that the base variable in question is substantially below average, below average, above average, or substantially above average. Figure 16–9 shows the set membership functions for inventory turnover in an industry for which the average figure is 6.

The system user must specify the points that define the four trapezoids of Figure 16–9 as well as those for the other base variables, 23 trapezoids in all. These trapezoids will depend on the averages for each industry and the amount of variation from the average that is typical for the industry.

Once the fuzzy set membership trapezoids have been specified, the user can enter financial values for a particular firm. The system will then use rules of the form

IF inventory turns are below average AND receivables turnover is not substantially below average AND fixed asset turnover is not substantially below average AND total turnover is above average or substantially above average AND the trend is strong, THEN efficiency is normal.

This system stores its fuzzy set membership factors in a table separate from the rules themselves, which makes it possible for a loan officer or other person to change these factors, perhaps for a new industry or perhaps to reflect a changed understanding of what "substantially above" ought to mean, without touching the rule base itself. This approach provides benefits, in terms of software clarity and in terms of protection against error, that resemble those of the expert system approach itself with its clear separation of knowledge from inference logic.

The Fuzzy Loan Evaluation System was written in the Pascal language because none of the expert system shells available to the authors supported fuzzy logic set membership functions in a "possibility base" separate from the inference rules. It runs on an IBM or compatible microcomputer under the MS-DOS operating system. A full evaluation of all 74 rules takes a negligible time, from a human perspective, even on the slowest hardware of this type.

[3]This example is condensed from [LEVY91].

FIGURE 16–8
Quantitative Factors in Loan Decision

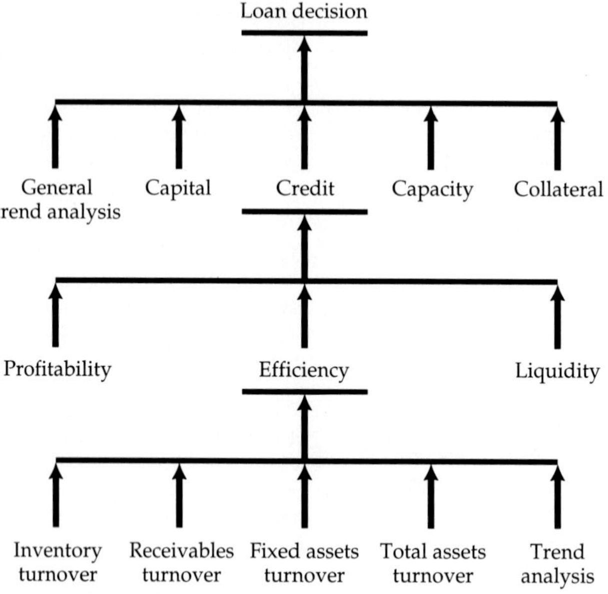

SOURCE: Based on Figure 1 of [LEVY91].

FIGURE 16–9
Inventory Turnover Fuzzy Set Membership Curves

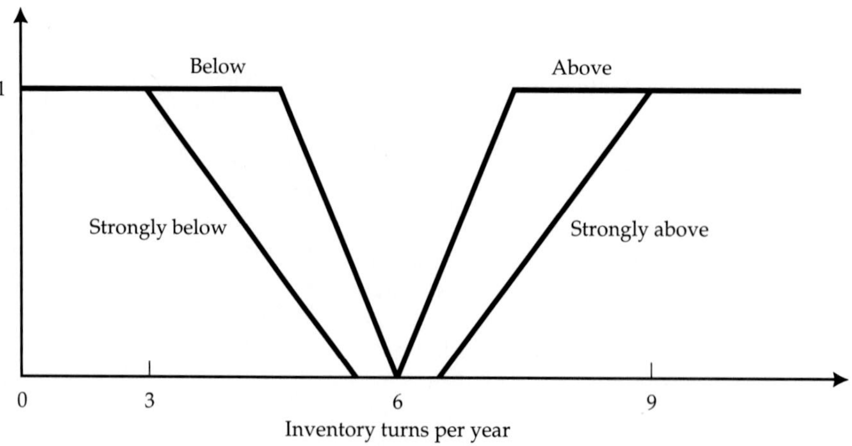

SOURCE: Based on Figure 3 of [LEVY91].

of parameter values: 15 rules for just these two parameters. The number of rules we would need to get a good match to the way humans deal with such data would get out of hand quickly. By using fuzzy logic, we effectively divide each parameter into an infinite number of segments. The rules of the expert system can carry out calculations based on membership grades without having the number of rules explode geometrically as it otherwise would. That simplifies an expert system a great deal. ("A great deal" is a fuzzy concept, too.)

Summary

Expert systems, despite some overall similarities, differ internally in several ways.

One difference among expert systems is in the way they represent facts: knowledge about the current problem and situation. The simplest approach is to represent facts by the values of variables in the workspace. Variables can take on Boolean (true or false) values, numeric values, character string values, or values chosen from a specific set of possibilities. Variables can be single valued or multiple valued.

Knowledge about how to solve a class of problems is usually represented in the form of production rules. Production rules are of the general form IF (antecedent), THEN (consequent if antecedent is true), ELSE (consequent if antecedent is false).

An expert system can process production rules via either backward chaining or forward chaining. For a given set of rules and input, both approaches will lead to the same conclusion, but one may reach it more efficiently than the other.

In backward chaining, the system begins with a goal which it tries to reach. If it does not have the facts that give a value for this goal, it establishes intermediate goals that might lead it toward its final goal. It keeps working backward until it reaches facts that it knows or can find out. It then uses these facts to derive its conclusion. Backward chaining is also known as goal-directed reasoning.

In forward chaining, the expert system begins with the facts it knows and sees what other facts it can derive from them. It continues this process until it derives the conclusion of the entire reasoning process. Forward chaining is also known as data-driven reasoning.

Production rules are modular and correspond in a straightforward manner with many experts' thought processes. They make it easy for an expert to explain its reasoning to its users. However, their lack of structure can create problems in large knowledge bases. Such knowledge bases need tools, such as frames, to structure their knowledge.

A frame is an object that represents knowledge in the form of semantic relationships. Here, an object is a software construct that includes both data about an entity and procedures for operating on its data. Semantic relationships are statements about the properties of an entity. In a frame, data about an entity are represented by values in slots. Frames support inheritance, by which a general type of frame can be used as the basis for several more specialized types of frames. Frames also support reasoning with the frame, whereby we can automatically draw conclusions from whatever facts we know about an entity. (This corresponds to forward chaining with production rules.) Frames are a good way to represent knowledge when a system deals with many items that have the same or similar attributes. Frames must be augmented by production rules to handle the expert's knowledge about solving the problem.

Predicate calculus is a branch of formal logic that supports reasoning from facts to conclusions. It can be used both to represent and to reason from them. In its ability to represent facts predicate calculus is equivalent to frames. Predicate calculus is not usually a good way to represent an expert's judgmental knowledge about solving a class of problems.

Many expert systems also store knowledge in databases or use knowledge that other applications have stored in databases. Database accessing capabilities are built into most expert system development tools.

Facts are not always known with certainty. Expert systems represent lack of certainty by associating confidence factors with facts. Confidence factors may also represent the value, or ranking, that an expert system associates with each of several possible conclusions.

Confidence factors may be entered with source data if there is uncertainty associated with those data. They may also be incorporated into a rule if the rule is known not to lead to its conclusion with total certainty. Once they enter a system via either of these routes, they are propagated forward through the reasoning process.

If a fact is true if any of several conditions is true, its confidence factor will be at least as high as the highest associated with any of the contributing conditions. If a fact is true only if all of several conditions are true, its confidence factor will be no higher than the lowest associated with any of the contributing conditions. Expert systems vary in how they combine confidence factors within these two general guidelines. One approach is that of statistical probability theory. This approach does not meet all needs, so other methods of merging confidence factors are often used as well.

Fuzzy logic provides another way of dealing with uncertain knowledge. Fuzzy logic provides a rigorous mathematical method to handle parameters that are defined subjectively. It does this by associating membership grades to different values of such parameters and carrying out calculations on those membership grades. Fuzzy logic is often a good match to the way people reason with subjective concepts.

Key Terms

backward chaining 512
Boolean variable 510
class (in object-oriented programming) 524
class library 526
confidence factor 532
dæmon 528
data-driven reasoning 516
default value 527
expectation-based reasoning 527
factual knowledge 529
firing a rule 515
forward chaining 516
frames 521, 526
fuzzy logic 536
goal-directed (or goal-driven) reasoning 512
inferencing methods 512
inheritance 523, 524
instance (of an object) 524
judgmental knowledge 529
membership grade 537
message (to an object) 524
method (in object-oriented programming) 524
multiple inheritance 523, 527
multivalued attribute 511
object 524
object-attribute-value (OAV) network 522
object-oriented programming 524
overriding (a default value) 527
partial set membership 537
polymorphism 524
possibility (in fuzzy logic) 538
predicate 530
predicate calculus 530
production rules 511
proposition 530
semantic networks 521
simple fact 510
single-valued attribute 510
slot 526
truth threshold 534
truth value 533
variables 510

Review Questions

1. What two basic types of knowledge must expert systems be able to represent?
2. What types of variables can be used to represent facts within an expert system?
3. What is a Boolean variable? An attribute variable?
4. What are the three basic components of a production rule? Which one(s) is(are) optional?
5. Give five advantages and five drawbacks of production rules.
6. What are the two basic inferencing methods? What is their fundamental difference?
7. What is another name for data-driven reasoning?
8. How would you decide which type of chaining to use in an expert system?
9. What is a semantic network? An OAV network?
10. Define an object. What are the two basic components of an object?
11. How does an object class differ from an instance of that class?

12. What happens when an object receives a message?
13. Define inheritance, multiple inheritance, and polymorphism.
14. What is a frame? Of the two basic types of knowledge in an expert system (review Question 1), which would be stored in frames?
15. Under what conditions are frames most useful in expert systems?
16. How can frame slots be filled with values?
17. Do frame-based systems have any use for production rules? If so, what?
18. What type of knowledge is best stored as predicates?
19. Do expert systems ever need to access a database? Why or why not?
20. What concept is used when an expert system cannot reach a single conclusion with absolute certainty?
21. State the two ways in which confidence factors can initially enter the reasoning process.
22. What is meant by "set membership" in fuzzy logic?

Exercises

1. Assuming your shell supported all types of variables, would you choose character string, numeric, Boolean, or set-valued variables to represent the following pieces of information in an expert system designed to help choose a vacation destination? Would each one take on a single value or multiple values? (Some of the pieces of information can be represented by more than one variable. For instance, you can represent the last line of a standard U.S. mailing address as either one character string, "Boston, MA 02192," or as three elements. Where you choose to use more than one data element, state what each one is.)
   a. The name of the traveler.
   b. The number of travelers in the group.
   c. The desired date of departure.
   d. The desired price range.
   e. Desired activities at the destination.
   f. Willingness to travel by air to reach the destination.
2. Write production rules that formalize the following English sentences. For each, also state if it is completely unambiguous.
   a. "I'm going to take the bus to class, unless it's late, and then I'll try to hitch a ride with Karen, but if I can't, then I'll have to take a taxi if I have the money, but if I don't have cab fare, I'll have to take the bus anyway."
   b. "I'm going to get a new toner cartridge for my laser printer if I have time before a 12:30 lunch meeting, unless I can print this report without too many light spots."

3. Do you think forward or backward chaining would work better in each of the following expert systems? In a few sentences, why?
   a. A system to help choose the best typeface to use in a laser-printed document.
   b. A system to recommend a weekly schedule for a work group, which has various requirements for meetings among different subsets of its members, where some of these meetings require facilities (e.g., a conference room equipped with a computer-linked overhead projector) whose supply is limited, and there are external schedule constraints on some of those group members.
   c. A system to recommend an approach to succeeding in a business negotiation.
   d. A system to recommend a production schedule based on existing orders and sales forecasts.
4. Show all the information in Figure 6–2, the college bookstore entity-relationship diagram, as an OAV network.
5. Define a parent frame and a child frame for the following entities. In each case, place at least four attributes in the parent frame. For the child frame, add some attributes that are not in the parent frame (because some entities that the parent might represent don't have them), and specify default values for some parent frame attributes that you could not specify in the parent frame.
   a. A student and a senior majoring in English.
   b. An airline flight number (e.g., Delta flight 211 from Boston to Bermuda) and a specific instance of that flight (e.g., the one leaving on March 17, 1993).
   c. A computer and an IBM PS/2 Model 57SX.
   d. A book and a hardcover book in your college or university library.
   e. A department store employee and a sales clerk (employed by the same store) paid on commission.
   f. An animal and a pedigreed show dog.
6. For each of the following possible expert systems, identify one piece of information that the user would have to enter, one piece of information that the system could (at least in theory) obtain from a suitable database, and one piece of information that it would be able to figure out as it worked:
   a. A system to help vacationers choose a travel destination.
   b. A system to recommend approval or rejection of loan applicants.
   c. A system to diagnose problems in office building air conditioning systems.
   d. A system to give driving directions from one place to another.
   e. A system to recommend a class schedule for college juniors.
7. Consider the example of deciding whether or not to drive the Jaguar convertible as it relates to OR'ed confidence factors in Section 16.6.2. Justify the statement at the end of the example that if the two decision factors

are correlated as stated, the probability of at least one of them being true (and hence of your wanting to drive the Jag) is lower than 96 percent. (*Hint*: Consider the limiting case of 100 percent correlation.)

References

DAVI77 Davis, R.; B. G. Buchanan; and E. H. Shortliffe. "Production Rules as a Representation of a Knowledge Base Consultation Program." *Artificial Intelligence* 8, pp. 15–45.

FROS86 Frost, Richard. *Introduction to Knowledge Base Systems.* Collins, London (1986).

KAND92 Kandel, Abraham, Ed. *Fuzzy Expert Systems.* CRC Press, Boca Raton, Fla. (1992).

LEVY91 Levy, Joshua; Efrem G. Mallach; and Peter Duchessi. "A Fuzzy Logic System for Commercial Loan Analysis." *Omega: International Journal of Management Science* 19, no. 6 (November–December 1991), pp. 651–69.

MOCK92 Mockler, Robert J. *Developing Knowledge-Based Systems Using an Expert System Shell.* Macmillan, New York (1992).

SUBB91 Subbart, Charles I. "Managerial Strategic Knowledge and Artificial Intelligence," in *Advances in Information Processing in Organizations,* vol. 4. James R. Meindl; Robert L. Cardy; and Sheila M. Puffer, Eds. JAI Press Inc., Greenwich, Conn. (1991).

WILL88 Williams, Tony, and Brian Bainbridge. "Rule Based Systems," in *Approaches to Knowledge Representation: An Introduction;* Gordon A. Ringland and David A. Duce, Eds. John Wiley and Sons, New York (1988).

ZADE65 Zadeh, Lofti A. "Fuzzy Sets." *Information and Control* 8, no. 3 (1965), pp. 338–53.

ZADE83 Zadeh, Lofti A. "The Role of Fuzzy Logic in the Management of Uncertainty in Expert Systems." *Fuzzy Sets and Systems* 11, no. 3 (1983), pp. 199–277.

Envoyance
Asbestos Abatememt Decisions[4]

"Hoo-boy!" exclaimed Miguel as Doug and Adrienne came in for their 4 P.M. appointment. "Seems I've just been appointed the resident expert on asbestos and what to do about it. In this business, if you see the same kind of problem once, you're ex-

[4]The technical information in this episode is from Chapter 18 of [MOCK92].

perienced; twice, you're a pro; three times, you're an expert. Maybe I'll get business cards that say 'Asbestos Abatement Guru' on them."

"It can't really be that bad, can it?" asked Adrienne.

"Well, no, not really," Miguel agreed. "There is such a thing as a real expert, I suppose. Still, there are so many problems and so few of us working on them, that it's hard to find someone who's been dealing with the same issue for years. It's not like sending pigs out to dig for truffles. That technology hasn't changed since the Middle Ages. Here, things keep changing. Every situation is different."

"How does that tie into asbestos?" asked Doug, not wanting to keep Miguel past normal quitting time.

"Well," said Miguel as he got back to the subject, "you know that asbestos can do a great deal of damage if you breathe it. Unfortunately, it's also a cheap, fireproof insulating material, so a lot of it got put in buildings before anyone knew it was dangerous. Now, the owners of these buildings have to do something to prevent their occupants from breathing the stuff.

"There are five factors you have to take into account in deciding what to do about an asbestos situation. On the engineering side you've got the type of asbestos and its condition. On the nontechnical side you've got your legal situation, your social pressure, and your business factors. Each of these gets broken down a lot more.

"There are five basic types of asbestos. The one called amosite is really nasty. You want to get rid of amosite absolutely, positively, and permanently. The others can sometimes stay around if they are dealt with in other ways. The 'sometimes' depends on the percentage of asbestos in the material, how crumbly the material is, and how much asbestos there is in total."

"Could you slow down a bit, please?" interjected Doug. "I don't want to keep you late, but I am trying to take notes."

"OK, I'll try. If you've got the types down, let's go on. Condition involves, first, the obvious: Is it in good shape, or is it falling apart because of water, abrasion, or any other reason? You also have to take into account how often people go near the asbestos, how long they stay there, whether air flow can take the asbestos from unoccupied areas into occupied space, and so on. For instance, say the asbestos is flaking off a bit. If it's flaking a little into a sealed space between two permanent concrete walls, that's one situation. If it's flaking into an operating room air conditioning intake duct, you've got an entirely different kind of problem.

"Then you get into the legal factors. There are rules and regulations at the federal, state, and, occasionally, the local levels. Several agencies can get into the act at each level: At the federal level, for example, you've got OSHA, EPA, and more. Each of these has rules on the books that are effective now, rules on the books that take effect at a future date, rules in the pipeline that we know about, and potential rules we can't foresee. A different kind of legal issue is the possibility of a lawsuit if someone comes down with an asbestos-related condition, thinks it was caused by conditions in a particular building, and thinks its owner should have done more about asbestos exposure. It's worth something to prevent a lawsuit even if you're sure you could win it.

"Social pressure can come from employees, from tenants, from community groups, from the media, and so on. Any of these kinds of pressure might motivate an owner to take an approach that isn't necessary for any technical or legal reason, but looks good in the press and can create positive PR. Or, an owner might want to do something to avoid the negative PR that people can generate on this issue. It can get real emotional. You'd be surprised, or maybe you wouldn't, how a clever radio talk show host can get people excited without knowing a darn thing and getting all the facts wrong.

"Finally, the owner's business situation is a factor. An owner who's short of funds might go for a short-term fix. This doesn't mean they'd jeopardize anyone's health, at least not if we have anything to say about it. It just means that they want something to tide them over for a few years, and then they'll have to revisit the issue. The owners can also be oriented toward economy or safety. Sometimes it's our job to convince them that the cheapest way out really isn't in the occupants' best interest. We lost a client over that once; they found someone else who would do a bare minimum to get them by the OSHA inspectors but didn't really solve the problem. Boy, does that ever frost me!"

"So," said Doug as he looked at his notes, "you end up with at least several dozen factors or levels of factors at the bottom. How does this come together in an action plan?"

"That's the bottom line," Miguel agreed. "The action plan is one of four things: remove it, coat it or cover it up—we call that encapsulation—enclose the area, or leave it alone."

"Leave it alone? Can you actually get away with that?" asked Adrienne, surprised.

"Once in a while, yes, and with a clear conscience. If the asbestos is in good condition and if it's in an area where people don't go and it won't be disturbed, the best thing to do is probably just to inspect it every couple of months. In a case like that, taking asbestos out or building walls next to it could disturb it more than 20 years of normal activity. That would create a bigger hazard than leaving it alone. Unfortunately—and I do mean unfortunately—legal and social factors sometimes force us to take action when leaving the asbestos alone really would be in everyone's best interest."

"Well, Miguel, this sounds like a perfect expert system application!" Adrienne exclaimed. "How would you like to be cloned by a microchip?"

Exercises

1. How does the asbestos abatement decision match the expert system selection factors in Section 16.2?
2. Is Miguel an "expert?" Would you use additional experts if you were to develop a system to make asbestos abatement recommendations? Why or why not? If you would, what characteristics would you want them to have?
3. How could you use variables in developing an expert system for this problem? How could you use frames?
4. Write, in English, a few example production rules that might be in this system.
5. Would you recommend forward or backward chaining for this system? Why?
6. What sort of database might be useful with this system?
7. How could you use confidence factors with this system?
8. How could you use fuzzy logic with this system?

CHAPTER 17 Building an Expert System

Chapter Outline

Introduction

Since expert systems of the type we are covering in this book are DSS, the discussions of the development process in Chapter 5 and of software tools and platforms in Chapters 6 and 7 apply in general. But because expert systems do have some unique characteristics that do not apply to other types of DSS, we can zero in more precisely on these aspects of their development and operation. Knowing as much as possible about expert systems, as specifically as possible, will put you in a better position to work with expert systems on the job.

Chapter Objectives

After you have read and studied this chapter, you will be able to:

1. Discuss how hardware platform considerations for expert systems differ from those for other types of information systems or decision support systems.
2. Describe the types of software tools that support expert system development.
3. Explain why using a shell is the most popular way to develop an expert system today.
4. Identify two specialized languages that lend themselves to expert system development.
5. Define knowledge acquisition and describe how engineers can help with knowledge acquisition.
6. Explain induction and when it can serve as an alternative to a human expert.
7. Summarize several key roles people must fill in order for an expert system to succeed.
8. Combine an expert system with the rest of a decision support system.

17.1 Hardware Platforms for Expert Systems

17.1.1 *Expert Systems and Microcomputers*

Many small and medium-sized expert system applications run quite well on desktop hardware. This was not true a few years ago, but today's microprocessors are quite capable of holding their own in this environment. Popular personal computer families have the advantage of a wide range of available software tools. Much of it is of the "low-end" variety and has significant functional limitations compared with what is available for more expensive platforms, but "industrial-strength" shells can be found at the desktop level as well.

Workstations, ever a popular environment for AI work because of their processing power, are now financially acceptable as an alternative to high-end PCs as well. Workstation prices dropped dramatically at the start of the 1990s as prices of bare-bones systems fell to below $5,000. Complete configurations are now available from several suppliers for well under $10,000. At those prices workstations are competitive with the higher members of popular PC lines. Since most workstations use the UNIX operating system, their software tools tend to have a minicomputer heritage. They therefore offer more application development functionality than does software that originated in the desktop environment.

The dividing line between a high-end PC and a low-end workstation is fuzzy and not getting clearer. The traditional distinction is based on the extensive high-performance graphics support built into most workstations. These capabilities are critical for applications such as three-dimensional computer-aided engineering design but far less important for expert systems work. Widespread use of a popular PC family in an organization argues for using that family as an expert system delivery platform. This is especially true if the intended users of that system already have PCs of sufficient power and if the available tools are sufficiently capable. A need for state-of-the-art hardware and software capabilities would tilt the decision toward products usually classed as workstations.

17.1.2 *Expert Systems and Minicomputers*

General-Purpose Minicomputers

The need for a high-powered system at each expert system user's desktop can make deploying a new microcomputer-based or workstation-based expert system to many users prohibitively expensive. If the system calls for a shared database, adding a LAN, supporting software, and a database server will increase the cost still further. Yet it is common for only a few of a system's "users" to be actually using the system at any given instant. The rest are planning their next step or performing an unrelated task. A minicomputer can concentrate substantial processing power on the few users who need it at that moment.

These factors often make minicomputers the platform of choice for expert systems. They spread the cost of a fast processor over many users and simplify shared database access. A wide range of expert system development tools is available for popular minicomputer software environments. Indeed, it is probably widest there, as AI workers have used minicomputers for years. Tools at this level have therefore reached a maturity that microcomputer-based tools do not yet have.

Symbolic Processors

In the 1980s several vendors developed specialized minicomputers for expert system applications. These systems are called "symbolic processors," or "LISP machines" after a popular language for artificial intelligence work. (The LISP language is discussed in Section 17.2.3.)

The instruction sets of symbolic processors are designed to work with lists of character strings. For example, a symbolic processor could find out in one instruction whether or not any of the names of foods in your pantry included the string "broccoli." It does this by storing the list of foods in a *list:* a compact, flexible data structure that occupies only the amount of memory that the foods you have call for, yet can adapt easily when you buy a new food or use one up. Other types of computers use software routines to deal with data stored in lists and must execute hundreds of instructions to search or to modify them. Since lists are a common data structure inside expert system inference engines, the idea of a computer designed from the ground up to handle them efficiently is attractive.

Symbolic processors were popular for dedicated expert system application environments during the mid-1980s. They are little used today but must be discussed because you may read about them elsewhere. They fell into disfavor for two reasons:

- Expert systems are increasingly integrated with other applications. Symbolic processors were poorly suited to other uses and did not have general-purpose software tools. Putting an expert system on a symbolic processor meant integrating two computers in order to get the entire job done. Users were willing to accept a cost-performance penalty in the expert system portion of a total application in order to avoid the complexities involved in getting two different machines to cooperate.
- The rapidly improving price performance of general-purpose microprocessors overcame the inherent design advantages of symbolic processors. A modern microprocessor requires a multimillion dollar investment in design work and fabrication facilities. Symbolic processors by their nature address a limited market and thus incur a high one-time cost per chip. While a

general-purpose chip has a higher fabrication cost for a given performance level than a specialized design, its lower one-time cost *per chip* more than makes up for this. Their lower overall cost, and hence lower price, makes them a more cost-effective choice for expert system builders.

For these reasons symbolic processors are rarely seen in the 1990s, although they continue to perform well where they were installed in the past. They have a small market as add-on boards to low-end general-purpose microcomputers, but these are boards not widely used either. You may occasionally see a symbolic processor on the job, but your future employer is not likely to buy one for a new application.

17.1.3 Expert Systems and Mainframes

Mainframes are not inherently well suited to expert system usage. Their high cost relative to their central processor power puts them at a disadvantage in applications, like expert systems, that require a great deal of processing power and not much of anything else. They do have one undeniable asset: in most large companies they store the corporate database. Where an expert system requires regular access to up-to-the-second data this factor can override other considerations. Other needs for integrating expert systems with mainframe applications can lead to the same conclusion, as can a situation where prospective expert system users already have mainframe terminals on their desks. If an expert system is not tied closely to an application that must be on the mainframe, to a database that must be on the mainframe, or to users who are already on and must remain on the mainframe, there is seldom a reason to use a mainframe as an expert system platform. The entire cost of buying and operating a more suitable platform will almost always be less than the cost of the mainframe processing power that the system will use.

17.1.4 Expert Systems and Parallel Processors

Expert systems require large amounts of central processor power. General-purpose microprocessors are the most cost-effective computing engines but offer limited power. Put these facts together, and they suggest a way to get the best of both worlds: use many microprocessors in one computer system.

This is easier said than done. Putting many microprocessors in one cabinet, attached to one power supply and one input/output bus, is realtively easy. Getting software to divide an application into small pieces for such a computer to process in parallel is a great deal harder.[1]

[1]The parallelizing task is simpler when all data elements are processed identically. Some scientific applications, such as weather prediction, work in a grid where each point is processed via the same equations as all other points. With such an application all the individual processors in a parallel computer can run the same program under central control. Unfortunately, expert systems don't work this way.

Expert systems are a nearly ideal application for parallel processing. Each rule in an expert system can, in principle, be processed independently:

- In backward chaining, an inference engine can conceptually examine all rules at the same time to see which ones can lead to the current goal.

  Suppose a knowledge base of 1,000 rules contains 50 that could potentially lead to its current goal (i.e., rules that contain the current goal in their consequent). If the inference engine can assign each such rule to one processor, the system can work through its current inference step in the time it takes one processor to process the longest single rule. This will usually be much less than the time it would take one processor, even a faster one, to examine all 50 rules.

  The degree of parallelism that can be exploited in a rule-based system using backward chaining is limited if we consider only one goal. However, in working back from its initial goal, the expert system is likely to find that several pieces of information could potentially lead it toward that goal. It then has several intermediate goals: one for each such piece of information. As it works back further, the goal tree broadens still more. As a result, such an expert system can eventually exploit a high degree of hardware parallelism.
- In forward chaining, the inference engine can conceptually examine all rules at the same time to see which ones can "fire" with the current state of the system's knowledge.

  Here, too, the speed advantage can be substantial. Out of the same 1,000 rules, there may again be 50 whose antecedents contain a newly discovered fact. The advantage of parallel processing is the same as with backward chaining since here too the tree of possibilities broadens at each step until it narrows to the solution.

Computers with limited amounts of parallelism, typically up to a few dozen processors, are now in regular commercial use. These computers support *coarse-grain* parallelism: the time devoted to each subtask is large enough to outweigh the substantial overhead these systems incur every time parallel threads must be created or must coordinate their activities with each other. Effective use of *massively parallel* computers (at least a few hundred, and up to several thousand, processors) for expert systems applications depends on fine-grain parallelism. The use of massive parallelism to improve expert system performance will be a commercial reality before you are far along in your career. It will be to your employer's advantage, and to yours, to be aware of their potential.

Parallel processing systems can also be used for the emerging AI field of neural nets, which we discussed in Section 14.2.4. Neural nets consist of many components, all of which carry out essentially the same process (albeit with different inputs and, hence, with different outputs) in parallel. Large arrays of simple microprocessors lend themselves well to cost-effective processing of neural nets. While neural nets have demonstrated impressive laboratory successes in areas such as pattern recognition, their commercial use as part of production DSS is still generally in the future as this book is written.

17.2 Software Tools for Expert Systems

A wide variety of software tools is available to support the developer of an expert system. They can be categorized as shown in Figure 17–1.

17.2.1 Packages

The easiest way for an organization to start using expert systems technology is for it to purchase a turnkey package developed with that technology.

At first this statement may seem both self-evident and pointless. After all, the easiest way to start using word processing (or any other) software technology is to buy a package—but few purchasers of word processors do so with the intention of writing their own word processing software as the next step. Why are expert systems different?

The answer lies in their behavior. Expert systems don't act like traditional MIS applications. They ask questions, and they provide answers. Beyond that, as we saw in Section 16.3.4, they can explain the reasons for their questions and the logic behind their answers. Using a system with this type of reasoning capability, asking it "how" or "why" and observing its answers, watching where it works and where it falls down, teaches a great deal about the capabilities of an expert system. Some of what one learns in this process is specific to the particular expert system package one is using, but much of its generalizes to other expert systems as well.

Expert system packages exist for a few applications. One example is com-

Figure 17–1

Diagram of Expert System Software Tools

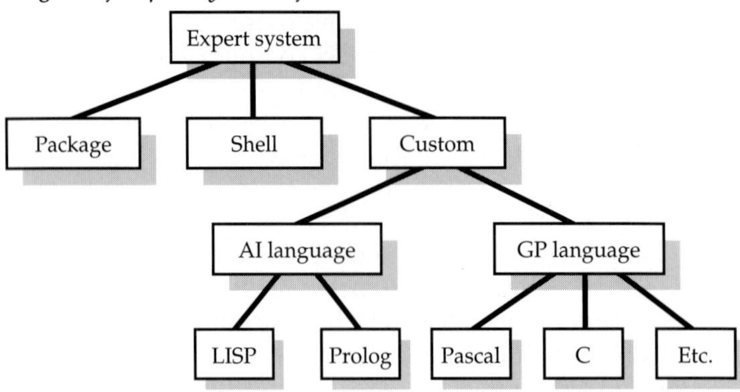

puter system performance tuning. Typical multi-user operating systems have many software- or operator-adjustable parameters that affect system performance. Such items as the amounts of processor time available to jobs of different priority levels, the number and types of jobs that will be allowed to run at the same time, the amount of physical memory to be made available to different jobs, the size and number of temporary storage areas for data read from disk drives, can all be set by system administrators. Setting these parameters optimally, or close to optimally, can allow an installation to achieve the necessary throughput from a smaller configuration than it would need if the parameters were not properly set. This can save money that would otherwise go to expensive hardware upgrades. In addition, since software and maintenance charges typically (for large multi-user systems) depend on the size of the computer, tuning provides on-going savings in these areas as well.

The best settings for one installation may be quite different than the best settings for another shop with a different job mix or user community. Performance experts can look at a dozen or so system performance indicators, all of them recorded by the operating system during normal operation, and determine which parameters should be adjusted. Since the indicators and their implications are essentially the same for all systems of a given hardware family using the same operating system, the same human expert can tune any of them. So can the same expert system. This creates a good market for expert systems designed to tune members of popular computer families for optimal performance.

System tuning is not a precise science. Even the best experts seldom achieve perfect results on their first try. They need a series of iterations, each followed by measurements. Each iteration generally improves matters. A company that hires a human expert to tune a computer must bring that expert back several times, at intervals of a week or so, before the process is complete. Expert systems, by contrast, are happy to wait in the wings from one weekly run to the next. They also don't charge extra to revisit a system every six months or so to make sure it's still running well.

Other expert system–based packages are available for common applications such as accounting and finance (including some specialized, but still widely useful, subareas of these fields), for analyzing the grammar of word processing documents, and for laying out display ads in a newspaper or magazine.

It is an unfortunate fact of life that most of these applications fall into the support category of corporate activities. Publicly available expert system packages that address mission-critical mainstream corporate functions hardly exist. Firms that have invested in their development consider them to be a factor in their competitive advantage and do not make them available to competitors. Software firms that might consider developing such a package for general sale will find that the truly valuable information about how important decisions are made is likewise closely guarded. The publicly available "textbook" version of decision-making wisdom would not give its adopter a competitive

Boole & Babbage Inc.'s DASD Advisor[2]

Of all the system areas to optimize, most mainframe installations will get the greatest return on their optimization investment by working on their mass storage products. Adding drives, at the five-figure prices of disk devices on large-scale mainframes, is one of the most expensive system upgrades. It is especially galling to have to add drives when the existing capacity is sufficient—but the inability of one drive to do more than one thing at a time is creating a performance bottleneck. According to IBM, performance considerations often cause as much as 30 percent of an installation's mass storage capacity to remain unused. With many large and even not-so-large installations spending well into seven figures for their mass storage subsystems, wasting 30 percent corresponds to a substantial sum.

The DASD Advisor product, from Boole & Babbage, is intended to help users of IBM ES/9000 and compatible mainframes (including its System/370 predecessors, as well as products from Amdahl and Hitachi Data Systems) running under the MVS operating system to optimize their mass storage configuration.

The DASD Advisor user begins by collecting data through volume problem analysis. This module uses rules to rank the individual disk volumes (drives) in order of their performance problems. The user can see at a glance which must be tuned first. As part of this analysis, DASD Advisor also assesses the potential effect of moving any number of files (data sets, in IBM mainframe terminology) from one volume to another.

DASD Advisor then recommends specific actions that will reduce conflicts for the resources involved in a data transfer (device, control unit, channel, cache, and the multiple paths that connect them) and thus improve performance. Potential solutions include moving data sets, redefining the way data sets are cached, changing application run schedules (not practical for on-line transaction processing), rearranging volumes onto different input/output paths to the processor, and more. Finally, it can simulate the effect of the changes so that user management can determine what performance improvement to expect.

advantage and therefore could not be the basis for a successful product. (The end of Section 13.4, on the Black-Scholes model used in investment options trading, gives an example of this phenomenon.)

Caution: Not every application that claims to use expert system technology actually does! Some software firms see the "expert system" label as a sales

[2]The author is grateful to Boole and Babbage, Inc., Sunnyvale, Calfornia, for their support in preparing this section.

Note: DASD, for Direct-Access Storage Device, is a common term for disk storage in IBM mainframe installations.

Boole and Babbage were 19th-century English contributors to what eventually became electronic computing. George Boole invented the true-and-false, or ones-and-zeroes, logic that computers use internally. Charles Babbage invented a mechanical precursor of today's computers, but he encountered mechanical problems in getting its gears and levers to function correctly and ran out of funds before these problems could be corrected.

aid, applying it to systems that do not truly qualify. Such systems may have an aspect of true expert systems: They may have been developed after studying human experts or may incorporate an explanation facility for their conclusions. They may do their jobs well and can be excellent solutions to real problems. However, these systems will not exhibit the characteristics of rule-based expert systems, for good or for bad. If you want a specific characteristic of rule-based systems, ask the right questions before you buy.

17.2.2 Shells

An inference engine, as we mentioned in Chapter 14, is a general-purpose program that can work with any set of rules we give it. The rules make the difference between one expert system and another. To the commercial user, the rules provide the business benefit or the competitive advantage that the user hopes to obtain.

Given these facts, many software firms have developed prepackaged inference engines to which a user can add any desired set of rules. A prepackaged inference engine is called an *expert system shell,* or (when context makes the meaning clear) simply a *shell.*

Each shell has a language in which its rules must be written and includes a user interface framework.[4] User interfaces vary in their sophistication, from simple text-based systems through graphic output to completely mouse-and-menu-driven systems. The nature of the operating system under which an expert system shell runs may determine, and will at least influence, the user interface that the shell provides.

Many shells provide complete expert system development environments, including text editors for the knowledge base, while others rely on the user to have a text editor or word processing package available. Shells may also provide interfaces to popular database packages and spreadsheets, plus additional features to support application integration with other aspects of a complete DSS.

As we mentioned at the beginning of Chapter 16, the syntax that a knowledge base developer must use varies from shell to shell. Figure 17–2 shows the three-rule knowledge base (hungry? homework? movie?), which you saw earlier, in three versions for two popular desktop microcomputer expert system shells: once as it would be written in VP-Expert (Figure 17–2A) and twice for two approaches to Level5 (Figures 17–2B and 17–2C).

You can see (at least) these differences between the two knowledge bases:

1. A VP-Expert consultation is controlled by a series of program-like commands in its "ACTIONS block." Level5 does not use a similar set of commands, so all its action must take place within rules. That's why each Level5 rule in Figure 17–2B has a command to display output, but the VP-Expert

---

[4]The language used to define a VP-Expert knowledge base is summarized in Appendix B.

FIGURE 17–2(A)

VP-Expert Form of Simple Knowledge Base

In VP-Expert

```
!This knowledge base recommends an evening activity

ACTIONS
DISPLAY "I will tell you what you should do."
FIND activity
DISPLAY "You should {activity}.";

RULE 1
IF hungry = yes
THEN activity = eat;

RULE 2
IF hungry = no
AND homework = yes
THEN activity = do_homework;

RULE 3
IF hungry = no
AND homework = no
THEN activity = see_a_movie;

ASK hungry: "Are you hungry?";
ASK homework: "Do you have homework?";

CHOICES hungry, homework: yes, no;
```

rules don't. We got around this restriction in the second Level5 version, in Figure 17–2C, but we had to add a new rule and a new goal to activate that rule.

2. VP-Expert's goals are determined by the FIND command. Those of Level5 are listed in an outline form. That gives Level5 more flexibility in controlling the simultaneous search for several goals and in defining subordinate goals to be sought, depending on which top-level goal is satisfied. (Admittedly, the simple knowledge base of Figure 17–2 doesn't take full advantage of this capability).

3. VP-Expert uses only character string variables, so the user's responses must be compared with "yes" and "no." Level5 also supports Boolean variables, which are a better choice in this case. They are inherently true or false so no comparison is necessary. Level5 also supports attribute variables, which we used in the second Level5 version of the knowledge base.

FIGURE 17–2(B)

First Level5 Form of Simple Knowledge Base

In Level5

```
TITLE Knowledge Base to Recommend an Evening Activity DISPLAY

                    I will tell you what you should do.

1. Recommendation is found

RULE 1
IF you are hungry
THEN Recommendation is found
AND DISPLAY "You should eat.".

RULE 2
IF NOT you are hungry
AND you have homework
THEN Recommendation is found
AND DISPLAY "You should do your homework.".

RULE 3
IF NOT you are hungry
AND NOT you have homework
THEN Recommendation is found
AND DISPLAY "You should see a movie.".

TEXT you are hungry
Are you hungry?
TEXT you have homework
Do you have homework?
```

The above three differences have a unifying thread: Level5 offers capabilities that VP-Expert does not, but these make Level5 more complex to use for simple knowledge bases where VP-Expert would suffice.

4. There are several cosmetic differences between the two knowledge bases. Level5 key words must be in all uppercase letters, whereas VP-Expert is case-insensitive. Level5 rules end with periods, while those of VP-Expert end with semicolons. Level5 allows spaces within variable names, while VP-Expert uses underscores where a human would normally put a space between words. Level5 uses the key word "TEXT" where VP-Expert uses "Ask." Taken as a group, these differences and others like them can make two knowledge bases look quite different when they are nearly identical in everything that matters.

FIGURE 17–2(C)

Second Level5 Form of Simple Knowledge Base

In Level5

```
TITLE Knowledge Base to Recommend an Evening Activity DISPLAY

                  I will tell you what you should do.

ATTRIBUTE activity

1. recommendation is found
     1.1. recommendation is displayed

RULE 1
IF you are hungry
THEN recommendation is found
AND activity IS eat.

RULE 2
IF NOT you are hungry
AND you have homework
THEN recommendation is found
AND activity IS do your homework.

RULE 3
IF NOT you are hungry
AND NOT you have homework
THEN recommendation is found
AND activity IS see a movie.

Rule 4
IF recommendation is found
THEN recommendation is displayed
AND DISPLAY "You should [activity].".

TEXT you are hungry
Are you hungry?

TEXT you have homework
Do you have homework?
```

In the 1990s the overwhelming majority of commercial expert systems are developed with packaged expert system shells. The job of developing a new inference engine is so large, the business benefit of having a unique inference engine (as opposed to unique expert system rules) so small, that firms with a bottom-line focus decide against developing their own inference engine nearly all the time.

If you are faced with an expert system development project on the job, you will in all likelihood use a shell as well. The characteristics of commercial expert system shells change rapidly. Most of the features that matter to a knowledge base developer would not show up in a summary table. For example, the way Level5 and VP-Expert handle goal setting could make a big difference in the ease of setting up a particular knowledge base, but either approach can in principle handle any situation. You can proceed as follows:

1. Scope out your system in general terms. How many rules will it have? (You won't know exactly, but you should be able to say "tens," "hundreds," or "thousands.") Will it access an existing database, a new one? How many people will use it, how often? Will they share a database? Will it require graphical output? Does the nature of its user community impose special requirements on its explanation interface? Will its user interface have other special characteristics? Do you expect it to use backward chaining, forward chaining, or both? Will it require frames to represent its knowledge?

2. Determine any constraints on the hardware you must use. If constraints exist, they will limit your choices to shells that run on that hardware. If there are no constraints, you may have a personal hardware preference that is suitable for the application. If you don't, you can probably at least determine the general type of hardware your system should use on the basis of the discussion in Section 17.1.

3. Based on the characteristics of your expert system and the hardware you expect to use, specify what you require of a shell. One survey found that experienced shell users consider the following features important [STYL92]. In reading the list, keep in mind that the 271 survey respondents probably used, on the average, more advanced features than you will need for your first projects. They averaged 12 years of computer experience, just over 3 years of expert system experience, and had been involved, on the average, with almost four projects. Their list suggests what you will find important in larger projects. The top few items from their list of 86, all of which were scored at 4 or higher on a 1-to-5 scale:

- Embeddability: the ability to embed an expert system developed with the shell in an overall application written in another language, usually a 3GL.
- Rapid prototyping: the ability to get a prototype of an application running quickly and add features to it later without rewriting what exists.
- Backward chaining. Forward chaining was also considered useful, ranking 13th of 86, but not quite as important as backward chaining.
- Explanation facility.
- Linkage to databases. The importance of this factor varies from one expert system (ES) to another and is usually an easily answered "yes or no" issue, but it is needed often. If you expect to use the same shell for several projects, keep database linkage in mind even if your first system won't use a database.

- Ability to customize explanations. The importance of explanations can be seen in the fact that explanation-related items took both fourth and sixth places.
- Documentation. Even experienced ES developers need good manuals!

4. Investigate the shells available for that system or that class of systems. Sources of products to investigate include software directories, trade press ads, magazine and newspaper articles and reviews, computer vendor or retail store sales representatives, and members of user groups.

Your employer may have already standardized on an expert system shell. If that is the case, evaluate it before you look for alternatives. Most corporate standards allow exceptions if the chosen product is demonstrably unable to meet a specific need—but be sure of your ground before you ask for a waiver!

5. Evaluate the shells you have identified versus your list of requirements.

- If only one of them meets your requirements and it seems to have no serious drawbacks, your choice is clear.
- If several do, you can study them in more detail, ask users of each how they like the product, perhaps try them out to see how well they fit your style, and let cost influence your choice to a degree. Don't be too swayed by package price, especially in the microcomputer world. The cost difference between a $99 package and a $695 package may seem large: after all, one costs seven times as much as the other! However, the $600 difference is negligible compared with the other costs of developing an expert system, especially the time of developers and human experts, or compared with the benefits the system is to provide.
- If none of them meet the requirements, you can keep looking, broaden your hardware options, or write your system from scratch. If you pick the third option, the next section is for you.

17.2.3 Languages

There are several reasons why you might develop an expert system without using a commercial shell:

1. *No commercial shell meets the requirements.* This is unlikely, unless one is constrained to use rare hardware or the expert system needs are unusual in some other way.

2. *To learn about expert systems by building one from the ground up.* This is a noble goal, often best achieved via a computer science–oriented course in expert systems. If you have the prerequisites for such a course, you will be in an excellent position to benefit from it after finishing the course you are in now.

3. *It's to be part of a larger system.* The expert system is part of a larger application that is to be written in some other language, and it's easier to

write inference routines in that language than it is to interface the overall application to a package or shell. (If the expert system is at all large or complex, it will probably be easier to use a shell and interface the two parts.)

4. *Because the programmer already knows another language and does not want to learn the language of a shell.* This may be a good reason if the expert system and its inference logic are simple, or if the language that the programmer knows is an AI-oriented language such as LISP or Prolog. Otherwise, the effort of learning a shell will more than pay for itself in reduced knowledge-base development time.

5. *Because the resulting system must be portable across multiple platforms, which do not all support the same shell or compatible shells.* (If the user community is small and not already committed to multiple platforms for other reasons, it may be less expensive to buy new equipment for some users than to reject the shell approach for this reason.)

6. *For improved performance.* This is seldom a valid reason even though the people who cite it believe it is true. The performance-critical portions of commercial shells are carefully coded by experts using efficient tools and algorithms.

In any of these situations you will have to write a program that processes knowledge according to rules. Your choice is then between specialized languages designed for AI applications and general-purpose languages meant to be used across a broad specturm of application areas. The advantage of a specialized lanugage is that, once mastered, it permits you to express expert system concepts quickly and concisely. However, the two most widely used AI languages differ in their underlying concepts from languages you are likely to use in other applications and may seem strange at first. General-purpose languages have the advantage of familiarity. The basic concepts of using any procedural language will be familiar to you if you have learned to program in any other, even if you do not have experience with a particular one. In terms of reason 3 above for not using a shell or package, the overall application will almost certainly be in a general-purpose language such as Pascal or COBOL.

Specialized AI Languages

Two languages have been developed by AI researchers for the specific purpose of developing AI applications and are in reasonably widespread use in 1993: LISP and Prolog. If you take a computer science course in expert systems, you will almost certainly use one, perhaps both, of these.

LISP

The LISP language, developed by John McCarthy and his MIT colleagues in the late 1950s for the vacuum-tube IBM 704, is one of the oldest programming languages still in use today. Its name, short for LISt Processing, refers to the use of structures called *lists* to store data. We mentioned lists briefly above when we discussed symbolic processors in Section 17.1.2. Storing data in lists is not, however, restricted to specialized hardware: This type of data structure goes back 40 years or more. In a list, each item contains *(a)* a data element and *(b)* an indication of where the next item on the list is located or that the item ends the list. Lists can thus grow and shrink as the data in them change. They differ in this regard from static data structures such as arrays, which must be planned for the maximum amount of data they will ever be required to hold.

The basic LISP data element is the *atom*. An atom corresponds to what is called a variable in other programming languages you may have studied.

Two atoms can be combined into a dotted pair as in (harry·jim). The functions *car* and *cdr* refer to the left and right members of the pair, respectively.[5]

Many collections of data have more than two elements, so they can't be represented directly by a dotted pair. Fortunately, an element of a dotted pair can itself be a dotted pair, so we can handle three elements like this:

```
(marketing·(finance·engineering))
```

This gets awkward rapidly, so LISP allows the shorthand notation of a list:

```
(marketing finance engineering)
```

The *car* of a list is its first element; the *cdr* of a list is the entire sublist after the first element. This is a generalization of the way these terms apply to dotted pairs. To see why the terms generalize in this way, consider the representation of the above three-element list as nested dotted pairs.

LISP computes with *symbolic expressions*. A symbolic expression, called an S-expression for short, is a list whose first element is a function. The function +, not surprisingly, adds numbers. The S-expression

```
(+ 3 8)
```

therefore returns 11. Symbolic expressions can be nested: the S-expression

```
(* (+ 2 3 ) 6)
```

has the value 30. (Why?)

The function *setq* is fundamental to most LISP programs. It assigns a value to an atom:

```
(setq x 4)
```

assigns the value 4 to the atom *x*. The S-expression

```
(setq x harry)
```

assigns the value of the atom *harry*, whatever that might be, to the atom *x*.

[5]These names are derived from hardware registers in the vacuum-tube IBM 704, for which LISP was first developed. They have outlasted even the most "modern" of its transistorized descendants—the 7094-II of the early 1960s—by decades.

If we want to assign the five-letter character string "harry" to *x*, we use a quotation mark:

```
(setq x 'harry)
```

We must also use quotes when we present a list of data elements to LISP to prevent it from attempting to interpret the list as an S-expression and complaining when its first element is not the name of a known function. For example, the S-expression

```
(car '(marketing finance engineering))
```

returns the atom "marketing." Had we left out the quotation mark, LISP would have thought we were using *marketing* as a function name. It would have complained that it does not know of any such function—unless, of course, we had defined a function called *marketing*.

Because of its extendability, LISP can easily provide a *pattern matching* capability for lists. If we have a list

```
(loves John Mary)
```

an easily defined function *match* (an example or a homework exercise in many introductory LISP texts) can attempt to find who loves Mary by matching it with the list

```
(loves ?x Mary)
```

The LISP interpreter will then bind the *pattern matching variable* "?x" to the atom "John."

LISP provides the *cond* function for conditional execution. It allows actions to be taken on the basis of a condition to be evaluated at run time, much as would be done by the *if . . . then . . . else* construct of most 3GLs. For example, we could define an absolute value function *abs* by

```
defun (abs (num)
    cond (   (< num 0)   (* num -1)
             (t num) )
```

This means: If *num* is less than 0 (the function < returns True if its first argument is less than its second), return the value of *abs* from the S-expression following that condition, that is, *num* multiplied by −1, and exit. Otherwise, *cond* continues to the next element of its list. The condition of this element is *t*, which is always True, so if the *cond* gets this far, *abs* takes the value *num*. (While *cond* is usually most useful inside function definitions, as in this example, it can be used anywhere.)

In general, the list following *cond* can have any number of elements, each of which contains a condition followed by any number of other S-expressions. The first group of expressions whose condition holds is executed.

At this point you are probably asking, "What is all this good for, how does it relate to expert systems, and why do AI professionals use LISP after nearly two generations?" There are several reasons:

- The basic LISP data type, the list built up from dotted pairs, matches the data structures used in AI and expert systems. The search tree of goal-directed programming can be constructed from lists whose components are other lists. A frame can be a list with slots in particular positions. (A shorthand notation replaces long sequences of *car*'s and *cdr*'s to get a specific element from a list. For example, *caddr* replaces *car-cdr-cdr*.) A set is easily modeled by a list whose elements can be scanned to see if a desired element is in the set. And, since LISP values are character strings, the developer isn't restricted to particular types of data elements.
- The LISP language is infinitely extensible in any direction a researcher wishes. The built-in *defun* (for DEfine FUNction, one of LISP's few concessions to function names that make sense) function allows users to define new functions at will. If your application requires a function to compute a new confidence factor from several existing ones, the system developer can define a function to do just that. To define a function to square a number, a LISPer can write

  ```
  (defun square(x)  (* x x))
  ```

  From that point on the function *square* behaves as if it was built into the language. Most functions are more complex than this, of course. They may be pages long, but the idea is the same.
- The pattern matching capability, easily added to any version of LISP, is often a natural way to scan a knowledge base for a desired fact or for values that make an assertion true.
- Since LISP programs themselves consist of lists, they can be created dynamically as they are being run. A system can actually create a statement and execute it. This esoteric-sounding feature is useful in practice: for instance, a LISP program can accept an input value and incorporate it into a program statement, which is then executed.
- The *cond* function can be used to create rules and reasoning capability of any desired type. It is particularly useful in conjunction with the *member* function, built into most dialects of LISP, which tests for set membership. A complex reasoning tree can be built into a set of nested *conds*.
- There are LISP interpreters for just about every combination of hardware and operating system one is likely to encounter.
- Finally, a great deal of AI work has been done in LISP over the past 30+ years. AI experts, especially in North America, are familiar with the language and are comfortable with it. The infrastructure of books, training courses, magazines and newsletters, "shareware" programs

to learn from and to modify already exists. This is not a conceptual reason to prefer a language, but it is an important practical one. It is nice to have company for one's first steps in an unfamiliar field.

There is, of course, some bad news as well:

- LISP is not well standardized. Dialects abound. There are interpreters for just about every system, to be sure, but they differ in myriad ways: some trivial, some significant.
- LISP programs tend to run slowly. Part of this is inherent in interpreted code. Perhaps alone among all programming languages, LISP must be at least partially interpreted if its full set of features (including dynamic program modification) is to be supported, although static portions of LISP code can be compiled. Some dialects of LISP, such as Common LISP, provide for improved performance—but at the expense of some of the linguistic purity that many LISP aficionados prize.
- As you have already noted, LISP requires a different mental view of what a program is about than do "conventional" Pascal, COBOL, etc. Some programmers find it hard to make the switch.

Prolog

Prolog was developed by Alain Colmerauer and his colleagues at the Université d'Aix-Marseilles, France, in the early 1970s. The name Prolog stands for LOGic PROgramming, using the French word order. For many years Prolog was considered to be "the European AI language," while LISP was "the American AI language." This distinction had blurred by the mid-1980s and is of purely historical interest today. Japan chose Prolog for its fifth-generation computing project and the language is now widely used for expert system development throughout the world.

As with LISP, Prolog concepts initially seem strange to a person trained in "conventional" programming languages but lend themselves well to expert systems. Programmers coming from COBOL, Pascal, etc., particularly miss the assignment statement at first: It has no real Prolog equivalent. Rather, a Prolog program consists of a set of assertions and a set of goals.

Prolog is usually interpreted. The interpreter works by identifying a goal and attempting to prove it (in the mathematical sense) from the assertions. The Prolog language thus parallels the structure of a goal-driven (backward chaining) expert system closely.

Examples of Prolog assertions are:

```
countryofstate(California,USA)

stateofcity(Sacramento,California)

countryofcity(X,Z) := stateofcity(X,Y),
  countryofstate(Y,Z)
```

The first two of these assertions are facts. The third is a rule. We can interpret these assertions to mean, respectively:

> The state California is in the country USA.
>
> The city Sacramento is in the state California.
>
> A city *X* is in a country *Z* if there is at least one state *Y*—we don't care what it is or they are—for which *(a)* city *X* is in state *Y*, and *(b)* state *Y* is in country *Z*.

The Prolog language does not force these interpretations. All it knows, using the first assertion as an example, is that we have defined a relationship we call *countryofstate* between the two strings "USA" and "California." The interpretation, which treats the name of the relationship as consisting of three English words run together and uses their standard meanings, is up to us. Prolog doesn't care.

Given these assertions, we can ask questions:

```
?- stateofcity(Sacramento,Y)
```

The Prolog interpreter will search its knowledge base for a *Y* that satisfies the stated relationship. It will then respond "California." We can also establish goals that require the interpreter to use both rules and assertions, such as this one to find out what country Sacramento is in:

```
?- countryofcity(Sacramento,Z)
```

The Prolog interpreter will respond "USA." It does so by establishing intermediate goals based on the rule *countryofcity*. This rule involves the two relationships *stateofcity* and *countryofstate*. The interpreter's first intermediate goal is to find some *Y* that satisfies the goal *stateofcity(Sacramento, Y)*. It finds California and assigns this value to *Y*. Having satisfied this goal, its next goal is to find some *Z* that satisfies the goal *countryofstate(California,Z)*. When it finds the answer USA, it has satisfied its top-level goal and responds with the answer.

Prolog will return multiple answers if it has them. If we had a more complete list of North American cities, generalizing the term "state" from the United States and Mexico to represent Canadian provinces as well, the goal

```
?- countryofcity(Sudbury,Z)
```

would return both "USA" (via, at least, Massachusetts) and "Canada" (via the "state," in this case province, of Ontario).

Prolog uses backtracking to implement goal-directed reasoning trees such as that of Figure 14–1. Suppose our program also had the fact

```
stateofcity(Sacramento,healthy)
```

but did not have a *countryofstate* fact for the state "healthy." Depending on the interpreter's search strategy and the order of the facts in its knowledge base, the interpreter might first find "healthy" as the state of Sacramento. It would next try to find a country having such a state and would fail. It would backtrack to its previous goal, which was to find the state of Sacramento, and continue through its knowledge base from the point at which it left off until it found California. This trial solution to the intermediate goal would lead to success as above.

Prolog also has built-in facilities for dealing with lists of data elements, written as [a,b,c, . . .]. Its built-in functions for finding if an item is an element of a given list help deal with systems that have many items in a given category.

Concluding Comments

A specialized AI language may be the best choice for a stand-alone expert system but may not be suitable for some part of that system. Perhaps your application has to access a database via SQL, or perhaps it must carry out extensive calculations that are best done in a compiled, numerically-oriented language such as FORTRAN.[6] Most LISP and Prolog interpreters can invoke subroutines written in other languages, allowing you to use each where it is most suitable.

General-Purpose Languages in Expert Systems

As mentioned above, most expert systems deal with symbolic knowledge that is often represented in the form of lists. The suitability of a general-purpose language for developing expert systems therefore often depends on how well it deals with symbolic data and with lists.

Handling knowledge effectively requires the ability to manipulate structured data and sets. FORTRAN and BASIC fall down in the area of data structures, but COBOL, PL/1, Pascal, and C all have facilities for this task. COBOL falls down in set handling relative to the other three.

Dealing with tree-structured data, such as search sequences, and with lists, such as ordered lists that do not lend themselves to a set representation, is greatly facilitated by the use of *pointers:* variables that, instead of containing a data value of interest, point to the location in memory where it can be found. With pointers, inserting an item into the middle of a list can be done by adjusting the pointer associated with the previous item to point to the new one and setting the pointer of the new item to point to the one that now comes after it. Deleting an item from the middle of a list is equally quick and simple. Without pointers, every item past the new or deleted list element must be physically moved. This process is so inefficient that it can make execution times unacceptable when items are inserted into lists and removed from them repeatedly. Here, again, Pascal, C, and PL/1 have the required

[6]The distinction between compiled versus interpreted languages is somewhat arbitrary. There is nothing inherent in FORTRAN that requires it to be compiled, nor is there anything in Prolog that inherently requires it to be interpreted. The fact remains that real-world FORTRAN systems generally do compile machine code, while real-world Prolog systems generally interpret the source code directly.

capabilities. FORTRAN, BASIC, and COBOL do not. Pointers can be mimicked in these languages by indexing into arrays. This is awkward and artificial, leads to code that is difficult to maintain, and is often inefficient as well.

The choice among Pascal, C, and PL/1 can be based on what programmers are familiar with and what runs on the available hardware. All have been used extensively for expert system development with good results. PL/1 is not widely supported compared with the other two, especially on micros. That may narrow your choices to Pascal and C.

If you are developing an expert system that is to be integrated with an existing application in, say, COBOL, one of your choices will be to use COBOL (or whatever). This is not out of the question: Good expert systems have been built in COBOL, FORTRAN, and almost every other language. However, you might first want to see if the main application can call and exchange data with routines written in a more suitable language. If it can, you will probably do better to use Pascal or C for your expert system work.

17.3 Knowledge Acquisition

17.3.1 *What Is Knowledge Acquisition?*

Knowledge acquisition is the process of identifying, obtaining, and organizing the knowledge that is to be incorporated into an expert system [KIM88]. Knowledge acquisition often involves working with subject matter experts to determine how they solve problems in their domain of expertise.

You may hear the term *knowledge elicitation* used in this context. Knowledge elicitation is one part of the knowledge acquisition process: working with a subject matter expert to extract problem-solving knowledge from his or her head, usually via a question-and-answer process. Knowledge acquisition is a broader concept as it also covers such methods as reading procedure manuals or observing an expert with no direct interaction. These may be used before, or concurrently with, the expert interaction.

Furthermore, knowledge acquisition continues after knowledge elicitation is complete. The knowledge must be organized, structured, and represented in a useful form before we can say it has been fully "acquired."

The goal of knowledge acquisition is to reproduce a suitable part of the expert's knowledge in the rule base of an expert system. There are two basic ways of doing this. The traditional approach has been to extract rules that an expert system can follow, even if the human expert uses somewhat different ones. The approach of *cognitive emulation,* by contrast, makes an explicit attempt to mimic the expert's mental data structures and thought processes in the expert system [SLAT87]. The distinction is often subtle: The traditional system developer will not limit the information-processing ability of an expert system to that of a human, whereas one who follows a strict cognitive emulation approach will. In most cases, and for most practical purposes, the end results will be the same. However, as you think about your representation of what the expert does, you should be aware of the difference.

Knowledge acquisition is often performed by specialists called *knowledge engineers.* Knowledge engineers are part subject matter professional, part computer specialist, and part psychologist. Their subject matter knowledge enables them to converse with an expert, their computer knowledge enables them to translate an expert's knowledge into a knowledge base, and their psychology training (or innate sensitivity to people) enables them to understand an expert's thought processes.

One difficulty with understanding an expert's thought process is that many experts don't truly understand their own thought processes. Many of their reasoning steps have become second nature to a point where the expert does not realize that they are taking place. We do this ourselves:

> "Betsy Ross made the first U.S. flag. Is she alive?"
>
> "Of course not, you dummy!"

The responder used the following knowledge, most of it subconsciously:

1. The United States is a nation.
2. The United States is 200+ years old.
3. A nation obtains its first flag at or near the start of the nation's existence.
4. Making a flag is the first step in that flag's existence.
5. "Betsy Ross" is a human name.
6. Creatures with human names are, unless stated otherwise, human.
7. A human must be alive in order to make something.[7]
8. The human life span is less than 200 years.

Change the question to this:

> "Tom Jones saw the first U.S. flag. Is he alive?"

The answer is now "maybe". A flag is made once, before it is used, but can be seen many times over years or centuries. There is no difference in the structure of the sentence, but there is a difference in the knowledge we use to answer it. If we use so many facts subconsciously to answer a trivial question, we should not be surprised that experts answering complex questions do so as well.

Large organizations often use professional knowledge engineers for major expert system applications. Their use is not, however, universal. Knowledge engineers are scarce. Being scarce, they are expensive. A smaller firm, a firm

---

[7]There are exceptions to this. Consider a 1992 newspaper article headlined "Christopher Columbus Still Making News After 500 Years." Can you think of others?

embarking on a smaller application, or a firm considering its first use of expert systems might not use a professional knowledge engineer. A DSS generalist such as yourself is often pressed into service to carry out a knowledge engineering job. The rest of this section should help you cope.

17.3.2 Finding the Expert(s)

At least one competent, willing, and cooperative expert must be available to develop an expert system. If such an individual cannot be found, an expert system cannot generally be developed—no matter how desirable it might be in terms of the criteria and checklists in Chapter 15. (See Section 17.3.7 for one minor exception to this rule.)

A subject matter expert must be chosen carefully. Good experts have these characteristics:

1. They must be experts. One criterion we stated in Section 15.2 for using the expert system approach was that we must be able to tell who the experts are. The person or people whom we choose as models for our expert system must fit the definition of expert as it applies to their specific field. Recognition of their expertise by professional colleagues is often a useful criterion. Where a field is changing rapidly, it is important to choose experts who are up to date rather than those whose reputation was established some time in the past but who may not be current with the latest approaches.

2. They must be willing to be "cloned" by the computer. Some experts take pride in this opportunity. Others see it as a threat to their control over what their firm does in their area of expertise.

3. They must be able to spend substantial time on the project. "Substantial" refers both to the fraction of their working day they will often devote to it and the number of weeks or months for which they will be involved with it.

4. They should be personally cooperative and easy to work with. Patience and cooperativeness will help.

5. They should be interested in computers. Many discussions with them will relate to how the computer is following (or not following) their rules and how the computer is handling its input data. A curiosity about this side of the project motivates experts to participate in this type of discussion and helps them contribute to it, even if they are not computer professionals themselves.

One Expert or Several?

Some expert system authorities [e.g., PRER90] advocate using only one subject matter expert in developing an expert system. One reason: doing so eliminates conflicts among the recommended approaches.

Using only one expert certainly does eliminate conflicts, but it does not guarantee the best results. As we saw in Section 15.1.2, expert systems tend to be "brittle": they work well within their range of expertise but may fail drastically the instant they pass their limits. Sets of rules derived from different human experts will tend to have different areas of applicability and to follow different lines of reasoning. They will therefore have different limits. When a problem passes outside the limitations of one expert, thus invalidating one line of reasoning the expert system might follow, other lines of reasoning derived from other human experts may still apply. The performance of such a system can degrade gracefully as it leaves its primary focus rather than "falling off a cliff."

Other advantages of using just one expert are cost and time. Where system sponsors agree that one expert's knowledge will suffice, there is no need to waste either of these by going to several. The other side of this coin is that one expert's time may be limited. If the approaches of several experts are sufficiently similar, this bottleneck can be relieved by using more than one.

If it has been decided to use several subject matter experts rather than one, they can be shadowed individually or solve problems as a group. Watching each expert individually and combining their methods in the system usually works better than gathering them into a group and expecting them to develop a composite approach to problem solution. Gathering them together may present logistical problems and will result in one compromise solution rather than displaying the spectrum of possible approaches. Even when logistics permit assembling all the experts in one place, group dynamics can cause problems that most subject matter experts and knowledge engineers are ill equipped to deal with. For example, the experts can spend more time arguing over how to solve a problem than actually solving it. Such problems can derail a project before it truly starts.

There are, however, situations where the experts should be assembled and work as a group. This may arise where the process of developing an expert system is intended to standardize the experts' approaches (a *multi-individual* system, as we discussed in Chapter 4), where it is necessary to bring them into agreement and the development project is a convenient way to do this, or where synergy among the experts makes the solution better than any one of them could develop individually. Alamo's RATE system, discussed in the box at the end of Chapter 14, is a good example of bringing experts together.

If the knowledge of several experts is combined in one system, the system can attempt to combine the knowledge of all the experts in solving every problem or can select one line of reasoning based on the specific problem. An expert system can combine several experts' knowledge by assigning a confidence factor (as discussed in Section 16.4.5) to the result obtained through each line of reasoning. Where different experts' lines of reasoning reach the same conclusion, the confidence factors will be merged and the system's conclusion will have a high confidence factor. Where the experts would disagree, the expert system will offer several conclusions, with a low confidence factor for each.

If each expert's line of reasoning is best applied to a specific part of the problem domain, the system can select one of them after a few general questions determine the domain in which the task at hand falls. A system that recommends vacation destinations may incorporate one expert's knowledge of Hawai'i and another's knowledge of the Alps. Once the system has determined if a prospective vacationer wants to surf or to ski, the consultation will follow either one expert's rules or the other's.

17.3.3 Characteristics of the Knowledge Engineer

You are probably not, at this stage in your MIS career, a professional knowledge engineer. You may, though, choose to become one: The need is growing as the usage of expert systems expands, and career opportunities are excellent. Even if you do not choose this path, you may be asked to perform a knowledge engineering task on a smaller scale than those projects that call for a full-fledged professional. The ideal knowledge engineer has these characteristics (summarized from [HART86]):

- *Intelligence* to understand expert systems technology and to learn enough about a new domain to discuss it intelligently with an expert.
- *Good communication skills* for many hours of discussion with correct interpretation of the written word, the spoken word, and unspoken body language.
- *Tact and diplomacy* to gain and maintain the cooperation of the subject matter experts.
- *Empathy and patience* to understand the problems that the expert faces and to work with him or her as a team.
- *Persistence,* because progress often comes slowly and includes periods where there are significant gaps in the knowledge base. The knowledge engineer must remain convinced that success will come.
- *Logicality,* because a human expert's thought processes, as expressed during problem-solving sessions, are not always logical. The knowledge engineer must structure fragments of knowledge into a coherent whole.
- *Versatility and inventiveness* to develop new ways to represent knowledge, both to represent the domain properly and to cope with shell or tool limitations.
- *Self-confidence and maturity* to remain in control of the knowledge acquisition process, without seeming patronizing.
- *Domain knowledge* to talk to the expert in the expert's terminology.
- *Programming knowledge* to understand how the result of the knowledge acquisition process will be put into a computer and to choose knowledge representations that lend themselves to the tools to be used.

Few if any people possess these characteristics fully. Fortunately, few if any situations demand them equally. If your job calls for you to serve as a knowledge engineer, reviewing this list in the context of your specific assignment will tell you where you are already equipped to do a good job, where you will need to learn new skills, and perhaps where you could use the help of another person.

17.3.4 Starting the Knowledge Acquisition Process

If you studied systems analysis, you probably learned about the four basic information-gathering methods: reading, direct observation, interviewing, and questionnaires. With a few modifications, these four methods apply to knowledge acquisition as well.

The first stage of the knowledge acquisition process consists of learning the basic concepts that are critical to the domain. You could not develop an expert system to navigate an automobile without understanding the fundamental concepts of street corners, traffic signs and signals, named and numbered roads, freeway interchanges, and more. The concepts that underlie most other domains are equally important, but you may be less familiar with them from daily life. You must, however, still know something about them in order to have an intelligent conversation with an expert. That means you must do some homework before you approach the human expert.

The best way to start learning the basic concepts of a subject area is usually through reading. Try to understand the nature of the problem to be solved, the information that is usually available to the person trying to solve it, alternative solutions that must be considered, the general approach or approaches that are commonly used to solve it, and the value of the solution to the person or organization with the problem. You should also know something of the terminology the expert will use and have a good idea of the typical expert's training and experience. It's a good idea to start out with a book that introduces you to the subject but not to stop there. Reading a few recent issues of a magazine or journal that focuses on the field will give you an idea of current issues, concerns, and procedures.

This background reading will not bring you to a level where you can perform the expert's job, but should prepare you to have an intelligent conversation with the expert about his or her specialty. Beware of the danger of trying to sound more informed than you are. A real expert will soon see how superficial your knowledge really is. Be honest with the expert: Explain that you have done some background reading in an effort to save his or her time, but that you don't really know the field.

Next, consider the second information-gathering method: direct observation. Sometimes you may be able to observe the process in which you are interested without disturbing anyone, such as by watching a travel agent talk to a client or watching a loan officer talk to a potential borrower. Observation in these cases might not tell you too much about the experts' decision methods, but it will tell you more about how the process really works than you could get out of books and policy manuals. In other cases, it won't: Watching a physician take notes while reading a patient folder as part of a medical diagnosis process would be a waste of time.

It may also be a good idea to use the interview method at the preparation stage, although not by interviewing the experts themselves. Suppose you're working on an expert system to help credit card company staffers decide whether to approve or reject an application and what credit limit to set for the card if the application is approved. You might spend time with a manager who will tell you about the business context of the problem and what the firm's objectives for the expert system are. Such background or context information will also be helpful as you work with the expert.

Once you've found out all you can about the problem on your own, it's time to approach your expert or experts.

17.3.5 Working with the Expert(s)

Begin working with your expert by continuing to elicit basic ideas and concepts in an initial interview or series of interviews. This gives you an opportunity to flesh out the initial understanding you have from your reading and to see how this specific expert's approaches fit in with what you have read. You may find that some of the ideas you learned are not useful in practice, are outmoded, or just don't fit that individual's approach. Depending on the complexity of the domain, on the completeness of your preliminary work, and on how well it matches your expert's sense of the domain, this step may take from a few minutes up to perhaps a day.

You are now in a position to watch that expert solve several problems associated with the expert system domain. As one problem may take several hours to solve—lengthened by the expert's need to explain each step to you, perhaps also by delays to obtain information from external sources such as medical tests—this step may take weeks or months to complete.

At each point in the shadowing process the subject matter expert must attempt to verbalize his or her reasoning process, the intermediate conclusions being reached, and the information, rules, and assumptions used to reach them. As this is going on, the knowledge engineer must understand how each conclusion is reached, why each additional fact was requested, and what would have happened if a question had been answered differently. If anything is unclear the knowledge engineer must ask for clarification. Needless to say, this process can try the subject matter expert's patience. Both members of the team must be sensitive to the other's feelings during this time.

Several methods have been developed to structure and analyze the information you obtain from the expert or experts. Some are designed for use with a single expert, while others help consolidate the knowledge of several experts. You can find a good summary with several references to in-depth descriptions in [LIOU92].

Not every subject matter expert is willing to undergo this type of extended scrutiny, nor does every willing one respond to it well. It is part of the knowledge engineer's job to be aware of the expert's feelings in this regard, to persuade and cajole as required, and finally to bring the situation to the attention of management if the expert's cooperation is deemed unacceptable.

17.3.6 From the Expert to the Computer

As you work with the expert, you can begin to put your rules into a prototype expert system. Working with this system, even though it may not solve many problems well (or at all), will be valuable in several ways:

- Working with the prototype will help you develop the user interface that your system will eventually use.
- If your system will have to access a database, the prototype can have this capability as well.
- In using the prototype on problems that the expert solved for you, you will be able to see where you might have misunderstood the expert or made a mistake in translating the expert's rules to the knowledge base.
- In using the prototype on problems that the expert has not solved for you, you will be able to identify gaps in the system's rules.

17.3.7 Induction: An Alternative to Knowledge Elicitation

Sometimes we might try to extract the rules an expert follows from a set of sample cases that the expert has worked on. This process is called induction. Many expert system shells, including some low-end shells such as VP-Expert, support induction from a "training set" of examples. For a more detailed discussion of induction, see, for example, [HART87] or [SHAW87].

Consider, for example, the excerpt from Harwich University's MBA program admissions data shown in Figure 17–3. The Harwich admissions staff must decide whether to accept, reject, or defer (place on the waiting list for possible later acceptance) each applicant. We might infer from this information that the Harwich admissions staff uses these rules:

- If GMAT is over 600, accept the applicant regardless of other factors.
- If the applicant has 10 or more years of work experience, accept regardless of GMAT and undergraduate record.
- If GMAT is over 550 and undergrad GPA is over 3.2, accept regardless of work experience.
- If GMAT is over 500 and undergrad GPA is over 3.0, defer, unless the undergraduate degree is from Princeton, in which case accept.
- If none of the above conditions are met, reject.

FIGURE 17–3

MBA Program Admissions Data, Harwich University

Name	*Undergraduate School*	*Undergrad GPA*	*GMAT Score*	*Years of Work Experience*	*Decision*
Abel	Princeton	3.1	570	2	Accept
Baker	Mid-State	3.6	510	0	Defer
Channing	Harvard	3.1	580	2	Reject
Davis	North-State	2.1	610	0	Accept
Erlich	Yale	2.9	480	8	Reject
Fowler	Stanford	3.9	730	5	Accept
Greene	Know-Nothing University	2.2	450	12	Accept
Hendler	Bucknell	3.1	580	4	Defer
Ibsen	Reed	2.7	470	7	Reject

Induction poses several difficulties in practice.

- The factors used in the induction may not include all the relevant factors in the decision. For example, Greene's acceptance may have been partly related to a $25 million donation from a family foundation to the Harwich School of Management. The data in the table do not enable us to find this out.
- The factors used in the induction may be correlated with each other. If we attempt to decide eligibility for retirement on the basis of age and hair color (black, brown, blond, grey, white, or bald) we will find that many grey-haired, white-haired, and bald people in the training set are declared eligible to retire while few of the others are. An induction process might conclude that hair color is a factor in determining eligibility.
- There may not be enough examples in the training set to induce all the relevant rules. Neural nets, whose development is in a sense an induction process, often use training sets with thousands of examples. While the training process for a neural net is not as structured as induction for expert system rules, the analogy is still

apt. The training set must include examples that bring out all the relevant factors and allow us to differentiate among all the relevant types of situations.
- The examples may leave room for error in the induced rules. In the above table, we know that Erlich and Ibsen were rejected, but Greene was accepted. The only visible difference in Greene's favor is that the others had 7 or 8 years of work experience while Greene had 12. Assuming that this factor was decisive, is the cutoff for acceptance on the sole basis of work experience 9 years, 10, 11, or 12? We can't be sure.

You may opt for induction where some of these conditions hold:

- A large number of representative examples is available.
- You would like a starting point to develop a more refined set of rules.
- The output of your system will be reviewed by people, or an occasional error is not critical to the application. (While an error in college admissions can be quite critical to the affected applicant, a system based on induction may make fewer errors than human admissions officers would.)
- You can use the results of the induction to screen out unambiguous cases and let humans focus on the borderline situations.

One rule of thumb is to use about two-thirds of the available examples as a training set and the rest to test the induced rules. If the examples can be subdivided into major categories, the training set should include about two-thirds of each category.

The quality of the induced rules depends strongly on the choice of attributes used to describe the examples in the training set. The attributes that an expert feels are appropriate to the problem will usually be suitable. A computer system can select the attributes that contribute most to differentiating among the different outcomes—in technical terms, those that have the highest information content—and work down to those that add little or nothing to the diagnosis or recommendation.

17.4 Beyond the Knowledge Engineer

Barker and O'Connor, based on experience at Digital Equipment Corporation, have identified seven key roles that people must play for the effective development of a large expert system [BARK89]. These roles are more specific than the DSS development roles we discussed in Section 5.2, as the category of expert systems is more specific than the broader category of all DSS of every type. As with those roles, it is not necessary that different people carry out all seven of these tasks: A given individual may play several roles, or several people may play the same role (such as users). The expert system development roles are:

1. The *champion,* with strategic vision, belief in the technology, and organizational influence.
2. The *sponsor,* who has the business problem, a commitment to solve it, and a position with authority and resources.
3. The *program manager,* who integrates the program and coordinates the other active players.
4. The *knowledge engineer,* who carries out the traditional tasks of knowledge acquisition and knowledge-base development.
5. The *software systems integration engineer,* who deals with non-knowledge-base aspects of the system such as the user interface and database access.
6. The *subject matter experts,* who provide domain knowledge and participate in quality assurance and verification.
7. The *users,* who provide business knowledge about the work being affected and how the system will fit into the organization.

As an example of how these roles might work, consider an airline that is developing an expert system to assign planes to airport gates. The roles might be as follows:

- Champion: Anyone at the airline with credibility to management, who thinks this would be a good expert systems application and is willing to speak up and say so. This person could come from the MIS organization if it is recognized as business oriented, not technically oriented.
- Sponsor: The manager in charge of assigning planes to gates. If this person does not support the project, it cannot possibly succeed.
- Program manager, knowledge engineer, and software systems integration engineer: As assigned by the MIS organization. A software systems integration engineer may not be required for this system.
- Subject matter experts: The people who now assign planes to gates. If there are many of them, the knowledge engineer(s) will probably only talk to some of them, although they might send out a questionnaire to the whole group.
- Users: The people who will assign planes to gates when the system is in use. Since the job will then not require the same level of expertise that it does now, these may not be the subject matter experts.

If an expert system project is initiated without clearly identified people in all these roles or a good reason why one or more of them are not necessary, it is likely to fail.

17.5 Combining Expert Systems and DSS

Expert systems can be useful by themselves. In a decision support context, they may be most useful when combined with other types of DSS.

Consider the Harwich University MBA admissions system we used as an example of induction. This expert system would produce a list of applicants with "accept," "reject," or "defer" attached to each name. Suppose we had also developed a group DSS for this department. It contained work flow logic to route applications to appropriate readers, a database with all available information and in which applicants who deserve special consideration (perhaps including, aside from the standard situations, people like Greene) were flagged, and a voting system for multiple readers to make joint decisions. If the total system combined the expert system and that database, it could produce three lists: applicants recommended for acceptance, applicants recommended for rejection, and applicants who would be rejected on the sole basis of their formal credentials but whose files should be reviewed by a human.

Summary

Despite the fact that expert systems are DSS, there are differences between their development process and the generic DSS development process.

One such difference is in selecting the hardware platform on which an expert system is to run. Because expert systems are "computationally intensive," workstations or high-end personal computers are often cost-effective platforms. Minicomputers are appropriate when an expert system is used within a group but when its use by any one group member is sporadic. Mainframes are usually not cost effective for expert systems.

The evolution of technology has affected the choice of platforms for expert systems. Symbolic processors, once widely touted for this purpose, are no longer a factor. Parallel processors are coming into use and are well suited to this application because they can process many rules at the same time. For this reason, parallel processors are also well suited to neural networks.

Software tools for expert systems can be categorized into applications, shells, and languages.

Application packages are an excellent choice where a suitable one is available. However, few packages are available for critical decision support applications.

Most expert system developers in business use commercial shells. A shell consists of an inference engine packaged with a user interface, to which the user must add a knowledge base. Most shells provide integrated development environments with editors and can read data from one or more database management systems. While shells differ in the precise way their rules must be written, all follow similar general concepts. Using a shell permits an organization to focus on the rules in their expert system rather than on programming the inference process.

Key Terms

assertion (in Prolog) 569
atom (in LISP) 566
car 566
cdr 566
champion 582
coarse-grain parallelism 555
cognitive emulation 572
dotted pair 566
induction 579
knowledge acquisition 572
knowledge elicitation 572
knowledge engineer 573
LISP 565
LISP machine 553
list 565
massively parallel computer 555
parallel processing, parallel processor 554
pattern matching, pattern matching variable 567
pointer 571
program manager 582
Prolog 569
shell 559
software systems integration engineer 582
sponsor 582
subject matter experts 574
symbolic expression (S-expression) 566
symbolic processor 553

Review Questions

1. Can desktop microcomputers be a viable platform for expert systems?
2. When might a minicomputer be a good choice as an expert system platform?
3. How could an expert system use parallel processing effectively?
4. Are canned packages that apply expert systems technology to critical business problems widely available? Why or why not?
5. What is a shell? What components of an expert system does one lack?
6. What are five key factors to consider when choosing a shell?
7. Give at least five reasons why one might write an expert system from scratch, without using a shell.

8. What are two programming languages that are especially suitable for developing knowledge-based systems?
9. What does the LISP *car* function do?
10. Give an example of a Prolog assertion.
11. Is the C language generally better or worse than COBOL for developing expert systems? Why?
12. What is the difference between knowledge acquisition and knowledge elicitation?
13. State five characteristics you would like a subject matter expert to have for working on an expert system development project.
14. What strengths should a knowledge engineer have?
15. Give three information-gathering methods you would use in knowledge acquisition for an expert system, and state the order in which you would use them.
16. What is induction? What conditions must hold for it to be useful?
17. State seven roles that someone must play in an expert system project.

Exercises

1. After reading the discussion of symbolic processors in Section 17.1.2 and the discussion of parallel processors in Section 17.1.4, a person might react thus:

   > First you told us that symbolic processors died out because they were too specialized to keep up with improvements in general-purpose systems. Then you told us that parallel processors are the way of the future—but they're a specialized design too. Won't they die out just as symbolic processors did?

   Do you agree or disagree with this statement? Why?
2. Consider the examples of expert system packages listed in Section 17.2.1. Why are these good applications for expert systems? What makes them suitable for standard packages?
3. Consider the Betsy Ross example in Section 17.3.1. Suppose the question were:
   a. "Betsy Ross made the first American flag. Is she still working?"
   b. "This sewing machine made the first American flag.[8] Is it still working?"
   What new or different "common sense" information did you use to answer these versions? What makes parts *a* and *b* different from each other?

[8]For purposes of this question, please pretend that sewing machines had been invented when the first U.S. flag was made.

4. Would you use one expert, several experts individually, or several experts as a group to develop the following expert systems? In each case, why?
   a. The Envoyance system to match cleanup methods to pollutants described in the case at the end of Chapter 15.
   b. A system to help car buyers choose the best way to pay for a new car.
   c. A system to recommend the best plastic to use for a particular application, given requirements for usage temperature, hardness, thermal conductivity, flammability, acid resistance, tensile strength, flexural strength (resistance to bending), and about 10 other similar application factors.
5. Represent the facts (just the ones about computers; you can skip Groucho's mustache) used as examples in Section 16.4 as Prolog assertions.
6. Reread the article "Who Is Liable? Just Ask the Experts" at the end of Chapter 15. Then, suppose an expert system shell was used to help develop an expert system to advise real estate developers where to build. The system gave poor advice, and a developer suffered financial losses by building in an inappropriate location. It is agreed the shell functioned properly and that the rules in the system's knowledge base were faulty. However, the developer's lawyer has read this article and has followed Attorney Newman's advice to sue everyone in sight. You have been called to testify as an expert witness defending the supplier of the shell. Explain why, in your opinion, the shell supplier should not be held liable. Target your explanation to a jury with no technical background.

References

BARK89 Barker, Virginia E., and Dennis E. O'Connor. "Expert Systems for Configuration at Digital: XCON and Beyond." *Communications of the ACM*, 32, no. 3 (March 1989), p. 298.

COOK89 Cooke, Nancy J. "The Elicitation of Domain-Related Ideas: Stage One of the Knowledge Acquisition Process," in *Expert Knowledge and Explanation: The Knowledge-Language Interface*. Charlie Ellis, Ed. Ellis Horwood Ltd., Chichester, England (1989).

HART86 Hart, Anna. *Knowledge Acquisition for Expert Systems*. McGraw-Hill, New York (1986).

HART87 Hart, Anna. "Role of Induction in Knowledge Elicitation," in *Knowledge Acquisition for Expert Systems*. Alison L. Kidd, Ed. Plenum Press, New York (1987).

KIM88 Kim, Jungduck, and James F. Courtney. "A Survey of Knowledge Acquisition Techniques and their Relevance to Managerial Problem Solving Techniques." *Decision Support Systems* 4, no. 3 (September 1988), pp. 269–284.

LIOU92 Liou, Yihwa Irene. "Knowledge Acquisition: Issues, Techniques and Methodology." *Data Base,* 23, no. 1 (Winter 1992), pp. 59–64.

PRER90 Prerau, D. S. *Developing and Managing Expert Systems.* Addison-Wesley, Reading, Mass. (1990).

SHAW87 Shaw, Michael J. "Applying Inductive Learning to Enhance Knowledge-Based Expert Systems." *Decision Support Systems* 3, no. 4 (December 1977), pp. 319–32.

SLAT87 Slatter, Philip E. *Building Expert Systems: Cognitive Emulation.* Ellis Horwood Ltd., Chichester, England (1987).

STYL92 Stylianou, Anthony C.; Gregory R. Madey; and Robert D. Smith. "Selection Criteria for Expert System Shells: A Socio-Technical Framework." *Communications of the ACM* 35, no. 10 (October 1992), pp. 30–48.

TYRA93 Tyran, Craig K., and Joey F. George: "The Implementation of Expert Systems: A Survey of Successful Implementations," *Database* 24, no. 1 (Winter 1993), 5–15.

ENVOYANCE
ASBESTOS ABATEMENT DECISIONS (*CONTINUED*)

In the previous episode, in Chapter 16, Miguel told Doug and Adrienne about asbestos abatement options. This episode picks up the story.

"So you really think you can develop an expert system to help make asbestos decisions for me?" asked Miguel when Doug and Adrienne returned the next day.

"Yes, we do," Adrienne answered. "In fact, it doesn't look like that difficult a problem from the technical point of view. We just have a few more questions before we get into the details."

"Go ahead!"

"Well, for one thing, last time you listed five categories of factors, five types of asbestos, and four methods of dealing with it. Are those pretty much the whole story?"

"Yes, they are, as far as they go. We didn't get into all the details, especially in terms of abatement methods. There are a few different encapsulation methods and materials. Enclosing the area containing the asbestos can mean just about anything, but that depends on the building configuration, and we can't generalize about it in advance."

"And as regards your breakdown of the social, legal, and the other factors?" Adrienne continued.

"You can really break those down as far as you want to go," responded Miguel in a meditative mood. "Take the question of how often people go into the area. What's 'often?' Once a week? Every five minutes? Somewhere between a year and five minutes is what most people would say. Then you get into how long they stay when they do go. Once a quarter for a full day's work with physical activity might be enough to justify pretty full-scale abatement. Once a month for 10 seconds to read a meter might not be."

"If we were going to build an expert system to advise you on these decisions," asked Doug as he changed the subject slightly, "we'd want it to run on hardware you have. I see you have a Compaq on your desk. It looks like a recent model. What configuration is it? What software do you use?"

"It's fairly new machine, but not top of the line," answered Miguel. "It's got a 486 chip inside—I forget the speed, but it's pretty fast. I've been running Microsoft Windows Release 3.1 for several months now. I still use MS-DOS for a few applications, though. As for the rest of the configuration, it's got 4MB of memory and a 120MB disk drive. Would any of those be a problem?"

"I don't really think so," said Doug. "Not for the size problem we seem to be talking about. The main reason I asked was because this information will help us narrow down the kinds of tools we'll be able to use. One last question: How often do problems like this arise?"

"Last time you were here, I would have said once every 10 minutes, because it was starting to feel like that!" Miguel joked. "Seriously, we might get a job in this area, or at least a chance to write a proposal, once every few weeks at the most. Each situation might call for anywhere from 1 to 20 evaluations. That makes the average one a day or less, but they come in bunches.

"Now I have a question for you. What do you plan to do next?"

Exercises

1. Do you agree with Doug, that Miguel's new Compaq is a suitable platform for developing an expert system for asbestos abatement decisions?
2. Suppose a decision similar to this had to be made every minute or two throughout a typical working day. Would this affect your choice of platform? If so, how? If not, why not?
3. Would you expect to find a ready-made expert system package that would help Miguel with this decision? Why or why not?
4. If you were going to use a shell to develop Miguel's system, what features would you want it to have?
5. If you, personally, were to program this expert system from scratch, which language would you use? Why? (There is no single right answer to this question.)
6. Who might fit each of the seven expert system development roles described in Section 17.4?

Chapter 18 Expert System Cases

Chapter Outline

Introduction

As we noted at the beginning of Chapter 13, to really understand decision support systems, it is important to see real DSS in action. The same is true of expert systems. For that reason, we present several such systems here. As with the DSS cases in Chapter 13, try to apply the principles you learned in the previous chapters to these real-life decision situations and systems. The review and discussion questions at the end of the chapter will help you do this effectively.

18.1 XCON[1]

Digital Equipment Corporation is one of the world's largest computer system manufacturers. Most of its shipments are custom-tailored configurations of the VAX line. This line starts with microcomputers for under $5,000 and extends to over a million dollars for a system to support hundreds of concurrent users.

Each VAX system typically incorporates tens to hundreds of parts from the 30,000+ in Digital's price list.[2] Configurable elements include processors, memory, tapes, disks, adapters, cables, cabinets, power supplies, terminals, communication and networking items, software (on any of several media), and documentation (likewise). The millions of combinations are subject to technical rules (using many adapters may call for an added power supply), marketing restrictions (the largest disk drives are not sold with the smallest models), and common sense rules (software on tape should not be ordered for a system with no tape drive).

When hardware configuration drawings were generated by hand from customer orders, the process took from five minutes to one hour of a specialist's time, with an average of 15 minutes. In addition, the likelihood of an error was high. In one internal check, fully 35 percent of the generated configurations had errors, although some of these errors were as minor as a cable length being one foot off. These mistakes were usually caught in final assembly and test, a process that generally added four to six weeks to customer delivery times. Finally, since each order was configured separately, it was common for customers who ordered several identical systems to receive systems with different internal configurations (for example, the physical relationship between the placement of a disk drive and of a tape drive) even though each was correct. This annoyed customers and hurt Digital's quality image.

In 1978, when the VAX line was new, Carnegie-Mellon University (CMU) computer science professor John McDermott came to work at Digital for a year. He suggested that a knowledge-based system might be able to automate the configuration task. Digital agreed to support a CMU project to develop such a system. McDermott and his colleagues began working on XCON (then called R1) in December 1978. In about a year it developed from an idea to a basic prototype to a system with true expertise.

XCON went through the following development phases in its first few years:

---

[1]Much of the material in this section is from [SCOW85], Chap. 6; [BARK89], and [SVIO90].

[2]Digital Equipment Corporation is often referred to as "DEC." However, the firm prefers "Digital" as the short form.

1. *Strategy formulation, initial prototype construction, and demonstration—December 1978 through April 1979.* During this period McDermott implemented a prototype with about 250 rules. Digital's Richard Caruso was the subject matter expert.

2. *Large-scale knowledge acquisition—May through September 1979.* McDermott consulted with Caruso to fill gaps in the prototype's knowledge and to refine it, eliciting information on exceptions that had not been articulated earlier.

3. *Testing—October through November 1979.* XCON processed 50 test cases with 2 major errors and 10 "low-level" errors—better than average performance for a technical editor—and was judged ready to use. At this point it had about 750 rules.

During this period Digital planned for the integration of XCON into their organization. Processes were put in place to add new products to its database and to add or modify rules.

4. *First installation—January 1980.* XCON was installed in Digital's Salem, New Hampshire, manufacturing plant and used on a daily basis. Its operation and output were closely monitored by the technician who had previously done the system configuration task.

5. *Integration and utilization—June through December 1980.* XCON was installed in more of Digital's final assembly and test plants. Digital software engineers extended the system to handle the second VAX model.

6. *Reimplementation—completed July 1980.* XCON was converted from its initial OPS4 language to the newer OPS5. OPS5 was easier to read and maintain, ran faster, and ran on the VAX rather than earlier hardware. McDermott and his CMU colleagues also streamlined the program in several ways.

7. *Utilization and expansion—January through July 1981.* The OPS5-based system was extended to a third VAX model and refined and expanded in other areas.

8. *Moving to BLISS-based version of OPS5—January 1982.* This conversion, to a new implementation of OPS5, was done entirely by Digital staff. Digital was now self-sufficient in XCON development. CMU settled into a consulting role.

9. *Further extensions—late 1982 through November 1983.* XCON was extended to configure all major Digital systems. Statistics and performance monitoring were added, the user interface was enhanced, and it was connected to databases for customer orders and problem reporting. By early 1985 XCON had over 4,000 rules.

In 1987 XCON was rewritten using Digital's RIME methodology [BACH88]. RIME helps knowledge engineers break down complex rules into sets of simpler ones, organize rules for easier modification and maintenance, and deal with the complexity of a large expert system. (By late 1988 XCON had over 10,000 rules, thus qualifying as "large" by any standard.)

18.1.1 How XCON Works

XCON accepts as input a list of items on a customer order, configures them into a system, notes any additions, deletions, or changes needed to make the system complete and functional, and prints out a set of detailed diagrams listing the configuration and showing the spatial relationships among the components as they should be assembled in the factory.

XCON's users now include:

- Technical editors who are responsible for seeing that only configurable orders are committed to production.[3]
- Assemblers and technicians in Digital's manufacturing organization who assemble the systems on the plant floor.
- Salespeople, who use XCON in conjunction with XSEL, an expert system that helps them prepare accurate quotes for customers. This can be done on a dial-up basis from a customer's or prospect's office.
- Scheduling personnel who use the information from XCON to decide how to combine options for the most efficient configurations.
- Technicians who assemble systems at the customer site.

Elements of the system include:

- The knowledge base, in the form of OPS5 condition/action rules.
- Working memory, which starts with the set of customer-ordered components and accumulates descriptions of partial configurations until the entire configuration is complete.
- The inference engine, which is the OPS5 interpreter.
- A component database with descriptions of all components that can be configured in systems. The knowledge base might have a rule that applies to any disk drive; the database would provide specific information such as capacity for each individual type of disk drive.
- User-interface software that allows the user to enter and modify orders interactively, to review XCON output for these orders, and to enter problem reports.
- Traditional software for database access, for collecting statistics on hardware resource utilization and functional accuracy, and for automatic routing of problem reports to the support organization.

XCON's four major subtasks are:

- Checking the order for gross errors, such as wrong voltage, no central processors, etc. This subtask also unbundles line item

---

[3] A technical editor, as Digital uses the job title in this context, is not an "editor" in the usual sense of a person who reviews and revises another person's writing.

packages to the configurable component level, assigns devices to controllers, and distributes modules among multiple busses.
- Placing the components in cabinets and finding an acceptable physical configuration of the physical components that go inside a cabinet: "card cages" to hold the printed circuit boards, backplanes to extend the system bus to them, etc.
- Configuring the rest of the components: panels, continuity cards, and unused backplanes. This subtask also computes the logical addresses (the identification numbers by which software will refer to them) of all modules.
- Developing a floor plan for the system and determining how to cable it together.

An example of a (pre-RIME) XCON rule rewritten from OPS5 into "normal" English is shown here.

```
RULE 1: Panel Space

IF the current active context is panel-space for
 module-x

AND module-x has a line-type that requires cabling

AND the cabling that module-x requires is to a panel

AND there is space for a panel in the current cabinet

AND there is no panel already assigned to the current
 cabinet with space for module-x

AND there is no partial configuration relating module-x
 to available panel space

THEN mark the panel space in the cabinet as used,

Assign it the same line type as module-x,

Create a partial configuration relating module-x to the
 panel space
```

XCON runs in batch mode. It takes from a fraction of a minute up to a few minutes to configure an order, depending on order complexity.

18.1.2 XCON Performance

Two measures of XCON success are its technical accuracy and its acceptance by its users. XCON's accuracy, as judged by human experts, was initially 75 percent and rose to 95 percent over a period of a year and a half. It currently creates a usable configuration 95 percent to 98 percent of the time. This compares with 65 to 90 percent correctness, pre-XCON, on the part of Digital's technical editors. (While Digital's top engineering specialists do much better than this, there are not enough of them to deal with a significant fraction of all orders, and they are needed for engineering work.) It is not practical to raise the accuracy much beyond 98 percent because new products are continually being added to the product line and because some of the "errors" reflect situations that may never recur. Technical editor productivity increased from 100 to 300 orders per editor per year in 1981 to more than 1,000 in 1986.

The technical editors and engineers in Digital's factories were originally unwilling to accept XCON as a tool. After the development team had run a large number of orders through XCON, they accepted the fact that the system worked. Today they do not see how they could perform their tasks without it.

18.1.3 XCON Benefits

- XCON has allowed Digital to avoid the costs of hiring more and more technical editors as the volume of systems sold increased.
- Before XCON, system configuration errors were sometimes discovered only after systems had been partially assembled. Those systems then had to be dismantled, reconfigured, and reassembled. This wasted time and floor space in the assembly plants. XCON reduces the incidence of assembly errors.
- Since all system elements must be taken into account to provide an accurate quote, configuration details should be dealt with at the time a system is ordered. XCON allows the sales force to obtain accurate configurations for quotes without forcing salespeople to become technical experts themselves.
- Experience with XCON has changed attitudes toward expert systems at Digital from skepticism to confidence, even enthusiasm. Digital has since developed many more expert systems and AI-based applications. Several of them are described in [KAEW90].
- XCON permitted Digital to restructure its system assembly, test, and shipment process. As noted above, pre-XCON, 80 to 90 percent of orders went through final assembly and test. With XCON's increased configuration accuracy, this step was no longer necessary. Once XCON was fully implemented, 80 to 90 percent of orders were shipped to customer sites as separate components and assembled there for the first time. This change, to which XCON made a major contribution, is credited with saving Digital $15 million per year.

In 1989 Digital estimated its overall return from XCON at over $40,000,000 per year.

There are, however, some negatives. Some orders cannot be fully processed by XCON, especially where new VAX models or nonstandard features are involved. In these cases, the technical editor must work through the entire XCON output, often 20 pages or more, to trace all the references to the items that must be changed, references to those references, etc. What's more, the

XCON output file must then often be changed on the computer with a text editor because salespeople expect to be able to see it on their screens. The technical editors find this new part of their job tedious and boring. In addition, the technical editors miss the regular contact they had with many parts of the company. Their job seems to have lost clout and become more technical.

18.1.4 Key Roles in XCON

In Section 17.4 you read about the seven key roles that Digital has identified for effective development of a large expert system. For XCON the roles were filled as follows:

1. The champion was, initially, McDermott.
2. The sponsor was, in principle, the manager in charge of assembling VAX systems. In practice, Digital's culture of that era allowed people a great deal of freedom to work on unusual projects. This would have been especially true of a visiting professor such as McDermott. The need for a formal sponsor was therefore small until it became time to put XCON into use.
3. The program manager was, initially, McDermott as well. As the XCON program grew in size, scope and usage, this became a formal, full-time job.
4. The knowledge engineer was also initially McDermott, as he was one of the few people who understood how expert systems worked. Digital now has several knowledge engineers working on XCON and related systems.
5. The software systems integration engineer became necessary as XCON evolved. In 1989 XCON and related configuration systems included five major databases and over 350 programs written in traditional languages such as Pascal and C and totaling over 50,000 lines of code.
6. The initial subject matter expert was Digital engineer Richard Caruso. The engineers who design current VAX models and know how their components should be configured continue to play that role.
7. The primary users were and are the technical editors.

These roles evolved considerably over XCON's first 10+ years of existence and continue to evolve today.

18.1.5 Lessons Learned from XCON

- Management support is absolutely necessary through the trials, tribulations, and pitfalls of getting the program started. With new technology we do not know exactly what path to follow in all cases.

We must learn from our mistakes and continue to make progress. Management must be willing to let a development team explore and see what they can and cannot do with the technology.

- Expert systems can be threatening to existing human experts, more so to human "subexperts" such as the technical editors. They must be introduced carefully and with sensitivity to these people's concerns.
- An expert system needs "mentors," experts who can evaluate its output. These people must know what the system is supposed to do and have some understanding of its high-level strategies if they are to report only actual errors and not "bogus problems," that is, the system's inability to solve problems it was never designed to solve in the first place.
- "When an expert system is implemented as a production system, the job of refining and extending the system's knowledge is quite easy" [MCDE80]. While some XCON team members feel that "easy" may be an overstatement, they are amazed that the amount of extension and refinement XCON has undergone over the years was possible at all.
- The typical expert system is never "complete" because the problems it solves are not static and because new rules to improve its performance can always be added.
- The process of ongoing modifications and extensions of the system's knowledge base is likely to lead to a juncture at which the whole base or some major part of it must be redesigned to eliminate redundancies, to make it more efficient, and to make it easier to read and maintain.

18.2 Expert System Calculates Space Shuttle Payload Configuration[4]

Calculating how a payload should fit in the cargo bay of a space shuttle takes considerable experience. So formidable is the task that only two men can do it with any certainty. One of those men retired recently, and the second is nearing the day when he will do the same. That thought worried the ground systems integration staff at Rockwell International Corporation's Space Systems Division enough that they developed an expert system to carry on when human experts are not available.

"The shuttle program now spans a generation," said James Engle, ground systems engineer. "One of our two experts for analyzing payload-to-ground

[4]This material is taken from [ALEX91]. Copyright 1991 by CW Publishing, Inc., Framingham, MA 01701. Reprinted from *Computerworld*.

systems compatibility has already retired, and the other is a senior member of the technical staff. It has become imperative that we capture the knowledge these men possess because otherwise, when they leave, their knowledge and skills leave with them."

The Rockwell staff members and Expertelligence Inc., a Santa Barbara, California, expert system shell developer, have created an expert system called G-Fit to capture the knowledge accumulated by Rockwell's configuration experts over the past 15 years.

G-Fit, short for Ground System to Flight Payload Integration Tool, is an object-oriented expert system that allows engineers to interactively configure a payload on screen and analyze it to see how well it fits in the cargo bay of a space shuttle.

The expert system, which runs on an Apple Macintosh II, includes a graphical user interface that engineers use to fit together pieces of a payload, like a jigsaw puzzle.

Payloads—satellites, telescopes, and gear needed for scientific experiments—must be stowed on board while the orbiter is in its vertical launch position. The entire cargo must be designed to slide flawlessly into place as a single unit so that nothing obstructs the closing of the payload bay doors. The trunnions, or pins, supporting each of the payload's components must slip into their holding fixtures within minute tolerances of only one one-hundredth of an inch.

Each payload configuration is unique, and it often takes weeks for experts at Rockwell's Space Systems Division to assemble payloads and try out each configuration on paper. "At any given time, there will be several different flights in work, and each flight requires at least four reviews," Engle said.

G-Fit has been used in configuration testing on several shuttle missions, although it is not the sole testing tool. "The overall task has required about 40 hours per week," Engle explained. "In automating the routine and repetitive manual activities, we have been able to recapture a large block of time that can be better used for creative problem solving."

On the Inside

The knowledge base contains two key components: the physical dimensions of the payload bay and mission-critical devices mounted on the bay's sides, as well as the rules governing the use of the available space and devices.

The G-Fit operator adjusts the overall configuration of the payload, drawing from a palette of objects representing payloads of different sizes, cameras, and other components. Payloads created on screen can be tested and refined until the knowledge base signals that the cargo bay can accommodate the configuration.

Once testing is completed, the operator produces a printed report and drawing of each payload for contractors, who determine whether the planned unit can be conformed to the payload configuration. If not, they propose alternatives and submit them to a new round of testing.

Eventually, the payload is assembled and inserted into an upright, cylindrical payload canister that is an exact duplicate of the orbiter's cargo bay. The payload is then transported to the launch site and loaded into the orbiter.

18.3 TRUCK BRAKE BALANCING[5]

Brake balancing is the art of adjusting the components of a truck's air brake system so that they operate in unison, with each contributing its share of the effort required to stop the truck. An unbalanced brake system causes the truck to handle poorly in emergencies and can cause other components of the vehicle to fail sooner than they otherwise would—often without indicating the root cause of their failure.

The importance of proper brake balancing grew dramatically during the years after the fuel crisis of the 1970s.[6] Trucks became more streamlined, reducing the braking effect of aerodynamic drag. Engine downsizing reduced its value in braking as well.

An "18-wheeler" truck has five axles, three on the tractor and two on the trailer (see Figure 18–1). Each has brake pads, which come in a range of sizes with a range of friction coefficients. The brake balancer must determine the proper values for both of these for each axle. The balancer must also consider air compressors, the length of the air lines, the number and type of hose fittings, and relay valve activation values. Further complicating the process is that tractors and trailers do not stay together but are exchanged frequently within a fleet. Balancing must therefore be performed on the fleet as a whole,

FIGURE 18–1
Schematic of 18-Wheeler Truck

[5]This case is summarized from [SMIT91].

[6]While the 1970s may be ancient history to most readers of this book, large trucks had been a fairly stable technology for the preceding two decades. Individual components changed significantly, but the overall truck design parameters and trade-offs did not.

or a tractor and trailer—each individually balanced—may be seriously out of balance when coupled together.

In 1988–1989, Eaton Corporation, a major manufacturer of truck brake components, developed a computer-based system to determine the balancing parameters for truck brake systems. This system was innovative in its use of two types of AI technology: neural networks and expert systems. It works in three stages:

1. A knowledge-based preprocessor performs a preliminary checking function. It records data observed by the brake-balance technician regarding the manufacturer of the installed components, their sizes, and their condition. It then uses preliminary test results to verify that the tractor and trailer are individually balanced. There is no point in proceeding with the overall truck balancing process if this condition is not met.

2. Neural networks input graphs of brake pressure or temperature versus time and determine if each graph is "good" or "bad." A typical graph plots brake pressure over time when the brakes are applied. There are six lines on this graph, one for each axle and one for the truck pressure control line. Classification factors include both the overall shape of the curves and how well they match each other.

3. A knowledge-based diagnostic system accepts data from the preprocessor knowledge base, from the neural networks, and from a model of a truck. It produces recommendations for adjusting the components of the brake system together with explanations of the reasoning behind those recommendations. A typical explanation is:

> The mismatched coefficients of the brake pads, combined with the oversized brakes and generally slow reaction of the brake system, will tend to cause the trailer brakes to do more work than the tractor brakes, creating excessive operating temperatures. In addition to wearing the brake pads prematurely, the brakes will quickly go out of adjustment, exaggerating the problem of a tardy brake system.

The knowledge-based components of the system were written using the LISP language and the KEE shell from IntelliCorp. They store data in frames. Slots are inherited statically from parent to child, for example, from trailer to axle. Values can be inherited dynamically in the other direction, from child to parent: once relay valve actuation values for both trailer axles are determined, a value for the trailer itself can be. Both knowledge-based subsystems together include a total of 120 methods (procedures associated with frame slots, which can behave like rules) and 40 freestanding rules not part of any frame. They use both forward and backward chaining where appropriate.

Neural networks were used for graph analysis because they can recognize patterns better than knowledge-based systems. The five neural nets were built with the Anza Plus board from HNC and its supporting software. (This board fits into an option slot of a workstation or microcomputer.) They use either three or four layers of neurons: an input layer, an output layer, and one or two hidden layers. The most complex network uses 11 neurons on each of two hidden layers and required a total of 50,000 iterations to converge three to five neurons on their single inner layer and converged after 1,000 iterations. Each of these networks is approximately 90 percent accurate in its classification of graphs: far better than either of two alternative approaches, a set of linear classifiers and a set of rules based on statistical data manipulation, could achieve. This is acceptable because there is some redundancy in the information contained in the five graphs. This allows the knowledge-based diagnostic system to correct a classification error made in any one of them. Also, an occasional balancing error on one rig in a large fleet is acceptable, as the system still performs better overall than all but the best few humans.

Interestingly, this 90 percent performance by the networks is higher than the system's developer expected. He surmises that, whether because of better design or better maintenance, today's truck brake systems are in better shape than were those of a few years ago when the training set data were obtained. Thus, he surmises, perhaps "some of the really awful tests that were seen in the training and test data won't be seen again." Training a neural network on examples that are more difficult than those it will see in real use is, he suggests, "a great trick if you can do it"—but one that can't be used in most practical situations.

The knowledge-based portions of this system were developed in less than four months: two months for knowledge acquisition and six weeks for design, development, and testing of the computer system. The total cost of this work was approximately $30,000 but would have been higher were it not for the use of college juniors and seniors working on the system for academic credit. The neural nets took about five months to develop at a cost of $50,000. Adding the cost of hardware and software brings the total cost of this system to $105,500, not including the cost of deploying additional systems to the field. This is offset by savings of $100,000 per year in direct travel expenses by Eaton's expert, plus the value of his time and the morale benefits of his not having to travel nearly every week. The system is thus well cost justified. Eaton cites these added benefits:

- Six times the former number of fleet brake balance appraisals can be conducted per year. As brake balancing is provided as a free service to large fleet customers to gain goodwill and hence do more business, this presumably spreads six times the goodwill.
- Extensive desk analysis is eliminated, thus giving the customer results in days or hours instead of weeks or months.
- The expert, freed from traveling to balance brakes, could be promoted to other, more challenging professional work. (Such a

potential opportunity can be a factor in obtaining an expert's cooperation.)

- The system is valuable for training inexperienced staff members.

Exercises

For Section 18.1, XCON

1. Evaluate XCON against the criteria for expert system development in Section 15.2. Is configuring VAX systems a good expert system application? Was XCON's development justified?
2. One criterion for expert system development (in Section 15.2) was the ability of the problem situation to accept solutions that may not be optimal in the mathematical sense or provably correct. How does XCON's intended purpose fit this criterion?
3. XCON uses forward chaining. Why do you think its developers chose this method? (After 15 years of use and all the public exposure that XCON has had, they would presumably have switched if they had made the wrong choice.) Why would backward chaining not be as suitable for it?
4. Could a system such as XCON use confidence factors meaningfully? Why or why not? If so, how could it use them? How about fuzzy logic?
5. Where could a system like XCON be useful outside the computer industry?
6. Some industry observers, while not questioning XCON's merits as an expert system, feel it reflects negatively on Digital's engineers. "How is it," they ask, "that all Digital's competitors of the late 1970s and early 1980s—Data General, Hewlett-Packard, Honeywell, Prime, Wang—introduced systems of the same performance level and configuration flexibility, using technology of the same era, that could be configured correctly by ordinary human beings? Why did Digital's engineers make the VAX so complicated that they needed XCON?" Do you agree with this criticism? Why might Digital have been right to develop XCON when its competitors did not choose to develop expert systems for the same purpose?

For Section 18.2, G-Fit

1. What was the major reason for developing G-Fit, in terms of the reasons for expert system development discussed in Section 15.2?
2. How does G-Fit match up with the task-related and expert-related criteria for expert system development discussed in Section 15.2?
3. What type of DSS would you consider G-Fit to be in terms of the DSS spectrum of Section 4.1?
4. Would a character-oriented user interface be suitable for G-Fit? Why or why not?
5. Which of the potential DSS benefits (see Section 1.4) does G-Fit provide?

6. Since Rockwell spent your (i.e., the taxpayers') money to develop G-Fit, it is reasonable for you to ask if that money was well spent. What could Rockwell and/or the National Aeronautics and Space Administration (NASA) do without G-Fit when the second payload configuration expert retires? Quantify the cost of that approach as closely as you can in terms of dollars, staff time, or schedule time. Do you feel that Rockwell was justified in developing G-Fit? Why or why not?

For Section 18.3, Truck Brake Balancing

1. Which of the criteria for expert system development (Section 15.2) does this system meet? Had you looked at those criteria before reading the list of benefits at the end of the case, do you think they would have justified its development?
2. What type of user interface would you recommend for this system? Why? (Who is the user?)
3. How do you think local brake technicians would react to the deployment of this system in their garages, if it were brought in without warning and they were simply told "Use it!"? What steps would you take to ensure a positive reception of the system on their part?
4. As mentioned above, much of the knowledge-based part of the system was developed by college juniors and seniors for academic credit after an experienced professional had designed them. According to [SMIT91], "they were relatively unfamiliar with programming, let alone LISP, KEE or AI." Do you think they should have received academic credit for their work on this project? Why or why not?

References

ALEX91 Alexander, Michael. "Expert System Calculates Space Shuttle Payload Configuration." *Computerworld,* 25, no. 15 (April 22, 1991), p. 21.

BACH88 Bachant, Judith. "RIME: Preliminary Work Toward a Knowledge-Acquisition Tool," in *Automating Knowledge Acquisition for Expert Systems.* S. Marcus, Ed. Kluwer Academic (1988).

BARK89 Barker, Virginia E., and Dennis E. O'Connor. "Expert Systems for Configuration at Digital: XCON and Beyond." *Communications of the ACM,* 32, no. 3 (March 1989), pp. 298–318.

KAEW90 Kaewert, Julie Wallin, and John M. Frost. *Developing Expert Systems for Manufacturing.* McGraw-Hill, New York (1990).

MCDE80 McDermott, John. "R1: A Rule-Based Configurer of Computer Systems." Report CMU-CS-80-119. Computer Science Department, Carnegie-Mellon University, Pittsburgh, Pa. (April 1980).

SCOW85 Scown, Susan J. *The Artificial Intelligence Experience: An Introduction.* Digital Equipment Corporation, Maynard, Mass. (1985).

SMIT91 Smith, Michael Lawrence. "Cooperating Artificial Neural and Knowledge-Based Systems in a Truck Fleet Brake Balance Application," in *Innovative*

Applications of Artificial Intelligence 2. Alain Rappaport and Reid Smith, Eds. AAAI Press, Menlo Park, Calif., and MIT Press, Cambridge, Mass. (1991).

SVIO90 Sviokla, John J. "An Examination of the Impact of Expert Systems on the Firm: The Case of XCON." *MIS Quarterly* 14, no. 2 (June 1990), pp. 127–40.

Part V Summary

CHAPTER

19 Pulling It All Together: Systems Integration and the Future of DSS

Chapter Outline

Introduction

You now understand several related types of systems: traditional decision support systems, expert systems, and executive information (or support) systems. Each type is useful by itself. Indeed, most real-world systems of all three types are built as separate projects. Yet organizations reap the greatest benefits from this sort of management support software when they are pulled together into a unified whole. This is the point of systems integration: pulling different systems, or parts of different systems, together to create a whole which is greater, in its value to the sponsoring organization, than the sum of its parts. While systems integration can be of value in many areas, not just in DSS, we'll focus on its use in a DSS context. We'll finish this chapter, and this book, with a few thoughts on where DSS is likely to go as you set out on your professional career in information systems.

Chapter Objectives

After you have read and studied this chapter, you will be able to:

1. Explain how decision support systems, group decision support systems, expert systems, and executive information (or support) systems relate to each other.
2. Explain how systems integration is important to users and decision support system specialists.
3. Identify the different types of systems integration.
4. Discuss current trends in systems integration, including the reasons users increasingly turn to outside systems integration firms.
5. Summarize factors to consider in selecting a systems integration firm.
6. Describe ways in which DSS is likely to evolve over the next several years.

19.1 Combining the Pieces

In the late 1960s, as immediate access to a database became practical, many information systems practitioners had a dream: the Management Information System. The MIS would provide managers with instant, up-to-date information on any business-related subject, processed and digested to their precise requirements. Truly, this would be the corporation of the late 20th century.

Things didn't work out that way. Many organizations invested vast sums in pursuit of this dream. They often found themselves, as a result, with better access to more information than they had previously had. But the payoff was less than they had hoped. The only remnant of the Management Information System concept today is the term: It is a common name for our field of study and, in many organizations, the title of the information-processing group.

Yet, in the 1990s, just about all the capabilities that were to have gone into this MIS exist individually. We have access to data across a network. We have easy-to-use financial modeling packages. We have graphs on demand, in our choice of formats and colors. What we do not have, as a single unified entity, is the MIS as a unit. Yet we are now in the position of being able to create much of it: not by installing a standard package or by developing a single monolithic "megasystem," but by integrating the pieces we have into a single functional whole.

We've discussed several of these pieces in the preceding chapters: decision support systems (DSS), group DSS (GDSS), executive information systems (EIS), expert systems, and variations on these themes. These types of systems all combine three characteristics to varying degrees: data, modeling, and communications. Figure 19–1 attempts, within the constraints of the two-dimensional printed page, to put each type of system in its appropriate place in this three-dimensional space:

- Decision support systems in the traditional sense incorporate varying degrees of database and model usage. However, their communications capability is incidental, usually limited to whatever is required in order to access the databases in question.
- Group decision support systems incorporate communications as an essential element. They also often incorporate a model, if only a model of how the group process is supposed to work. Their use of a database, however, is normally limited.
- Executive information systems focus on communications and data. Since their primary purpose is to support unpredictable and unstructured decisions, complex models are usually not found there.
- Expert systems focus on the model aspect: Indeed, their essence is the process model built into their rules. Some use databases as a

FIGURE 19–1

Three-Dimensional Data/Modeling/Communications Diagram

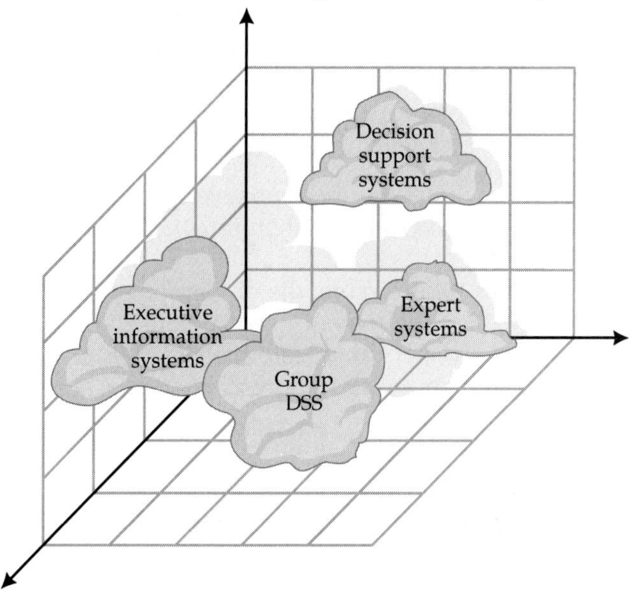

source of facts; others don't. Communications aspects tend to be incidental.

The "total MIS" must incorporate aspects of all these. Indeed, it must do more: It must bring them together into a unified whole. Such a system, even if it falls short of the 1960s' Management Information System concept, is often called a *management support system* or MSS. There are several good reasons for not calling it an MIS:

- The term MIS has another meaning today.
- The objectives of an MSS really are different. We are not trying to computerize the world. We are trying specifically to support managers in their decision-making and communication tasks.
- The term MIS, used in this narrow context, might bring back memories of unfulfilled promises and thus turn people against a new, fully achievable, system.

A management support system includes:

- Access to internal databases reflecting the financial, marketing, production, R&D project, etc., status of the organization.
- Access to external databases containing economic data, technology information, and the text of key business and industry publications.

- An easy-to-use interface by which any of these can be queried.
- Processing capabilities to perform statistical and other analyses of the data so retrieved and to display it in tabular or graphical form.
- Modeling capabilities to help make decisions on the basis of these data.
- Communication capabilities to discuss and share this information with other managers in the organization.

The professional discipline that pulls elements of an information system together into a whole is called system integration. We now discuss its impact on DSS.

One note of caution: While the discussion of systems integration focuses on technical issues, the overall need to consider nontechnical ones during implementation has not disappeared. Refer back to Chapter 9, in particular to Section 8.4.2, if you wish to refresh your memory.

19.2 WHAT IS SYSTEMS INTEGRATION?

A decision support application is seldom useful in a vacuum. Some DSS, usually of the model-oriented sort, receive all their inputs directly from human users via a keyboard and return their outputs to humans via a printer or display screen. Those are, however, the exceptions. It is more common for a DSS to communicate in some fashion with other applications or computer systems: not necessarily to the exclusion of interaction with human users, but at least to supplement it.

The ability of different applications or computer systems to communicate meaningfully with each other is not, unfortunately, automatic. Each subsystem, each part of the overall system, must be designed to provide the outputs that other subsystems need and/or to accept inputs that other systems can provide. Once this is done, technical issues of data representation, file structure, and database organization must be resolved. Issues of data communication and networking must also be dealt with if, as is often the case, parts of the overall system reside on different computers. At a higher level, issues relating to the partitioning of an application across systems must be considered early in the application design stages.

Systems integration (SI) is the design and development of information systems that combine several hardware and/or software components to cooperate to carry out a joint task that would be beyond the capabilities of any one of them individually.

This definition has a few points worth noting:

1. SI is a process, an activity that takes place over a period of time. It is not a one-time event.

2. SI can take involve hardware, software, or both:

- At the software level, SI can mean enabling several software packages to cooperate on one computer.
- At the combined hardware/software level, SI may mean assigning one part of a task to one program on one computer and another part to another program on another computer. A DSS might obtain data from a mainframe database and manipulate it on a microcomputer. An organization could create a client-server application from components that were not originally designed to function in that mode. Combined hardware/software integration, usually involving data communication, is what most people think of when they use the term SI.
- At the hardware-only level, a user organization could buy a package that comes in parts intended to run on different, networked computers. The Pilot EIS, which you read about in Chapter 12, works that way. The user doesn't have to integrate the software; Pilot has already done that. The user is still, however, responsible for creating the necessary communication link between the mainframe and the micro.

3. The statement "beyond the capabilities . . ." doesn't mean that the task must be beyond the capabilities of a single hardware or software component in principle. It might be possible, in theory, to design a single component to do the entire job. In the SI case, however, we didn't. We chose to combine several components. Doing that is SI. Whether or not another approach could have worked in principle—or might have worked better in practice—is beside the point. It's like driving your car to visit your next-door neighbor. If you chose to drive your car, you're driving your car. Whether or not that was the ideal mode of transportation for your purpose is a separate issue.

A similar definition comes from ADAPSO, the Association of DAta Processing Service Organizations. It defines SI as "the process of identifying and bringing together various technologies in order to define and deliver a complete information system that will fulfill specific design, operational, and/or management objectives."

19.3 A Systems Integration Example

Consider a supermarket chain with electronic cash registers that read universal product code (UPC) bar codes on package labels. The cash registers look up product prices in files kept at a store controller. This is a high-speed microcomputer or small minicomputer connected to all the cash registers. The store controller also collects data on each product's sales for inventory management and for management analysis.

Buyers and managers at chain headquarters must know how well each product is selling in order to plan orders from their suppliers. They can do this with a DSS that looks at recent sales trends. It must also take prior years' records into account because many products' sales follow seasonal trends or depend on holidays. (A buyer who tried to predict the sales of cranberry sauce in the United States in the last half of November by extrapolating from October would be in for a big surprise.) It must also accept user input about planned sales and other promotional activities.

It is quite impractical for this DSS to run on an in-store controller. For one thing, that computer doesn't have the capacity; for another, it's in the wrong place; for a third, it doesn't have access to all stores' data; and finally, it was probably not designed to run user applications. It is equally impractical to take the system on which the DSS runs—most likely, a mainframe or large mini at corporate headquarters—and expect it to control cash registers. Hence, we need a network to connect the DSS system to the stores. We must also make sure our DSS can understand the data transmission formats used by the store controller.

A low-tech approach to accomplishing this end would be to obtain sales data printouts in every store, ship them to headquarters, and then type them into the DSS system. This would be labor intensive, time consuming, and error prone to the point of absurdity. It is not surprising, then, that before integrated DSS, supermarket managers made most of their own ordering decisions. They were often "helped" in this regard by "friendly" supplier representatives. Each of these representatives would suggest that ordering more of his or her product would be a good idea. No wonder that decisions were often not optimal. One branch of a chain might have a sale to get rid of surplus perishable goods while another branch, two towns over, is out of stock on the same item.

A modern supermarket chain would take a systems integration approach to this project. They would start with the existing store systems. These systems probably have some flexibility in configuring their data communication capability but are otherwise fixed. Along the lines of the prototyping approach we discussed in Section 5.2.2, they would also determine what managers require of their DSS. This step of the project would tell them what had to be in the DSS database. They would then choose either an existing database management system or a platform and DBMS to use in building the required new one. The DBMS would be chosen at least in part for the availability of query and analysis tools that the supermarket chain's managers will need.

The previous paragraph, by the way, glossed over a topic that is often a key issue in DSS development because it does not arise in this particular example. That issue is data availability. The data managers need in order to make decisions may not be available on any of the organization's computers.

In that case the DSS developer must first determine whether the data in question—or alternative data, perhaps less ideal, but more easily obtained—can be brought into the system and, if so, how. Until the developer knows where all the necessary data are coming from, proceeding with system development is a risky activity.

Having determined the end points of their system, store personnel would look for a data communication protocol and file format that are common to both the store controllers and the database environment. Should they fail in this quest, they would reconcile themselves to writing file conversion routines and look for, at least, a common data communication protocol. This search should succeed. Most systems on which the DSS would run support a wide variety of communication protocols, and the people who develop store controllers know which protocols are popular. The DSS team would then be in a position to pull all the pieces together and bring consolidated sales data to decision makers' desks.

19.4 Types of Integrated Systems

There are, as we hinted in Section 19.2, several possible approaches to developing an integrated system. They differ along three principal dimensions, as portrayed in Figure 19–2. The three issues that correspond to the three axes of this cube are discussed in the next sections.

19.4.1 Single-System Visibility versus Multiple-System Visibilities

Does the system appear to its user as one integrated system or as multiple systems with the ability to transfer data among them? This can determine how easy it is to use a decision support system.

As a simple example, consider an integrated spreadsheet package such as Lotus 1-2-3, Excel, etc. It combines the ability to perform spreadsheet-style calculations with the ability to graph their output. Using such a system is easier than performing the calculations in a single-function spreadsheet package and then transferring its output to a single-function graphing package. Even with semi-automated data transfer approaches such as the Object Linking and Embedding (OLE) of Microsoft Windows or the Publish and Subscribe of the Macintosh, the user must still deal with two packages rather than one. This may be worth the effort if one or both of the single-function packages provides needed capabilities that integrated packages don't support, but it is still an added effort.

Executive information systems represent a situation where developers typically go to a great deal of trouble to provide single-system visibility. EIS

FIGURE 19–2

Integrated Systems Cube

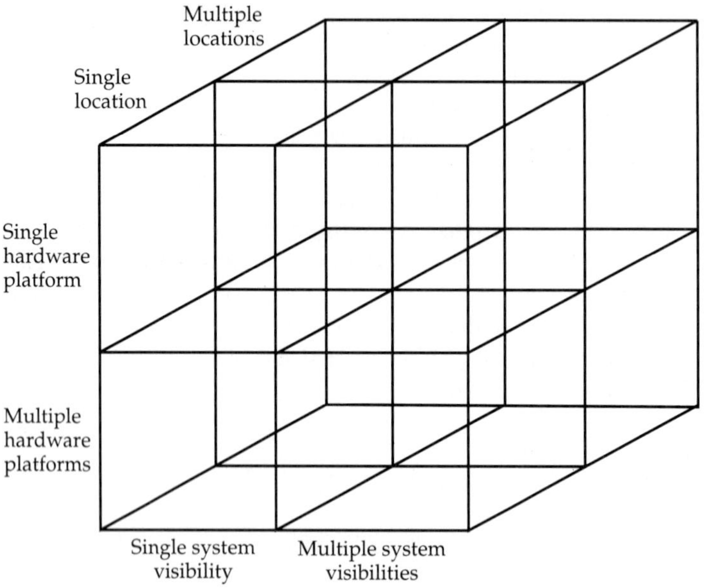

commonly allow the executive to access electronic mail, external databases, models, and more, all through a single interface. Here the trade-off is this: The executive's time is so valuable that the added development effort needed to reduce his or her learning time is worthwhile.

If the parts of a system are seldom or never used as a unit, creating single-system visibility may be a waste of time. In the supermarket example of Section 19.3, the people who update current selling prices in the store controller look-up tables are not the ones who make purchase decisions. There is no need to provide the appearance of a single system in this case.

19.4.2 *One Hardware Platform versus Multiple Hardware Platforms*

It is a fact of life that some applications are developed for some hardware architectures, whereas other applications are developed for other architectures. The user who wishes to use data from an existing mainframe database as input to a desktop publishing program on a microcomputer has no choice but to deal with two different platforms. In the supermarket example of Section 19.3, using a single platform for both systems might have been a theoretical possibility but was far from a practical one.

In other cases, using a single hardware and software platform is a practical option. Expert system development tools are available for a wide range of hardware types, quite possibly including the one that holds the database that an expert system will eventually have to access. In situations such as these, putting all parts of a total system on the same type of hardware, running in the same software environment (operating system, DBMS, etc.), will simplify the systems integration task.

The advantages of using compatible hardware may be a factor in package selection. Package A might be best for the job, but package B runs on the existing hardware. Package B will therefore be easier to integrate with other existing applications. We might select it for that reason. Is this a compromise? Yes, but either choice would be a compromise. (Indeed, most business decisions are compromises.) The people charged with package selection must weigh the benefits of having the capabilities of package A against the costs of integrating it. These costs may include a delay in making any capabilities available since package B could perhaps be brought up in a matter of days whereas package A would take weeks or months.

Using a combination of hardware platforms does not necessarily mean losing the benefits of a single, uniform system visibility to the user. The client/server approach to computing, which we discussed in Section 7.4, allows the client to invoke the assistance of the server as necessary. The user interface is entirely through the client, although much of the application may be executed on the server system.

Client/server integration is common when specialized processors are used to perform a specific part of a complex task. High-performance supercomputers may be the best way to process a complex financial model. Such systems are also totally unsuited to giving managers an easy way to access this model and, in any case, would not be cost effective in end-user interaction. Integrating a microcomputer or workstation client with a supercomputer server is a way to get the best of both worlds. Symbolic processors, which we discussed in Section 16.1.2, were often used in this way. (This was not referred to as client/server computing at that time, as symbolic processors fell into disuse before the phrase "client/server" became current, but the essence of client/server operation was there.)

Running software written for different architectures usually means using more than one computer, but it doesn't necessarily have to. It is possible for a computer to run programs originally written for a different architecture. This can be done via hardware or software:

- In the hardware approach, at the microprocessor level, the designer includes all of the necessary microprocessors in the system. Rare today, this approach is occasionally found as the last holdout of symbolic processors: A symbolic processing chip is added to an otherwise conventional microprocessor-based system to improve its performance in knowledge-based applications.
- A central processor can be designed to operate in more than one mode. This approach, called emulation, involves both hardware and

software [MALL72, MALL75]. It is usually used as a transition tool from one generation of computers to the next. Since the processor's older operating mode is considered out of date, using it for new DSS is not a practical approach.

- In the software approach, a simulator program is written for the *host computer* to mimic what the central processor of the *target computer* would do: fetch instructions, analyze them for operation codes and operands, carry out the requested operation, and repeat with the next instruction. This is a slow process. It is practical only when the host computer is fast and there is a strong reason to need software written for a different system.

None of these approaches is likely to surface as ideal in your next system integration job. Proceed under the assumption that if software written for different architectures must be run, it will run on different computers. You'll be right more than 99 percent of the time.

19.4.3 One Location versus Multiple Locations

The complexity of system integration is affected by the locations of the systems to be integrated. Communications or networking of any type makes the integration job more complex. The more complex the network, the more it increases the complexity of the integration task.

Systems that run on different hardware/software platforms almost always require some form of communication interface. (We discussed some exceptions in the previous section, but, as we noted there, these are rare.) Integrating systems via data communications involves the communication protocol and data interchange at the application level.

Communication protocols are becoming standardized, but new ones emerge to handle new requirements and technologies as fast as the older ones turn into widely used standards. This situation is not likely to stabilize during the current century. You will almost always be able to find a common local area or wide area protocol that all components of your system support.[1] Difficulties will emerge only if your application is one of those that gives rise to the aforementioned new requirements. If you have to send full-motion digital color video in real time, traditional networking technologies won't do the job. Before committing to a critical corporate application that depends on unproven technologies, look for an alternate way to meet the business need.

Data interchange may be more of a challenge. Sequential text files can usually be sent without much difficulty. You may have to write conversion

[1]During Honeywell Information Systems' transition from an older product line to a new one in the late 1970s, the only communication protocol via which its product lines could communicate with each other was IBM's binary synchronous protocol. While this was a source of short-term embarrassment to HIS salespeople, it got the job done.

routines at one or both ends to get data into and out of a useful interchange format and a common character set. Graphics, geographic data, voice, and video are far more of a challenge. There are few standards in these areas, and none have yet received general support. It is often easiest to process graphical data as completely as possible on its originating platform and transmit it in a "lowest common denominator" format for screen display at the user's desk. In more complex situations, often involving multimedia, consider standardizing on one vendor's products across the board even if they are not ideal for some part of the overall requirement. If this would mean too much of a compromise in application functionality, prepare yourself for a big SI job.

19.5 Trends in Systems Integration

Systems integration is growing in importance during the 1990s because information systems, and the issues surrounding information system development, are becoming more complex. Much of the reason for this, in turn, involves DSS and expert systems.

When systems were used solely for transaction processing, a user organization could pick a computer and develop its systems to run on that computer. Its systems were not necessarily simple, but at least they were all in one place. With DSS, one often has a transaction processing database in one place and managers who require access to it on another system. DSS, by requiring data gathered in one place for one purpose to be made available in another place for another purpose, has driven the need for SI.

A second reason for the growing importance of SI is the enormous proliferation of incompatible pieces of hardware and software throughout most organizations. Rapidly dropping prices have enabled every part of even a modest firm to obtain its own information-processing capability. Proper corporate planning can keep this mixture under a semblance of control but has seldom, if ever, been able to prevent it from occurring. (Even if it is under control, a merger or acquisition can come along to upset the carefully planned applecart.)

Other widespread trends are also increasing the need for SI. On-line databases require the integration of data from multiple sources. (The need for on-line databases, in turn, is often driven by decision support requirements.) Mission-critical systems that link firms with their suppliers and customers impose integration requirements. Attaching computers to functional devices such as cash registers and production equipment imposes such requirements also. In short, there are several driving forces in the expansion of SI.

SI allows an organization to accomplish information-processing tasks that it could not have accomplished, or could not have accomplished cost effectively, otherwise. The whole is worth, in many cases, more than the sum of its parts. The real value of an integrated information system is in bringing the parts together.

The major drawback of SI is equally clear if we think about it. The whole is also more complex than the sum of its parts. To develop a simple integrated system that combines two components, an organization must first be able to use the two parts individually. It must, in addition, be able to connect them to each other so that they can communicate. It must then be able to connect them in such a way that the resulting assemblage presents a single, or at least a uniform, interface to its users.

Major computer manufacturers have all developed architectures that attempt to unify their own products and make it easier to integrate them than to integrate products from multiple vendors. Thus, IBM's System Application Architecture has Common User Access, Common Programming Interface, Common Communications Support, and more. The intent is that a user who wishes to integrate a mainframe computer with several workstations will find it easier to do so with IBM products in these two categories than with, say, an IBM mainframe and workstations from Sun Microsystems. Other vendors have developed their own architectures with approximately the same intention. [FOLE90] summarizes 10 such architectures. Most of these architectures embody a degree of openness; that is, they are designed to accommodate both the vendor's products and those that conform to widely used standards such as the UNIX operating system. Adopting a vendor's overall architecture, especially where it does not restrict the user to that vendor's products, can simplify many low-level aspects of the systems integration task.

One way or another, with a vendor's architecture or the user's own, the user must pay to make all parts of its system work together. There are tradeoffs in choosing the way its components will be integrated:

- A user can obtain only compatible systems from the same firm. In this case the user pays via product compromises: No firm's offerings are best for every single part of almost any large-scale, enterprise-wide system. This approach corresponds to a home buyer choosing an existing house from those on the market at the time the choice is made.
- A user organization can perform the system integration task itself. In this case it pays by hiring (or engaging on a contract basis) the necessary specialized professionals and by devoting management time and energy to supervising their work. This corresponds to a home buyer acting as general contractor and building a house: finding and hiring carpenters, plumbers, electricians, roofers, etc.
- The third is for the organization to call in a systems integrator. This corresponds to the home buyer hiring a general contractor to find and supervise the specialized workers.

Systems integration requires skills that the average user organization does not possess—and does not need, at least on a full-time, permanent basis. Therefore, it also does not have managers who understand these skills well enough to supervise them properly. As a result, many user organizations contract with specialized systems integration firms. You may well find yourself working with a systems integration firm as you develop DSS on the job. In many cases your DSS will be one component of a larger system. Your employer will have engaged the SI firm, with its specialized skills, to develop some of the more complex pieces and to fit them all together.

The preference of user organizations to go outside for specialized skills accounts for the dramatic increase, during the late 1980s and early 1990s, in the number and size of firms offering systems integration services on a contract basis. According to *Computer Systems News*, the SI revenues of the top 50 U.S. firms totaled $10.7 billion in 1990 [ALPE91]. What's more, these firms were responsible for an additional $15 billion worth of purchases on the part of their customers. Clearly, SI is big business—and it's getting bigger. The top 25 systems integration firms, according to the Gartner Group of Stamford, Connecticut, are listed in Figure 19–3. Gartner Group estimates that the top 25 firms did $6.6 billion worth of SI work in 1992. Other firms have different estimates: SI is often one of many corporate activities, many SI firms do not disclose precise figures, and there is no universally accepted definition of what constitutes SI. All observers agree that the figure is large and growing.

Hiring a Systems Integrator

Information technology executives, as Mark Fischetti reports in [FISC92], offer these guidelines for selecting an outside systems integration firm:

1. Before seeking outside help, define—*on paper*—the business problem you are trying to deal with. "If you can't write it down," writes Fischetti, "no one will be able to solve it."
2. Get ideas from colleagues, from other companies in the same line of work as yours, and by asking in user groups.
3. Get a list of each contender's experience, and check references.
4. Test to see which of the contenders best understands your business. Knowing the technology is important but not as important as handling your kinds of applications. Watch out for those who know the answer before they study the question, who try to sell a preset package.
5. Make sure the candidates are willing to work at your location, with your people. Eventually you will have to maintain the system. Make sure the SI firm is willing to transfer its knowledge to you for this purpose.
6. Try to reach a comfortable level of rapport with the finalists.
7. Draw up a written contract with specific milestones and timetables.
8. Form an integrated team that includes both your firm's employees and those of the systems integrator.

FIGURE 19–3
List of Largest SI Firms (by 1992 revenues)

Company	SI Revenues*
1. IBM Corporation	1,623
2. Andersen Consulting	1,105
3. Electronic Data Systems (EDS)	1,094
4. Digital Equipment Corporation	650
5. Cap Gemini	246
6. Groupe Bull	145
7. American Management Systems	132
8. Siemens Nixdorf	123
9. SEMA Group	116
10. FINSEIL	107
11. SHL Systemhouse	99
12. Computer Sciences Corporation	95
13. LOGICA	95
14. Control Data Corporation	93
15. Ernst & Young	92
16. SLIGOS	89
17. Deloitte and Touche	87
18. SYSECA	86
19. Coopers & Lybrand	86
20. NYNEX	83
21. Olivetti Information Systems	79
22. General Electric Information Systems	74
23. Hughes Aircraft	74
24. Price Waterhouse & Company	70
25. Perot Systems	68

*All figures in millions of U.S. dollars
SOURCE: *InformationWeek*, November 30, 1992. Estimates by Gartner Group.

Since strategic information systems often involve networking—how else can one communicate among the different parts of a large firm or between a firm and its customers?—the growth in usage of strategic information systems has contributed to the growth in systems integration. To the extent that DSS are a part of strategic information systems, they too bear some responsibility for this phenomenon.

19.6 THE FUTURE OF DSS

We began this chapter with a look back at the "Management Information System" pipedream of the late 1960s. As we study decision support systems in the 1990s, we too can envisage the information systems world of the future.

In some ways it resembles that MIS. In other ways it does not. As this book is being written, it seems likely to evolve in these directions:

DSS capability will become a standard and expected part of information systems.
The history of information systems shows that new capabilities are first introduced as separate modules then incorporated into "regular" applications. You've seen this in graphing: once the task of separate programs, since the mid-1980s it has been an expected component of commercial spreadsheet software. As companies develop new applications in the future, decision support needs will increasingly be taken into account when they are planned rather than being added on (more or less well integrated) after the fact. This will impact the way databases are planned and organized, the way access to a system is controlled, the way an application uses standard interfaces and the "open systems" approach to computing.

Decision makers will become more computer literate.
You are personal evidence of this. It is already impossible to graduate from an accredited bachelor's or graduate program in management without having used spreadsheets and studied information systems. More and more programs go beyond this. They incorporate industry databases and management simulation "games" into strategic planning courses, statistical analysis into market research courses, project planning tools into operations management courses, and groupware technologies into organizational behavior courses. The managers you work with during your career will have a solid grounding in information technology and what it can do for them. They will increasingly be eager to cooperate in prototyping new applications to support their work.

Hardware technology will continue to evolve.
This is not news. Each time "experts" predict that the end of rapid progress is at hand, something comes along to prove them wrong.[2] As soon as supercomputers encounter fundamental physical limits in their speed, with each new gain obtained only at great cost, massively parallel computing comes along with a totally new way of achieving the same goal. This will continue. While no one can predict the precise direction in which technology will evolve, we can be sure that its evolution will not stop. You must keep an open mind for new approaches and be willing to try them.

"New" software technologies will enter the mainstream.
So-called new or emerging software technologies such as expert systems and voice recognition already proven their value in commercial use. Their users

---

[2]The head of the U.S. patent office in the 1890s urged Congress to shut that organization down because "everything useful has already been invented."

have been the pioneers or early adopters who first try any new technology: They gain the most if it succeeds but lose the resources they put into the attempt if it doesn't.

Usage will continue to evolve away from character-based interfaces.
The trend to graphical user interfaces is already clear. Microsoft is estimated to have shipped over eight million copies of Windows before the end of 1992, although it is not clear how many of these are in regular use.[3] Pen-based computing is a 1993 reality for specialized applications and is being rapidly enhanced by several vendors, large and small. Voice interaction is the foreseeable next step.

The job market for information systems professionals with a business perspective will remain strong.
The intelligent use of technology has reshaped human enterprises for thousands of years. Farming technology reshaped the lifestyle of our hunter-gatherer ancestors. Printing technology, then telegraph and telephone technology, reshaped communication. Steam technology reshaped transportation—after which internal combustion technology reshaped it again. Assembly lines reshaped manufacturing (which, in many firms today, is being reshaped again by taking assembly lines out).

The technology that is changing most rapidly always offers the most opportunities to redesign business processes to achieve organizational objectives more effectively. Today, the technology that is changing most rapidly is information systems technology. People who can harness that technology to the needs of the organization—people who understand both the technology and the business imperatives—will be those who create corporate success.

In Conclusion

The 19 chapters you have just completed took you on a journey through the world of decision support systems—from the concepts of decision making, through the ways in which computers can support decision making through some specific technologies (expert systems, executive information systems) that are used for this purpose. In this last chapter you looked at the ways in

[3]A large number of copies were shipped "bundled" with computers from several vendors. Nobody knows how many of the users of these systems actually use this software since the computers in question also come with MS-DOS and can operate without Windows. Other copies were purchased to try out and, after a trial, were put back on the shelf—often because the cost of upgrading the hardware for adequate Windows performance was prohibitive. Still others were bought to run one specific, rarely used, application that requires Windows. Whatever the true figure, the trend toward GUIs of all types is nonetheless clear.

which the pieces can be put together and some directions in which the field may evolve in the future.

You are now ready to take what you know and put it to use. Your other courses have taught you, or will teach you, about programming languages, database management, and the other technologies that the modern information systems professional must understand. When you combine these with what you now know about DSS, you will be able to make a real contribution to your employer's "bottom line."

Good luck!

Summary

Decision support systems are not, by themselves, the answer to management's information systems prayers. They are an important part of the piece, as are executive information systems, expert systems, group DSS, and all the other elements of the corporate information systems picture. For management to obtain the maximum benefit from its investment in information systems, they must be combined into an integrated whole.

That integrated system can be called a management support system. Such an MSS would provide easy-to-use access to internal and external databases, to a variety of useful models, to analysis and display capabilities, and to communications networks.

The process of pulling disparate systems together into such a unified whole is called systems integration. Systems integration, or SI, can be done at the hardware level, the software level, or both. The resulting system can appear to its users as one system or as several, can run on single or on multiple hardware platforms, and can be in a single location or in multiple locations.

Systems integration calls for the short-term use of skills that many firms do not possess. For that reason, information systems users with a need for SI often call on a specialized systems integration firms. Using them does not necessarily represent an added cost to the user since the user would otherwise have to assemble staff with those skills and also have to supervise their work with often-unfamiliar technologies. Systems integration firms are therefore growing rapidly.

Selecting a systems integration firm, if one is to be used, should be done as carefully as any other major corporate decision is made. The problem must be defined, each contender carefully evaluated, and references checked. The agreement with the SI firm must be based on a mutual understanding of the business problem and a sense of rapport, but it must still include a carefully written contract.

Decision support systems will grow in importance in the future, as expansion and standardization of communications and distributed databases make information more easily accessible from the manager's office. New hardware and software technologies will make DSS both easier to develop and easier to use. The information systems professional who works in this area will find himself or herself a valuable, and valued, contributor to organizational success.

Key Terms

emulation 617
host computer 618
Management Information System 610
management support system 611
systems integration 612
target computer 618

Review Questions

1. Of the three major components of most management information systems—databases, models, and communications—which do traditional decision support systems emphasize?
2. Which do group decision support systems emphasize? Executive information systems?
3. What is a management support system?
4. Define systems integration.
5. What does systems integration have to do with MSS?
6. When doesn't it matter if the parts of an integrated system don't "look integrated?"
7. How can you run software that was originally written for two different computers on one computer? Give three approaches.
8. How are DSS contributing to the growth in systems integration?
9. What do specialized systems integration firms offer that information systems users find of value?
10. Approximately how large is the total U.S. systems integration market?
11. Will decision support systems continue to be used in the future?
12. Are decision makers becoming more or less computer literate? Why?
13. When will computer hardware stop evolving?
14. Is it possible to find work supporting managers by developing decision support systems?

Exercises

1. Call the local sales offices of a few computer manufacturers or systems integration firms. (Use Figure 19–3, or a reference service in your college or university library, as a starting point for the names of SI firms.) Obtain their definitions of systems integration. Compare and contrast them with each other and with the two definitions at the start of Section 19.2. What common themes emerge from all their definitions?
2. Consider the supermarket systems integration example in Section 19.4. What type of decision(s) is(are) being made here? What type of DSS, in terms of the DSS hierarchy, is this? Is the statement that this DSS "most likely [runs on] a mainframe or large mini at corporate headquarters" reasonable? Why or why not?
3. The SoftPC package (Insignia Solutions Inc., Mountain View, California) runs on a Macintosh computer. It mimics the behavior of an Intel-family microprocessor, as used in IBM-compatible PCs, and of those computers' built-in input/output routines. It thus enables Macintosh users to run programs written for MS-DOS. Where does this fit into the spectrum of approaches to running programs written for different computers, discussed in Section 19.4.2? How might you use such a program if you had a Macintosh database and an MS-DOS cross-tabulation program that you wanted to use on the data it contained?
4. Pick a firm with which you are familiar. How could this firm benefit from pen-based computing? From voice recognition? How could you combine these technologies with its existing information systems? How difficult a job do you feel this would be?

References

ALPE91 Alper, Alan, Ed. "The Top 50 1991 Systems Integrators." special edition of *Computer Systems News,* June 3, 1991.

FISC92 Fischetti, Mark. "Hiring the Right Consultant." *Beyond Computing,* May/June 1992, p. 14.

FOLE90 Foley, Mary Jo. "10 Architectures That Will Boost Your Business." *Systems Integration* 23, no. 6 (June 1990), pp. 26–42.

MALL72 Mallach, Efrem G. "Emulation: A Survey." *Honeywell Computer Journal* 6, no. 4 (April 1972), pp. 287–97; reprinted in *Advances in Microprogramming.* Efrem G. Mallach and Norman E. Sondak, Eds. Artech House, Dedham, Mass. (1983).

MALL75 Mallach, Efrem G. "Emulator Architecture," *Computer* 8, no. 8 (August 1975), pp. 24–32; reprinted in *Advances in Microprogramming.* Efrem G. Mallach and Norman E. Sondak, Eds. Artech House, Dedham, Mass. (1983).

ENVOYANCE
FUTURE PLANS

"Surprise!" called out Dan, Sandra, Miguel, Bob, Chris, Jackie, Kareem, and the rest of the Envoyance staff as Adrienne and Doug came in for their regular Thursday afternoon visit. The conference room was decorated with "Congratulations" ribbons and there was a cake, with a college graduation cap and diploma in dark blue icing under an excellent rendition of the Harwich University seal.

"We know it's a few weeks early, but we're not really worried about you two making it," explained Dan. "Besides, with your project report due next week, you might not be coming back."

"How can you say that? How could we not come back?" asked Adrienne, astonished. "And just drop everything? We at least have to see how things come out on some of those bids!"

"Well, we were hoping you'd say something like that," said Sandra. "Actually, we were hoping for a bit more. Do you two have jobs yet?"

"Sorry, but I do," answered Adrienne with evident regret. "I interviewed with several companies that came to campus last semester, before this project started, and accepted a job right around the beginning of this term. I'll start their training program in early July."

"Well, Doug, how about you?" Dan followed up.

"Actually, Dan, I had been planning to go to graduate school and get by MBA. I've been accepted here at Harwich. I think I need more general business education to go with the technical stuff I've been focusing on until now. As soon as I got into Professor Khan's business strategy course, I realized that a few more electives in marketing and human behavior might have been at least as useful as the extra programming courses I took. If I get an MBA, I'll have the best of both worlds."

"Have you considered working for a few years and getting your MBA then?" Dan persisted.

"Now that you mention it, the MBA program people told me that most of their new students *do* have three or four years of work experience, and that it helps them in the classroom. It might not be a bad idea. Can I talk to you about it next week?"

APPENDIX A Data Flow Diagrams

Introduction

Data flow diagrams, or DFDs, are a clear and unambiguous way to record how data moves through an information system. That makes them a valuable communication tool for systems analysts: to users to make sure they understand an existing system, again to users to make sure a proposed system meets their needs, or to programmers to describe how a proposed system is to function.

This appendix will enable you to draw data flow diagrams. Its material applies whether you draw them by hand or, as is increasingly common, use computer-based tools to take care of the mechanics. These tools fall into a software category called CASE, for Computer-Aided System (or Software) Engineering. While CASE tools can prevent certain types of errors in drawing DFDs, the analyst must still describe the system to them in DFD terms. No CASE tool can make sure the diagrams truly reflect the system which the analyst meant to describe!

A.1 ABOUT DATA FLOW DIAGRAMS

A data flow diagram is a pictorial representation of how information flows through a system. Figure A–1 repeats the DFD of payroll processing you saw in Chapter 3. You don't have to be a payroll expert to see what's going on here. Employees submit time sheets. If nothing is wrong with a time sheet, it is put on the time sheet pile. Earnings are computed from the time sheets on the pile, checks are issued, and files are updated with new year-to-date totals. Also, cost reports are prepared for management and tax reports for government agencies. Armed with this diagram, you could study this system in more detail, computerize it, or—if you're the payroll manager—review someone else's plans to computerize it.

Data flow diagramming is important because data flow diagrams are the most common way of describing precisely how information flows through a system. As a DSS specialist or a professional in another field, you'll have to communicate with other people about the way DSS work, the way they should

FIGURE A–1

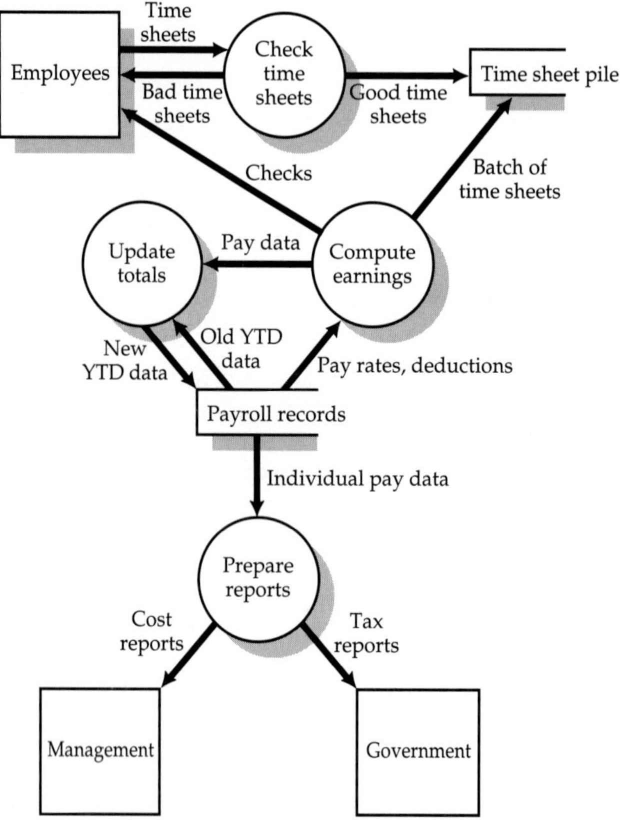

work, or the way they will work. Understanding data flow diagramming helps make this possible. Other means of describing system behavior exist, but they are imprecise (English), highly technical (HIPO diagrams), or less widely used.

Data flow diagramming is a *language*. It isn't a general-purpose language. You can't use it to order a pizza. But it *is* a language in the broad sense of the word: a structured means of communication with a *vocabulary* and a *grammar*. You'll see its vocabulary and its grammar below.

Written languages developed as a way to represent something else. Written human languages originally evolved as a more permanent representation of speech. Musical notation was developed to represent sounds. Programming languages represent processes a computer will carry out. Data flow diagrams represent an existing, planned, or possible information system.

Just as we can create combinations of words in human languages that are not sentences, we can create nonsense data flow diagrams. Studying language rules (grammar) can prevent this both in English and in data flow diagrams.

It is also possible in human languages to write sentences that are technically correct but are not meaningful—"I fed the chair"—or to write sounds in musical notation that can be created on an instrument but are unpleasant to hear. Likewise, we can draw a data flow diagram of an inefficient information system or one that does not produce the desired results. An advantage of using DFDs is that we can study and improve systems on paper, without having to build them in order to try them out.

A.2 THE DATA FLOW DIAGRAMMING VOCABULARY

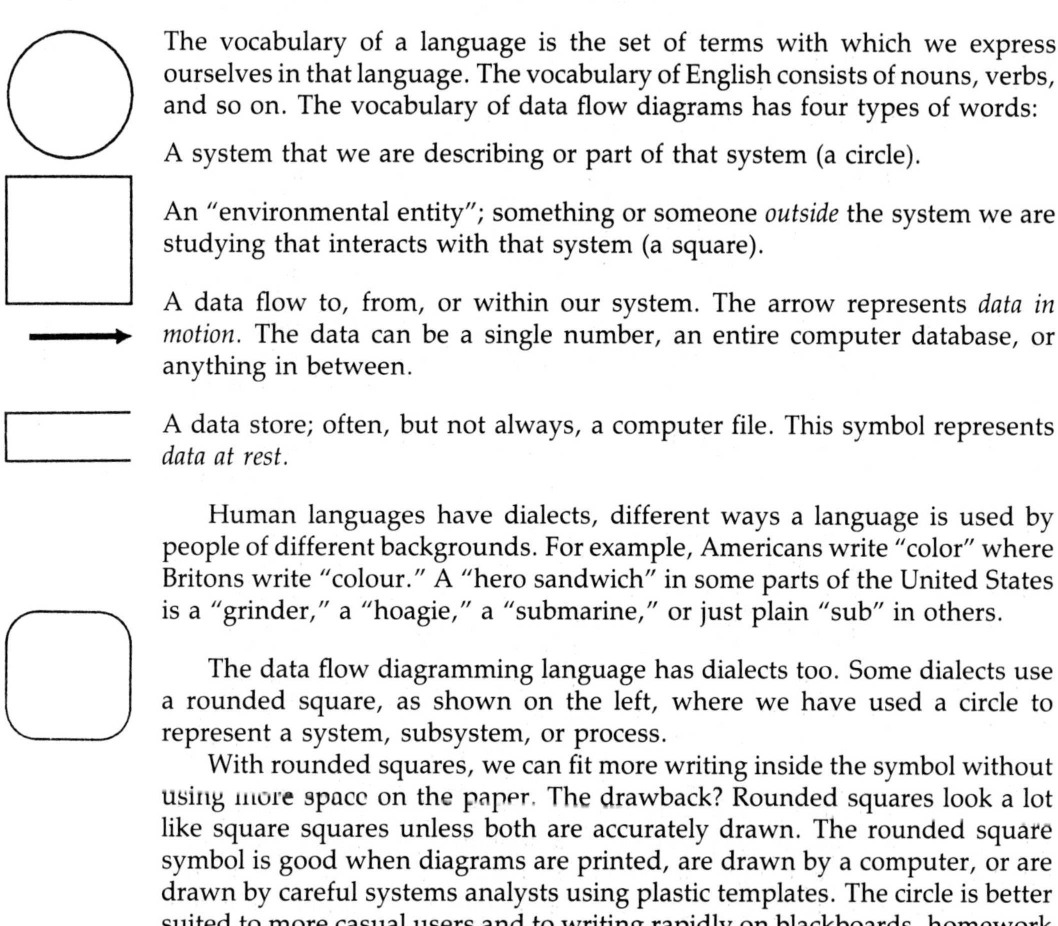

The vocabulary of a language is the set of terms with which we express ourselves in that language. The vocabulary of English consists of nouns, verbs, and so on. The vocabulary of data flow diagrams has four types of words:

A system that we are describing or part of that system (a circle).

An "environmental entity"; something or someone *outside* the system we are studying that interacts with that system (a square).

A data flow to, from, or within our system. The arrow represents *data in motion.* The data can be a single number, an entire computer database, or anything in between.

A data store; often, but not always, a computer file. This symbol represents *data at rest.*

Human languages have dialects, different ways a language is used by people of different backgrounds. For example, Americans write "color" where Britons write "colour." A "hero sandwich" in some parts of the United States is a "grinder," a "hoagie," a "submarine," or just plain "sub" in others.

The data flow diagramming language has dialects too. Some dialects use a rounded square, as shown on the left, where we have used a circle to represent a system, subsystem, or process.

With rounded squares, we can fit more writing inside the symbol without using more space on the paper. The drawback? Rounded squares look a lot like square squares unless both are accurately drawn. The rounded square symbol is good when diagrams are printed, are drawn by a computer, or are drawn by careful systems analysts using plastic templates. The circle is better suited to more casual users and to writing rapidly on blackboards, homework assignments, and tests. We use circles in this book. You may find rounded squares in other books or on the job.

Some data flow diagram dialects use two parallel horizontal lines to represent a data store, where we used a rectangle open on the right.

There are two major DFD dialects. Gane-Sarson DFDs use rounded rectangles for processes and open-ended rectangles for data stores. Yourdon-DeMarco DFDs use circles for processes and parallel lines for data stores. Most CASE packages will let the user generate either from the same system description but will not produce a hybrid such as using circles for processes and open-ended rectangles for data stores.

A.3 Data Flow Diagramming Grammar

The grammar of a language tells how to combine vocabulary elements into correct sentences. In English we can say, "Feed the cat," but we cannot properly say, "Feed cat the." Data flow diagram grammar has four rules:

1. ○, □, and [are connected via →.
2. If one end of → is □ or [, the other end must be ○.
3. Every ○, □, and [must connect to at least one →.
4. Every symbol of any type must be labeled.

Some DFD dialects change these rules slightly. One variation modifies rule 4 to allow unlabeled → data flows if their content is "obvious." Unfortunately, one person's "obvious" is another person's "what on earth is going on here?" What's obvious to a trained systems analyst, who has studied a billing system for weeks, may not be obvious to a shipping dock supervisor seeing a data flow diagram for the first time in his or her life.

A second variation adds rule 5: *All subsystems and processes must be numbered for reference.* This is necessary when several diagrams are related to each other. Since most systems take up more than one diagram, this rule is widely used in real-world data flow diagramming. In a free-standing DFD, not related to any other diagrams, we may leave the numbers off. Numbering processes can never hurt. It's a good habit to get into.

A.4 A Simple Data Flow Diagram

Figure A–2 represents a computerless information system in which you and a friend decide when to see a movie. It's drawn from your friend's viewpoint; she's the information processing system. She receives information from you about when you can see the movie and from her calendar about when she isn't busy. She then picks a time to see the movie and tells you when it will be. You are outside the system and are drawn as a square symbol. She is inside the system—in fact, she is the only component of this system—and is drawn as a circle. The calendar is a data store with information about her schedule.

FIGURE A–2
Example of Computerless Information System

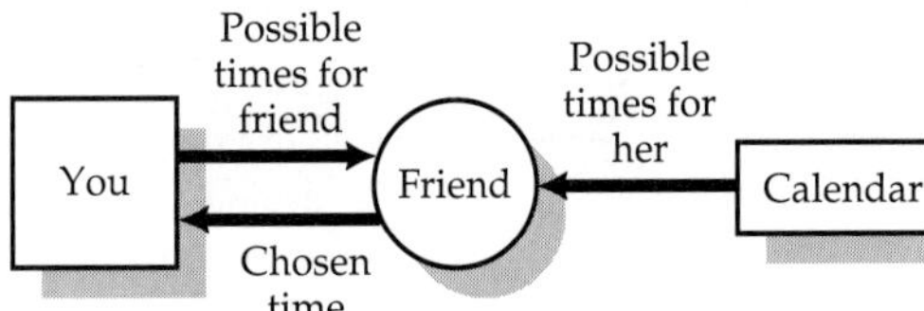

Data flow diagrams do not show timing. Here we understand the timing relationships among the data flows intuitively. First, you activate the system by suggesting possible times. Second, your friend checks those times on her calendar and picks one. Third, she tells you which of the times you suggested is best. These timing relationships must be described somewhere other than the data flow diagram.

In a more complex system, several data flows may be going on at once. In a large company, one person may write a purchase order, while another person enters payroll data into a computer, and a third records items that are out of stock in the warehouse. The fact that all these things can go on at the same time is also not shown on a data flow diagram.

This is an example of an important principle. *One system description method can't tell us everything we might want to know about an information system.* Data flow diagrams can't. Neither can any other method. Methods that provide timing information fall short in other ways. In any situation, we must choose description methods that convey the information we need in that situation. Most of the time, to communicate between information systems professionals and knowledge workers in other fields, data flow diagrams are part of the answer.

A.5 A More Complicated Data Flow Diagram

Figure A–3 repeats the diagram we used at the beginning of this appendix. One difference: We've numbered the processes because we'll split some of them into more detailed DFDs in the next section. Process numbers help us see how diagrams relate to each other in describing different aspects of a system.

As with the previous example, this DFD doesn't show timing. Employees may submit time sheets at various times during the week. They might be checked at once, or at the end of the day for all the time sheets that came in during the day, or all in a batch at the end of the week. The DFD doesn't (and can't) say. Earnings are computed all at once for a batch of time sheets, probably weekly. Totals are presumably updated right after the earnings are computed and the checks sent out. Different reports may have different

FIGURE A–3

DFD of Payroll Processing with Process Numbers Added

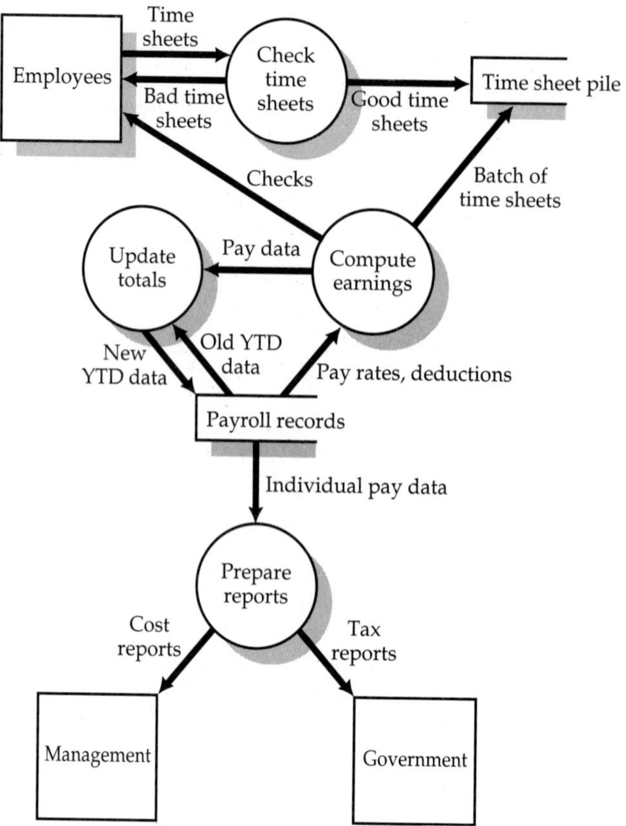

schedules: management reports weekly or monthly; government reports monthly, quarterly, or annually. A more detailed breakdown of process 4, prepare reports, could show different categories.

There are two data stores in this DFD. One, the time sheet pile, is not in a computer. This data store exists to deal with the timing difference between the approval of a time sheet and its processing. If earnings were computed immediately after a time sheet was checked, we would never have *data at rest*. Consequently, we would not have a data store.

The other data store, payroll records, may or may not be in a computer. Most firms use computers to process payroll, but some small ones do not. All must keep payroll records. The content of the records is the same in either case. This DFD does not show the physical form in which we store the data; it merely records the fact that we store it. Technically, that makes our data flow diagram a *logical data flow diagram.* Had we shown the physical form of the data stores and flows, it would be a *physical data flow diagram.*

Data stores exist for either or both of the above two reasons: because of a timing mismatch between two processes or because we need to retain data after its creation for later use.

Three environmental entities interact with our system: employees, management, and the government. Before you start a DFD you must decide what is inside the system and what is an environmental entity. Here we decided that employees and managers are not part of the system we are studying.

You may ask, "Aren't managers employees too?" They are. Some people may both submit time sheets and receive reports. However, they do these things in two different roles. We are concerned with the jobs people do in a data flow diagram, not with their actual identity. In submitting a time sheet, a person is playing the role of an employee; in receiving a report, the role of a manager.

When you first draw a data flow diagram with this many symbols, you'll find that your lines cross, your paper is crowded in one corner but empty in another, and the whole thing doesn't look nearly as nice as the printed examples in this book. That's normal! Data flow diagramming skill improves with practice. Even seasoned pros revise DFDs several times before they are satisfied with the way those diagrams look.

A.6 Leveled Data Flow Diagrams

Many systems are too complicated to fit into one data flow diagram. We could try, but the DFDs would be so cluttered with tiny symbols that it would be impossible to follow. In this case, we use a set of DFDs. We begin with a *top-level data flow diagram* to show its major subsystems and the data flows among those subsystems. These tend to be the most important data flows in the system. Then, we draw a data flow diagram showing each subsystem in more detail. This diagram shows the data flows into and out of that subsystem. It also shows the processes that take place within that subsystem and the data flows among those processes.

Consider process 2, compute earnings, in the payroll DFD. It consists of several subprocesses shown in the *second-level DFD* (Figure A–4). Process 2 has been broken down into four subprocesses, numbered 2.1 through 2.4. By using this consistent numbering scheme, we can relate this diagram to process 2 in the top-level DFD.

Every input to process 2 in the original diagram is an input to at least one subprocess in the new one. Similarly, every output from the original process 2 is an output from some subprocess here. This is important. Inputs and outputs cannot appear out of nothing or disappear into nothing as we go from one level to

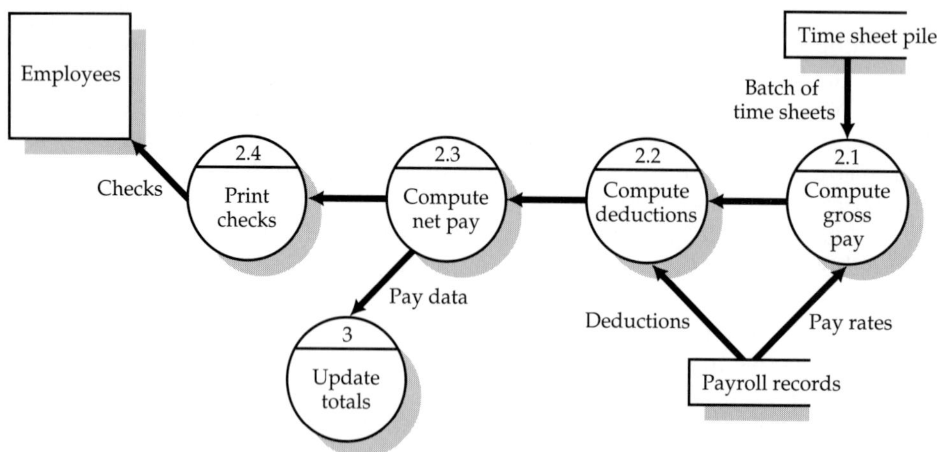

the next. Since subprocesses 2.1 through 2.4, as a group, add up to the original process 2, they must have the same aggregate inputs and outputs as it did. In addition to the processes into which we have broken down the original process 2, our second-level DFD shows the sources of every input to process 2 and the destinations of every output from it. CASE systems can often enforce this rule, thus preventing mistakes.

Sometimes an exception is made for "minor" data flows that are not important enough to show in a top-level DFD. This should be done with caution and only when a particular data flow is rare in practice. For example, an occasional time sheet mistake might make it past the checking process and be caught in process 2, compute earnings. We wouldn't want to clutter up the top-level DFD with this rare event, but we might want to show it at the next level of detail.

This particular second-level data flow diagram has no internal data stores. However, there can be data stores used only within a process and not visible outside it. Such data stores appear in a second-level (or even lower level) data flow diagram for the first time. They need not be shown in the top-level DFD.

Sometimes we want to break down one of the subprocesses in a second-level data flow diagram still further. Suppose we wanted to break down process 2.2, compute deductions, into separate processes for insurance, retirement, and taxes. We would number those 2.2.1, 2.2.2, and 2.2.3. Or, the earnings computation could be quite complex. It might involve hourly, weekly, piecework, commission, and bonus pay. Each of these might use data from different sources. Figuring commissions, for example, could require data from a sales database.[1] It could easily take one or two more levels to describe these data flows fully.

How far down should you go in drawing a leveled set of DFDs for a system? At some level you will find calculation or decision making, not data flow, to be the essence of a process. When you reach this level, don't break that process down any further. Describe the calculations or decisions by another method. You might use English, structured English, a decision table, a decision tree, or a mathematical formula. The choice depends on what you are describing.

You may want to go down to different levels for different parts of your system. In our original payroll example, the process of updating the year-to-date totals in the payroll file is quite simple. You might break it down one more level or not at all. However, it might take two more levels to describe the data flows for computing earnings and deductions fully. You need not take every process to the same level.

Individual data flow diagrams are related via the numbering scheme. A person looking at a DFD containing processes 3.1.4.1, 3.1.4.2, 3.1.4.3, and so on, knows that this DFD amplifies process 3.1.4. He or she can find the DFD for process 3.1 to see how 3.1.4 fits into the overall picture.

A.7 Another Look at Grammar Rule 2

Data flow diagramming grammar rule 2 was:

2. If one end of → is □ or ⊏⊐, then the other end must be ○.

The reason for this rule is that exceptions to it can't make sense. If one of your diagrams violates this rule, you have a problem at that point. This may mean you have left out a process. Let's see what it can mean if you violate rule 2. There are four ways to violate it:

a. □ → □ means one environmental entity sends data to another. In the real world, perhaps it does. In a DFD, such a data flow is entirely outside the boundaries of the system we're describing. It is therefore not relevant to our system. Any data flow that does not directly involve a process in our system should not be in its DFD.

b. □ → ⊏⊐ means that an environmental entity enters data directly into a data store in our system. This is impossible. There

[1]If we need the sales database for this purpose, this database must be shown on this data flow diagram. It would appear at this level, sending data to process 2.1. It could also appear at the top level, sending data to process 2, compute earnings.

must be a process of some sort—even if it's trivial—to accept data from the outside world and store it away.

c. ▭ → □ is the reverse of part *b.* Again, we need a process to generate the reports or to send the data that leave our system. Data can't get up and leave by themselves.

d. ▭ → ▭ means that one data store is sending data directly to another. Data stores are inanimate objects. They can't do that. A process must exist to move the data. Even if the process doesn't change the content of the data store, it has to be there for the motion to take place.

A.8 The Context Diagram

A top-level data flow diagram shows the major processes within a system and how data flows among these processes. Sometimes we want even a more simplified view than that: a "bird's-eye view" of how our system fits into its environment, with no internal details at all. That's the purpose of the *context diagram*. Think of the context diagram as an extra-high-level DFD. The context diagram of our payroll system is shown in Figure A–5.

In terms of our system's relationship to the outside world, this diagram is *exactly* the same as the top-level DFD. It shows the same time sheets coming from employees, the same bad time sheets and checks going to them, the same reports going to management and the government. Every external entity, every data flow that enters or leaves the system in the top-level DFD is in the context diagram and vice versa. The difference is that the internal processes, data stores, and data flows have been replaced by one circle representing the entire system.

A.9 Drawing a Set of Data Flow Diagrams

The context diagram is a good place to begin drawing a set of data flow diagrams. Drawing the context diagram forces you to decide precisely what's inside your system and what isn't. It forces you to decide what data flows enter and leave your system. Once you know these, you can go on to the top-level DFD. Here, put in the processes that accept the inbound data flows and the processes that generate the outbound data flows. Then, add the rest of the internal processes and data stores until the system is complete.

This diagramming procedure is essentially the same for documenting an existing system or describing one that does not yet exist. There is one difference in how you approach it, however.

FIGURE A–5

Context Diagram of Payroll System

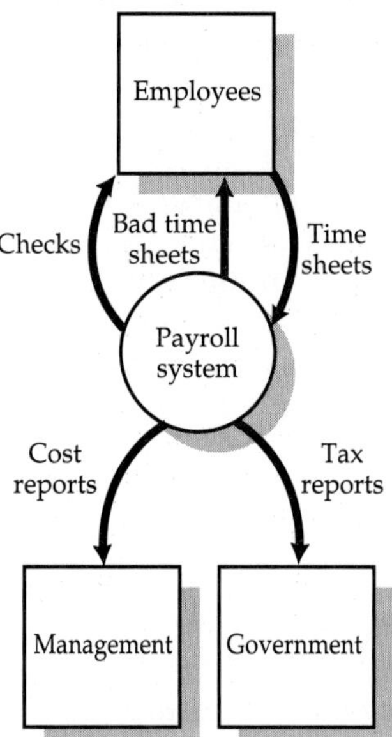

When you document an existing system, you will start by studying the system or reading about it. (On the job, you'll usually study a system. In college, you'll usually read about it.) In either case you'll make a list of processes and data stores that form the bottom level of your system. These processes and data stores now have to be organized, from the bottom up, into a layered set of DFDs. If you try to put them all into the same DFD, that DFD will be so crowded it will be almost useless. You have to collect sets of processes into subsystems. If you still have too many subsystems, group them into larger subsystems. Eventually you will have few enough subsystems to create a top-level data flow diagram. The individual processes, or perhaps lower level subsystems, will form the lower levels of the set of DFDs.

How is designing a system from scratch different? You can't study the system or read about it because it doesn't (yet) exist. When you design a system from scratch, you usually start with an overall idea of how the system will work. This gives you its major subsystems right away. Then, you can go into each subsystem in detail and define its processes. This is a "top-down" procedure. It's usually easier to create a well-structured system via a top-down procedure than it is with a bottom-up procedure.

There's no fixed rule about how to cluster processes into subsystems. Different analysts will do this differently, ending up with different sets of DFDs for the same system. A good guideline to follow is, as much as possible, to group processes that communicate mostly with each other. Keep the number of data flows between subsystems to a minimum. If two processes have several data flows between them, or if three processes share a data store that no other processes use, use these groups and others like them as a starting point for your subsystems. Systems analysis and software engineering courses can provide more guidance.

How many processes or subsystems should be on one DFD? Let clarity and legibility guide you. About 15 or 20 symbols (processes, data stores, and external entities) on a full-page, carefully drawn DFD is the maximum. If data flows are few and simple, put in a few more. If there are many data flows connecting the processes, with arrows running all over the page and crossing each other, use fewer. When in doubt, try your diagram on a friend to see if it's reasonably clear. If the friend says it's too crowded, don't argue! Group processes into subsystems and draw another.

APPENDIX B VP-Expert

Introduction

This appendix introduces VP-Expert and lists its commands with brief explanations of each. It is not a full textbook on VP-Expert. That would be as large as this book. This appendix has a more modest goal: to provide you with a reference to the most important VP-Expert commands and operations.

VP-Expert is a low-end shell but supports most important expert system features. It has forward and backward chaining and database access. With its integrated editor and the simple structure of its knowledge base, it provides an easy way to learn about expert systems. Its major limitation is that it supports only character string-valued variables. When your needs grow and VP-Expert no longer suffices, you will be able to learn a more feature-rich system easily.

VP-Expert operates in two modes: editing and consultation. You create a knowledge base in editing mode and run it in consultation mode. We'll start by looking at a short consultation. Then we'll go over to editing mode and look at the knowledge base that this consultation used. Finally, we'll cover the commands you can use to create a more complicated knowledge base.

B.1 A SAMPLE CONSULTATION

Our "mini-consultation" is shown on the screen in Figure B–1. (This consultation uses the same knowledge base as Section 14.3.2.) The screen is divided into three parts. The consultation window is across the top. Your program displays its output here. When you type information into your program, it also goes here. You can make this window occupy the whole screen and create additional consultation windows, if you wish. The bottom left window shows the rules in your system as they are being evaluated. The bottom right window shows the facts that your system gathers as it runs. The two bottom

FIGURE B–1
Sample Consultation Display

```
[ KBS: SAMPLE ]
I will tell you what to do. Press any key.

Are you hungry?
 yes                     no◀

Do you have any homework?
 yes                     no◀

You should see a movie.
```

```
[ RULES ]
Finding is_hungry
Testing 2
RULE 2 IF
is_hungry = no and
has_homework = no
THEN
activity = see_a_movie CNF 100
Finding has_homework
```

```
[ FACTS ]
is_hungry = no CNF 100
has_homework = no CNF 100
activity = see_a_movie CNF 100
```

```
1Help    2Go    3WhatIf   4Variable 5Rule   6Set    7Edit    8Quit
1Help 2How? 3Why? 4Slow 5Fast 6Quit
```

windows can be a blur, but you can slow VP-Expert to read them as they go by.

The top window of our sample consultation starts with a line describing the system. The system then asked two questions: Are we hungry?, and Do we have homework? We answered "no" to both. In the bottom right window, the system assigned the value "no" to the variables *is_hungry* and *has_homework.* Using its rules, part of which can be seen in the bottom left window, the system then suggested that we should see a movie.

B.2 THE KNOWLEDGE BASE

Figure B–2 shows the knowledge base behind this consultation. It's short but has all the elements of a full-scale knowledge base:

1. The ACTIONS block, which directs the overall consultation process.
2. The rules, which reflect "expert" knowledge.
3. Additional specification statements that control how the system behaves.

FIGURE B–2

Sample Knowledge Base (same as FIGURE 17–2A)

```
!This knowledge base recommends an evening activity

ACTIONS
DISPLAY "I will tell you what to do. Press any key ~"
FIND activity
DISPLAY "You should {activity}.";

RULE 1
IF hungry = yes
THEN activity = eat;

RULE 2
IF hungry = no
AND homework = yes
THEN activity = do_homework;

RULE 3
IF hungry = no
AND homework = no
THEN activity = see_a_movie;

ASK hungry: "Are you hungry?";
ASK homework: "Do you have homework?";

CHOICES hungry, homework: yes, no;
```

The ACTIONS block of this expert system has three commands:

1. DISPLAY. The text between the two sets of quotation marks appeared on screen at the top of the consultation window in Figure B–1.
2. FIND. This command starts the backward chaining process by instructing VP-Expert to find a value for a variable called *activity*. The VP-Expert inference engine decides which rules may help it find the needed value and invokes them in the order it sees fit.
3. A second DISPLAY command to display the result of the consultation. The text in quotation marks says `{activity}` where the consultation window displayed `see a movie`. Braces around a variable name tell VP-Expert to substitute the value of that variable before displaying the text. Since rule 2

assigned the value `see a movie` to the variable *activity,* VP-Expert displayed `see a movie` as part of its answer.

Our knowledge base has three rules. They fit situations where you (1) are not hungry and have homework, (2) are not hungry and don't have homework, and (3) are hungry. Each rule assigns a value to the output variable *activity*. In a more complex knowledge base, most rules assign values to intermediate variables. Such a knowledge base takes several steps to get from its inputs to its output.

The ASK statements at the end of the knowledge base tell VP-Expert how to phrase its questions if it needs values for *is_hungry* and *has_homework.* You can see these questions in the consultation window in Figure B–1. VP-Expert asks these questions automatically when it decides it needs values for these variables and can't get the values from other rules. The CHOICES statement after the ASK statement constrains the user's answers. Because of this statement, "Yes" and "No" were on the screen after each question. In the absence of a CHOICES statement in the knowledge base, VP-Expert allows the user to enter any character string as the value of a variable.

About VP-Expert Variables

Variable names in VP-Expert may be up to 40 characters long and may not contain spaces. Use the underscore, as in the names *is_hungry* and *has_homework* above, to make multiword names and values more legible to humans while satisfying the "no spaces" rule.

VP-Expert variables take character strings as their values. You can assign a variable the value "true," "yes," "pepperoni," "Susan," or "3.1416." Values, like variable names, may be up to 40 characters long and may not contain spaces. Use underscores instead of spaces here as well. When VP-Expert displays the value of a variable on the screen, it replaces underscores by spaces to improve legibility.

Some variables in VP-Expert can take on several values at the same time. Variables that can have several values are called *plural variables*. You must tell VP-Expert that a variable is a plural variable. The PLURAL command that you use to do this is described later in this appendix, along with additional information about plural variables. New values for plural variables are added to those it already has. A new value for a single-valued variable (i.e., those that are not plural) replaces any value that the variable already has.

Unlike some expert system shells and most programming languages, VP-Expert does not have numeric or Boolean (true or false) variables. If you try to use a non-numeric string in an arithmetic calculation, VP-Expert will complain—but the error will be detected when you try to use the improper value,

---

[1]You can constrain user input to numeric values in a given range by the RANGE command. It is described in Section B.6.2.

not when you enter it.[1] The lack of Boolean variables can cause confusion: "true" is not, to VP-Expert, the opposite of "false." It is simply a different value. Not being "true" isn't the same, in VP-Expert's world, as being "false."

B.3 Navigating the VP-Expert System

VP-Expert is quite simple to use once you understand its structure. This section will give you enough information to proceed. It assumes that you already know basic MS-DOS commands and operations. If you don't, you can learn enough to get in and out of VP-Expert in a few minutes or find someone to help you.

VP-Expert starts with the screen shown in Figure B–3. It resembles the consultation window of Figure B–1, but it has a welcoming message instead of a consultation. Below the three windows are two rows of menus. VP-Expert uses a multilevel menu system similar to those you might have used in Lotus 1-2-3 or other programs. The upper menu line is active. The lower line tells you what will happen, or what further menus you will find, if you select the currently highlighted entry on the upper line. When you invoke an entry that shows a menu on the lower line, that line moves up to the upper level and a new lower line appears.

Figure B–3

VP-Expert Welcome Screen

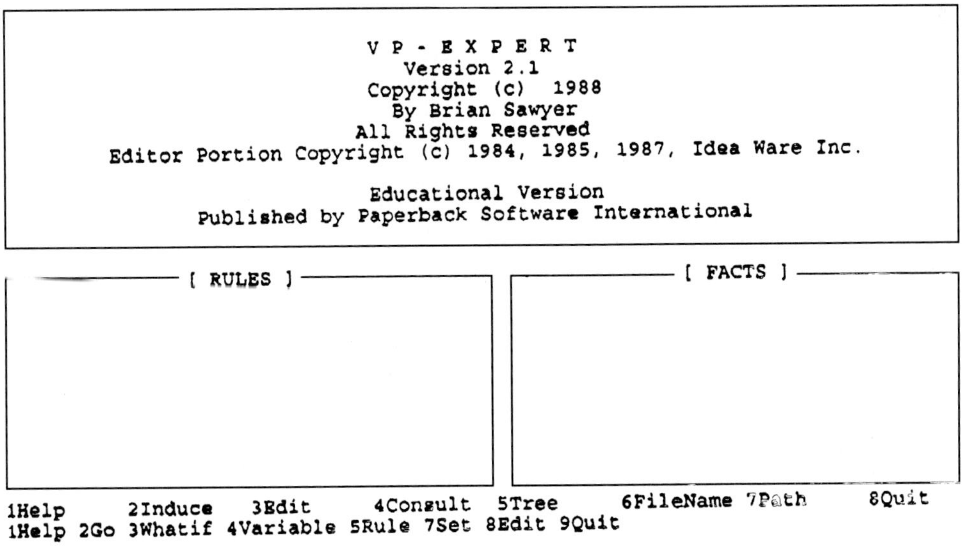

```
                          V P - E X P E R T
                             Version 2.1
                          Copyright (c)  1988
                            By Brian Sawyer
                          All Rights Reserved
      Editor Portion Copyright (c) 1984, 1985, 1987, Idea Ware Inc.

                          Educational Version
               Published by Paperback Software International

 ------------- [ RULES ] ------------    ----------- [ FACTS ] ----------

1Help     2Induce    3Edit     4Consult  5Tree     6FileName 7Path     8Quit
1Help 2Go 3Whatif 4Variable 5Rule 7Set 8Edit 9Quit
```

You can invoke menu commands in four ways: by pressing the corresponding function key, by pressing the corresponding number key, by typing the first letter of the command, or by highlighting a desired command via cursor control (arrow) keys and then pressing <Enter>. To go to the editor from the top-level menu you can press 3, press F3, press E, or press <Cursor Right> and <Cursor Left> until Edit is highlighted and then press <Enter>. It makes no difference which you choose. (This does not apply to menus in Edit mode. Menus work differently in that mode. Edit mode is described, with its menus, in Section B.4.) The eight top-level menus described below appear from left to right on your screen. All VP-Expert menu commands are listed hierarchically in Section B.7.

Help Not useful with the student edition of VP-Expert. It doesn't come with Help files. Try it if you want to see. You won't hurt anything.

Induce Lets VP-Expert figure out rules that could produce a set of decisions that you present to it. While this capability can be useful, as you can read in Section 17.3.7, it's not a good way to learn about how expert systems work, so we don't cover it here.

Edit Switches the VP-Expert system to Edit mode, described in the next section. If you are working with a knowledge base, the editor will display that one. You can choose to edit a different one via Filename (below). If you haven't told it which knowledge base to use yet, it will ask you. In either case, you can only specify a knowledge base in your current working directory. To edit a knowledge base in a different directory, you must first make that directory the current working directory via Path (below).

Consult Runs a consultation. As with Edit, this command continues to use the knowledge base you are using unless you instruct VP-Expert to change. If you are starting a run and haven't told it which knowledge base to use yet, it will ask you. Again as with Edit, you can only specify a knowledge base in your current working directory. To use a knowledge base in a different directory, make that directory the current working directory via Path (below).

Trace Tells you, after a consultation, which rules were used. For this to work you must activate tracing via the Set menu entry: after you choose Consult and before you start the actual consultation by choosing Go. The best way to learn what Trace does is to try it.

Filename Tells VP-Expert which knowledge base to use. When you choose Filename, you will see a list of the knowledge bases in your current working directory. Use the arrow keys to highlight one and then press <Enter>. If you realize, as you look at this list, that the knowledge base you want to use is in a different working directory, press <Escape> to close the window, use Path to select the proper directory, and then invoke Filename again. To start a new knowledge base, type its name when the Filename window opens. It will be given a .KBS extension, if you didn't type an extension yourself, and will be placed in your current working directory.

Path Lets you change to a different working directory. You must use Path before Filename in order to access a knowledge base that is not in the current working directory. Provide the full pathname of the desired directory, including its disk, as in `C:\MYDIR\PROJECT.` (The period there ends the sentence. It is not part of the MS-DOS pathname.)

Quit Exits VP-Expert and returns to MS-DOS. When Quit appears in lower level menus, it brings you up a level each time you press it until you reach the top level. Pressing <Escape> is the same as choosing Quit.

Here's how to do some of the common things you will want to do with VP-Expert:

To run an existing knowledge base in your current working directory: Choose Filename, select the knowledge base you want with the arrow keys, press <Enter>, choose Consult to get the consultation mode menu, and choose Go. If you choose Consult directly after starting VP-Expert, before you have selected any knowledge base, it will, in effect, invoke Filename automatically for you.

To run an existing knowledge base in a different working directory: Choose Path, type the pathname of the working directory that has the knowledge base you want, and press <Enter>. Then continue as above.

To modify an existing knowledge base: Identify it by using Path (if necessary) and Filename as above. Then select Edit to enter the editor.

To create a new knowledge base: If it is to be in a different working directory than the one you are now in, choose Path, and type the pathname of that directory. Then choose Filename. Instead of using the arrow keys to choose an existing knowledge base, type the name of the new one. If you don't type the .KBS extension, VP-Expert will add it for you. Press <Enter>, then choose Edit. You will see a blank editor screen with the name of your knowledge base in the top right corner. Start typing.

B.4 THE VP-EXPERT EDITOR

You use the VP-Expert editor to create and modify your knowledge base. You can also use a word processor or text editor if you give your file name the extension .KBS. Using the built-in editor is usually easier because you can move easily between editing mode and consultation mode without leaving VP-Expert.

To create a knowledge base in VP-Expert, just enter Edit mode and type it. Use cursor keys to move around the screen. Navigation commands are similar to those of most MS-DOS word processing programs. The <Page Up>

and <Page Down> keys move you through your program a screenful at a time. <Page Up>, if pressed with <Control> held down, takes you to the start of your program. Similarly, <Control> <Page Down> takes you to its end.

You should also know these three control commands:

1. <Control><Enter> creates a new blank line above the current cursor position. Use it to enter new lines in the middle of an existing knowledge base. The cursor should usually be at the start of the line before you issue this command. If it's in the middle of a line, VP-Expert will split the current line in two at the cursor position. This is occasionally, but only rarely, useful. Note that <Control><Enter> does not move the cursor to the new blank line. The cursor stays with the line of text where it had been. This is now the line below the new blank line you created. Follow <Control><Enter> with <Up Arrow> to enter text into the blank line you have just created.
2. <Control>T erases from the cursor position to the end of the line.
3. <Control>Y erases the entire line containing the cursor, from beginning to end.

Additional editor commands are in a menu at the bottom of the screen. This menu changes when you press the <Alt> key, the <Control> key, or the Shift key, for a total of four different menus. Three important menu commands are:

1. <Alt>F5 (pressing function key 5 while you hold down the <Alt> key) saves changes you have made so far and keeps VP-Expert in editing mode. Do this every few minutes in a long editing session, as you never know when the power will fail or some other disaster will befall your machine. Whenever VP-Expert saves a new version of your program, it appends the file name extension .KBS to that version and saves the previous version with the same file name and the extension .BAK. The previous .BAK file—that is, the next-to-last version—is discarded.
2. <Alt>F6 saves your program and returns VP-Expert to consultation mode to run it. If you answer "N" when it asks if you want to save your knowledge base under its current name, you will be able to type a new name. This lets you save a new version of your knowledge base without changing the old one. If you decide after pressing <Alt>F6 that you don't want to leave the editor after all, press <Escape>.
3. <Alt>F8 discards any changes you have made and returns VP-Expert to consultation mode. It gives you a chance to change your mind before discarding your work.

Editor mode menu commands can only be invoked by pressing the appropriate function key. Pressing the appropriate numeric key, the first letter of the menu name, or the arrow keys, won't work. That's because all those keys are used to edit the knowledge base itself in editor mode.

Anyone who is familiar with common PC word processing commands can show you want the other menu commands do and how they work, or you can try them. Formatting commands, such as boldface, center, and underline, affect how your knowledge base listing will appear when you print it but not how your knowledge base will behave.

B.5 USING VP-EXPERT IN CONSULTATION MODE

You run a VP-Expert consultation through commands listed in menus at the bottom of the screen and by entering data in the consultation window.

At times VP-Expert will ask you to provide a value for a variable. If it offers you a list of choices, use cursor keys to highlight the desired value and press <Enter>. A triangle will appear next to that value. If the variable is of the plural variety, which can take more than one value, you can continue to select more values as you press <Enter> for each one. If you make a mistake and select a value you didn't want, highlight it again and press <Delete>. Finally, press <End> to enter your selection(s) into VP-Expert and proceed with the run.

If you do not have a menu of choices, or when a variable takes numeric values, type in a value for the variable and press <Enter>.

In either case, you can type a question mark to give a variable status UNKNOWN. This status can be tested in the knowledge base itself.

Whenever VP-Expert pauses for input, you may press / (slash) to invoke this menu:

1. Help (Not functional in the student version of VP-Expert.)
2. How? (See below.)
3. Why? (See below.)
4. Slow (See Section B.7.)
5. Fast (See Section B.7.)
6. Quit (Ends the consultation run and returns you to the Consult menu.)

How? and Why? allow you to ask questions about the reasoning process of your knowledge base. How? asks VP-Expert how it reached a particular conclusion. Why? asks why it wants an input value.

When you ask How?, VP-Expert will show a menu of all the variables in your knowledge base. You then select, using the arrow keys, the variable you are asking How? about. If you select a variable that has not yet been given a value, VP-Expert will tell you so. If you select a variable whose value you entered via the keyboard, it will respond with "You said so." If you select a variable whose value was assigned by a rule that has a BECAUSE clause, it will display the text of that clause. Otherwise—that is, if you select a variable whose value was assigned by a rule that has no BECAUSE clause—it will display a blank line as its answer.

Asking Why? does not require you to select a variable because Why? always refers to the variable that VP-Expert has paused to accept. If it needs the value because of a rule with a BECAUSE clause, it will display the text of that clause. Otherwise, Why? will display a blank line as its answer.

B.6 Creating Your Knowledge Base

B.6.1 The General Idea

Creating a knowledge base is similar to writing a program, but VP-Expert differs from other programming languages you may know. If you can program in Pascal or another procedural (third-generation) language, part of what you know will help. Part may get in your way, especially if you expect VP-Expert to provide full programming language facilities such as nested loops.

A VP-Expert knowledge base consists of statements, each of which ends with a semicolon. Statements may appear in any order, but some orders make the knowledge base easier to understand and modify than others. Each statement must follow precise rules of spelling and grammar. We'll cover those later. The statements fall into three major categories.

1. *The ACTIONS block.* There is one ACTIONS block per knowledge base: no more, no fewer. It controls the progress of the consultation and is the closest thing in VP-Expert to a conventional computer program. It consists of commands (technically, *clauses*) to be executed one at a time, in the sequence in which they are entered, except as modified by looping commands. A FIND statement in the ACTIONS block starts the VP-Expert inference process. Loop commands can tell VP-Expert to repeat a group of statements until a termination condition is met. You can also use loop commands to execute statements conditionally. (This conditional execution capability is more awkward, less flexible, than those of "real" programming languages.) The ACTIONS block ends with a semicolon.

2. *Rules that define the system's logic.* (The word "rule," when used here in lowercase, includes those headed by both RULE and WHENEVER as described below.) Each rule has an antecedent (a set of conditions) to be evaluated as true or false. The antecedent is followed by commands to be executed if the conditions are true and others to be executed if they are false. Backward-chaining rules, such as the ones in Figure B–2, are headed by the key word

RULE. VP-Expert tries these rules when it feels that they might help it determine the value of a variable it has been asked to FIND. Forward-chaining rules are headed by the key word WHENEVER. VP-Expert tests them when a variable that might affect their truth or falsity changes. Each rule ends with a semicolon.

3. *Control statements.* These supply VP-Expert with information that it uses to control its execution of the consultation. The ASK and CHOICES statements that we've seen are examples of these. When VP-Expert decides that its user must supply a value for the variable *is_hungry,* it uses the ASK statement for that variable to phrase its request. Each control statement ends with a semicolon.

You use clauses within the ACTIONS block and the rules to direct VP-Expert to take specific actions, such as assigning a value to a variable or displaying a message on the screen. DISPLAY is a clause. So are FIND and the commands that assigned values to *activity* in the rules of the above mini-knowledge base. Clauses are not freestanding elements of a knowledge base. They can only appear where stated: that is, within the ACTIONS block and the rules. They do not end with a semicolon unless they happen to be the last clause of their enclosing unit. In that case they end with the semicolon that terminates the enclosing unit.

Many commands, such as RULE, allow (or require) you to state a condition. The condition must be of the form <variable><relation> <expression>. The <relation> can be any of the following:

=	Equal to.
>	Greater than.
<	Less than.
>=	Greater than or equal to.
<=	Less than or equal to.
<>	Not equal to.

The <expression> on the right-hand side of the <relation> can be a constant, a variable, or the result of a calculation. Variable names and expressions to be calculated must be put in parentheses to allow VP-Expert to tell them from constants. The condition

```
IF food = eggs
```

will be true if the variable *food* has the value "eggs," but the condition

```
IF food = (eggs)
```

will be true if the variables *food* and *eggs* have the same value.

The word UNKNOWN is a special type of constant for the right side of a condition. The condition `variable = UNKNOWN` will test as True if *variable* has never been assigned a value, if it has been RESET, or if the user entered a question mark when asked for its value. This allows a knowledge base to deal explicitly with missing information.

The rest of this section summarizes the VP-Expert commands you will need. As noted earlier, it is not a complete text on the VP-Expert language. In particular, these notes do not cover graphics output, file input/output (except FDISPLAY and REPORT), data transfer to and from spreadsheets, inducing a knowledge base from a decision table, and a few other topics.

VP-Expert is case insensitive: It doesn't care if you use capital or lowercase letters. <Angle brackets> in these notes indicate items you supply or are used, as above, around the names of control keys on the keyboard. Don't type the <>. When they are used to indicate items you must supply, replace the angle brackets and the "placeholder" word between them with the actual variable name, value, or other component of your knowledge base.

Annotate your system with comments. VP-Expert treats anything after ! in a line as a comment. (This does not apply to exclamation points in text between quotation marks.) If a line starts with ! the entire line is considered a comment. Multiline comments need a ! on each line.

A practical constraint on annotation is the 16KB limit of the VP-Expert student edition on the total size of your .KBS file, including comments. The ideal of full annotation may have to yield to the need to squeeze your knowledge base into this limit.

B.6.2 Statements

Statements are the highest level unit within a VP-Expert knowledge base. Statements may not be nested inside other statements. Each is a free standing unit that begins with the appropriate key word (listed alphabetically below) and ends with a semicolon. Semicolons may only appear inside a statement within a comment or a quoted string.

Statement order doesn't matter. VP-Expert scans them all as it loads a knowledge base before starting a consultation. Arrange your statements to make the knowledge base as easy as possible for people to understand when they read its listing. The function of control statements such as AUTOQUERY, BKCOLOR, and ENDOFF is usually clearest if you put them before the ACTIONS block, but they work equally well anywhere. ASK statements can be placed near rules that invoke them or grouped at the end of the knowledge base. RANGE statements and CHOICES and PLURAL statements that refer to only one variable may go near the ASK statement for that variable. CHOICES and PLURAL statements that refer to several variables can be grouped in one place.

ACTIONS begins the Actions block, which controls the overall execution of your system. Follow ACTIONS by command clauses as required. There is one Actions block per knowledge base. The entire Actions block ends with a semicolon.

ASK <variable>: "text"; displays *text* in the active window and allows the user to enter the value of *variable.* ASK is invoked automatically whenever VP-Expert needs a value for *variable* and can't get that value from rules. You can't force VP-Expert to ask for input by using ASK. To force VP-Expert to request a value for *variable,* put FIND *variable* in the Actions block or in the consequent of a rule. Use CHOICES or RANGE to constrain user input.

AUTOQUERY; asks VP-Expert to supply a standard query whenever a variable value is needed if the knowledge base does not contain an ASK statement for that variable. AUTOQUERY helps get a knowledge base running quickly because you don't have to write all the ASK statements in order to test your expert system. It also provides a "backstop" capability in case you forgot one or more ASK questions. Using it should therefore become a habit. As you perfect your knowledge base you will want to write user-oriented ASK statements to replace the standardized queries that AUTOQUERY produces.

BKCOLOR = <n>; sets the background color of the display per the table:

0	Black (initial setting when you start VP-Expert).
1	Blue.
2	Green.
3	Light blue.
4	Red.
5	Magenta.
6	Brown.
7	White.

No more than one BKCOLOR statement should be in a knowledge base. Consultation windows can have different background colors as specified by WOPEN. On a monochrome display, all values except 7 yield black. A color set by BKCOLOR stays in effect through further consultation runs and knowledge bases until you run a knowledge base with a different BKCOLOR or restart VP-Expert from MS-DOS.

CHOICES <variable list>: <value list>; supplies alternative values for VP-Expert to display as a menu when ASK is issued for a variable in the list.

ENDOFF; eliminates the need to press <End> to finalize menu selection for single-valued variables. If ENDOFF is in effect, pressing <Enter> chooses the highlighted value. Menus for plural variables are not affected: you must still press <End> to finalize their selections. Since ENDOFF is a control statement, not a command, it controls an entire consultation. There is no way to switch between the two modes of operation during a consultation.

EXECUTE; tells VP-Expert to begin a consultation at the main menu CONSULT command, rather than switching to the consultation menu and waiting for a subsequent GO command, and to return to MS-DOS at the end of a consultation. If you use EXECUTE while you are still developing your knowledge base, you'll have to restart VP-Expert after each consultation run.

PLURAL: <variable list>; specifies that the listed variables (up to 10, separated by commas) can be assigned multiple values during a consultation. You can use more than one PLURAL statement if you have more than 10 plural variables. Access a single value of a plural variable by removing it via POP.

When a plural variable is used on the right side of a comparison, only its top value (the one that would be removed via POP) is tested. When a plural variable is used on the left side of a comparison, all its values are tested to see if any of them makes the comparison true. For example, suppose the single-valued variable `food` has the value `pizza` and the plural variable `many_foods` has the values `chips` (on top) and `pizza` (below it). Then

```
food = (many_foods)
```

is false because the top value of `many_foods` does not match `food`, but

```
many—foods = (food)
```

is true because one value of `many_foods` does match `food`. This means that you cannot test two plural variables against each other directly to see if they have any matching value pairs. Use POP in a WHILEKNOWN loop to do this.

RANGE <variable: lowvalue, highvalue>; limits input for *variable* to numeric values in the specified range. Both limiting values are accepted as input. A user attempt to enter a value outside this range, or a non-numeric value, will result in an error message with a request to enter a value in the given range.

RULE <label> IF <conditions> THEN <commands> ELSE <commands> BECAUSE <"text">; defines the backward-chaining logic of your knowledge base. The label is for your reference and is not meaningful to VP-Expert. The ELSE and BECAUSE parts are optional. The THEN and ELSE parts contain command clauses. These are executed in the order in which they appear if the condition of the rule is tested and found to be true (or, for ELSE, false) during a consultation. Because rules are so important to a knowledge base, Section B.6.4 has more information about their components. Section B.6.5 discusses the use of confidence factors in reaching conclusions.

RUNTIME; removes the Rules and Facts windows from the screen during a consultation, enlarging the consultation window to occupy the entire screen. Using RUNTIME makes VP-Expert run faster because it doesn't have to spend time displaying rules and facts in the two bottom windows.

WHENEVER <label> IF <conditions> THEN <commands> ELSE <commands> BECAUSE <"text">; monitors all variables in <conditions>. It evaluates <conditions> whenever (hence its name!) any variable in them changes. It then executes the <commands> following THEN if <conditions> are true, those following ELSE if <conditions> are false and the optional

ELSE component is present. The <commands> can change the values of other variables. This, in turn, can trigger other WHENEVER statements.

WHENEVER provides forward chaining to complement the backward chaining capability of RULE. If the <commands> change a variable that is tested in the conditions of the same WHENEVER statement, the loop may run forever. You can also get into an endless loop via a closed cycle of WHENEVERs if each one changes a variable that is tested in the next.

The only difference between <commands> in WHENEVER and in RULE is that FIND may not be used with WHENEVER. The information about rules in Sections B.6.4 and B.6.5 applies to WHENEVERs as well.

B.6.3 Command Clauses

Command clauses may appear within ACTIONS, RULE, and WHENEVER statements (with one exception: FIND, as noted just above). They are executed sequentially within their enclosing unit except as specified by loop control commands. Unlike statements, which are scanned when a knowledge base is loaded, command clauses do nothing until they are activated as part of their enclosing unit.

Clauses are not terminated by semicolons. A semicolon is used only to terminate the enclosing unit. That semicolon may look like part of the last command clause in the unit, but it really isn't.

ACTIVE <n> makes a window from 0 to 9 the active window. Text displayed by the DISPLAY clause, from that moment until another ACTIVE with a different window number, appears in window *n*. When VP-Expert starts, only window 0 is available. Additional windows are opened on the screen by WOPEN and removed from the screen by WCLOSE.

Assignment clauses assign value to variables. Their format is **<variable> = <value>.** If *value* is the value of another variable or an arithmetic expression, it must be enclosed in parentheses to avoid being treated as a character string constant. The four basic arithmetic operations are represented by

- \+ Addition.
- − Subtraction.
- * Multiplication.
- / Division.

In common with most programming languages, VP-Expert does not indicate multiplication via the algebraic convention of writing two variable names next to each other. You must separate them by *. You may use additional parentheses in an expression to control the order in which operations are evaluated.

Confidence factors (see Section B.6.5) of variables appearing on the right side of the equal sign are ignored in assignment clause. That is, those variables are treated as though they have CNF (confidence factor) 100. The value given to the variable on the left side of an equal sign will have CNF 100 unless another CNF is explicitly assigned to it in the assignment clause. If a plural variable appears on the right side of the equal sign, only its top value (the value that would be removed by POP) will be used in the calculation. If you want to use all the values of a plural variable in a calculation, you must embed the calculation inside a WHILEKNOWN loop and use POP to retrieve each value of the variable individually. (See the POP command below for a simple example of this use.)

You may use the following functions in arithmetic expressions, where the @ is part of each function name and an expression having a numeric value is to be substituted for *x:*

@ABS(x)	Absolute value.
@EXP(x)	Exponential function; *e* to the power *x*.
@LOG(x)	Natural (base *e*) logarithm of *x*.
@SQRT(x)	Square root.
@COS(x)	Cosine (angle in radians here and below).
@SIN(x)	Sine.
@TAN(x)	Tangent.
@ACOS(x)	Arccosine.
@ASIN(x)	Arcsine.
@ATAN(x)	Arctangent.

CLS clears the active consultation window. The two bottom windows (for rules and facts) and any open but inactive consultation windows (if you used WOPEN) are not affected.

COLOR = <n> sets the text color on a color monitor. Colors 0 through 7 are defined in the BKCOLOR table above. Add 8 to a color value for a light color: for example, Color 0, black, becomes gray. Add 16 to a color value for blinking text. Text already on the screen when COLOR is executed is not affected. COLOR affects all text displayed until another COLOR statement with a different color value is executed. While you can have only one BKCOLOR per run, you can execute COLOR any number of times to get multicolored text.

COUNT <variable1, variable2> counts the number of values assigned to plural *variable1* and puts that number in *variable2*.

DISPLAY <"text"> displays up to 1,000 characters in the active window. The <text> may include semicolons, which will not terminate the enclosing statement when used between quotation marks. If a tilde (~) immediately precedes the closing quotation mark, the system will pause after the text is displayed until the user presses any key. Names of variables enclosed in curly brackets ({ }) within <text> are replaced by their values. If a variable name is preceded by a pound sign (#) within the curly brackets, its confidence factor is also displayed. If a variable name is preceded by an integer within the curly brackets, its value will be displayed right justified in a field of the specified width. If both a width specification and # are used, # comes first. See FORMAT for more control over number formats.

EJECT causes the printer to feed the paper to the top of the next page.

END is used with FOR, WHILEKNOWN, and WHILETRUE to define the scope of a repetition. Loops of any type may *not* be nested within each other. You can accomplish functional nesting, if not physical nesting, by using a FIND in the outer loop to invoke a rule that contains the inner loop in its consequent. This may offend purists, but it works. For example, this will execute the inner loop once for each execution of the outer loop (which, as written here, must be embedded within a statement such as the ACTIONS block):

```
dummy1 = true      !sets condition for inner loop rule to fire
FOR i = 1 TO 5     !starts outer loop
FIND dummy2        !to invoke inner loop
RESET dummy2       !so FIND will look for dummy2 anew each time
END                !ends outer loop

RULE inner_loop
IF dummy1 = true
THEN
dummy2 = foo       !so that FIND dummy2 will invoke this rule
FOR j = 1 TO 5     !starts inner loop
. . .              !code inside the nested loops goes here
. . .              !it will be executed 25 times
END;               !ends inner loop and the rule
```

You can also accomplish the same thing with a WHENEVER to control the inner loop.

FDISPLAY <filename, "text"> sends *text* to the specified file; <filename> may include a DOS pathname if desired. If the file does not exist it is created. If it does exist, *text* is appended to it. Send values of variables by enclosing the variable names in curly brackets.

FIND <variable> instructs the VP-Expert inference engine to find a value (or values, if *variable* is plural) for *variable.* The next command clause is executed after the value(s) is(are) found or after VP-Expert exhausts the rules without being able to assign it a value. If FIND does not assign a value to *variable,* it remains unchanged: either UNKNOWN or as previously assigned. FIND may appear in the consequent of a RULE statement but not in the consequent of a WHENEVER statement. An attempt to FIND a single-valued variable for which VP-Expert already has a value will be ignored. To be sure VP-Expert gets a new value for such a variable, RESET the variable before you FIND it again.

FOR <variable> = <startvalue> TO <stopvalue> causes following commands up to END to be executed repetitively. On the first execution, *variable* has the value *startvalue*. It is incremented by 1 for each execution of the loop. The loop is not executed and control passes to the command following END as soon as the value of *variable* exceeds *stopvalue*. The value of *variable* may be changed by assignment within the loop.

Both *startvalue* and *stopvalue* must be numeric constants. This is a problem when the number of times a loop should repeat depends on user input or on a value that your knowledge base calculates as it runs. To get around this problem, use two variables. One is your "real" index variable. You will have to set and increment this variable by hand. The other is a dummy variable, one that has no real meaning to your problem, for FOR to use. Use a *stopvalue* larger than the real ending value could possibly be. Inside the loop, set the dummy variable to a value that will end the loop when your real index variable reaches its limit. For example, if you would like to do this but can't because *max* is not a numeric constant.

```
FOR x = 1 TO max              !not legal in VP-Expert
. . .                         !body of loop goes here
END
```

do this instead:

```
x = 0                         !initialize real loop variable
FOR dummy = 1 TO 9999         !assume x will never reach 9999
x = (x+1)                     !increment real loop variable
. . .                         !body of loop goes here
dummy = (9999 - max + x)      !FOR will terminate when x=max
END
```

FORMAT <variable, n.m> specifies the format for a numeric variable in subsequent DISPLAY or PDISPLAY commands. *Variable* is displayed in a field of width *n* with *m* digits after the decimal point. The field width *n* must, if applicable, allow for the decimal point itself and for a minus sign. Since FORMAT is a clause, it takes effect when executed. Be sure it will be executed before the first (P)DISPLAY command it should affect.

GETCH <variable> pauses execution until the user presses a key. The character corresponding to the key is placed in *variable*, and execution resumes. GETCH differs from DISPLAY with a tilde (~) in that GETCH lets you find out what key the user pressed.

LENGTH <variable1, variable2> causes the value of *variable2* to be set to the length, in characters, of the value of *variable1*.

LOCATE <row,column> causes text produced by the next DISPLAY statement to start at the specified position in the active window. This text will overwrite existing text if present. Rows and columns are counted from the top left corner of the active window, not of the screen.

PDISPLAY <"text"> is the same as DISPLAY except that the text is sent to the printer.

POP <variable1, variable2> removes one value of *variable1*, which must be a plural variable, and places it in *variable2*, which may be single valued or plural. POP removes the most recently assigned value of *variable1* unless *variable1* was SORTed. If several values from a CHOICES statement were assigned to a plural variable, they are stored in the reverse of the order in which they were listed in CHOICES: the last one in the CHOICES list is on the top of the plural variable stack and will be the first removed via POP. (The order in which the user selected the values on the screen doesn't matter.) If *variable1* was SORTed, the value with the highest confidence factor is on top and will be removed. POPping its last value gives *variable1* status UNKNOWN. Use POP in a WHILEKNOWN–END loop to repeat a series of commands for each value of a plural variable. For instance, this loop will assign all values of the plural variable *rhs* to the plural variable *lhs*, on top of any values that *lhs* already has when the loop is entered:

```
WHILEKNOWN rhs
POP rhs, lhs
END
```

This process will reverse the order of the values of *rhs* as they are stored in *lhs;* the value that was on the bottom of *rhs* will end up on the top of *lhs*, and so on. If the source variable *rhs* was sorted by confidence factors (see SORT, below in this section and in Section B.6.5) the value having the lowest confidence factor will now be on top of *lhs*.

PRINTOFF causes the printer not to echo the text of DISPLAY commands. VP-Expert starts in this mode.

PRINTON causes the printer to echo the text of DISPLAY commands. Other screen output (ASK, CHOICES lists, etc.) is not echoed to the printer. Print that output via PDISPLAY if you want a printed record of it.

REPORT <filename> creates a file to contain the BECAUSE text of rules that are executed during a consultation. This file will replace any existing file of the same name, so rename or relocate the existing REPORT file via MS-DOS commands between consultations if you want to save it.

RESET <variable> removes any value or values assigned to *variable* and returns it to UNKNOWN status. It is often used inside a WHILEKNOWN loop to make sure the control variable of the loop is UNKNOWN if a FIND command fails.

SORT <variable> sorts the current values of a plural variable by descending confidence factor so that the value with the highest CNF is on the top of the stack. SORT is useful for POPping the most likely candidates for a conclusion first. SORTing a single-valued variable does not accomplish anything.

TRUTHTHRESH = <integer> sets the minimum confidence factor that the antecedent of a rule must have to be considered true. An antecedent that evaluates to true with a lower confidence factor is considered false. The default threshold is 20.

WCLOSE <window number> closes the specified window. The contents of the closed window are lost. They do not reappear if the window is re-opened.

WHILEKNOWN <variable> causes following commands up to END to be executed repetitively as long as *variable* is not UNKNOWN. The value of *variable* must be changed by an assignment command within the loop or by a rule triggered by the loop. Variables become UNKNOWN in four ways: initially, before they have been assigned a value; when a user enters "?" as their value; when the last value of a plural variable is removed by POP; and when they are RESET. Assigning the character string "UNKNOWN" as the value of a variable does *not* make it UNKNOWN. *Variable* is tested at the end of the loop before repeating it, so a WHILEKNOWN loop is executed at least once even if *variable* is UNKNOWN on entry. *Note:* WHILEKNOWN does not take THEN before the repeated commands, although WHILETRUE does.

WHILETRUE <condition> THEN causes following commands up to END to be executed repetitively as long as *condition* is true. AND and OR may be used inside *condition*. You can execute commands conditionally by using a WHILETRUE . . . END loop that is executed either once or not at all. For example, suppose you have assigned either "Yes" or "No" to the variable `display_it`. The following "loop" will execute its DISPLAY statement only if `display_it` has the value "Yes" when the WHILETRUE is reached.

```
WHILETRUE display_it = Yes
THEN
DISPLAY "This line is displayed at most once."
display_it = No !or any value except Yes to avoid looping
END
```

Setting `display_it` to "No" after the DISPLAY command keeps the loop from repeating forever. *Note:* WHILETRUE takes THEN before the repeated commands, as shown, even though WHILEKNOWN does not.

WOPEN <number, row, column, height, width, BGcolor> opens, but does not activate, consultation window *number*. *Row* and *column* give the position of its top left corner on the screen. *Height* and *width* give its size in rows and columns. *BGcolor* gives its background color per the table in the description of BGCOLOR. An ACTIVE clause must be executed for output to appear in the newly opened window.

B.6.4 Rules

Rules describe the problem-solving logic of a VP-Expert knowledge base. In principle, each rule in a knowledge base ought to represent an independent chunk of knowledge, so their order shouldn't matter. However, VP-Expert scans its rules sequentially when it tries to satisfy a Find command. If the variable it is trying to Find is single valued, it will stop its scan as soon as it succeeds. Other rules, which might have led to assigning that variable a different value with a higher confidence factor, will not be tested. One way around this problem is to use a plural variable. VP-Expert will scan all rules and assign it all possible values. You can then Sort the plural variable and Pop the value with the highest confidence factor into a single-valued variable for later use.

The following items, listed alphabetically, are part of RULEs or WHENEVERs.

AND combines conditions in rules. A compound condition joined by AND is true only if all its components are true. OR (see below) takes precedence over AND if both are present in the same rule.

BECAUSE <**"text"**>; provides an answer to Why? or How? from the screen menu. More information on Why? and How? is in Section B.5. The semicolon shown at the end of the BECAUSE clause here is the semicolon that terminates the entire rule.

ELSE separates the conclusions to be reached if the premise of a RULE or a WHENEVER is true from the conclusions to be reached if it is false.

IF precedes the antecedent (conditions) of a rule. Conditions may be combined via AND and OR. There is a limit of 20 conditions in an antecedent.

OR combines conditions in rules. A compound condition joined by OR is true if any of its components are true. OR takes precedence over AND. That is, the compound condition

```
a AND b OR c
```

is evaluated as if it were written

```
a AND (b OR c)
```

and not as if it were written

```
(a AND b) OR c
```

If *a* is false and *c* is true, the two interpretations yield different answers.

THEN precedes the commands to be executed if the premise of a RULE or a WHENEVER is true.

B.6.5 Confidence Factors

Confidence factors express the concept that some conclusions may be more likely than others or that some recommendations may be more suitable than others. Confidence factors range from 0 to 100. A CNF of 100 represents absolute certainty, while 0 represents absolute uncertainty.

Because VP-Expert variables contain only character strings, uncertainty in one value of a variable is not the same as certainty in what humans would consider its opposite. If humans know a statement is not true, we also know it is false. VP-Expert, however, does not consider the four-letter string "true" to be the opposite of the five-letter string "false" any more than "Dave" is the opposite of "Karen." Knowing that a person's name is not Dave does not tell us that it is Karen. Similarly, knowing that a variable's value is not "true" does not tell VP-Expert that its value is "false." If you want a variable to have the value "false," you must assign that value to it. Assigning "true CNF 0" won't do the job. Some shells do support truth-valued, or Boolean, variables, but VP-Expert does not.

Confidence factors can be assigned to values of variables in three ways:

1. *User input.* After an item is highlighted in a CHOICES menu or typed, press <Home>. Type a confidence factor for that value and press <Enter>. Repeat this process as often as necessary to assign more than one value to a plural variable, each with its own confidence factor. If the user does not assign a confidence factor to a value, VP-Expert will give it CNF 100. It is never necessary to type CNF 100, although it doesn't do any harm.

2. *Direct assignment.* Follow an assignment command in a knowledge base with CNF <integer>. If the CNF clause is absent, CNF 100 is assumed. For example, to assign `food` the value `pizza` with CNF 80, use

```
food = pizza CNF 80
```

As mentioned in the discussion of the assignment statement, one plural variable cannot be assigned directly to another. You must use a WHILEKNOWN loop with POP. However, POP cannot assign confidence factors. You must use an intermediate variable to assign one plural variable to another with a confidence factor. To assign all values of the plural variable *rhs* to the plural variable *lhs* with a confidence factor of 80, use a loop such as this:

```
WHILEKNOWN rhs
POP rhs, temp
lhs = (temp) CNF 80
END
```

3. *Assignment as a result of uncertainty in the conditions of a rule.* The confidence factor of a rule's conditions applies to any assignment statements within the rule. When comparing the values of two variables, the CNF of the variable on the left side of the comparison determines the CNF of the result. If `food_1` has the value `pizza` with CNF 80 and `food_2` has the value `pizza` with CNF 70, then

```
IF food_1 = (food_2)
```

is true with CNF 80, but

```
IF food_2 = (food_1)
```

is true with CNF 70.

If CNFs figure both in the conditions and in the conclusion of a rule, they are multiplied to give the final CNF of the variable in the conclusion. For example, if `food` has the value `pizza` with CNF 80:

```
IF food = pizza
THEN go_for_pizza CNF 75
```

will assign CNF 60 to `go_for_pizza` since $0.80 \times 0.75 = 0.60$.

After applying a series of confidence factors in assignments, variables may reach confidence factors well below 20. If you would like these values to still test true in conditions, use TRUTHTHRESH to lower the threshold for considering a condition "true."

When two or more comparisons with confidence factors are combined via AND in the antecedent of a rule, the confidence factor of the result is the lowest of the confidence factors of all the ANDed conditions.

When two comparisons with confidence factors are combined via OR in the antecedent of a rule, the confidence factor of the result is higher than either of the contributing confidence factors. In effect, VP-Expert applies one confidence factor to the uncertainty remaining after the other factor. For example, consider two ORed conditions with confidence factors of 70 and 80. Applying the confidence factor 80 leaves an "uncertainty" of 20. The remaining confidence factor of 70, applied to that uncertainty, adds $0.7 \times 20 = 14$ to the overall confidence factor of the conclusion. The final confidence factor is $80 + 14 = 94$. The result is the same if you take the factors in the other order. (Try it.)

If more than two comparisons are combined via OR, VP-Expert first uses the above formula with the first two comparisons. This gives the CNF that it combines with that of the third comparison. It then uses that CNF with the CNF of the fourth comparison, if there is one, and so on for the rest. The order doesn't affect the result here either.

If the same value is assigned to a variable more than once, the ORing formula is used to compute the resulting CNF. This applies to single-valued variables and to each member of the set of values of a plural variable. The following sequence of two (identical) commands:

```
name = Fred CNF 80
name = Fred CNF 80
```

will give the variable *name* the value "Fred" with CNF 96.

See also *(a)* the discussion of the DISPLAY command for information on displaying the confidence factor of a variable and *(b)* the discussion of the assignment command on the use of confidence factors in numerical expressions.

B.6.6 Database Access

VP-Expert can read and write files created with dBase II, dBase III, VP-Info, or any other program that creates compatible files. Create your file and enter data outside VP-Expert. Make sure your file name has a .DBF extension.

Four VP-Expert commands access a database: APPEND, GET, CLOSE, and PUT. All are command clauses that can go in the ACTIONS block or in the consequents of RULEs and WHENEVERs.

Each field in your file is automatically associated with a single-valued VP-Expert variable of the same name. Use that variable name only to access that field, and not in any other way.

APPEND <filename> adds one record to the file. Before APPENDing a record you must FIND or otherwise assign values to all the relevant fields in the record.

GET <condition>,<file name>,<field name> retrieves one record from a file. The <condition> looks like a rule condition. Use it to select records to be retrieved. For example, suppose there is a field *first_name* in your file and a variable *fname* in your program. To retrieve a record for an employee whose fist name equals the value of *fname,* use

```
GET fname = first_name, . . .
```

To retrieve the next record in a file regardless of its content, use the condition ALL.

You cannot test a database field for a constant value directly because the left side of a VP-Expert condition must be a variable. For example, you cannot retrieve records with the value "catcher" in the field "position" by a command such as

```
GET position = catcher, . . .
```

Assign the constant to a variable and then use that variable in the GET condition. To retrieve information about only catchers, use a variable such as *pos* like this:

```
pos = catcher
GET pos = position, . . .
```

<file name> is the name of your data file. Include its DOS pathname if it is not in the current directory. Don't include its .DBF extension here. VP-Expert will supply it.

<field name> tells VP-Expert which field to retrieve from the selected record. Use ALL for the field name to retrieve all fields. You can retrieve one field or all the fields in the record. You cannot retrieve more than one, but less than all, fields in one GET command.

Searching first starts with the first record of your file. Successive GETs start with the record after the last one retrieved and continue through the file, stopping at and retrieving the first record that meets your condition.

Variables associated with fields to be retrieved are set to UNKNOWN status when a GET command begins execution. If there are no more records in the file, or no more that meet your retrieval condition, they remain UNKNOWN. This lets you use a WHILEKNOWN loop to process all the records in a file, stopping when there are no more records.

CLOSE <file name> resets the file pointer so the next retrieval operation starts with the first record in the file again. (Note to experienced programmers: There is no OPEN command in VP-Expert. If necessary, GET will perform the job of OPEN in other languages.)

PUT <file name> rewrites the most recently read record. Use PUT to update your file after changing the value of one or more fields.

B.6.7 Using Database Contents with ASK Commands

ASK can offer the user a choice of values based on the content of a file as an alternative to the CHOICES statement. To use this feature, create a file as above. There are then two commands and one system-defined variable you can then use:

MENU <variable>,<condition>,<file name>,<field name> executed before ASK is encountered, causes ASK to display a menu of choices for a variable based on the content of a file. <variable> is a VP-Expert variable for which a menu is to be created. <condition> determines which records in the file should be used to create the menu. As with GET, a condition of ALL means "use all records." <file name> is as above. <field name> is the name of a database field whose contents are used in the menu. MENU does not display anything when it is executed. It prepares data to be used the next time ASK is invoked for the variable in question.

MRESET <variable> where <variable> was previously used in a MENU statement, frees up the memory used for its menu. This can be considerable. Place MRESET after any statements, such as FIND, which might cause the menu to be used. Once MRESET is executed, it is as if MENU had never been executed.

MENU_SIZE is a system variable that contains the number of entries in the most recently generated menu. It can be useful for deciding if you want to display the menu as is or take some other action.

What's the difference between CHOICES and MENU? CHOICES gives VP-Expert information when a knowledge base is loaded, while MENU is a command that must be executed before ASK can use it. If a knowledge base has both CHOICES and MENU for the same variable, it will use CHOICES if MENU has not yet been executed or has been canceled by MRESET. Once MENU has been executed for a given variable, the menu it created from the file contents takes precedence over a CHOICES statement for the same variable. You can use CHOICES for some input variables and MENU for others.

B.6.8 Chaining

The student version of VP-Expert limits knowledge base size to about 16,000 characters. The regular version is limited by the available RAM up to a maximum of 640 KB. (VP-Expert does not use either extended or expanded memory.) In either case a bigger knowledge base than these limits allow is often needed. Chaining knowledge bases lets you build a larger expert system by passing the results of one consultation to another. To chain, use the following three clauses. As clauses, they can appear in the ACTIONS block or in the consequents of RULEs or WHENEVERs.

CHAIN <kbname> tells VP-Expert to switch to the knowledge base *kbname*. This knowledge base starts running at the beginning of its ACTIONS block. You need not supply the .KBS extension. The student version of VP-Expert limits the length of a chain to three knowledge bases. (The regular version has no limit in this regard.) The limit applies to CHAIN commands that are actually executed during a run. You can have any number of CHAIN commands in your knowledge-base listing. The first one that is executed will switch to the knowledge base <kbname>. The others won't count against the limit of three.

LOADFACTS <filename> loads a set of facts previously saved by a SAVEFACTS clause. Use it at the beginning of the ACTIONS block of a knowledge base after the first. If <filename> has an extension, you must supply it both here and in SAVEFACTS.

SAVEFACTS <filename> saves the current values of all VP-Expert variables in a file named *filename* in the current working directory. SAVEFACTS normally precedes CHAIN.

SAVEFACTS and LOADFACTS are optional, but omitting them means that each knowledge base in the chain must start without the information ascertained by its predecessors. This may be appropriate, such as when the first module exists only to figure out which of several possible subsequent modules it should chain to.

The use of SAVEFACTS and LOADFACTS is not limited to chains. SAVEFACTS creates a text file of assignment statements to all the variables in your system, complete with their confidence factors. You can read this file via the MS-DOS Type command or any word processing program to review a knowledge base run. You can also use SAVEFACTS and LOADFACTS to get around the student edition of VP-Expert's three-segment limit per chain manually, by doing this:

- Put SAVEFACTS at the end of the third segment of the chain, where you would put CHAIN to the fourth segment if the student version of VP-Expert allowed you to.
- Put a matching LOADFACTS at the start of the ACTIONS block of the fourth segment of the chain.
- Program the third segment to terminate normally after its SAVEFACTS. (It's a good idea to follow SAVEFACTS by a DISPLAY statement to remind the user to start the fourth segment.)
- When the third segment terminates, start the fourth segment manually via Filename, Consult, and Go. Because of your SAVEFACTS and LOADFACTS, the fourth segment will start with all the facts that the third segment had when it terminated. Since you have just started a new chaining sequence, the student edition of VP-Expert will be happy to chain to the fifth and sixth segments by itself. If you need more than six segments in your chain, you can chain any number of segments together by repeating this manual process after every third segment. (If you *really* need more than six segments in your chain, making the modest investment in the full version of VP-Expert is probably a good idea.)

SAVEFACTS and LOADFACTS have a side effect on plural variables: They reverse the order of their values. That is, the value that was on top before SAVEFACTS will be on the bottom after LOADFACTS, and so on. This happens because SAVEFACTS creates a series of assignment commands starting with the value on top of the plural variable. When these commands are executed by LOADFACTS, the first value in the list—the one that had been on top before SAFEFACTS—is loaded into the plural variable first and therefore ends up on the bottom. If the order of values is important, SORT the plural variable if appropriate, or use a loop such as the one described under POP above to reverse their order again.

Chaining has another use in addition to allowing you to develop a knowledge base that exceeds 16,000 source characters in size. It lets you create modules that apply only to a particular part of your knowledge-processing task. For example, suppose your expert system is intended to help people pick a vehicle to buy. You might start with some basic questions to decide if they need a car or a truck. From that point on, all your rules would have to look like

```
   IF vehicle_type = car
   AND . . . [continue with rest of conditions and
consequents]
```

If, however, you chain either to a module that deals only with cars or a module that deals only with trucks, the first condition in the antecedent will automatically be taken care of. You won't have to worry about a truck rule being fired by mistake when the customer wants a car.

B.7 VP-Expert Menu Commands

This section lists the commands you will see at the bottom of a VP-Expert screen. VP-Expert has a hierarchical menu structure. That is, the menus form a tree. When you make a selection from the top menu level, you get the next menu level with another set of selections you can make. This may continue to more levels. If no subentries are listed indented below a menu entry, that's the lowest level entry. When you choose a bottom-level entry, VP-Expert carries out the task in question.

1. Help (not functional at this or any other level in student version)
2. Induce (induce rules that created a set of examples; not covered in these notes)
3. Edit (has its own menu and command structure; see Section B.4)
4. Consult (loads previously selected knowledge base automatically)
    1. Help
    2. Go (start the run)
    3. WhatIf (change the value of a variable directly)
    4. Variable (inspect the current value of a variable)
    5. Rule (inspect a rule)
    6. Set
        1. Help
        2. Trace (have VP-Expert create a trace file for subsequent inspection)
        3. Slow (cut VP-Expert's speed in half each time this is chosen)
        4. Fast (reset VP-Expert's speed to its initial value)
        5. Windows (move and resize screen windows with arrow keys)
            1. Help
            2. Consult (move/resize Consultation window)
            3. Rules (move/resize Rules window)
            4. Values (move/resize Facts window)
            5. Save (save current window positions and sizes)
            6. Quit (return to Set menu)
    7. Edit (same as item 3 in top-level menu)
    8. Quit (return to top-level menu)

5. Tree (only works if VP-Expert previously created a trace file)
   1. Help
   2. Text (displays rule trace as indented text tree)
   3. Graphics (display rule trace as graphic tree)
   4. Quit (return to top-level menu)
6. Filename (select a knowledge base from current working directory or create a new one)
7. Path (change current working directory)
8. Quit (exit VP-Expert and return to MS-DOS)

Glossary

accounting model the fourth DSS level in Alter's hierarchy; accounting model DSS incorporate deterministic models, often of accounting relationships. (3, 4)

action bar same as menu bar. (5)

***ad hoc* DSS** a DSS developed for one-time use, often by a single individual, with the expectation of discarding it after the need for it has gone away. (4)

adverse consequences in the Kepner-Tregoe decision-making method, the potential negative effects of a particular decision. (2)

alternatives the set of possible choices facing a decision maker. (2)

analysis information system the third DSS level in Alter's hierarchy; analysis information systems can access a database and provide limited modeling capability. (4)

antecedent in an expert system using production rules, that part of a rule that expresses the conditions for the rule to apply; see also consequent. (14)

architecture (of an information system) a written expression of the desired future for information use and management in an organization that creates the context within which people can make consistent decisions. (5)

artificial intelligence "the science of making computers do things that would require intelligence if done by people" (Minsky); generally used today to encompass expert systems, robotics, machine vision, natural language understanding, neural networks, and occasionally a few other areas of investigation. (14)

assertion (in Prolog) a statement that indicates that the user believes a certain relationship among data elements is true. (17)

atom in the LISP language, an elementary data item consisting of a character string. (17)

audit (of a spreadsheet) examination of a spreadsheet's formulas to detect any errors. (6)

autocorrelation the tendency of the output of one part of a simulation run to be correlated with the output of other parts of the same run. (9)

automatic data processing early term for data processing. (1)

backtracking the process of discarding successively higher level goals and selecting new ones when it becomes apparent, through attempting to reach all lower level goals that could lead to the higher level goal now being pursued, that that higher level goal cannot possibly be reached. (14)

backward chaining in expert systems, an inference method in which a specified goal is used to select rules, which will in turn call for additional information and eventually work back to information that is available to the system. (16)

NOTE: The number in parentheses indicates the chapter in which the term is discussed.

blackboard in an expert system, same as workspace. (14)

Boolean variable variable that can take on only two values, often expressed as True and False. (16)

boundary the conceptual separation between a system and its environment. (3)

Box's method numerical optimization method in which the lowest of several function values is discarded and replaced by another value, taken at a point where it will hopefully be higher. (10)

builder same as DSS builder. (5)

bulletin board system (BBS) an information system in which users can leave messages to be read by other interested users, with provisions to search for messages of interest by subject matter, discussion thread, and so forth. (11)

business analyst in the intermediary mode of DSS usage, an assistant who contributes business knowledge or management science expertise to the computer-aided decision-making process. (4)

calculus a branch of mathematics dealing with the rate of change of functions and allowing one to find their maxima. (This refers specifically to differential calculus. Integral calculus deals with other, albeit related, topics.) (10)

calendar program a computer program that keeps track of the schedules of several users and can schedule activities for times that are convenient for the greatest possible number of participants. (11)

capacity planners people who analyze computing system loads versus the capacity of those systems and suggest modifications to handle present or anticipated future loads effectively. (7)

car in the LISP language, a reference to the first element of a list. (17)

cardinal utility an approach to utility theory in which the utility of alternatives is assessed in utils and the alternative having the highest value in utils is chosen. (2)

cdr in the LISP language, a reference to all elements of a list beyond the first. (17)

cell an element of a spreadsheet, typically identified by its column-and-row location coordinates, which can contain text, a number, or a formula that carries out a computation using the content of other cells. (6)

centroid the "center of gravity" of a set of points, each of whose coordinates is the arithmetic mean of the corresponding coordinate values of the given points. (10)

champion a highly placed executive who provides visible support to an information system project (8); in particular, an executive information system project (12) or an expert system project (17), where the champion has a belief in the strategic value of expert system technology.

change in the context of this book, moving from habitual use of one decision-making method to habitual use of another. (8)

charting software package same a graphing software package. (6)

chauffeured (meeting style) a form of electronic meeting in which group communication is primarily verbal, with one person using the computer as a recording device; contrast with interactive and supported (meeting styles). (11)

choice phase the third of Simon's three stages of decision making, in which alternatives developed in the design phase are evaluated and one of them is chosen. (2)

class in object-oriented programming, a set of objects having similar characteristics but different data values. (16)

class library in object-oriented programming, a collection of class definitions that programmers can use as necessary. (16)

clerk mode a DSS usage mode in which the decision maker decides how a problem is to be presented to a computer, but the mechanical work of presenting it is done by another person. (4)

client (*a*) in client/server computing in general, the system closest to the user, which provides the user interface and often performs computations on data supplied by the server; (*b*) in the X Windows system, the computer that describes to the X server how the user interface is supposed to appear and behave; contrast with server. (7)

client/server computing (*a*) in general, execution of computer programs in which a computing task is partitioned over two or more systems, each handling the part of the program to which it is best suited; (*b*) often used specifically to mean execution of computer programs in which a server computer provides access to a database and a client computer performs computations on data from that database. (7)

closed loop system a system that incorporates feedback, generally to help it adjust its output to a desired objective; contrast with open loop system. (3)

closed system a system that does not receive input from, or send output to, its external environment. (3)

coarse-grain parallelism parallel processing in which the program is decomposed into large elements for parallel execution. (17)

CODASYL (COnference on DAta SYstems Languages) database (*a*) a standard for a particular type of network database; (*b*) informally, same as network database. (6)

cognitive emulation an approach to expert system development that attempts to mimic the internal cognitive (mental) processes of the expert, including all its human limitations and fallibilities, as opposed to an idealized version that is only appropriate for computers. (17)

cognitive skills problem-solving skills that involve only intellectual capability, not physical activity. (15)

command-line interface a method of controlling a computer system by entering commands from the keyboard. (5)

communication management system a system at the second level of the group DSS hierarchy, which provides facilities for user control over information flow. (11)

complete enumeration an optimization method in which all possible alternatives are evaluated and compared. (10)

complex method same as Box's method. (10)

compound document a document that incorporates several types of information, such as text, graphics, animation, and sound. (11)

confidence factor a numerical assessment of the degree to which an input value, intermediate result, or recommendation is considered appropriate in an expert system. (15, 16)

connection management system a system at the first level of the group DSS hierarchy, which provides a basic mechanism through which people involved in a decision can communicate. (11)

consequent in an expert system using production rules, that part of a rule that describes what action the system should take, or what facts should now be asserted, if the rule does or does not apply; see also antecedent. (14)

constraint (*a*) in general optimization, a limit on the value that an independent variable can take on; (*b*) in linear programming, the maximum quantity of a resource that may be used in a feasible solution. (10)

content management system a system at the third level of the group DSS hierarchy, which is programmed with information about the decision process and is able to handle different types of messages appropriately to their role in that process. (11)

context-sensitive help on-line help that reflects the activity that the user was performing at the time help was requested. (5)

continuous model an information-based model of a system in which quantities vary continuously (as a computer approximates continuous variation) over their range of values; contrast with discrete-event model. (3)

continuous speech human speech in which the speaker does not pause deliberately between words in order to facilitate computer recognition of what is being said. (14)

continuous-system simulation the process of simulating a continuous system via a continuous model (see separate listing). (9)

control interface the way in which a user controls an expert system. (15)

controllable variable in a simulation model, a variable that the user sets in order to specify the characteristics of a given run or set of runs. (9)

conversion the process of replacing user access to one system by user access to its successor. (8)

correlation a statistical statement of the degree to which one quantity generally varies when another is known to vary. (6)

crisp logic a form of reasoning in which an entity either does or does not have a particular characteristic; contrast with fuzzy logic. (16)

criteria (singular: criterion) what a decision maker is trying to optimize via the decision. (2)

Critical Success Factor (CSF) one of a small number of pieces of information that are crucial in evaluating an executive's or manager's job performance. (12)

cumulative distribution function a statement of the probability that a randomly selected value from a specified distribution falls below or equals the given value. (9)

cut-over the act of switching one or more users off one system and onto its successor; the critical moment in the conversion process. (8)

dæmon (*a*) in an expert system, a rule that is triggered automatically whenever a slot in a frame is filled; (*b*) in general, a program that checks periodically for certain conditions and runs whenever those conditions exist. (16)

data analysis system the second DSS level in Alter's hierarchy; data analysis systems allow data retrieval and limited operations on the retrieved data. (4)

data cube historical financial and marketing information of a firm, broken down by several variables (product type, time period, geographic region), in an executive information system. (12)

data flow diagram (DFD) a graphical representation of the processes and data stores in an information system and of the data flows that connect them with each other and with the environment of the system. (3)

data interface the way in which a user supplies data to an expert system. (15)

data manager software designed to organize a single file at a time, allow users to store information in it, and allow them to retrieve that information; contrast with database management system. (6)

data model a specification of the entities about which a database contains data and the ways in which these entities are related; often illustrated as an entity-relationship diagram. (6)

data processing (DP) originally, all computer-based information processing; today, also used to refer specifically to routine, repetitive computations. (1)

data store in a data flow diagram, a part of a system where data are at rest for a period of time. (3)

data-driven reasoning same as forward chaining. (16)

data-oriented DSS any DSS from the three lowest levels of Alter's hierarchy: file drawer systems, data analysis systems, or analysis information systems; contrast with model-oriented DSS. (4)

database A structured set of information stored in a computer that consists of multiple files whose contents are in some way related. Also used loosely to refer to any set of information stored in a computer. (1, 6)

database management the activity of organizing a database and providing controlled access to it. (6)

database management system software designed to organize a database comprising multiple files, allow users to store information in it, and allow them to retrieve that information; contrast with data (or file) manager. (6)

decision a reasoned choice among alternatives. (2)

decision analyst a person who understands the available tools in a decision conference facility, can explain them, and can aid the decision makers in choosing and using the appropriate ones. (11)

decision conference an electronic meeting augmented by task support tools. (11)

decision statement a clear statement of what a person or group is trying to decide. (2)

decision support system (DSS) an information system whose primary purpose is to provide knowledge workers with information on which to base informed decisions. (1, 2)

decision tree a graphical representation of a decision process in which possible decisions and states of nature (which affect the outcome of the decisions) alternate at the nodes of the tree. (2)

decisional guidance help provided to a user by a DSS in choosing an appropriate decision method for a particular problem. (5)

default value a value supplied by the system for a data element, expected to be correct in most cases, but capable of being overridden by software or by a user. (16)

defensive DSS use using a DSS to justify, retroactively, the correctness of a decision that was taken in the past; contrast with offensive DSS use. (1, 4)

Delphi technique a means of reaching group consensus about the most likely future by several cycles of individual estimates followed by group discussion. (11)

derivative in calculus, the slope of a function at a specified point. (10)

descriptive model a system model that describes how a system behaved in the past or is behaving at present; contrast with prescriptive model. (3)

design phase the second of Simon's three phases of decision making, in which alternatives are developed and objectives for the decision are stated. (2)

deterministic model a system model in which all the relationships among quantities in the model are fixed; contrast with stochastic model. (3)

direct conversion, direct cut-over a conversion strategy in which an entire organization uses one information system until the moment of cut-over and uses its successor from that time forward. (8)

disconnected speech human speech in which the speaker pauses deliberately between words in order to facilitate computer recognition of what is being said. (14)

discrete-event model an information-based model of a system in which quantities are considered to change instantaneously from one value to a different one; contrast with continuous model. (3)

discrete-event simulation simulation of a process represented by a discrete-event model. (9)

domain expert in expert system development, a person who is familiar with the problem to be solved and the methods used to solve it but is not necessarily familiar with expert systems or computers. (14)

dominant function the personality function that an individual prefers to use in his or her preferred (internal or external) world. (2)

dotted pair in the LISP language, a list of two elements, represented by writing the elements between parentheses and separated by a dot. (17)

drill down the capability of an executive information system (or, in principle, any DSS) to investigate an apparent problem area in increasing levels of detail. (12)

DSS builder (development role) a technical expert who makes decisions about software tool(s) to use, hardware platform(s) to use, models and/or databases to incorporate into a DSS, and how they will be integrated with each other. (5)

DSS generator a program that can be customized or modified to create a specific DSS. (6)

DSS tool (*a*) originally, a program that can be used to create a DSS generator; (*b*) today, a program that can become part of, but not all of, a DSS. (6)

dynamic model an information-based model of a dynamic system that follows the changes over time that result from system activities; contrast with static model, sense *b*. (3)

dynamic system a system that incorporates cause-and-effect relationships between activity in one time period and the state of the system in subsequent periods. (3)

economic feasibility a determination, with respect to an information system project, that its expected benefits justify the necessary financial investment; compare with operational feasibility, technical feasibility. (15)

electronic boardroom same as electronic meeting room. (11)

electronic bulletin board same as bulletin board system. (11)

electronic data processing early term for data processing; while little used by itself today, it remains in the phrase "EDP auditing," referring to an accounting audit of an organization's information processing. (1)

electronic meeting a problem-solving session that uses electronic meeting room facilities. (11)

electronic meeting room a meeting room equipped with computers for each participant, linked in a network, with software to facilitate the use of these computers in reaching a group decision. (11)

electronic meeting systems software intended for use in an electronic meeting room. (11)

emulation (*a*) the addition of hardware and/or microcode to one computer (the host computer) to enable it to run programs originally written for another computer (the target computer) (19); (*b*) also used to refer to programming a computer so that it appears to be a terminal to another computer with which it is communicating.

end-user computing, end-user development the development of information systems directly by the person or people who will also ultimately use them to solve their business problems. (1, 5)

endogenous event in a simulation model, an event that results from activity within the system being modeled; contrast with exogenous event. (9)

entity-relationship diagram a graphical description of a data model. (6)

environment (of a system) those entities outside a system that interact with it. (3)

equations of balance in queuing theory, the equations that represent the balancing of transitions into and out of a state when the system is at rest. (9)

Erlang distribution a distribution of events in time characterized by smaller variance than the exponential distribution and modeled by two or more processes, each having exponential service time, through which a transaction proceeds serially. (9)

Ethernet 10 Mbit/sec local area network communication protocol originally developed jointly by Intel, Xerox, and Digital Equipment Corporation; now standardized by the IEEE (Institute of Electrical and Electronics Engineers). (7)

event an activity that is considered to change the state of a system instantaneously. (3, 9)

evolutionary prototyping a system development methodology in which a prototype is developed and then modified and enhanced to create the final system. (5)

executive one of the top managers of an organization, typically in charge of a large part of that organization and responsible for major, strategic decisions. (12)

executive information system (EIS) an information system designed to provide executives with the type of information they need for decision making. (1, 12)

executive support system (ESS) an executive information system enhanced by the addition of communication and/or modeling capabilities. (12)

exogenous event in a simulation model, an event that results from activity outside the system being modeled; contrast with endogenous event. (9)

expectation-based reasoning in expert systems, giving data elements the values they are most likely to have on the basis of other known facts, with the capability of changing these values on the basis of user input or later facts. (16)

expediting problem solving (DSS benefit) enabling a person or organization to solve an overall problem more quickly than it could without a suitable DSS. (1)

expert system an information system that follows rules derived from the knowledge of human experts in order to recommend a decision. (1, 14)

expert-related criteria factors related to the availability and characteristics of experts in making a particular decision that may or may not make that decision suitable for support by an expert system; contrast with task-related criteria. (15)

explanation interface the means by which an expert system explains to its user the reasons for its recommendations and for its information requests. (15)

exponential distribution a distribution of events in time in which knowing the time since the last event of a given time does not help predict when the next one will take place. (9)

external entity anything outside an information system that exchanges information with that system. (3)

external feedback feedback that takes place in whole or in part outside the boundaries of a system; contrast with internal feedback. (3)

extraversion a behavioral preference in which individuals prefer to direct their energy toward the outer world; contrast with introversion. (2)

facilitating interpersonal communication (DSS benefit) improving decision quality by helping people involved in the decision communicate with each other. (1)

facilitator (development role) same as DSS builder. (5)

factual knowledge knowledge of specific facts that pertain to the current decision situation; contrast with judgmental knowledge. (16)

feasible region in linear programming, that part of the solution space that does not violate any resource constraints. (10)

feedback in a system, the use of system output (perhaps after processing or modification) as system input. (3)

feeling a behavioral preference for weighing personal values and others' reactions in making a decision; contrast with thinking. (2)

file drawer system the lowest DSS level in Alter's hierarchy; file drawer systems allow immediate access to individual data items. (4)

file manager same as data manager. (6)

file server a computer that stores files to be accessed by multiple users across a network. (7)

filter criteria same as Must objectives. (2)

financial modeling software programs designed to create financial models of a firm. (6)

fine-grain parallelism parallel processing in which the program is decomposed into small elements for parallel execution; fine-grain parallelism imposes demanding requirements on system software, because each element must be started with minimal overhead or else the potential gains of parallelism will not be achieved. (17)

firing a rule testing the antecedent of a rule and taking appropriate action on the basis of its being true or false. (16)

flexibility the extent to which decision makers free themselves from tradition and structure in making a decision. (2)

forecasting the process of predicting future values of a quantity on the basis of its past values and other available information. (6)

forecasting software a computer program designed to perform forecasting. (6)

form (for work flow systems) a screen display in which the user is to enter information into specified locations; this is a functional, if not always a graphical, equivalent of a paper form. (11)

formula in a spreadsheet, a specification of a calculation that will determine the content of a cell. (6)

forward chaining in expert systems, an inference method in which known facts are used to select rules, which will provide additional facts and thus, eventually, the solution to the problem. (16)

fourth-generation (programming) language (4GL) a computer programming language in which the programmer specifies the result the computer must produce but need not specify the steps via which it will be produced. (6)

frame in an expert system, a data structure that can hold several data elements related to the same entity. (16)

future events queue in a simulation model, a computer data structure that contains information about events that have been scheduled for future occurrence in the model. (9)

fuzzy logic a form of reasoning in which an entity may have a characteristic partially but not totally; contrast with crisp logic. (16)

global maximum the highest point anywhere on a surface; contrast with local maximum. (10)

goal-directed (or goal-driven) reasoning same as backward chaining. (14, 16)

GPSS a programming language for developing discrete-event simulation models. (9)

graphical (user) interface (GUI) a user interface in which computer commands are given by pointing at icons and by selecting commands from menus that are likewise selected by pointing. (5)

graphical model a description of an object or system via pictures and diagrams. (3)

graphing software package a program designed to create graphs of data supplied to it by the user or by another program. (6)

group decision support systems (Group DSS, GDSS) decision support systems designed to support the information flow and group decision process of an organization; contrast with individual DSS, multi-individual DSS. (1, 4, 11)

groupthink the tendency of members of a group to fall into similar thought patterns and to deprecate any departure from those thought patterns by a member. (11)

groupware software, including but not limited to DSS, designed to support the work of a group. (1, 4, 11)

GUI acronym for graphical (user) interface. (5)

help desk an organizational entity designed to provide assistance in the use of one or more specific information systems. (8)

heuristic searching following a heuristic in order to reach a goal, as opposed to following an algorithm that always yields a solution. (14)

heuristics "rules of thumb" that generally reach an adequate decision but may not always do so and are not guaranteed to reach the best one. (10)

hierarchical database database structure in which records of one type are explicitly linked to records of another type in a hierarchy in which each lower level record belongs to one record at the next level up; contrast with network database, relational database. (6)

hill-climbing an optimization method in which function values are used to determine a direction along a surface in which higher values are expected to lie. (10)

host computer see emulation, sense *a*. (19)

hot line a telephone number through which end users can obtain quick answers to problems that impede their use of a computer system; the people who answer a hot line may be part of a help desk (see separate listing). (8)

hot spot a screen location to which a computer can point in order to activate a computational process. (12)

"How?" explanations in an expert system, output messages that explain how the system reached a particular conclusion. (15)

hyperexponential distribution a distribution of events in time characterized by larger variance than the exponential distribution and modeled by two processes, each having exponential service time, whereby a transaction proceeds through either one or the other. (9)

hypermedia hypertext extended to include graphics, sound, animation, and other media. (5)

hypertext an electronic document whose parts are electronically linked in a nonlinear fashion. (5)

icon in a graphical user interface, a small on-screen picture intended to represent an object such as a program or a data file. (5)

image processing computer applications in which scanned images represent a significant fraction of the information that is stored and communicated. (11)

implementation the process through which an information system, tested and considered ready for use, is made available to its user community. (8)

improving personal efficiency (DSS benefit) enabling an individual to carry out part of a decision-making task more quickly than he or she would have been able to without a suitable DSS. (1)

increasing organizational control (DSS benefit) use of a DSS to ensure that decisions are made consistently with management policies and/or with each other. (1)

indifference curve the line connecting all points on a graph that represent combinations of goods, money, or other valuable items that a decision maker considers to have the same total value as the other combinations along the curve. (2)

individual DSS a decision support system designed to be used by one person and whose design, therefore, does not reflect any need to make the decision in conjunction with other people; contrast with multi-individual DSS, group DSS. (4)

induction the process of deriving decision-making rules for an expert system from examples in which humans have previously made the corresponding decision. (17)

inference engine a software component of an expert system that applies facts about the current situation to the rules in the system's rule base. (14)

inferencing method the specific process that an inference engine uses in applying rules to facts about the current situation. (16)

information base a read-only database derived from the business database(s) of an organization and used to provide data to decision support systems. (7)

information center a component of an organization whose purpose is to help users carry out end-user computing projects. (5)

information reporting systems (IRS) information systems whose purpose is to provide members of an organization with information on transactions that have taken place. (1)

information retrieval package a program designed to facilitate the retrieval of information from a database, normally by end users. (6)

information system a system whose purpose is the storage, processing, and communication of information. (3)

information-based model a representation of reality by information about reality. (3)

inheritance in object-oriented programming and frame-based expert systems, defining an object or frame on the basis of an existing object or frame, where the newly defined entity retains those characteristics of the existing one that are not explicitly overriden in its definition. (16)

initial state the values of all state variables that define a system at the instant a simulation or other modeling process starts. (9)

input interface combined term for the control interface and the data interface of an expert system. (15)

installation the process of making computer hardware ready to run programs. (8)

instance in object-oriented programming, a particular member of a class; often corresponds to a particular real-world entity. (16)

institutional DSS decision support systems that are used regularly, often as a matter of formal policy, by many members of an organization. (4)

intelligence phase the first of Simon's three phases of decision making, which consists of finding, identifying, and formulating the problem or situation that calls for a decision. (2)

interarrival time the statistically defined time between the arrival of one entity (customer, order, etc.) at a system and the arrival of the next entity of the same type. (9)

interactive (meeting style) a form of electronic meeting in which virtually all interaction among the participants is via the computer, with little or no speech; contrast with chauffeured, supported (meeting styles). (11)

intermediary (development role) in intermediary usage mode (see separate listing) the individual who will help the user or users use the DSS. (5)

intermediary mode a DSS usage mode in which a decision maker describes a problem to another person, who uses his or her professional expertise in presenting it to the computer. (4)

internal feedback feedback that takes place entirely within the boundaries of a system; contrast with external feedback. (3)

introversion a behavioral preference in which individuals prefer to direct their energy toward the inner world; contrast with extraversion. (2)

intuition a behavioral preference to perceive patterns or relationships among ideas, people, and events; contrast with sensing. (2)

join (in a relational database) combining corresponding records from more than one table on the basis of a match among specified fields in those records. (6)

judgment a behavioral preference to tend to let one's judgment process (thinking or feeling) run one's outer life; contrast with perception. (2)

judgmental knowledge knowledge of general rules or procedures that apply to many similar decisions, even though the facts in each situation and, hence, the correct decision may vary from one to another; contrast with factual knowledge. (16)

Kepner-Tregoe method a systematic, multi-stage decision-making method. (2)

key attributes in a file or database, fields in a record by which the entity described in that record can be identified. (6)

keyboard shortcut in a GUI, a keystroke or combination of keystrokes that can be used as an alternative to pointing and clicking. (5)

knowledge acquisition the process of identifying, obtaining, and organizing the knowledge that is to be incorporated into an expert system. (17)

knowledge base the set of rules used by an expert system. (14)

knowledge elicitation the process of working with a subject matter expert to extract problem-solving knowledge from his or her head, usually via questions and answers; part of the knowledge acquisition process. (17)

knowledge engineer a knowledge acquisition specialist who has some knowledge of computers, psychology, and the subject matter of the expert system. (14, 17)

knowledge-based system same as expert system. (14)

linear programming an optimization method that deals with objective functions that are linear combinations of system outputs, outputs that are linear combinations of system inputs, and constraints on the available quantities of those inputs. (10)

LISP a programming language widely used in artificial intelligence work. (17)

LISP machine same as symbolic processor. (17)

list a data structure in computer storage whose elements can be stored in arbitrary storage locations with each element containing, in addition to its data value, an indication of where the next element is located. (In a double-threaded list, each element also contains an indication of where the preceding element is located.) (17)

local area network (LAN) a computer network in which maximum communication distance (typically restricted to less than 2 km) is sacrificed for high communication speed at low cost. (7)

local maximum a point on a surface that is higher than any other point in its immediate vicinity but not higher than all other points on the surface; contrast with global maximum. (10)

LocalTalk 230 Kbit/sec local area network communication protocol developed by Apple. (7)

Loebner prize an annual prize awarded since 1991 by David Loebner for progress in passing the Turing test. (14)

machine intelligence same as artificial intelligence; term is often used in the United Kingdom. (14)

machine vision programming computers to recognize objects on the basis of visual (typically video camera) input. (14)

mainframe computer a large commercial computer system, typically costing over $1 million, designed for high overall throughput and intended to be used as the central information processing facility of a medium-sized or large organization. (7)

Management Information System (*a*) originally, a system to provide information to management about all aspects of a firm's operations; (*b*) in all lowercase letters, a general term for business-oriented computation as a whole. (1, 19)

management support system an information system that provides managers with access to internal and external databases, and to processing, modeling, and communication capabilities, via an easy-to-use interface. (19)

managing change the process of ensuring that change takes place in a positive manner that will support the goals of the organization. (8)

Markov process any process whose state depends only on its previous state and not on its earlier history. (9)

massively parallel computer a parallel computer having at least hundreds, often thousands, of central processing units. (17)

mathematical model (*a*) same as information-based model; (*b*) a description of a system via equations that define its behavior. (3)

meeting facilitator in an electronic meeting or decision conference, a neutral individual who is trained in the technology of the electronic meeting room and in group processes but is not a member of the decision-making group. (11)

membership grade in fuzzy logic, the degree to which an entity is a member of a fuzzily defined set. (16)

menu (interface) a user interface style in which the system presents the user with a set of choices and the user must then select one of them. (5)

menu bar in a GUI, a row of menu names across the top of a screen or window from which the user can choose to select a menu and then can invoke one of the elements of that menu. (5)

message in object-oriented programming, a command to an object that invokes a method associated with that object. (16)

method in object-oriented programming, a program associated with an object class that responds to a particular message directed to an instance of that class. (16)

minicomputer a multi-user computer smaller and less expensive than a mainframe; as minicomputers blend into microcomputers at one end of the spectrum and into mainframes at the other, a generally accepted precise definition does not exist. (7)

model (*a*) a replica of a real system or object; (*b*) in a DSS, a computer representation of a system or decision-making process. (1, 3, 9)

model-oriented DSS any DSS from the upper four levels of Alter's hierarchy: accounting models, representational models, optimization systems, and suggestion systems; contrast with data-oriented DSS. (4)

modeling software package a program designed to ease the creation of computer models of a particular type. (6)

Monte Carlo simulation simulation where the behavior of the simulated system is determined in part by random or pseudo-random numbers. (9)

mouse a device held under a computer user's hand and moved on a flat surface, with its movement translated into corresponding movement of a pointer on the computer screen. (5)

Motif a GUI standard based on X Windows, developed by the Open Software Foundation.

moving the second phase in the Lewin-Schein theory of change, which constitutes the change itself: putting the new system into operation to replace the old. (8)

multi-attribute decision problem a decision-making situation in which the alternatives are described by several attributes that cannot be optimized simultaneously. (2)

multi-individual DSS a DSS intended for use by individuals but designed to allow those individuals to coordinate decisions of the same type with each other in order to achieve organizational consistency or conformity to organizational policy. Contrast with individual DSS, group DSS. (4)

multi-valued attribute in an expert system, a variable that can take on more than one value at a time; contrast with single-valued attribute. (16)

multiple inheritance inheritance (see separate listing) in which the newly created object or frame retains characteristics of more than one existing object or frame. (16)

multiprocessing executing computer programs on a multiprocessor computer. (7)

multiprocessor a computer system having more than one central processing unit; these CPUs may be working on different user-visible tasks; contrast with parallel processors, in which multiple CPUs work on the same task. (7)

Must objectives in the Kepner-Tregoe decision-making method, attributes of a solution that it absolutely must have in order to be considered further; contrast with Want objectives. (2)

narrative model a description of an object or system through sentences in a natural language such as English. (3)

natural language interpretation (*a*) programming computers to recognize sound waves as text (same as speech recognition); (*b*) programming computers to interpret text strings that are in the form of natural language expressions or sentences. (14)

network database a database structure in which records of one type are explicitly linked to related records of another type without regard for hierarchy of relationships; contrast with hierarchical database, relational database. (6)

neural network an information system whose structure is modeled after that of the brain. (14)

neuron (*a*) in a living creature, a cell in the nervous system that processes and transmits neural impulses; (*b*) in a neural network, a computer (hardware or software) component that accumulates inputs signals until a threshold is reached and then sends outputs signals to prespecified destinations. (14)

numerical optimization methods optimization methods that depend on our ability to calculate the value of a function at any given point but not on our ability to express that function as a mathematical formula or to differentiate it. (10)

object a logical entity that combines, or encapsulates, its data and programs (called methods) to operate on that data. (16)

object-attribute-value (OAV) network a semantic network using only "has-a" and "is-a" arcs. (16)

object-oriented DBMS a database management system designed to store information about objects. (6)

object-oriented programming programming methods that make maximum effort to deal with data in the form of objects rather than traditional data structures; often uses specialized languages that facilitate this effort. (16)

objective function a function whose value will be determined by one or more decisions to be made, where the purpose of the decision is to maximize (or minimize) this value. (10)

off-line EIS an executive information system in which information that might be of interest to executives is preprocessed into tables or graphs in order to be ready if and when it is requested; contrast with on-line EIS. (12)

offensive DSS use using a DSS to persuade people that a particular decision should be made now or in the future; contrast with defensive DSS use. (1, 4)

office information system (OIS) information system designed to improve information handling in an office. (1)

on-line EIS an executive information system in which information is not processed into tables or graphs until it is requested; contrast with off-line EIS. (12)

on-line help information about how to use a system, which is available through the computer at the time the system is being used. (5)

open loop system a system that has no feedback; contrast with closed loop system. (3)

open system (*a*) system that receives input from and/or sends output to its external environment (3); (*b*) a computer system whose external interfaces are based on vendor-independent standards. (7)

open software environment software-based open system in sense *b*. (7)

operating sponsor a trusted, high-level subordinate of an executive information system sponsor who takes over the sponsor's responsibility for providing overall direction to system development efforts. (12)

operational decision a decision that affects activities taking place in the organization right now but either has little or no impact on the future or is made within the confines of a controlling policy. (2)

operational feasibility a determination, with respect to an information system project, that it can work within the existing or planned organizational structure and culture; compare with economic feasibility, technical feasibility. (15)

optimization the mathematical process of finding the highest (or, sometimes, the lowest) value of a function. (10)

optimization system the sixth DSS level in Alter's hierarchy; optimization systems generate mathematically optimal solutions to decision problems. (4)

ordinal utility an approach to utility theory in which individual decision factors are not valued in utils but where combinations of factors that have the same utility to the decision maker are determined and the decision options compared with those. (2)

organizational decision making an approach to decision making that recognizes and attempts to reconcile the goals, priorities, and "rights" of people and organizational subunits. (2)

output interface the way in which an expert system presents its conclusions and its explanations to its users. (15)

overcoming resistance in system implementation, the process of persuading people who might be reluctant to change that it is in fact in their best interest to do so. (8)

overriding changing a default value via user input or software action. (16)

parallel conversion a conversion strategy in which an organization uses both an old information system and its replacement concurrently, comparing their results until it is determined that the new one is functioning properly. (8)

parallel processing the execution of different parts of one program by more than one CPU at the same time. (7, 17)

parallel computer, parallel processor a computer having more than one central processing unit and designed for parallel processing; contrast with multiprocessors, which have more than one CPU but which cannot generally assign more than one to a given task. (17)

parameter (of a simulation model) same as controllable variable. (9)

partial derivative in calculus, the slope of a function of more than one variable at a specified point with all but one of the variables held constant. (10)

partial set membership in fuzzy logic, a statement that an entity has a characteristic to a partial but not a total degree. (16)

pattern matching in the LISP language, the process of attempting to match values with a pattern-matching variable in order to make an expression true. (17)

pattern-matching variable in the LISP language, a variable that is to be matched with a value that will make an expression true. (17)

pattern recognition programming computers to distinguish between objects inside a set of interest and objects not in that set, where the programmer cannot define rigorously what characteristics define set membership. (14)

perception a behavioral preference to tend to let one's perception process (sensing or intuition) run one's outer life; contrast with judgment. (2)

personal information systems information systems developed and used by one individual to improve his or her personal productivity and effectiveness. (1)

phased conversion a conversion strategy in which an organization uses some parts of an old information system and some parts of its replacement, replacing parts of the old with corresponding parts of the new until the entire new system is in use. (8)

physical model a simplified, often smaller, reproduction of a real object. (3)

pilot conversion a conversion strategy in which part of an organization uses an old information system while other parts of the organization use its replacement, moving organizational units from the old to the new until the entire organization is using the new system. (8)

platform the hardware-software base on which application programs run. (7)

pointer in programming, a variable whose value indicates the location of another variable in computer memory. (17)

pointing device input device that allows a user to indicate position on the display screen; most often a mouse, but alternatively a trackball, joystick, etc. (5)

political decision making a decision-making process in which bargaining among the participants is decisive. (2)

politicality the extent to which a decision involves competition among decision makers and depends on the distribution and use of organizational power. (2)

polymorphism in object-oriented programming, the ability of a message to invoke different actions depending on the type of object to which it is sent. (16)

POSIX a set of operating system interfaces based closely on UNIX, standardized by the IEEE (Institute of Electrical and Electronics Engineers), supported by several computer vendors. (7)

possibility same as membership grade. (16)

predicate a logical statement whose truth is known and that can therefore be used as a basis for reasoning to a conclusion. (16)

predicate calculus a formal method of reasoning from known statements to logical conclusions. (16)

predictive model same as prescriptive model. (3)

prescriptive model a system model that describes how a system is expected to behave in the future; contrast with descriptive model. (3)

probability (of an adverse consequence) in the Kepner-Tregoe decision-making method, the likelihood that an adverse consequence will occur; typically rated using a 1 to 10 scale, with 10 indicating the highest probability, and where the numbers do not correspond to statistical probabilities. (2)

probe in spreadsheet auditing, determining the cells whose formulas use the value contained in a given cell; contrast with trace. (6)

process (in a DFD or system) an activity that takes place in a system. (3)

process management system a system at the fourth level of the group DSS hierarchy that is able to handle different messages of the same type differently on the basis of their content. (11)

process model an information-based model of the process people use to reach a particular type of decision; contrast with system model. (3)

process structure in Nunamaker's categorization of group DSS, any techniques or rules that direct the pattern, timing, or content of group communication. (11)

process support in Nunamaker's categorization of group DSS, the communication infrastructure among participants in a group decision. (11)

process oriented DSS a DSS whose behavior is based on a process model; typically a suggestion system in Alter's DSS hierarchy. (4)

production rule in an expert system, a decision rule of the form IF . . . THEN . . . ELSE. (14, 16)

program manager in expert system development, the person who coordinates the work of the various specialized professionals on the project. (17)

Prolog a programming language widely used in artificial intelligence work. (17)

promoting learning or training (DSS benefit) helping a decision maker learn to make better decisions unaided by showing him or her how a particular decision should usually be made. (1)

proposition a statement whose truth is not known but that we would like to validate from known predicates. (16)

proprietary system, proprietary software environment an information system whose user and application programming interfaces are defined by one vendor without consultation with other vendors or standards bodies; one that is not freely available for other system vendors to use. (7)

prototyping determining the specifications of an information system by allowing its prospective users to experiment with possibilities and to suggest improvements until agreement is reached. (5)

pseudo-random number a number created by a computational process, which can therefore be predicted by a person aware of the process being used, but a series of which has the same statistical characteristics as a corresponding series of random numbers. (9)

psychological type one of 16 personality categories determined by a person's four behavioral preferences. (2)

question-and-answer dialogue a user interface style in which the system asks for each input data item as it is required and the user then enters its value. (5)

queuing theory a branch of mathematics that enables us to find the steady-state probabilities of a system being in any given state, given the average transition rates among the states. (9)

quick-hit DSS a decision support system developed from existing components, in order to be available when needed, often for one-time use and often at the expense of computational efficiency. (5)

random number a number whose value cannot be predicted by any computational method. (9)

random search an optimization method in which a function is evaluated at several randomly selected points, with the highest (or lowest) value found at those points taken as the maximum (or minimum) value of the function. (10)

rapid application development same as evolutionary prototyping. (5)

rational decision making the classical assumption about how managers make decisions—obtaining all possible facts, weighing the likelihood of alternative outcomes, and choosing the one with the highest expected value. (2)

rationality the extent to which a decision is based on collecting and analyzing information objectively, then choosing among alternatives based on their relationship to predetermined objectives. (2)

refreezing the third phase in the Lewin-Schein theory of change, which involves making the new system part of the organizational fabric. (8)

regression calculating the parameters of a function of a specified type (often, but not always, a straight line) that best matches a supplied set of data. (6)

relational database a database structure in which data are stored in two-dimensional tables, with no visible links among related records in different tables; contrast with hierarchical database and network database. (6)

renormalization in Markov process computations, forcing the sum of the elements of the state vector back to 1 after they drift off because of accumulated computational errors. (9)

replication providing access to a database at multiple sites by creating copies of that database on a local computer at each site. (11)

representational model the fifth DSS level in Alter's hierarchy; representational model DSS generally incorporate stochastic models. (3, 4)

robotics programming computers to activate a physical mechanism to perform the motions or manipulations required to achieve a certain purpose, where the programmer specifies only the goal and not the necessary motions to achieve it. (14)

rule (in an expert system) same as production rule. (14)

rule base same as knowledge base. (14)

rule trace a listing or representation of the rules that an expert system used to solve a given problem. (15)

rule-based system same as expert system. (14)

satisficing making a decision that is "good enough" when further analysis might yield a better one. (2)

scratchpad in an expert system, same as workspace. (14)

scripting language an easy-to-use language that enables users to create hypertext documents. (5)

scripts (for work flow systems) instructions that define how a form is to be routed by the system. (11)

semantic network a representation of factual knowledge as a network of relationships among objects connected by labeled, directed arcs. (16)

semistructured decision a decision for which one or two of the three phases (intelligence, design, and choice) is or are structured. (2)

sensing a behavioral preference for finding out about things through the senses and through careful, detailed observation; contrast with intuition. (2)

seriousness (of an adverse consequence) in the Kepner-Tregoe decision-making method, the impact of an adverse consequence if it does occur; typically rated using a 1 to 10 scale, with 10 indicating the highest impact, where the numbers are not related mathematically to any numerical measure of impact seriousness. (2)

server (*a*) in client/server computing in general, a system with which the user has no direct contact, which often provides data for use by the client; (*b*) in the X Windows system, the computer or terminal that provides the user interface; contrast with client. (7)

service time the statistically defined time between the beginning of a service process and its end. (9)

shell an expert system development tool consisting of an inference engine, user interface software, and rules for creating a knowledge base. (17)

simple fact in an expert system, same as single-valued variable. (16)

simplex method a method for solving linear programming optimization problems that works by moving around the edges of the feasible region, from one vertex to an adjacent vertex, until no such move can improve the result. (10)

simplification (in a model) the omission of details of the real system that are not important for the purpose for which the model is to be used. (3)

Simscript a programming language for developing discrete-event simulation models. (9)

simulation the process of using a simulation model to study a system. (9)

simulation model a model, generally expressed as a computer program, that follows the behavior of a system over time in order to draw conclusions about how it is likely to behave in actuality. (9)

simulation study a series of simulations intended to determine how a system is likely to behave for particular values of its controllable variables. (9)

simulator a DSS generator intended to simulate a particular type of system. (9)

single-valued attribute in an expert system, a variable that can only take on one value at a time; contrast with multi-valued attribute. (16)

slot in a frame, a position for a data element of a particular type. (16)

software systems integration engineer in expert system development, the person who deals with non-knowledge-base aspects of the system such as the user interface and database access. (17)

sparse matrix a matrix whose elements are almost all zero. (9)

speaker-dependent said of a speech recognition system, requiring training for each speaker that it is to understand and hence able to understand only speakers whose voices it has been trained to recognize; contrast with speaker-independent. (14)

speaker-independent said of a speech recognition system, able to understand any speaker within broad limits and hence not requiring training for each speaker it is to understand; contrast with speaker-dependent. (14)

speech (sound) recognition programming computers to recognize sound waves as text; same as natural language interpretation, sense *a*. (14)

speed governor nonfunctional code added to a system to slow down its response time in order to prevent the initial users of a system from developing performance expectations that will not be sustainable when the system is fully loaded. (8)

sponsor (*a*) of an executive information system,

same as champion (12); (*b*) of an expert system, the person who has the business problem, a commitment to solve it, and a position with authority and resources but not necessarily the commitment to expert systems technology that the champion has. (17)

spreadsheet a computer program that presents the user with a grid of cells, each of which can contain text, a number, or a formula that carries out a computation using the content of other cells. (6)

SQL (Structured Query Language) a language for retrieving information from relational databases. (6)

staff assistant in the intermediary model of DSS usage, an assistant who saves a decision maker's time by presenting a problem to a computer. (4)

state (of a system) the set of values of all state (uncontrollable) variables. (9)

state transition in queuing theory and Markov process analysis, the movement of a system from one state to another. (9)

state transition matrix in Markov process analysis, a statement of the probability that a system will go from any given state to any given state in the next time interval. (9)

state transition rate in queuing theory and Markov process analysis, the average rate of transitions from one specified state to another specified state, expressed in transitions per unit time. (9)

state variable in a simulation model, a variable whose value is determined by activity within the model rather than being set by the user. (9)

static model (*a*) an information-based model of a static system; (*b*) an information-based model of a dynamic system that shows the values that system attributes take when the system is in balance. In sense *b*, contrast with dynamic model. (3)

static simulation model a simulation model of a static system. (9)

static system a system whose behavior is not affected by the passage of time. (3)

statistical software programs that carry out statistical calculations on supplied data, such as means, correlations, regression, and analysis of variance. (6)

steady state the equilibrium condition of a dynamic system. (3, 9)

stochastic model a system model in which some of the relationships among quantities in the model are described statistically; contrast with deterministic model. (3)

strategic decision a decision that will affect an entire organization, or a major part of it, for a long period of time. (2)

strategic information system (SIS) an information system intended to given the organization that deploys it a strategic competitive advantage over its rivals. (1)

structured decision a decision for which a well-defined decision-making procedure exists; a decision is structured if all three of its phases are structured. (2)

structured decision phase a decision phase (intelligence, design, or choice) whose inputs, outputs, and internal procedures can all be specified. (2)

subject matter expert same as domain expert. (14, 17)

subscription mode a DSS usage mode in which a decision maker receives decision support information on a regular basis without requesting it each time. (4)

subsystem a system that is also a component of another system. (3)

suggestion system the seventh (highest) DSS level in Alter's hierarchy; suggestion systems suggest which decision a person might be advised to make. (4)

supported (meeting style) a form of electronic meeting in which interaction among the participants is partly verbal and partly electronic, with all group members able to write on the computer "blackboard;" contrast with chauffeured, interactive (meeting styles). (11)

symbolic expression (S-expression) in the LISP language, a list that is interpreted as a function name followed by its operands. (17)

symbolic model same as information-based model. (3)

symbolic processor a computer whose instruction set is designed to process symbols and lists of symbols. (17)

synapse a signal pathway between neurons. (14)

sysop short for SYStem OPerator; the person responsible for operating a bulletin board system. (11)

system a group of interacting elements having a purpose and a boundary. (3)

system development life cycle (SDLC) a series of standard steps to be followed in system development, typically beginning with a feasibility study or needs analysis and continuing through implementation and maintenance. (5)

system model a model, in DSS usually an information-based model, of a system to be studied; contrast with process model. (3)

systems integration the design and development of information systems that combine several hardware and/or software components to cooperate to carry out a joint task that would be beyond the capabilities of any one of them individually. (19)

tactical decision a decision that will affect how a part of the organization does business for a limited time into the future. (2)

target computer see emulation, sense *a*. (19)

task structure in Nunamaker's categorization of group DSS, the use of models. (11)

task support in Nunamaker's categorization of group DSS, the use of data-oriented DSS without models. (11)

task-related criteria factors related to the nature of a decision-making task that may or may not make it suitable for support by an expert system; contrast with expert-related criteria. (15)

technical feasibility a determination, with respect to an information system project, that it can be completed with currently available hardware and software tools; compare with economic feasibility, operational feasibility. (15)

technical support person (development role) a programmer who integrates existing packages into one overall system and carries out custom programming that contributes directly to DSS functionality. (5)

technical support staff in the intermediary mode of DSS usage, an assistant who contributes computer-related technical expertise to the decision-making process. (4)

temperament a set of psychological types having similar decision support needs. (4)

terminal mode a DSS usage mode in which the decision maker presents a problem directly to a computer himself or herself. (4)

test cases (for neural networks) example problems for which the correct answer is known but on which the network has not been trained. (14)

thinking a behavioral preference for considering pros and cons or consequences and then coming to a logical choice, decision, or conclusion; contrast with feeling. (2)

third-generation programming language (3GL) a computer programming language in which the programmer must specify the steps of the process via which a computer will produce a desired result. (6)

throwaway prototyping a system development methodology in which a prototype is developed and then used as a specification for the final system. (5)

time-sharing a mode of computer use in which multiple users perform unrelated activities while sharing the hardware resources of one computer. (7)

Token ring 4 or 16 Mbit/sec local area network communication protocol originally developed by IBM, now standardized by the IEEE (Institute of Electrical and Electronics Engineers). (7)

toolsmith (development role) an expert on tools and packages who focuses on creating underlying DSS capabilities, often not visible to the user but important for system development. (5)

trace (*a*) in spreadsheet auditing, determining the cells whose values are used in the formula contained in a given cell; contrast with probe (6); (*b*) in expert systems, same as rule trace. (15)

training (*a*) in the implementation of a computer system, teaching its prospective user community how to use it effectively (8); (*b*) in a neural network, the process of giving the network example problems for which the answer is known and adjusting its internal structure to increase the probability that it will give the correct answer. (14)

transaction processing recording and processing information about significant events, usually financial in nature, that take place in the organization. (1)

transaction processing system (TPS) an information system that performs transaction processing. (1)

truth threshold in an expert system, the confidence level above which the antecedent of a rule is considered to be true. (16)

truth value the characteristic of a data element as being true or false. (16)

Turing test a test proposed by Alan Turing in which a computer would be considered intelligent if it could fool a person into thinking that he or she was communicating with another human. (14)

uncontrollable variable same as state variable. (9)

unfreezing the first phase in the Lewin-Schein theory of change in which conditions and attitudes that are necessary before meaningful change can take place are created. (8)

UNIX a multi-user operating system originally developed at AT&T Bell Laboratories that is the basis for many international standards and operating systems today. (7)

unstructured decision a decision for which none of the three phases (intelligence, design, and choice) is structured. (2)

user (development role) a person or group responsible for solving the problem that a DSS is to help with. (5)

user interface (*a*) the way in which a DSS (or information system in general) communicates with its user; sometimes used to refer only to the way in which a user tells the information system what to do next (5); (*b*) of an expert system, the way in which the system communicates both with its users and with its developers. (14)

user profile a set of user characteristics that a computer uses to offer that user the most appropriate type of interface in terms of prompting, length of messages, and nature of menus. (15)

util an arbitrary unit of measure for cardinal utility. (2)

utility in economics, a measure of the value to a person of an additional amount of something. (2)

utility curve a curve defining the relationship between the amount of something a person has and its value to that person. (2)

utilization ratio in queuing theory and Markov process analysis, the average service time of a facility divided by the average interarrival time of demands for that facility; actual utilization may be less than this if some arrivals, finding the facility busy, do not join its queue. (9)

validity rating same as confidence factor. (15)

variables (*a*) in general, named storage locations in a computer that hold data useful for the problem now being solved; (*b*) in an expert system, named storage locations in the workspace that hold elements of factual knowledge. (16)

virtual reality technology that gives the user the impression of interacting physically with a computer-created environment. (5)

Want objectives in the Kepner-Tregoe decision-making method, attributes of a solution that are desirable but that an acceptable solution may lack; contrast with Must objectives. (2)

war room same as electronic meeting room. (11)

"What If" explanations in an expert system, output messages that explain what the system would recommend if one or more input data elements were changed. (15)

"Why?" explanations in an expert system, output messages that explain why the system is requesting the user to supply a particular piece of information. (15)

work flow systems (also written as one word: "workflow" systems) information systems that are programmed to handle the information flow of a given work process or decision. (11)

work group information system an information system designed with the objective of being shared by a group of co-workers. (1)

workspace in an expert system, a part of computer storage in which factual knowledge about the current situation is kept. (14)

X server same as server, sense *b*. (7)

X Windows a standard computer-to-terminal communication protocol for the creation and use of graphical user interfaces. (5)

yield management the practice of setting different prices for the same product or service under different terms and conditions to maximize total revenue. (4)

Index